W9-AFS-594

Theory and Applications of Ultraviolet Spectroscopy

Theory and Applications of Ultraviolet Spectroscopy

H. H. Jaffé and Milton Orchin

Professors of Chemistry
University of Cincinnati

John Wiley and Sons, Inc.

New York   London

48, 256
Nov. '64

SECOND PRINTING, MARCH, 1964

Library of Congress Catalog Card Number: 62-15181
Printed in the United States of America

Preface

This book is an outgrowth of two courses which were given independently at the graduate level at the University of Cincinnati during the past several years. One course, "Molecular Spectra," was directed primarily to students majoring in the physical and theoretical chemistry programs. The second course, "Applications of Ultraviolet Spectrophotometry," attracted primarily graduate students in the organic chemistry program. The frequent consultations between professors as well as between students in the two courses indicated the desirability of preparing a textbook which would incorporate both theory, based on the molecular-orbital approach, and a range of applications appealing to organic chemists with a broad interest in structure determination.

The frequently successful utilization of resonance theory by organic chemists in the correlation and integration of a host of chemical facts without resort to the mathematical aspects of the theory has demonstrated the value of a working or qualitative knowledge of resonance. The application of the theory has been particularly successful in the description of molecules in the ground state. Electronic absorption spectroscopy requires not only a description of the ground state, but a knowledge and description of the excited state as well. A description of the excited state is most satisfactorily given in molecular-orbital terminology, and consistency then requires a similar description of the ground state.

The growing interest of organic chemists in understanding the molecular-orbital theory and their desire to use it as a qualitative tool served as a further stimulus to prepare a textbook in which this theory could be developed and applied.

The purpose of the book may be stated simply: to facilitate an understanding of electronic absorption spectra. In order to achieve this goal our basic problem was to organize the vast empirical knowledge of ultraviolet spectra around a framework of theoretical concepts that would neither offend the molecular spectroscopist nor appear incomprehensively complex to the great number of practicing organic chemists who desire a firm foundation for understanding and using absorption spectroscopy. Our

v

different backgrounds, interests, approaches, and temperaments were an advantage in the attempts to solve this problem. The principal device for effecting the necessary compromise between mathematical theory and qualitative development in this book is the use of fine-print sections. Where the logical development of certain basic concepts required a rigorous mathematical justification, this elaboration has been placed in fine print. Occasionally, descriptive material not immediately pertinent to the topic but possessing broad relevance has also been set in reduced type. The large print, then, is intended as a continuous, coherent presentation.

The book is necessarily incomplete in many respects. In order to keep the theoretical part within bounds, many of the topics not commonly encountered in experimental investigations of a nonspectroscopic nature, such as singlet-triplet absorption and spin-orbit coupling, although briefly touched upon, have not been given the space their theoretical importance might have suggested. Similarly, the profusion of experimental material has required very strong selectivity of literature references. Platt has counted as many as 500 papers on spectra appearing in a single year, and estimates indicate that about every third page in the *Journal of the American Chemical Society* contains spectroscopic information. The selections frequently have been arbitrary; familiarity with the literature, the authors' own work and interests, the desirability of developing certain thought processes—these criteria rather than complete and systematic coverage guided the selection. Material of equal or possibly greater worth may have been omitted. In the discussion of theory no specific attempt has been made to give a historical development or to distribute credit to individuals for their specific contributions; rather the primary effort was directed toward producing a unified, homogeneous picture of the present state of the theory, as far as it was believed necessary for an understanding of the experimental material. In the discussion of applications, a similar, rather arbitrary selection of references was made. The number of workers who have contributed to this picture is so tremendous that proper credit is impracticable. We sincerely hope that in this approach we have not done too many injustices to authors and work not included in this version.

Acknowledgments

It is a pleasure to acknowledge the help and understanding of the many people who contributed to the book. Mrs. Edna Penn typed virtually the entire manuscript, often from practically indecipherable notes, and Mrs. E. Ennis was helpful with the preparation of index material. On the scientific side we must first acknowledge our indebtedness to all the workers who have contributed to the state of the knowledge in this field and who are indeed, in a very real sense, responsible for the book. In particular we wish to thank S. Bratož, J. R. Platt, L. F. Fieser, W. T. Gilbert, J. Hinze, and D. McDaniel for reading various chapters and contributing constructive criticisms, and Jerome Collins, Joe Roberts, and William Layne for providing some of the data and doing literature searching; and R. A. Friedel for furnishing a large number of spectra. One of us (M. O.) is grateful to E. Gil-Av and to the Weizmann Institute of Science for a Visiting Lectureship during which some of the material in the early chapters was discussed in a series of lectures. Finally we wish to thank our patient families, whose routines were so frequently interrupted and without whose understanding encouragement it would have been impossible to devote the time and effort required for reading and writing.

H. H. JAFFÉ
MILTON ORCHIN

Cincinnati, Ohio
June, 1962

Contents

1 Light absorption and its measurement

1.1 The Electromagnetic Spectrum and Its Classification

Many apparently different forms of radiant energy such as radio waves, sunlight, x-rays, and gamma rays have similar properties, and are called *electromagnetic radiation*. All such forms of radiant energy can be considered as wave motion which travels at the same velocity (approximately 186,000 miles per second in air or 186,284 miles per second in vacuum). The wavelength, a convenient classification of electromagnetic waves, is the distance, measured along the line of propagation, between the crests or any two points which are in phase on adjacent waves. In absorption spectroscopy the wavelength, λ, is most frequently expressed in microns (μ), millimicrons (mμ), or angstrom (A) units:

$$1 \ \mu = 1000 \ \text{m}\mu = 10{,}000 \ \text{A}$$

The definitions of units of length have now been internationally accepted in terms of the wavelength of the red cadmium line, placed at 6438.4696 A. Thus 1 A is equal to 1/6438.4696 of the wavelength of the red cadmium line in vacuum.

A diagram of the electromagnetic spectrum is shown in Fig. 1.1. The light of shortest wavelength is found at the blue end, that of longest wavelength at the red end, of the spectrum.

Electromagnetic radiation is classified not only by wavelength but also very frequently by the number of waves per unit distance, usually a centimeter. The number of waves per centimeter is called the *wavenumber*, $\tilde{v}$ or $\bar{v}$, and is expressed in reciprocal centimeters, cm^{-1}. The longer is the wavelength, the smaller the number of waves per centimeter: $\tilde{v} = 1/\lambda$. Thus a wavelength of 2000 A is equivalent to $\dfrac{10^8}{2 \times 10^3} = 5 \times 10^4 \ \text{cm}^{-1} =$ 50,000 cm^{-1} or 50,000 reciprocal centimeters (sometimes inaccurately called 50,000 wavenumbers). Since the magnitude of $\tilde{v}$ in the ultraviolet

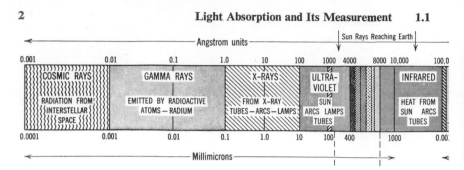

region is >25,000, the unit kilokayser (kK), equal to 1000 cm^{-1} is occasionally employed. Thus, in the above example

$$2000 \text{ A} \cong 50 \text{ kK}$$

The third common classification of radiation is by frequency, ν, the number of waves that pass a particular point per unit time, or the number of cycles per unit time, usually the second. In all electromagnetic waves, the frequency or number of waves passing a point per second multiplied by the wavelength equals the velocity of light (about 3×10^{10} cm/sec):

$$\text{frequency} = \frac{\text{velocity of light (cm/sec)}}{\text{wavelength of light (cm)}}$$

The dimensions of frequency are then seconds^{-1}. For example, 3000 A is converted to frequency as follows:

$$\nu = \frac{3 \times 10^{10} \text{ cm/sec}}{3000 \text{ A}} = \frac{3 \times 10^{10} \text{ cm/sec}}{3 \times 10^{-5} \text{ cm}} = 10^{15} \text{ sec}^{-1}$$

Because frequencies are such large numbers in the range of wavelengths of interest to absorption spectroscopists, the unit called the *fresnel* (f) is used. One fresnel is equal to 10^{12} oscillations per second or, in the above example, 3000 A $\cong$ 1000 fresnels. In general,

$$\nu \text{ (f)} = \frac{3 \times 10^6}{\text{(A)}}$$

Although physicists have defined the symbol $\tilde{\nu}$ to denote wavenumbers, and ν to denote frequency, in much of the literature on spectroscopy ν is used to denote *either* frequency *or* wavenumbers. The fact that frequency and wavenumbers are directly related by the equation, frequency = wavenumbers × speed of light, probably accounts for the use of the same symbol to denote either.

The region of the electromagnetic spectrum of interest to spectroscopists extends from about 100 to 3,000,000 A. Definitions of the various regions

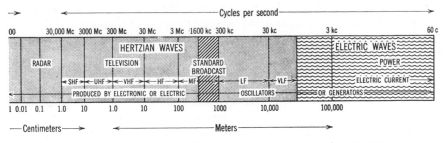

Fig. 1.1   A schematic diagram of the electromagnetic spectrum.

in this range have been proposed by the Joint Committee on Nomenclature in Applied Spectroscopy[1] and are given in Table 1.1. It is clear from this

TABLE 1.1
The Regions of the Electromagnetic Spectrum

Region	Wavelength		Wavenumber, cm^{-1}	Frequency, f
	μ	A		
Far ultraviolet	0.01–0.2	100–2000	1,000,000–50,000	30,000–1500
Near ultraviolet	0.20–0.38	2000–3800	50,000–26,300	1500–787
Visible	0.38–0.78	3800–7800	26,300–12,800	787–385
Near infrared	0.78–3	7800–30,000	12,800–3333	385–100
Middle infrared	3–30	30,000–300,000	3333–333	100–10
Far infrared	30–300	300,000–3,000,000	333–33.3	10–1
Microwave	300–1,000,000	3,000,000–10,000,000,000	33.3–0.01	1–0.0003

listing that the use of different units in different regions of the spectrum is convenient. The adjectives near and far, when used to modify ultraviolet and infrared, relate to the visible region as a reference point. Thus the near ultraviolet is the region of the ultraviolet nearest to the visible and hence refers to the longer wavelengths in the ultraviolet region, whereas the near infrared, which describes the infrared region closest to the visible, is the infrared region of shortest wavelength.

1.2   The Classification and Origin of Spectra

EMISSION SPECTRA.   When atoms or molecules are subjected to intense heat or an electric discharge, they may absorb energy and become "excited." On return to their "normal" state, they may emit radiation. Such emission is the result of a transition of the atom or molecule from a high-energy or "excited" state to one of lower energy, usually the normal or ground state. The energy lost in the transition is emitted in the form of light. Excited *atoms* usually produce line spectra, which are very valuable

[1] Report No. 6 of the Joint Committee on Nomenclature in Applied Spectroscopy, *Anal. Chem.*, **24,** 1349 (1952).

for identification purposes. Determination of the composition of celestial bodies, for example, has been aided by spectroscopic examination of their light emissions. "Excited" molecules produce band spectra. Flame spectra and arc and spark spectra are examples of such emission spectra. Other examples are fluorescence and phosphorescence spectra, which are discussed in Chapter 19.

ABSORPTION SPECTRA. When continuous radiation (i.e., light of all wavelengths) passes through a transparent material, a portion of the radiation may be absorbed and the residual radiation, when passed through a prism, may yield a spectrum with gaps in it. Such a spectrum is called an absorption spectrum. During the absorption process the atoms or molecules pass from a state of low energy (the initial or ground state) to one of higher energy (the excited state).

According to the laws of classical mechanics governing the energies of moving bodies, no restrictions are placed on the energy content of molecules or atoms. Application of these laws would lead to the conclusion that energy can be absorbed in any arbitrary quantity, and, accordingly, that all substances should have continuous spectra. However, the experimental evidence is contrary to this prediction, and the Bohr theory (named for the Danish physicist Niels Bohr) was developed to account for the fact that energy changes produced by light absorption occur only in integral multiples of a unit amount of energy called a *quantum*, which is characteristic of each absorbing species.

In both emission and absorption spectra, the relation between the energy changes in the molecule and the frequency of the light emitted or absorbed is given by the so-called Bohr condition:

$$h\nu = E_f - E_i$$

where h is Planck's constant, ν is the frequency, and E_f and E_i are the energies of a single molecule in the final and the initial states. When $E_f - E_i$ is negative, the negative value of the frequency corresponds to emission; when the frequency is positive, absorption of light is occurring. Although the changes in "internal" or potential energy of a molecule are quantized, the kinetic or "external" energy manifested by molecular translational motion is quantized in such small units that it appears unquantized, and the molecule may gain or lose translational energy in virtually any finite quantity.

Absorption spectra may be further classified into three types: rotation, rotation-vibration, and electronic. The third type includes rotational and vibrational interaction.

The *rotation* spectrum of a molecule is associated with changes which occur in the rotational states of the molecule without simultaneous changes in the vibrational and electronic states. The energies of the various rotational states differ by only a relatively small quantity, and hence the energy difference $E_i - E_f$ is a small number. Accordingly, the frequency of the light which is necessary to effect the change in rotational levels is very small and the wavelength of this light is very large. Pure rotation spectra are observed, accordingly, in the far infrared and microwave regions, experimentally difficult regions within which to work. Until the rather recent developments of microwave spectroscopy, rotational spectra were comparatively little investigated.

Rotation-vibration spectra are associated with transitions in which the vibrational states of the molecule are altered and may be accompanied by changes in rotational states. Since the energy difference between the initial and final vibrational state of a molecule is greater than that between rotational states, absorption occurs at larger frequencies or shorter wavelengths. Therefore vibration-rotation spectra occur in the middle infrared region.

Electronic spectra arise from transitions between electronic states and are accompanied by simultaneous changes in the vibrational and rotational states. Relatively large energy differences $(E_f - E_i)$ are involved, and hence absorption occurs at rather large frequencies or relatively short wavelengths. Virtually all electronic transitions occur in the ultraviolet and visible regions.

The relations between the various energy levels and corresponding spectra can be illustrated by means of Fig. 1.2, which shows the energy states of a diatomic molecule.

The two heavy lines on the left, *G* and *H*, represent the electronic energy levels of two electronic states. *H* may be considered the energy level of the molecule under normal conditions and is called the ground state. *G* may be considered the energy level of the first excited state. These levels represent the energies of the two states if it is assumed that the nuclei of the two atoms are held in fixed positions, i.e., that no rotational or vibrational motion occurs. The horizontal lines in the center of the figure represent energies of a few of the lowest vibrational states associated with each electronic state. These energy levels represent states in which it is assumed that no rotations are occurring. The series of lines at the right of the figure represent a few of the rotational levels associated with the two electronic levels and the various vibrational levels in each state. The rotational levels are represented by broken lines.

The vertical line *AB* corresponds to a transition in the pure rotation spectrum of the substance, since the electronic and vibrational levels do not change. The line *CD* corresponds to a transition in the vibration-rotation spectrum and, being longer than *AB*, represents a greater change

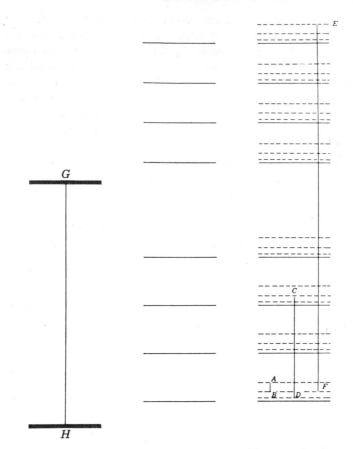

Fig. 1.2 Energies of a diatomic molecule in (*left to right*) electronic, vibrational, and rotational states. (Reprinted by permission from G. W. Wheland, *Resonance in Organic Chemistry*, John Wiley and Sons, New York, 1955, p. 246.)

in energy and therefore absorption of light of shorter wavelength. The line *EF* corresponds to a transition in the electronic spectrum and, since it is longer than *CD*, represents absorption at still shorter wavelength.

Each electronic state is associated with a large number (nearly infinite) of vibrational and rotational states. A transition between two electronic states does not correspond to only a single change in energy and does not result in only a single spectral line. A large number of lines result from the transition, and these are not widely spaced from each other. In the absorption spectra of gases, it is possible, with spectrographs of high resolution, to separate the individual lines, and much information about molecules has been obtained from such analyses. In absorption spectra of liquids, solutions, and solids, it is not possible to separate rotational lines, and only rarely possible to separate vibrational bands, i.e., the superposition of the various rotational lines belonging to a single vibrational transition. Hence only relatively broad absorption bands are observed. It is usually difficult to decide, without a detailed analysis of the spectrum, the exact value of the wavelength that corresponds to the electronic transition alone, which corresponds to GH in Fig. 1.2.

1.3   Energies Associated with Absorption Spectra

It is of fundamental importance to be able to evaluate the energy associated with absorption in any specific region of the spectrum. Since ultraviolet spectra are of particular interest here, the energies will be evaluated in terms of millimicrons. The fundamental equation is the Bohr equation:

$$\epsilon = h\nu$$

ϵ is the energy per molecule, and the energy per mole (E) is ϵN; the values of the constants which are employed in the calculation are as follows:

$$h = 6.6242 \times 10^{-27} \text{ erg sec}$$

$$1 \text{ kcal} = 4.1840 \times 10^{10} \text{ ergs}$$

$$N = \text{Avogadro's number} = 6.023 \times 10^{23}$$

$$c = \text{velocity of light} = 2.9979 \times 10^{10} \text{ cm sec}^{-1}$$

$$E \text{ (kcal/mole)} = \frac{6.6242 \times 10^{-27}}{4.1840 \times 10^{10}} \times \frac{c \text{ (cm/sec)}}{\lambda \text{ (cm)}} \times 6.023 \times 10^{23}$$

$$= \frac{28.635 \times 10^{3}}{\lambda \text{ (m}\mu)}$$

For example, if we wish to calculate the energy corresponding to absorption at 400 mμ, substitution into the above equation gives a value of 71.6 kcal/mole. The amount of energy absorbed by a mole of a compound at any particular wavelength corresponds to the energy of Avogadro's number of photons (light quanta), and this energy, in kilocalories, has been called an *einstein*. An einstein of 400 mμ light is thus 71.6 kcal, or the energy associated with absorption at 400 mμ can be denoted as 71.6 kcal/einstein.

Since wavenumbers are directly proportional to energy, there is a linear relation between the two. Wavelength, however, is inversely proportional to energy, and the nonlinear relationship between the two is shown in

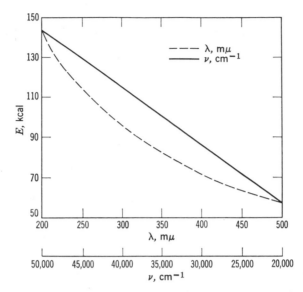

Fig. 1.3   Relation between energy, wavenumbers, and wavelength.

Fig. 1.3 and compared with the linear wavenumber-energy relation. The linear relationship is the principal reason why wavenumber (or frequency) is the classification of radiation preferred by many spectroscopists. Wavenumbers of 70,000, 700, and $7\ cm^{-1}$ correspond, respectively, to electronic, vibrational, and rotational excitations and also, respectively, to approximately 195, 1.95, and 0.0195 kcal/mole.

Also, a spectral shift of $700\ cm^{-1}$ anywhere in the spectrum corresponds to 1.95 kcal/mole. A change of 1.95 kcal/mole, however, corresponds to a shift of 2.7 mμ at 200 mμ but to a shift of 41.5 mμ at 800 mμ.

1.4   Laws of Light Absorption

There are two principal laws of light absorption of interest to the spectroscopist. The first of these, Bouguer's or Lambert's law,[2] states that the proportion of light absorbed by a transparent medium is independent of the intensity of the incident light and that each successive layer of the medium absorbs an equal fraction of the incident light. For example, if the intensity of light incident upon any transparent medium is unity, and the fraction of the incident light absorbed by each unit thickness of the medium is equal to one-tenth, the light intensity will be diminished

---

[2] This law has been attributed to both Bouguer (1729) and Lambert (1760); it appears that the former first stated it unequivocally.

successively to the following values: 1, 0.9, 0.81, 0.729, 0.6561, etc. These numbers are values from the following sequence: $(0.9)^0$, $(0.9)^1$, $(0.9)^2$, $(0.9)^3$, $(0.9)^4$. The relationship may be generalized in the expressions

$$I = I_0 \times e^{-\alpha b} \quad \text{and} \quad \log_e I_0/I = \alpha b$$

where $I =$ the intensity of light transmitted
   $I_0 =$ the intensity of incident light
   $b =$ the thickness of the layer (in centimeters)
   $\alpha =$ an absorption coefficient characteristic of the medium
   $e =$ the base of the natural logarithms.

When the logarithm to the base 10 is used, α is converted to the so-called Bunsen and Roscoe extinction coefficient, K, and $\log_{10} I_0/I = Kb$, where K is a constant depending only on the medium examined and is equal to $(\log I_0/I)/b$. Hence K is the reciprocal of the thickness required to weaken the light to one-tenth of the incident intensity, and $\alpha = 2.303K$.

The absorption coefficients α and K contain no concentration factor and are applicable only to pure materials. The second important law, Beer's law, deals with the concentration factor.

A photon of light can be absorbed by a molecule only if it collides with this molecule. The probability of such collision occurring is directly proportional to the number of absorbing molecules in the light path. Accordingly, Beer's law states that the amount of light absorbed is proportional to the number of absorbing molecules through which the light passes. The absorption of the solution, if the absorbing substance is dissolved in a transparent medium, will be proportional to its concentration.[3] The proportionality to concentration can be incorporated into the Bouguer or Lambert law to give the expression

$$I = I_0 10^{-abc} \quad \text{or} \quad \log I_0/I = abc$$

where $a =$ absorptivity, a molecular property characteristic of the substance under examination and independent of concentration, c, and b is cell length. Either of these expressions or the equivalent one, $\log 1/T = abc$, where T is the transmittance, describes the absorption laws.

[3] Beer's law [A. Beer, *Ann. physik. Chem.* (2), **86**, 78 (1852)] applies to the absorption of a beam of parallel, monochromatic radiation in a homogeneous isotropic medium. A substance is isotropic if the velocity of light (and hence the index of refraction) is the same in all directions for the substance. Gaseous, liquid, and amorphous media (such as glass) have this property, and crystalline substances belonging to the cubic system also are isotropic. Crystals of all systems other than the cubic are anisotropic, and the velocity of light is not uniform in all directions. Hence such crystals exhibit double refraction or birefrigence. Since the crystalline character of solids is of course destroyed on solution, this particular limitation to Beer's law is of no concern in solution spectra.

Although Bouguer, Lambert, Bunsen, and Roscoe, as well as Beer, all made contributions to the absorption law, the law is most frequently and conveniently referred to as Beer's law, since the concentration of the absorbing species is the aspect which has most importance in applied spectroscopy.

The quantity that is actually measured with the usual spectrophotometer is called the *absorbance*, A (or, less desirably, the optical density). It is related to the quantities discussed in the above paragraph by:

$$\log I_0/I = A = abc$$

When the concentration is expressed in moles per liter and the cell length, b, in centimeters, the absorptivity, a, is called the *molar absorptivity* and is denoted by ϵ. Accordingly ϵ is expressed as follows:

$$\epsilon = \frac{A}{b\,(\text{cm}) \times c\,(\text{moles/liter})} = \frac{A}{bc} \times \frac{1000\ \text{cm}^2}{\text{moles}}$$

Invariably, ϵ is given without units, although, as indicated, it has units of $1000\ \text{cm}^2/\text{mole}$, i.e., area per mole;[4] it is also called the molar extinction coefficient.

1.5 Plotting and Comparison of Spectra

Spectral data are usually presented as graphs in which extinction is the ordinate and wavelength or frequency the abscissa. The spectra of pure compounds are most commonly plotted with the absorption intensity, in terms of the molar absorptivity, ϵ, or log ϵ, as ordinate, and the wavelength, increasing from left to right as abscissa. Some authors plot absorbance and indicate the concentrations used for each absorbance plot. The unit $E_{1\,\text{cm}}^{1\%}$ has been used in the literature as the ordinate. This unit is the absorptivity of the material for a 1-cm cell length at a concentration of 1g of solute per 100 ml of solution. Since this unit is not a function of the molecular weight, no assumption as to the molecular structure of the substance is necessary.

The units most commonly employed for the abscissa are $m\mu$ and A. Some authors prefer $m\mu$ because the one less significant figure as compared to A gives a better indication of the true reliability of the experimental data; the former unit will be generally used in this book. Most theoretical spectroscopists probably prefer a frequency unit as the abscissa, and the wavenumber (cm^{-1}) is most often used. Absorption bands of

---

[4] For an interesting kinetic interpretation of Beer's law see H. A. Liebhafsky and H. G. Pfeiffer, *J. Chem. Educ.*, **30**, 450 (1953), and J. H. Goldstein and R. A. Day, *J. Chem. Educ.*, **31**, 417 (1954).

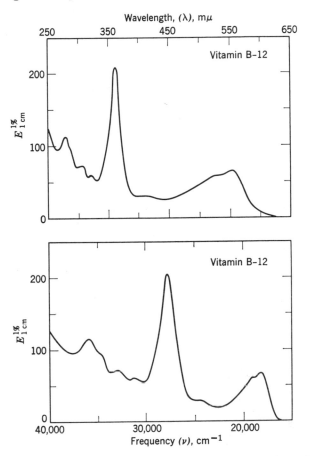

Fig. 1.4 Comparison of wavelength and wavenumber plots of vitamin B-12 in water. (Reprinted by permission from A. E. Gillam and E. S. Stern, *An Introduction to Electronic Absorption Spectroscopy in Organic Chemistry*, E. Arnold, London, 1954, p. 13.)

substances in solution plotted on a wavenumber scale tend to be more symmetrical and more uniformly spaced along the abscissa than plots on a wavelength scale. The plot on a wavelength scale tends to compress the short-wavelength bands and expand the long-wavelength bands as compared to the wavenumber plot. These differences can be noted by comparing the spectra shown in Fig. 1.4.

The spectrum of phenanthrene is shown in Fig. 1.5, plotted on different sets of coordinates. The low-intensity structure at the long-wavelength end apparent in Figs. 1.5*d* and *f* is practically obscured in the plot using molar absorptivity, ϵ (Fig. 1.5*b*). The greatest advantage of the log plots

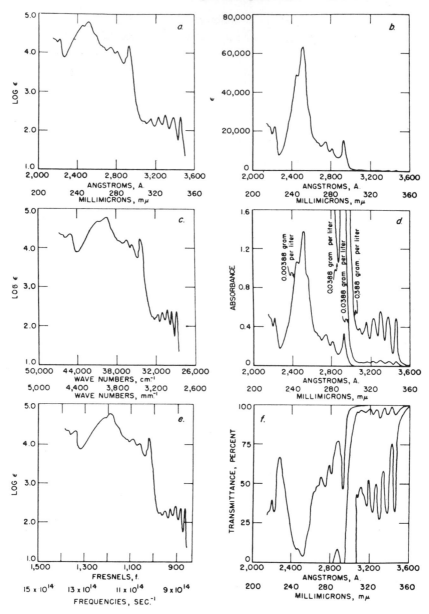

Fig. 1.5 The spectrum of phenanthrene in various coordinate systems. (Reprinted by permission from R. A. Friedel and M. Orchin, *Ultraviolet Spectra of Aromatic Compounds*, John Wiley and Sons, New York, 1951, p. 6.)

(a, c, e) is the expansion of these weak bands, although they result in some distortion and obliteration of fine structure. Spectra may also be presented using different ordinate scales for different parts of the wavelength scale (see, e.g., Fig. 17.10).

1.6   Instruments

Practically all ultraviolet spectrophotometers possess a photoelectric device for measuring the radiant energy. There are four essential components of such spectrophotometers: (1) a source of radiant energy; (2) the spectrometer or monochromator; (3) the absorption-cell assembly; and (4) the photometer or detecting device. A schematic diagram of the arrangement of these components in the Beckman D.U. Quartz Spectrophotometer is shown in Fig. 1.6.

The hydrogen-discharge lamp is the most suitable source of a virtually continuous spectrum in the ultraviolet region of 200–400 mμ. The lamp consists of a tube containing two electrodes and hydrogen gas at low pressure (5-10 mm Hg). Bombardment of the hydrogen and return of the excited molecules to the ground state result in emission of a continuous spectrum. A collimating lens or mirror is attached to the lamp in order that radiant energy of all wavelengths be transmitted in a parallel path to the entrance slit of the spectrometer. For the longer-wavelength region of the near ultraviolet and visible a tungsten-filament lamp is usually employed. A continuous spectrum characteristic of a black-body radiator, at

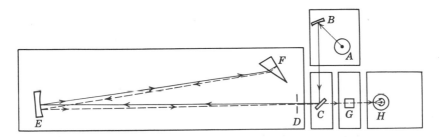

Fig. 1.6 The optical system of the Beckman D.U. Quartz Spectrophotometer. An image of the light source A is focused by the condensing mirror B and diagonal mirror C on the entrance slit at D. The entrance slit is the lower of two slits placed vertically over each other. Light falling on the collimating mirror E is rendered parallel and reflected toward the quartz prism F. The back surface of the prism is aluminized so that light refracted at the first surface is reflected back through the prism, undergoing further refraction as it emerges from the prism. The collimating mirror focuses the spectrum in the plane of the slits D, and light of the wavelength for which the prism is set passes out of the monochromator through the exit (upper) slit, through the absorption cell G to the phototube H.

a temperature of about 3000°C is generated when the filament is heated to incandescence. Larger current is required for the tungsten lamp than for the hydrogen-discharge lamp. Usually the tungsten lamp is employed in the range 320–800 mμ.

The spectrometer component permits the selection of radiant energy of the desired wavelength. A quartz prism or a ruled grating is usually employed as the dispersive element to separate a continuous spectrum into its constituent wavelengths. The optical system of the spectrometer is designed to give different angles of incidence so that radiant energy of a desired wavelength can be selected to emerge from the exit slit of the spectrometer. In addition to the prism the spectrometers possess entrance and exit slits, and adjustment of slit width is important. The entrance slit is necessary to ensure that the light entering the spectrometer be parallel, although at the same time limiting its intensity; the exit slit limits the spectral width of the radiant energy emerging from the spectrophotometer in order to make this emergent beam as monochromatic as possible. With entrance-slit widths small relative to exit-slit widths, the spectral range is narrower, but the intensity of the emergent light is weak. Increasing the width of the entrance slit relative to that of the exit slit widens the spectral range, but the relative intensity at the nominal wavelength is much higher. To have sufficient intensity for photometric measurements with prism spectrometers it is necessary to vary the slit width as the wavelength changes; this requires synchronous adjustment of the two slit widths.

Glass absorption cells can be used in the 350–800 mμ region, but quartz windows or fused silica cells are necessary for measurements below 350 mμ.

The photometer, which measures the relative intensity of the radiant energy transmitted by the solution, is usually a photoelectric cell or a photomultiplier.

Excellent descriptions of spectrophotometric instrumentation for the ultraviolet region are available in a number of books and articles and in brochures from the several manufacturers of manual and recording ultraviolet spectrophotometers.[5]

The performance of an instrument can be readily checked for accuracy in both wavelength and intensity measurements. The spectrum of mercury affords a convenient and accurate check on the wavelength calibration, and intensity measurements can be verified with a standard potassium chromate solution.

[5] T. R. Hogness, F. P. Zscheiler, Jr., and A. E. Sidwell, Jr., *J. Phys. Chem.*, **41**, 379 (1937); K. G. Gibson, *Natl. Bur. Standards Circ.* 484 (1949); A. C. Hardy, *J. Opt. Soc. Am.*, **25**, 305 (1935); H. H. Cary and A. O. Beckman, *J. Opt. Soc. Am.*, **31**, 682 (1941); H. H. Cary, *Rev. Sci. Instr.*, **17**, 558 (1946).

GENERAL REFERENCES

F. Twyman and C. B. Allsopp, *The Practice of Absorption Spectrophotometry*, A. Hilger, London, 1934.

T. R. P. Gibb, *Optical Methods of Chemical Analysis*, McGraw-Hill Book Co., New York, 1942.

G. F. Lothian, *Absorption Spectrophotometry*, A. Hilger, London, 1949.

M. G. Mellon, *Analytical Absorption Spectroscopy*, John Wiley and Sons, New York, 1950.

W. R. Brode, *Chemical Spectroscopy*, John Wiley and Sons, New York, 1943.

R. A. Sawyer, *Experimental Spectroscopy*, Prentice-Hall, Englewood Cliffs, N.J., 1944.

G. R. Harrison, R. C. Lord, and J. R. Loofbourow, *Practical Spectroscopy*, Prentice-Hall, Englewood Cliffs, N.J., 1948.

David F. Baltz, editor, *Selected Topics in Modern Instrumental Analysis*, Prentice-Hall, Englewood Cliffs, N.J., 1952.

2 Atomic orbitals and elementary wave mechanics

2.1 Introduction

According to the Bohr condition, the wavelength of a spectral transition depends on the energy difference between two states. This problem thus becomes one of describing the various states of molecules, and of evaluating the energy differences between them. Since in electronic spectra the contributions from vibrational, and particularly from rotational, motion are quite small, it is practical, in most spectroscopic work, to ignore such motion and to be concerned primarily with the electronic states of molecules. It is, furthermore, a convenient, although rather rough, approximation to consider electrons in molecules independent of one another, and hence to consider excitation as the promotion of one or more electrons.

Most of organic chemistry is concerned with the ground state of molecules, and conventional valence-bond structures and the formal rules of resonance suffice for most descriptions of molecules. For discussions of the excited state, it is often more convenient and more satisfactory to use molecular orbital (MO) descriptions, and in order to be consistent both the ground and excited states should be described in terms of MO theory. Before considering MO theory, it is desirable to review some of the basic concepts that are presently employed to describe the distribution of electrons in atoms.

2.2 Atomic Orbitals

In 1913 Niels Bohr introduced the first satisfactory dynamic model of an atom. In this theory, the electron (for example, of hydrogen) was presumed to move in an orbit around the nucleus under the action of classical laws of motion, and certain quantum conditions were introduced to restrict the number of permitted orbits. This is the kind of motion that is exhibited by the planetary system, and so this model may be called the planetary atom.

16

There are two objections to this planetary theory which need not be considered when the motion of planets is studied, but which are important when the theory is applied to atomic behavior. The theory presumes that the velocity and the position of each electron may be simultaneously determined, and that the motion or orbit of each electron can be followed. In 1927, Heisenberg[1] showed that there is no way of measuring exactly and simultaneously the velocity and the position of an electron. Since the electron cannot be followed in its orbit, an alternative description of its motion was developed. In 1924, de Broglie showed that waves could be associated with particles; if equations are available for the description of light, sound, and water waves, they should be available also to describe electron waves. Such a description was provided by the wave mechanics introduced in 1926 by Erwin Schrödinger.

Schrödinger's wave mechanics rested upon two lines of argument: (*a*) the wave character of an electron, and (*b*) the probability or statistical character of the knowledge of very small particles, perhaps best expressed by the statement that, although the exact location of an electron cannot be determined, its position can be defined by the probability of finding it in any given region. The electron's position is thus defined by a probability function usually denoted by $\rho(x, y, z)$, where x, y, z are the Cartesian coordinates describing a location. The electron will thus be found in those regions where ρ is greatest, and $\rho\,dx\,dy\,dz \equiv \rho\,d\tau$ is the probability that the particle is in the infinitesimally small volume $dx\,dy\,dz$ ($\equiv d\tau$) surrounding the point (x, y, z). Accordingly, ρ is sometimes called the probability density, and, since the particle must be somewhere, the probability integrated over all space equals unity: $\int \rho\,d\tau = 1$. Before attempting to connect the probability density ρ with the wave equation, it is instructive to consider the methods available for representing the probability of finding an electron in certain regions around the nucleus. The simplest atom, the hydrogen atom, will be used as an example.

We can visualize the electron of the hydrogen atom as moving randomly in all directions but being more frequently in some places than in others. If we could locate the electron at a particular moment, place a dot at that point in space, and then repeat the process many, many times after equal but very minute intervals of time, the relative density of the dots would represent the probability of finding the electron in space. This relative density, called the *charge distribution* or *charge cloud* of the electron, is represented by Fig. 2.1.

The distribution of the electron cloud can be illustrated in a variety of

[1] W. Heisenberg, *Physical Principles of the Quantum Theory*, University of Chicago Press, 1930.

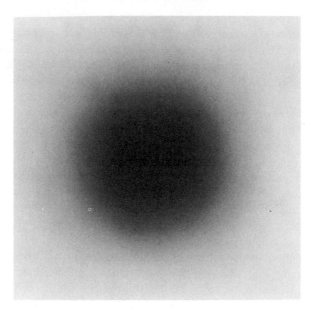

Fig. 2.1 Representation of the distribution of an electron about a hydrogen nucleus.

ways; the two equivalent ways shown in Fig. 2.2 are particularly attractive.[2] In part *a* of this figure, the probability P that the distance between the electron and the proton is less than r is plotted against r. In Fig. 2.2b the seven concentric circles are cuts in the plane of the paper of seven concentric spheres (not circles); the values listed along the horizontal axis are equal to the distances (in angstroms) from the proton, depicted by the + sign. The values listed on the individual circles are equal to the probabilities that the electron will be found somewhere within the corresponding spheres. Still another method of representation is a single circle, with a dot in the center to represent the nucleus (Fig. 2.3). The circle can be identified with any of the circles in Fig. 2.2b. If, for example, the outermost circle is chosen, the electron is nineteen times as likely to be inside the corresponding sphere, with a radius of 1.7 A, as it is to be outside that sphere. This circle is the boundary surface of the sphere in which the electron is most likely to be, i.e., the atomic orbital (AO) of the hydrogen atom. This spherically symmetrical orbital is called an s orbital.

The probability of finding an electron in a particular element of space has been portrayed above in several ways. It is desirable now to relate this

[2] G. W. Wheland, *Resonance in Organic Chemistry*, John and Wiley Sons, New York, 1955, pp. 58 f.

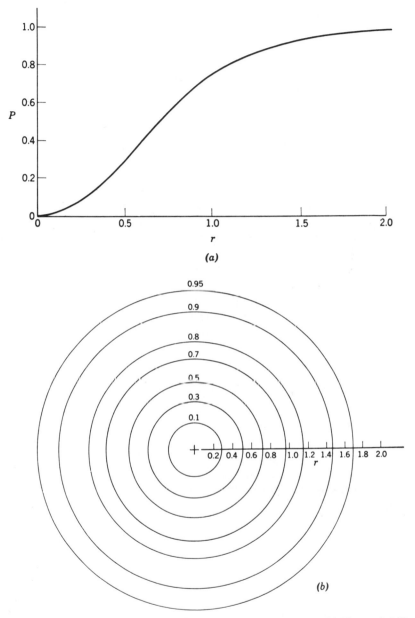

Fig. 2.2 The charge distribution in the normal hydrogen atom. (*a*) The probability *P* that the electron is at a distance less than *r* from the nucleus, plotted against *r*. (*b*) Contours of equal probability. (Reprinted by permission from G. W. Wheland, *Resonance in Organic Chemistry*, John Wiley and Sons, 1955.)

probability function to the wave behavior of an electron. All wave motion, whether it is the readily visualized vibration of a string or the difficultly imagined electromagnetic waves of light radiation, is characterized by a transmission of energy from one point to another without permanent displacement of the intervening medium. Another characteristic of all waves is that they can be described by similar equations, one feature of which is that the amplitude of the wave is a function of the distance along the wave path. The behavior of electrons has been found to have characteristics similar to those of a standing or stationary wave, for example, that produced by a vibrating string stretched between two fixed points. The amplitude is a function of the distance along the wave in the lengthwise direction of the wave. At certain integral values of the distance along the standing wave, the amplitude will be zero; at periodic intervals of the distance, the amplitude will be a maximum. Acceptable solutions for values of the amplitude as a function of the distance along the wave path satisfy what are known as "continuity" and "boundary" conditions. According to these conditions, for every value of x between given boundaries, the function of x or $f(x)$, which determines the amplitude, must be continuous, finite, and single valued. Figure 2.4 shows (a) unacceptable and (b) acceptable solutions of the wave equation for vibrations of a stretched string.[3] Acceptable solutions are called *eigenfunctions*.

Fig. 2.3 The 1s atomic orbital of hydrogen in cross section.

The equation that describes the motion of an electron is called a *wave equation* and is analogous to the equation used in mechanics to describe a standing wave. However, the electron, instead of moving in only one direction like the standing wave, can move in any direction and is located by the three Cartesian coordinates or, more profitably, the three polar coordinates r, θ, and φ. The relation between Cartesian and polar coordinates is shown in Fig. 2.5. The location of the electrons can then be expressed by the wave function, written $\phi(r, \theta, \varphi)$.

In most wave phenomena it is the square of the amplitude of a wave that has significance rather than the amplitude itself. If this generalization is applied here, it may be expected that $\rho(r, \theta, \varphi) \equiv \phi^2(r, \theta, \varphi)$,[4] and by the

---

[3] E. Cartmell and G. W. A. Fowles, *Valency and Molecular Structure*, Butterworth's Scientific Publications, London, 1956, pp. 27 f.

[4] Although no complex wave functions will be used in this book, the reader should realize that the function ϕ may be a complex number. In that case the definition $\rho \equiv \phi^2$ must be replaced by $\rho = \phi^*\phi$, where ϕ^* is the complex conjugate of ϕ; i.e., if $\phi = a + ib$, where $i = \sqrt{-1}$, $\phi^* = a - ib$, and $\phi^*\phi = a^2 + b^2$.

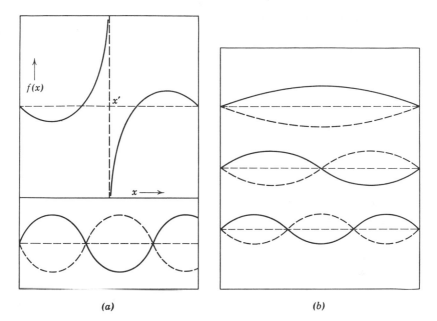

Fig. 2.4   Solutions of the wave equation for the vibrations of a stretched string, (a) unacceptable and (b) acceptable solutions. (Reprinted by permission from E. Cartmell and G. W. A. Fowles, *Valency and Molecular Structure*, Butterworth's, London, 1956.)

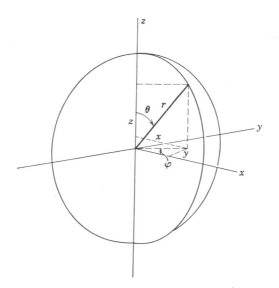

Fig. 2.5   The relation between Cartesian and polar coordinates.

choice of a proper constant which is incorporated in the ϕ:

$$\rho(r,\, \theta,\, \varphi) = \phi^2(r,\, \theta,\, \varphi) \quad \text{and} \quad \int \phi^2 \, d\tau = 1$$

This wave function is said to be normalized. If ϕ is not already normalized, it may be made so by multiplication by a number N such that the integral is equal to unity. There is a simple reason why ϕ^2 and not ϕ must be associated with the probability density. The solution of the wave equation usually gives some regions of space in which ϕ is positive and others in which it is negative. The probability, however, must always be zero or some positive number, and thus ϕ^2 rather than ϕ must be employed in order to relate the wave function and the density.

According to the wave equation, a moving particle is represented by a wave function ϕ such that $\phi^2 \, d\tau$ is the probability that the electron is found in the volume $d\tau$. In Fig. 2.2b we may regard each contour or circle as representing the probability of finding the electron within the appropriate distance r from the nucleus. We may say that the largest circle represents the contour for the wave function ϕ such that 95 per cent of the charge lies within this contour. This can be called the boundary surface for the electron and thus represents the 1s orbital. The shapes of the various boundary surfaces (or orbitals) largely determine the stereochemical disposition of the atoms in a polyatomic molecule, and hence it is of importance to appreciate these shapes. In the normal or ground state, the electron of the hydrogen atom will occupy the 1s orbital. The electron can be made to occupy other orbitals by "exciting" it in some manner. These higher orbitals are best considered in the framework of the periodic classification of the elements.

The state of the electron in the hydrogen atom is expressed in terms of three so-called quantum numbers, n, l, and m. The principal quantum number, n, determines the (average) distance of the electron from the nucleus and the energy of the electron; it may have any positive integral value. The other two quantum numbers, l and m, are related to the rotational motion of the electron around the nucleus. The azimuthal quantum number, l, determines the total angular momentum of the electron due to its rotation about the nucleus and may have any integral value between 0 and $n-1$, i.e., $l = 0, 1, 2, \ldots, n-1$. For the ground state of H, where $n = 1$, l therefore is zero, and the electron has no angular momentum. This corresponds to a wave function $\phi(r,\, \theta,\, \varphi)$ and an associated probability function $\rho(r,\, \theta,\, \varphi) = \phi^2$, which is independent of the polar angles θ and φ (i.e., a straight line if $\phi(r,\, \theta,\, \varphi)$ was plotted against θ or φ) and hence to a spherically symmetrical ρ.

Although quantum numbers were introduced in the Bohr theory on an empirical basis in order to explain the observed spectra, they arise logically in the quantum-mechanical treatment of the hydrogen atom. The postulation of the Schrödinger equation and the definition of the wave function ϕ as a function which, when squared, gives a probability, produce three restrictions on ϕ: it must be (1) continuous, (2) single valued, and (3) finite or normalizable. Condition (1) means that the function must have no discontinuities; an infinitesimal change of the value of one of the coordinates must give an infinitesimal change of ϕ. If ϕ is to be a probability, it must at any point in space have only a single value, hence condition (2). Finally, the probability of finding a particle anywhere in space must be unity if the particle exists, and therefore the sum over all space (or better the integral) must be unity; this is condition (3). The Schrödinger equation is a second-order differential equation and has an infinite number of solutions. Among these, however, many do not satisfy the three conditions and hence are unsatisfactory. Only those solutions, still infinite in number, which obey the three conditions are acceptable wave functions. The solution of the Schrödinger equation, which is a three-dimensional differential equation, involves its separation into three one-dimensional second-order differential equations, one in each of the three polar coordinates, r, θ, and φ. In the solution of each of these equations one quantum number is introduced. In the equation in φ, the quantum number m is introduced to ensure singlevaluedness; in the equations in r and θ, n and l, respectively, are introduced to ensure normalizability.

A rotating electron possesses a magnetic moment, just as all electric current has associated with it a magnetic field. If the electron is placed in a magnetic field, the axis about which it is rotating will tend to orient itself with respect to this field and precesses about the direction of the field in the same way that a top precesses about the direction of the field of gravity when its motion is disturbed. According to quantum mechanics, the axis precesses at only certain angles with the direction of the field. Each of these orientations is associated with another quantum number called the magnetic quantum number, m, which may have any integral value between $+l$ and $-l$: $m = l, l - 1, \ldots, -(l - 1), -l$.

As indicated above, the value for l in the hydrogen atom, where $n = 1$, is zero. Orbitals with $l = 0$, such as that of the hydrogen electron, are spherically symmetric and are called s orbitals. Orbitals with $l = 1, 2,$ and 3 are called p, d, and f orbitals, respectively. This terminology is taken from atomic emission spectroscopy, and the letters used are the initial letters of the words sharp, principal, diffuse, and fundamental, which describe lines observed in atomic spectra.

The three quantum numbers considered thus far, then, may be described as having the following significance: n largely determines the energy associated with the orbital, l indicates the geometrical shape of the orbital, and m is associated with different orientations of the orbital with reference to some defined direction. There is a fourth quantum number, called the spin quantum number, s. The existence of this quantum number was first proposed by Goudsmit and Uhlenbeck in 1925 to account for the "double"

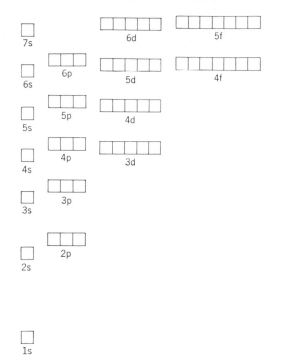

Fig. 2.6 Approximate stability sequence of atomic orbitals.

lines in the spectra of some alkali metals. The electron in, for example, the hydrogen atom was assumed to have axial (spin) as well as orbital angular momentum resulting from its motion in orbit. Both motions produce a magnetic field, but the field resulting from the spin can either reinforce or oppose the field resulting from the orbital rotation, depending upon whether the direction of spin is clockwise or counterclockwise. The spin quantum number may have values of $\pm\frac{1}{2}$.

In building up the periodic classification of the elements and the arrangement of the electrons around the nucleus, two important principles must be observed. One is the *Pauli exclusion principle*, which states that no two electrons in the same atom can possess the same values of the four quantum numbers. Thus, if two electrons in an atom have identical values of n, l, and m, it follows that their spins must be opposed or antiparallel. Each orbital can thus accommodate a maximum of two electrons with antiparallel spins. The other principle is the *Aufbau principle*. It states that, in determining the electronic structure of the ground state of an atom, all electrons may be thought of as removed from the nucleus, and then fed back into the atom, filling up the available orbitals in the order of their energies. Thus the first two electrons go into the 1s orbital, with anti-parallel spin. According to the Pauli principle, no further electrons can be accommodated by this orbital, and other electrons, if any, must then go into higher orbitals. The electrons go into these orbitals in such a way that the orbitals are filled up in order of increasing energy.

Since l can have any integral value between $n - 1$ and 0, for $n = 1$, l must be 0, and hence m (which has integral values between $+l$ and $-l$) must be 0. Accordingly, the $n = 1$ shell, the K shell, is completely filled when it possesses two electrons, i.e., in helium. In lithium, therefore, with three electrons, one electron must go into a higher orbital with $n = 2$ in the so-called L-shell. For $n = 2$, l may be 0 or 1; the $l = 0$ orbital is the 2s orbital and has lower energy than the $l = 1$ orbitals, the p orbitals. For $l = 1$, m may be 0, $+1$, or -1, so that there are three 2p orbitals, designated $2p_x$, $2p_y$, and $2p_z$. The number of subshells in a shell is equal to the principal quantum number, and the total number of orbitals in a shell is equal to the square of the principal quantum number. Thus the M shell with the principal quantum number 3 contains three subshells and nine orbitals, one 3s, three 3p, and five 3d orbitals. The approximate stability sequence of AO's is given in Fig. 2.6.

Electrons in the ground state of the atoms occupy orbitals of the lowest energy. From Fig. 2.6 it is apparent that there is a greater tendency to occupy a 1s orbital than a 2s, and a 2s than a 2p. If more than one electron is available for a given set of p orbitals which have the same energy, the electrons do not pair but occupy separate orbitals until each of the three p orbitals has at least one electron. This rule is incorporated in the generalization known as Hund's rule, which states that two electrons do not occupy a given orbital in a subshell until all the orbitals of the subshell have at least one electron and all of these possess parallel spin.

The electron distribution of the elements from lithium to neon, which constitute the second period of the periodic table, is shown in Fig. 2.7,

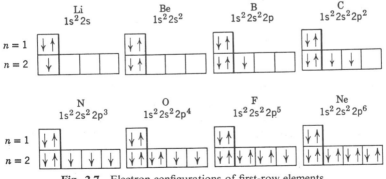

Fig. 2.7   Electron configurations of first-row elements.

where the boxes represent orbitals, and the arrows (arbitrary) direction of spin.

It is of interest to observe from Fig. 2.7 that the elements have the following numbers of unpaired electrons:

Li	Be	B	C	N	O	F	Ne
1	0	1	2	3	2	1	0

Since a covalent chemical bond is usually considered to be formed by the pairing of two electrons, one from each of the bonded atoms, the number of unpaired electrons indicates the valence of the element. For beryllium, boron, and carbon, however, there appears to be no relationship between the chemically observed valence and the number of unpaired electrons. In the case of beryllium a divalent structure can be written by promoting one of the 2s electrons to a 2p orbital: Be $(1s^22s^2) \rightarrow$ Be* $(1s^22s2p)$. This promotion requires the relatively small energy of 62 kcal/mole. Similar $2s \rightarrow 2p$ promotions with boron and carbon would give the following excited-state structures:

Be*   B*   C*

$1s^22s2p$ $1s^22s2p^2$ $1s^22s2p^3$

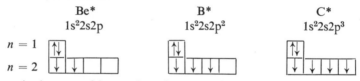

The excited atom of boron has three unpaired electrons, and carbon has four. Thus the numbers of unpaired electrons may now be written:

Li	Be*	B*	C*	N	O	F	Ne
1	2	3	4	3	2	1	0

This order now follows the familiar valences of these elements. The promotion energy for carbon $(1s^22s^22p^2 \rightarrow 1s^22s2p^3)$ is 122 kcal/mole, and for boron $(1s^22s^22p \rightarrow 1s^22s2p^2)$ it is 106 kcal/mole.[5] The energy required for such promotions is more than compensated for by the extra strength and larger number of the bonds that are formed with tetravalent carbon and trivalent boron.

The description of the electronic structure presented here is an approximate one; it assumes that the total wave function (Φ) of the atom, which is a function of the coordinates of *all* the electrons, can be factored into a product of functions ϕ each of which is a function of one electron only. Such functions ϕ are called one-electron orbitals, and also, since they are taken in the form derived from the solution of the wave equation of the hydrogen atom, hydrogen-like orbitals. A wave function Φ written in this form as a product of one-electron orbitals ϕ is called a configuration. Thus we speak of the configuration $1s^22s^22p^2$ and of the configuration

[5] H. H. Jaffé, *J. Chem. Educ.*, **33**, 25 (1956).

$1s^22s2p^3$ of a carbon atom, and such a description implies knowledge of the angular momentum of each electron. The angular momenta of individual electrons cannot even in principle be determined experimentally, but the resultant angular momentum of the entire atom can be determined. The angular momenta of the individual electrons are coupled together according to certain rules[6] to produce, from each configuration, one or more states which are characterized by the total orbital and total spin angular momentum of the atom.

The analysis of the coupling of individual electron orbital angular momenta and spin angular momenta can be elaborated in more detail as follows.

Just as the angular momentum of each electron is quantized by the quantum numbers l and m (or m_l), the angular momentum of the entire atom is quantized according to quantum numbers L and $M_L = L, L - 1, \ldots, -L$. The quantum number M_L is the sum of the m_l values of all the electrons; and, since a single configuration such as $1s^22s^22p^2$ can correspond to various combinations of m_l's, it leads to several values of M_L. In many cases all these correspond not to a single L, but to several of them, and the energies of atoms with different L's are different. These different energy levels of an atom, corresponding to different L values, several of which may belong to the same configuration, are called the *states* of the atom.

This discussion can best be illustrated by detailed examination of a special case. The configuration $2p^2$, for example, includes all fifteen of the wave functions listed in Table 2.1. In this table the m or m_l values are given by arrows in the appropriate column, and the spin quantum number m_s is indicated by an appropriate arrow (up for $+\frac{1}{2}$, down for $-\frac{1}{2}$). The reader can readily convince himself that the arrangements given in Table 2.1 are the only ones compatible with the Pauli principle. Addition of the m_l values gives the M_L values listed, and similarly addition of the m_s's gives M_S. These values represent the z components of the orbital and spin angular momentum, respectively, of the atom. Since there is a wave function with $M_L = 2$, it follows that there must be a state with $L = 2$, a D state, to which must correspond values of M_L of 2, 1, 0, -1, and -2. Since for $M_L = +2$ and -2, $M_S = 0$, in this D state the spins are paired. The same must then be true in all its components. The nomenclature of states involves the resultant orbital angular momentum (L), just as the nomenclature for individual electrons follows their individual orbital angular momenta (l). Thus the state with $L = 2$ is called a D state, just as an electron with $l = 2$ is called a d electron. The lack of a resultant spin angular momentum is expressed by the preceding superscript 1, which is the "multiplicity," given by $2S + 1$, where S is the total spin.

After the wave functions corresponding to the ^{1}D state (i.e., one each wave function with $M_L = 2, 1, 0, -1, -2$ and $M_S = 0$), there remain ten functions. The highest value of M_L remaining is 1 (with other values of M_L of 0 and -1), and it is associated with values of M_S as high as 1 (with other values of M_S of 0 and -1). Consequently a state with $L = 1$, $S = 1$, a ^{3}P state, must exist. Corresponding to this state there must be the following nine wave functions, indicated by the given M_L and M_S values: 1, 1; 1, 0; 1, -1; 0, 1; 0, 0; 0, -1; -1, 1; -1, 0; -1, -1. After these are removed, there remains only one wave function, $M_L = 0$, $M_S = 0$, corresponding to a ^{1}S state.

---

[6] Russel-Saunders coupling for light elements, and $j - j$ coupling for heavy elements; cf. J. C. Slater, *Quantum Theory of Matter*, McGraw-Hill Book Co., New York, 1951, p. 171.

It will be noted in Table 2.1 that two wave functions have the identical quantum numbers $M_L = 1$ and $M_S = 0$, and thus both belong to ^1D and ^3P states. It is impossible to assign one of these wave functions to ^1D and the other to ^3P because the two cannot be distinguished. Similarly, there are three wave functions with $M_L = M_S = 0$, and these three belong to ^1D, ^3P, and ^1S. Again, however, a specific assignment of which belongs to which cannot be made.

Addition to the p^2 configuration of two 2s electrons to give $2s^2 2p^2$ does not change this result, since $m_l = 0$ for both 2s electrons, while $m_s = +\frac{1}{2}$ for one and $-\frac{1}{2}$ for the other, and hence M_L and M_S are both zero. Therefore the same three states, ^1D, ^3P, and ^1S, arise.

TABLE 2.1

The Wave Functions Corresponding to the Configuration p^2

$m_l =$			M_L	M_S	Component of
1	0	−1			
↑↓			2	0	^1D
↑	↑		1	1	^3P
↑	↓		1	0 ⎫	
↓	↑		1	0 ⎬	^1D, ^3P
↓	↓		1	−1	^3P
↑		↑	0	1	^3P
↑		↓	0	0 ⎫	
↓		↑	0	0 ⎬	^1D, ^3P, ^1S
	↑↓		0	0 ⎭	
↓		↓	0	−1	^3P
	↑	↑	−1	1	^3P
	↑	↓	−1	0 ⎫	
	↓	↑	−1	0 ⎬	^1D, ^3P
	↓	↓	−1	−1	^3P
		↑↓	−2	0	^1D

Thus, for example, the configuration of the carbon atom described by $2s^2 2p^2$ corresponds to three states. Two of these describe a situation in which the two electrons in the p orbitals have antiparallel spins and can be in any one of the three p orbitals together or separately, although which p orbital(s) are occupied cannot be specified. One of these two states has a total orbital angular momentum (L) of 2 and is designated as ^1D, and the other of zero (^1S). The third state corresponding to the configuration $2s^2 2p^2$, describes a situation in which the two electrons are

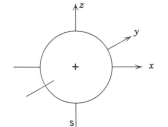

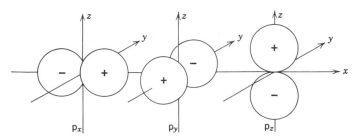

Fig. 2.8 s and p atomic orbitals; boundary surfaces. (Reprinted by permission from C. A. Coulson, *Valence*, Oxford University Press, 1952, p. 25.)

never in the same p orbital, but have parallel spins, and therefore must occupy any two of the three p orbitals; this state is designated as ^{3}P.

To return to the shape of various orbitals, it has already been stated that the 1s orbital is spherically symmetrical. The charge-cloud density on the s type of orbital is a function only of r. All other types of orbitals have lower symmetry. There are three p-type AO's in which the boundary surface consists of two regions which together resemble two spheres touching at a surface. There is a very marked directional character in these orbitals, which is indicated by a subscript designating the Cartesian coordinate around which the orbital is centered, p_x, p_y, p_z. Figure 2.8 shows approximate boundary surfaces for these AO's.

Each of the p orbitals is cylindrically symmetrical around one of the coordinate axes, and the orbitals are entirely independent. One half, or lobe, of the wave function is positive, and the other half negative. These signs are placed in the regions where ϕ is positive or negative. There is no physical significance whatever in the signs, since they can be reversed by multiplication by -1. The difference in sign may be regarded as similar to amplitudes in a wave:

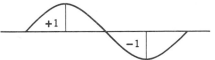

Another feature of the p atomic orbitals is that the regions where ϕ is of opposite sign are separated by a "nodal plane," in which $\phi = 0$ or in which there is zero probability of finding the electron. The nodal plane in the orbital p_x is the yz plane. The plus and minus character of the two lobes makes the p orbital antisymmetrical with respect to reflection on the nodal plane, even though the orbital has cylindrical symmetry around its axis.

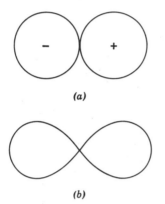

(a)

(b)

Fig. 2.9   Cross section of a p orbital, (a) ϕ; (b) ϕ^2.

It is also important to note that the three p orbitals are at right angles to each other.

The surfaces shown for the s and p orbitals represent wave functions, ϕ. Surfaces showing ϕ^2 rather than ϕ are identical for an s orbital but are slightly different for the p orbitals. Figure 2.9 shows ϕ and ϕ^2 for the p orbitals. The ϕ surface is that of two spheres in contact. The same general properties remain in the ϕ^2 surface (i.e., the same orientation of the p_x, p_y, and p_z orbitals and the same nodal planes), but the shape is different, and, of course, there are no positive and negative regions. The probability patterns, ϕ^2, are the physically significant ones; and the orbital patterns, the mathematically useful ones.

There are five d-type AO's. The surfaces of these orbitals are shown in Fig. 2.10. These d orbitals have two nodal planes.

It must be emphasized that each orbital can accommodate a maximum of two electrons. Thus each of the d orbitals shown in Fig. 2.10 can accommodate at most two electrons. When there are several AO's which are completely equivalent, they correspond to the same energy value. In such a case the energy level is spoken of as *degenerate*, and the number of equivalent atomic orbitals as the *degree of degeneracy*. Thus the d orbitals are five-fold degenerate, the p orbitals three-fold degenerate, and the s orbital singly degenerate or nondegenerate. The s, p, or d character of the orbital determines its geometrical character. The s, p, or d character also determines the number of nodal planes through the origin, this being 0, 1, or 2, respectively.

2.3   Hybridized Atomic Orbitals

It has already been pointed out that the lowest configuration of the carbon atom is $1s^2 2s^2 2p^2$; in order to obtain a tetravalent carbon atom, one of the $2s^2$ electrons must be excited into the empty 2p orbital to give the electronic configuration, $1s^2 2s 2p_x 2p_y 2p_z$. In this state, three of the electrons

Fig. 2.10 d atomic orbitals. [Reprinted by permission from R. G. Pearson, *Chem. & Eng. News*, June 29, 74 (1959).]

are in p orbitals and the fourth in an s orbital. One might expect that carbon would form, with univalent groups such as hydrogen, three bonds of identical character and a fourth bond different from the other three. This is manifestly not the case in a molecule such as methane, which is tetrahedral. Four equivalent bonds can be secured by mixing or *hybridizing* the one s and three p orbitals to give four equivalent orbitals, each of which

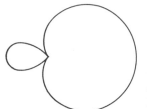

is called an sp^3 hybrid orbital. The boundary surface or cross section of one of the sp^3 orbitals is shown in Fig. 2.11.

An approximate way of showing the formation of an sp^3 hybrid orbital from the combination of an s orbital and a p-type orbital is shown in Fig. 2.12.

Fig. 2.11 The sp^3 (tetrahedral) hybrid orbital. (Reprinted by permission from C. R. Noller, *Chemistry of Organic Compounds*, Saunders, Philadelphia, Pa., 1952, p. 11.)

The sp^3 hybrid is a strongly directional orbital, and the large positive lobe means that it can overlap very effectively with an orbital of another atom. Since good overlap is one of the most important aspects of the formation of a strong bond,[7] a hybrid orbital can thus form much stronger bonds than either pure p or pure s orbitals. Although energy is expended, first in the promotion of an electron from an s to a p orbital and then further in the hybridization, the gain in bonding power because of the increased number of bonds and directional character of the hybrid orbital, and the consequent increase in bond energy, is sufficient to more than offset the promotion and hybridization energy.

It should be noted that the hybrid orbital (or rather its charge distribution) has a lower symmetry than the charge distribution of the unhybridized orbitals. The s electron cloud has the highest possible degree of symmetry, spherical symmetry: it has a center of symmetry, and any conceivable symmetry operation can be performed on it. The symmetry of the charge cloud of the p electron is lower; the center of symmetry is retained, but only one infinite-fold axis remains: the lengthwise axis of the orbital, and rotation about it by any angle leads to no detectable change. The sp^3 hybrid-orbital charge distribution still retains this axis, but has lost the center of symmetry. Both the p orbital and the hybrid orbital are said to have cylindrical symmetry, which indicates that they have the axis described. It should be pointed out that the four sp^3 hybrid orbitals are directed toward the corners of a tetrahedron, and hence four groups attached to carbon are separated by approximately $109\frac{1}{2}°$.

When three groups are attached to carbon (as, for example, each carbon

---

[7] L. Pauling, *The Nature of the Chemical Bond*, Cornell University Press, 1960; R. S. Mulliken, *J. Am. Chem. Soc.*, **72**, 4493 (1950).

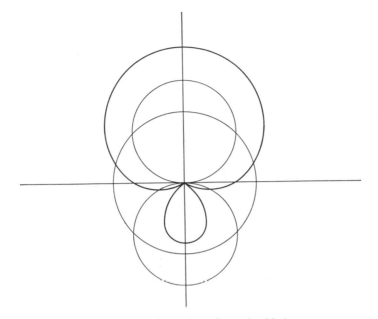

Fig. 2.12   The formation of an sp³ orbital.

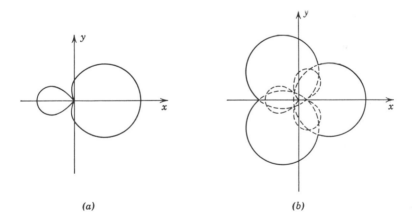

Fig. 2.13   The sp² (trigonal) hybrid orbitals: (*a*) cross section; (*b*) three orbitals in a plane. (Reprinted by permission from C. R. Noller, *Chemistry of Organic Compounds*, Saunders, Philadelphia, Pa., 1952, p. 11.)

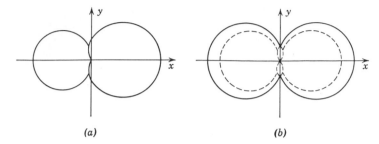

Fig. 2.14 The sp (digonal) hybrid orbital: (a) cross section; (b) two orbitals in a line. (Reprinted by permission from C. R. Noller, *Chemistry of Organic Compounds*, Saunders, Philadelphia, Pa., 1952, p. 10.)

in ethylene, which will be discussed later), the carbon atom utilizes three hybrid orbitals, made by mixing one s orbital and two p orbitals to give three equivalent sp^2 orbitals, which are all in a plane and directed at 120° from each other. Figure 2.13a shows the cross section of a single sp^2 hybrid AO; and Fig. 2.13b, the three sp^2 hybrid orbitals. Hybridization to form the sp^2 orbitals is called *trigonal* hybridization.

When carbon is attached to only two groups (as, for example, each carbon in acetylene), two hybrid orbitals resulting from mixing one s and one p orbital are utilized by the carbon atom. This is called *digonal* hybridization. Figure 2.14 shows the cross section of such orbitals. Trigonal and digonal orbitals also have cylindrical symmetry.

GENERAL REFERENCES

L. Pauling and E. B. Wilson, *Introduction to Quantum Mechanics*, McGraw-Hill Book Co., New York, 1935.

J. C. Slater, *Quantum Theory of Matter*, McGraw-Hill Book Co., New York, 1951.

E. U. Condon and G. H. Shortley, *Theory of Atomic Spectra*, Cambridge University Press, London, 1951.

3 Elementary molecular-orbital theory

In the molecular-orbital description of molecules, it is assumed that the atoms comprising the molecule do not preserve their individual characters. The individual AO's are combined into a set of wave functions (molecular orbitals, MO's) that encompass the whole molecule. The inner electrons of the atoms are considered to remain in unperturbed orbitals on their respective atoms. However, the valence electrons from all the joined atoms are stripped and pooled and then placed into the MO's following, as in the case of AO's, the Aufbau principle and the Pauli exclusion principle; i.e., the electrons are assigned to the MO's so that each of those of lower energy is filled with two electrons before any electron is assigned to an orbital of higher energy. In the case of orbitals of equal energy (degenerate orbitals) Hund's rule applies just as it does for AO's; i.e., one electron is assigned to each of the degenerate orbitals before the second electron is assigned to any one of them.

3.1 The Hydrogen-Molecule Ion, H_2^+, and the Hydrogen Molecule, H_2[1]

The simplest of all molecular structures is the hydrogen-molecule ion, H_2^+, which consists of two hydrogen nuclei or protons and one electron. If the two protons of H_2^+ are at a great distance from each other, the system is described as consisting of a hydrogen atom plus an isolated proton, and the average distribution of electronic charge can be represented by either Fig. 3.1a or Fig. 3.1b, in each of which the two plus signs represent the two protons and the closed curve represents the sphere within which the single electron is most likely to be found. Now, if the two

---

[1] Since the discussion in this chapter is meant to pave the way for a qualitative treatment of MO's, and hence of spectra of large molecules, it will be based entirely on the crudest, semiempirical, so-called LCAO (linear combination of atomic orbitals) theory, often called *Hückel theory*. In Chapter 8 on the comparison of MO and VB (valence-bond) theory, it will be necessary to go much deeper into the refinements necessary to complete the theory, and the interested reader is referred to that chapter for the details of a more adequate treatment of H_2^+ and H_2.

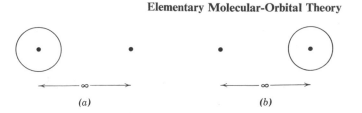

Fig. 3.1   The atomic orbitals of H_2^+ at large internuclear distance. (Reprinted by permission from G. W. Wheland, *Resonance in Organic Chemistry*, John Wiley and Sons, New York, 1955, p. 57.)

protons are brought closer together and reach the equilibrium distance characteristic of the stable H_2^+ molecule ion, the electron does not belong uniquely to either one or the other of the protons but belongs equally to both. The resulting charge distribution can be represented by the closed surface of Fig. 3.2. The electron is now concentrated in the region between the nuclei, and the electrostatic interactions lead to attraction and hence to bond formation. The electron is said to be in the bonding MO. In MO parlance the electron is described by a certain wave function, ψ, which represents the orbit of the electron in the molecule and is therefore called a *molecular orbital*. In the neighborhood of one of the protons, A, the wave equation resembles the wave equation of the isolated hydrogen atom, so that the MO wave function ψ resembles the AO wave function ϕ_A. In the neighborhood of the other proton, B, the MO wave function resembles ϕ_B. Since the complete MO has characteristics separately possessed by ϕ_A and ϕ_B, it may be written as a linear combination of the AO's (LCAO); in the present example the wave function of the bonding and lowest-energy MO can be represented[2] as $\psi_b = \phi_A + \phi_B$, where ϕ_A and ϕ_B are the AO's of atoms A and B. The subscript b in ψ_b refers to bonding.

The bonding MO is not spherical like the atomic s orbital, but it does have cylindrical symmetry about the internuclear axis; when the MO possesses this kind of symmetry, it is called a σ (sigma) orbital because of its similarity to the symmetry of the s atomic orbital. The valence bond that is formed by the σ orbital is called a σ (or sigma) bond.

It was pointed out at the beginning of this chapter that molecular orbitals ψ, according to MO theory, are formed from the AO's of the constituent atoms without consideration of the electrons they have to accommodate. It follows therefore that the MO's for the hydrogen-molecule ion, H_2^+, and for the hydrogen molecule, H_2, are identical. Accordingly, the bonding MO of lowest energy for the hydrogen molecule will also be $\psi_b = \phi_A + \phi_B$. In the case of the hydrogen molecule, this orbital will be occupied by the maximum of two electrons (which are

[2] The sum of $\phi_A + \phi_B$ should be multiplied by a constant called the *normalization factor*; for simplicity this factor is omitted unless numerical calculations require its use.

paired, i.e., have opposite spin), but the wave function of this orbital is identical with the MO of the H_2^+ and hence is also described by Fig. 3.2.

Thus far, one MO, the lowest-energy or bonding MO, has been described. There is a second MO, which results from the combination of the two AO's. The necessity for a second MO can be accounted for on the following basis; if two AO's, each of which can accommodate a maximum of two electrons, (i.e., a total of four electrons) combine to form MO's, two MO's must result in order to accommodate the same maximum of four electrons. According to a principle of wave mechanics, the second orbital formed from ϕ_A and ϕ_B should be orthogonal to the first. This means that the product of the two MO's when integrated (i.e., summed) over all space should vanish (be equal to zero). This can be assured by choosing the first orbital so that, corresponding to each point in space for which the product $\psi_A\psi_B$ has a certain value, there is a corresponding point in space for which the product has an equal absolute value but is of opposite sign. A wave function which fulfills this condition relative to $\psi_b = \phi_A + \phi_B$ is $\psi_a = \phi_A - \phi_B$. The orbital described by $\phi_A - \phi_B$ is called the antibonding orbital, and the subscript a in ψ_a refers to antibonding. The orthogonality of the two wave functions is readily verified by multiplying them together: $(\phi_A + \phi_B) \times (\phi_A - \phi_B) = \phi_A{}^2 - \phi_B{}^2$. The integral over all space of the square of a wave function (which is, of course, the probability of finding the electron anywhere) is unity, and hence $\int(\phi_A{}^2 - \phi_B{}^2)\,d\tau = 0$. The antibonding MO for the hydrogen molecule is shown in Fig. 3.3.

Another way of representing graphically the molecular orbital ψ_b is shown in Fig. 3.4b, where the value of ψ_b is plotted along the internuclear axis A-B. This plot results from the addition of ϕ_A and ϕ_B, which are plotted separately in Fig. 3.4a. The plot of the antibonding orbital ψ_a along the internuclear axis is shown in Fig. 3.4c and results from subtraction of ϕ_B from ϕ_A. The ordinate values below the abscissa in $\phi_A - \phi_B$ represent minus values or the values in the negative lobe of the antibonding orbital in Fig. 3.3. Now the condition of orthogonality requires that the product of the two molecular orbitals ψ_a and ψ_b formed from the two atomic

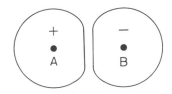

Fig. 3.2 The bonding molecular orbital of H_2^+ or H_2. (Reprinted by permission from G. W. Wheland, *Resonance in Organic Chemistry*, John Wiley and Sons, New York, 1955, p. 59.)

Fig. 3.3 The antibonding molecular orbital of H_2^+ or H_2.

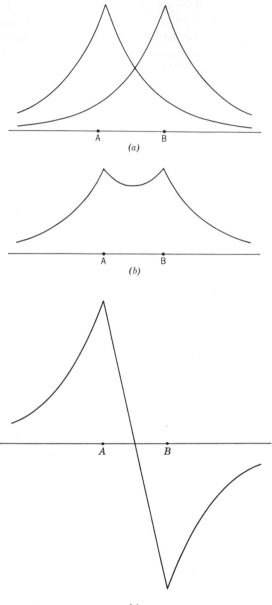

Fig. 3.4 Plots of values of orbitals along the internuclear axis: (a) ϕ_A and ϕ_B; (b) $\psi_b = \phi_A + \phi_B$; (c) $\psi_a = \phi_A - \phi_B$. (H. H. Jaffé in *Comprehensive Biochemistry*, Vol. I, edited by M. Florkin and E. Stotz, Elsevier Publishing Co., Amsterdam, 1961.)

orbitals ϕ_A and ϕ_B when integrated over all space be equal to zero.   The product $\psi_a\psi_b$ (obtained by multiplying values in Fig. 3.4b by those in Fig. 3.4c) has a form very similar to ψ_a and could also be represented schematically by Fig. 3.4c.   This plot shows that the area under the curve in the upper half (positive) is just equal to and hence cancels the area under the curve in the lower half, and accordingly the integral of the product is indeed zero as required by the orthogonality relationship of the two wave functions.

It is instructive to consider the two molecular orbitals ψ_a and ψ_b in more detail.   The wave functions for the hydrogen-molecule ion have been written $\psi_b = \phi_A + \phi_B$ and $\psi_a = \phi_A - \phi_B$.   Each of these functions should have been multiplied by a normalization factor, so that they would read $\psi_b = N_b(\phi_A + \phi_B)$ and $\psi_a = N_a(\phi_A - \phi_B)$. Absolute values for N_b and N_a may be found from the normalization equation (see footnote 2), which has the form

$$\int \psi_b{}^2 \, d\tau = 1$$

$$= N_b{}^2 \int (\phi_A + \phi_B)^2 \, d\tau$$

$$= N_b{}^2 \left[\int \phi_A{}^2 \, d\tau + \int \phi_B{}^2 \, d\tau + 2 \int \phi_A\phi_B \, d\tau \right] \tag{3.1}$$

Here, each of the first two integrals is equal to 1, since ϕ_A and ϕ_B are separately normalized.   The last integral, $\int \phi_A\phi_B \, d\tau$, is abbreviated S_{AB}, and is called the *overlap integral*; it represents the degree of overlap of the orbitals ϕ_A and ϕ_B, and extensive tabulations of such integrals exist.[3]   Accordingly, equation (3.1) becomes

$$N_b{}^2(1 + 1 + 2S) = 1$$

$$N_b = \frac{1}{\sqrt{2(1 + S)}}$$

$$\psi_b = \frac{1}{\sqrt{2(1 + S)}} (\phi_A + \phi_B)$$

Similarly, $\int \psi_a{}^2 \, d\tau = 1$, and hence

$$N_a{}^2 \int (\phi_A - \phi_B)^2 \, d\tau = N_a{}^2 \left[\int \phi_A{}^2 \, d\tau + \int \phi_B{}^2 \, d\tau - 2 \int \phi_A\phi_B \, d\tau \right]$$

$$= N_b{}^2(1 + 1 - 2S) = 1$$

$$N_a = \frac{1}{\sqrt{2(1 - S)}}$$

$$\psi_a = \frac{1}{\sqrt{2(1 - S)}} (\phi_A - \phi_B)$$

[3] R. S. Mulliken, C. A. Rieke, D. Orloff, and H. Orloff, *J. Chem. Phys.*, **17**, 1248 (1949);   H. H. Jaffé and G. O. Doak, *J. Chem. Phys.*, **21**, 196 (1953);   H. H. Jaffé, *J. Chem. Phys.*, **21**, 258 (1953);   D. P. Craig, A. Maccoll, R. S. Nyholm, L. E. Orgel, and L. Sutton, *J. Chem. Soc.*, 332 (1954);   J. L. Roberts and H. H. Jaffé, *J. Chem. Phys.*, **27**, 883 (1957).

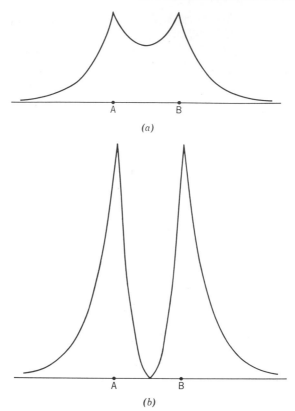

Fig. 3.5 The value of ψ^2 along the internuclear axis; (a) $\psi_b{}^2$; (b) $\psi_a{}^2$. (Reprinted by permission from H. H. Jaffé in *Comprehensive Biochemistry*, Vol. I, edited by M. Florkin and E. Stotz, Elsevier Publishing Co., Amsterdam, 1961.)

It is theoretically impossible to make actual physical measurements of the quantity ψ. On the other hand, ψ^2 or properties directly related to ψ^2 are amenable to physical measurement, and hence it is interesting to plot the value of ψ^2 along the internuclear axis for the bonding and antibonding MO's of the hydrogen molecule. Such plots are shown in Figs. 3.5a and b, and represent the probability of finding an electron, or, alternatively, the density of electrons, at any place along the internuclear axis.

Examination of Figs. 3.4b and 3.5a shows that the molecular orbital ψ_b corresponds to a concentration of electronic charge in the area between the nuclei and hence to especially high Coulombic attractive forces. These forces cause an electron in the orbital ψ_b to bond or hold the nuclei together, and therefore ψ_b is called the bonding MO. The orbital $\psi_a = \phi_A - \phi_B$, on the other hand, has a specially low charge density between the nuclei (Figs. 3.4c and 3.5b). On the average, electrons in ψ_a are farther from the nuclei than they would be in ϕ_A or ϕ_B (isolated atoms), and hence the atoms would be in an energetically more favorable condition if they were far separated; consequently $\psi_a = \phi_A - \phi_B$ is called the antibonding orbital. The potential-energy diagrams corresponding to the bonding and antibonding orbitals, and thus to the bonding and antibonding states of H_2^+, may be represented by Fig. 3.6. Here the potential energy is plotted against internuclear distance. The left curve representing the bonding orbital has a minimum which corresponds to the equilibrium bonding distance of the two atoms. At distances greater than this, bonding is less, and at distances smaller than that corresponding to the minimum energy, repulsions of the two nuclei become important and the energy rises steeply. The right curve represents the $\phi_A - \phi_B$ orbital and is called a *repulsive state.*

The antibonding orbital, Figs. 3.3 and 3.4c, has cylindrical symmetry relative to the bond axis, just as the bonding orbital does. Accordingly, the antibonding orbital is also a σ orbital; however, to indicate its antibonding character, an asterisk is frequently added and ψ_a is designated σ^* (sigma starred). Since ψ_a changes sign between the nuclei, it must vanish (go through a value of zero) somewhere between the two atoms; because

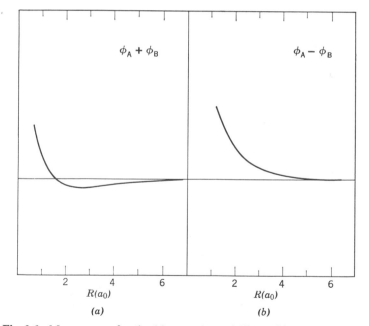

Fig. 3.6   Morse curves for the (a) attractive and (b) repulsive states of H_2^+.

the two atoms are indistinguishable, this must occur on the plane defined by all the points equidistant from both nuclei. Such a plane, in which the probability of finding an electron is zero, is called a *nodal plane*.

Since atoms A and B in the hydrogen molecule (or H_2^+) are equivalent, it follows that the molecule and hence the charge distribution must have a center of symmetry (see Chapter 4). Accordingly, every *observable* property of the hydrogen molecule must be symmetric with respect to this center; this includes the square of the wave function, ψ^2, although it does not apply to the wave function ψ itself. The restriction that its square must be symmetric implies that ψ itself can only be symmetric or antisymmetric with respect to the center and cannot be unsymmetric.[4]

Functions which do not change sign when reflected from a center are called *gerade* (German for even) or *g*, and functions that do change sign are called *ungerade* (German for odd) or *u*. Inspection of Fig. 3.2 shows that ψ_b is gerade and hence called σ_g, and Fig. 3.3 shows that ψ_a is ungerade, σ_u^*.

One of the difficulties that puzzle persons unfamiliar with quantum mechanics is to understand the physical significance of the nodal plane or nodal surface, as in an atomic p orbital or an antibonding MO. Thus the question is frequently asked, How does the electron get past the nodal plane; i.e., how can the electron in one lobe of the orbital in Fig. 3.3 get into the other lobe? The answer is that it is a fallacy to look at an orbital as an orbit describing the physical motion of an electron. Following the uncertainty principle, the only information available is a probability distribution of the electronic charge. The existence of a nodal plane indicates the presence of a plane at which the charge density vanishes. No simple physical picture of this situation exists, since all of our physical pictures are based on classical mechanics, which breaks down in the case of the description of an electron.

3.2 Energies of Molecular Orbitals

Application of the Aufbau principle (i.e., the assignment of electrons into MO's) requires a knowledge of the various energies of the MO's so that assignments may be made into orbitals of lower energy before those of higher energy become occupied. Furthermore, in spectroscopy we are generally interested in the differences between the energies of the various orbitals, since these differences determine the wavelength of light absorbed

---

[4] A function is *symmetric* with respect to a symmetry operation if, upon application of the symmetry operation, it remains unchanged; it is *antisymmetric* if its absolute value remains unchanged but the function changes sign; it is *unsymmetric* if its absolute value changes upon application of the symmetry operation. For a more detailed discussion of symmetry operations, see Chapter 4.

or emitted. Hence it is important to be able to calculate these energy differences as accurately as possible.

In the case of the hydrogen molecule, where ϕ_A and ϕ_B are equal, the approximate energies of ψ_b and ψ_a are given by:

$$\epsilon_b = \alpha + \beta \quad \text{and} \quad \epsilon_a = \alpha - \beta \qquad (3.2)$$

where α is the Coulomb integral, and β the resonance integral. The Coulomb integral represents approximately the energy required to remove an electron from an orbital on the isolated hydrogen atom. The resonance integral represents the degree of interaction of the orbitals ϕ_A and ϕ_B in the hydrogen molecule. Since these two orbitals are identical and overlap strongly, we may expect this interaction to be relatively large and the resonance integral to be large.

The above formulas [equation (3.2)] can be developed as follows. To calculate the energy required to remove an electron from a molecular orbital ψ, or, as is generally said for short, to calculate the energy ε of ψ, reference must be made to the wave equation,

$$H\psi = \varepsilon\psi \qquad (3.3)$$

where H is the Hamiltonian operator, a mathematical quantity the exact form of which does not need to be specified in detail at this point. If ψ were the exact wave function, equation (3.3) would be an identity, and ε could be evaluated by substituting the value of ψ at any point. But since the ψ's of the preceding section are only approximate, equation (3.3) is an approximation, and the best value of ε is obtained by averaging over all space. According to a well-known principle of quantum mechanics, such an average is obtained by multiplying both sides of equation (3.3) by ψ, and integrating over all space:

$$\int \psi H\psi \, d\tau = \int \psi \varepsilon \psi \, d\tau = \varepsilon \int \psi^2 \, d\tau = \varepsilon \qquad (3.4)$$

Here the second equality follows, since ε is a constant average, independent of the coordinates of integration; and the third equality is valid, since $\int \psi^2 \, d\tau$ is the normalization integral and hence $= 1$ because the ψ's are supposed to have been normalized. Substituting the MO $\psi_b = N_b(\phi_A + \phi_B)$, where N_b is the normalization factor, into equation (3.3) and calling the associated energy ε_b gives

$$\varepsilon_b = N_b^2 \int (\phi_A + \phi_B) H(\phi_A + \phi_B) \, d\tau$$

$$= N_b^2 \int \phi_A H\phi_A \, d\tau + N_b^2 \int \phi_B H\phi_B \, d\tau + 2N_b^2 \int \phi_A H\phi_B \, d\tau \qquad (3.5)$$

The first two of these integrals are numerically equal, since ϕ_A and ϕ_B are identical orbitals, and are abbreviated as α; they are the *Coulomb integrals* and represent approximately the energy required to remove an electron from an atomic orbital ϕ_A on an isolated atom. The last integral in equation (3.5) is usually abbreviated by the

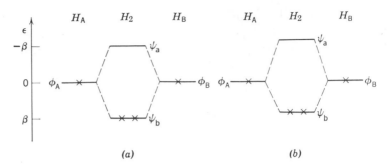

Fig. 3.7 The energy levels in the H_2 molecule, (a) assuming $S_{AB} = 0$ [equation (3.2)]; (b) assuming $S_{AB} \neq 0$ [equation (3.7)].

symbol β and is called the *resonance integral*. With these symbols and the value for N_b, derived on p. 39, equation (3.5) becomes

$$\varepsilon_b = \frac{1}{2(1 + S)}(2\alpha + 2\beta)$$

$$= \frac{\alpha + \beta}{1 + S} = \frac{\alpha + \alpha S + \beta - \alpha S}{(1 + S)}$$

$$= \alpha + \frac{\beta - \alpha S}{1 + S} \tag{3.6}$$

Similarly, for $\psi_a = N_a(\phi_A - \phi_B)$,

$$\varepsilon_a = \alpha - \frac{\beta - \alpha S}{1 - S} \tag{3.7}$$

One further very common approximation is to neglect the overlap integral S; then the final equations for the energies are those in equation (3.2).

The energy levels resulting from these calculations are shown in Fig. 3.7; Fig. 3.7a represents the approximation $S_{AB} = 0$. This figure shows that the molecular orbitals ψ_b and ψ_a are above and below ϕ_A and ϕ_B by equal amounts with ε increasing upward; ε_b is the lowest energy because β is a negative quantity. The simple relation between ε_b and ε_a disappears when

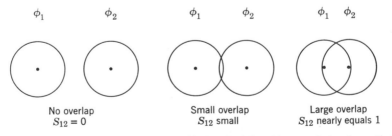

Fig. 3.8 The overlap of two identical orbitals. (Reprinted by permission from C. A. Coulson, *Valence*, Oxford University Press, 1952, p. 60.)

S is not neglected (cf. Fig. 3.7b), since equations (3.6) and (3.7) show that, when S is positive as it normally is, ε_a is higher above α than ε_b is lower below it. For a better picture of the significance of the overlap integral, the overlap possibilities are shown in Fig. 3.8.

3.3   The Electronic Configuration of the Hydrogen-Molecule Ion, H_2^+, and the Hydrogen Molecule, H_2, and Their States

Now that the procedures for constructing MO's have been considered and the calculations of the energy levels of the various MO's have been illustrated, the electronic structures of simple molecules will be described. In the ground state, the electrons will occupy the orbitals of lowest energy; excitation (for example, by ultraviolet light of appropriate wavelength) will promote an electron from the occupied MO of highest energy to the unoccupied level of lowest energy. Such a transition would occur with the least energy (longest-wavelength radiation). It is apparent that the MO's of both states need to be described in order to understand spectra.

In accordance with the Aufbau principle, in the ground state of H_2^+ the single electron in the system is placed in the MO of lowest energy, i.e., the orbital ψ_b formed from the combination of the 1s atomic orbitals of the two hydrogen atoms. The electronic structure of the ground state of H_2^+ is described as σ_g(1s) and is shown in Fig. 3.2. The σ_g describes the MO, and (1s) describes the AO's which combined to form the MO. In the lowest-energy excited state, the electron is placed into the excited MO of lowest energy, which is the orbital $\psi_a[\sigma_u{}^*(1s)]$, also formed from the 1s orbitals of the hydrogen atoms. This orbital is shown in Fig. 3.3. Higher-energy MO's are of course possible, as, for example, the MO's σ_g(2s) and $\sigma_u{}^*$(2s) formed from 2s orbitals. These excited states, which frequently interest physicists and astronomers, are of only minor concern to chemists. The energies of the various MO's in increasing order of magnitude are probably

$$\sigma 1s < \sigma^*1s < \sigma 2s < \sigma^*2s < \sigma 2p < \pi_y 2p$$

$$= \pi_x 2p < \pi_y{}^*2p = \pi_x{}^*2p < \sigma^*2p$$

In the hydrogen molecule there are two valence electrons; again using the Aufbau principle, these two electrons are accommodated in the lowest MO, ψ_b (Fig. 3.2), leading to the configuration $\sigma_g{}^2$(1s). Here the superscript 2 indicates that the σ_g(1s) orbital contains two electrons. According to the Pauli exclusion principle, the electrons must have opposed or antiparallel spins; i.e., they are paired. This is a description of the ground state of the hydrogen molecule. When the electrons are paired, the state is called a *singlet state*.

The notation used here merits a little closer scrutiny. What is actually desired is an expression for the total wave function, Ψ, of the hydrogen molecule, which, at fixed internuclear distance, is a function of the coordinates (x, y, and z, or r, θ, and φ) of each of the electrons. In the approximation used here, this function is expressed as a product of individual, so-called one-electron functions ψ, each of which is a function of the coordinates of one electron only. Thus:

$$\Psi(r_1, \theta_1, \varphi_1, r_2, \theta_2, \varphi_2) = \psi_1(r_1, \theta_1, \varphi_1)\psi_2(r_2, \theta_2, \varphi_2)$$

In the case under discussion (the hydrogen molecule), ψ_1 and ψ_2 are both $\sigma_g(1s)$, and hence the symbol $\sigma_g{}^2(1s)$ really closely approaches the meaning of a squaring process: $\sigma_g{}^2(1s)$ means that Ψ is a product of two terms, both of which are the $\sigma_g(1s)$ function, *but* they are functions of the coordinates of different electrons.

This type of notation has been encountered previously, when sp³ was written to characterize an atomic configuration, the wave function Φ of which is a product of one s and three p functions.

To form excited states of hydrogen, one or both electrons are promoted to higher-lying MO's. In the first excited state, one electron is promoted from the ψ_b to the ψ_a orbital. The electronic configuration of this state may be indicated by $\sigma_g(1s)\sigma_u{}^*(1s)$. Since now the electrons are in different orbitals, the Pauli exclusion principle produces no restriction, and the spins of the two electrons may be parallel or antiparallel. If the spins are antiparallel (i.e., the electrons are paired), the state is again a singlet, as in the case of the ground state, where both electrons are in the ψ_b orbital. If, however, the spins of the two electrons are parallel, three states are possible. The z component of the clockwise or counterclockwise spin of an electron[5] may have a value of $+\frac{1}{2}$ or $-\frac{1}{2}$, so that the z components of the spins of the two electrons both may be $+\frac{1}{2}$, or both may be $-\frac{1}{2}$, or one may be $+\frac{1}{2}$ and the other $-\frac{1}{2}$. The z components of the resulting angular momentum due to spin may then have the values $+1$, -1, or 0. There are thus three possible states; they all have the same energy (in the absence of an applied magnetic field) and are jointly called a *triplet state*.

The relationship between configuration and states perhaps requires additional elaboration and clarification. Just as a single configuration of an atom can lead to several states (cf. p. 28), so a single electronic configuration of a molecule can lead to several observable states. To examine this possibility, it is necessary to write the total wave function in more detail. Omitting the symbol 1s after σ as unnecessary, we can write for the orbital function $\sigma_g(1)\sigma_u{}^*(2)$, where the numerals in parentheses refer to electrons #1 and #2. But unfortunately it is impossible to tag electrons, and hence we cannot specify which electron belongs to the orbital σ_g and which to $\sigma_u{}^*$. Therefore it is necessary to write each wave function so that every observable quantity is independent of the way in which the two electrons are assigned to the two orbitals. Since the

[5] The z component of the spin is the projection of the spin angular momentum, which, like all angular momenta, is a vector quantity, on the z axis; the z axis is customarily considered fixed by the application of a homogeneous magnetic field, which has lines of force parallel to the z axis.

observable quantities always depend on the square of the wave function, the function itself must be either symmetric or antisymmetric in the coordinates of the two electrons; i.e., exchanging the two electrons must either leave the function exactly as it was, or leave it as it was except for a change in sign. Corresponding to the configuration $\sigma_g\sigma_u^*$, there are two such functions:

$$\sigma_g(1)\sigma_u^*(2) + \sigma_g(2)\sigma_u^*(1), \quad \text{and} \quad \sigma_g(1)\sigma_u^*(2) - \sigma_g(2)\sigma_u^*(1)$$

The first of these is symmetric, the second antisymmetric, in exchange of the electrons, as can readily be verified by exchanging the numerals (1) and (2).[6] Thus, for example, if the numerals were changed in the second expression, the result would be $\sigma_g(2)\sigma_u^*(1) - \sigma_g(1)\sigma_u^*(2)$, which is equivalent to the result obtained by multiplying the original by -1; hence this function is said to be antisymmetric in exchange of electrons.

However, the given orbital functions still must be multiplied by spin functions. If the spins in the two directions are denoted by the spin functions α and β, respectively, then the possible spin functions of the molecules are

$$\alpha(1)\alpha(2); \quad \beta(1)\beta(2); \quad \alpha(1)\beta(2); \quad \beta(1)\alpha(2)$$

Each of the functions α and β is supposed to be normalized, and the functions are orthogonal to each other. The first two combinations are already symmetric in the electrons. The last two can be combined in two ways:[7]

$$\alpha(1)\beta(2) + \alpha(2)\beta(1); \quad \alpha(1)\beta(2) - \alpha(2)\beta(1)$$

of which the first is symmetric, the second antisymmetric, with respect to exchange of electrons. Each of the four spin functions can then be multiplied by each of the two orbital functions. As can be readily verified, this leads to eight functions, of which four are symmetric and four antisymmetric in exchange of electrons. Now, it can be shown that there is no possible interaction between systems the wave functions of which are symmetric and systems the wave functions of which are antisymmetric with respect to exchange in any pair of elementary particles; and hence, in a world in which one type of symmetry holds, systems of the other type cannot be observed even if they were present. In the universe known to man all wave functions are antisymmetric with

[6] Actually, both these functions should be multiplied by a normalizing factor $(2)^{-\frac{1}{2}}$, which can be seen by evaluating the normalization integrals:

$$\tfrac{1}{2}\iint [\sigma_g^2(1)\sigma_u^{*2}(2) + \sigma_g(2)\sigma_u^*(1)]^2 \, d\tau_1 \, d\tau_2 = 1$$

$$\tfrac{1}{2}\left[\int \sigma_g^2(1)\,d\tau_1\int \sigma_u^{*2}(2)\,d\tau_2 + \int \sigma_g^2(2)\,d\tau_2\int \sigma_u^{*2}(1)\,d\tau_1 \right.$$
$$\left. \pm 2\int \sigma_g(1)\sigma_u^*(1)\,d\tau_1\int \sigma_g(2)\sigma_u^*(2)\,d\tau_2 \right] = 1$$

Here, $d\tau_1$ and $d\tau_2$ are the elements of volume in the coordinates of electrons #1 and #2, respectively, and the integrals can be separated because each function depends on the coordinates of only a single electron. But the first four integrals are normalization integrals, and hence equal to 1; the last two orthogonality integrals, and hence equal to 0. Therefore the equation given is an identity.

[7] Again, these should be multiplied by a normalizing factor $(2)^{-\frac{1}{2}}$, as can be shown exactly in footnote 6.

respect to exchange of elementary particles; this statement is equivalent to the Pauli principle. Accordingly, only the four antisymmetric combinations are possible; these are

$$\psi_1 = [\sigma_g(1)\sigma_u{}^*(2) + \sigma_g(2)\sigma_u{}^*(1)][\alpha(1)\beta(2) - \alpha(2)\beta(1)]$$

$$\psi_2 = [\sigma_g(1)\sigma_u{}^*(2) - \sigma_g(2)\sigma_u{}^*(1)]\alpha(1)\alpha(2)$$

$$\psi_3 = [\sigma_g(1)\sigma_u{}^*(2) - \sigma_g(2)\sigma_u{}^*(1)]\beta(1)\beta(2)$$

$$\psi_4 = [\sigma_g(1)\sigma_u{}^*(2) - \sigma_g(2)\sigma_u{}^*(1)][\alpha(1)\beta(2) + \alpha(2)\beta(1)]$$

ψ_1 has an orbital part symmetric and a spin part antisymmetric in exchange of electrons, ψ_2, ψ_3, and ψ_4 have the opposite type of symmetry. In the absence of a magnetic field ψ_2 to ψ_4 have equal energy (are degenerate) but different energy from ψ_1. Since ψ_2 to ψ_4 are degenerate, they belong to one state; and, since there are three such functions, the state is called a *triplet*. ψ_1, on the other hand, alone represents another state called a *singlet*. It is obvious that the spin functions of ψ_2 and ψ_3 represent parallel spins of the two electrons; that the same is true for ψ_4 is not obvious and must be taken on faith. ψ_1, on the other hand, corresponds to antiparallel spins of the two electrons.

In the $H_2{}^+$ ion, there is no problem of exchange of electrons; however, the orbital function, be it σ_g or $\sigma_u{}^*$, can be multiplied by either of the two spin functions α and β. Hence, in the absence of a magnetic field, there are always two degenerate wave functions for each state; accordingly these states are called *doublets*.

A further excited state of H_2 arises if both electrons are in the molecular orbital ψ_a, giving the configuration $[\sigma_u{}^*(1s)]^2$; this again is a singlet, since the two spins must be antiparallel. Further excited states can, of course, be formed by use of higher-lying AO's but are again unimportant because their energy is very high. Further discussions of electronic states arising from various configurations will be postponed to Chapter 5.

3.4 Molecular-Orbital Descriptions of Other Homonuclear Diatomic Molecules[8]

DILITHIUM, Li_2. The simplest stable diatomic molecule after H_2 is Li_2. The formation of the MO's from the AO's of two lithium atoms is shown in Fig. 3.9, where the ordinate is an arbitrary energy scale and the horizontal lines represent relative energy levels, the lowest levels representing the most stable or lowest-energy orbitals. Each lithium atom has three electrons, two in the 1s and one in the 2s orbital. The two 1s orbitals combine to form two MO's, the $\sigma_g(1s)$ and the $\sigma_u{}^*(1s)$, and both are doubly occupied. As a first approximation, it can be assumed that the splitting of the MO's is equal; i.e., the energy of the bonding MO, σ_g, is as much below the atomic 1s as the energy of the antibonding MO, $\sigma_u{}^*$, is above it. This approximation is equivalent to saying that the overlap is neglected or the overlap integral is zero, i.e., $S_{AB} = 0$. Accordingly, no stabilization arises out of the combination of 1s orbitals into bonding and

[8] An extensive tabulation of more detailed calculations of diatomic molecules is given by L. C. Allen and A. M. Karo, *Rev. Mod. Phys.*, **32**, 275 (1960).

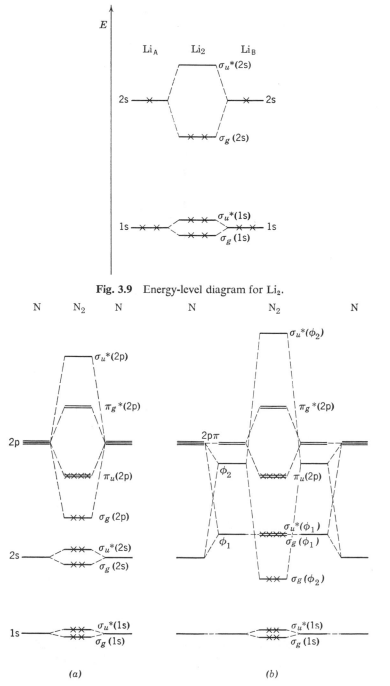

Fig. 3.9 Energy-level diagram for Li_2.

Fig. 3.10 Energy-level diagram of N_2: (*a*) no hybridization; (*b*) sp hybridized.

antibonding orbitals; and, as far as interaction of the K shells is concerned, the molecule is no more stable than the isolated atoms. Similarly the two 2s AO's combine to form an MO, $\sigma_g(2s)$. It is customary to write the Li_2 structure as $K_A K_B \sigma_g{}^2(2s)$, where K_A and K_B refer to the 1s electrons of each of the lithium atoms, respectively. If the assumption $S_{AB} = 0$ is not made for the K shell, it is found that the antibonding electrons destabilize more than the bonding electrons stabilize, and this excess repulsion is often referred to as inner-shell repulsion. The abbreviated notation for the electronic configuration of the molecule is still retained. The spatial extension of the 1s orbitals is small; hence S_{AB} is small, as is the resonance integral, β, and the inner-shell repulsion is not very important. All the bonding energy in the Li_2 molecule comes from the $\sigma_g(2s)$ molecular orbital.

THE NITROGEN MOLECULE. The formation of the MO's of the N_2 molecule from the nitrogen atoms in terms of energy levels is shown in Fig. 3.10. Attention should first be focused on Fig. 3.10a. The problem is to combine the seven electrons (two 1s, two 2s, and three 2p) of each nitrogen atom into MO's and to place the fourteen electrons of the N_2 molecule in MO's of lowest energy in accordance with the Aufbau and Pauli principles. As in the Li_2 molecule, the four electrons of the 1s orbitals are placed in $\sigma_g(1s)$ and $\sigma_u{}^*(1s)$, and these MO's are of little concern, since they are involved neither in chemical properties nor in the commonly observed spectroscopic states. Next to be considered is the 2s orbital of each atom, whose combination (assuming no hybridization as in Fig. 3.10a) results in two MO's, $\sigma_g(2s)$ and $\sigma_u{}^*(2s)$, into each of which two electrons are placed, thus accounting for four more of the electrons and leaving six to be accommodated. The wave functions of the MO's from the 2s orbitals may be written:

$$\psi_1 = 2s_A + 2s_B = \sigma_g(2s)$$

$$\psi_2 = 2s_A - 2s_B = \sigma_u{}^*(2s)$$

The contours of ψ_1 and ψ_2 are shown in Figs. 3.11a and b. The next MO to be filled is the one formed from the single 2p orbital of each atom which has cylindrical symmetry around the bond axis (this can arbitrarily be chosen as the z axis). This MO is called $\sigma_g(2p)$, since it has cylindrical symmetry around the bond axis. The wave function may be written:

$$\psi_3 = 2p_A\sigma + 2p_B\sigma = \sigma_g(2p)$$

The contour of ψ_3 is shown in Fig. 3.11c. The atomic p orbital used for the formation of this MO is one of three degenerate (equal-energy) p atomic orbitals in the isolated atom. As another atom is brought into the force

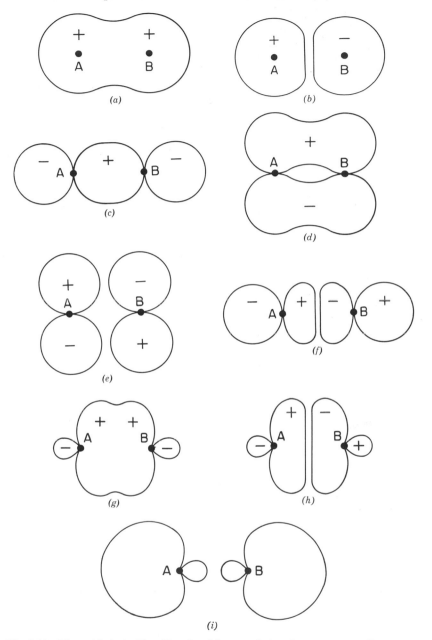

Fig. 3.11 The orbitals in N_2. (Reprinted by permission from H. H. Jaffé in *Comprehensive Biochemistry*, Vol. I, edited by M. Florkin and E. Stotz, Elsevier Publishing Co., Amsterdam, 1961.)

field of the first atom, this degeneracy splits, and the p orbital to be used for σ-bond formation goes to a higher level than the remaining pair, which are also raised but to a lesser extent and remain degenerate. The pσ level is higher because of repulsion by the electrons of the second atom.[9] However, when the atoms are within bonding distance, the pσ electrons overlap effectively in the bonding MO, leading to a lower-energy MO, ψ_3, than the MO's formed from the other p electrons. With the filling of $\sigma_g(2p)$, only four electrons remain to be placed. The next two MO's are degenerate. They result from the combination of pπ electrons in the two atoms; and, since the pπ atomic orbitals occur as degenerate pairs (i.e., $2p_y$ and $2p_x$ have the same energy), the molecular π orbitals also occur as degenerate pairs. The wave functions of the π MO's are identical and can be written:

$$\pi_{4,5} = 2p_A\pi + 2p_B\pi = \pi_u(2p)$$

The contour of one of these wave functions is shown in Fig. 3.11d. Examination of this figure shows that ψ_4 (and ψ_5), the bonding MO's, are ungerade, since reflection at the center of symmetry changes the sign; this is true in general of the lowest bonding π orbital. The bond axis lies in the nodal plane of the orbitals, which can be thought of as "sausages" lying above and below, and in front of and in back of, the bond axis.

The combination of the two degenerate pπ orbitals of each atom leads to four MO's. The bonding MO's, ψ_4 and ψ_5, called $\pi_u(2p)$, have been described. The corresponding antibonding MO's from this combination are also degenerate and are called $\pi_g*(2p)$. The wave functions of these orbitals are $\psi_{6,7} = 2p_A\pi - 2p_B\pi = \pi_g*(2p)$, and the contour of ψ_6 is shown in Fig. 3.11e. The gerade character of this antibonding MO is obvious. In the ground state $\psi_{6,7}$ are not occupied, since the fourteen electrons have already been accommodated in MO's of lower energy. The antibonding MO resulting from the combination of the pσ electrons is denoted as $\sigma_u*(2p)$, and $\psi_8 = 2p_A\sigma - 2p_B\sigma = \sigma_u*(2p)$. The contour of this wave function is shown in Fig. 3.11f. The electronic structure of N_2 (if hybridization is neglected) is denoted by $K_A K_B \sigma_g^2(2s)\sigma_u*^2(2s)\sigma_g^2(2p)\pi_u^4(2p)$.

In considering the AO's of each atom and their combination into MO's, only the equivalent AO's of the two nitrogen atoms were combined. Although the 2s and $2p_z$ electrons do not have the same symmetry properties with respect to each nitrogen atom, they do have the same symmetry properties with respect to the N_2 molecule, which is of course less symmetrical (i.e., contains fewer symmetry elements; see Chapter 4) than the atom. It is thus possible to hybridize or mix the 2s and 2p orbitals and

---

[9] This may be considered as the simplest example of what is often called a *ligand-field* (or a *crystal-field*) *effect*.

to replace them by two hybrid orbitals given by some linear combinations
of the two:

$$\phi_1 = \lambda 2s + 2p\sigma \quad \text{and} \quad \phi_2 = 2s - \lambda 2p\sigma$$

where λ is a weighting factor. This weighting factor would be unnecessary
if the hybrid orbitals were made of equal parts of s and p, but one orbital
has more s than p character, and the other less. The new MO's are now:

$$\psi_1 = \phi_{1A} + \phi_{1B} = \sigma_g(\phi_1)$$
$$\psi_2 = \phi_{1A} - \phi_{1B} = \sigma_u{}^*(\phi_1)$$
$$\psi_3 = \phi_{2A} + \phi_{2B} = \sigma_g(\phi_2)$$
$$\psi_8 = \phi_{2A} - \phi_{2B} = \sigma_u{}^*(\phi_2)$$

The relative energies of the new MO's are shown schematically in Fig.
3.10b. The energetics of the hybridization process are of interest. If the
2s and 2pσ orbitals were each doubly occupied, hybridization to ϕ_1 and ϕ_2
would involve no change in energy. However, 2s is doubly occupied
whereas 2pσ has only a single electron. Hybridization to a doubly
occupied ϕ_1 and a singly occupied ϕ_2 involves promotion of a fraction of an
electron (determined by λ) from a 2s to a 2p atomic orbital. This promotion
from one AO to another is energetically expensive (cf. Chapter 2). The
energy expended, however, is more than compensated for by two factors:
(1) increased binding energy due to $\sigma_g(\phi_2)$, for which the overlap integral
and the resonance integral are much larger than for $\sigma_g(2p)$; i.e., the
hybridized orbitals overlap much better than unhybridized orbitals, or, in
the words of Mulliken, "a little hybridization goes a long way"; and
(2) greatly reduced repulsion of ϕ_1 electrons. The reduced repulsion arises
out of the fact that S and β for the ϕ_1 orbitals are much smaller than for
the unhybridized 2s orbitals, which means that the excess of antibonding
by $\sigma_u{}^*(\phi_1)$ over bonding by $\sigma_g(\phi_1)$ (where the approximation $S = 0$ is not
made) is much smaller than the same excess for $\sigma_u{}^*(2s)$ and $\sigma_g(2s)$. The
orbitals ϕ_1 and ϕ_2 are similar to sp orbitals of the carbon atoms that
combine to form acetylene (Fig. 3.17). The orbitals ϕ_{2A} and ϕ_{2B} overlap
to form the strong σ bond shown in Fig. 3.11g. The corresponding
antibonding hybrid MO, $\sigma_u{}^*$, which is ψ_8, is shown in Fig. 3.11h. The
orbitals ϕ_{1A} and ϕ_{1B} barely overlap; they have their small negative lobes
between the two atoms and their large positive lobes directed away from
the bond. These two orbitals, shown in Fig. 3.11i, which correspond to ψ_1
and ψ_2 in the unhybridized case, have almost the same energy. They are
nonbonding orbitals and contain the lone-pair electrons. The electronic
structure of N_2 then is

$$K_A K_B \sigma_g{}^2(\phi_1)\sigma_u{}^{*2}(\phi_1)\sigma_g{}^2(\phi_2)\pi_u{}^4(2p)$$

or, again abbreviated,

$$K_A K_B \phi_{1A}{}^2 \phi_{1B}{}^2 \sigma_g{}^2 (\phi_2) \pi_u{}^4 (2p)$$

In the N_2 molecule there is thus one doubly occupied bonding σ orbital and two doubly occupied bonding π orbitals, each representing a bond and giving the well-known triply bonded electronic structure $:N \equiv N:$. The electron distribution of the four π electrons in the two π orbitals represents a distribution of charge cylindrically symmetrical about the N-N axis.

THE OXYGEN AND FLUORINE MOLECULES. The energy diagrams of Fig. 3.10 were derived only by consideration of the interaction of the AO's of two nuclei for which we needed to consider the K and L shells, and without any reference to the number of electrons they would eventually have to accommodate. They can, therefore, be used immediately to derive the electronic structure of O_2 and F_2. In O_2, two more electrons must be added. According to the Aufbau principle, they should go into ψ_6 and $\psi_7 [\pi_g*(2p)]$; and, since these are degenerate, Hund's rule indicates that one electron should be assigned to each, with parallel spins. Accordingly, the electronic structure of O_2 is $K_A K_B \phi_{1A}{}^2 \phi_{1B}{}^2 \sigma_g{}^2 (\phi_2) \pi_u{}^4 (2p) \pi_g{}^{*2}(2p)$, and since the last two electrons have equal spin, the ground state of O_2 should be a triplet, as it actually is. The two electrons in $\pi_g*(2p)$ are antibonding. There are thus six electrons in bonding and two electrons in antibonding orbitals, leaving a net of four bonding electrons, i.e., a "double bond."

Addition of two more electrons leads to the structure

$$K_A K_B \phi_{1A}{}^2 \phi_{1B}{}^2 \sigma_g{}^2 (\phi_2) \pi_u{}^4 (2p) \pi_g{}^{*4}(sp)$$

of F_2. Here, the bonding character of $\pi_u{}^4$ is essentially balanced by the antibonding character of $\pi_g{}^{*4}$, except for closed-shell repulsion, and these orbitals may formally be replaced by $2p\pi_A{}^4 2p\pi_B{}^4$, leading to the single bond in F_2 $[\sigma_g{}^2 (\phi_2)]$ and to the three lone pairs in each F $(\phi_1{}^2 2p\pi^4)$ and the familiar structure $: \overset{..}{\underset{..}{F}} : \overset{..}{\underset{..}{F}} :$.

3.5   The Molecular-Orbital Description of Heteronuclear Diatomic Molecules, LiH and CO

Heteronuclear diatomic molecules are a little more difficult to handle. Here the symmetry requirements are much less and do not so readily determine the molecular orbitals. In LiH, for example, the bonding MO, ψ_b will be a combination of the 1s orbital of H and the 2s orbital of Li (although some hybridization with 1s and 2pσ orbitals should really be considered). Hydrogen is more electronegative than lithium, however, and hence the electron density near H should exceed that near Li. Thus the bonding orbital becomes[10] $\sigma = N_b (\lambda_b 1s_H + 2s_{Li})$, and ψ_a, the antibonding

---

[10] Since the molecule has no center of symmetry, no g, u classification is possible.

orbital, becomes $\sigma^* = N_a(1s_H - \lambda_a2s_{Li})$, where λ_a and λ_b are two constants, both larger than 1, the values of which are so far unknown, and N_a and N_b are the usual normalization factors.

In the evaluation of λ_a and λ_b, use is made of the variational principle. This principle states that the energy value obtained from the true wave function is lower than that obtained from any approximate wave function, provided the complete Hamiltonian operator is used in the evaluation of the energy.[11] Consequently, it is necessary to find only the value of λ_b for which ε_b is a minimum, and this value of ε_b is the best energy value obtainable with a wave function of the form given. It is then generally assumed, although not necessarily true, that the function so obtained is the best wave function of that form. The application of standard methods of calculus gives two equations:

$$(\alpha_H - \varepsilon)N\lambda + (\beta - \varepsilon S)N = 0$$
$$(\beta - \varepsilon S)N\lambda - (\alpha_{Li} - \varepsilon)N = 0$$

These equations, called the secular equations, have solutions for λ and ε only when the determinant of the coefficients, the so-called secular determinant, vanishes:

$$\begin{vmatrix} (\alpha_H - \varepsilon) & (\beta - \varepsilon S) \\ (\beta - \varepsilon S) & (\alpha_{Li} - \varepsilon) \end{vmatrix} = 0$$

Expansion of this determinant gives

$$(\alpha_H - \varepsilon)(\alpha_{Li} - \varepsilon) - (\beta - \varepsilon S)^2 = 0$$
$$\varepsilon^2(1 - S^2) - \varepsilon(\alpha_H + \alpha_{Li} - 2\beta S) + \alpha_H\alpha_{Li} - \beta^2 = 0$$

$$\varepsilon = \frac{1}{2(1 - S^2)} \{\alpha_H + \alpha_{Li} - 2\beta S \pm [(\alpha_H + \alpha_{Li} - 2\beta S)^2 - 4(1 - S^2)(\alpha_H\alpha_{Li} - \beta^2)]^{\frac{1}{2}}\}$$

Using the common approximation $S = 0$,

$$\varepsilon = \tfrac{1}{2}\{\alpha_H + \alpha_{Li} \pm \sqrt{(\alpha_H + \alpha_{Li})^2 - 4(\alpha_H\alpha_{Li} - \beta^2)}\}$$
$$= \tfrac{1}{2}\{\alpha_H + \alpha_{Li} \pm \sqrt{(\alpha_H - \alpha_{Li})^2 + 4\beta^2}\}$$

When $\alpha_H - \alpha_{Li}$ is small compared to 2β, which is one condition of effective interaction of orbitals, this becomes approximately

$$\varepsilon \approx \tfrac{1}{2}\{\alpha_H + \alpha_{Li} \pm (2\beta + \alpha_H - \alpha_{Li})\}$$

and hence

$$\varepsilon_b \approx \alpha_H + \beta \quad \text{and} \quad \varepsilon_a \approx \alpha_{Li} - \beta$$

It is seen that this method gives two values of the energy. One of these corresponds to ψ_b, the other to an orbital orthogonal to ψ_b and hence identifiable with ψ_a. Substitution of these values of ε, one at a time, into the secular equations, then, permits solution for ψ_b and ψ_a, and finally the N are found by normalization.

The value of λ so obtained estimates the distribution of the charge between the two atoms involved in the bond, and hence permits evaluation of the dipole moment. Alternatively, λ is often estimated from experimental

---

[11] This statement is proved in Appendix 2, where the mathematics involved in its application is outlined.

dipole moments. The energies of ψ_b and ψ_a are shown schematically in Fig. 3.12. It should particularly be noted that, in the approximation used, the bonding orbital is stabilized by the resonance integral β with respect to the AO of the hydrogen atom, while the antibonding orbital is destabilized by an equal amount with respect to the AO of lithium.

The last diatomic molecule to be considered in this discussion will be CO.[12] Following the procedure used for N_2, the 2s and 2p orbitals are hybridized into ϕ_1 and ϕ_2; but, since ϕ_{1A} and ϕ_{1B} refer to C and O atoms, there is no need that both involve the same mixture of 2s and $2p\sigma$ character, and they undoubtedly do not. Just as in LiH, the MO's are formed from unequal amounts of the AO's of the two atoms.

In the case of carbon monoxide, since the AO's of the two atoms which form the σ bond need not be equivalent, as they must be in N_2, their relative energies must also be considered. It is well known that two AO's, other things being equal, form the stronger bond the closer their energies. Inspection of the energy-level diagram (Fig. 3.13b) shows that this criterion of similar energies in CO can be met only if ϕ_1 of carbon interacts with ϕ_2 of oxygen to form the σ bond (the comparable energy-level diagram of N_2 is shown in Fig. 3.13a), and these orbitals have the form:

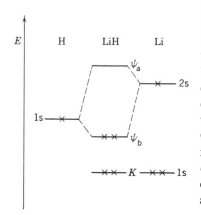

Fig. 3.12   The energy-level diagram of LiH.

$$\sigma = \phi_{1C} + \lambda_\sigma \phi_{2O}$$
$$\sigma^* = \lambda_\sigma \phi_{1C} - \phi_{2O}$$

As a result, the lone pair of the carbon atom in $:C\equiv O:$ will be in a ϕ_{2C} orbital and have largely p_z character, and the lone pair of the oxygen atom will be in ϕ_{1O} and have largely s character.

The bonding and antibonding π orbitals in CO resemble those in N_2, except for one major difference. Just as, in the LiH σ orbitals, the contributions of the Li and H orbitals were different and were determined by a constant λ evaluated through solution of a secular equation, so, in the π orbitals of CO (as well as in the bonding and antibonding σ orbitals), such unequal mixing occurs. Thus the π orbitals of CO take the form

$$\pi = 2p\pi_C + \lambda_\pi 2p\pi_O$$
$$\pi^* = \lambda_\pi 2p\pi_C - 2p\pi_O$$

[12] R. S. Sahni, *Trans. Faraday Soc.*, **49**, 1246 (1953), has a more complete MO treatment of CO.

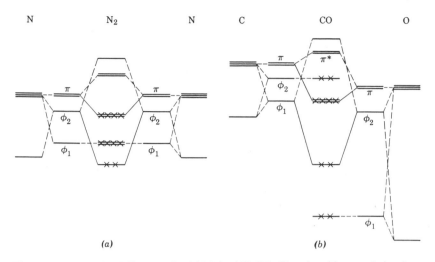

Fig. 3.13   Energy-level diagrams for (a) N_2 and (b) CO. [Reprinted by permission from H. H. Jaffé and M. Orchin, *Tetrahedron*, **10**, 212 (1960).]

Since the energy of $2p\pi_O$ is lower than that of $2p\pi_C$, $\lambda_\pi > 1$, and the bonding π orbital is concentrated more on O (polarized toward O) and the antibonding orbital more on C. The π and π^* levels are shown in Fig. 3.13b.

The term-level diagram in Fig. 3.13b is of value in interpreting the chemical properties of CO, and their relation to those of N_2.[13] The ionization potential of the carbon lone pair in ϕ_{2C} is quite low, making it a relatively basic lone pair. This relativley high energy level of the lone pair and the fact that it is largely p in character and thus strongly directional must be responsible for the many reactions in which CO acts as a nucleophile. The ionization potential of the oxygen lone pair is relatively high, and these electrons are thus unavailable chemically; furthermore, the orbital has predominantly s character and is accordingly not strongly directional. The lone-pair electrons on the nitrogen atoms in N_2 are similar to those on the oxygen atom in CO. These facts explain why the reactivity of CO resides on the carbon atom and is so much greater than that of N_2.[13]

The energy-level diagram of CO further serves to explain its reactivity toward nucleophilic reagents (e.g., ^-OR) as well as its unusual ability to accept back-donation from filled d orbitals in transition-metal carbonyls. The lowest unoccupied orbital is a π^* orbital. Inspection of the MO diagram shows that this orbital receives a predominant contribution from the carbon $p\pi$ orbital and a much lesser contribution from the corresponding oxygen orbital. Accordingly nucleophilic attack occurs exclusively on carbon, and overlap of the π^* orbital with a π or $d\pi$ orbital of a metal is favorable. The relatively low energy of the orbital contributes to its acceptor ability. Hence both λ_σ and $\lambda_\pi > 1$, thus placing more of the charge of the bonding MO's on O than on C.

[13] H. H. Jaffé and M. Orchin, *Tetrahedron*, **10**, 212 (1960).

3.6 Polyatomic Molecules: Methane and Ethane

In the saturated molecule methane, CH_4, the carbon atom is attached to four groups and uses sp^3 hybrid orbitals. Each of these orbitals has cylindrical symmetry around the bond axis and hence is a σ bond. Each bond is made by the overlap of the sp^3 orbital of carbon with the 1s orbital of hydrogen. The formation of one such bond is shown in Fig. 3.14. Four such s-sp^3 bonds are present in methane and form a tetrahedron with carbon at the center. There is, of course, an antibonding σ^* orbital present as well for each bond, but these are unoccupied and, because they lie at quite high energy levels, are rarely of interest.

The problem of finding an MO description for polyatomic molecules is considerably more difficult than for diatomics. But by making full use of symmetry properties, the problem can be solved readily. In the treatment of methane, e.g., the AO's of the hydrogen atoms are combined linearly with those of the central carbon atom to give functions of the form

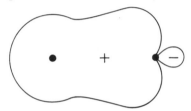

$$\psi = c_1\phi_C + c_2 1s_A + c_3 1s_B + c_4 1s_C + c_5 1s_D$$

where $1s_A$, $1s_B$, $1s_C$, and $1s_D$ are the AO's of the hydrogen atoms A, B, C, and D, and ϕ_C are the AO's of carbon. But the individual 1s orbitals of the hydrogen atoms do not have the symmetry of the molecule (tetrahedral), and hence c_2, c_3, c_4, and c_5 must obey certain relations, $c_2 = \pm c_3 = \pm c_4 = \pm c_5$. Table 3.1 gives the various possible relations of c_2 to c_5 and lists the corresponding AO's of the carbon atom having the same symmetry as the combination

Fig. 3.14 A bonding localized orbital. (Reprinted by permission from H. H. Jaffé in *Comprehensive Biochemistry*, Vol. I, edited by M. Florkin and E. Stotz, Elsevier Publishing Co., Amsterdam, 1961.)

of hydrogen orbital (the so-called group orbital) with the c's given. Having performed this classification, it is readily possible to write down the various bonding MO's:[14]

$$\psi_1(a_1) = 2s_C + \lambda_a(1s_A + 1s_B + 1s_C + 1s_D) = a_1$$
$$\psi_2(t) = 2p_x + \lambda_t(1s_A + 1s_B - 1s_C - 1s_D) = t$$
$$\psi_3(t) = 2p_y + \lambda_t(1s_A - 1s_B + 1s_C - 1s_D) = t$$
$$\psi_4(t) = 2p_z + \lambda_t(1s_A - 1s_B - 1s_C + 1s_D) = t$$

and the four antibonding orbitals in which $\psi_5(t) = \lambda_t 2p_x - (1s_A + 1s_B - 1s_C - 1s_D)$, etc. ψ_2 to ψ_4, and ψ_5 to ψ_7, are degenerate. The electronic structure of methane then is $\psi_1^2\psi_2^2\psi_3^2\psi_4^2$ or $a_1^2t^6$. This description, unfortunately, is of little help to the chemist. It can, however, be readily transformed into an expression which represents chemical thinking. Assuming $\lambda_a = \lambda_t$ and adding $\psi_1 + \psi_2 + \psi_3 + \psi_4$, i.e. making a linear transformation, a procedure which is always possible with a set of equally occupied orbitals, we obtain

$$\psi_A = 2s_C + 2p_x + 2p_y + 2p_z + 4\lambda 1s_A$$

[14] For completeness, symmetry characters are given for these wave functions. These characters are explained in Chapter 4.

Similarly, adding any two and subtracting the other two, we obtain

$$\psi_B = 2s_C + 2p_x - 2p_y - 2p_z + 4\lambda 1s_B$$
$$\psi_C = 2s_C - 2p_x + 2p_y - 2p_z + 4\lambda 1s_C$$
$$\psi_D = 2s_C - 2p_x - 2p_y + 2p_z + 4\lambda 1s_D$$

But the combinations of the form $2s_C + 2p_x + 2p_y + 2p_z$ are just the four hybrid sp^3 orbitals of carbon, and thus the MO's have the form

$$\psi_b = sp^3{}_C + \lambda 1s_H$$

and there is just one such orbital for each C-H bond. Such orbitals are called *localized* molecular orbitals, as distinguished from the *nonlocalized* molecular orbitals ψ_1 to ψ_4 above. The four orbitals ψ_b are bonding, and a typical one is illustrated in Fig. 3.14.

TABLE 3.1

Relation of the Relative Signs of the Constants c_2 to c_5 and the Associated Carbon Orbitals in Methane

Character[a]	C	c_2	c_3	c_4	c_5
a_1	s	+	+	+	+
t	p_x	+	+	−	−
	p_y	+	−	+	−
	p_z	+	−	−	+

[a] These are discussed in Chapter 4.

Application of the same operations to the four antibonding molecular orbitals ψ_5 to ψ_8 leads to the localized antibonding orbitals $\psi_a = \lambda sp^3{}_C - 1s_H$.

α's for the 2s and 2p orbitals of carbon are not identical. S and β for the interaction of the 2s and 2p orbitals of carbon with hydrogen orbitals are not the same, and the 1s orbitals of the hydrogen atoms overlap slightly so that their interactions make some contribution to the secular equations. Accordingly, the assumption $\lambda_a = \lambda_t$ is not quite valid. However, construction of the same linear combinations leads to the orbitals

$$\psi_b = sp^3{}_C + (\lambda_a + 3\lambda_t)1s_A + (\lambda_a - \lambda_t)(1s_B + 1s_C + 1s_D)$$

where $\lambda_a + 3\lambda_t \gg \lambda_a - \lambda_t$. Again four such bonding orbitals and four corresponding antibonding orbitals are formed; following Lennard-Jones, they are called *equivalent* orbitals, since they are equivalent to each other except that they involve the hydrogen orbitals in different order. Since $\lambda_a + 3\lambda_t \gg \lambda_a - \lambda_t$, the equivalent orbitals are very nearly, though not completely, localized in the various bonds.

A description of ethane in terms of nonlocalized MO's could be given in a manner similar to that for methane, but it will be sufficient from here on to discuss σ bonds in terms of localized MO's. In this approximation, the four sp^3 hybrid AO's of each carbon atom, pointing to the corners of a tetrahedron, overlap, respectively, another sp^3 orbital of the other carbon atom, and the 1s orbitals of three hydrogen atoms. Thus the electronic structure and σ-bond skeleton is made up of six MO's of the form $\psi = sp^3{}_C + \lambda 1s_H$ and one MO of the form $\psi = sp^3{}_{CA} + sp^3{}_{CB}$.

3.7 Ethylene and Acetylene

In ethylene each carbon atom is attached to three other atoms; hence carbon utilizes sp² orbitals.[15] These orbitals are directed at 120° to each other. Each carbon atom makes two sp²-s σ bonds with hydrogen and one sp²-sp² σ bond with the other carbon atom. All six atoms are in one plane. The electrons involved in the formation of these five bonds are very tightly bound and are of no spectroscopic interest. There is left on each carbon atom one electron in the p_x orbital.[16] This orbital is perpendicular to the plane of the carbon-hydrogen bonds; a schematic picture is shown in Fig. 3.15. The two electrons in the p_x orbitals have identical symmetry and can overlap to form MO's. This type of MO is called a π (or pi) orbital. Its formation can be represented by Fig. 3.16. This π bond decreases the distance between carbon atoms; compare the distance in a C-C single bond of 1.54 A to the double-bond distance of 1.34 A.[17] Because the overlap of the two p orbitals is not as great as the σ sp³-sp³ overlap, the π bond is weaker (60 kcal/mole) than the σ bond (80 kcal/mole), and accounts for the greater reactivity and the unsaturated character of the double bond. The orbital can be represented by two fat "sausages" above and below the plane of the molecule. The wave function ψ has different signs in each region, and the original nodal plane of the AO's in the yz plane remains a nodal plane for the MO. It is important to realize that the two "sausages" go together and together they represent the MO. This orbital does not

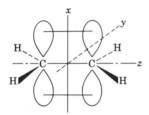

Fig. 3.15 The σ-bond skeleton and π atomic orbitals in ethylene. (C. R. Noller, *Chemistry of Organic Compounds*, Saunders, Philadelphia, Pa., 1952, p. 30.)

[15] It is usually assumed that all three σ-bonding orbitals of carbon are equally hybridized, i.e., are equal mixtures of s and p orbitals. This is not necessary and probably is incorrect. The fact that the ∡HCH in ethylene is about 116°, not the expected 120°, suggests strongly that the orbitals forming bonds with hydrogen have more p character, and that consequently the orbital forming the C-C σ bond has more s character than a pure sp² hybrid.

[16] This designation is not the one to which most chemists are accustomed. However, it should be realized that the selection of coordinates is arbitrary and is made throughout this book in accord with the report adopted by The Joint Commission for Spectroscopy of the International Astronomical Union and The International Union of Pure and Applied Physics [*J. Chem. Phys.*, **23**, 1997 (1955)], which is explained in Appendix 1.

[17] Actually it is now believed that the π bond is responsible for only part of this shortening. Any sp²-sp² C-C bond, without an accompanying π bond, is believed to be only about 1.48 A long [C. A. Coulson, *Chem. Soc. Spec. Publ.* 12, Bristol, 1958, pp. 89 ff.; M. J. S. Dewar and H. N. Schmeising, *Tetrahedron*, **11**, 96 (1960)], and hence the shortening due to the π bond accounts only for the reduction from 1.48 to 1.34 A.

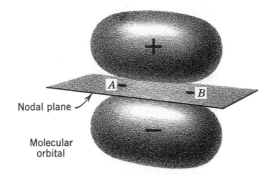

Nodal plane

Molecular
orbital

Fig. 3.16 Formation of a π-type molecular orbital. (Reprinted by permission from C. A. Coulson, *Valence*, Oxford University Press, 1952, p. 89.)

have cylindrical symmetry. Furthermore, it is ungerade because of the different signs in each lobe. This bonding orbital may be denoted by $\pi_u(2p)$, and written $\psi_u = \phi_A(2p_x) + \phi_B(2p_x)$.

The combination of the two p_x AO's results in two MO's. Since only two electrons are involved, according to the Aufbau principle they are placed in the lower-energy MO, which is the one just described. The second MO is of great interest, not only to spectroscopists but also to all chemists interested in problems of bonding, especially carbon-metal bonding, where an olefinic linkage acts as an acceptor of electrons. This second, antibonding, MO must be orthogonal to $\psi_u = \phi_A + \phi_B$; its trace is shown in Fig. 3.17, where it is seen to have π-type symmetry and hence is designated as a π^* orbital. This orbital has two nodal planes, one in the same plane as that of the original AO's, and the second at right angles to the first. The importance of the signs in each region becomes manifest here, since examination reveals that this MO is gerade. The wave function may be written $\psi_g{}^* = \phi_A(2p_x) - \phi_B(2p_x)$ and denoted as $\pi_g{}^*(2p)$.

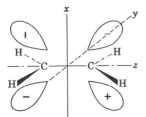

Fig. 3.17 An antibonding π-type molecular orbital.

The mathematical treatment of the orbitals and their energies is identical to the one given for H_2, except that the appropriate symmetry symbols for the wave functions are used. In the approximation neglecting overlap (more justifiable here, since for the $2p\pi$ orbitals of ethylene $S = 0.27$, much less than for the 1s orbitals of H_2), the energy of π_u is $\alpha_C + \beta$ and that of $\pi_g{}^*$ is $\alpha_C - \beta$. The energy-level diagram is again that given in Fig. 3.7. Excited states are $\pi_u(2p)\pi_g{}^*(2p)$ and $\pi_g{}^{*2}(2p)$; the former is possible as a singlet or a triplet.

As in ethylene, the orbitals in acetylene can be discussed in terms of σ and π orbitals. Only one p orbital of each carbon atom has σ character (e.g., the $2p_z$ if the C-C bond axis is the z axis), while the nodal planes of $2p_x$ and $2p_y$ include the z axis and hence have π character. The σ orbitals of carbon are hybridized to the diagonal sp orbitals. Each carbon forms an s-sp bond with the hydrogen attached to it, and the carbon atoms form an sp-sp bond as represented in Fig. 3.18. The three σ bonds are formed along the molecular axis. The two p orbitals, p_x and p_y, remaining on each carbon atom are combined, as in N_2, to form two bonding, $\pi_u(2p)$, and two antibonding, $\pi_g^*(2p)$, orbitals. A cross section of the complete orbital system is shown in Fig. 3.19a, and the bonding combination of the pπ orbitals is shown in Figs. 3.19b and c. Actually the superposition of the two perpendicular bonding orbitals around the same axis leads to cylindrical symmetry. The electronic structure of the ground state, omitting σ electrons, then, is $\pi_u^4(2p)$, and the following excited states exist: $\pi_u^3\pi_g^*$ (singlet and triplet); $\pi_u^2\pi_g^{*2}$ (singlet, triplet, and quintuplet); $\pi_u\pi_g^{*3}$ (singlet and triplet); π_g^{*4} (singlet). Except for the first and last, each of these electron configurations can give rise to several states in each multiplicity, since π_u and π_g^* each represent a pair of degenerate orbitals, and different possible distributions between these are possible. This matter will be further discussed in Chapter 5.

The two π bonds are responsible for shortening the distance between carbon atoms from 1.54 A in ethane to 1.20 A in acetylene (except for hybridization shortening[17]). The digonal hybridization (i.e., the utilization of sp bonds) makes acetylene a linear molecule. The greater s character of the sp bond of carbon to hydrogen in acetylene, as compared to the sp^2 bond in ethylene and the sp^3 bond in ethane, draws the electrons of the C-H bond closer to the carbon in acetylene as compared to its analogs and hence makes the hydrogen easier to remove as a proton, thus accounting for the known greater acidity of acetylene.

Just as the π-bonding MO's of acetylene are analogous to those of nitrogen and result from the coalescence of two π bonds at right angles to each other, the two antibonding π orbitals of acetylene are analogous to those of nitrogen. The antibonding orbital $\pi_g^*(2p)$ of ethylene was represented as being in the plane of the paper when the plane of the molecule was

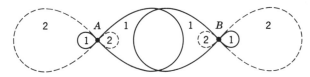

Fig. 3.18 Overlapping sp hybrid orbitals in acetylene. (Reprinted by permission from C. A. Coulson, *Valence*, Oxford University Press, 1952, p. 193.)

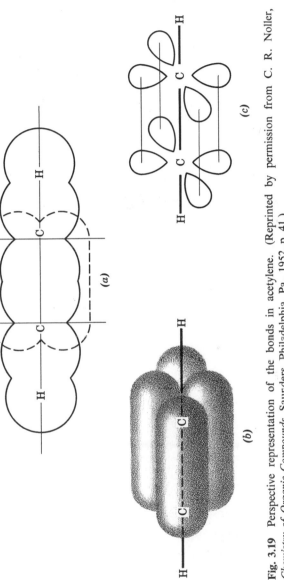

Fig. 3.19 Perspective representation of the bonds in acetylene. (Reprinted by permission from C. R. Noller, *Chemistry of Organic Compounds*, Saunders, Philadelphia, Pa., 1952, p. 41.)

perpendicular to the paper (Fig. 3.17). Nitrogen and acetylene have two such antibonding orbitals which are degenerate and resemble the anti-bonding orbital of ethylene, but are perpendicular to each other.

3.8 Butadiene

The orbitals in a conjugated system like butadiene are conveniently discussed in terms of the σ and π symmetry classifications, just as in ethylene. Each carbon atom in butadiene is attached to three other groups, and hence sp² hybrid orbitals of carbon are used. The σ orbitals are formed into localized MO's and then into a σ-bond skeleton which determines the geometry of the molecule but which is of little further spectroscopic interest. There remain four electrons, one from each carbon atom, each of which is in a pπ orbital. The four pπ orbitals combine to form four MO's which are delocalized over all four carbon atoms.

The wave function of each π electron is the weighted sum of the four $2p_x$ orbitals of the four carbon atoms: $\psi = c_1\phi_1 + c_2\phi_2 + c_3\phi_3 + c_4\phi_4$. Here, however, symmetry alone is insufficient to determine the c's, and recourse must be had to the secular equations. These are readily set up (cf. Appendix 2):

$$c_1(\alpha_1 - \varepsilon) + c_2 H_{12} + c_3 H_{13} + c_4 H_{14} = 0$$

$$c_1 H_{12} + c_2(\alpha_2 - \varepsilon) + c_3 H_{23} + c_4 H_{24} = 0$$

$$c_1 H_{13} + c_2 H_{23} + c_3(\alpha_3 - \varepsilon) + c_4 H_{34} = 0$$

$$c_1 H_{14} + c_2 H_{24} + c_3 H_{34} + c_4(\alpha_4 - \varepsilon) = 0$$

This already assumes neglect of overlap integrals. Now, since all atoms are carbon atoms, $\alpha_1 = \alpha_2 = \alpha_3 = \alpha_4$, and by symmetry $c_1 = \pm c_4$, $c_2 = \pm c_3$. Also, it is customary to neglect H_{AB} if A and B are not neighboring atoms and to assume the other H_{AB} equal, implying equal bond lengths. Making these substitutions, one obtains for $c_1 = +c_4$, $c_2 = +c_3$, i.e., for the symmetric wave functions

$$c_1(\alpha - \varepsilon) + c_2\beta = 0$$
$$c_1\beta + c_2(\alpha - \varepsilon + \beta) = 0$$

(3.8)

and hence the determinant

$$\begin{vmatrix} \alpha - \varepsilon & \beta \\ \beta & \alpha - \varepsilon + \beta \end{vmatrix} = 0$$

which can be expanded into the quadratic equation

$$(\alpha - \varepsilon)(\alpha - \varepsilon + \beta) - \beta^2 = 0$$

$$\varepsilon^2 - (2\alpha + \beta)\varepsilon + \alpha^2 + \alpha\beta - \beta^2 = 0$$

This equation in turn leads to the solutions:

$$\varepsilon = \tfrac{1}{2}[(2\alpha + \beta) \pm \sqrt{(2\alpha + \beta)^2 - 4(\alpha^2 + \alpha\beta - \beta^2)}]$$

$$= \alpha + \tfrac{1}{2}(1 \pm \sqrt{5})\beta$$

Substituting these values back into equation (3.8) gives

For ψ_1: $-\frac{1}{2}(1 + \sqrt{5})\beta c_1 + \beta c_2 = 0$

$c_1/c_2 = \frac{1}{2}(1 + \sqrt{5})$

For ψ_3: $-\frac{1}{2}(1 - \sqrt{5})\beta c_1 + \beta c_2 = 0$

$c_1/c_2 = \frac{1}{2}(1 - \sqrt{5})$

Similarly, for the antisymmetric functions, $c_1 = -c_4$; $c_2 = -c_3$,

$$c_1(\alpha - \varepsilon) + c_2\beta = 0$$
$$c_1\beta + c_2(\alpha - \varepsilon - \beta) = 0$$
$$(\alpha - \varepsilon)(\alpha - \varepsilon - \beta) - \beta^2 = 0$$
$$\varepsilon^2 - (2\alpha - \beta)\varepsilon + \alpha^2 - \alpha\beta - \beta^2 = 0$$
$$\varepsilon = \frac{1}{2}[2\alpha - \beta \pm \sqrt{(2\alpha - \beta)^2 - 4(\alpha^2 - \alpha\beta + \beta^2)}]$$
$$= \alpha - \frac{1}{2}\beta(1 \pm \sqrt{5})$$

For ψ_2: $c_1/c_2 = \frac{1}{2}(1 - \sqrt{5})$

For ψ_4: $c_1/c_2 = \frac{1}{2}(1 + \sqrt{5})$

Finally, normalization is achieved by assigning absolute values to the c's such that

$$c_1^2 + c_2^2 + c_3^2 + c_4^2 = 1$$

and the MO's and their energies are given by:

$$\psi_1 = 0.373(\phi_1 + \phi_4) + 0.602(\phi_2 + \phi_3); \quad \varepsilon_1 = \alpha + 1.618\beta$$
$$\psi_2 = 0.602(\phi_1 - \phi_4) + 0.373(\phi_2 - \phi_3); \quad \varepsilon_2 = \alpha + 0.618\beta$$
$$\psi_3 = 0.602(\phi_1 + \phi_4) - 0.373(\phi_2 + \phi_3); \quad \varepsilon_3 = \alpha - 0.618\beta$$
$$\psi_4 = 0.373(\phi_1 - \phi_4) - 0.602(\phi_2 - \phi_3); \quad \varepsilon_4 = \alpha - 1.618\beta$$

In deriving the expressions for the wave functions of each of these orbitals it is important to note that carbon atoms 1 and 4, and 2 and 3, in butadiene are equivalent. The four MO's are thus combinations in which the functions associated with carbons 1 and 4 are either added or subtracted, and this sum (or difference) is added to or subtracted from the sum (or difference) of the C_2, C_3 combination. The four wave functions (equating all numerical coefficients) are then of the form:

$$\psi_1 = (\phi_1 + \phi_4) + (\phi_2 + \phi_3) = (\phi_1 + \phi_2 + \phi_3 + \phi_4)$$
$$\psi_2 = (\phi_1 - \phi_4) + (\phi_2 - \phi_3) = (\phi_1 + \phi_2) - (\phi_3 + \phi_4)$$
$$\psi_3 = (\phi_1 + \phi_4) - (\phi_2 + \phi_3) = \phi_1 - (\phi_2 + \phi_3) + \phi_4$$
$$\psi_4 = (\phi_1 - \phi_4) - (\phi_2 - \phi_3) = (\phi_1) - (\phi_2) + (\phi_3) - (\phi_4)$$

The π MO's are shown schematically in Fig. 3.20. It is apparent from this figure that ψ_1 and ψ_3 are ungerade (u) and ψ_2 and ψ_4 gerade (g). Also, ψ_1 does not change sign, or has no nodes, between any two atoms; hence the charge density is relatively high between each pair of atoms, and an electron occupying this orbital tends to hold all the nuclei together. Accordingly, ψ_1 is a bonding orbital and makes a bonding contribution for each pair of neighboring atoms. Similarly, ψ_2 has no nodal planes between the two pairs of outside atoms (1 and 2, 3 and 4), and hence is bonding with respect to these; however, ψ_2 has a nodal plane between the two middle atoms, and hence is antibonding with respect to them. Since ψ_2 makes two bonding contributions and one antibonding contribution, it has an over-all bonding character, although much less so than ψ_1. Since both ψ_1 and ψ_2 are doubly occupied in the ground state, and both contribute bonding to the 1-2 and 3-4 bonds, these bonds are considerably shorter and stronger than a single bond; such bonds are represented as double bonds in the principal resonance structures, and are called *essential double bonds*. The bonding contribution to the 2-3 bond of the two electrons in ψ_1, is, however, largely canceled by the antibonding contribution of the two electons in ψ_2, and hence the 2-3 bond is only very slightly shorter[17] and slightly stronger than a single sp^2-sp^2 bond; such bonds are represented as single bonds in the principal resonance structure, and are called *essential single bonds*. Figure 3.20 shows that ψ_3 has nodal planes between atoms 1 and 2, and between 3 and 4, and hence makes two antibonding and one bonding contribution and is weakly antibonding, whereas ψ_4 makes three antibonding contributions and is accordingly strongly antibonding. The bonding character of ψ_1 and ψ_2 can alternately be obtained from the energy of the AO's given above. Since α is the energy of the free AO's and β is a negative quantity, ψ_1 and ψ_2 have energies

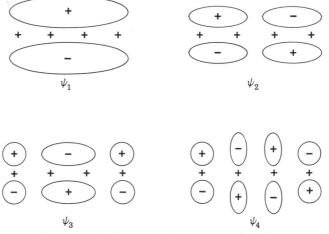

Fig. 3.20 The four molecular orbitals in butadiene.

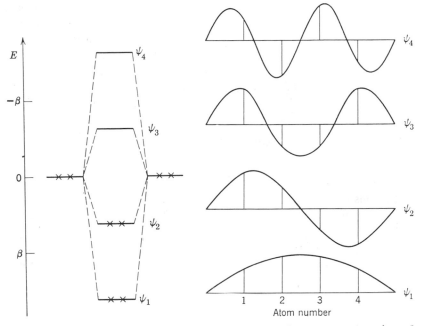

Fig. 3.21 The energy-level diagram for butadiene.

Fig. 3.22 An alternate representation of the molecular orbitals of butadiene.

lower than the AO's from which they are formed, but this lowering is greater for ψ_1 than ψ_2. The same argument shows ψ_3 and ψ_4 to be antibonding, ψ_3 less so than ψ_4.

The energy-level diagram for the butadiene system is shown in Fig. 3.21. It should be noted that the MO's occur in pairs having energies equally spaced on either side of the energy of the free AO's (provided only that the overlap S is neglected). This situation is general for all acyclic hydrocarbon molecules, and all cyclic ones not having an odd-membered ring (i.e., all so-called alternant hydrocarbons), and is part of the Coulson-Rushbrooke theorem.[18]

The electronic structure of the π-electron system of the ground state of butadiene is then given (setting π_u for ψ_1, π_g for ψ_2, π_u^* for ψ_3, and π_g^* for ψ_4) as $\pi_u^2\pi_g^2$, and for excited states it can be written $\pi_u^2\pi_g\pi_u^*$, $\pi_u^2\pi_g\pi_g^*$, $\pi_u\pi_g^2\pi_u^*$, etc.

An alternate method[19] of representing the MO's of a linear conjugated molecule such as butadiene is shown in Fig. 3.22. This method of representation brings out the analogy of the wave functions of the MO's to

[18] C. A. Coulson and G. S. Rushbrooke, *Proc. Cambridge Phil. Soc.*, **36**, 193 (1940).
[19] H. H. Jaffé, *J. Chem. Phys.*, **21**, 1287 (1953).

standing waves in a vibrating string. The figure is constructed by arranging the atoms of the conjugated system along a horizontal line, and then plotting the values of the c's up or down according to their signs, at the point representing the respective atoms. Finally a smooth curve is drawn through the ends of the line segments representing the c's and allowed to join the abscissa one bond length beyond the extreme atoms of the conjugated system. When the wave functions in adjacent atoms have opposite signs, there is a node between the atoms; when they have the same sign, they combine and are bonding.

In connection with the MO treatment of butadiene, it is worth while to introduce a few quantities readily calculated from the MO's which are of considerable interest, not only in spectroscopy but also particularly in discussions of structure and reactivity of molecules.

The first of these is the *charge density q*. This quantity is readily defined in terms of the simple MO theory, neglecting overlap, although in better approximations it becomes much more difficult to define. According to the basic postulates of quantum mechanics (cf. Chapter 2), the probability of finding an electron having a wave function ψ_j, or alternately the density of the electron in the element of volume $d\tau$, is given by $\psi_j{}^2\, d\tau$ (or $\psi_j{}^*\psi_j\, d\tau$ if complex wave functions are used). Summing this over all electrons in a molecule means summing such expressions over all occupied orbitals.

Since each MO of a molecule may accommodate 0, 1, or 2 electrons, this gives $\sum_j n_j\psi_j{}^2\, d\tau$, where n_j is the number of electrons, 0, 1, or 2, having wave function ψ_j. Then, substituting the MO's in LCAO form, $\psi_j = \sum_s c_{js}\phi_s$, where the running index s specifies the atoms, into this expression gives

$$\sum_j n_j \left(\sum_s c_{js}\phi_s \right)^2 d\tau = \sum_j n_j \left[\sum_s c_{js}{}^2\phi_s{}^2 + \sum\sum_{s \neq t} c_{js}c_{jt}\phi_s\phi_t \right] d\tau$$

for the charge density in the element of volume $d\tau$. To obtain the density of charge near atom r, or less accurately at atom r, we must integrate in the neighborhood of this atom; then

$$q_r = \sum_j n_j \left[\sum_s c_{js}{}^2 \int_r \phi_s{}^2\, d\tau + \sum\sum_{s \neq t} c_{js}c_{jt} \int_r \phi_s\phi_t\, d\tau \right] \qquad (3.9)$$

Now ϕ_s is small everywhere except near atom s, and hence in the first sum over s all terms except that for r are very small. Second, the assumption of neglect of overlap integrals suggests that $\int_r \phi_s\phi_t\, d\tau$ can be neglected. Finally, since ϕ_r is small except near r, we can replace $\int_r \phi_r{}^2\, d\tau$ by $\int \phi_r{}^2\, d\tau$ $= 1$, where the integration extends over all space and the value of 1 arises because ϕ_r is normalized. Furthermore, any contributions from $\int_r \phi_s^2 \, d\tau$, with $s \neq r$, which are neglected are partially balanced by contributions from $\int \phi_r^2 \, d\tau$ outside the immediate neighborhood of r. Hence equation (3.9) reduces to

$$q_r = \sum_j n_j c_{jr}^2 \tag{3.10}$$

Equation (3.10), which is readily evaluated, is the definition of the charge density. It should be noted that the normalization conditions require that $\sum_r q_r = n$, the total number of π electrons.

It is interesting to note that for alternate hydrocarbons (i.e., for all compounds containing only chains and even-membered rings, having all Coulomb integrals equal, and having as many π electrons as atoms in the conjugated system) $q_r = 1$ for all atoms r.[18]

The second quantity is the *bond order*, p.[20] This is a measure of the amount of double-bond character of a given bond, and is related to the charge density in the bond. Quite analogously to the above arguments it can be shown that the bond order p_{rs} (due to π electrons) of the bond between atoms r and s is given by

$$p_{rs} = \sum_j n_j c_{jr} c_{js} \tag{3.11}$$

p_{rs} has significance only for adjacent atoms. The total bond order, including σ bonds, is of course $1 + p_{rs}$.

In higher approximations, similar though more complicated definitions are possible. For the case of one-electron MO theory, but not neglecting overlap, these have been given by Coulson and Chirgwin[21] and by Löwdin,[22] and for higher approximations Mulliken has introduced the population analysis,[23] which achieves a similar end.

The third quantity of interest is the *free valence number*, F. This is a quantity which is supposed to measure the extent to which the maximum valence of an atom is *not* satisfied by bonds, and is given by

$$F_r = F_{\max} - \sum_s p_{rs} \tag{3.12}$$

where the summation extends over all atoms adjacent to atom r. $F_{\max}$ is a maximum value, for which the quantity $\sqrt{3} = 1.732$ frequently is used (this is good only if no triple bonds occur).[20]

[20] C. A. Coulson, *Valence*, Oxford University Press, 1952, p. 254.
[21] B. H. Chirgwin and C. A. Coulson, *Proc. Roy. Soc. (London)*, **A201**, 196 (1950).
[22] P.-O. Löwdin, *J. Chem. Phys.*, **18**, 365 (1950).
[23] R. S. Mulliken, *J. Chem. Phys.*, **23**, 1833, 1841, 2338, 2343 (1955).

In the ground state of butadiene, equations (3.10)–(3.12) give $q_1 = q_2 = q_3 = q_4 = 1$, $p_{12} = p_{34} = 0.894$, $p_{23} = 0.447$, $F_1 = F_4 = 0.838$, and $F_2 = F_3 = 0.391$, as the reader can readily verify with pencil and paper. This information, particularly about p's and F's is frequently summarized in so-called molecular diagrams, in which p is written on each bond (or usually only on one bond of a group of symmetrically equivalent ones) and F at the end of a short arrow starting at an atom of each type. The molecular diagram for butadiene would then be:

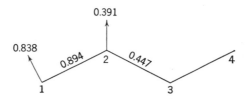

Quantities similar to this can be defined in valence-bond (resonance) theory and are briefly discussed in Chapter 8. It should be noted, however, that they do not have the same numerical values, although in comparisons between different atoms and bonds within a molecule, or between different molecules, the same trends are almost universally observed.

GENERAL REFERENCES

C. A. Coulson, *Valence*, Oxford University Press, 1952.

A. Streitweiser, *Molecular Orbital Theory for Organic Chemists*, John Wiley and Sons, New York, 1961.

R. Daudel, R. Lefebvre, and C. Moser, *Quantum Chemistry: Methods and Applications*, Interscience Publishers, New York, 1959.

J. D. Roberts, *Molecular Orbital Calculations*, W. A. Benjamin, New York, 1961.

4 Symmetry operations, point groups, and symmetry species

4.1 The Basic Symmetry Operations and Associated Symmetry Elements

Many organic chemists tend to view problems of symmetry in terms of optical activity and dipole moments. On the other hand, spectroscopists regard symmetry in a much broader frame of reference. Thus, for example, the organic chemist tends to look at a compound like *trans*-dichloroethylene in terms of its plane of symmetry (the plane of the molecule), which immediately rules out optical activity, and its center of symmetry, which accounts for the zero dipole moment. The spectroscopist, however, is interested in all elements of symmetry, including the two-fold rotation axes (see later) in order to assign the molecule to a point group. He is also interested in the symmetry properties of the molecular orbitals (or wave functions), the occupied as well as unoccupied ones, so that he may understand the probabilities of certain transitions. The need for a knowledge of symmetry elements and properties should have become evident in reading Chapter 3, where reference to them was frequently made. In view of the great importance of symmetry considerations, it is worth while to devote considerable space to a discussion of symmetry elements, symmetry operations, point groups, and symmetry species.

Although many molecules do not possess elements of symmetry in many of their conformations, it is frequently possible and convenient to treat such molecules as though they did have symmetry elements. Thus, for example, the symmetry properties of *trans*-2-butene depend strongly on the relative rotational orientation of the methyl groups to each other and to the plane of the molecule defined by the carbon skeleton. Because of the free rotation of the methyl groups and hence the changing orientation of the hydrogens in these groups, in few of the vast number of possible conformations is there a plane of symmetry. For most purposes, however, it is quite satisfactory to treat this molecule as if the methyl groups were single atoms (pseudoatoms) and as if the molecule consequently had the symmetry of *trans*-dichloroethylene. A not altogether dissimilar situation prevails in some familiar considerations of optical activity. Thus, for example, of the infinite number of possible conformations of ethane produced by rotation of the carbon-carbon bond, only the completely staggered and completely eclipsed conformations possess planes of symmetry. The molecule is, however, optically inactive, because for every asymmetric conformation there is a statistically equal probability that its mirror image exists to cancel the activity that might have been produced by the first conformation.

The symmetry properties of a molecule are best described in terms of the symmetry operations which can be performed on the molecule. A symmetry operation (such as rotation about an axis or reflection in a mirror) is an operation which, when applied to an object, results in a new object which is indistinguishable from the original one and hence superimposable on it. There are many different symmetry operations. However only five of these are basic types of operations; any others can be described in terms of successive applications of some combination of these five.

Each symmetry operation implies the existence of an element of symmetry, and the symmetry properties of an object may be indicated by specifying the symmetry elements which the object possesses. The five basic types of symmetry operations and the associated symmetry elements will now be described.

1. ROTATION ABOUT A SYMMETRY AXIS. If upon rotation of a molecule about some axis by an angle of $360°/p$ (the operation), an orientation of the molecule results which is indistinguishable from the original one, the axis is called a *p*-fold symmetry or rotational axis (the symmetry element), usually designated C_p, where C stands for cyclic.[1] The case where $p = 1$ is obviously trivial, since rotation about an axis of $360°$ restores any rotated molecule to its original position. The water molecule (Fig. 4.1*a*) has a two-fold or C_2 axis, since rotation by $180°$ about the axis in the plane of the molecule and bisecting the HOH angle leads to an orientation indistinguishable from the starting one. Methyl chloride (Fig. 4.1*b*) has a C_3 axis along the C-Cl bond. Clockwise rotation along this axis by $360/3 = 120°$ places H^1 at H^3, H^2 at H^1, and H^3 at H^2. The resulting orientation is equivalent to and indistinguishable from the original one. A second $120°$ rotation produces another equivalent orientation, and a third $120°$ rotation restores the molecule to its original position. The molecules cyclobutane and benzene possess C_4 and C_6 axes, respectively, these axes being perpendicular to the plane of the molecule. A linear molecule (i.e., a molecule in

---

[1] Wherever clarity dictates, the Cartesian coordinate coincident with the C axis will be indicated by a superscript on C_p, as $C_p{}^z$ for a C_p axis along the z coordinate.

which all atoms lie on a straight line, such as acetylene or hydrogen cyanide) can be rotated around the lengthwise axis by any angle and hence in a linear molecule $p = \infty$, and the axis is C_∞. In a molecule having a C_p axis, for any atom not lying on this axis, there must be $p - 1$ equal atoms located at equivalent positions with respect to the axis.

A molecule may have several rotational axes. Thus the planar molecule ethylene (Fig. 4.1c) has three two-fold axes of symmetry. If the center of the molecule is placed at the center of the Cartesian coordinate system, and all atoms are placed in the yz plane, the x, y, and z axes are the three C_2 axes, $C_2{}^x$, $C_2{}^y$, $C_2{}^z$.

2. INVERSION (OR REFLECTION) AT A CENTER OF SYMMETRY.   If in a poly-atomic molecule a straight line is drawn from each atom through the center of the molecule, is then continued, and always meets an equal atom at the same distance from the center but on the opposite side, the molecule possesses a center of symmetry, designated as i, for inversion. The symmetry operation thus consists of reflecting each point of the molecule from

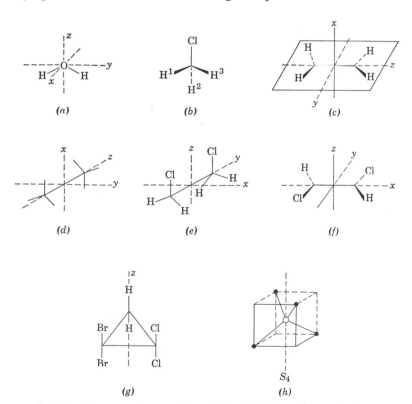

Fig. 4.1 The symmetry operations illustrated with various molecules.

the center of the molecule, whereby an equivalent point is found in the reflection. The staggered form of ethane (Fig. 4.1d) has a center of symmetry which is the center of the C-C bond. The operation may also be described by placing the coordinate system at the center of the molecule, then moving each atom from x, y, z to $-x$, $-y$, $-z$, If the resulting molecule is identical with the original one, the center of the molecule is a center of symmetry. Only one center of symmetry can exist in any one molecule, and if such a center exists, it must coincide with the center of gravity. Any atoms not at the center must occur in pairs. Ethylene (Fig. 4.1c) has a center of symmetry at the intersection of the three C_2 axes.

3. REFLECTION AT A PLANE OF SYMMETRY (MIRROR PLANE). If a plane mirror can be imagined as bisecting a molecule so that one half of the object coincides with (is superimposable upon) the reflection in the mirror of the other half, the plane is called a *plane of symmetry* or *mirror plane* and is designated by σ. In a molecule having a plane of symmetry, all atoms except those in the plane occur in pairs; for every atom on one side of the plane there is an equal atom on the other side in a corresponding position. If, for example, in eclipsed dichloroethane (Fig. 4.1e) the yz plane is a mirror plane bisecting the chlorine atoms, each point x, is transformed into $-x$ by reflection at that plane. All planar molecules have at least one plane of symmetry, the molecular plane. The planes of the HOH and $CH_2{=}CH_2$ molecules are planes of symmetry, but HOH has a second plane of symmetry perpendicular to the first, and ethylene has two additional planes both perpendicular to the plane of the molecule. A molecule may have any number of planes of symmetry; for example, a linear molecule has an infinite number, namely, all those planes that include the C_∞ axis.

4. ROTATION ABOUT AN AXIS, FOLLOWED BY REFLECTION AT A PLANE NORMAL TO THIS AXIS. In some molecules, rotation about an axis by $360°/p$ may lead to a new orientation; but if this rotation is followed by a reflection at a plane at right angles to this axis, the resulting orientation may then be equivalent to the original one. For example, in *trans*-dichloro-ethylene (Fig. 4.1f), the axis joining the carbon atoms is a two-fold rotation-reflection axis.[2] Rotation of the molecule by 180° around this axis, followed by reflection at a plane perpendicular to this axis, gives the original molecule. A second 180° rotation and reflection restores the molecule to the original arrangement. These operations are shown in Fig. 4.2. Thus, for example, if in *trans*-dichloroethylene all atoms are assumed to lie in the xy plane and are numbered as in Fig. 4.2a, rotation of the molecule by 180° around the x axis gives the arrangement in Fig. 4.2b, which on reflection at the yz plane perpendicular to the x axis gives

---

[2] Actually, the same is true for any other axis through the center of symmetry.

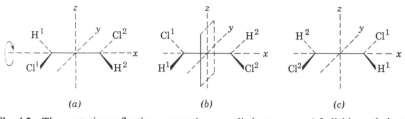

(a) (b) (c)

Fig. 4.2 The rotation-reflection operation applied to *trans*-1,2-dichloroethylene. (*a*) The original molecule; (*b*) after rotation about x; and (*c*) subsequent reflection on *yz*.

Fig. 4.2*c*; this is equivalent to the original. Now the second 180° rotation of Fig. 4.2*c* about the x axis, followed by reflection on the *yz* plane perpendicular to the axis, restores the molecule to the original arrangement (Fig. 4.2*a*). The *p*-fold rotation-reflection axis is designated S_p, and in the above example the x axis[1] is S_2^x. This axis is also called an alternating axis, since equivalent points lie alternately in front and behind (or above and below) the plane of reflection. The S_2^x axis in the above example is not a C_2 axis, and the plane of reflection is not a σ plane. It will be noted that *trans*-dichloroethylene also has a center of symmetry, i; as a matter of fact, a two-fold rotation-reflection axis is always identical with a center of symmetry ($S_2 = i$), since the same pair of atoms is exchanged in the two operations. It is also of interest to note that an S_1 axis is equivalent to a plane of symmetry. Thus for example, 1,1-dibromo-2,2-dichlorocyclopropane (Fig. 4.1*g*) has an S_1 axis perpendicular to the plane of the ring, since rotation of the molecule by 360° around this axis and reflection at the plane perpendicular to this axis give the original molecule.

Some brief mention of the relationship between optical activity and symmetry elements is appropriate here. The test for optical activity of a molecule is that its mirror image be nonsuperimposable on the original. In molecules possessing reasonably "free" rotation around single bonds, no possible conformation should have a superimposable mirror image if the molecule is to be optically active. Mathematical analysis has shown that an object is identical with its own mirror image if, and only if, it possesses an alternating axis of some order (including an S_1 axis); i.e., the single criterion of whether a molecule is optically active or not is the possession or absence of an S_p axis, and only those molecules lacking this element of symmetry are optically active.[3] In

[3] K. Mislow and R. Bolstad, *J. Am. Chem. Soc.*, **77**, 6712 (1955), reported the synthesis of (*dextro*)-menthyl-(*levo*)-menthyl-2,6,2′,6′-tetranitro-4,4′-diphenate:

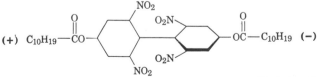

(*Footnote continued on p. 76*)

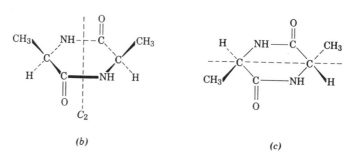

(a)

(b)

(c)

C_2

Fig. 4.3 Some molecules illustrating the relation between symmetry and optical activity.

stereochemistry this rule finds its only important applications in those instances in which the molecules have planes of symmetry (equivalent to an S_1 axis) or centers of inversion (equivalent to an S_2 axis). A compound[4] (Fig. 4.3a) has been prepared which has neither a plane nor a point of symmetry and which has been shown to be optically inactive because of the presence of a four-fold alternating axis of symmetry, which, together with the C_2 axis implied by S_4, is the only symmetry element present. Many molecules possess four-fold alternating axes (e.g., methane, Fig. 4.1h), but they frequently possess several other symmetry elements as well. Molecules which do not possess an S axis of any order (in addition to being optically active) are said to be *dissymmetric*. The word *asymmetric* means without symmetry. However, some molecules that are not *asymmetric* may be *dissymmetric* and hence optically active. Thus the *cis* form of planar dimethylketopiperazine (Fig. 4.3b) is not asymmetric but is dissymmetric and optically active, since it possesses only a C_2 axis perpendicular to the ring plane as shown. The *trans* isomer (Fig. 4.3c) has an $S_2 = i$ element of symmetry and hence is not active. A somewhat simpler molecule possessing a C_2 axis which despite this element of symmetry is optically active is *trans*-1,2-cyclohexanedicarboxylic acid.

which is optically inactive despite the fact that it lacks an alternating axis of symmetry. No possible conformation has a mirror image superimposable on itself; rotation around the 4,4′ bonds is essential for mirror-image superimposability, and such rotameric interconversions ensure statistically equal populations of enantiomeric conformations and thus account for the observed optical inactivity.

[4] G. E. McCasland and S. Proskow, *J. Am. Chem. Soc.*, **78**, 5646 (1956).

5. IDENTITY.   The identity operation (I) is really not an operation at all; it may be regarded as a pseudo operation which leaves the molecule unchanged. This symmetry element is introduced for mathematical reasons. Its inclusion allows us to say that, if two symmetry operations are carried out in succession, the result is the same as that of one other possible symmetry operation of the molecule. Thus, for example, in *trans*-dichloroethylene as seen in Fig. 4.2, a rotation by 180° about the z axis, C_2 (which corresponds to conversion of x, y, z to $-x, -y, z$) followed by a reflection at $\sigma_h(-x, -y, z$ to $-x, -y, -z)$ is equivalent to i (conversion of x, y, z to $-x, -y, -z$) or, expressed mathematically, $C_2{}^z \times \sigma_h = i$. Similarly two successive inversions, two successive reflections on σ_h, or two successive 180° rotations about $C_2{}^z$ give back the original configuration, and these operations may be expressed as $i^2 = I$, $\sigma_h{}^2 = I$, $(C_2{}^z)^2 = I$.

4.2 Multiple Symmetry Operations

As we have shown, certain of the symmetry elements are merely combinations of others, and in such instances only the independent elements need be specified. For example, any four-fold symmetry axis, C_4, is always a C_2 axis as well, and hence the C_2 axis need not be specified. *trans*-Dichloroethylene has i as a symmetry element and hence, because $i = S_2$, the S_2 axes are not basic symmetry elements. Any alternating axis of odd order is equivalent to a simple axis of the same order plus a plane of symmetry perpendicular to it; as an example, the S_3 axis of cyclopropane is the combination of the C_3 axis and the plane of the ring (Fig. 4.4*a*). An alternating axis of order $4p + 2$, where p is an integer, always implies a simple axis of order $2p + 1$ and a center of inversion. Thus, for example, the chair form of cyclohexane (Fig. 4.4*b*) has a six-fold alternating axis of symmetry, S_6, perpendicular to the ring and passing through the center of it; it also has a C_3 axis (the same axis) and a center of inversion.

4.3 Point Groups

In general, molecules have several symmetry elements. By combining more and more of these elements, systems of higher and higher symmetry

(a)   (b)

Fig. 4.4 Examples of molecules having multiple symmetry elements.

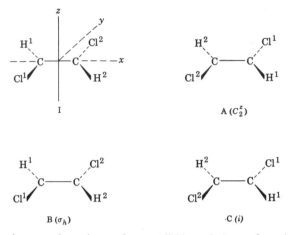

Fig. 4.5 The four configurations of *trans*-dichloroethylene after the symmetry operations.

are obtained. Not all combinations of symmetry elements are possible; on the other hand, the presence of certain symmetry elements implies the presence of certain others, as has been shown in Section 4.2. Two mirror planes at right angles to each other, as in HOH, means that the molecule also has a C_2 axis which is the intersection of the two planes. A two-fold axis, C_2, and a plane of symmetry perpendicular to this axis, as in *trans*-dichloroethylene (Fig. 4.2), implies a center of symmetry, i, and an infinite number of S_2 axes.

A possible combination of symmetry operations is called a *group*. The concept of a group may be grasped better by using a specific example,[5] and for this purpose *trans*-1,2-dichloroethylene will again be chosen. The molecule will be oriented perpendicularly to the plane of the paper with the center of the molecule at the center of the coordinate system as in Fig. 4.5, I. This molecule possesses four basic elements of symmetry; these elements and the symmetry operations associated with them are:

(1) The two-fold rotation axis, $C_2{}^z$. Rotation of configuration I by 180° around this axis produces configuration A, which is superimposable on and identical with I.

(2) A plane of symmetry, σ_h, the xy plane. Reflection at the xy plane produces configuration B, which is identical with the original configuration I. The z coordinate of every point in the molecule is changed to $-z$ by the operation.

[5] A. B. F. Duncan in *Chemical Applications of Spectroscopy*, Vol. IX of *Technique of Organic Chemistry*, edited by A. Weissberger, Interscience Publishers, New York, 1956, pp. 208 ff.

(3) A center of inversion, i. In this operation Cl^1 in the original goes to the Cl^2 position and vice versa, and a similar inversion occurs with the hydrogen atoms, producing configuration C, in which the signs of the coordinates of all points have been reversed. (Since $S_2 = i$, the S_2 axes are not included.)

(4) The identity, I. This consists of leaving the molecule unchanged and is only a pseudo operation.

The four operations transforming the initial configuration I into the four superimposable configurations I, A, B, and C, namely, the identity, C_2, σ_h, and i operations, are called a group, and, since they all leave the center of gravity of the molecule unchanged, a *point group*.[6] A molecule to which *all* the symmetry operations of a point group are applicable, or which possesses all the symmetry elements belonging to a point group, is said to belong to that point group. Thus, *trans*-1,2-dichloroethylene belongs to point group C_{2h}. All molecules with identical symmetry properties belong to the same point group.

It will be noted in the above example that the symmetry elements in a point group are not all independent. Successive application of any two of $C_2{}^z$, σ_h, and i results in the third. Thus, for example, the presence of the plane σ_h and the $C_2{}^z$ axis perpendicular to this plane requires the presence of a center of inversion. This can be demonstrated by considering only signs of the coordinates of a typical point under the operations; reflection in the σ_h plane converts x, y, z to x, y, z, and rotation around z converts x, y, z to $-x$, $-y$, z. Thus reflection and rotation results in the conversion of x, y, z to $-x$, $-y$, $-z$, which is precisely equivalent to the change of signs produced by the single operation of inversion.

There is an infinite number of point groups; these can, however, be grouped into a few types, and every molecule fits into one and only one of these groups, depending on the number and the kind of symmetry elements it possesses. A molecule belonging to a given point group possesses all the symmetry elements of that group and only these elements.

In considering the symmetry of a molecule it is always assumed that an axis of symmetry (if only one is present) or the axis of the highest order (if several are present) is set up vertically. The planes through this axis are given the subscript v, and the plane perpendicular to this axis is denoted by the subscript h. If these were mirror planes, they would be σ_v and σ_h, respectively. The possible point groups of interest in molecular structure are discussed below under several headings.

---

[6] Groups which also involve translation of the center of gravity are of interest in crystallography and are called *line*, *plane*, and *space* groups.

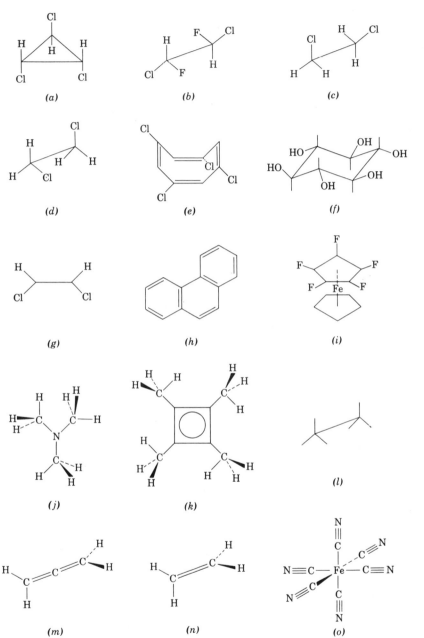

Fig. 4.6 Examples of molecules belonging to various point groups.

TYPE I: NO ROTATIONAL AXIS (EXCEPT SINGLE-FOLD).

Point group $I = C_1$ has no elements of symmetry.

Point group $\sigma = C_s = S_1$ has only a single plane of symmetry. All planar compounds that lack further symmetry elements belong to this point group (e.g., HOCl, mono- or unsymmetrically polysubstituted naphthalenes). A molecule such as 1,2,3-trichlorocyclopropane (Fig. 4.6a) with one chlorine atom *trans* to the other two also belongs to this class, since the only symmetry element the molecule possesses is a plane perpendicular to the plane of the ring. An axis perpendicular to the plane of symmetry is also an S_1 axis, as pointed out earlier.

Point group $i = C_i = S_2$ has a center of inversion (equivalent to an infinite number of S_2 axes) as the only symmetry element. Staggered, *trans*-ClCHF—CHClF (Fig. 4.6b) is an example.

TYPE II: ONLY ONE AXIS OF ROTATION, C_p, $p > 1$.

Point groups C_p: The only element of symmetry is a p-fold axis of rotation. Both the staggered (Fig. 4.6c) and eclipsed *gauche* (Fig. 4.6d) forms of 1,2-dichloroethane are C_2 (the axis halfway between the Cl atoms and bisecting the C-C bond), and all-*cis*-1,2,3-trichlorocyclopropane would be C_3 if the CH-Cl groups were twisted with respect to the plane of the three-membered ring by less than 90°, and all in the same direction.

Point groups S_p: Since $S_1 = \sigma$, $S_2 = C_i$, and S_p with p odd also has C_p, only S_4 and S_6 need be considered. Although these imply C_2 and C_3, respectively, the reverse is not the case, and S_4 and S_6 are higher point groups (have more symmetry elements) than C_2 and C_3. Examples of S_4 are 1,3,5,7-tetrachlorocyclooctatetraene (Fig. 4.6e) and the spiran (Fig. 4.3a) previously discussed; and of S_6, a hexahydroxycyclohexane in the chair form (Fig. 4.6f), with all the OH's in equatorial positions and OH hydrogens turned to parallel the nearest C-C bond.

Point groups C_{pv}, with the symmetry elements C_p and p "vertical" mirror planes (σ_v) intersecting in the axis: Molecules in these point groups are very common. Examples of C_{2v} are H_2O, *cis*-1,2-dichloroethylene (Fig. 4.6g), eclipsed *cis*-1,2-dichloroethane (Fig. 4.1e) and phenanthrene (Fig. 4.6h); of C_{3v}, chloroform, NH_3; of C_{5v}, ferrocene (eclipsed or staggered), in which one ring is perfluoro substituted (Fig. 4.6i); of $C_{\infty v}$, any heteronuclear diatomic molecule or any linear molecule without a center of symmetry.

Point groups C_{ph} have the symmetry element C_p and, at right angles to it, a "horizontal" mirror plane (σ_h). When p is even, C_p and σ_h also imply a center of symmetry. An example of C_{2h} is *trans*-dichloroethylene (Fig. 4.5); of C_{3h}, planar trimethylamine in the conformation shown in Fig. 4.6j; and of C_{4h} tetramethylcyclobutadiene, assuming delocalization in the ring and the conformation shown in Fig. 4.6k.

TYPE III: ONE p-FOLD AXIS AND p TWO-FOLD AXES.

Point groups D_p have only these axes. These groups are not common. Ethylene in an orientation neither planar nor perpendicular is D_2; cyclopropane with partially twisted CH_2 groups is D_3.

Point groups D_{ph} arise when a horizontal plane is added to D_p, and consequently $p\sigma_v$, each the plane of one C_2 and the C_p axis, also must arise, and for p even a center of symmetry i is implied. The case D_{2h} (as D_2) is complicated because no one of the axes stands out over the others. Hence a special designation V_h (V for D_2) is often used. Ethylene (Fig. 4.1c), for example, is D_{2h}. The z axis may be considered the one p-fold axis in this case, and hence there are 2 two-fold axes as well, the x and the y axes. In addition to the horizontal plane xy, there are $p\sigma_v = 2\sigma_v$, the xz and yz planes. Naphthalene is also D_{2h}. Other examples are: of D_{3h}, cyclopropane (Fig. 4.4a), and eclipsed ethane (Fig. 4.6l); of D_{4h}, cyclobutane; of D_{5h}, eclipsed ferrocene; of D_{6h}, benzene; of $D_{\infty h}$, all homonuclear diatomic molecules and all linear molecules with a center of symmetry (carbon dioxide, acetylene).

Point group D_{pd}: Besides the axes defining D_p, D_{pd} has p "diagonal" planes (σ_d) which bisect the angles between successive two-fold axes. These elements also imply, if p is even, a $2p$-fold rotation-reflection axis (S_{2p}); if p is odd, there also is a center of inversion, i. Examples of D_{2d} ($= V_d$) are allene (Fig. 4.6m) and the perpendicular excited state of ethylene (Fig. 4.6n); of D_{3d}, staggered ethane; of D_{5d}, staggered ferrocene.

TYPE IV: MORE THAN ONE AXIS HIGHER THAN TWO-FOLD.

Point group T_d: the common tetrahedral molecules, such as CH_4 and CCl_4. The symmetry elements are 4 three-fold (C_3) and 3 two-fold (C_2) axes, which are also four-fold rotation-reflection axes (S_4), and 6 mirror planes (σ).

Point group O_h: the point group of the symmetrical octahedral molecule, such as $Fe(CN)_6^{3-}$ (Fig. 4.6o). It has the symmetry elements $3C_4$, $4C_3$, $6C_2$ (other than the C_4), i, and 9σ.

The point groups T (as T_d without the planes), T_h (as T plus i), O (as O_h less the center and planes), I ($6C_5$, $10C_3$, $15C_2$), and I_h (as I with i, and additionally planes and S axes) have been omitted because they are of little importance in dealing with chemical compounds.

Point group K_h: the centrosymmetric point group of all free atoms. All possible symmetry elements belong to this point group.

Although molecules can occur in any of the infinite number (since p in C_p, C_{pv}, etc., can have any value from 2 to ∞) of possible point groups, only 32 point groups can occur in crystals, since, in these, space must be completely filled by the unit cells, and hence p is restricted to the values 2, 3, 4, and 6.

4.4 Symmetry Species and Character Tables

trans-Dichloroethylene belongs to the point group C_{2h}, and the four symmetry operations, I, C_2^z, σ_h, and i, making up this group have been discussed in detail in section 4.3; the effect of these operations on the initial configuration I is shown in Fig. 4.5. Any product[7] (i.e., succession) of these operations must be equal to another operation; thus, $C_2^z \times i = \sigma_h$, and $C_2^z \times C_2^z = I$. In this way a multiplication table of symmetry elements of the group may be constructed which shows the results of successive operations. The multiplication table for the point group C_{2h} is given in Table 4.1, where the letters I, A, B, and C are used for the operations I, C_2^z, σ_h, and i. The first operation in a product (successive) operation is looked for in the top row, and the following operation in the first left-hand column outside the table. The result (product) is found at the intersection of the row and column. Thus $A \times B = C$, $C \times A = B$, etc.

TABLE 4.1

A Group Multiplication Table

	I	A	B	C
I	I	A	B	C
A	A	I	C	B
B	B	C	I	A
C	C	B	A	I

The various symmetry operations which can be applied to molecules have been described, as well as the manner in which these symmetry operations depend on each other and combine into point groups. Some properties of molecules, as well as the molecules themselves, are subject to the same symmetry operations.

Static properties of molecules are subject to the symmetry operations, but dynamic properties (i.e., properties changing with time) need not be subject to the same symmetry operations; such dynamic properties are, for example, the motion or, more specifically, the velocities of individual parts of the body. It is, nevertheless, always possible to analyze any *dynamic property* into several components in such a manner that the individual components, under the possible symmetry operations, either remain unchanged (i.e., are *symmetric*) or retain their absolute magnitude but change their sign (this behavior is called *antisymmetric*). As an example, consider a molecule which has as the only symmetry element a mirror plane (σ), such as 1-bromo-2-chloroethane (see Fig.

[7] It should be noted that multiplication of symmetry operations is not generally commutative, and consequently the order of application of the operations is important. By convention, the order is from right to left, since the symbols actually represent operators, operating on an operand to the right of the symbols.

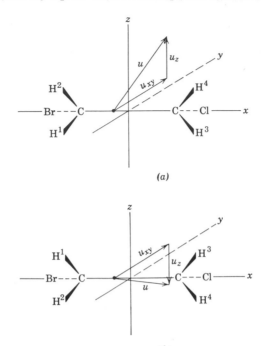

(a)

(b)

Fig. 4.7 Behavior of a velocity under reflection at a plane (*a*) before and (*b*) after reflection.

4.7*a*). Let this molecule move in an arbitrary direction with a velocity u. Then it is always possible to separate u into two components, u_{xy} and u_z, parallel and normal to the mirror plane, respectively, so that $u^2 = u_{xy}^2 + u_z^2$. If the motion of the molecule is such that the distances between all pairs of atoms in the molecule remain constant (i.e., there is no vibrational motion), and the molecule has no angular momentum (i.e., no rotational motion), then it follows that u_{xy} and u_z are the same for all atoms. Now u_{xy} and u_z, being velocities, have not only magnitude, but also direction. The direction of u_{xy} is fixed parallel to σ_{xy}, and hence reflection at σ leaves u_{xy} unchanged (see Fig. 4.7*b*). However, u_z has direction normal to σ_{xy}, and reflection of necessity inverts the direction. Hence u_{xy} would be called symmetric, and u_z antisymmetric, with respect to the mirror plane.

The arguments presented in the preceding paragraphs are not of too much direct concern in electronic spectra; they do apply directly, however, to vibrational motion and hence are of prime interest in infrared and Raman spectra, and in considerations of the interaction of vibrations and electronic states. The classification into symmetric and antisymmetric types is, however, equally important in electronic states for the simple reason that we are always dealing with wave functions which are not, in the sense discussed, static properties of a system (molecule), since they describe the motion of the electrons. The observable static properties, such as the charge distribution, must, as pointed out above, be subject to each symmetry operation (i.e., be symmetric under each of them). These properties, however, arise uniformly as squares of wave functions or as products of them. Now it is obvious that the square of an antisymmetric function must be symmetric, since the negative sign, the only difference between the values of the function at corresponding points, is lost in squaring. Consequently, a wave function, just like the dynamic variables, may be either symmetric or antisymmetric with respect to each symmetry operation applicable to the molecule to which the wave function belongs.

The particular property of interest in electronic spectra is the wave function. The symmetry operations that are performed on the molecule can be performed on the wave function, and it remains to be determined whether under a particular symmetry operation the wave function remains unchanged (i.e., is symmetric) or retains its absolute magnitude but changes its sign (i.e., is antisymmetric). Cases where the behavior is neither symmetric nor antisymmetric will be discussed below.

The wave function in *trans*-dichloroethylene, $\psi_b = \phi_A + \phi_B$, can be represented by the familiar "sausage" above and below the plane of the molecule, the top sausage having the positive sign and the bottom one the negative sign; and the symmetric or antisymmetric behavior of the wave function on application of a particular symmetry operation is easily visualized in terms of the sausage picture. Thus, if the $C_2{}^z$ operation is performed on *trans*-dichloroethylene, the wave function described above remains unchanged or is symmetric with respect to the symmetry operation. However, if the symmetry operation σ_h is performed, reflection of the positive lobe encounters the negative lobe and vice versa; accordingly the wave function is antisymmetric with respect to this symmetry operation. This is equivalent to saying that the wave function after the symmetry operation is equal to -1 times the wave function before the operation. When the behavior is symmetric, however, the result of the operation may be described as multiplying the wave function by $+1$. These factors of $+1$ (for symmetric) and -1 (for antisymmetric behavior) are known as the character associated with the wave function with respect to the operation.

The bonding π MO in *trans*-dichloroethylene is symmetric $(+1)$ with respect to the $C_2{}^z$ axis, but antisymmetric (-1) with respect to the σ_h plane. With respect to the other symmetry elements, the wave function is symmetric with respect to I $(+1)$ and antisymmetric (-1) with respect to i. Thus the wave function has been analyzed with respect to the symmetry operations appropriate to point group C_{2h}. In accordance with its behavior, the wave function is classified into what is called a *symmetry species*. In this example, the wave function was $+1$, $+1$, -1, and -1, with respect to I, C_2, σ_h, and i. The symmetry species to which the wave function with this behavior belongs is denoted by A_u. The A stands for a species symmetric with respect to the rotational axis. The subscript u stands for ungerade, since the wave function is antisymmetric with respect to i.

Other wave functions will have different patterns of behavior with respect to the four symmetry operations. Four distinct patterns are possible; they are called the four symmetry species of the point group C_{2h} and are listed in Table 4.2. This table is called a character table because each

TABLE 4.2

Symmetry Species and Characters for the Point Group C_{2h}

C_{2h}	I	C_2^z	σ_h	i
A_g	+1	+1	+1	+1
A_u	+1	+1	−1	−1
B_g	+1	−1	−1	+1
B_u	+1	−1	+1	−1

entry is the character (symmetric or antisymmetric) of a wave function under a given symmetry operation.

It can be readily verified that the characters conform to the multiplication table for point group C_{2h} (see Table 4.1). Actually it is quite simple to develop character tables for the simple point groups. All properties of a molecule, including the wave function, will always be symmetric with respect to the I operation. Now in C_{2h} only two symmetry operations are independent; we may choose the C_2^z and σ_h; the operation i is then equivalent to $C_2^z \times \sigma_h$. If there are two independent symmetry operations, there are only four possible permutations of symmetric and antisymmetric behavior. The four possibilities (or symmetry species) with respect to the two symmetry elements are $++$, $+-$, $-+$, and $--$. The sign of the i operation will always be the sign of the product of $C_2^z \times \sigma_h$. Hence the whole of Table 4.2 is readily constructed. In the symmetry species notation, B is used to designate a species antisymmetric with respect to the C_2 operation, and g means gerade or symmetric with respect to i. If a wave function has no i, the symmetry species will not carry the u or g notation.

To further illustrate the determination of symmetry species in simple molecules, the water molecule will be examined. The HOH molecule is oriented in the coordinate system as shown in Fig. 4.8. The molecule has a C_2^z axis, $\sigma_v(xz)$ and $\sigma_v(yz)$. It belongs to point group C_{2v}. Since $C_2^z \times \sigma(xz) = \sigma(yz)$, readily verified by

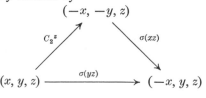

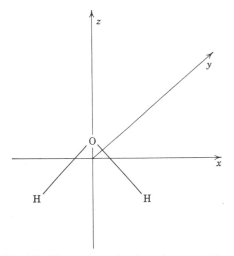

Fig. 4.8   The water molecule, point group C_{2v}.

only two of the symmetry operations are independent and need be specified; for instance, C_2^z and $\sigma(xz)$. Again there are four symmetric-antisymmetric possibilities and four symmetry species, as shown in Table 4.3. Here again the species is denoted by A if it is symmetric, and by B if it is antisymmetric, with respect to the rotational axis. The subscripts 1 and 2 are necessary to

TABLE 4.3

Symmetry Species and Characters for the Point Group C_{2v}

C_{2v}	I	C_2^z	$\sigma_v(xz)$	$\sigma_v(yz)$
A_1	$+1$	$+1$	$+1$	$+1$
A_2	$+1$	$+1$	-1	-1
B_1	$+1$	-1	$+1$	-1
B_2	$+1$	-1	-1	$+1$

distinguish species which are similar with respect to the rotational axis but differ with respect to the other symmetry operations. The totally symmetric species is designated as A_1.

Derivation of the symmetry species for point groups which have no rotational axis greater than two-fold is rather straightforward. The symmetry species appropriate to these point groups are given in Appendix 3, Tables A3.1–A3.3. Point groups which have a p-fold axis with $p > 2$ among their symmetry elements cannot be treated in the simple way outlined above. Thus, for example, if a molecule has a three-fold axis, three successive rotations by 120° represent a rotation by 360° or a superposition over the original.

Antisymmetric behavior with respect to this operation would imply a change of sign for the first 120° rotation; a second change, returning to the original sign, for the second 120° rotation; and a third change of sign for the third 120° rotation. Thus rotation by 360°, resulting in restoration of the original configuration, and equivalent to the identity operation, would correspond to a change of sign, which is obviously not possible. In this situation new types of symmetry species exist, in which wave functions occur in degenerate pairs or groups of three. If only one axis is higher than two-fold, doubly degenerate species, denoted by the symbol e, arise. If several axes are higher than two-fold (point groups T_d and O_h primarily), in addition, species with triply degenerate wave functions appear; these are generally denoted by the symbol t or f.

Degenerate wave functions have one very important property. If χ_1 and χ_2 are degenerate eigenfunctions of the Hamiltonian operator H, so that

$$H\chi_1 = E_1\chi_1 \qquad (4.1)$$

and

$$H\chi_2 = E_1\chi_2 \qquad (4.2)$$

then it is obvious that any linear combination of χ_1 and χ_2, say $\alpha_1\chi_1 - \alpha_2\chi_2$, is also an eigenfunction of H, since multiplication of equations (4.1) and (4.2) by α_1 and α_2, respectively, and addition leads to the identity

$$H(\alpha_1\chi_1 - \alpha_2\chi_2) = E_1(\alpha_1\chi_1 - \alpha_2\chi_2) \qquad (4.3)$$

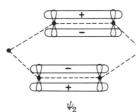

ψ_2

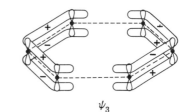

ψ_3

(a)

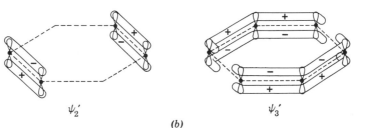

ψ_2'

ψ_3'

(b)

Fig. 4.9 The rotation of the orbitals ψ_2 and ψ_3 of benzene about C_6 by $\pi/6$.

This property of degenerate wave functions becomes important in the point groups under consideration: while a single one of a set of degenerate wave functions may be neither symmetric nor antisymmetric under a given symmetry operation, it is always possible to find a linear combination of the set of degenerate functions which, after the symmetry operation, is equivalent to one of the functions of the original molecule.

The π-electron system of benzene has a pair of degenerate energy levels (ψ_2 and ψ_3) shown in Fig. 4.9a, which can be used to illustrate this point:

$$\psi_2 = \tfrac{1}{2}(\phi_2 + \phi_3 - \phi_5 - \phi_6) \tag{4.4}$$

$$\psi_3 = \frac{1}{\sqrt{12}} (2\phi_1 + \phi_2 - \phi_3 - 2\phi_4 - \phi_5 + \phi_6) \tag{4.5}$$

It is then claimed that we can always find functions ψ_2' and ψ_3' equivalent to ψ_2 and ψ_3, but rotated by a multiple of $2\pi/6$. These are obtained as linear combinations of ψ_2 and ψ_3:

$$\psi_2' = d_{22}\psi_2 + d_{23}\psi_3 = \frac{2}{\sqrt{12}} d_{23}\phi_1 + \left(\tfrac{1}{2}d_{22} + \frac{1}{\sqrt{12}} d_{23} \right)\phi_2$$

$$+ \left(\tfrac{1}{2}d_{22} - \frac{1}{\sqrt{12}} d_{23} \right)\phi_3 - \frac{2}{\sqrt{12}} d_{23}\phi_4 - \left(\tfrac{1}{2}d_{22} + \frac{1}{\sqrt{12}} d_{23} \right)\phi_5$$

$$- \left(\tfrac{1}{2}d_{22} - \frac{1}{\sqrt{12}} d_{23} \right)\phi_6 \tag{4.6}$$

$$\psi_3' = d_{32}\psi_2 + d_{33}\psi_3 = \frac{2}{\sqrt{12}} d_{33}\phi_1 + \left(\tfrac{1}{2}d_{32} + \frac{1}{\sqrt{12}} d_{33} \right)\phi_2$$

$$+ \left(\tfrac{1}{2}d_{32} - \frac{1}{\sqrt{12}} d_{33} \right)\phi_3 - \frac{2}{\sqrt{12}} d_{33}\phi_4 - \left(\tfrac{1}{2}d_{32} + \frac{1}{\sqrt{12}} d_{33} \right)\phi_5$$

$$- \left(\tfrac{1}{2}d_{32} - \frac{1}{\sqrt{12}} d_{33} \right)\phi_6 \tag{4.7}$$

Functions ψ_2' and ψ_3', obtained by rotating ψ_2 and ψ_3 by $2\pi/6$, and illustrated in Fig. 4.9b, must be [cf. equations (4.4) and (4.5)]

$$\psi_2' = \tfrac{1}{2}(-\phi_1 + \phi_3 + \phi_4 - \phi_6) \tag{4.8}$$

$$\psi_3' = \frac{1}{\sqrt{12}} (\phi_1 + 2\phi_2 + \phi_3 - \phi_4 - 2\phi_5 - \phi_6) \tag{4.9}$$

Comparison of equations (4.8) and (4.6) shows that $d_{22} = \tfrac{1}{2}$, $d_{23} = \dfrac{-\sqrt{12}}{4}$. Similarly, equations (4.9) and (4.7) lead to $d_{32} = \dfrac{3}{\sqrt{12}}$, $d_{33} = \tfrac{1}{2}$. Similar arguments lead immediately to values of the d's for various other rotations by $n2\pi/6$, which are given in Table 4.4.

In general, then, the pair of degenerate wave functions χ_a and χ_b of an original molecule, upon application of a symmetry operation, become equivalent to the functions

$$\chi_a' = d_{aa}\chi_a + d_{ab}\chi_b$$
$$\chi_b' = d_{ba}\chi_a + d_{bb}\chi_b \tag{4.10}$$

in the resulting molecule.[8] Simple symmetric or antisymmetric behavior is just a limiting case of these equations, with d_{aa} and $d_{bb} = +1$ or -1, and $d_{ab} = d_{ba} = 0$.

When sets of three functions are degenerate, as happens if more than one axis is higher than two-fold, linear transformations equivalent to (4.10), but involving three equations giving $\chi_a{}'$, $\chi_b{}'$, and $\chi_c{}'$ in terms of χ_a, χ_b, and χ_c, represent the behavior of the functions under symmetry operations.

TABLE 4.4

Matrix Elements d_{ab} for Rotations by $\dfrac{n2\pi}{6}$

n		d_{22}	d_{23}	d_{32}	d_{33}	$d_{22} + d_{33}$
1	C_6	$\frac{1}{2}$	$\dfrac{-\sqrt{12}}{4}$	$\dfrac{3}{\sqrt{12}}$	$\frac{1}{2}$	1
2	$C_6{}^2 \equiv C_3$	$-\frac{1}{2}$	$\dfrac{-\sqrt{12}}{4}$	$\dfrac{3}{\sqrt{12}}$	$-\frac{1}{2}$	-1
3	$C_6{}^3 \equiv C_2$	-1	0	0	-1	-2
4	$C_6{}^4 \equiv C_6{}^{-2} \equiv C_3{}^2 \equiv C_3{}^{-1}$	$-\frac{1}{2}$	$\dfrac{\sqrt{12}}{4}$	$\dfrac{-3}{\sqrt{12}}$	$-\frac{1}{2}$	-1
5	$C_6{}^5 \equiv C_6{}^{-1}$	$\frac{1}{2}$	$\dfrac{\sqrt{12}}{4}$	$\dfrac{-3}{\sqrt{12}}$	$\frac{1}{2}$	1
6	$C_6{}^6 \equiv C_3{}^3 \equiv C_2{}^2 \equiv I$	1	0	0	1	2

Even degenerate functions are symmetric or antisymmetric with respect to the "simple" symmetry operations (inversion, reflection, rotation about a *two*-fold axis), or at least can always be transformed into a form in which they are either symmetric or antisymmetric with respect to them.

The complete equations (4.10) are not required to characterize the symmetry behavior of a function. It has been shown[8] that the sum of the diagonal elements ($d_{aa} + d_{bb}$ for two-fold, and $d_{aa} + d_{bb} + d_{cc}$ for three-fold, degenerate species) is sufficient to characterize the behavior, and accordingly it has become customary to list these sums in the character tables. Tables for degenerate symmetry species are given in Appendix 3.

Linear molecules, with their C_∞ axis, produce some slight complications in this scheme, in so far as an infinite number of species is possible. However, all except the ones symmetric with respect to rotation about C_∞ are doubly degenerate. The species are characterized in the manner described in the preceding paragraphs, but a special notation applies. This notation is based on one introduced for diatomic molecules in

[8] G. Herzberg, *Molecular Spectra and Molecular Structure*, D. Van Nostrand Co., Princeton, N.J., 1945, p. 86.

analogy with the customary notation for atoms, and uses as primary criterion the angular momentum around the axis. The angular momentum 0 is represented by Σ (just as S represents 0 momentum in atoms); then Π stands for 1, Δ for 2, Φ for 3, etc. Σ functions, in addition, may be symmetric or antisymmetric with respect to reflection in a plane including the C axis, and are accordingly classified as Σ^+ or Σ^-. If the linear molecule has a center of symmetry, such as acetylene, the g and u classification also applies. The species for linear molecules are given in Tables A3.18 and A3.19.

GENERAL REFERENCES

G. Herzberg, *Infrared and Raman Spectra of Polyatomic Molecules*, Vol. II in *Molecular Spectra and Molecular Structure*, G. Van Nostrand Co., Princeton, N.J., 1945.

P. J. Wheatley, *The Determination of Molecular Structure*, Oxford University Press, 1959.

5 Electronic states and absorption spectra

5.1 Electron Correlation

In Chapter 3 the MO description of molecules was developed; this involved the formation of MO's from the AO's of the constituent atoms and the assignment of electrons to these MO's. In this way certain so-called "electron configurations" were formed. When the assignment of electrons to orbitals is done in accordance with the Aufbau principle, the lowest possible configuration (i.e., the ground-state configuration) results. When violations of the Aufbau principle are allowed, excited configurations result. In the process of deriving the configurations, however, no account has been taken of the interaction of various electrons, except as far as their spins are concerned. This interaction of electrons, often called *electron correlation*, is the greatest stumbling block to all accurate calculations in atomic and molecular quantum mechanics. Electron correlation is responsible for the fact that wave equations are not accurately soluble, and evaluation of the integrals needed to take adequate account of electron correlation remains one of the major computational problems, even when large electronic computers are available. Fortunately, much can be done without mathematical evaluation, and electron correlation will be dealt with only qualitatively in this book.

The most important aspect of the interaction of electrons for the present purpose of understanding electronic spectra lies in the fact that a single electronic configuration can give rise to several electronic states, depending on the relative orientation of the electrons. It was shown in Chapter 3 that, depending on the relative orientation of the spins of two electrons, singlet or triplet states arise.[1] In atomic spectra the various possible combinations of orbital angular momenta of the electrons of one configuration give rise to various states with different total orbital angular momenta;

---

[1] Although in atomic spectroscopy higher multiplets are of tremendous importance, they rarely if ever play any role in molecular spectra. In free radicals, doublets and possibly quartets occur.

thus a configuration p^2 gives rise to S, P, and D states, where the notation S, P, and D represents the total orbital angular momenta of 0, 1, and 2 units, respectively, in the same way as the s, p, d notation applied to individual electrons specifies their individual orbital angular momenta.

Electrons in linear molecules also can be classified according to orbital angular momentum, only now the angular momentum is around the internuclear axis. Classification according to this angular momentum is the basis of distinguishing the symmetry species of the point groups $D_{\infty h}$, to which all symmetrical linear molecules belong, and $C_{\infty v}$, to which all unsymmetrical linear molecules belong, and hence is the origin of the well-known σ, π, δ classification,[2] indicating angular momenta of 0, 1, and 2 units around the axis.[3] This short discussion now permits the classification of molecular electronic states.

5.2 The Hydrogen Molecule

It was seen in section 3.1 that the two 1s orbitals of the hydrogen atoms in H_2 give rise to the two MO's $\sigma_g(1s)$ and $\sigma_u^*(1s)$. The two MO's involving two electrons then give rise to three configurations: σ_g^2, $\sigma_g\sigma_u^*$, $(\sigma_u^*)^2$. Since the σ electrons have no orbital angular momentum around the bond axis, the resultant angular momentum of all three configurations is zero, and all correspond to what are called Σ states. Owing to the operation of the Pauli exclusion principle, the configurations σ_g^2 and $(\sigma_u^*)^2$ must have antiparallel (paired) spins, and hence correspond to singlet states, but the configuration $\sigma_g\sigma_u^*$ gives rise to both a singlet and a triplet. Finally, the product of two functions of equal parity (i.e., g, u character) always is gerade (even), but the product of two functions of unequal parity is ungerade (odd). Hence the spectroscopic states of H_2 are:

$$^1\Sigma_g{}^+(\sigma_g{}^2); \quad ^3\Sigma_u{}^+(\sigma_g\sigma_u{}^*); \quad ^1\Sigma_u{}^+(\sigma_g\sigma_u{}^*); \quad ^1\Sigma_g{}^+(\sigma_u{}^{*2})$$

The + superscripts to the Σ's indicate that reflection at a plane including the bond axis does not change the sign of the wave function.

The ground state of H_2 is, accordingly, $^1\Sigma_g{}^+(\sigma_g{}^2)$. In the absorption spectrum we might anticipate transitions from the ground state to any of the excited states:

$$^3\Sigma_u{}^+(\sigma_g\sigma_u{}^*) \leftarrow {}^1\Sigma_g{}^+(\sigma_g{}^2); \qquad T \leftarrow N$$
$$^1\Sigma_u{}^+(\sigma_g\sigma_u{}^*) \leftarrow {}^1\Sigma_g{}^+(\sigma_g{}^2); \qquad V \leftarrow N$$
$$^1\Sigma_g{}^+(\sigma_u{}^{*2}) \leftarrow {}^1\Sigma_g{}^+(\sigma_g{}^2); \qquad Z \leftarrow N$$

[2] This notation has been usurped by chemists to denote bonds and orbitals in non-linear molecules which, without reference to angular momentum, have similar symmetry properties, as the σ, π, and δ orbitals of linear systems. The similarity consists in having the same number of nodes which include the axis of reference (usually the bond axis).

[3] Note that the molecular classification consists simply of the Greek alphabet analogs of the Roman letters used for the same angular momenta in the atomic classification.

These three transitions are of rather different types and can be used to illustrate some principles of notation and spectral classes. The most complete and satisfactory notation is unquestionably the one just given; usually, however, the parenthetical indication of the configuration can be omitted and the transition written $^3\Sigma_u{}^+ \leftarrow {}^1\Sigma_g{}^+$, etc.[4] The first of these transitions obviously involves the excitation from a singlet to a triplet, a singlet-triplet transition; as discussed in Chapter 6, such transitions are always weak and are called *forbidden*, since their probability is zero in the first approximation. The last of the three transitions involves the excitation of two electrons at once; such transitions are also forbidden and give rise to bands of low intensity. Through most of this book their consideration can be safely ignored. Both of the first two transitions involve the excitation of one electron from a bonding MO to the corresponding antibonding MO.

The first of these transitions, involving excitation from a singlet to a triplet state, has been called $T \leftarrow N$ (triplet from normal) by Mulliken, and the second $V \leftarrow N$ (V for valence);[5] $V \leftarrow N$ transitions are generally intense and usually the most prominent in an absorption spectrum.

A third notation of spectra is commonly used, one based on electron configurations alone, but very convenient in the framework of the simple MO theory. Thus a $^1\Sigma_u{}^+ \leftarrow {}^1\Sigma_g{}^+$ transition can be called a $\sigma_g \rightarrow \sigma_u{}^*$ transition, indicating the nature of the electron being excited. This type of notation is not applicable to the third of the H_2 transitions listed above, which involves two electrons being excited; also it is not usually applied to singlet-triplet transitions.

In Fig. 3.7 an energy-level diagram for H_2 was given. This diagram, which is reproduced as Fig. 5.1a, obviously shows only a single transition, $\sigma_g \rightarrow \sigma_u{}^*$. This is due to the fact that any diagram of the energy levels of one-electron functions, or MO's, suggests only one-electron excitations, and, since it ignores electron-electron repulsions, fails to take cognizance of the singlet-triplet separations in excited configurations which can occur as states of either multiplicity. A better, though less simple, representation of the conditions in the hydrogen molecule is shown in the *term-level*

---

[4] As a general convention in spectroscopy, in any transition expressed in terms of atomic or molecular states, the higher-energy state, the "upper" state, is listed first, the lower-energy or "lower" state last, and the direction of the arrow indicates whether the transition is accompanied by absorption (arrow from lower to higher, i.e., pointing to left) or emission (pointing to right). Thus the expression given above, $^3\Sigma_u{}^+ \leftarrow {}^1\Sigma_g{}^+$, read as "triplet sigma u plus from singlet sigma gee plus", indicates that absorption occurs, raising the molecule from the $^1\Sigma_g{}^+$ state to the $^3\Sigma_u{}^+$. The expression has the advantage that, if the state symbol is replaced by the energy of the state, the arrow by a minus sign, it represents the energy associated with the transition.

[5] R. S. Mulliken, *J. Chem. Phys.*, **7**, 20 (1939).

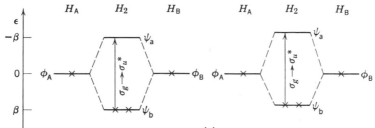

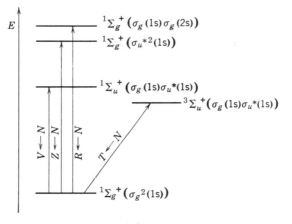

(b)

Fig. 5.1 (a) One-electron energy level and (b) term-level diagrams for the hydrogen molecule.

diagram in Fig. 5.1b, where the molecular *states* are indicated. Comparison of Figs. 5.1a and 5.1b further serves to focus on the different notations introduced. The state notation of Fig. 5.1b is the more general and acceptable. The one-electron, or configuration, notation of Fig. 5.1a, however, has the advantages of the simple LCAO MO theory. The associated notation, like $\sigma_g \rightarrow \sigma_u^*$ of the preceding paragraph, always implies, even though the arrow is to the right, that one deals with *absorption from the ground state*; i.e., that the electrons not specifically stated are in the lowest possible configuration, and only the single electron being excited is specified.

Molecular orbitals can also be formed from AO's of higher quantum numbers, and *one* electron in the ground state can be excited into such MO's. The most characteristic aspect of the resulting absorption spectra is that they occur in series with systematically narrowing spacings toward the high-frequency (short-wavelength) side of the spectrum. They are called *Rydberg transitions* or *Rydberg series* in analogy with the corresponding series in atomic spectroscopy, and are referred to by Mulliken as $R \leftarrow N$ (for Rydberg) bands; see Fig. 5.1*b*.

5.3 Ethylene and Acetylene

In ethylene, a total of twelve valence electrons, besides the four K-shell electrons of the two carbon atoms, has to be considered. As outlined in section 3.7, these twelve valence electrons are customarily divided into (*a*) ten σ electrons, occupying MO's which are symmetrical with respect to reflection in the plane of the molecule, and which can be transformed into localized orbitals or into equivalent orbitals largely localized in individual bonds, and (*b*) two π electrons occupying a π MO which has a node in the plane of the molecule, and which is antisymmetric with respect to this plane.[2] The ten σ electrons, when assigned appropriately to the five single or σ bonds of the molecule, form what is often called the *σ-bond framework* of the molecule; they are not generally involved in spectroscopic phenomena in the visible and near ultraviolet regions since they are very tightly bound. They are similarly not generally involved when unsaturated, conjugated, and aromatic compounds undergo the reactions characteristic of these classes of compounds. Hence only the two π electrons need be considered.

There are only two π orbitals available in ethylene, the bonding (ψ_1) and antibonding (ψ_2) combinations of the $2p\pi$ AO's of the two carbon atoms A and B:

$$\psi_1 = 2p\pi_A + 2p\pi_B = \pi_u$$
$$\psi_2 = 2p\pi_A - 2p\pi_B = \pi_g{}^*$$

whereas in linear molecules these orbitals, and the resulting electronic states, are classified according to the angular momentum around the internuclear axis and the symmetry properties with respect to the symmetry elements of the point group of linear molecules ($C_{\infty v}$ and $D_{\infty h}$), in nonlinear molecules orbitals and states are classified only according to the symmetry properties. Ethylene belongs to the point group D_{2h}, the character table for which is given in Table A3.3, and the symmetry elements of ethylene are apparent from Fig. 5.2.

In general, one-electron orbitals are abbreviated by the appropriate symmetry symbol in lower case, and electronic states by the capital symbol of the symmetry species of the total wave function. This distinction will become clearer in the discussion that follows.

The molecular orbital ψ_1 of ethylene with the $(+)$ "sausage" above the nodal yz plane and the $(-)$ "sausage" below this plane is antisymmetric with respect to $\sigma(yz)$ but symmetric with respect to $\sigma(xz)$ and $\sigma(xy)$.

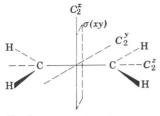

Fig. 5.2   Symmetry elements in ethylene.

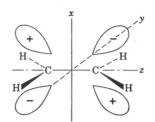

Fig. 5.3   The antibonding orbital, ψ_2, of ethylene.

Reference to Table A3.3 shows that this wave function with -1, $+1$, $+1$ for the respective σ's belongs to the species b_{3u}. The lower-case symbol is employed because the orbital rather than the state is under discussion. The b indicates that the orbital is antisymmetric with respect to at least one C_2 axis (in this case the $C_2{}^z$ as well as the $C_2{}^y$ axis), and the u indicates that the wave function or orbital is antisymmetric (ungerade) with respect to the center of inversion, i. The molecular orbital ψ_2 of ethylene, which is the antibonding orbital, has been described in Chapter 3, and is shown in Fig. 5.3. This orbital or wave function is antisymmetric with respect to $\sigma(xy)$, symmetric with respect to $\sigma(xz)$, and antisymmetric with respect to $\sigma(yz)$. This combination of $+1$, -1, $+1$ for the respective σ's is called $b_{2g}{}^*$; b because of antisymmetry (-1) with respect to the $C_2{}^x$ and $C_2{}^z$ axes, g because of the (gerade) symmetry with respect to the center of inversion, and the asterisk as superscript because of the anti-bonding character of the orbital. The subscript 2 is necessary to distinguish this b_g species from two other b_g species. The number is arbitrary but follows the assignments given by Herzberg.[6a]

In the ground state of ethylene the two π electrons are assigned to ψ_1, so that the configuration is $\psi_1{}^2 = b_{3u}{}^2$. Since now the wave function $\Psi = \psi_1{}^2$ is in effect the square of the b_{3u} function, it must be symmetric with respect to every symmetry element. The same is true for the part of Ψ due to all the σ electrons, since they occur in pairs in the same orbitals. In addition, the spins of the two π electrons must be paired because of the Pauli exclusion principle. The state is thus completely symmetric and is described as ^1A_g. This discussion illustrates the usage of the lower-case and capital letters; $b_{3u}{}^2$ specifies the configuration, but the state is symmetric and hence is denoted by A. The symmetry species of the many-electron function (the state) is readily obtained by some rather simple rules[6b] from the species of the one-electron functions involved in it. With

[6] G. Herzberg, *Molecular Spectra and Molecular Structure*, D. Van Nostrand Co., Princeton, N.J., 1945, (a) p. 108, (b) pp. 126 ff.

few exceptions, the ground states of stable organic chemical compounds belong to the totally symmetric symmetry species, meaning that they are symmetric with respect to each symmetry operation; the symbol used always involves A (except in linear molecules, where it is Σ) and, depending on the appropriate point group, may be A_1, A_g, A_{1g}, A', etc.

Excitation of one of the π electrons of ethylene gives rise to the configuration $\psi_1\psi_2 = b_{3u}b_{2g}$. This configuration belongs to the B_{1u} species, as can be verified in a simple manner by multiplying together the symmetry behavior of the one-electron orbitals. Thus b_{3u} in respect to the three σ's (see Table A3.3) is $+1$, -1, $+1$ and b_{2g} is -1, $+1$, -1. The product is $\sigma(xy)-1$, $\sigma(xz)+1$, $\sigma(yz)+1$, and reference to Table A3.3 shows that this symmetry species is B_{1u}. The configuration $\psi_1\psi_2$ or $b_{3u}b_{2g}{}^*$ can give rise to either a singlet or triplet state, and the multiplicity of the state is indicated by a superscript in front of the symmetry species. Thus the excited states under discussion are $^3B_{1u}$ and $^1B_{1u}$. Excitation of both electrons from the bonding MO of ethylene would give rise to the configuration $\psi_2{}^2 = b_{2g}{}^{*2}$, which must be a singlet state. This state must also be completely symmetric for the same reasons given above for the ground state, and hence the excited state $b_{2g}{}^{*2}$ also belongs to the symmetry species ^1A_g.

The absorption spectrum of ethylene may thus be expected to show three transitions:

$$^3B_{1u}(\psi_1\psi_2) \leftarrow {}^1A_g(\psi_1{}^2)$$
$$^1B_{1u}(\psi_1\psi_2) \leftarrow {}^1A_g(\psi_1{}^2)$$
$$^1A_g(\psi_2{}^2) \leftarrow {}^1A_g(\psi_1{}^2)$$

The first of these is a singlet $\rightarrow$ triplet transition, and hence forbidden (section 6.3). The second, $^1B_{1u} \leftarrow {}^1A_g$ is the $V \leftarrow N$ transition; it occurs at 165 mμ and is very intense. It may also be called $b_{3u} \rightarrow b_{2g}{}^*$ or, more generally, $\pi \rightarrow \pi^*$ to indicate that it is a transition from a bonding to an antibonding π-type orbital. The last of these transitions, $^1A_g \leftarrow {}^1A_g$, is also $V \leftarrow N$, but as a two-electron transition it is forbidden and expected to be quite weak. This transition has been observed at 200 mμ; this fact is quite surprising, since we might have anticipated that excitation of two electrons from ψ_1 to ψ_2 would have required much more energy (roughly twice as much) as excitation of only one electron, rather than considerably less. Careful MO calculations, including electron correlation (and configuration interaction; cf. Chapter 8), however, have shown that the wavelength is not unreasonable.[7]

Application of the same principles to acetylene is considerably more complicated. Of the ten valence electrons, six are σ electrons (since the molecule is linear, the $\sigma\pi\delta$

[7] F. A. Matsen in *Chemical Applications of Spectroscopy*, Vol. IX of *Technique of Organic Chemistry*, edited by A. Weissberger, Interscience Publishers, New York, 1956, has a discussion with references on this subject on pp. 648 ff.

classification is strictly applicable, and the σ electrons have 0 angular momentum around the molecular axis); they are again ignored in what follows. The other four are π electrons and have available to them a degenerate pair of bonding π_u orbitals and a degenerate pair of antibonding π_g^* orbitals. The ground state is $\pi_u^4 = {}^1\Sigma_g^+$. Excited configurations are $\pi_u^3\pi_g^*$, $\pi_u^2\pi_g^{*2}$, and $\pi_u\pi_g^{*3}$. The last, involving excitation of three electrons, may be safely ignored. Each of the other two excited configurations, however, gives rise to several states, because of the degeneracy of the orbitals involved.

Consider first the singly excited configuration $\pi_u^3\pi_g^*$. Since three electrons are assigned to the two (degenerate) π_u orbitals, two electrons must have spins paired, but the spins of the other two may be paired or unpaired, and hence there should be singlet and triplet states. The orbital angular momentum of π electrons is either $+1$ or -1; since in π_u two electrons must occupy one orbital, and the third electron the other orbital, the resulting angular momentum may be $+1$ or -1. The angular momentum of the π_g^* electron is also $+1$ or -1, and hence the total orbital angular momentum is ± 2, or 0, so that Σ and Δ states should result. In this case, the Σ states may be either symmetric or unsymmetric with respect to reflection from a plane through the bond axis, and hence are Σ^+ or Σ^- states. Thus six states are expected: ${}^1\Sigma_u^+$, ${}^3\Sigma_u^+$, ${}^1\Sigma_u^-$, ${}^3\Sigma_u^-$, ${}^1\Delta_u$, ${}^3\Delta_u$; they are all ungerade, since the product of the three u and the one g functions must be u.

The situation in the $\pi_u^2\pi_g^{*2}$ configuration is even worse. Since now no two electrons need be in the same orbital, we may have singlets, triplets, and quintets. But if all electrons are in different orbitals, the orbital angular momenta must be $+1$, -1, $+1$, -1, with a sum of 0, giving rise to a ${}^5\Sigma_g^+$, three ${}^3\Sigma_g^+$, and two ${}^1\Sigma_g^+$ states. If the two π_u electrons occupy the same orbital, but the π_g^* electrons different ones, we may have singlets or triplets which may, however, have two units of angular momentum (i.e., ${}^1\Delta_g$ and ${}^3\Delta_g$). Another set of ${}^1\Delta_g$ and ${}^3\Delta_g$ states arises from π_u electrons in different, π_g^* electrons in the same, orbitals. Finally, with both the π_u electrons in one orbital and the π_g^* electrons in one orbital, the angular momenta may be $+1$, $+1$, $+1$, $+1$, leading to a ${}^1\Gamma_g$ state, and $+1$, $+1$, -1, -1, leading to two ${}^1\Sigma_g^+$ states. As a result we obtain a ${}^1\Gamma_g$, a ${}^5\Sigma_g^+$, a ${}^3\Sigma_g^+$, a ${}^1\Sigma_g^-$, two each ${}^1\Delta_g$, ${}^3\Delta_g$, and ${}^3\Sigma_g^-$, and three ${}^1\Sigma_g^+$ states.

Considering the tremendous array of available states, it does not appear surprising that the theoretical interpretation of the acetylene spectrum has not been very successful to date.[8]

5.4   Butadiene

A consideration of the geometry of butadiene is a necessary prelude to a discussion of its electronic states and absorption spectrum. There are two extreme configurations of planar butadiene, which are distinguished by the geometry around the C_2-C_3 bond. Because of the partial double-bond character of this bond, the two vinyl groups may be represented as being *trans* or *cis*, as in *b* or *c*.

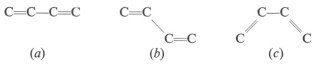

$$C{=}C{-}C{=}C \qquad\qquad C{=}C \qquad\qquad C{-}C$$

$$(a) \qquad\qquad\qquad (b) \qquad\qquad\qquad (c)$$

[8] J. R. Platt, H. B. Klevens, and W. C. Price, *J. Chem. Phys.*, **17**, 466 (1949); C. K. Ingold and G. W. King, *J. Chem. Soc.*, 2702, 2704, 2708, 2725, 2745 (1953); H. Howard and G. W. King, *Can. J. Chem.*, **37**, 700 (1959).

Configuration b is called *s-trans*-butadiene and c is called *s-cis*-butadiene; the lower-case s refers to the fact that the distinction arises from *cis* and *trans* configurations around an essential single bond. Molecule b belongs to point group C_{2h} and c to C_{2v}. Crude MO theory (as outlined in section 3.9) makes no differentiation between b and c and actually treats butadiene as though it were the linear molecule a and belonged to point group D_{2h}, just like ethylene. It is worth while, however, to consider the MO's of butadiene in terms of each of the configurations. The symmetry types or species of the MO's of butadiene are summarized in Table 5.1. In order to explain the construction of this table one example will be given in detail, using molecule c.

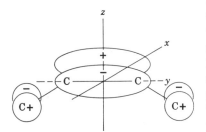

Fig. 5.4 *s-cis*-Butadiene in the yz plane showing the orbital ψ_3.

s-cis-Butadiene must be oriented with all carbon atoms in the plane of the paper as in Fig. 5.4 in order for the C_2 axis to be vertical and the molecule thus lies in the yz plane. The character table for point group C_{2v} is given in Table 4.3. In order to illustrate a simple method for determining

TABLE 5.1

The π Molecular Orbitals of Butadiene

Orbital	LCAO Representation	Symmetry Type in		
		D_{2h}	C_{2h}	C_{2v}
ψ_1	$c_1(\phi_1 + \phi_4) + c_2(\phi_2 + \phi_3)$	b_{3u}	a_u	b_1
ψ_2	$c_2(\phi_1 - \phi_4) + c_1(\phi_2 - \phi_3)$	b_{2g}	b_g	a_2
$\psi_3{}^*$	$c_2(\phi_1 + \phi_4) - c_2(\phi_2 + \phi_3)$	$b_{3u}{}^*$	$a_u{}^*$	$b_1{}^*$
$\psi_4{}^*$	$c_1(\phi_1 - \phi_4) - c_2(\phi_2 - \phi_3)$	$b_{2g}{}^*$	$b_g{}^*$	$a_2{}^*$

the symmetry species of a particular configuration, the configuration $\psi_1{}^2\psi_2\psi_3{}^*$ will be considered. The wave function ψ_1 is antisymmetric (-1) with respect to $C_2{}^z$, has a node in the yz plane, and hence is antisymmetric (-1) with respect to $\sigma(yz)$ and is symmetric $(+1)$ with respect to $\sigma(xz)$; therefore it is b_1. With respect to the same symmetry elements, ψ_2 is $+1$, -1, -1, respectively, and is thus a_2. With respect to $C_2{}^z$, $\sigma(xz)$, and $\sigma(yz)$, ψ_3, which is sketched in Fig. 5.4, is -1, $+1$, -1, and hence is $b_1{}^*$. The configuration $\psi_1{}^2\psi_2\psi_3{}^*$ for C_{2v} can then be written $b_1{}^2a_2b_1{}^*$, and the symmetry behavior of this configuration is readily obtained. Thus the sign under C_2^z may be obtained from the product $(+1)$ (in b_1^2) $\times$ $(+1)$ (in a_2) $\times$ (-1) (in b_1) and hence is -1. Similarly $\sigma(xz)$ is $(+1)$ in (b_1^2) $\times$ (-1) (in a_2) $\times$ $(+1)$ (in b_1) $= -1$, and $\sigma(yz)$ is $(+1)$ in (b_1^2) $\times$ (-1) (in a_2) $\times$ (-1) (in b_1) $= +1$. The state corresponding to $-1, -1, +1$ is B_2.

The ground-state configuration of butadiene, ignoring σ electrons, is $\psi_1^2\psi_2^2$. The fact that each of the orbitals again occurs squared means that the state is totally symmetric, and that it must be a singlet. In the three point groups it becomes:

$$b_{3u}^2 b_{2g}^2 = {}^1A_g; \quad a_u^2 b_g^2 = {}^1A_g; \quad \text{and} \quad b_1^2 a_2^2 = {}^1A_1$$

A number of excited configurations arise from one-electron promotions, of which the lowest is $\psi_1^2\psi_2\psi_3^*$ (described in detail for s-cis-butadiene above), followed by $\psi_1^2\psi_2\psi_4^*$, $\psi_1\psi_2^2\psi_3^*$, and $\psi_1\psi_2^2\psi_4^*$. Further configurations result from two-electron promotions (e.g., $\psi_1^2\psi_3^2$). States arising from the lower excited configurations, and their appropriate symmetry species, are listed in Table 5.2. Excitation to these five excited states could

TABLE 5.2

Configurations and Symmetry Species of Excited States of Butadiene[a]

Configuration	D_{2h}	C_{2h}	C_{2v}
Ψ_{f1} $\psi_1^2\psi_2\psi_3^*$	$b_{3u}^2 b_{2g} b_{3u}^* = B_{1u}$	$a_u^2 b_g a_u^* = B_u$	$b_1^2 a_2 b_1^* = B_2$
Ψ_{f2} $\psi_1^2\psi_2\psi_4^*$	$b_{3u}^2 b_{2g} b_{2g}^* = A_g$	$a_u^2 b_g b_g^* = A_g$	$b_1^2 a_2 a_2^* = A_1$
Ψ_{f3} $\psi_1\psi_2^2\psi_3^*$	$b_{3u} b_{2g}^2 b_{3u}^* = A_g$	$a_u b_g^2 a_u^* = A_g$	$b_1 a_2^2 b_1^* = A_1$
Ψ_{f4} $\psi_1\psi_2^2\psi_4^*$	$b_{3u} b_{2g}^2 b_{2g}^* = B_{1u}$	$a_u b_g^2 b_g^* = B_u$	$b_1 a_2^2 a_2^* = B_2$
Ψ_{f5} $\psi_1^2\psi_3^{*2}$	$b_{3u}^2 b_{3u}^{*2} = A_g$	$a_u^2 a_u^{*2} = A_g$	$b_1^2 b_1^{*2} = A_1$

[a] There is, of course, a triplet state corresponding to each singlet except $\psi_1^2\psi_3^{*2}$.

give rise to five absorption bands corresponding to two ${}^1B_{1u} \leftarrow {}^1A_g ({}^1B_u \leftarrow {}^1A_g$ or ${}^1B_2 \leftarrow {}^1A_1)$ transitions and three ${}^1A_g \leftarrow {}^1A_g ({}^1A_g \leftarrow {}^1A_g$ or ${}^1A_1 \leftarrow {}^1A_1)$ transitions. The latter are forbidden except for molecule c (cf. section 6.3) and, if observed at all, will be of low intensity. The first ${}^1B_{1u} \leftarrow {}^1A_g$ transition is a $V \leftarrow N$ transition; it is observed at 2200 A. The second ${}^1B_{1u} \leftarrow {}^1A_g$ transition occurs at considerably shorter wavelength.

5.5   Benzene

The benzene molecule belongs to the point group D_{6h}, which, like the point group $D_{\infty h}$ of acetylene (cf. section 5.3), involves degenerate symmetry species and accordingly represents a considerably more complicated case than ethylene or butadiene. Ignoring the σ-bond skeleton of the

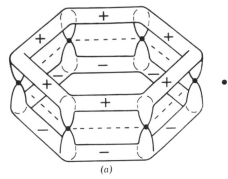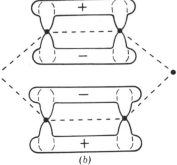

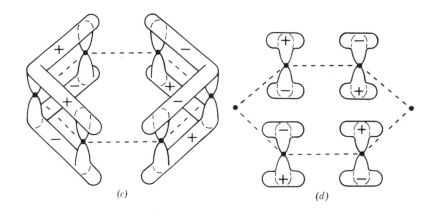

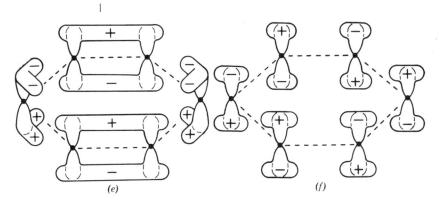

Fig. 5.5   The molecular orbitals of benzene. (Reprinted by permission from H. H. Jaffé in *Comprehensive Biochemistry*, Vol. I, edited by M. Florkin and E. Stotz, Elsevier Publishing Co., Amsterdam, 1961.)

molecule, we need to consider in the electronic structure of benzene only
the six $p\pi$ orbitals (ϕ_1 to ϕ_6) of the six carbon atoms, which are occupied by
six π electrons. Since all atoms are equivalent, one MO can be written down
immediately as $\psi_1 = 1/\sqrt{6}(\phi_1 + \phi_2 + \phi_3 + \phi_4 + \phi_5 + \phi_6)$ (cf. Fig. 5.5a),
which is symmetric with respect to the six-fold axis, and the two- and
three-fold axes coincident with it, and with respect to the six σ_v and σ_d, but,
since all the ϕ_i are p_z orbitals, is antisymmetric with respect to σ_h, and the
six C_2 normal to C_6, and hence is of species a_{2u}. In addition, a second
orbital immediately appears of the form $\psi_6 = 1/\sqrt{6}(\phi_1 - \phi_2 + \phi_3 - \phi_4 + \phi_5 - \phi_6)$ (cf. Fig. 5.5b), which is antisymmetric with respect to C_6 and the
coincident C_2, symmetric with respect to C_3 (also coincident with C_6),
symmetric with respect to the σ_v through the atoms, and the C_2 normal to
C_6 between atoms, antisymmetric with respect to the σ_d between atoms and
the C_2 through them, and, of course, antisymmetric with respect to σ_h, and
hence of species b_{2g}. The other four orbitals, as can be shown readily by
group theory or can be found by solution of the secular equation, belong
in pairs to the species e_{1g} and e_{2u}. The orthogonal degenerate pair of
orbitals ψ_2 and ψ_3 are both gerade (cf. Figs. 5.5b and c); the subscript 1
designates the functions which are antisymmetric with respect to the symmetry operation $C_2 = C_6^3$ (i.e., a rotation by 180° about the six-fold axis),
which applies to ψ_2 and ψ_3, and hence together they belong to species e_{1g}.
A detailed analysis of their behavior under the symmetry operation C_6 is
given in section 4.4. ψ_4 and ψ_5 are also an orthogonal degenerate pair.
They are shown in Figs. 5.5d and e. Inspection shows that these functions
are ungerade and symmetric with respect to the symmetry operation
$C_2 = C_6^3$ and hence together belong to symmetry species e_{2u}. When
orbitals occur in degenerate pairs, no unique forms can be assigned them;
any pair of linear combinations of one set of these functions is also a
satisfactory set, provided they are orthogonal. However, it has become
customary to write them in the form given in Table 5.3. This form is
particularly attractive because the orbitals have the symmetry properties
required of orbitals in the point groups of substituted benzenes (monosubstituted, unsymmetrically *para*-disubstituted, symmetrically *ortho*- or
meta-disubstituted, all C_{2v}, or symmetrically *para*-disubstituted, D_{2h}, etc.).

The ground state of benzene has then the electronic configuration
$\psi_1^2\psi_2^2\psi_3^2$ or $a_{2u}^2e_{1g}^4$; and, since all orbitals are completely filled, the
electronic state is a singlet and belongs to the totally symmetric species $^1A_{1g}$.

The configuration $\psi_1^2\psi_2^2\psi_3^2$, together with the degeneracies of ψ_2 and ψ_3,
and of ψ_4 and ψ_5, suggests that four low-energy excitations should be
possible with the same energy leading to the excited configurations:
$\psi_1^2\psi_2^2\psi_3\psi_4$, $\psi_1^2\psi_2^2\psi_3\psi_5$, $\psi_1^2\psi_2\psi_3^2\psi_4$, and $\psi_1^2\psi_2\psi_3^2\psi_5$, all of which can be
represented by $a_{2u}^2e_{1g}^3e_{2u}$. It may be shown by methods of group theory

that this configuration gives rise to three states, of species, B_{1u}, B_{2u}, and E_{1u}, respectively, all of which are ungerade, since each arises from the multiplication of three gerade functions and one ungerade function. Thus theory predicts three absorption bands, $^1B_{2u} \leftarrow {}^1A_{1g}$, $^1B_{1u} \leftarrow {}^1A_{1g}$, and $^1E_{1u} \leftarrow {}^1A_{1g}$, and, of course, the corresponding singlet-triplet transitions, since there may be two electrons with parallel spins in the excited states.

TABLE 5.3

The Benzene Molecular Orbitals

Symmetry	Orbital[a]	E (in β)[a]
a_{2u}	$\psi_1 = \dfrac{1}{\sqrt{6}}(\phi_1 + \phi_2 + \phi_3 + \phi_4 + \phi_5 + \phi_6)$	2
e_{1g}	$\psi_2 = \tfrac{1}{2}(\phi_2 + \phi_3 - \phi_5 - \phi_6)$	1
	$\psi_3 = \dfrac{1}{\sqrt{12}}(2\phi_1 + \phi_2 - \phi_3 - 2\phi_4 - \phi_5 + \phi_6)$	1
e_{2u}	$\psi_4 = \tfrac{1}{2}(\phi_2 - \phi_3 + \phi_5 - \phi_6)$	-1
	$\psi_5 = \dfrac{1}{\sqrt{12}}(2\phi_1 - \phi_2 - \phi_3 + 2\phi_4 - \phi_5 - \phi_6)$	-1
b_{2g}	$\psi_6 = \dfrac{1}{\sqrt{6}}(\phi_1 - \phi_2 + \phi_3 - \phi_4 + \phi_5 - \phi_6)$	-2

[a] The normalization factors and energies given apply to calculations in which overlap integrals are assumed negligible. Lack of this assumption changes the normalization factors and energies but not the form of the orbitals.

Simplest theory would, because of the degeneracies, lead to the prediction that all these bands occur at the same wavelengths. However, as a result of different electron correlation in the various configurations, some energy differences occur. It is readily seen from Table 5.3 that the charge distributions due to ψ_2 and ψ_4 are identical, as is true of those due to ψ_3 and ψ_5. Hence the configurations $\psi_1{}^2\psi_2{}^2\psi_3\psi_5$ and $\psi_1{}^2\psi_2\psi_3{}^2\psi_4$ involve the same repulsions, and consequently might jointly be assigned to the E_{1u} state. The three predicted absorptions actually occur in the spectrum of benzene.

The longest-wavelength band in the spectrum of benzene occurs at 256 mμ with a molar absorptivity, ϵ, of about 160, which indicates that it corresponds to a forbidden transition. Of the three transitions expected, $^1B_{2u} \leftarrow {}^1A_{1g}$ and $^1B_{1u} \leftarrow {}^1A_{1g}$ are forbidden (cf. section 6.3), and $^1E_{1u} \leftarrow {}^1A_{1g}$ is allowed. Analysis of the vibrational structure of the 256 mμ band suggests that it is the $^1B_{2u} \leftarrow {}^1A_{1g}$ transition, which, in Platt's notation (cf. section 13.2), is called $^1L_b \leftarrow {}^1A$. Then, the 200 mμ band almost certainly is $^1B_{1u} \leftarrow {}^1A_{1g}$ ($^1L_a \leftarrow {}^1A$), and the 180 mμ band, $^1E_{1u} \leftarrow {}^1A_{1g}$ ($^1B \leftarrow {}^1A$ in Platt's notation).

5.6 Formaldehyde

The σ-bond skeleton of CH_2O may be described in terms of three localized MO's, the familiar σ orbitals formed by combination of sp²-s orbitals for the two C-H bonds and sp²-sp orbitals for the C-O bond. An alternative and, for many purposes, preferable treatment consists of describing the σ-bond skeleton in terms of three nonlocalized orbitals, two of which will be of species a_1 and one of species b_2 of the point group C_{2v} appropriate to formaldehyde (see Table 4.3). Since the nonlocalized orbitals extend over several atoms, they cannot be directly correlated with specific bonds in the way localized (or even equivalent) orbitals can be. However, the nonlocalized orbitals can be transformed into localized (or equivalent) orbitals by simple linear transformations.

In the point group C_{2v} the s and p_z orbitals of the C and O atoms belong to species a_1 (see Table 5.4 and Fig. 5.6a). The p_x orbitals of both atoms belong to species b_1, and the p_y orbitals to species b_2. The 1s atomic orbital of each of the H atoms does not separately reflect the symmetry properties of the molecule; i.e., a single 1s orbital of one of the H atoms is neither symmetric nor antisymmetric with respect to the symmetry

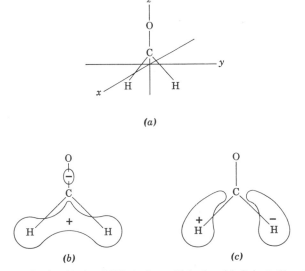

(a)

(b)   (c)

Fig. 5.6 Nonlocalized orbitals of CH_2 in formaldehyde. (a) Orientation of the molecule. (b) The σ-bonding MO of species a_1 and (c) of species b_1.

elements. However, the two 1s orbitals can be combined into two group orbitals (GO's) which are symmetric and antisymmetric linear combinations: $\phi_s = \dfrac{1}{\sqrt{2}}$ [1s(H$_1$) + 1s(H$_2$)], the symmetric GO, and $\phi_a = \dfrac{1}{\sqrt{2}}$ [1s(H$_1$) − 1s(H$_2$)], the antisymmetric GO.[9] The first of these AO's belongs to species a_1, and the second to b_2.

TABLE 5.4
Symmetry Classification of the Atomic Orbitals of CH$_2$O

Species	O	C	H$_2$
a_1	s, p$_z$	s, p$_z$	$\dfrac{1}{\sqrt{2}}(s_1 + s_2)$
a_2	...	...	...
b_1	p$_x$	p$_x$	...
b_2	p$_y$	p$_y$	$\dfrac{1}{\sqrt{2}}(s_1 - s_2)$

In an accurate MO treatment we would now form and solve a secular determinant for each of the species: a 5×5 for a_1, a 3×3 for b_2, and a 2×2 for b_1. These solutions would lead to five MO's of species a_1, two of which are bonding, two are antibonding, and one is approximately nonbonding; all of them would extend over all four atoms. Similarly, in species b_2, a bonding, an antibonding, and a nonbonding MO extending over all four atoms would result. In species b_1, only a bonding and antibonding π MO extending over C and O are formed. However, an approximate partially localized treatment will suffice for the present discussion.

The s and p$_z$ orbitals of C and of O can be combined into hybrid orbitals, one of the hybrids on each pointing up (s + p$_z$) and one on each pointing down (s − p$_z$). Combination of s − p$_z$ of O and s + p$_z$ of C forms a σ-bonding a_1 molecular orbital, ψ_1, between these atoms. (There is of course a corresponding antibonding MO, ψ_6, which must also be of species a_1, since it is generated from two AO's of this species.) The other hybrid of C, the s − p$_z$ orbital, combines with the group orbital ϕ_s of the hydrogen atoms to form the σ-bonding a_1 molecular orbital, ψ_2 (and the corresponding antibonding orbital). This bonding MO is shown in Fig. 5.6b. It can be represented approximately by

$$\psi_2 = 2s(C) - 2p_z(C) + \lambda_2\phi_s$$

[9] This formulation of the group orbitals ϕ_a and ϕ_s is based on the not-quite-correct assumption that no interaction between the 1s orbitals of the nonbonded H atoms exists, and assumes that the energy levels of ϕ_a and ϕ_s are equal, and equal to the energy of each 1s. If account is taken of the interaction, ϕ_a and ϕ_s are multiplied by factors $1/\sqrt{1 + S}$ and $1/\sqrt{1 - S}$, respectively, and the energies are adjusted for the interaction energy.

The p_y atomic orbital of C (species b_2) combines with the second of the GO's of the hydrogen atoms ϕ_a (species b_2) to form the bonding b_2 molecular orbital, ψ_3, shown in Fig. 5.6c. This MO can be represented approximately as

$$\psi_3 = 2p_y + \lambda_3\phi_a$$

A simple linear transformation $\psi_2 \pm \psi_3$, assuming $\lambda_2 = \lambda_3$, leads to localized orbitals as follows:

$$\psi_+ = \psi_2 + \psi_3 = 2s(C) + 2p_z(C) - 2p_y(C) + \lambda(\phi_s + \phi_a)$$
$$= sp^2(C) + \lambda 1s(H_1)$$

where the last step follows by substituting the definition of $\phi_a + \phi_s$ given above. Similarly

$$\psi_- = \psi_2 - \psi_3 = 2s(C) - 2p_z(C) - 2p_y(C) + \lambda(\phi_s - \phi_a)$$
$$= sp^2(C) + \lambda 1s(H_2)$$

Thus it is seen that ψ_+ and ψ_-, which are here written without regard to normalization factors, are localized on the C and on the H atom each. A more realistic approach would have been to assume $\lambda_2 \neq \lambda_3$; this would have led to orbitals which were largely but not completely localized and are often called equivalent orbitals. They would then be of the form

$$\psi_\pm = sp^2(C) + (\lambda_2 \pm \lambda_3)1s(H_1) + (\lambda_2 \mp \lambda_3)1s(H_2)$$

In order to complete the description of formaldehyde, the two lone pairs on oxygen and the π bond of the carbonyl group must be introduced. One lone pair on oxygen is in the $s + p_z$ orbital of oxygen in the z axis pointing up from O and hence of species a_1. The other lone pair on oxygen is in the p_y orbital and hence belongs to b_2. The C-O π bond, ψ_4, is anti-symmetric with respect to the C_2^z axis and with respect to $\sigma(yz)$ and hence belongs to species b_1.

In addition to these occupied MO's described above, the following antibonding unoccupied MO's are of interest: b_1^*, the antibonding π-type orbital, ψ_5, corresponding to the b_1 π-type filled orbital; and possibly a_1^*, ψ_6, the antibonding σ-type orbital corresponding to the C-O bonding a_1-type orbital. The energy-level scheme is shown in Fig. 5.7a. The ground state is then described (omitting the two a_1 and the b_1, σ-bonding orbitals) as:

$$a_1^2 b_1^2 b_2^2 : {}^1A_1$$

The following excited states can be written, each involving excitation of one electron only:

(1) $a_1^2 b_1^2 b_2 b_1^* : \quad {}^1A_2, \quad {}^3A_2$

(2) $a_1^2 b_1^2 b_2 a_1^* : \quad {}^1B_2, \quad {}^3B_2$

(3) $a_1^2 b_1 b_2^2 b_1^* : \quad {}^1A_1, \quad {}^3A_1$

(4) $a_1 b_1^2 b_2^2 b_1^* : \quad {}^1B_1, \quad {}^3B_1$

(5) $a_1^2 b_1 b_2^2 a_1^* : \quad {}^1B_1, \quad {}^3B_1$

(6) $a_1 b_1^2 b_1^2 a_1^* : \quad {}^1A_1, \quad {}^3A_1$

and hence the following singlet-singlet transitions (Fig. 5.7a) may be considered: (1), $^1A_2 \leftarrow {}^1A_1$; (2), $^1B_2 \leftarrow {}^1A_1$; (3) and (6), two $^1A_1 \leftarrow {}^1A_1$; (4) and (5), two $^1B_1 \leftarrow {}^1A_1$. According to the selection rules (cf. section

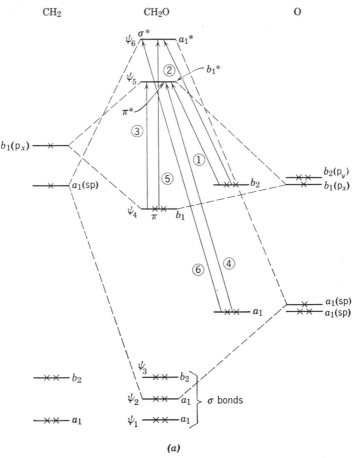

(a)

Fig. 5.7 (a) The energy-level diagram and (b) term-level diagram of formaldehyde.

6.3) all these transitions are allowed except the first, $^1A_2 \leftarrow {}^1A_1$. Transition (3) is the typical $V \leftarrow N$, $\pi \rightarrow \pi^*$ type of transition previously described, and is consequently expected to occur with high intensity. It is believed to contribute to the observed band at 1850 A in formaldehyde, and at somewhat higher wavelengths in other carbonyl compounds.

Transition (5) is a $\pi \rightarrow \sigma^*$ transition. It probably occurs at quite short wavelength, and has not been identified. The other four transitions involve some new features. They all involve the excitation of lone-pair electrons of the oxygen atom. Such transitions have been called $Q \leftarrow N$ or $A \leftarrow N$ and $B \leftarrow N$ transitions by Mulliken.[5] In two of them [(1) and (4)] the electron is excited into a π^* orbital, and such transitions are frequently called $n \rightarrow \pi^*$, or simply $n \rightarrow \pi$, transitions, following Kasha.[10] The other two [(2) and (6)] involve excitation of the electron to a σ^* orbital, and are hence referred to as $n \rightarrow \sigma^*$ transitions.

The first of the $Q \leftarrow N$ transitions, $^1A_2 \leftarrow ^1A_1$, is forbidden by symmetry (cf. section 6.3) but, because of vibrational interaction, is observed at low intensity. This transition is observed in formaldehyde at about 270 mμ with relatively low intensity ($\epsilon_{max} = 100$)[11] and is in general characteristic of carbonyl compounds. The intensity is always low even when, in carbonyl compounds belonging to a different point group, the transition is not forbidden. In order to stress this point, Platt[12] has introduced the notion of local symmetry, which, he specifies, forbids this transition.

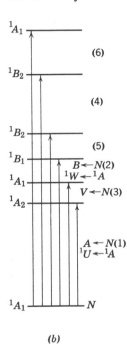

(b)

The concept of local symmetry is based on the consideration that, in determining the intensity of a transition, only that part of the π^* orbital is important which arises from the 2pπ orbital of the oxygen atom; and hence not the symmetry of the MO, but only that of the 2pπ and the n orbitals at the centrosymmetric O atom, need be considered. The upper state of such a transition is, in Platt's notation, assigned the symbol U for unallowed, and the transition is called $^1U \leftarrow ^1A$.

The transition $^1B_2 \leftarrow ^1A_1$ is also a $Q \leftarrow N$ transition, but it is allowed both by the symmetry of the molecule and by local symmetry. It is referred to as $^1W \leftarrow ^1A$ (W for allowed) by Platt, and is believed to be responsible for the band at 185 mμ. Alternately, it seems quite possible that the $^1W \leftarrow ^1A$ transition observed at 185 mμ corresponds to transition (4), which is another $n \rightarrow \pi^*$ transition, involving excitation of one of the hybrid σ lone-pair electrons of oxygen, and is allowed by molecular symmetry.

Figure 5.7b gives a term diagram for formaldehyde. This should further serve, in comparison with Fig. 5.7a, to focus on the distinction between

[10] M. Kasha, *Discussions Faraday Soc.*, **9**, 14 (1950); cf. J. Sidman, *Chem. Revs.*, **58**, 689 (1958).

[11] R. S. Mulliken, *J. Chem. Phys.*, **3**, 564 (1935).

[12] J. R. Platt, *J. Chem. Phys.*, **18**, 1168 (1950); *J. Opt. Soc. Am.*, **43**, 252 (1953).

configuration (one-electron) notation and molecular-state notation. In particular, it should be noted that the one-electron notation implies that transitions (1), (3), and (4), $b_2 \rightarrow b_1{}^*$, $b_1 \rightarrow b_1{}^*$, and $a_1 \rightarrow b_1{}^*$, involve excitation of electrons from different orbitals in the *same* ground state to the same orbital in excited states, which, as states, are different, as is seen from their configurations. This is probably clearer in Fig. 5.7b, where the ground states all have the same symbol, N.

6 Intensities

6.1 General

It is customary in ultraviolet spectrophotometry to discuss and to describe the intensities of absorption bands in terms of the molar absorptivities, ϵ_{max} (frequently called the *molar extinction coefficients*). These quantities are of great convenience, since they are readily obtainable from the determination of the wavelength of maximum absorption, and from accurate measurement of the absorbance at this *one* wavelength. Unfortunately, however, the value of ϵ_{max} is not directly related to any quantity obtainable from theory.

A spectral transition (i.e., an absorption line) corresponds to the energy difference between two well-defined states of the absorbing molecule. If the molecule absorbed light only at a single wavelength, the spectrum would consist of individual lines, like the emission spectra of atoms, and band widths would depend predominantly on the resolving power of the monochromator. Unfortunately, however, the situation is complicated by the fact that molecules possess, in addition to electronic energy, vibrational and rotational energy. Changes in these energies accompany the changes in electronic energy and give rise to the familar band spectra. Thus a single electronic transition comprises many individual lines (bands), and the quantity of interest, the total energy transferred, must be the sum of the contribution from all these lines (bands).

In the case of liquids and solutions, discussed predominantly in this book, the matter is further complicated because, in the liquid state, the energy levels are broadened (cf. section 6.8), and thus the band spectrum, which in the vapor state frequently consists of a multitude of rather sharp lines, is broadened into diffuse bands.

The quantity of interest in theory thus is not ϵ_{max} but is the integrated (absolute) intensity (I), which is the area under the absorption curve; its evaluation requires that the band under consideration be isolated from all other bands, and that the area under the absorption curve be measured. Such measurement can readily be achieved by the usual methods of counting

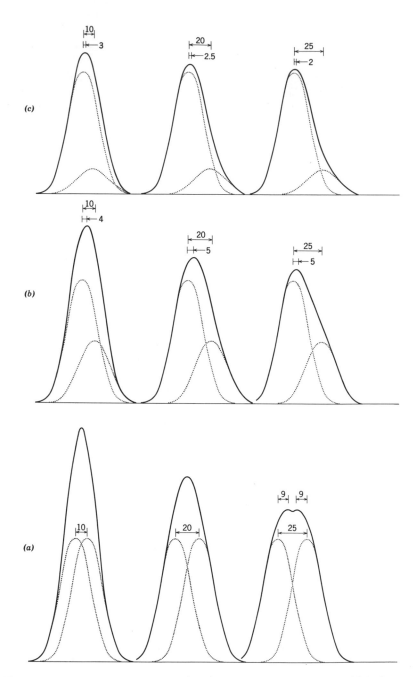

Fig. 6.1 Band shape to be expected from a two-component band in which the components have (*a*) equal intensity, (*b*) an intensity ratio of 1:2 and (*c*) of 1:5.

112

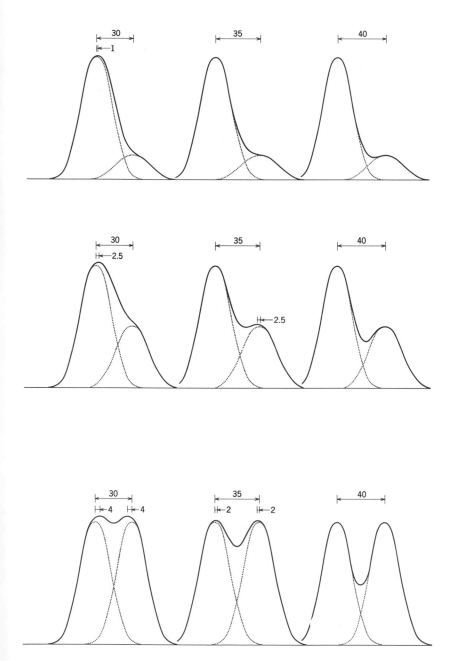

[Reprinted by permission from J. M. Vandenbelt and C. Henrich, *Appl. Spectroscopy*, **7**, 173 (1953).]

squares (when the spectrum is plotted on graph paper), cutting out and weighing, or using a planimeter. The segregation and isolation of an absorption band is much more difficult than measuring the area under it. Ultraviolet spectra rarely contain isolated bands, and we must generally extrapolate the band to the abscissa in a somewhat arbitrary manner. Since the experimental integrated intensity is mathematically defined by the integral

$$I = \int \epsilon \, d\nu$$

it is obvious that the spectrum must be plotted with an abscissa linear in frequency (or wavenumbers) and an ordinate linear in ϵ.

When comparing experimental and theoretically estimated intensities, it is often practical to use ϵ_{max} as a measure of integrated intensities. Particularly when comparing the "same" band (i.e., bands of substantially the same electronic origin) in the spectra of a series of closely related compounds, we frequently assume that the shapes or widths of the bands in the spectra under comparison are so similar that ϵ_{max} and I are proportional. A very good approximation to the integrated intensity in these cases is achieved by multiplying ϵ_{max} by $\Delta\nu$, where $\Delta\nu$ is the so-called half-band width, i.e., the width of the band in cm^{-1} where $\epsilon = \frac{1}{2}\epsilon_{max}$.

In the ultraviolet region, strongly overlapping bands are frequently encountered. The evaluation of the integrated intensity of such bands then requires analysis into separate bands, which is always somewhat arbitrary. The molar absorptivities of such bands are customarily taken to be measured values. Although this is a satisfactory procedure for empirical identification purposes, provided the "spectral width" of the light beam is reasonably constant, such intensities are quite questionable for theoretical purposes, since they represent a superposition of ϵ_{max} for the main band, plus a contribution from one or more overlapping bands. The problem is particularly serious in discussing intensities of partly submerged bands appearing in the spectrum only as shoulders or inflection points. The analysis[1] of such two-component bands into their separate components is illustrated in Fig. 6.1. In part a, where the two component bands (dotted lines) are of equal intensity, distinct peaks first appear in the summation or observed band (solid line) when the components have maxima 30 mμ apart. The observed maxima, however, are shifted 4 mμ from their true value. One of the component (standard) bands in Fig. 6.1b and c is identical with those in a, but the second band in b is one-half and in c one-fifth the intensity of the standard.

Much of the older literature contains data for ϵ_{min} (and λ_{min}). These

[1] J. M. Vandenbelt and C. Henrich, *Appl. Spectroscopy*, **7**, 176 (1953).

quantities are devoid of theoretical significance; furthermore they are so sensitive to a number of extraneous factors (purity of sample and solvent, slit width, and other details of spectrophotometric technique) as to be virtually useless.

6.2 Theoretical Calculation of Absorption Intensity

In principle, the problem of the calculation of the absolute intensity of an absorption (or emission) band is not difficult. It has been shown[2] that the probabilities of emission (A) and absorption (B) between two electronic states, i (initial) and f (final), are given by

$$A_{if} = (64\pi^4 v^3 e^2 / 3h) G_f D_{if}$$

and

$$B_{if} = (8\pi^3 e^2 / 3h^2 c) G_f D_{if}$$

where e is the charge of an electron, h Planck's constant, c the velocity of light, v the frequency of the emission, G_f the statistical weight of the final state (i.e., the number of degenerate wave functions to which absorption or emission can lead), and D_{if} the dipole strength elaborated below. Mulliken[2] has transformed the quantity B_{if} into a measure of intensity, the oscillator strength f, which is given by:

$$f = (8\pi^2 mc/3h) G_f v D_{if} = 1.096 \times 10^{11} G_f v D_{if}$$

and is related to the absolute intensity by

$$f = 0.102(mc^2/N\pi e^2) \int \epsilon \, dv = 4.315 \times 10^{-9} \int \epsilon \, dv$$

where m is the mass of the electron, N is Avogadro's number, ϵ is the molar absorption coefficient, and the integration extends over the entire, absorption band. In the spectra with which most of this book is concerned, the statistical factor G_f is unity and need not be considered further.

The dipole strength D thus is proportional to the intensity, and is the square of a relatively simple-appearing integral:

$$\sqrt{I} \propto \sqrt{D} = \int \Xi_i \mathbf{M} \, \Xi_f \, dT \qquad (6.1)$$

where Ξ_i and Ξ_f are the total wave functions of the initial and final states of the molecule, respectively, dT represents the product of the volume elements in the coordinates of all the nuclei and electrons, and $\mathbf{M}$ is the so-called dipole-moment vector, which needs some elaboration. The dipole moment of a molecule is defined as the distance between the centers

_____

[2] See R. S. Mulliken, *J. Chem. Phys.*, **7**, 14 (1939).

of gravity of the positive and negative charges multiplied by the magnitude of these charges. Since, in the approximation usually used, location of the nuclei produces no problem, the center of gravity of positive charge is readily fixed. Electrons, however, cannot be located, but are described by a probability function, and the center of gravity of the electrons is consequently an average over the probability function. The average distance between the centers of gravity of the positive and negative charges is evaluated by averaging the distance (with direction, i.e., the radius vector) $\mathbf{r}$ from the center of gravity of positive charge to the electron. According to quantum mechanics, the desired average is given by the integral

$$\int \Psi_i' \, \Sigma \, e\mathbf{r} \, \Psi_i \, dT = \int \Psi_i' \, \mathbf{M} \, \Psi_i \, dT$$

where the summation extends over all electrons. For this reason the quantity $\mathbf{M} = \Sigma \, e\mathbf{r}$ is called the dipole moment vector. Equation (6.1) does not represent a dipole moment exactly but may be thought roughly to represent a charge migration or displacement during the transition; it is frequently called the *transition moment*.

The symmetry properties of the dipole moment vector $\mathbf{M}$ are of considerable interest. This vector, like all vectors, can be analyzed into three components, $M^2 = M_x^2 + M_y^2 + M_z^2$ in the direction of the three Cartesian coordinate axes. Application of a given symmetry operation will either leave such a component unchanged, in which case the component is symmetric, or reverse the direction of the component, in which case the component is antisymmetric with respect to the operation. Perhaps an example will make this clearer. Consider the operations in point group C_{2v}, namely, $C_2{}^z$, $\sigma(xz)$, $\sigma(yz)$, and I. The three components of a vector $\mathbf{M}$, namely, M_x, M_y, and M_z, may be represented by arrows parallel to the x, y, and z axes, respectively. The symmetry operations of the point group can now be performed on these arrows. The operation $C_2{}^z$ transforms the arrows representing M_x and M_y into arrows pointing in the opposite directions but leaves the arrow representing M_z unchanged. Both operations σ_v leave the arrow M_z unchanged; $\sigma(xz)$ inverts M_y but not M_x, while $\sigma(yz)$ inverts M_x but not M_y. The identity operation leaves all arrows unchanged. If each inversion is represented by -1 and each lack of inversion by $+1$, the character of each of the components M_x, M_y, and M_z in the point group C_{2v} becomes identical with the character of each of symmetry species B_1, B_2, and A_1, respectively. Consequently it can be said that M_x, M_y, and M_z belong to these symmetry species or, in the terminology of the mathematician, transform as these symmetry species. The assignments of the components of $\mathbf{M}$ to the appropriate symmetry species are indicated in the last column of each of the character tables (Appendix 3) by placing M_x, M_y, and M_z opposite the symmetry species to which they belong. The usual difficulties occur when discussing symmetry and antisymmetry with respect to rotation by more than two-fold axes (cf. section 4.4), and in these cases the components of $\mathbf{M}$ belong in pairs to doubly degenerate, or in groups of three to triply degenerate, species.

Equation (6.1) permits the evaluation of the intensity, provided the total wave functions Ξ_i and Ξ_f are known. This is, however, never the case, and a long series of approximations is required. First, it is assumed that rotational and vibrational wave functions can be factored out, and equation (6.1) reduces to

$$\sqrt{D} = \int \Psi'_i \, \mathbf{M} \, \Psi'_f \, d\tau \tag{6.2}$$

where Ψ'_i and Ψ'_f are the total electronic wave functions of initial and final states, and $d\tau$ is the product of the volume elements in terms of the coordinates of all the electrons.

Integrals of the form of equation (6.2) can be evaluated, and the calculations have been performed for a series of simple molecules.[3] Unfortunately, however, such numerical computations become prohibitive in complexity for all but the simplest molecules, and further approximations become necessary. Equation (6.2) can, nevertheless, be used in a qualitative or semi-quantitative way, as outlined in section 6.3.

Next, we frequently assume that (1) the Ψ' can be factored into a series of one electron functions (orbitals), ψ_j, (2) only a single electron is excited, and (3) the ψ_j are the same in the ground and excited states. Assumption (2) is generally valid and is further discussed below, but assumptions (1) and (3) are quite serious approximations. They do, however, permit reduction of the problem to manageable proportions, and in particular permit far-reaching qualitative and semiquantitative conclusions. In addition, the approximation frequently made, that the geometries of ground and excited states are equal, is serious. The vibronic interaction will be discussed in section 6.6. With these assumptions, and arbitrarily letting the electron being excited be number 1, equation (6.2) reduces to

$$\sqrt{D} = \int \psi_{i1} \, \mathbf{M}_1 \, \psi_{f1} \, d\tau_1 \tag{6.3}$$

Equation (6.3) can be evaluated numerically, but the assumptions made above, and the approximate nature of the available ψ_j, mean that the results are very crude. Fortunately, however, the right-hand side of equations (6.2) and (6.3) frequently vanish identically, and this fact alone yields most important information. A more detailed discussion of the approximate numerical evaluation of equation (6.3) is given in section 6.4.

[3] R. S. Mulliken and C. A. Rieke, *Repts. Progr. in Phys.*, **8**, 231 (1941).

An interesting semiempirical theory of absorption intensity has been proposed by Braude,[4] based largely on the fact that ϵ is expressed in the units 1000 cm²/mole. Since ϵ for a typical allowed transition is of the order of 10^5, this corresponds to 10^8 cm²/mole, or 1.7×10^{-16} cm²/molecule. The dimensions of most molecules are of the order of a few angstroms, i.e., 10^{-8} cm, and hence their areas are of the order of 10^{-16} to 10^{-15} cm, which is just the order of magnitude of ϵ. Braude has suggested that, for an allowed transition, all light falling on the molecule or, better, the effective chromophore area a of the molecule, is absorbed, and on the basis of this postulate arrives at an expression

$$\epsilon = 0.87 \times 10^{20} a$$

The effective chromophore area of a π-electron system is assumed to have the length of the system (i.e., the sum of the lengths of all the C-C bonds in a conjugated system) and to have a width of 1.5 A, a value reasonable on the basis of x-ray data. On the basis of these assumptions, Braude calculates an effective area a of 2.02 A², and an ϵ of 17,400, for ethylene, in fair agreement with the observed value of 15,000. Although the calculated values for the polyenes exceed the observed values by increasing amounts, up to a factor of 5 for $C_{22}H_{24}$, the agreement is exceedingly good, considering the simplicity of the theory. As a further slight approximation it can be considered that the area is proportional to the number, n, of conventional double bonds; then $\epsilon = 0.87 \times 10^{20} \times 2 \times 10^{-16} n = 1.74 \times 10^4 n$.

6.3   Selection Rules

The most useful property of integrals of the type of equations (6.2) and (6.3) is that they frequently vanish identically; i.e., the integral is equal to zero. If this is the case the transition is called *forbidden*, and should, according to the *approximate* theory, not occur at all. Actually, forbidden transitions do occur; and, as might have been expected, calculation by more refined theories gives small but nonvanishing values for the intensities. Observed intensities of forbidden transitions are generally quite small, much smaller than those of allowed transitions [for which equations (6.2) and (6.3) give nonvanishing intensities].

Fortunately it is usually possible to tell, from the symmetry properties of wave functions, whether or not equation (6.2) and (6.3) will vanish. Relatively simple rules can be established which predict the vanishing or nonvanishing of the intensity integral; these rules are referred to as *selection rules*. The next few paragraphs will deal with the manner in which such selection rules may be established.

[4] E. A. Braude, *J. Chem. Soc.*, 379 (1950).

It is a well-known fact of mathematics that $\int y\,dx$ represents the area under the curve if y is plotted against x, areas below the abscissa being counted negative. Now, assume functions $y(x)$ such that y^2 is symmetric in x; i.e., $y^2(x) = y^2(-x)$. One such function $y = x^2$ is shown in Fig. 6.2a. In this case $y(x) = y(-x)$ (i.e., for two identical values of x which differ only in sign, y has the same value); such a function is called *even*. The (shaded) area under the parabola can be expressed by the integral $\int_{-a}^{+a} y\,dx = 2\int_{0}^{a} y\,dx$, since the areas under the two halves of the curve both are above the abscissa and are equal. A plot of the equation $y = x^3$ is shown in Fig. 6.2b, where it can be seen that for every positive value of x there is a positive y value, and for every negative value of x a corresponding negative value of y. Here $y(x) = -y(-x)$; such a function is called an *odd* function. Integration of $y = x^3$ gives $\int_{-a}^{+a} y\,dx = 0$, since the (shaded)

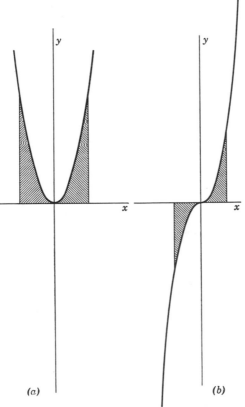

(a)   (b)

Fig. 6.2 Even (a) and odd (b) functions $y(x)$.

areas under the curve for positive and negative x are equal but above and below the abscissa, respectively, and thus cancel. The product of an even and an odd function is always odd, while the products of two even or of two odd functions are always even. The integral over all space of an odd function always vanishes identically, whereas the integral over all space of an even function may or may not vanish, but generally does not.

The integrals of equations (6.2) and (6.3) can be expanded into the sum of a series of integrals, each involving only one coordinate (i.e., one of the components of **M**), and it is necessary only to demonstrate that the integrand is an odd function of the integration coordinate to demonstrate that the integral vanishes. Provided the molecule has some elements of symmetry,[5] it is possible to demonstrate that equation (6.3) vanishes for certain transitions.

The first selection rule to be discussed is concerned only with molecules which have a center of symmetry (e.g., ethylene). All wave functions (orbitals) are either symmetric or antisymmetric with respect to the center [i.e., either gerade (g) or ungerade (u)], and all components of the vector **M** are of necessity ungerade. The product of two functions is ungerade only if one is gerade and the other ungerade. Hence the integrand of equation (6.3) can be gerade only if **M** is multiplied by an ungerade quantity, which can happen only if ψ_i, the ground-state wave function (orbital), and ψ_f, the excited-state wave function, are of unequal parity (gerade-ungerade character). Hence the selection rule $g \rightarrow u$ or $u \rightarrow g$; but $g \nleftrightarrow g$ and $u \nleftrightarrow u$. The crossed arrows indicate that the transitions are forbidden.

The second selection rule to be considered is concerned with the multiplicity of states. Thus a transition from a singlet to a triplet state, a so-called singlet $\rightarrow$ triplet transition, will be considered. It is assumed that the initial wave function (electron configuration) is given by ψ_k^2, and the final one by $\psi_k \psi_j$. In ψ_k^2, the spins of the two electrons, since they occupy the same orbital, must be antiparallel; this is indicated by writing $\psi_k^2 \alpha\beta$, where α and β are spin wave functions of opposite direction. In the excited triplet state, the function will be $\psi_k \psi_j \alpha^2$ (or β^2), since now the spins are parallel.[6] Equation (6.3) becomes[7]

$$\int \psi_i \alpha \mathbf{M} \psi_f \beta \, d\tau \, d\sigma = \int \psi_i \mathbf{M} \psi_f \, d\tau \int \alpha\beta \, d\sigma$$

[5] This is a more exact condition than is absolutely necessary. Since rough approximations are customarily made, it is necessary only that the parts of the molecule, or the wave functions considered have elements of symmetry.

[6] A further spin function, $\alpha(1)\beta(2) + \alpha(2)\beta(1)$, also corresponds to parallel spins and makes up the third component of the triplet.

[7] In singlet $\rightarrow$ singlet transitions the spin functions can be safely neglected, since they reduce to a factor $\int \alpha^2 \, d\sigma = 1$.

($d\sigma$ is the element of volume in the spin coordinates), and the integrand $\alpha\beta$ in the last integral is odd; hence the intensity vanishes, and singlet $\rightarrow$ triplet transitions are forbidden.

The third selection rule deals with the symmetry of states. Operation of this rule can be effectively illustrated by consideration of formaldehyde. As discussed in detail in section 5.6, the ground-state configuration of formaldehyde, ignoring the σ-bond skeleton, may be represented by $a_1^2 b_1^2 b_2^2$ and hence belongs to species $^1A_1$. Transitions 1, 2, and 3 shown in Fig. 5.6 may be designated as follows:

$$(1)\ n \rightarrow \pi^* \quad \text{or} \quad Q \leftarrow N \quad \text{or} \quad {}^1A_2 \leftarrow {}^1A_1$$
$$(2)\ n \rightarrow \pi^* \quad \text{or} \quad Q \leftarrow N \quad \text{or} \quad {}^1B_2 \leftarrow {}^1A_1$$
$$(3)\ \pi \rightarrow \pi^* \quad \text{or} \quad V \leftarrow N \quad \text{or} \quad {}^1A_1 \leftarrow {}^1A_1$$

In the point group C_{2v}, to which formaldehyde belongs, the three components M_x, M_y, and M_z of $\mathbf{M}$ belong to the symmetry species B_1, B_2, and A_1, respectively. For the three transitions listed above, the products $\Psi_i'\Psi_f$ belong to the species $A_1 A_2 = A_2$, $A_1 B_2 = B_2$, and $A_1 A_1 = A_1$, respectively. Since none of the components of $\mathbf{M}$ belongs to species A_2, the integrand $\Psi_i' \mathbf{M} \Psi_f$ in the intensity-determining integral, equation (6.2), is an odd function and hence the integral vanishes. Thus, the longest-wavelength $n \rightarrow \pi^*$ transition is forbidden, thus explaining the low intensity observed. The $\pi \rightarrow \pi^*$, the $V \leftarrow N$ transition, is very intense; the $\Psi_i'\Psi_f$ product belonging to species A_1 makes this transition allowed, and the geometric rough coincidence of the π and π^* orbitals leads to very large values of $\Psi_i'\Psi_f$ and hence to the usual high intensity of $V \leftarrow N$ transitions. It is apparent that the first selection rule, the $g \rightarrow u$ rule, is just a special case, although a particularly important one, of this third selection rule.

To demonstrate further the operation of the selection rules, the possible transitions in butadiene in two approximations will be considered. As mentioned in the earlier discussion in section 5.4, butadiene exists in an *s-trans* form and an *s-cis* form, and it can be treated in MO theory as though it had a linear configuration. The point group to which each of these configurations belongs and the symmetry species of the excited states were given in Table 5.2. The effect of the selection rules on the transitions is summarized in Table 6.1. The ground-state Ψ_i in all models of butadiene is a singlet state, and accordingly all transitions to the triplet states are multiplicity forbidden. Two transitions in the linear model are forbidden by the $g \rightarrow u$ selection rule; and, since the center of symmetry remains unchanged in going from D_{2h} to C_{2h} symmetry, the parity-forbidden transitions remain forbidden in the *s-trans* model. The C_{2v} point group has no center of symmetry, and hence there are no $g \rightarrow u$

transitions and no parity forbiddenness. The distortion from D_{2h} symmetry to C_{2v} symmetry makes the $\Psi'_i \to \Psi'_{f2}$ and $\Psi'_i \to \Psi'_{f3}$ transitions in the *s-cis* model allowed; but, since this distortion is not large and does not greatly affect the wave functions, it is a logical inference that these transitions in *s-cis* butadiene will be weak. No transitions in either the *s-cis* or *s-trans* models are symmetry forbidden.

TABLE 6.1

Selection Rules (SR) in Butadiene
(A = allowed; F = forbidden)

	Linear (D_{2h})		*s-trans* (C_{2h})		*s-cis* (C_{2v})	
Ψ_i	A_{1g}		A_g		A_1	
Transition	Ψ_f	SR	Ψ_f	SR	Ψ_f	SR
$\Psi_i \to \Psi_{f1}$	B_{1u}	A	B_u	A	B_2	A
$\Psi_i \to \Psi_{f2}$	A_g	F	A_g	F	A_1	A
$\Psi_i \to \Psi_{f3}$	A_g	F	A_g	F	A_1	A
$\Psi_i \to \Psi_{f4}$	B_{1u}	A	B_u	A	B_2	A

In discussions of spectral behavior of particular compounds we frequently encounter statements such as the following: "Because of the high symmetry, many of the transitions in this molecule are forbidden." The statement is seldom amplified and might seem puzzling because the relationship between high symmetry and forbiddenness is not immediately obvious. Accordingly an explicit discussion of this relationship is desirable.

In order for a transition to be allowed, the product $\Psi'_i \Psi'_f$ must belong to the same symmetry species as at least one of the components of **M**. A molecule with no elements of symmetry belongs to point group I, in which there is only one symmetry species. The product $\Psi'_i \Psi'_f$ *must* belong to the same species as all the components of **M**, and hence all transitions are allowed. In point groups C_s and C_2 at least one component of **M** belongs to each of the two symmetry species, and again the product $\Psi'_i \Psi'_f$ must belong to the same species as one of the components of **M** and all transitions are allowed. In point group C_{2v} there are four symmetry species; and, as shown in section 6.2, the three components of **M**, namely, M_x, M_y, M_z, belong to (or transform as) symmetry species B_1, B_2, A_1, respectively. Since each of the three components of **M** can belong to only one symmetry species and there are a total of four, there must be at least one species to which no component of **M** belongs. Then some products of $\Psi'_i \Psi'_f$ may belong to this species and hence correspond to a forbidden transition. In point group C_{2v} no component of **M** belongs to species A_2; if the product of the wave functions of an initial and a final state of a molecule in this point group belonged to species A_2, the transition between these states would be symmetry forbidden. It follows that the "higher" the symmetry of a molecule, the larger the number of symmetry species.[8] Products of $\Psi_i'\Psi_f$ in no more than three symmetry species can lead to allowed transitions, since the three components of $\mathbf{M}$ can at most belong to three species (actually, frequently two components belong to one species, usually a doubly degenerate species, or all three belong to a single triply degenerate species); hence the larger the number of symmetry species, the greater the probability of finding $\Psi_i'\Psi_f$ products belonging to a species to which no component of $\mathbf{M}$ belongs and accordingly corresponding to forbidden transitions.

Summarizing the selection rules, there are at least three basic types of forbidden transitions: (1) parity-forbidden transitions, i.e., $g \nleftrightarrow g$ and $u \nleftrightarrow u$. The visible spectra of simple transition-metal ions are examples: the molar absorptivities (extinction coefficients) usually are of the order of <3; (2) spin-forbidden transitions, as the singlet-triplet transitions in ethylene; their intensity is very low, generally $\epsilon < 1$; and finally (3) symmetry-forbidden transitions, such as the 260 mμ band of benzene, with intensities up to ~300. Furthermore, there are transitions which have low intensities, even though they are not forbidden in the sense discussed; as long as the product $\Psi_i'\Psi_f$ of equation (6.2) is small everywhere, the intensity must be low.

So far the discussion has been restricted to transitions involving the excitation of a single electron. It can be shown that the integral in equation (6.2) vanishes when Ψ_i and Ψ_f, expressed as products on one-electron functions ψ, differ in more than one of the ψ's, and hence many-electron excitations are forbidden. Only the fact that the many-electron configurations cannot strictly be expressed as products of one-electron orbitals ψ_j, but are linear combinations of such (configuration interaction; cf. Chapter 8) leads to a nonvanishing probability of many-electron excitations. As a corollary, the less the states involved in a transition are involved in configuration interaction, the lower is the intensity of the corresponding transition.

The proof that two electron excitations are forbidden goes as follows. Using

$$\Psi_i = \varphi_1(1)\varphi_2(2) \ldots \varphi_{n-1}(n-1)\varphi_n(n)\varphi_{n+1}(n+1)$$

$$\Psi_f = \varphi_1(1)\varphi_2(2) \ldots \varphi_{n-1}(n-1)\varphi_{n+2}(n)\varphi_{n+3}(n+1)$$

and

$$\mathbf{M} = \mathbf{M}(1) + \mathbf{M}(2) + \ldots + \mathbf{M}(n-1) + \mathbf{M}(n) + \mathbf{M}(n+1) = \Sigma\,\mathbf{M}(j)$$

[8] It is of course not strictly possible to assign a unique scale of increasing degree of symmetry but, in general, the number of symmetry species increases with increasing symmetry.

equation (6.2) becomes the integral over two products of wave functions multiplied by the sum of the $M(j)$. This can be separated into a sum of integrals, each of which has the form

$$\int \varphi_1(1)\varphi_2(2) \ldots \varphi_{n-1}(n-1)\varphi_n(n)\varphi_{n+1}(n+1)M(j)$$

$$\times \varphi_1(1)\varphi_2(2) \ldots \varphi_{n-1}(n-1)\varphi_{n+2}(n)\varphi_{n+3}(n+1) \, d\tau_1 \, d\tau_2 \ldots d\tau_{n-1} \, d\tau_n \, d\tau_{n+1}$$

Each of this set of integrals may be factored into a product of integrals, of which the one for $j = n$ is

$$\int \varphi_1(1)\varphi_1(1) \, d\tau_1 \int \varphi_2(2)\varphi_2(2) \, d\tau_2 \ldots \int \varphi_{n-1}(n-1)\varphi_{n-1}(n-1) \, d\tau_{n-1}$$

$$\times \int \varphi_n(n) \, \mathbf{M}(n)\varphi_{n+2}(n) \, d\tau_n \int \varphi_{n+1}(n+1)\varphi_{n+3}(n+1) \, d\tau_{n+1}$$

In this product, the first $n-1$ integrals are normalization integrals, and hence unity, but the last one is an orthogonality integral, and hence zero, and consequently the whole product vanishes. The same is true for $j = n + 1$; if $j < n$, there will be two vanishing terms. Consequently each term of the sum partial integrals vanishes, the predicted intensity is zero, and the transition is forbidden.

6.4   Calculation of Intensities by LCAO Molecular-Orbital Theory

A crude calculation of intensities by simple LCAO MO theory can be achieved, and for illustrative purposes the linear model of butadiene (cf. section 5.4) will be used. The wave functions are (cf. Table 5.1)

$$\psi_{1,4} = c_1(\phi_1 \pm \phi_4) \pm c_2(\phi_2 \pm \phi_3)$$

$$\psi_{2,3} = c_2(\phi_1 \mp \phi_4) \pm c_1(\phi_2 \mp \phi_3)$$

(6.4)

where the upper signs belong to the bonding orbitals ψ_1 and ψ_2, the lower ones to the antibonding orbitals ψ_3 and ψ_4. ϕ_1, ϕ_2, ϕ_3, and ϕ_4 are again the AO's of the carbon atoms 1 to 4, and $c_1 = 0.373$, $c_2 = 0.602$ were obtained in section 3.9.

Consider now the three transitions

$$\Psi_i \to \Psi_{f1} \, (^1A_g \to {}^1B_{1u}, \psi_2 \to \psi_3{}^*)$$

$$\Psi_i \to \Psi_{f2} \, (^1A_g \to {}^1A_g, \psi_2 \to \psi_4{}^*)$$

$$\Psi_i \to \Psi_{f4} \, (^1A_g \to {}^1B_{1u}, \psi_1 \to \psi_4{}^*)$$

(cf. Tables 6.1 and 5.2). Since the simple LCAO MO theory deals strictly with one-electron orbitals, it is necessary only to substitute the appropriate orbitals ψ_i and ψ_f (as listed in the parentheses above) into equation (6.3), using the functions listed in equations (6.4). Thus we obtain for:

(1)

$$\int \psi_2 \mathbf{M} \psi_3{}^* \, d\tau = \int [c_2(\phi_1 - \phi_4) + c_1(\phi_2 - \phi_3)]\mathbf{M}$$

$$\times [c_2(\phi_1 + \phi_4) - c_1(\phi_2 + \phi_3)] \, d\tau$$

$$= e \int [c_2{}^2(\phi_1{}^2 - \phi_4{}^2) - c_1{}^2(\phi_2{}^2 - \phi_3{}^2)$$

$$- 2c_1 c_2(\phi_1\phi_3 - \phi_2\phi_4)]\mathbf{r} \, d\tau$$

(6.5a)

(2)
$$\int \psi_2 M \psi_4^* \, d\tau = \int [c_2(\phi_1 - \phi_4) + c_1(\phi_2 - \phi_3)]M$$

$$\times \, [c_1(\phi_1 - \phi_4) - c_2(\phi_2 - \phi_3)] \, d\tau$$

$$= e \int \{c_1 c_2[(\phi_1 - \phi_4)^2 - (\phi_2 - \phi_3)^2] - (c_1{}^2 - c_2{}^2)$$

$$\times \, (\phi_1 \phi_2 - \phi_1 \phi_3 - \phi_2 \phi_4 + \phi_3 \phi_4)\} \mathbf{r} \, d\tau \qquad (6.5b)$$

(3)
$$\int \psi_1 M \psi_4^* \, d\tau = \int [c_1(\phi_1 + \phi_4) + c_2(\phi_2 + \phi_3)]M[c_1(\phi_1 - \phi_4) - c_2(\phi_2 - \phi_3)] \, d\tau$$

$$= e \int [c_1{}^2(\phi_1{}^2 - \phi_4{}^2) - c_2{}^2(\phi_2{}^2 - \phi_3{}^2) - 2c_1 c_2(\phi_1 \phi_3 - \phi_2 \phi_4)]\mathbf{r} \, d\tau$$

$$(6.5c)$$

In the last step M has been replaced by $e\mathbf{r}$, where $\mathbf{r}$ is the vector distance of the electron from the center of positive charge (i.e., the center of gravity or the center of symmetry) of the molecule. In order to avoid complicated integrations, and in keeping with the assumptions general to LCAO MO theory, a series of approximations is now made. The subsequent steps are given in detail only for transition (1). Equation (6.5a) can be rewritten as follows:

$$\int \psi_2 M \psi_3^* \, d\tau = e \left[c_2{}^2 \left(\int \phi_1{}^2 \mathbf{r} \, d\tau - \int \phi_4{}^2 \mathbf{r} \, d\tau \right) - c_1{}^2 \left(\int \phi_2{}^2 \mathbf{r} \, d\tau - \int \phi_3{}^2 \mathbf{r} \, d\tau \right) \right.$$

$$\left. - 2c_1 c_2 \left(\int \phi_1 \phi_3 \mathbf{r} \, d\tau - \int \phi_2 \phi_4 \mathbf{r} \, d\tau \right) \right] \qquad (6.6)$$

Just as the overlap integrals $S_{AB} = \int \phi_A \phi_B \, d\tau$ are neglected, the last two integrals in equation (6.6) are neglected. The integrals $\int \phi_A{}^2 \mathbf{r} \, d\tau$ represent roughly the charge of an electron at the atom A and are replaced by $z_A \int \phi_A{}^2 \, d\tau$, where $\int \phi_A{}^2 \, d\tau$ is a normalization integral and equal to unity, and z_A is the z coordinate of the atom A. Hence, equation (6.6) becomes

(1)
$$\int \psi_2 M \psi_3^* \, d\tau = e[c_2{}^2(z_1 - z_4) - c_1{}^2(z_2 - z_3)] \qquad (6.7a)$$

Similarly, equations (6.5b) and (6.5c) give

(2)
$$\int \psi_2 M \psi_4^* \, d\tau = e[c_1 c_2(z_1 + z_4 - z_2 - z_3)] \qquad (6.7b)$$

(3)
$$\int \psi_1 M \psi_4^* \, d\tau = e[c_1{}^2(z_1 - z_4) - c_2{}^2(z_2 - z_3)] \qquad (6.7c)$$

But $z_1 = -z_4$ and $z_2 = -z_3$ follow from the symmetry of the molecule (the origin of the z axis is at the center). A further approximation is now made. In setting up the secular equation (section 3.9), resonance integrals (H_{AB}) were taken equal for the three bonds, thus implying that the bonds were assumed of equal lengths. Calling this bond length d, we readily see that

$$z_1 = 3z_2 = 3d/2$$

Substituting these identities and the values for c_1 and c_2 into equations (6.7) yields

(1) $$\sqrt{D} = (3c_2{}^2 - c_1{}^2)ed = 0.981ed \qquad (6.8a)$$

(2) $$\sqrt{D} = 0 \qquad (6.8b)$$

(3) $$\sqrt{D} = (3c_1{}^2 - c_2{}^2)ed = 0.041ed \qquad (6.8c)$$

Equations (6.8) are revealing. First, equation (6.8b) shows that the $^1A_g \leftarrow {}^1A_g$ transition gives a 0 intensity, as required by the selection rule. It can be shown without difficulty that the neglected terms of equation (6.5b) also vanish identically, as expected. The calculation was not done for the other $^1A_g \leftarrow {}^1A_g$ ($\Psi_{f3}, \leftarrow \Psi_i \; \psi_1 \rightarrow \psi_3{}^*$) transition, but the result would have been the same. Second, the longest-wave-length $V \leftarrow N$ transition (1) has a predicted intensity much larger (by a factor of 20) than the other such transition (3). Although it can hardly be hoped that the crude calculations given here accurately and quantitatively reflect intensities, the calculated intensity ratio is qualitatively correct. The method described has considerable merit for rough comparisons because of its simplicity.

In the light of the selection rules and the methods of calculating intensities, a further discussion of local symmetry in $Q \leftarrow N$ transitions (cf. Section 5.6) seems indicated. Take as an example the $Q \leftarrow N$ transitions in formaldehyde. Transitions (1), (2), (4), and (6) were written as

(1) $\qquad a_1{}^2b_1{}^2b_2b_1{}^*(^1A_2) \leftarrow a_1{}^2b_1{}^2b_2{}^2(^1A_1) \quad$ or $\quad b_2 \rightarrow b_1{}^*$

(2) $\qquad a_1{}^2b_1{}^2b_2a_1{}^*(^1B_2) \leftarrow a_1{}^2b_1{}^2b_2{}^2(^1A_1) \quad$ or $\quad b_2 \rightarrow a_1{}^*$

(4) $\qquad a_1b_1{}^2b_2{}^2b_1{}^*(^1B_1) \leftarrow a_1{}^2b_1{}^2b_2{}^2(^1A_1) \quad$ or $\quad a_1 \rightarrow b_1{}^*$

(6) $\qquad a_1b_1{}^2b_2{}^2a_1{}^*(^1A_1) \leftarrow a_1{}^2b_1{}^2b_2{}^2(^1A_1) \quad$ or $\quad a_1 \rightarrow a_1{}^*$

where b_2 is a p_y orbital of O, a_1 is an sp^2 hybrid orbital of O [$2s(O) + 2p_z(O)$], $b_1{}^*$ is a π^* orbital of the form $2p_x(O) - \lambda_\pi 2p_x(C)$, and $a_1{}^*$ is a σ^* orbital of the form $2s(O) - 2p_z(O) - \lambda_\sigma[2s(C) + 2p_z(C)]$. The intensity-determining integrals for these four transitions hence are:

(1) $$\int p_y(O)\mathbf{M}[p_x(O) - \lambda_\pi p_x(C)] \, d\tau$$

(2) $$\int p_y(O)\mathbf{M}\{s(O) - p_z(O) - \lambda_\sigma[s(C) + p_z(C)]\} \, d\tau$$

(4) $$\int [s(O) + p_z(O)]\mathbf{M}[p_x(O) - \lambda_\pi p_x(C)] \, d\tau$$

(6) $$\int [s(O) + p_z(O)]\mathbf{M}\{s(O) - p_z(O) - \lambda_\sigma[s(C) + p_z(C)]\} \, d\tau$$

Each of these integrals can be expanded into a series of integrals [two for (1), four for (2) and (4), and eight for (6)]. A transition is forbidden by *molecular* symmetry whenever *all* terms vanish because the integrands are odd, and this occurs for transition (1) only. But, the various wave functions of the oxygen atom occupy regions in space considerably distant from those occupied by the carbon orbitals, and hence integrals over an oxygen and a carbon function are very small and may be neglected. What remains are terms involving oxygen atoms only, and such integrals vanish or fail to vanish only according to the *local* centrosymmetric symmetry around the oxygen atom. In transition (1) the only such integral is $\int p_x(O)\mathbf{M}p_y(O) \, d\tau$, which vanishes since p_x, p_y, and $\mathbf{M}$ each are ungerade, and hence the integrand is ungerade. In transition (2), $\int p_y(O)Mp_z(O)\,d\tau$ vanishes for the same reason, but $\int p_y(O)Ms(O)\,d\tau$ does not, since p_y and M are ungerade, s is gerade, and hence the integrand is gerade. In the remaining transition, the integrals involving two s or two p functions vanish, but those involving one each s and p orbitals do not. Hence transition (1) is forbidden, but the others are allowed, by local symmetry. But in transition (4) only the s part of the lone-pair orbital contributes to the intensity. Similarly, in transition (2) only the s part of the oxygen atom of the antibonding σ^* orbital contributes.

These results are quite general. In $n \rightarrow \pi^*$ transitions, excitation of lone-pair electrons in p orbitals is forbidden, excitation of s electrons allowed, and in excitation of hybrid electrons only the s part contributes to the intensity. Results for $n \rightarrow \sigma^*$ are less simple, since σ^* orbitals are usually hybrids.

6.5   Polarization of Absorption Bands[9]

The theory so far developed applies to ordinary electromagnetic radiation. If the incident radiation is polarized (say by passage through a Nicol prism), the dipole moment vector **M** in equation (6.1) (and subsequent equations) must be replaced by only its component in the direction of polarization of the light. Since, normally, molecules are oriented randomly with respect to the incident light, all possible relations between the axis of the light and of the molecules occur, and the intensity is unaffected. But by use of a single crystal or of a monomolecular film of oriented molecules, it is possible to achieve a fixed relation between the axis (or plane) of the molecule and the direction of polarization of the incident light. Consequently it is of interest to consider the absorption of light polarized in different directions with respect to the molecular symmetry elements.

Integrals of the form of equation (6.3) can be separated into three components:

$$\int \psi_i M_x \psi_f\,d\tau, \quad \int \psi_i M_y \psi_f\,d\tau, \quad \int \psi_i M_z \psi_f\,d\tau$$

where M_x, M_y, and M_z are the three components of the vector **M**. As long as the least one of these components is not zero, the transition is called allowed, and nonpolarized light is absorbed. Imagine now a particular transition in a molecule for which $\int \psi_i M_z \psi_f\,d\tau \neq 0$, but $\int \psi_i M_y \psi_f\,d\tau$ and $\int \psi_i M_y \psi_f\,d\tau = 0$, and further imagine that all the molecules are so arranged, say in a single crystal, that their z axes are parallel. If we now shine light polarized in the z direction at this crystal, the light will be absorbed. If, however, the crystal is rotated so that its z axis becomes perpendicular to the direction of polarization of the light, no light is absorbed. The particular absorption band would be called polarized in the z direction.

The argument can be illustrated by application to formaldehyde. In

[9] For a recent review, see F. Dörr and M. Held, *Angew. Chem.*, **72**, 287 (1960).

section 6.3 the $^1A_2 \leftarrow {}^1A_1$, $^1A_1 \leftarrow {}^1A_1$, and $^1B_2 \leftarrow {}^1A_1$ transitions were discussed, and it was shown that M_z is of species A_1, M_y of species B_2; consequently the $^1A_1 \leftarrow {}^1A_1$ transition is z polarized, the $^1B_2 \leftarrow {}^1A_1$ transition y polarized. Since the $^1A_2 \leftarrow {}^1A_1$ transition is forbidden, all three component integrals vanish, and the polarization of this band will depend on the nature and symmetry species of the vibration which makes this transition slightly allowed (see section 6.6). It is usually possible to make such a choice of Cartesian axes that only one of the three component integrals is nonzero, and every absorption band is polarized.

To determine which of the component integrals for an electronic transition vanish, it is necessary only to compare the symmetry species of the $\Psi_i^o \Psi_f$ product with those of the components of **M**. Hence we can readily determine the expected polarization of any predicted absorption band, and polarization measurements thus should be of great help in interpreting spectra in terms of the underlying electronic transitions.

Unfortunately, however, polarization measurements are experimentally very difficult,[9] and the data obtainable are not always readily interpreted. The first, and probably least serious, problem is to obtain sources of plane-polarized light of sufficient intensity. It is much more difficult to obtain samples of appropriately oriented molecules, but this can sometimes be achieved by using a single crystal, if all molecules are aligned parallel in the crystal, a situation fortunately approximated in many polynuclear aromatic hydrocarbons. An alternative method of obtaining oriented molecules consists of utilizing very thin layers. The interpretation of data so obtained is then complicated by the fact that the molecules so oriented are not free, but are in the field of the crystal, which appreciably affects spectra. The above elementary theory fails to take account of vibrational interaction, which is particularly important for forbidden transitions.

A number of other, special methods have been devised to measure polarization. A solute, frozen in a hydrocarbon glass, although not preferentially oriented, retains its orientation. With plane-polarized light, only appropriately oriented molecules are excited, and by observing their fluorescence spectra inferences are drawn about the relative polarizations of several transitions.

Figure 6.3 shows the spectrum of a single crystal of anthracene oriented with its b axis parallel and perpendicular to the direction of polarization of the incident light.[10] Two bands, at 268.0 and 259.5 mμ, corresponding to two vibrational subbands of a $B_{3u} \leftarrow A_g$ transition, which are theoretically predicted to be polarized parallel to the long axis of the molecule, are observed strongly when the b axis is normal to the plane of polarization, but are absent when the b axis is parallel to this plane.

[10] D. P. Craig and P. C. Hobbins, *J. Chem. Soc.*, 539 (1955).

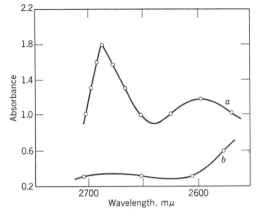

Fig. 6.3   The spectrum of anthracene under light polarized (*a*) parallel, (*b*) perpendicular, to the *b* axis. [Reprinted by permission from D. P. Craig and P. C. Hobbins, *J. Chem. Soc.*, 539 (1955).]

6.6   Vibrational Interaction

In the discussion of the intensities of absorption bands the assumption was made that the wave function of a molecule can be factored into a vibrational and an electronic component. This assumption is not strictly valid, but an accurate treatment of the interaction of vibrational and electronic motion is beyond the scope of this book.[11] However, there are cases in which this interaction is of extreme importance, and some qualitative discussion seems indicated.

Benzene is a highly symmetrical molecule (D_{6h} symmetry), and because of this symmetry some of its spectral transitions are forbidden (cf. section 6.3). Thus, in particular, one of the transitions which may be ascribed to the excitation of one of the electrons occupying the highest MO to the lowest unoccupied orbital, the lowest $\pi \rightarrow \pi^*$ transition ($^1B_{2u} \leftarrow {}^1A_{1g}$), is forbidden by symmetry. However, the statement that "the benzene molecule is of D_{6h} symmetry" is not quite correct. The molecules are constantly undergoing vibrations; and, although some of the vibrational modes are symmetric, during others the symmetry is distorted. Since electronic phenomena are vastly more rapid than the motion of nuclei, benzene behaves with respect to light absorption as if it were a mixture of many different molecules; depending on their vibrational states, some have D_{6h} symmetry, but others are vibrationally distorted. However, since, in the lower vibrationally excited states, the nuclei never move very far from their equilibrium positions, the molecules always behave approximately as if they had D_{6h} symmetry; i.e., while the first $\pi \rightarrow \pi^*$ transition

[11] Such calculations have been discussed, e.g., by A. D. Liehr, *Ann. Rev. Phys. Chem.*, (in press); *Advances in Chem. Phys.*, (in press).

is not completely forbidden for the individual molecules in vibrational states distorting the D_{6h} symmetry, the transition remains of low intensity. Consequently the longest-wavelength absorption is not completely forbidden, and the weak band of benzene near 260 mμ is this forbidden band, which becomes weakly allowed by vibrational interaction.

A quantitative treatment of vibronic interaction indicates that the weakly allowed character of this transition exists if the electronic excitation is accompanied by vibrational excitation of the particular mode which appropriately distorts the symmetry (cf. section 6.7). One of the outstanding features of the spectrum of benzene in solution (cf. Fig. 12.3) is the structure of the long-wavelength band, arising from the transformation of varying numbers of quanta into vibrational energy. Actually, the band corresponding to no vibrational excitation (the so-called 0-0 band) is missing from the spectrum.

A particularly interesting example of a forbidden transition occurring with considerable intensity because of vibrational interaction is shown in Fig. 6.4, where the spectra of I and II in hexane are shown.[12] Although I

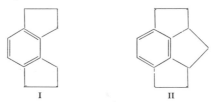

I   II

belongs to point group C_{2v}, the π-electron system is that of an isolated benzene ring only slightly perturbed by the fused five-membered rings, and hence the long-wavelength transition should still be nearly forbidden. Vibrational interaction, the result of which is quite prominent in Fig. 6.4, undoubtedly contributes considerably to the intensity. In compound II, the vibrational motion is considerably inhibited by the rigidity imparted to the molecule by the third fused five-membered ring, and by distortion of the benzenoid ring. As a result, the structure has disappeared from the spectrum of II, and the total intensity is considerably reduced.

Vibrational structure in benzene and in I are observed in many compounds of high total or local symmetry, but the present level of understanding is rarely adequate to make a detailed analysis. The fact that parity- and symmetry-forbidden transitions can be observed at all is usually due to the vibrational interaction discussed.

Vibrational interaction also is of considerable interest in relation to the polarization of symmetry-forbidden bands. In such bands, all three components of the intensity-determining integral vanish, and hence

[12] H. Rapoport and G. Smolinsky, *J. Am. Chem. Soc.*, **82**, 1171 (1960).

polarization cannot directly be determined by the methods outlined in the preceding section. Forbidden bands are observed because of vibrational interaction, and the intensity-determining integral [equation (6.1)] fails to vanish completely because of this interaction. The separation of the intensity-determining integral [equation (6.1)] into a product of two integrals, one over the electronic coordinates only and containing the Ψ"s, the other over the nuclear coordinates and involving the vibrational wave functions χ only [see equation (6.9) below], assumes equal geometry of ground and excited states and Ψ"s independent of the nuclear coordinates.

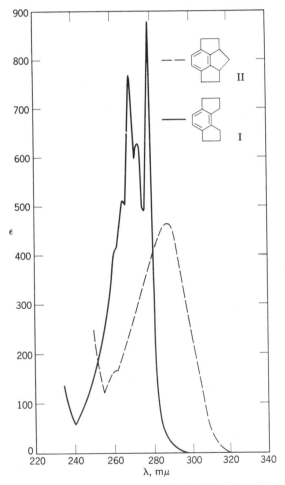

Fig. 6.4   The spectra of compounds I and II, showing the effect of vibronic interaction. [Reprinted by permission from H. Rapoport and G. Smolinsky, *J. Am. Chem. Soc.*, **82,** 1171 (1960).]

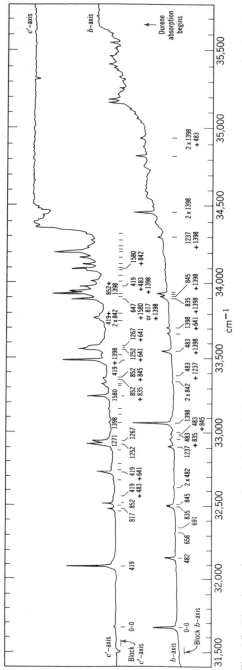

Fig. 6.5 The absorption spectrum of naphthalene *d*-8 in durene, single crystal at 20° K, *b*- and *c'*-polarized. [Reprinted by permission from D. S. McClure, *J. Chem. Phys.*, **24**, 1 (1956).]

132

If this assumption is not made, the Ψ"s are dependent on the nuclear coordinates. For an evaluation of intensity and polarization of forbidden bands this separation thus cannot be made. Each wave function Ξ_i and Ξ_f, however, may be treated as a product of a vibrational and an electronic function, χ_i and Ψ'_i, χ_f and Ψ'_f, respectively. The Ξ will then belong to the symmetry species of the product of the appropriate χ and Ψ'.

As an example the forbidden $^1A_2 \leftarrow {}^1A_1$ transition of formaldehyde will be considered. This molecule has $3n - 6 = 6$ normal vibrations, of which three belong to species a_1, one to b_1, and two to b_2. In the nondegenerate point groups, the vibrational wave functions for even vibrational quantum numbers belong to the totally symmetric species, a_1 in the case of C_{2v}, and for odd quantum numbers to the species characteristic of the vibration which they describe. Consider first one of the vibrations belonging to species a_1. All χ belong to a_1, and the product $\Psi'_i\Psi'_f$ to A_2, hence $\Xi_i\Xi_f = \Psi'_i\chi_i\Psi'_f\chi_f$ belongs to A_2. Since neither M_x, M_y, nor M_z belongs to A_2, all three components of equation (6.1) vanish, even under vibronic interaction. But for excitation of one of the b_1 or b_2 vibrations, the products $\Xi_i\Xi_f$ belong to B_2 and B_1, respectively, and hence one component of (6.1) is nonzero. Consequently, interaction of the $^1A_2 \leftarrow {}^1A_1$ transition with b_1 vibration leads to vibronic bands which are y polarized, and interaction with the b_2 vibrations to x-polarized components. No z-polarized bands occur, since no a_2 vibrations exist, which would give a $\Xi_i\Xi_f$ product of a_1 symmetry.

These arguments then show that a single forbidden electronic transition may give rise to vibrational subbands of different polarization. This is commonly observed, particularly because many polarization measurements have been made on aromatic hydrocarbons in which the long-wavelength bands (^1L_b and ^1L_a in Platt notation; see section 13.2) are forbidden. A typical example is shown in Fig. 6.5.

The preceding arguments require some further refinement. Because the wave functions Ψ' of electronic states discussed in Chapter 5 are not exact solutions of the Schrödinger wave equation, even assuming the Born-Oppenheimer approximation, best theory requires further improvement of these functions. One way of achieving such improvement consists of forming new state functions as linear combinations of the various Ψ', so-called configuration interaction, which will be discussed in more detail in Chapter 8. For the present purpose it is sufficient to point out that such configuration-interaction functions consist of linear combinations of a set of Ψ's all of which belong to the *same* symmetry species. In a similar manner the Ξ's under discussion in this section are only approximate solutions and can be improved by configuration interaction, but now with wave functions of the same symmetry species as the Ξ. In this way the Ξ's are admixed, albeit slightly, by other electronic states, which have different symmetry from the Ψ' part of Ξ.

A treatment of formaldehyde along the lines of these arguments has been given by Pople and Sidman.[13] The Ξ functions for the excited state belong to the species B_1 and

[13] J. A. Pople and J. W. Sidman, *J. Chem. Phys.*, **27**, 1270 (1957)

B_2; and admixture to the vibronic states of the $^1A_2$ electronic state by $^1B_1$ and $^1B_2$ states, (4) or (5), and (2), of section 5.6, is possible. Since transitions to these states are allowed, this admixture should contribute to the intensity. Calculations by Pople and Sidman show that the admixture of the $^1B_1$ state should be by far the more important. As shown above, it should lead to x-polarized components. In agreement with this expectation, vibrational analysis of the formaldehyde spectrum shows prominently vibrational structure of the b_2 vibration, the out-of-plane bending mode; and, in accord with the arguments developed, only odd numbers of vibrational quanta appear. The observation of the b_2 vibration is also consistent with the statement that the mode transforming the molecule from the ground-state to the excited-state geometry should appear, since the $^1A_2$ state is known to be nonplanar and the b_2 mode is the only out-of-plane vibration, and hence the only nuclear motion which can transform the planar ground state into the nonplanar excited state. The b_1 vibrations, asymmetric CH stretching and CH rocking, do not seem to have been identified in the spectrum. Surprisingly, however, careful analysis of the formaldehyde spectrum has demonstrated z-polarized component bands in the forbidden $^1A_2 \leftarrow {}^1A_1$ transition. Since there is no a_2 vibration, this could arise only by vibronic interaction from a combination band of the b_1 and b_2 vibrations, a possibility which can, however, be excluded here. The calculations of Pople and Sidman suggest that we deal here with rotational electronic interaction.

6.7   The Franck-Condon Principle

One additional factor affecting the intensities of absorption bands has been completely neglected so far. Since nuclear motion is much slower than electronic phenomena, the geometry of a molecule after absorption must be almost identical to its geometry before absorption. Similarly, it is necessary that the momentum (or the kinetic energy of the motion) of the nuclei remain substantially unchanged during the transition. These statements, due to Franck[14] and elaborated by Condon, are known as the Franck-Condon principle.[15]

The principles involved are simply illustrated by examining a diatomic molecule. The potential energy U of such a molecule is a function of the internuclear distance r, and this functional relationship is approximated by the so-called Morse curve,[16] examples of which for the ground state are shown in the lower curves of Fig. 6.6.

The potential energy of the diatomic molecule has a minimum at the "equilibrium internuclear distance" r_e; at shorter distances the curve rises with increasing steepness because of nuclear repulsion, and goes to infinity since it is impossible to let the nuclei approach to zero distance. At distances longer than r_e, corresponding to stretching the bond, the potential energy increases, but sooner or later, when the atoms become substantially separated, U approaches a final value asymptotically; this

[14] J. Franck, *Trans. Faraday Soc.*, **21**, 536 (1925).

[15] E. U. Condon and P. M. Morse, *Quantum Mechanics*, McGraw-Hill Book Co., New York, 1929, pp. 164 ff.

[16] W. West in *Chemical Applications of Spectroscopy*, Vol. IX of *Technique of Organic Chemistry*, edited by A. Weissberger, Interscience Publishers, New York, 1956, pp. 18 f.

value corresponds to the energy of the separated atoms and is commonly used as the zero point of the energy scale. The difference between U at r_e, $U(r_e)$, and U at $r = \infty$, $U(\infty)$, is, except for the zero-point energy, the energy required to dissociate the molecule (dissociation energy).

The potential energy of excited states can, of course, also be plotted against internuclear distance. If the excited state is stable to dissociation, the resulting curve also has the appearance of a Morse curve. For the special case in which this equilibrium internuclear distance is identical in ground and excited states, the curves are given in Fig. 6.6a.

The much greater speed of electronic motion (as little as 10^{-15} second may be required for excitation of an electron), compared with nuclear or vibrational motion (appreciable displacement of atoms does not occur in less than about 10^{-10} to 10^{-12} second), indicates that the bond distance cannot change appreciably during excitation. At room temperature the vast majority of molecules of a diatomic compound are in the lowest (0, zero) vibrational level of the electronic ground state, and hence the atoms are at a distance r between a and b in Fig. 6.6a. Then, following excitation to the lowest (0) vibrational level of the excited state, the $0 \rightarrow 0$ transition, the distance r between the atoms will have changed only infinitesimally and hence will be between c' and d'. Since it was assumed that the potential-energy curve for the excited state is the same (except for the vertical displacement) as that for the ground state, there is a point on

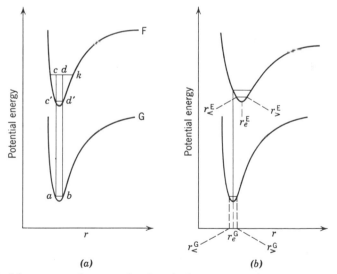

(a)   (b)

Fig. 6.6 Morse curves for ground and excited states, assuming $U(r)$ (a) identical and (b) different in the two states. [Reprinted by permission from J. A. Pople and J. W. Sidman, *J. Chem. Phys.*, **27**, 1270 (1957).]

the line $c'd'$ representing the 0 level of the excited state directly above each point between a and b of the line representing the 0 level of the ground state, and the kinetic energy is identical for such corresponding points. The kinetic energy, which is the difference between the total energy (given by the horizontal line representing the state) and the potential energy (given by the point on the appropriate Morse curve at the appropriate value of r), is the vertical distance of the line representing the state from the Morse curve at the particular value of r. Thus, a molecule may be excited from any point on its ground state to a corresponding point in its excited state, and the Franck-Condon principle produces no limitation for the $0 \rightarrow 0$ transition.

Consider next the transition from the same ground state to the kth vibrational level of the excited state, the $0 \rightarrow k$ transition (Fig. 6.6a). According to the Franck-Condon principle, the internuclear distance after excitation must be somewhere between c and d. But examination of Fig. 6.6a shows that the kinetic energy in this region is appreciably larger than for corresponding points in the ground state. Thus the kinetic energy of a molecule in the kth vibrational level of the excited state at point d' is equal to the distance dd', whereas the kinetic energy of the molecule in the 0 level of the ground state at b is 0. Because of this difference in kinetic energy, the $0 \rightarrow k$ transition is forbidden by the Franck-Condon principle.

In the example discussed above (Fig. 6.6a), the equilibrium internuclear distances were equal in the ground and excited states, the $0 \rightarrow 0$ transition was intense, and excitations corresponding to $0 \rightarrow 1$, $0 \rightarrow 2$, $\ldots$, $0 \rightarrow k$ were forbidden. Usually, however, in going from a ground to an excited state an electron is promoted from a bonding or nonbonding orbital to an antibonding orbital; consequently the bond of the molecule in the excited state is weakened, and the equilibrium bond distance in this state is greater than the corresponding distance in the ground state (i.e., $r_e^E > r_e^G$). The resulting pattern is shown in the upper curve of Fig. 6.6b, where the shallower and broader minimum reflects the loosening of the binding forces. In the transition to such an excited state, the Franck-Condon principle becomes of great importance both for the wavelength of absorption and for its intensity. The transition from the lowest vibrational level of the ground state to the lowest vibrational level of the excited state can, of course, occur only when the photon strikes the molecule at a moment in which the internuclear distance r corresponds to a classically allowed distance in the excited state, i.e., if r is between $r_<^E$ and $r_>^G$ where $r_<^E$ refers to the minimum internuclear distance r in the excited state and $r_>^G$ to the maximum r in the ground state (see Fig. 6.6b). Since part of the time r is less than $r_<^E$, not all collisions with photons, but only that fraction occurring while the molecule is in the favorable geometric arrangement, can be effective. Hence it is important to examine the probability of finding the molecule at any given value of r.

The molecule has least kinetic energy and hence moves slowest near $r_<^G$ and $r_>^G$, and has highest kinetic energy and moves fastest at r_e^G. Accordingly the probability curve is that given in Fig. 6.7a, and the probability that the molecule is in the favorable geometry $r_<^E < r < r_>^G$ is equal to the ratio of the shaded area in Fig. 6.7a to the total area under the curve.

On the basis of the above argument of overlapping of the classically allowed r values of the ground state and the particular vibrational level of the excited state, we would expect, in the case pictured in Fig. 6.6b, an increase of the intensity for successively higher vibrational levels, i.e., the $0 \rightarrow 1$, $0 \rightarrow 2$, etc., transitions. However, the simultaneous restrictions provided by the conservation of momentum further modify the argument, and usually produce the highest probability for certain selected vibrational jumps accompanying electronic excitation.[17]

Although the foregoing classical argument serves well to illustrate the principle, and is adequate for high vibrational levels, the classical distribution of Fig. 6.7a is not valid for low vibrational levels. According to quantum mechanics,[18] the distributions of r for the first four vibrational levels are given by the graphs in Fig. 6.7b. Application of the classical argument now leads to similar ratios, which will, however, have quite different values because of the different form of the probability curve.

An even better evaluation of the effect of the Franck-Condon principle is given by a completely quantum-mechanical description, which states that the intrinsic probability of Equation (6.3) must be multiplied by an integral of the form $\int \chi_i \chi_f \, dr$, where χ_i and χ_f are the vibrational wave functions of the molecule before and after the transition, respectively.

The way in which this factor $\int \chi_i \chi_f \, dr$ arises can be demonstrated readily. The intensity is given by

$$\sqrt{D} = \int \Xi_i \mathbf{M} \Xi_f \, dT \tag{6.1}$$

where the Ξ are the complete wave functions. If, as is usually done, it is assumed that Ξ can be factored into an electronic function Ψ and a vibrational function χ (Born-Oppenheimer approximation),

$$\sqrt{D} = \int \Psi_i \chi_i \mathbf{M} \Psi_f \chi_f \, dT$$

$$= \int \Psi_i \mathbf{M} \Psi_f \, d\tau \int \chi_i \chi_f \, dr \tag{6.9}$$

since $\mathbf{M}$ depends only on the electronic coordinates, and assuming the same for Ψ.

[17] See W. Kauzman, *Quantum Chemistry*, Academic Press, New York, 1957, p. 665, for a more detailed discussion.

[18] L. Pauling and E. B. Wilson, *Introduction to Quantum Mechanics*, McGraw-Hill Book Co., New York, 1935, Chapter III.

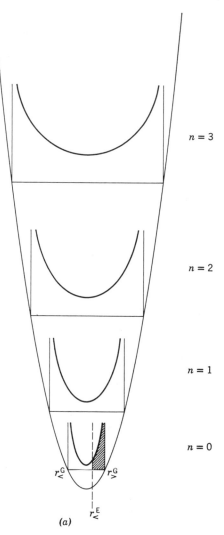

(a)

Fig. 6.7 The distribution function for a harmonic oscillator (a) classically at the values of the energy of the first four quantum levels, and (b) quantum mechanically (i.e., χ^2) for the first four quantum levels.

It was stated above that the Franck-Condon principle is of considerable importance in connection with intensities. This statement is true only if the extinction coefficient at the maximum wavelength is used as the measure of intensity. The absolute intensity is independent of the Franck-Condon restriction. This fact can be demonstrated as follows. The total intensity of a transition is the sum over the intensities of all the vibrational subbands. For the total intensity arising from all transitions originating from a single vibrational level of the ground state, but ending in the different vibrational levels

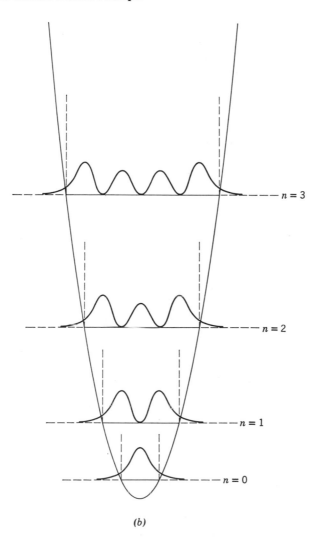

(b)

of the excited state (having wave functions χ_{fj}), we thus obtain a sum over an infinite number of terms in which the basic integral of equation (6.2) is multiplied successively by the vibrational part of equation (6.9):

$$\Sigma_j \left(\int \chi_i \chi_{fj}\, dr \right)^2 \qquad\qquad (6.10)$$

Now, it is always possible to expand any given function in terms of some other functions, provided an infinite expansion is used and the expansion functions form what mathematicians call a complete set; all the vibrational wave functions for any given vibration of any molecule provide such a complete set. Calling χ_{ik} the infinite set of vibrational functions of the ground state (with k as a running index indicating the quantum number), each χ_{fj} can be expanded in terms of the χ_{ik}:

$$\chi_{fj} = \sum_{k=1}^{\infty} a_{jk}\chi_{ik} \tag{6.11}$$

The transformation of one complete set of orthonormal functions into another obeys the conditions

$$\Sigma_j a_{jk}^2 = \Sigma_k a_{jk}^2 = 1$$

Substitution of equation (6.11) into equation (6.10) leads to

$$\Sigma_j \left(\int \chi_i \Sigma_k a_{jk}\chi_{ik} \, dr \right)^2 = \Sigma_j \left(\Sigma_k a_{jk} \int \chi_i \chi_{ik} \, dr \right)^2$$

but the last integrals vanish when χ_{ik} is not the same function (i.e., does not correspond to the same vibrational quantum number) as the ground-state vibrational function χ_i, and is equal to unity when the two are identical. Hence equation (6.10) reduces to

$$\Sigma_j a_{jk}^2 = 1$$

Thus it is seen that Franck-Condon effects can influence not the total, integrated intensity of a band, but only the relative importance of various vibrational subbands.

One additional inference can be drawn from the Franck-Condon principle. As shown above, where the potential-energy curves of ground and excited states are identical, χ_i and χ_f are orthogonal and all vibrational bands except the 0-0 band are forbidden. Although this extreme is probably never realized, in many cases the potential-energy diagrams of the ground and excited states resemble each other closely, and the $\int \chi_i \chi_f \, dr$ will decrease rapidly with increasing difference in vibrational quantum number. However, the larger the difference in the potential-energy curves between the two electronic states involved in a transition, the further will the χ's deviate from orthogonality, the larger will be the probability that vibrational excitation occurs simultaneously with electronic transitions, and consequently the more complex will be the vibrational structure.

The arguments up to this point apply to the vibration of a diatomic molecule and its interaction with electronic excitation. It now remains to generalize the discussion of polyatomic molecules. In a molecule having n atoms, $3n$ coordinates (e.g., x, y, and z for each atom) must be fixed to define completely the position of each atom in space, or, equivalently, to define the position and orientation of the molecule in space, and the relative positions of the atoms with respect to each other. The position of the molecule in space alone is determined by the three coordinates of its center of gravity, and the orientation of the molecule can be fixed by specifying three angles [in the case of a linear molecule, only two angles, since rotation about the lengthwise (C_∞) axis is not determinable]. Thus there remain $3n - 6$ coordinates, so-called *degrees of freedom* (in the case

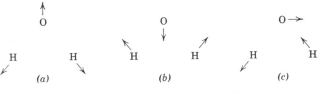

Fig. 6.8   The normal vibrations of H_2O.

of the linear molecule, $3n - 5$ of them), to specify the relative positions of the atoms with respect to one another.   An infinite number of possibilities for choices of these coordinates exist, but the treatment of vibrations and vibrational spectra has led to the almost universal selection of one particular set, the so-called *normal coordinates*, which make the treatment of vibrations particularly attractive.[19]   These coordinates are in general denoted by the symbol ξ_i, with subscripts specifying the $3n - 6$ (or $3n - 5$) different ones.   The particular simplicity of the normal coordinates lies in the fact that they permit factoring the total vibrational wave function X into a product of functions each of which is a function of only one of the ξ_i: $X = \Pi_i \chi_i(\xi_i)$.

A direct physical interpretation of the ξ is not always simple.   Some of them represent bond distances directly;   others represent bond angles. Thus, in H_2O there are two totally symmetric normal vibrations, which are shown in Figs. 6.8a and b: in the symmetric stretching vibration (Fig. 6.8a), ξ represents the (equal) lengths of the two OH bonds; in the bending vibration (Fig. 6.8b), ξ represents the $\sphericalangle$HOH. In other vibrations, such as the unsymmetrical stretching vibration (Fig. 6.8c), no such simple interpretation of ξ can be given; it represents the simultaneous motion of the three atoms along the path followed in the vibration.

The potential energy U of an n-atomic molecule is a function of all $3n - 6$ (or $3n - 5$) normal coordinates ξ_i, and should be presented in a $3n - 5$ (or $3n - 4$) dimensional plot. Since such a plot is not readily produced, it is customary to give $3n - 6$ (or $3n - 5$) sections, each indicating the dependence of U on one ξ_i, while holding all other ξ_i's constant at their equilibrium values. Some of these plots, particularly when the appropriate ξ can be given a simple physical interpretation, are readily constructed. For example, for the symmetric stretching vibration of H_2O, the potential-energy diagram will have the form of a simple Morse curve. For the bending vibration of H_2O, the potential-energy curve is given in Fig. 6.9. It is obvious that, for $\xi = 0$ (i.e., for the $\sphericalangle$HOH = 0°), the potential energy becomes infinite, since the H atoms would be superimposed. Furthermore, the curve must be symmetric with respect to an angle of 180° (i.e., a linear conformation of H_2O) and have a minimum for $\sphericalangle$HOH of 104° (the equilibrium angle).

[19] For example, see G. Herzberg, *Molecular Spectra and Molecular Structure*, D. Van Nostrand Co., Princeton, N.J., 1945, pp. 70 ff.

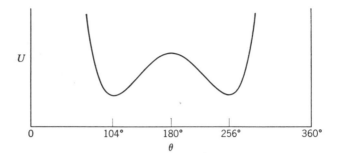

Fig. 6.9 The potential-energy curve for the bending vibration of H_2O.

Application of the above arguments to equation (6.1) then leads to the following results:

$$\sqrt{D} = \int \Psi_i \mathbf{M} \Psi_f \, d\tau \int X_i X_f \Pi_j \, d\xi_j$$

$$= \int \Psi_i \mathbf{M} \Psi_f \, d\tau \, \Pi_j \int \chi_{ij} \chi_{fj} \, d\xi_j$$

so that the intensity involves a product of $3n - 6$ (or $3n - 5$) integrals, each having the form of the single one involved in the diatomic molecule, but each involving a different one of the normal coordinates ξ_i. Now, following the arguments developed above for the diatomic molecule, if the potential-energy curve for a given ξ_j does not change upon electronic excitation, all bands involving a change in vibrational quantum number are forbidden. The more the potential-energy curve for a given ξ_j differs between the electronic ground and the excited states of a molecule, the farther removed from orthogonality are the χ_{ij} and χ_{fj} for different quantum numbers v_j, and the greater is the probability of changes of vibrational quanta accompanying electronic transitions. The potential-energy curve for a vibrational coordinate ξ_j will change particularly strongly if there is a pronounced change in the equilibrium value ξ_{je} between the electronic ground and the excited states, corresponding to different geometries of the two states. Hence the vibration by which the geometry of the ground state is converted into that of the excited state appears particularly strongly in the spectrum of such a molecule.

One specific case illustrating these arguments is ethylene. The ground state of ethylene is planar, since in the planar state the overlap of the p_x orbitals of the two C atoms is at a maximum. In the first excited state, with one electron occupying the antibonding π^* orbital, however, the most stable configuration is that in which the planes defined by the two CH_2 groups are at right angles. The angle θ between these planes is one of the normal coordinates discussed, and potential-energy curves with respect to this angle are shown in Fig. 6.10a. It is immediately apparent that absorption from the ground vibrational (torsional) level must occur to an excited vibrational level of the electronically excited state; i.e., that the 0-0 band is forbidden.

Next, consider a substituted ethylene in which there is sufficiently strong steric repulsion between the substitutent groups to twist the molecule somewhat out of plane. The potential-energy curve then will look somewhat like Fig. 6.10*b*. Because of the Franck-Condon principle, absorption from the torsional ground state can now go to a lower torsionally excited state. Statements about the effect of this substitution on the wavelength of the absorption, illustrated by the length of the vertical line, are difficult to make, since these effects depend on the raising of the lowest vibrational state of the electronic ground state *and* on the raising of the energy of the twisted configuration in the excited state (although, because of the greater C-C distance in the excited state, the latter should be relatively smaller than the former). But the intensity should be increased, since less vibrational excitation is required, and since the proportion of ground-state

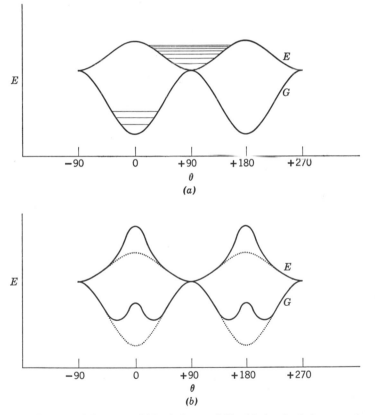

Fig. 6.10   The potential energy of (*a*) ethylene and (*b*) a hindered ethylene as a function of angle of twist. G = ground state; E = excited state.

molecules geometrically in position to be excited to low vibrational levels of the electronically excited states is larger in the substituted ethylene than in the parent compound.

6.8 Band Shapes

The various factors determining the intensity at any particular wavelength can now be summarized. The discussion will first be given in terms of vapor (band) spectra and then be generalized to spectra in the condensed (solution) phase. The wavelength of the light absorbed by any given molecule is determined by the state in which it is found before the transition, and the state to which it is raised during the transition. We may normally assume that all molecules are in the lowest electronic state, but are distributed between a few low vibrational levels and a number of rotational sublevels of this state. Upon absorption of a quantum, the molecule may be raised to any of the various vibrational levels and rotational sublevels of the excited state. Each of these transitions will involve a somewhat different energy and different wavelength, and hence there arise the large number of individual lines appearing in the typical band spectrum. The intensity of each of these lines can now be discussed in terms of a number of factors.

THE INTRINSIC INTENSITY.   A common factor of all the individual components of a band system having common electronic ground and excited states is the integral given in equation (6.3), the square of which may be called the *intrinsic intensity* I_o.

THE FRANCK-CONDON TERM.   A second factor involved in the intensity of the components of a band system is the square of the integral $\int \chi_i \chi_j \, dr$ discussed in section 6.7. This quantity will be denoted by I_v to indicate that it involves the vibrational wave functions.

THE POPULATION DISTRIBUTION.   A third factor involved in the intensity of absorption is the fraction of molecules present in the rotational sublevel of the vibrational level of the ground state from which the molecule is excited. This fraction is given by a Boltzmann factor $N_i/N_o = e^{-\varepsilon_i/kT}$, where N_i is the number of molecules having an energy ε_i above the lowest vibrational and rotational level, N_o is the number in the lowest state, and k is the Boltzmann constant.

The intensity is then given by

$$I_\lambda = C I_o I_v e^{-\varepsilon_i/kT} \tag{6.12}$$

where C is a proportionality constant. The factor I_o is constant within a band system. The Boltzmann factor is the same for all transitions originating from a single rotational sublevel of a vibrational level, but is dependent on temperature (T). The factor I_v incorporates the Franck-Condon restrictions. The use of equation (6.12) then permits the estimation of the intensities of the individual components of a band system.

In the condensed phase molecules generally cannot rotate freely, and hence the rotational energy levels have lost their meaning. The rotational degrees of freedom become a form of rather ill-defined vibrations (libations) and consequently, instead of definite quantized energy levels, broad bands of allowed energy are encountered. As a consequence, the sharp lines of the band spectra of vapors become broadened and merge into regions of continuous absorption. Furthermore, the vibrational energy levels also are broadened because of the varying interactions of molecules with their neighbors, which occur in a more or less random arrangement. This broadening often is sufficient to obscure most or all of the vibrational structure of absorption bands, although in many cases such structure is clearly observed (e.g., in benzene, Fig. 12.3). However, roughly the appearance of an absorption band in a spectrum in solution should be approximated by a smoothed curve drawn through the intensities of the individual lines of the band spectrum of the vapor. In vapor spectra at high pressures, broadening of rotational levels also occurs.

6.9 Spin-Orbit Coupling

It was shown in section 6.3 that singlet → triplet transitions are forbidden. Nevertheless, such transitions are frequently observed. It remains to ask what makes these transitions observable, since it had appeared that the selection rule forbidding them had particularly strong validity. Kasha[20] has suggested that so-called "spin-orbit coupling" is involved.

Normally, the angular momentum of electronic motion is considered to consist of two independent parts, the orbital and the spin angular momenta. Actually, the only observable quantity, which is a physical constant of a real system, is the total angular momentum, and accordingly wave functions should represent states of given total angular momentum. To the extent that such separation is legitimate, distinction of states on the basis of multiplicity is valid. However, the separation is not completely legitimate; there is a small but not negligible interaction between wave functions of different multiplicities but the same *total* angular momentum. Call $^1\Psi'$ and $^3\Psi'$ two wave functions derived on the basis of the assumption that separation of orbital and spin angular momenta is complete; i.e., that integrals of the sort of $\int {}^1\Psi' H {}^3\Psi'\, d\tau$ vanish identically. Since this assumption is only approximately correct, evaluation of these integrals (the spin-orbit

---

[20] For a review see M. Kasha and S. P. McGlynn, *Ann. Rev. Phys. Chem.*, **7**, 403 (1956).

coupling) and their use in the appropriate secular equation lead to two final wavefunctions of the form

$$\Psi = \alpha \, ^1\Psi + \beta \, ^3\Psi$$

of which one has predominantly, but not completely, singlet, the other triplet, character. When the excited state in a transition is such a wave function, the admixture of a slight amount of triplet character to the function which is basically a singlet is of little importance, since it results only in a slight reduction of intensity. However, the small admixture of the singlet function to the predominant triplet function is of tremendous importance, since it leads to an intensity integral which, instead of vanishing identically, has a small but finite value, thus explaining why singlet-triplet transitions, though very weak, are observed.

7 Geometry and physical properties of ground and excited states

7.1 Geometry of Ground States

Much information about the geometry of ground states of molecules is available today. From the experimental point of view the geometry of ground states can be investigated and relatively precise measurements of bond distances and angles can be obtained by the methods of diffraction (x-ray, electron, and neutron diffraction).[1] More indirect, but frequently much more accurate, information is obtainable from spectroscopic measurements, particularly by means of microwave, infrared, and Raman spectroscopy.[1] Although a discussion of these techniques is well beyond the scope of this book, it is obvious that their application requires the availability of significant quantities of compounds in a relatively pure state.

Having thus considerable information about the arrangements of atoms in the ground states of molecules, it is a great temptation to assume that identical arrangements persist in the excited states. This assumption is unfortunately incorrect. It will be shown in the following paragraphs how the geometry of ground states can be predicted, at least qualitatively, by simple valence theory. Application of the same arguments to excited states (see section 7.2) will show that, in many cases, the excited states must have considerably different geometry. Such changes are of considerable spectroscopic interest, particularly in connection with the Franck-Condon principle (cf. section 6.7).

Theoretical evaluation of the geometry of molecules is a difficult problem. Unfortunately, wave functions and molecular energies cannot generally be expressed as explicit functions of bond distances and bond angles, and hence the evaluation of the point of minimum energy on a potential-energy surface requires the separate evaluation of the energy for several values of the bond length or angle, and subsequent evaluation of the minimum, possibly by use of a theoretical or empirical potential function.

[1] P. J. Wheatley, *The Determination of Molecular Structure*, Clarendon Press, Oxford, 1959.

Moreover, the exact position of the minimum is rather sensitive to certain assumptions necessary for the calculations, and accordingly molecular calculations are frequently made for a single value of the geometric parameters taken from experimental information.

Qualitative predictions about major geometric features can, however, be made from theory. Thus the knowledge that the electronic structure of oxygen and sulfur in the ground state is s^2p^4 immediately suggests that two bonds formed by these atoms in such compounds as R_2O and R_2S should be formed by p electrons in orbitals at right angles, and hence be not linear, but nearly at right angles. This argument is found to be correct for sulfur; in oxygen, hybridization and repulsion of the bonded groups open the angle to about 105°, or 15° above the right angle. For mercury, with electronic structure s^2, which requires for formation of two bonds that one electron be promoted to give the configuration sp, the same type of argument predicts a linear structure with sp hybridization in agreement with the experimental findings.

The angle between the two HOO planes in HOOH is another example of simple qualitative theoretical arguments that give information about ground-state geometry. Each single bond in this molecule may be considered as being formed from pure p orbitals of the oxygen atoms.[2] Then the two lone pairs of each oxygen atom must be assigned to an s and a p orbital. Because of the spherical symmetry around the oxygen nuclei of s orbitals, the s electrons do not affect the geometry of the molecule. If the molecule had a planar structure, the p orbitals holding the four electrons, or two lone pairs, would be able to interact, leading to a bonding and an antibonding MO. Each of these would be occupied by two electrons. It is, however, a result of the quantum-mechanical treatment that, when two AO's combine to form a bonding and an anti-bonding MO, the stabilization by the bonding orbital is always less than the destabilization by the antibonding one.[3] Thus the total energy of the planar structure must be higher than that of a structure in which the lone-pair p electrons do not interact, a condition realized in a structure (Fig. 7.1) in which the two HOO planes are at right angles. Consequently, it may be predicted from theory that H_2O_2 should have a structure with these planes at an angle close to 90°. Experiment indicates[4] the actual angle to be 94° in solid H_2O_2.

Another example of the prediction of the geometry of a molecule,

[2] Correctly, allowance for hybridization should be made, but the over-all argument would not be affected thereby.

[3] This statement does not hold for the lowest approximation, the LCAO method with neglect of overlap integrals, in which the two quantities are identical. Inclusion of overlap, however, leads to factor $1/(1 + S)$, in the first of them, $1/(1 - S)$ in the second, and thus to the stated inequality.

[4] S. C. Abrahams, R. L. Collin, and W. N. Lipscomb, *Acta Cryst.*, **4**, 15 (1951).

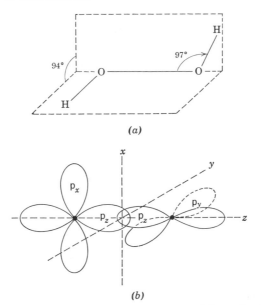

Fig. 7.1 The H_2O_2 molecule, showing (a) the geometry of the molecule and (b) the bonding and lone-pair p orbitals at right angles to each other.

based on a consideration of the orbitals involved, is the case of allene, $CH_2=C=CH_2$. The middle carbon of this molecule uses sp hybrid orbitals and hence the three carbon atoms must lie in a straight line. The remaining two pπ orbitals on the middle carbon atom are at right angles to each other and may arbitrarily be designated the p_x and p_y orbitals. These orbitals will overlap the p_x and p_y orbitals of carbons 1 and 3, respectively, which have similar symmetry. In order to form the two π bonds at right angles, the terminal CH_2 groups must be forced into positions at right angles to each other. The alternative possibility of a completely planar structure in which one MO overlaps the three carbon atoms and two electrons remain in an AO would lead to a structure of higher energy.

These three examples illustrate how qualitative theory may be applied in making important predictions about the geometry of ground states of atoms. Further cases have been treated in a long series of papers by Walsh[5] and by many other authors.

Aside from such quantum-mechanical arguments predicting the geometric structure of molelules, innumerable less sophisticated methods have been devised, some on empirical bases, others in classical or quasi-quantum-mechanical terms. For a wide variety of compounds, such

[5] A. D. Walsh, *J. Chem. Soc.*, 2260, 2266, 2288, 2296, 2301, 2306, 2318, 2321, 2325, 2330 (1953).

arguments have been found to be successful. That several, sometimes apparently widely differing, theories lead to identical results or qualitatively equal conclusions is a common observation in theoretical chemistry; it implies that frequently which theory is used to explain results is immaterial but at the same time indicates the need for caution in interpreting agreement between theory and experiment as verification of theory. It is very possible that many of the apparently different arguments leading to the same result are actually not basically conflicting, but only focus on substantially similar phenomena in semantically or mathematically different ways. A prime example of this equivalence of different theories is the comparison of MO and VB (valence-bond) theories discussed in Chapter 8.

One of the prime classical approaches to predicting the geometry of molecules is electrostatic. It is based on the concept of repulsion of valence electrons and predicts that the geometry about any atom should be such that all electron pairs are as far distant from one another as possible. Such maximum distance is achieved by a linear configuration for two electron pairs, a planar triangular one for three, a tetrahedral one for four, a trigonal bipyramidal one for five, and an octahedral one for six.[6] As is well known, these are the favored configurations about atoms with the appropriate numbers of electron pairs, provided lone pairs are counted and considered to occupy one apex each of the appropriate figures. Theories such as this are distinguished by their simplicity, but are not likely to be as successful as the more sophisticated quantum-mechanical ones in dealing with finer structural details, although many refinements in these simple theories are possible and have been suggested.

7.2   Theory of the Geometry of Excited States

Since theoretical considerations do not require availability of the material under consideration, a theoretical treatment of excited states is exactly analogous to a theoretical treatment of the ground state. Thus, in ethylene, excitation of a bonding π electron to the antibonding π orbital implies that the planar state is stabilized by one bonding π electron, but destabilized by one antibonding π electron. As discussed in section 7.1, this results in a net destabilization of the planar state with respect to a state in which the p orbitals do not interact. Consequently this excited state of ethylene is nonplanar, as indicated by the upper potential-energy curve of Fig. 6.10a. This further means that the excited state of ethylene does not belong to the same point group (D_{2h}) as the ground state, but to the point group D_{2d}. Characterization of excited states in terms of the symmetry species of the ground state, hence, is only an approximation, and in very careful work

[6] N. V. Sidgwick and H. M. Powell, *Proc. Roy. Soc.* (*London*), **A176**, 153 (1940).

we would characterize the excited state in terms of the symmetry species appropriate to its own point group.

However, in the excited state of ethylene, the minimum for $\theta = \pi/2$ is lower than the maxima at $\theta = 0$ and π only by twice the difference in stabilization and destabilization of the bonding and antibonding orbitals, a quantity which is relatively small. The minimum in the ground-state potential-energy curve at $\theta = 0$ (compared to $\theta = \pi/2$), however, represents twice the stabilization of the bonding π orbital, and accordingly is much greater. This is indicated schematically by the relative depth of the potential-energy minima in Fig. 6.10a.

Another interesting case in which the geometry of the excited state has been considered in detail is the first excited state of acetylene, in which one bonding π electron is excited to an antibonding π orbital. The electronic structure will then involve, besides the σ bonding electrons, three bonding and one antibonding π electrons. Two of the bonding π electrons will hold the molecule in a plane. The other two electrons, one bonding and the other antibonding, will try to occupy orbitals which have minimum interaction. This is achieved by rehybridization, removing some s character from the σ bonds and admixing it with the AO's of the last two π orbitals. Consequently, the σ bonds acquire a character resembling that of sp^2 orbitals, and the linear structure of acetylene is distorted to an ethylene-like structure, except that each carbon atom has one instead of two C-H bonds, and in place of the other C-H bond of ethylene an orbital occupied by one electron.[7] This consideration of the structure of the excited state of acetylene suggests that there should be a *cis* and a *trans* isomer of this state. The interaction of orbitals is smaller in the *trans* isomer (point group C_{2h}), which has accordingly the lower energy and is believed to represent the excited state reached by the longest-wavelength transition of acetylene. Another analogous transition to the *cis* isomer of C_{2v} symmetry is believed to occur at considerably shorter wavelength.[8]

Another molecule of interest in this regard is formaldehyde which, in the ground state, is planar. Two transitions, the $n \rightarrow \pi^*$ ($^1A_2 \leftarrow {}^1A_1$) and the $\pi \rightarrow \pi^*$ ($^1A_1 \leftarrow {}^1A_1$), are of interest and lead to different excited states. The excited $^1A_2$ state has two electrons in the bonding π orbital and one in the antibonding π^* orbital. The antibonding character of the electron in the π^* orbital reduces the resistance to distortion from the planar configuration, but does not cancel the effect of the two bonding electrons which make the molecule planar; hence, this excited state is planar and belongs

[7] C. K. Ingold and G. W. King, *J. Chem. Soc.*, 2702, 2704, 2708, 2725, 2745 (1953).

[8] H. Howard and G. W. King, *Can. J. Chem.*, **37**, 700 (1959), who have made numerical calculations for the *cis* and *trans* structures; L. Burnelle, *J. Chem. Phys.*, **35**, 311 (1961).

to the point group C_{2v}, just as does the ground state. The excited $^1A_1$ state, however, has one electron each in the bonding and antibonding π orbitals. In this configuration the planar conformation again is subject to a net destabilization which, as in acetylene, is at least partially overcome by a rehybridization, transforming the σ-bonding orbitals of carbon further toward sp³ character and the molecule to a pyramidal configuration of point group C_s.

Thus it is seen that excited states frequently, if not usually, have different geometry from ground states, and excited states of a single compound corresponding to different transitions may have different geometry.

In some cases, at least, these considerations can be generalized. Thus the first excited state of any symmetrical alternant molecule is twisted by 90° about any essential double bond at its center. Consequently, the lowest excited state of molecules such as stilbene and azobenzene must have the planes of the two benzene rings at right angles.

A more detailed discussion of the geometry of stilbene and its sterically hindered derivatives[9] is given in section 15.4 in connection with steric effects on spectra and applications of the Franck-Condon principle. The discussion found there will further serve to illustrate how valence theory (in either the MO or VB form) can be used to make qualitative and semi-quantitative statements about potential-energy curves, and hence about the geometry of various states. It will be seen there that, even when the gross geometry of a molecule remains unchanged upon excitation, minor changes in bond distances may generally be expected.

7.3   Experimental Approaches to the Geometry of Excited States

It has been pointed out that the customary experimental techniques for dealing with the geometry of molecules require significant amounts of such materials over considerable lengths of time, and usually in a reasonable degree of purity. Since it is ordinarily not possible to obtain the requisite quantities of the excited states for the time needed, entirely different techniques are required for their study.

Excited states are, of course, formed in all light-absorption processes. The concentrations so formed, under the usual experimental conditions, are so microscopically small as to be useless for making direct physical measurements. With special exciting sources, however, sufficient numbers of excited molecules can be generated to observe some of their properties. The most common observations relate to the manner in which the molecule returns to the ground state. One mode of return is by emission of radiation, which can frequently be observed as either fluorescence or phosphorescence

[9] H. H. Jaffé and M. Orchin, *J. Chem. Soc.*, 1078 (1960).

spectra (Chapter 19), depending on whether the time elapsed between absorption and re-emission is relatively short or long, respectively. Since little information concerning the geometry of the excited state is obtained from these spectra, they will not be discussed further.

A special technique recently developed for the generation of significant quantities of excited molecules involves excitation by the flash from an exploding wire. Sufficient quantities of excited molecules can thus be produced to obtain considerable information about excited states and their decay, but the technique has not yet been extensively used to obtain information about molecular geometry.

Much information concerning the symmetry, and the evaluation of bond lengths and angles in stable molecules, comes from infrared and microwave spectra (i.e., from vibrational and rotational excitation). This type of information cannot be directly obtained for excited molecules, but it is accessible through a careful analysis of absorption spectra. Electronic excitation is accompanied by vibrational and rotational excitation, and the breadth of absorption lines has been, at least in part, ascribed to this fact. Also, as shown in section 6.6, certain forbidden transitions are observable only because of the concomitant vibrational and electronic excitation. Since, at room temperature, molecules are predominantly in the lowest vibrational level, the spacings of vibrational energy levels of the ground state do not appear very prominently in the spectra. But since electronic excitation can end in many vibrational levels of the excited state (consistent with the Franck-Condon principle), the vibrations of the excited state appear prominently in the spectra.

Unfortunately, it is rarely possible to resolve sufficient vibrational structure in spectra of dissolved compounds or of compounds in condensed phases. Even if such resolution could be achieved, the information would not be of much use, since the vibrational motion is modified in such phases through the proximity of solvent molecules. The spectra of gaseous compounds at low pressure, however, can usually be resolved sufficiently so that individual vibrational bands are observed, and these in turn can sometimes be further resolved to show the rotational fine structure. Such vapor spectra can then be analyzed to permit identification of various vibrational modes and rotational constants of the excited states. This information can be used roughly in the same manner as that obtained from infrared and microwave spectra of stable molecules. Although the accuracy of such information is not as great as can be obtained by direct observation of the vibrational and rotational spectra, useful data frequently result.

One additional piece of information is available from analysis of the vapor spectra. It was seen in section 6.6 that the vibration which distorts a molecule so that a forbidden transition is observed figures prominently in the absorption spectrum. Similarly, the vibration which transforms the geometry of the ground state to that of the excited state appears prominently in the spectrum. Thus, observation of the dominant vibration in the vapor spectrum frequently is sufficient to pinpoint the particular distortion which occurs upon excitation, and thus gives important clues to the structure of the excited state. In this problem the operation of the Franck-Condon principle is again of prime importance, since it specifies the particular vibrational energy levels accessible from the ground state by vertical excitation.

In a series of papers, Ingold and King[7] have investigated the geometries of excited states of acetylene; the details of their treatment are, however, too involved to repeat here.

7.4 Physical Properties of Excited States

The geometry of excited states was discussed in sections 7.2 and 7.3. Vibrational frequencies for such states are obtainable from analysis of vapor spectra, where the vibrational frequencies give rise to progressions of bands; such information is, however, generally obtainable only for relatively small molecules with reasonably high vapor pressure, and requires observation of vapor spectra under high resolution. When the spectrum is sufficiently resolved, vibrational analysis then permits calculation of force constants. With very small molecules, particularly diatomics and triatomics, even the vibrational bands have quite frequently been resolved, and the rotational structures analyzed. Spectroscopic properties of certain excited states, generally the lowest excited singlet and particularly the lowest triplet, are also commonly observed, and will be discussed in Chapter 19. In addition, some other properties of excited states have been inferred from spectroscopic observations, and considerably more activity in this area may be anticipated in the future.

Lippert[10] has been able to make rough calculations of the dipole moments of the first excited singlet states of some appropriately substituted aromatic molecules from the solvent dependence of the $V \leftarrow N$ transition in absorption and the $V \rightarrow N$ transition in fluorescence, which in the cases treated has substantially the character of an intramolecular-charge transfer transition. The solvent dependence in these compounds is, in nonpolar solvents, due to dipole-induced dipole forces, and, in polar solvents, to dipole-dipole forces (cf. section 9.7). Examples of dipole moments calculated in this way for the V state of some molecules are given in Table 7.1.

[10] E. Lippert, *Z. Elektrochem.*, **61**, 962 (1957); see also N. Mataga, Y. Kaifu, and M. Koizumi, *Bull. Chem. Soc. Japan*, **29**, 465 (1956).

An especially interesting case is compound I, where the dipole moment in the ground state is 33 D.U. and *decreases* on excitation, probably to some-

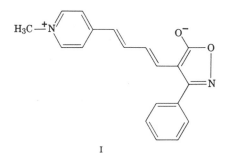

I

where around 20 D.U. In this case, the effect of increasing solvent polarity is a hypsochromic shift, contrary to usual experience, with $V \leftarrow N$ transitions.

Another method to determine dipole moments of excited states is based on the effect of external electric fields on the degree of polarization of

TABLE 7.1

Dipole Moments of Some Compounds in the Ground and Excited States

Dipole Moment, DU

| | | Excited State | |
| | | Lippert | Czekalla |
Compound	Ground State	(footnote 10)	(footnote 11)
4-Amino-4′-nitrobiphenyl	6.4	18	20
2-Amino-7-nitrofluorene	7	25	19–20
4-Dimethylamino-4′-nitrostilbene	7.6	32	20.7–23.7
4-Amino-4′-nitrostilbene	...	...	...
4-Amino-4′-cyanobiphenyl	...	...	9–12
I	33	20	...

fluorescence spectra.[11] This method depends basically on a reorientation of molecules in an electric field, and the consequent change in the polarization of the fluorescence emission. Results obtained by this method are also shown in Table 7.1 and are seen to be in rough agreement with those obtained by Lippert, although generally somewhat lower.

[11] J. Czekalla, *Z. Elektrochem.*, **64**, 1221 (1960).

Since Förster[12] has shown that excited molecules can undergo acid-base reactions without simultaneous electronic deactivation, these reactions have received considerable attention. Observation in media of varying pH of the fluorescence spectra of molecules having acidic or basic functional groups showed that there is a drastic change in the spectra at a pH which is considerably different from the pH at which the compound in the ground state undergoes acid-base reactions. Several inferences were made from this observation: (1) the excited-state molecules underwent an acid-base reaction (i.e., a base picked up a proton from the solvent or an acid lost a proton to the solvent); (2) this process does not greatly disturb the

TABLE 7.2

pK's of Some Molecules in the Ground (pK_G), Lowest Singlet (pK_S), and Lowest Triplet (pK_T) States

Compound	pK_G	pK_S	pK_T
2-Naphthol	9.5	3.1	8.1
2-Naphthoic acid	4.2	10–12	4.0
1-Naphthoic acid	3.7	10–12	3.8
Acridine	5.5	10.6	5.6
Quinoline	5.1	. . .	6.0
2-Naphthylamine	4.1	−2	3.3
N,N-Dimethyl-1-naphthylamine	4.9	. . .	2.7

electronic structure of the excited molecule; (3) the process is extremely rapid, occurring in less than 10^{-8} to 10^{-7} second, since this is the lifetime of the fluorescent state. On the basis of these initial observations, Weller[13] has measured the pK of a number of compounds in their fluorescent states i.e., the lowest excited singlet. Some typical data are shown in Table 7.2. The pK values obtained vary widely from those of the ground state, frequently by as much as six powers of ten in K. Such measurements have also been made at different temperatures, thus permitting estimation of ΔH and ΔS for the reactions of the excited state. In addition, determination of the fluorescence quantum yield permits estimation of the individual rates of the acid-base reactions.[12] Many of the protonation reactions are shown to be diffusion controlled, but the reverse reactions, although also very fast, are frequently too slow for diffusion control.

Acid-base reactions of excited triplet states cannot be measured by an

[12] T. Förster, Z. Elektrochem., 54, 42 (1950).

[13] A. Weller, Z. Elektrochem., 56, 662 (1957); Z. physik. Chem. (Frankfurt), 3, 238 (1955); 18, 163 (1958).

analogous technique using phosphorescence measurements, because phosphorescence is generally not observed in liquid solutions. However, the method of triplet-triplet absorption lends itself to pK determination.[14] By the use of flash photolysis, high concentrations of the lowest triplet are generated in solutions of varying pH, and the absorption spectra are determined during the lifetime of the triplet. Typical results obtained by this method are shown in Table 7.2; surprisingly, the pK of the lowest triplet seems to be close to that of the ground state rather than to that of the excited singlet state, which has the same electronic configuration. Confirmation of the data is obtained from a calculation of the pK difference between ground and triplet states from the phosphorescence spectra.[13]

[14] G. Jackson and G. Porter, *Proc. Roy. Soc. (London)*, **A260,** 13 (1961).

8 Comparison of molecular-orbital and valence-bond (resonance) theories

8.1 General

Molecular orbital theory is best suited for a quantitative treatment and, in many cases, even for a qualitative understanding of the spectra of many molecules. At the same time, chemists have little practice in visualizing MO's, which are basically descriptions of the orbitals of one electron at a time. A mental summation over all occupied orbitals is required to achieve a qualitative picture of the molecule as a whole. Partly because it became widely used earlier than MO theory, partly because it provides a more easily visualized picture of a molecule, resonance theory is more familiar to chemists, and has been used in much of the work of interpreting spectra. Consequently resonance theory will be used considerably in subsequent chapters and will, in this chapter, be introduced and placed in its proper relation to MO theory. This will be achieved by first recapitulating and extending the *complete* MO treatment, then outlining the *complete* valence-bond (VB) treatment, and finally contrasting the two. The hydrogen molecule will serve as a first example. It should be noted that the two *complete* treatments, as outlined here, necessarily lead to the same result, provided the same AO's are used as starting point, and that any differences arise only because the two methods are not carried to completion. The complete results are, however, not necessarily correct, since many assumptions are common to the two theories.

As a starting point, it will be well to restate the problem, to find the allowed values of the energy W_j and the associated functions Ξ_j which satisfy the equation

$$\mathcal{H}\Xi_j = W_j\Xi_j \tag{8.1}$$

where $\mathcal{H}$ is the complete Hamiltonian operator of the system, involving kinetic- and potential-energy terms for all particles (nuclei and electrons) in the system, and the Ξ are functions of the coordinates of all these particles, i.e., of three-space coordinates and, in addition, the spin coordinate. The problem of the exact solution of this differential equation is hopeless; to make any progress a long series of approximations and assumptions is necessary. It is beyond the scope of the present book to treat and justify all these assumptions, but a few will merit short comment.

The first concerns the separation of the differential equation (8.1) into several separate ones. It has been pointed out that the "motion" of electrons is several orders of magnitude faster than the motion of nuclei. Consequently, it is a good approximation, when discussing the motion of electrons, to assume the nuclei to be stationary—this assumption has become known as the Born-Oppenheimer approximation[1]—and when discussing the motion of nuclei to treat the electrons as an average charge cloud. This approximation permits factoring of the wave equation into nuclear and electronic parts, thereby greatly simplifying the process of obtaining an electronic wave function.

The next simplification involves the spin coordinates. The nonrelativistic Hamiltonian operator contains no terms *simultaneously* involving both the spin and the space coordinates, and hence the Schrödinger differential equation (8.1) may be separated into two. The first of these equations involves spin coordinates only, and usually is trivial and contributes no information. The other involves the three coordinates defining the position of each electron in space. This approximation amounts to assuming that there is no interaction or coupling of spin and orbital angular momenta, and is also involved in the assumption made in Russell-Saunders coupling in the corresponding atomic case.

With these assumptions which are common to VB and MO theory, equation (8.1) reduces to

$$H\Psi_i = E_i\Psi_i \qquad (8.2)$$

where the Ψ_i depend on the coordinates of the electrons only, H is the Hamiltonian operator containing the nuclei only as constant terms and containing spin and space coordinates separated, and E_i are the electronic energy levels. From this point on, the two theories treat the problem differently, and will be dealt with in turn.

8.2   The Hydrogen Molecule in Molecular-Orbital Theory

The next approximation of MO theory is to assume that the function Ψ_i of equation (8.2) can be factored into a product of one-electron functions:

$$\Psi_i = \Pi_j\psi_j \qquad (8.3)$$

This approximation of necessity involves either the complete neglect, or a crude approximation, of electron correlation (cf. section 5.1). In addition, the assumption is commonly made that each of the ψ_j is independent of which other one-electron orbitals are occupied,

[1] M. Born and J. R. Oppenheimer, *Ann. Physik.*, **84**, 457 (1927).

an assumption which is undoubtedly not good and can be at least partially circumvented by the use of self-consistent field (SCF) methods,[2] but one that is made in most qualitative and semiquantitative work. In Chapter 3 the orbitals ψ_j were derived by solution of the secular equation, and in Chapter 5 were assembled qualitatively into electronic states. Completion of the MO treatment involves the construction of the total electronic wave function Ψ_i from the one-electron functions ψ_j.

STEP I is the calculation of the ψ_j from the atomic orbitals ϕ_r by use of the variational principle and the secular equation, if needed. In the case of H_2 this leads to[3]

$$\psi_+ = (2 + 2S)^{-\frac{1}{2}}(\phi_1 + \phi_2)$$

and

$$\psi_- = (2 - 2S)^{-\frac{1}{2}}(\phi_1 - \phi_2)$$

STEP II is the formation of configurations (Ψ^C) from the ψ_j; three configurations of the two electrons of H_2 and the two orbitals ψ_+ and ψ_- are possible:

$$\Psi_1{}^C = \psi_+{}^2$$
$$\Psi_2{}^C = \psi_+\psi_-$$
$$\Psi_3{}^C = \psi_-{}^2$$

STEP III. As discussed in the treatment of triplet states in Chapter 3, it is now necessary to (1) consider the spin functions, and (2) assure that each wave function is antisymmetric with respect to the exchange of any two electrons.

The possible spin functions for two electrons are (cf. p. 47)

$$\alpha(1)\alpha(2)$$
$$\beta(1)\beta(2)$$
$$2^{-\frac{1}{2}}[\alpha(1)\beta(2) + \alpha(2)\beta(1)]$$
$$2^{-\frac{1}{2}}[\alpha(1)\beta(2) - \alpha(2)\beta(1)]$$

The first three of these are symmetric, the last antisymmetric, in the exchange of electrons.

The configurations

$$\Psi_1{}^C = \psi_+{}^2 = \psi_+(1)\psi_+(2) = (2 + 2S)^{-1}[\phi_1(1) + \phi_2(1)][\phi_1(2) + \phi_2(2)]$$

and

$$\Psi_3{}^C = \psi_-{}^2 = \psi_-(1)\psi_-(2) = (2 - 2S)^{-1}[\phi_1(1) - \phi_2(1)][\phi_1(2) - \phi_2(2)]$$

are symmetric in exchange of electrons 1 and 2 (as specified in the parentheses) and hence can be combined only with the antisymmetric spin function, yielding the two state functions (Ψ^S):

$$\begin{aligned}\Psi_1{}^S &= (2)^{-\frac{3}{2}}(1 + S)^{-1}[\phi_1(1) + \phi_2(1)][\phi_1(2) + \phi_2(2)] \\ &\quad \times [\alpha(1)\beta(2) - \alpha(2)\beta(1)] \\ &= (2)^{-\frac{3}{2}}(1 + S)^{-1}[\phi_1(1)\phi_1(2) + \phi_2(1)\phi_2(2) + \phi_1(1)\phi_2(2) + \phi_1(2)\phi_2(1)] \\ &\quad \times [\alpha(1)\beta(2) - \alpha(2)\beta(1)]\end{aligned}$$

and

$$\begin{aligned}\Psi_4{}^S &= (2)^{-\frac{3}{2}}(1 - S)^{-1}[\phi_1(1) - \phi_2(1)][\phi_1(2) - \phi_2(2)][\alpha(1)\beta(2) - \alpha(2)\beta(1)] \\ &= (2)^{-\frac{3}{2}}(1 - S)^{-1}[\phi_1(1)\phi_1(2) + \phi_2(1)\phi_2(2) - \phi_1(1)\phi_2(2) - \phi_1(2)\phi_2(1)] \\ &\quad \times [\alpha(1)\beta(2) - \alpha(2)\beta(1)]\end{aligned}$$

---

[2] C. C. J. Roothaan, *Revs. Modern Phys.*, **23**, 69 (1951); **32**, 179 (1960).

[3] In this chapter the normalization factors will be written explicitly.

The configuration $\Psi_2'^C = \psi_+\psi_-$ can be written in two ways: $\psi_+(1)\psi_-(2)$ and $\psi_+(2)\psi_-(1)$. Neither of these is satisfactory, since they both imply an ability to specify which electron is in ψ_+ and which is in ψ_-, and they should be replaced by symmetric and antisymmetric linear combinations:

$$\Psi_2'^C = 2^{-\frac{1}{2}}[\psi_+(1)\psi_-(2) - \psi_+(2)\psi_-(1)]$$
$$= 2^{-\frac{3}{2}}(1 - S^2)^{-\frac{1}{2}}\{[\phi_1(1) + \phi_2(1)][\phi_1(2) - \phi_2(2)] - [\phi_1(2) + \phi_2(2)]$$
$$\times [\phi_1(1) - \phi_2(1)]\}$$
$$= 2^{-\frac{1}{2}}(1 - S^2)^{-\frac{1}{2}}[\phi_1(2)\phi_2(1) - \phi_1(1)\phi_2(2)]$$
$$\Psi_2'^{C'} = 2^{-\frac{1}{2}}[\psi_+(1)\psi_-(2) + \psi_-(1)\psi_+(2)]$$
$$= 2^{-\frac{3}{2}}(1 - S^2)^{-\frac{1}{2}}\{[\phi_1(1) + \phi_2(1)][\phi_1(2) - \phi_2(2)] + [\phi_1(1) - \phi_2(1)]$$
$$\times [\phi_1(2) + \phi_2(2)]\}$$
$$= 2^{-\frac{1}{2}}(1 - S^2)^{-\frac{1}{2}}[\phi_1(1)\phi_1(2) - \phi_2(1)\phi_2(2)]$$

where $\Psi_2'^C$ is antisymmetric, $\Psi_2'^{C'}$ symmetric, with respect to exchange of electrons, and must consequently be multiplied by symmetric and antisymmetric spin functions, respectively, giving the state functions:

$$\Psi_2'^S = 2^{-\frac{1}{2}}(1 - S^2)^{-\frac{1}{2}}[\phi_1(1)\phi_2(2) - \phi_2(1)\phi_1(2)]\begin{cases}\alpha(1)\alpha(2)\\ \beta(1)\beta(2)\\ 2^{-\frac{1}{2}}[\alpha(1)\beta(2) + \alpha(2)\beta(1)]\end{cases}$$

$$\Psi_3'^S = 2^{-1}(1 - S^2)^{-\frac{1}{2}}[\phi_1(1)\phi_1(2) - \phi_2(1)\phi_2(2)][\alpha(1)\beta(2) - \alpha(2)\beta(1)]$$

As indicated in Chapter 3, and again above, each of the functions $\Psi_1'^S$, $\Psi_3'^S$, and $\Psi_4'^S$ involves only a single function, each an antisymmetric spin function, and hence all are singlets; They may now be called $^1\Psi_1'^S$, $^1\Psi_3'^S$, and $^1\Psi_4'^S$. However, $\Psi_2'^S$ involves three functions, which are degenerate in the absence of a magnetic field since they are distinguished only by the three different symmetric spin functions, and accordingly is a triplet: $^3\Psi_2'^S$. Thus we have the four states already given in Chapter 5:

$$^1\Psi_1'^S, {}^3\Psi_2'^S, {}^1\Psi_3'^S, \text{ and } {}^1\Psi_4'^S$$

STEP IV. Since the molecule H_2 belongs to the point group $D_{\infty h}$, each of these state functions must belong to one of the symmetry species of this point group. Since all states are derived from the 1s functions of the two H atoms (ϕ_1 and ϕ_2), all states are Σ^+ states. Inspection of the functions shows that $\Psi_1'^S$ and $\Psi_4'^S$ are gerade, $\Psi_2'^S$ and $\Psi_3'^S$ ungerade, and thus there are the four state functions:

$$^1\Psi_1'^S = {}^1\Sigma_g^+; \quad {}^3\Psi_2'^S = {}^3\Sigma_u^+; \quad {}^1\Psi_3'^S = {}^1\Sigma_u^+; \quad {}^1\Psi_4'^S = {}^1\Sigma_g^+$$

Each of the functions corresponds to a single configuration, and although their energies, including electron correlation, can be evaluated, each function still encompasses the assumption that Ψ_i' is a product of one-electron functions [cf. equation (8.3)]. This assumption must now be abandoned, by finding the linear combination of the various state functions which has the lowest energy, and others orthogonal to it. Use is again made here of the variational principle. We might now set up a secular determinant, in which the diagonal elements are the integrals

$$H_{ii} = \int \Psi_i'^S H \Psi_i'^S \, d\tau,$$

which are just the energy values of these state functions, and the off-diagonal elements are the integrals

$$H_{ij} = \int \Psi_i'^S H \Psi_j'^S \, d\tau \tag{8.4}$$

Since H is a totally symmetric operator, these integrals vanish unless the product $\Psi_i^S \Psi_j^S$ is also totally symmetric; this is possible only if Ψ_i^S and Ψ_j^S belong to the same symmetry species. Further, since H does not involve the spin coordinates, the integral (8.4) vanishes if the spin coordinates are orthogonal, i.e., if Ψ_i^S and Ψ_j^S are of different multiplicities. Consequently, the off-diagonal elements connecting wave functions of either different symmetry or different multiplicity vanish, and the secular determinant factors into a product of determinants involving the interaction of states of equal symmetry and multiplicity.

In the present case, the secular determinant thus factors into two 1×1 determinants for the $^1\Sigma_u^+$ and $^3\Sigma_u^+$ states, and these states are accordingly unaffected. The two $^1\Sigma_g^+$ states, however, lead to a 2×2 determinant and interact. The process of calculating their interaction is called *configuration interaction* because states having the same symmetry, but arising from *different configurations*, are allowed to interact. The result of configuration interaction then is the mixing of $^1\Psi_1^S$ and $^1\Psi_4^S$ and yields:

$$\Psi_a(^1\Sigma_g^+) = 2^{-3/2}\{(1 + S)^{-1}[\phi_1(1)\phi_1(2) + \phi_2(1)\phi_2(2) + \phi_1(1)\phi_2(2)$$
$$+ \phi_1(2)\phi_2(1)] + (1 - S)^{-1}\mu'[\phi_1(1)\phi_1(2) + \phi_2(1)\phi_2(2) - \phi_1(1)\phi_2(2)$$
$$- \phi_1(2)\phi_2(1)]\}[\alpha(1)\beta(2) - \alpha(2)\beta(1)]$$
$$= \{\mu_1^a[\phi_1(1)\phi_2(2) + \phi_1(2)\phi_2(1)] + \mu_2^a[\phi_1(1)\phi_1(2) + \phi_2(1)\phi_2(2)]\}$$
$$\times [\alpha(1)\beta(2) - \alpha(2)\beta(1)]$$

Similarly,

$$\Psi_b(^1\Sigma_g^+) = \{\mu_1^b[\phi_1(1)\phi_2(2) + \phi_1(2)\phi_2(1)] + \mu_2^b[\phi_1(1)\phi_1(2) + \phi_2(1)\phi_2(2)]\}$$
$$\times [\alpha(1)\beta(2) - \alpha(2)\beta(1)]$$

with

$$\mu_1^a = 2^{-3/2}[(1 + S)^{-1} - \mu'(1 - S)^{-1}]$$
$$\mu_2^a = 2^{-3/2}[(1 + S)^{-1} + \mu'(1 - S)^{-1}]$$
$$\mu_1^b = 2^{-3/2}[(1 + S)^{-1} - \mu''(1 - S)^{-1}]$$
$$\mu_2^b = 2^{-3/2}[(1 + S)^{-1} + \mu''(1 - S)^{-1}]$$

where μ' and μ'' are coefficients determined by solution of the secular equation.

Introducing the notation (ab, cd) for $\phi_a(b)\phi_c(d)$, and α_a for $\alpha(a)$, etc., the four final wave functions of MO theory are

$$\Psi_a(^1\Sigma_g^+) = \{\mu_1^a[(11, 22) + (12, 21)] + \mu_2^a[(11, 12) + (21, 22)]\}[\alpha_1\beta_2 - \alpha_2\beta_1]$$

$$\Psi_2(^3\Sigma_u^+) = 2^{-1}(1 - S^2)^{-1/2}[(11, 22) - (21, 12)]\begin{cases} \sqrt{2}\alpha_1\beta_2 \\ \sqrt{2}\beta_1\beta_2 \\ \alpha_1\beta_2 + \alpha_2\beta_1 \end{cases}$$

$$\Psi_3(^1\Sigma_u^+) = 2^{-1/2}(1 - S^2)^{-1/2}[(11, 12) - (21, 22)](\alpha_1\beta_2 - \alpha_2\beta_1)$$

$$\Psi_b(^1\Sigma_g^+) = \{\mu_1^b[(11, 22) + (12, 21) + \mu_2^b[(11, 12) + (21, 22)]\}[\alpha_1\beta_2 - \alpha_2\beta_1]$$

Further possible wave functions will be considered briefly in section 8.4.

8.3   The Hydrogen Molecule in the Valence-Bond Method

In contrast to the MO method, VB theory analyzes the wave function Ψ_i as a linear combination of *atomic* many-electron functions, which, in turn, are generally considered constructed from products of one-electron functions.

STEP I. In the usual procedure, the VB treatment of H_2 starts with the assumption that two neutral H atoms interact, and that the wave function of the molecule is the product of the wave functions of the two atoms, each with its electron. Calling the states[4] of the two H atoms Φ_1 and Φ_2, with $\Phi_1 = \phi_1(1)$ and $\Phi_2 = \phi_2(2)$, we obtain

$$\Psi_1 = \Phi_1 \cdot \Phi_2 = [\phi_1(1) \cdot \phi_2(2)]$$

STEP II. This involves again the indistinguishability of the electrons, and hence considers $\Psi_{II} = \phi_1(2)\phi_2(1)$ a function equally as good as Ψ_I, and states that the actual wave function must be a linear combination of Ψ_I and Ψ_{II}:

$$\Psi_A = (2)^{-\frac{1}{2}}(\Psi_I + \Psi_{II}) = 2^{-\frac{1}{2}}(1 + S^2)^{-\frac{1}{2}}[\phi_1(1)\phi_2(2) + \phi_2(1)\phi_1(2)]$$

Similarly, the combination

$$\Psi_B = (2)^{-\frac{1}{2}}(\Psi_I - \Psi_{II}) = 2^{-\frac{1}{2}}(1 - S^2)^{-\frac{1}{2}}[\phi_1(1)\phi_2(2) - \phi_2(1)\phi_1(2)]$$

is a satisfactory wave function. This step is often referred to as electron exchange, and the binding energy arrived at in this process as the exchange energy; however, it must be kept in mind that no physical exchange of electrons is involved, and that the separation of the exchange energy is merely a matter of mathematical convenience.

Next the spin functions must be combined with Ψ_A and Ψ_B. It is readily seen that Ψ_A is symmetric, Ψ_B antisymmetric in exchange of electrons, and consequently Ψ_A is multiplied by an antisymmetric spin function, $2^{-\frac{1}{2}}[\alpha(1)\beta(2) - \alpha(2)\beta(1)]$, and Ψ_B by the set of three symmetric spin functions, $\alpha(1)\alpha(2)$, $\beta(1)\beta(2)$, and $2^{-\frac{1}{2}}[\alpha(1)\beta(2) + \alpha(2)\beta(1)]$. Hence Ψ_A is a singlet, Ψ_B a triplet.

STEP III. Next, consideration must be given to the fact that the functions Ψ_A and Ψ_B are not the only possible ways of assigning two electrons to two nuclei. It is also possible, although less likely, to have the molecule made up of an H^+ and an H^- ion, i.e., to assign both electrons to the same nucleus. If this is done, naturally it is again necessary to consider the two nuclei as equivalent, and two functions, $\Psi_{III} = \phi_1(1)\phi_1(2)$ and $\Psi_{IV} = \phi_2(1)\phi_2(2)$, must be considered, and considered as equivalent. This leads to the two structures

$$\Psi_C = (\Psi_{III} + \Psi_{IV}) = 2^{-\frac{1}{2}}[\phi_1(1)\phi_1(2) + \phi_2(1)\phi_2(2)]$$

and

$$\Psi_D = (\Psi_{III} - \Psi_{IV}) = 2^{-\frac{1}{2}}[\phi_1(1)\phi_1(2) - \phi_2(1)\phi_2(2)]$$

Again Ψ_C and Ψ_D are to be multiplied by the appropriate spin functions. Both are symmetric with respect to exchange of electrons and hence must be multiplied by the antisymmetric function, $2^{-\frac{1}{2}}[\alpha(1)\beta(2) - \alpha(2)\beta(1)]$.

STEP IV. It remains to combine the functions Ψ_A, Ψ_B, Ψ_C, and Ψ_D into appropriate orthogonal wave functions. Inspection shows that Ψ_B and Ψ_D belong to the species Σ_u^+ and are, respectively, identical to the $^3\Sigma_u^+$ and $^1\Sigma_u^+$ functions obtained by the MO method. Ψ_A and Ψ_C are both $^1\Sigma_g^+$ functions and are linearly combined to give

$$\Psi_1(^1\Sigma_g^+) = N_1(\Psi_A + \lambda_1\Psi_C)$$
$$= \{\lambda_1{}^a[(11, 22) + (21, 12)] + \lambda_2{}^a[(11, 12) + (21, 22)]\}$$
$$\times [\alpha_1\beta_2 - \alpha_2\beta_1]$$

and

$$\Psi_4(^1\Sigma_g^+) = N_4(\Psi_A + \lambda_4\Psi_C)$$
$$= \{\lambda_1{}^b[(11, 22) + (21, 12)] + \lambda_2{}^b[(11, 12) + (21, 22)]\}$$
$$\times [\alpha_1\beta_2 - \alpha_2\beta_1]$$

[4] In the present case, Φ_1 and Φ_2 appear to be one-electron functions; this, however, is due to the nature of the H_2 molecule and is not the normal case in VB theory.

using the abbreviations introduced at the end of section 8.2. The λ_1^a, λ_1^b, λ_2^a, λ_2^b are appropriate combinations of the normalization factors and the variational coefficients, and can be shown to be numerically equal to the corresponding μ's of section 8.2. Thus, the wave functions are the same in both theories.

8.4   Comparison of Molecular-Orbital and Valence-Bond Treatments for H_2

First, it will be instructive to analyze the meaning of the various terms in the wave functions. Inspection of the VB development shows that the (11, 22) and (21, 12) terms correspond to covalent structures, i.e., to structures in which both electrons are equally shared by both nuclei. The terms (11, 12) and (21, 22), however, arise from the ionic structures Ψ'_{III} and Ψ'_{IV}. Although these contributions from the covalent and ionic structures are the same in both methods when the treatment is complete, it is noteworthy that, in the MO method, before configuration interaction covalent aud ionic structures make *equal* contributions to the ground state, whereas, in the VB method, in the common approximation of neglecting ionic structures, or at least some ionic structures, their importance is underestimated. Thus it is seen that the two methods approach the same final result from different directions: MO theory overestimates ionic structures; VB theory, if anything, underestimates them.

In order to assure that both theories give identical results it is also necessary to ensure that the assumptions made in both are the same. This is particularly important with regard to the basic wave functions used. The MO treatment must, by its nature, start from atomic one-electron orbitals, although various possible approximations of such orbitals might be used. The VB method, on the other hand, can start from atomic functions of any desired complexity. Only if the atomic functions used are developed as products of the same one-electron orbitals is the agreement between the methods assured.

Finally, some comment concerning the lack of completeness of even this treatment is called for. In the case of H_2, for example, only 1s orbitals were considered, largely because the next higher orbitals, the 2s orbitals, are of very much higher energy. Inclusion of configurations involving just one electron in a 2s orbital gives rise, in addition to the two $^1\Sigma_g^+$ states and the $^1\Sigma_u^+$ and $^3\Sigma_u^+$ states, to four new $^1\Sigma_g^+$, two new $^3\Sigma_g^+$, and three each $^1\Sigma_u^+$ and $^3\Sigma_u^+$ states. Inclusion also of the 2p orbitals (which are, in H, degenerate with the 2s orbitals and should probably be considered at the same time) gives rise, in addition to six $^1\Sigma_g^+$, four $^3\Sigma_g^+$, five $^1\Sigma_u^+$, five $^3\Sigma_u^+$, two $^1\Sigma_g^-$, two $^3\Sigma_g^-$, one $^1\Sigma_u^-$, one $^3\Sigma_u^-$, six each $^1\Pi_g$, $^3\Pi_g$, $^1\Pi_u$, $^3\Pi_u$, two $^1\Delta_g$, and one each $^1\Delta_u$ and $^3\Delta_u$ states.

The new states listed are of little interest in themselves, since their energy is very high. Their importance for the present purpose lies in the contribution they make, through configuration interaction, to the ground state, and to the low excited states, of the molecule. Since all these lower states belong to the species Σ_g^+ and Σ_u^+, the Σ^-, Π, and Δ states are of no interest. However, the ten $^1\Sigma_g^+$ states arising from wave functions involving one electron in the $n = 2$ shell could appreciably affect the two $^1\Sigma_g^+$ states (discussed above) arising from the configurations $\sigma_g^2(1s)$ and $\sigma_u^{*2}(1s)$; similarly, the six $^1\Sigma_u^+$ and six $^3\Sigma_u^+$ states of the $n = 2$ shell could affect the low excited states $^1\Sigma_u^+$ and $^3\Sigma_u^+$ of the configuration $\sigma_g(1s)\sigma_u^*(1s)$. Similar considerations, although usually neglected, become more and more important in the study of heavy atoms, where the number of valence electrons is larger, the higher shells are energetically less unaccessible, and the number of states is generally even much larger.

In the VB method, similar considerations will apply. In this case, consideration of higher AO's will necessitate writing further functions, similar to Ψ'_A, Ψ'_B, Ψ'_C, and Ψ'_D, but involving instead of the 1s orbitals (represented by ϕ_A or ϕ_B in these wave functions the appropriate higher orbitals. Then, in Step IV, the linear combination needs to be carried over the increased number of structures, involving so many more variational coefficients, λ.

8.5   Generalization of the Valence-Bond and Molecular-Orbital Methods to Larger Compounds

It now remains to generalize both treatments for larger molecules. In the MO method, the first step (Step I on p. 160) always involves the formation of the one-electron MO's, as was illustrated for many molecules in Chapter 3.

$$\psi_j = \Sigma_r c_{jr} \phi_r$$

The next step (Step II on p. 160) is the generation of the configuration function, as previously shown in Chapter 5.

$$\Psi'^C_i = \Pi_j \psi_j^{n_{ij}} = \Pi_j (\Sigma_r c_{jr} \phi_r)^{n_{ij}}$$

where n_{ij} represents the number of electrons occupying the jth MO in the ith configuration, 2, 1, or 0 as long as ψ_j is nondegenerate, and $\Sigma_j n_{ij} = n$, the total number of electrons in the molecule.

The third step (Step III on p. 160) in the development involves the assignment of spins. Each product function configuration, $\Psi'^C_i = \Pi_j \psi_j^{n_{ij}}$, is multiplied, successively, by each of the 2^n possible (not necessarily all different) combinations of spin functions $\Pi_k \sigma_k$, leading to a set of 2^n functions of the form

$$\Pi_k \psi_j(k) \sigma(k) \tag{8.5}$$

where k refers to the various electrons and takes the values 1 to n, σ is either of the spin functions α and β (2^n combinations of α's and β's are possible), and the electrons have now been assigned to the various functions ψ_j, so that the product is more readily taken over the various electrons. Since, however, the electrons are indistinguishable, the wave function must be either symmetric or antisymmetric in them; furthermore, it can be shown[5] that an alternative expression of the Pauli principle is that any wave function *must* be antisymmetric in the exchange of electrons (i.e., must change sign if two electrons are exchanged). This can be achieved by generating the determinant of the products (8.5)

$$\frac{1}{\sqrt{n!}} \left| \Pi_k \psi_j(k) \sigma_k \right|$$

i.e., a determinant of the form

$$\begin{vmatrix} \psi_1(1)\sigma_1(1) & \psi_1(2)\sigma_1(2) & \psi_1(3)\sigma_1(3) & \cdots \\ \psi_2(1)\sigma_2(1) & \psi_2(2)\sigma_2(2) & & \\ \psi_3(1)\sigma_3(1) & & & \end{vmatrix}$$

Finally, these determinental wave functions must be orthogonalized, which is achieved by setting up and solving a secular equation for their interaction.

The over-all process will be illustrated for two electrons and two wave functions; the configuration is $\psi_1 \psi_2$. Upon multiplication by the possible spin functions we obtain

$$\text{I} = \psi_1(1)\alpha(1)\psi_2(2)\alpha(2)$$
$$\text{II} = \psi_1(1)\alpha(1)\psi_2(2)\beta(2)$$
$$\text{III} = \psi_1(1)\beta(1)\psi_2(2)\alpha(2)$$
$$\text{IV} = \psi_1(1)\beta(1)\psi_2(2)\beta(2)$$

[5] J. C. Slater, *Quantum Theory of Matter*, McGraw-Hill Book Co., New York, 1951, section 7.5.

The four product functions I–IV lead, then, to the four determinants

$$\text{I} = \frac{1}{\sqrt{2}} \begin{vmatrix} \psi_1(1)\alpha(1) & \psi_1(2)\alpha(2) \\ \psi_2(1)\alpha(1) & \psi_2(2)\alpha(2) \end{vmatrix} = \frac{1}{\sqrt{2}} [\psi_1(1)\alpha(1)\psi_2(2)\alpha(2) - \psi_2(1)\alpha(1)\psi_1(2)\alpha(2)]$$

$$= \frac{1}{\sqrt{2}} [\psi_1(1)\psi_2(2) - \psi_2(1)\psi_1(2)]\alpha(1)\alpha(2)$$

$$\text{II} = \frac{1}{\sqrt{2}} \begin{vmatrix} \psi_1(1)\alpha(1) & \psi_1(2)\alpha(2) \\ \psi_2(1)\beta(1) & \psi_2(2)\beta(2) \end{vmatrix} = \frac{1}{\sqrt{2}} [\psi_1(1)\alpha(1)\psi_2(2)\beta(2) - \psi_2(1)\beta(1)\psi_1(2)\alpha(2)]$$

$$\text{III} = \frac{1}{\sqrt{2}} \begin{vmatrix} \psi_1(1)\beta(1) & \psi_1(2)\beta(2) \\ \psi_2(1)\alpha(1) & \psi_2(2)\alpha(2) \end{vmatrix} = \frac{1}{\sqrt{2}} [\psi_1(1)\beta(1)\psi_2(2)\alpha(2) - \psi_2(1)\alpha(1)\psi_1(2)\beta(2)]$$

$$\text{IV} = \frac{1}{\sqrt{2}} \begin{vmatrix} \psi_1(1)\beta(1) & \psi_1(2)\beta(2) \\ \psi_2(1)\beta(1) & \psi_2(2)\beta(2) \end{vmatrix} = \frac{1}{\sqrt{2}} [\psi_1(1)\beta(1)\psi_2(2)\beta(2) - \psi_2(1)\beta(1)\psi_1(2)\beta(2)]$$

$$= \frac{1}{\sqrt{2}} [\psi_1(1)\psi_2(2) - \psi_2(1)\psi_1(2)]\beta(1)\beta(2)$$

I and IV are orthogonal to each other and to II and III, and are satisfactory wave functions; they are identical to two of the three functions $\Psi_2{}^S$ written down in section 8.2 for H_2. II and III are not orthogonal. By setting up and solving the appropriate secular equation, it is shown that $\frac{1}{\sqrt{2}}$ (II $\pm$ III) are the appropriate combinations, as might have been suspected from symmetry arguments, and simple algebra then leads to the functions

$$\tfrac{1}{2}[\psi_1(1)\psi_2(2) - \psi_2(1)\psi_1(2)][\alpha(1)\beta(2) + \beta(1)\alpha(2)]$$

and

$$\tfrac{1}{2}[\psi_1(1)\psi_2(2) + \psi_2(1)\psi_1(2)][\alpha(1)\beta(2) - \beta(1)\alpha(2)]$$

which are equal to the third of the functions $\Psi_2{}^S$ and to $\Psi_3{}^S$ of section 8.2.

This process, which is called *antisymmetrization*, and the result of which are so-called antisymmetrical molecular orbitals (ASMO), thus leads to the functions:

$$\Psi_i{}^S = \Sigma_l a_{il} \frac{1}{\sqrt{n!}} |\Pi_k \psi_j(k)\sigma(k)|_l = \Sigma_l a_{il} \frac{1}{\sqrt{n!}} |\Pi_k \sigma(k)\Sigma_r c_{jr}\phi_r(k)|$$

which are sometimes abbreviated as

$$\Psi_i{}^S = |\Psi_i{}^C| = |\Pi_k \sigma(k)\Sigma_r c_{jr}\phi_r(k)|$$

Thus the state function $\Psi_i{}^S$ will be represented by

$$\Psi_i{}^S = |\Psi_i{}^C|$$

Finally, the last step (Step IV on p. 161) consists of introduction of configuration interaction, by taking a weighted sum over all states of the same symmetry species, with the coefficients determined by the variational principle:

$$\Psi_k = \Sigma_i a_{ik} \Psi_i{}^S = \Sigma_i a_{ik} |\Psi_i{}^C| = \Sigma_i a_{ik} |\Pi_j \Psi_j^{n_{ij}}|$$

$$= \Sigma_i a_{ik} |\Pi_j [\Sigma_r c_{jr}\phi_r]^{n_{kj}}|$$

The VB method in the first step also starts with the AO's, just as the MO method. But, whereas in the MO method, the AO's are combined into one-electron MO's, in the VB method the AO's of each atom are combined into many-electron atomic functions:

$$\Phi_{jr} = \Pi_j \phi_{jr}^{n_{jr}}$$

for each atom r, where n_{jr} is again the population number, i.e., the number of electrons occupying the atomic orbital ϕ_j of atom r in the state Φ_{jr}. Thus, for example, in Li_2 the atomic functions $\Phi_A = 1s_A{}^2 2s_A$ and $\Phi_B = 1s_B{}^2 2s_B$ of atoms A and B would be formed. These atomic functions are then multiplied together to form the many-electron molecular function, a so-called structure:

$$\Psi_i{}^{ST} = \Pi_r \Phi_{jr} = \Pi_r \Pi_j \phi_{jr}^{n_{jr}}$$

or in the case of Li_2

$$\Psi_i{}^{ST} = \Phi_A \Phi_B = 1s_A{}^2 2s_A 1s_B{}^2 2s_B$$

The n_{jr} of course must obey the condition $\Sigma_{jr} n_{jr} = n$, the total number of electrons. The above structure is a covalent one, since Φ_A and Φ_B are wave functions of neutral lithium. Ionic structures are similarly formed; for example, $\Phi_A = 1s_A{}^2 2s_A{}^2$ and $\Phi_B = 1s_B{}^2$, corresponding to Li^- and Li^+, multiplied together give $\Psi^{ST} = 1s_A{}^2 2s_A{}^2 1s_B{}^2$, one possible ionic structure Li^-Li^+.

In each structure, again, all electrons must be made indistinguishable, spins must be assigned, and the wave function must be made antisymmetric in exchange of electrons. This is again achieved by specifying, with each ϕ_{jr}, the electron k which occupies this ϕ, multiplying the ϕ by a spin function $\sigma(k)$, $\alpha(k)$, or $\beta(k)$, and developing the determinant over the products, just as was done in MO theory. We then obtain

$$\Psi_i{}^{ST} = |\Pi_r \Phi_{jr}| = |\Pi_r \Pi_j \phi_{jr}(k)\sigma(k)|$$

or, equivalently,

$$\Psi_i{}^{ST} = |\Pi_k \phi_{jr}(k)\sigma(k)|$$

In the final step, the variational principle is used to form the appropriate linear combination over all possible structures $\Psi_i{}^{ST}$:

$$\Psi_k = \Sigma_i \lambda_i |\Pi_k \phi_{jr}(k)\sigma(k)|$$

Summarizing, then, the wave function in MO theory has the form:

$$\Psi = \Sigma_i a_{ik} |\Pi_j [\Sigma_r c_{jr} \phi_r]^{n_{ij}}|$$

and in VB theory

$$\Psi = \Sigma_i \lambda_i |\Pi_k \phi_{jr}(k)\sigma(k)|$$

Both theories involve substantially the same steps, but in different order. In MO theory, a summation over all atoms is followed by a multiplication with a factor for each electron, formation of a determinant to antisymmetrize, and a summation over states, using the variational principle. Valence-bond theory involves first a multiplication over electrons (and atoms), followed by antisymmetrization by formation of the determinant, and summation over the structures, using the variational principle.

8.6   Common Approximations

The general method outlined in section 8.5 again will lead to the same results, independently of whether the MO or VB method is used, provided only that the same sets of AO's, ϕ_r, are used and that all steps are carried out adequately. The amount of labor involved in this process is, however, ordinarily prohibitive. A series of additional approximations is usually made. Thus, the MO treatment is frequently cut off at the stage of the Ψ_i^C. Even in arriving at this stage many simplifications are often employed. Thus certain integrals are evaluated empirically, and many terms, such as all resonance integrals between nonadjacent ("nonbonded") atoms and even overlap integrals between adjacent atoms, are neglected (the so-called *Hückel approximation*).

In VB theory, two simplifications are made; the first is predominantly one of notation, not of new approximations. As developed above, VB theory involved writing down the wave function for each structure in terms of the atomic functions involved, and then permitting exchange. Thus the function of the simplest stable molecule, H_2, was of the form

$$\Psi_A = (2)^{-\frac{1}{2}}(1 + S^2)^{-\frac{1}{2}}[\phi_1(1)\phi_2(2) + \phi_2(1)\phi_1(2)]$$

and eventually had to be multiplied by a spin function; for more complex molecules, such functions would be considerably more complicated. For the purpose of qualitative descriptions, such wave functions are replaced by a single symbol, Ψ(H—H) (i.e., the wave function of the structure), and the electron exchange is considered as implied in such expressions. In this form, VB theory becomes what is generally known as *resonance theory*[6] and is then equivalent with Ingold's theory of mesomerism.[7] This type of abbreviation obscures, to some extent, the mathematical processes involved in a VB treatment, and consequently the various conditions necessary for interaction between structures must be stated explicitly. These have been excellently summarized by Wheland,[6] and the reader is referred to his treatment. With this simplification, the total wave function is simply a linear combination of structures, with the relative weights to be determined by the variational principle.

The second simplification made in VB theory is one of approximation. However, it is quite different in nature from the approximation made in MO theory. Whereas the main simplification of MO theory consisted of truncating computation before it is complete, in VB (or resonance) theory the corresponding approximation consists in a limitation on the number of structures to be included.

As an example, it may be profitable to consider briefly the VB description of benzene. Just as in MO theory, the σ-electron framework, forming the six C-H bonds, and the six C-C bonds of the ring will be ignored, except

[6] G. W. Wheland, *Resonance in Organic Chemistry*, John Wiley and Sons, New York, 1955.

[7] C. K. Ingold, *Structure and Mechanism in Organic Chemistry*, Cornell University Press, Ithaca, N.Y., 1953.

that their presence is considered to have determined the gross geometry of the molecule. Attention will be focused exclusively on the six π electrons, occupying the six $\pi(2p_z)$ orbitals, one from each carbon atom. Instead of writing down the wave functions Ψ^{St} for the various structures, it will suffice to depict each structure by a structural formula, which is to imply one of the determinantal forms of Ψ^{St}. The molecular wave function is then formed by a weighted sum over these structures.

In the very lowest approximation, benzene may be considered as a mixture of, or a resonance hybrid of the two structures of lowest energy, the Kekulé structures, I:

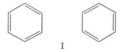

I

Three further purely covalent structures, the so-called Dewar structures, II, may be drawn:

II

and should be included in a reasonably adequate treatment of benzene.

Beyond these purely covalent structures, a large number of ionic structures are possible; these generally have higher energy and hence are not very important in the ground state. The lowest in energy among these ionic structures are III and the 11 others equivalent to it; next comes IV

III   IV   V

and 5 equivalent ones. Of considerably higher energy are V and 23 equivalent structures. In addition, there are possible 72 structures each with two positive and two negative charges, and 20 structures each with three positive and three negative charges.

These then are *all* possible structures involving only 2p electrons, and for complete equivalence between MO and VB theory all would have to be included. It is quite certain that no one of the structures beyond III makes any appreciable contribution to the ground state, and probably also not to the spectroscopically interesting low-lying excited states. Even all these structures together probably do not greatly affect the energy of any state of interest, although this is not quite so certain, since obviously there is a tremendous number. However, the larger and more complex the molecule becomes, the larger the number of ionic and high-energy structures. At the same time the number of low-energy structures does not increase nearly so rapidly, and hence the importance of the high-energy ionic structures becomes increasingly greater, while at the same time their inclusion with anything approaching completeness becomes progressively more difficult.

In summary, then, neither method can readily be carried through to completion, and hence calculations or even qualitative conclusions from the two methods may well disagree. It is unfortunately not possible to single out one of the methods as superior in reliability over the other; and hence, when the two lead to different results, a choice between them is at least difficult, if not impossible. Fortunately, however, in many cases both methods lead, if not to quantitatively equal, to qualitatively very similar, results, and then these results can usually be accepted as having a high degree of probability. Where the results quantitatively disagree, it is a good rule of thumb to assume that the true result will lie between them, since, as pointed out above, they tend, as they are refined, to converge on the identical result from opposite sides; i.e., where MO theory overestimates ionic structures, VB theory neglects them.

8.7   Excited Spectroscopic States in Valence-Bond Notation

It finally remains to attempt to find in an approximate fashion the VB equivalents of the MO descriptions of the excited states of the various types of electronic transitions. Although it appears theoretically sounder to approximate an excited state by the MO configuration to which it belongs (omitting configuration interaction), the chemical implications of VB structures and the qualitative pictures they convey make a description of excited states in terms of the structures desirable.

In some cases no difficulty is involved. For example, the singlet-triplet transition in the hydrogen molecule or ethylene[8] has as an excited state the only triplet considered in either the MO or the VB method, and hence the excited state is clearly defined. Similarly, the $V \leftarrow N$ transition in both compounds has an upper state ($^1\Sigma_u{}^+$ in H_2, $^1B_{1u}$ in ethylene)[8] which is identical in the two methods. In H_2 this state was described as $\Psi_D = \Psi_{III} - \Psi_{IV} = [(11,12) - (21,22)][\alpha_1\beta_2 - \alpha_2\beta_1]$ and hence is obviously an ionic state. It cannot be simply described as $H_1{}^+H_2{}^-$ but, because of the equivalence of the two H atoms, must be a mixture of equal contributions from $H_1{}^+H_2{}^-$ and $H_1{}^-H_2{}^+$; consequently, even though it is an ionic state, it involves a symmetric distribution of charge. This result is general for $V \leftarrow N$ transitions, the upper state of which generally represents either

---

[8] No VB description of ethylene has been given, but to the extent that only the two π electrons are involved, the VB treatment is quite analogous to that for H_2 except for differences in the symmetry symbols.

essentially pure ionic structures or, in more complex compounds, mixtures of structures in which the ionic ones predominate. In butadiene, for example, the upper state of the transition which by MO theory was described as $V \leftarrow N\ (b_{2g} \rightarrow b_{3u}{}^*$, or $\pi \rightarrow \pi^*)$ would contain as main contributions the structures C^+—C=C—C^- and C^-—C=C—C^+. The VB description of the upper states of $Q \leftarrow N\ (n \rightarrow \pi^*)$ transitions, such as in carbonyl compounds, also is not too difficult, although complicated by the less straightforward ground states. Because of the lower symmetry and the electronegativity difference between C and O, the ground state of the carbonyl group $>$C$=$O is not made up predominantly of the structure $>$C$=$O, but contains an important (in aldehydes and ketones estimated to approach 50 per cent) contribution from the structure $>$C$^+$—O^-. The electron shift, as can be seen from an MO treatment, is predominantly due to the bonding π orbital b_1. The nature of the excited electron (i.e., the nature of the n and the π orbitals) makes it obvious that excitation involves a shift of electron from the O to the C atom (i.e., that, in the excited state, structures like $>$C$^-$—O^+ must make a considerable contribution). But to the extent that the $>$C$^+$—O^- structure contributes to the ground state, the same shift leads only to $>$C$=$O in the excited state. Furthermore, to the extent that the π^* orbital involves a contribution from the $2p\pi\ (b_1)$ orbital of the O atom, no shift of electrons away from O is involved. As a net result it is possible only to say that the excited state will contain some contribution from $>$C$^-$—O^+, $>$C$=$O, and $>$C$^+$—O^-, and that there is a net migration of charge from O to C. Spectra which are due in large extent to such charge migration occurring intramolecularly have sometimes been called *intramolecular charge-transfer spectra*, and $n \rightarrow \pi^*$, or in general $Q \leftarrow N$ transitions, can be considered as one of simpler types of such spectra.

8.8   Charge Density, Bond Order, and Free Valence

In Chapter 3 several quantities obtainable from MO theory were briefly discussed. These were, in particular, the total π electron energy $\mathscr{E}$, the charge density q, the bond order p, and the free valence F. All these, with the exception of $\mathscr{E}$, have analogues in VB theory. The charge density q is the weighted average of the formal charges occurring in the various structures. The weighting factors are the weights of the particular structures in the complete wave function. Thus, if a molecule A-B has a wave function made up of 60 per cent covalent structure AB, 30 per cent ionic structure A^+B^-, and 10 per cent ionic structure A^-B^+, the charge density on A is $0.6 \times 1 + 0.3 \times 0 + 0.1 \times 2 = 0.8$; on B it is $0.6 \times 1 + 0.3 \times 2 + 0.1 \times 0 = 1.2$. In conjugated and aromatic compounds, resonance theory, just like MO theory, ignores the σ-bond skeleton and considers only π electrons. In alternant hydrocarbons, ionic structures generally occur in equivalent pairs, such as structures H_2C^+—C^-H_2 and H_2C^-—C^+H_2 of ethylene, which make canceling contributions to q so that q for alternant hydrocarbons is unity at each C atom, just as in MO theory.

The bond order p is evaluated in a similar manner. The order of a given bond (1 for single, 2 for double, and 3 for triple) in each structure is multiplied by the weight of the structure and summed over all structures. Thus, in benzene, considering only the two Kekulé structures I, which, because of symmetry, must have equal weights, the bond order of any bond is $p = 0.5 \times 1 + 0.5 \times 2 = 1.5$, since each bond is single in one structure, double in the other. If the three Dewar structures, II, are considered, with a combined weight of 22 per cent, the bond order becomes $p = 0.39 \times 1 + 0.39 \times 2 + 0.07 \times 1 + 0.07 \times 1 + 0.07 \times 2 = 1.46$.

The free valence F in resonance theory can be defined in two alternate ways. The simpler definition assumes that any electron involved in a long bond, such as the long bond through the center of the molecule in Dewar structures II, is essentially free to form other bonds. Hence, the free valence at an atom is the sum of the weights of the structures in which long bonds terminate at this atom. Thus, in benzene, considering only Kekulé structures leads to $F = 0$; considering also Dewar structures, again with a combined weight of 22 per cent, leads to $F = 0.07$. The alternate definition of F is analogous to the one used in MO theory. The sum of the bond orders of all bonds terminating at an atom is subtracted from the maximum valence F_{max} to give the free valence of the atom. By this definition, and using $F_{max} = 4.732$, we obtain for benzene $F = 4.732 - 2 \times 1.5 - 1 = 0.732$ and $F = 4.732 - 2 \times 1.46 - 1 = 0.740$ in the two approximations considered above.

Calculation of bond orders, charge densities, and free valences by MO and VB theory does not lead to identical values because of basic differences in the definitions. These quantities have, however, little absolute significance; their primary importance lies in permitting comparisons between different compounds, and different positions in the same compound. It is fortunate and gratifying that such comparisons are generally independent of which of the theories is used, as long as one or the other is employed consistently.

GENERAL REFERENCES

C. A. Coulson, *Valence*, Oxford University Press, 1952.

A. Streitwieser, *Molecular Orbital Theory for Organic Chemists*, John Wiley and Sons, New York, 1961.

R. Daudel, R. Lefebvre, and C. Moser, *Quantum Chemistry: Methods and Applications*, Interscience Publishers, New York, 1960.

9 Simple chromophores and solvent effects

9.1 Compounds with No Chromophores

Compounds in which all valence-shell electrons are involved in the formation of single bonds, such as the saturated hydrocarbons, do not absorb light in the near and middle ultraviolet regions of the spectrum. The excitations which do occur in such molecules involve promotion of σ-bonding electrons to either σ^* orbitals or to higher shells than the valence shell; the energy for these excitations is large, and hence absorption occurs in the vacuum ultraviolet. Such spectra are difficult to observe and are of little general interest except to the professional spectroscopist.

The situation is slightly different in compounds having atoms bearing lone-pair electrons, or other electrons of relatively high energy (loosely bound electrons). The excitation of such electrons to antibonding σ^* orbitals requires less energy than the excitation of bonding σ electrons, and the resulting spectra show some absorption at wavelengths greater than 200 mμ. Typical examples of such compounds are water, alcohols, ammonia, amines, and the halogen compounds. The spectra of these compounds are not readily observed, since the peaks usually occur in the region below 200 mμ.

The vapor spectrum of methanol shows λ_{max} at about 183 mμ ($\epsilon \sim 500$), and the spectrum of water has λ_{max} at about 167 mμ ($\epsilon \sim 7000$). Since absorption by these compounds occurs near the short-wavelength end of the region customarily accessible, and the absorption usually increases with decreasing wavelength, these absorptions are frequently referred to as *end absorption*. End absorption has a tremendous practical, although nonconstructive, importance, since it occurs in most of the common solvents—water, alcohols, ethers, halocarbons—and thus limits the range of wavelength in which these are practical as spectroscopic solvents. Thus, it is quite difficult, if not impossible, to balance a Beckman DU Quartz Spectrophotometer with 1 cm silica cells with water as solvent below about 201–203 mμ, with ethanol below 209 mμ, with ether below

215 mμ, with chloroform below 250 mμ, and with carbon tetrachloride below 260 mμ.

It is interesting to note that there appears to be a regular relationship between the spectra of the compounds with lone pairs of electrons and the ionization energies of such compounds. Thus the ionization energies of HCl, HBr, HI, CH_3Cl, CH_3Br, CH_3I, H_2O, CH_3OH, H_2S, CH_3SH, NH_3, and CH_3NH_2 parallel[1] their absorption spectra; the lower the ionization energy, the longer the wavelength of absorption. This correlation is to be expected, since the energy required to remove an electron from an atom is the ionization energy, and the higher the energy level of the electron, the more readily it can be removed (ionization) or promoted (spectra). The fact that end absorption becomes increasingly more serious with increasing atomic weight of the element responsible for it is rationalized on the same basis. Thus, in the halogens, the wavelength at which end absorption becomes serious increases in the order F < Cl < Br < I. Actually, in the alkyl iodides and bromides, distinct absorption bands occur

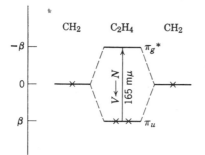

Fig. 9.1   One-electron energy levels for ethylene.

above 200 mμ, which have been assigned to n → σ* transitions (cf. section 17.3). This fact suggests that in the heavier atoms excitation of lone-pair electrons, from np orbitals (where n is the quantum number of the valence shell) to $(n + 1)$ and higher orbitals, contributes strongly to end absorption. It should be noted that end absorption is often accompanied by predissociation or photodecomposition; see section 19.1.

In heavier atoms, the presence of lone pairs in the valence shell is not a prerequisite for end absorption. Thus, dialkylmercury compounds show end absorption beginning near 235 mμ, undoubtedly because of excitation of d electrons of the penultimate electron shell of the Hg atom. Similar phenomena are observed with all elements in the lower rows of the periodic system.

9.2   Ethylene

The MO description of ethylene was given in section 3.7, and the symmetry species for the point group D_{2h} to which ethylene belongs is given in Table A3.3. The one-electron energy levels for the combination of the

[1] F. A. Matsen, in *Chemical Applications of Spectroscopy*, Vol. IX of *Technique of Organic Chemistry*, edited by A. Weissberger, Interscience Publishers, New York, 1956, p. 659.

p_x AO's of carbon are given in Fig. 9.1. In the approximation which neglects overlap integrals, the π_g* level lies as much above the isolated atom level as the π_u level lies below, and the energies of the two levels are $(\alpha + \beta)$ and $(\alpha - \beta)$, respectively (see section 3.2), where α is the Coulomb integral and β the resonance integral. The $V \leftarrow N$ transition occurs at 165 mμ and is the $^1B_{1u}(\psi_1\psi_2) \leftarrow {}^1A_{1g}(\psi_1{}^2)$ transition described in section 5.3. The reader is referred to this section for a complete description, including the origin of the 200 mμ band.

9.3   Lone-Pair Electron Atoms on Ethylene

The substitution of an oxygen, nitrogen, or chlorine atom for a hydrogen in ethylene causes a bathochromic shift of both ethylene bands. Groups which cause such bathochromic effects are called *auxochromes*. The group responsible for the absorption (C=C in this case) is called the *chromophore*. The atom with the lone pair produces both a resonance and an inductive effect.

It is frequently convenient to discuss the influence of a group or substituent on an organic molecule in terms of the well-known *inductive* and *resonance effects*, with the implication that part of this influence occurs by displacement of electrons by a substantially electrostatic mechanism (the inductive effect) and that the other part occurs by the charge delocalization explained only in terms of quantum-mechanical resonance or MO theory, but qualitatively adequately described by Ingold's well-developed concept of mesomerism (the resonance effect). The implication is further made that, at least with sufficient ingenuity, the two effects could be separated. Careful consideration, however, will show that the two effects are so closely interrelated that no such separation is possible. Thus, because of the "resonance effect" certain charge displacements occur; these exert electrostatic forces or, better, cause a change in the electrostatic force field, and hence certain inductive effects. Similarly, any inductive charge displacement leaving nuclei with partial charges must inevitably modify their attraction for electrons (measured, e.g., by the Coulomb integral of MO theory) and hence affect the mesomeric charge distribution. This interrelation is reflected in quantum-mechanical calculations by the need for arriving at a charge distribution which is self consistent.

Recognizing this interrelation and inseparability of inductive and mesomeric effects, we customarily resort to a somewhat different definition of these effects as an aid in their evaluation. A substituent attached to a saturated group can exert no resonance effect. Hence we define as inductive effect the influence of groups in such systems. Then, considering conjugated systems, we define as the inductive effect that part of the over-all effect which is proportional to the effect in a saturated system, and all that remains is defined as the resonance effect. The concept of the two separate effects is very useful if these restrictions are kept in mind.

It can be shown, by application of elementary MO theory, that the participation (resonance effect) of a lone pair of electrons on an atom B attached to the vinyl group strengthens the C-C bond. Since one AO from each carbon and an AO from B combine, a description in terms of three MO's is necessary. The energy-level diagram of such a system is shown in

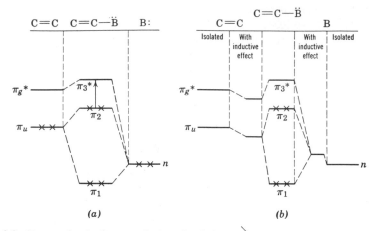

Fig. 9.2 Energy levels for a substituted ethylene, $\rangle C{=}C{-}B:$, showing (a) the resonance effect alone and (b) inductive and resonance effects.

Fig. 9.2a. The interaction of the lone-pair orbital, n, which lies below the π level in ethylene, with the two ethylene π orbitals results in three molecular levels designated as π_1, π_2, and π_3^* in Fig. 9.2. The level π_1 is much lower relative to n than π_2 is above π_u, because of interaction with the antibonding orbital π_g^* of ethylene, and hence the interaction imparts a net (resonance) stabilization to the system. A further effect of the interaction of the lone pair of B with the ethylene electrons is that the level π_2, the highest occupied orbital, and the level π_3^*, the lowest unoccupied level, are both raised. Since, however, the energy of the lone-pair level of B is closer to π_2 than to π_3^*, π_2 is raised more (the interaction of B with π_2 is greater) than π_3^*. Accordingly, substitution of an atom with a lone pair for hydrogen on ethylene lowers the excitation energy and causes a red shift in the spectrum relative to unsubstituted ethylene. At the same time, the raising of π_2 decreases the ionization potential, and it is easier to remove an electron from the substituted ethylene than from ethylene itself.

The inductive effect arises whenever atoms of differing electronegativity are bonded to each other. The electrons comprising such a bond are not equally shared. When an atom such as nitrogen, oxygen, or chlorine, which is more electronegative than hydrogen, is substituted for a hydrogen atom bonded to carbon, this atom withdraws electrons from the carbon atom and thus produces a negative inductive effect, frequently denoted by the symbolism $^{+\delta}R \rightarrow B^{-\delta}$. The negative inductive effect of a substituent B in R—B increases the ionization potential (i.e., makes it more difficult to remove an electron) of R and decreases the ionization potential of the substituent B, since B is richer in electronic charge than it would be if it were not attached to a group R from which it can "withdraw" electrons. This inductive effect will tend to lower both π levels of ethylene and raise the substituent level, as shown in the first step in the level changes in Fig. 9.2b. The lowering of the ethylene levels will lower π_2 and $\pi_3{}^*$ by about equal amounts; and, since the location of the absorption band depends on the difference between these levels, the inductive effect has only a small influence on the spectrum. The net result of both inductive and resonance effects of the substituent B is to produce a red shift in the spectrum of ethylene. The substitution of Cl, OH, SH, and NH_2 all cause such a red shift, and OH and NH_2 have a greater effect than Cl because of the greater ease of participation of the lone pair of the first-row elements.

9.4 Alkyl Substitution in Ethylene

The substitution of alkyl groups for hydrogen on ethylene also results in a bathochromic shift. Although the alkyl groups do not possess a lone pair of electrons, in many instances they behave as though they did. Thus, for example, participation of a methyl group with the ethylene linkage can be represented by the resonance

$$H_3\overset{\frown}{\equiv}C\overset{\curvearrowleft}{\longrightarrow}CH\overset{\frown}{\equiv}CH_2 \longleftrightarrow \overset{+}{H_3}=C=CH-\overset{-}{CH_2}.$$

The methyl group may be considered as furnishing an electron pair, or it

may be thought of as $\overset{..}{C}=H_3$. In either case there is a formal analogy to an atom with a lone pair of electrons. The participation of electron pairs in C-H bonds with an adjacent unsaturated linkage is called *hyperconjugation*, a name suggested by Mulliken, Rieke, and Brown[2] in 1941 to describe the delocalization of C-H bond electrons. In the same way as atoms attached to a chromophore and having a lone pair of electrons on them were described as auxochromes, so the methyl group may be called an auxochrome, since it similarly intensifies the ethylene absorption band, shifts it to the red, decreases the ionization potential, and imparts resonance stabilization to the ground state.

The MO description of hyperconjugation starts with formation of three group orbitals (GO's) from the AO's of the three hydrogen atoms.[2] One of these GO's belongs to the symmetry species a_1 of the point group C_{3v} appropriate for an isolated methyl group, and may be considered as a pseudo-σ orbital. The other two GO's belong to species e of C_{3v} and have nodes through the symmetry axis at right angles to each other. Because of these nodes, these GO's may be considered as pseudo-π orbitals. Formation of MO's from the GO's of the pseudo atom H_3 and the AO's of carbon then leads to a description of the methyl group quite analogous to $C\equiv N$, and in particular involves two π-type MO's at right angles to one another. The binding energy of electrons in such

[2] R. S. Mulliken, C. A. Rieke, and W. G. Brown, *J. Am. Chem. Soc.*, **63**, 41 (1941).

MO's is relatively low because the H_3 π-type GO's are destabilized by H—H inter-action, and such electrons are consequently relatively readily delocalized.

The possibility of C—H electron delocalization was first suggested by Baker and Nathan[3] in 1935 to account for the greater effect of *para* substitution by methyl than by *tert*-butyl on certain reactions of benzyl halides. The order of reactivity $CH_3 > C_2H_5 > (CH_3)_2CH > (CH_3)_3C$, which is presumed to be the order of electron release from the alkyl group, is called the Baker-Nathan order. On the other hand, the reverse order is presumed to be the order of decreasing inductive effect. Many suggestions have been made for modification of the original theory of Baker and Nathan.[4] One of the most important departures is based on a study of the vapor spectra of *p*-alkylnitrobenzene and *p*-alkylphenols,[5] from which it was concluded that electronic transitions that demand electrons from a substituent satisfy this demand in the reverse of the Baker-Nathan order, i.e., $(CH_3)_3C > (CH_3)_2CH > C_2H_5 > CH_3$. The Baker-Nathan order, which is generally found to hold for rate and equilibrium constants found in solution studies, is then ascribed to steric hindrance to solvation of electron-deficient sites in the near proximity of the alkyl group, thus making the small CH_3 group the apparent best elec-tron-release group. The importance of the hyperconjugative effect, especially in relation to the inductive effect, is still under vigorous study.

9.5 The Carbonyl, Substituted Carbonyl, and Thiocarbonyl Groups

A detailed treatment of the simplest carbonyl compound, formaldehyde, was given in section 5.6. However, in order to discuss in later chapters the effect of substitution and of steric effects on the carbonyl chromophore and its interaction with other chromophores, an abbreviated and simplified treatment will be given here.

The ground-state configuration of the carbonyl group is $s^2\pi^2y_O^2$, which indicates that, aside from the two C-O σ-bonding electrons, there are two electrons in the C-O π bond and two lone pairs, one in the s and the other in the p_y orbital of oxygen; the internuclear axis is oriented along the z axis and the molecule lies in the yz plane. The lowest unoccupied orbital of the carbonyl group is the antibonding or π^* orbital of the C-O group. The electrons in the highest occupied orbital are the lone-pair electrons on the oxygen; this is reasonable, since nonbonding electrons are generally held more loosely than any electrons used in bonding. The energy-level diagram is shown in Fig. 9.3; for the complete diagram of formaldehyde see Fig. 5.6. The excitation requiring the least energy (or the absorption band at longest wavelength in the ultraviolet spectrum of the carbonyl group) is the promotion of an electron from the nonbonding p_y orbital to the antibonding π^* orbital:

$$s^2\pi^2y_O^2 \rightarrow s^2\pi^2y_O\pi^*$$

---

[3] J. W. Baker and W. S. Nathan, *J. Chem. Soc.*, 1844 (1935).

[4] See Conference on Hyperconjugation, *Tetrahedron*, **5**, 105 (1959).

[5] W. M. Schubert, J. M. Craven, R. G. Minton, and R. B. Murphy, *Tetrahedron*, **5**, 194 (1959).

This is the $Q \leftarrow N$ or $n \rightarrow \pi^*$ transition. This symmetry-forbidden transition (see section 6.3) occurs at 270 mμ in formaldehyde, and the $V \leftarrow N$ transition occurs at 185 mμ. Both transitions are associated with the π-bond structure of the carbonyl group and will be discussed later.

The effect of alkyl substitution on the spectrum of ketones[6] is illustrated by Table 9.1. The introduction of the larger and more branched alkyl groups causes a bathochromic shift. Apparently in the methyl ketones the inductive effect is more important than the resonance effect, probably because one methyl group furnishes most of the electrons that can participate in the carbonyl chromophore, and the other group attached to the carbonyl plays principally an inductive role. However, as already noted, it is very difficult to separate these effects, especially in solution spectra.

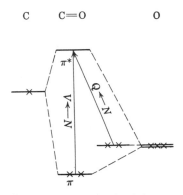

Fig. 9.3   Energy levels of the carbonyl group.

Substitution of a group with a lone pair of electrons, such as NR_2, OR, or X, into the carbonyl group, as in an amide, acid, ester, or acid chloride,

TABLE 9.1

Effect of Alkyl Groups on the Long-Wavelength Absorption
Band in Methyl Ketones, $CH_3COCRR'R''$,[6] in $CHCl_3$

R	R'	R''	λ_{max}, mμ	ϵ_{max}
H	H	H	275	17.1
H	H	CH_3	277	19.4
H	H	C_2H_5	279	21.2
H	H	C_3H_7	279	21.2
H	CH_3	CH_3	281	21.2
CH_3	CH_3	CH_3	285	21.2

results in pronounced effects on the position of the long-wavelength $n \rightarrow \pi^*$ transition, illustrated in Table 9.2. The atoms with the lone-pair electrons influence the carbonyl group both by the resonance and by the inductive effect. The resonance interaction is similar to that described earlier for the similar substitution on ethylene, and accordingly both the π and π^* levels will be raised but the π level will be raised more (cf. Fig. 9.2),

[6] F. O. Rice, *J. Am. Chem. Soc.*, **42**, 727 (1920).

TABLE 9.2

The n $\to \pi^*$ Transition in Simple Carbonyl Compounds

Compound	λ_{max}, mμ	ϵ_{max}	Solvent
CH$_3$—C $\overset{O}{\underset{H}{<}}$	293.4	11.8	Hexane
CH$_3$—C $\overset{O}{\underset{OH}{<}}$	204	41	Alcohol
CH$_3$—C $\overset{O}{\underset{OC_2H_5}{<}}$	204	60	Water
CH$_3$—C $\overset{O}{\underset{NH_2}{<}}$	214		Water
CH$_3$—C $\overset{O}{\underset{Cl}{<}}$	235	53	Hexane
CH$_3$—C $\overset{O}{\underset{CH_3}{<}}$	279	14.8	Hexane

with a resulting bathochromic effect. However, in the case of a carbonyl chromophore, the bathochromic effect on the $V \leftarrow N$ transition caused by the lone-pair substituent is not large enough to bring this transition into the accessible ultraviolet, and hence it is not observed. Even in the absence of an inductive effect, the lone-pair substituent should give rise to a hypsochromic effect in the n $\to \pi^*$ level, since the π^* level has been raised by the resonance interaction and the n level is largely unaffected by such inter-action. All the lone-pair atoms, O, N, and Cl, are more electronegative than carbon, and hence the lone-pair electrons on the carbonyl oxygen are held more firmly than they would be in the absence of an inductive effect. Thus all the compounds listed in Table 9.2 show a hypsochromic effect relative to acetaldehyde. The electron-release effect of methyl, as in acetone, apparently does not exert an inductive effect large enough to overcome the raising of the π level by the resonance effect, and hence acetone absorbs at shorter wavelength than acetaldehyde.

An α-halogen atom in an acyclic ketone, as in chloroacetone, does not have a large effect on the carbonyl n $\rightarrow$ π^* transition. In cyclic ketones, however, α-halogen atoms do influence this transition; the influence is greater for axial than for equatorial halogen. Extensive data on α-halo-cycloalkanones[7] and on the steroid series[8] indicate that equatorial chlorine or bromine produces a small hypsochromic shift ($\sim$5 mμ) in the n $\rightarrow$ π^* transition of the unsubstituted ketone. However, axial bromine and chlorine produce 20–30 mμ and 11 mμ bathochromic shifts, respectively, accompanied by a strong hyperchromic effect. The infrared spectra of the α-halocycloalkanones are also significant.[9] In cyclohexanones, the introduction of an equatorial α-bromo substituent shifts the carbonyl frequency about 15–22 cm^{-1} to higher frequency, but an axial bromo substituent has no effect. The observations suggest that equatorial halogen is interacting inductively with the carbonyl group, shortening and strength-ening the C-O double bond and making it more difficult to promote the n electron of the carbonyl oxygen. Axial halogen appears to have little inductive effect on the carbonyl group, but there does seem to be some electronic interaction. This interaction might be expressed by no-bond structures involving halogen or by neighboring group interaction:

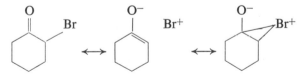

Such participation of halogen is more important in the excited state, Q, than in the ground state, N, and accordingly would facilitate the $Q \leftarrow N$ transition, in consistency with the observed bathochromic effect.

[7] N. J. Leonard and F. H. Owens, *J. Am. Chem. Soc.*, **80**, 6039 (1958).

[8] R. C. Cookson, *J. Chem. Soc.*, 282 (1954); L. F. Fieser and M. Fieser, *Steroids*, Reinhold Publishing Corp., New York, 1959, p. 176; R. N. Jones, D. A. Ramsay, F. Herling, and K. Dobriner, *J. Am. Chem. Soc.*, **74**, 2828 (1952); C. W. Bird, R. C. Cookson, and S. H. Dandegaonker, *J. Chem. Soc.*, 3675 (1956).

[9] E. J. Corey and H. J. Burke, *J. Am. Chem. Soc.*, **77**, 5418 (1955).

Thioketones, $R_2C{=}S$, absorb at much longer wavelength than their oxygen analogs. The lone-pair electrons in sulfur are in a $3p_y$ orbital, and this level lies much higher than the $2p_y$ orbital in oxygen because electron shielding of the nuclear charge is more effective in sulfur than in oxygen. The π^* level is probably not raised nearly as much as the lone-pair level, and the over-all effect facilitates the electron promotion, accounting for the longer-wavelength absorption in thioketones.

9.6   Nitro and Azo Groups

The *nitro group* may be represented by the two principal and equivalent resonance structures:

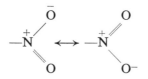

These structures imply that nitrogen is bonded to three other atoms, the two oxygen atoms and a third atom, usually carbon, as in CH_3NO_2. In the σ-bond skeleton of RNO_2, nitrogen uses three sp^2 hybrid orbitals for bonding with the three atoms. This leaves an unshared electron pair on nitrogen in a $p\pi$ orbital, p_x.

Each oxygen has one $p\pi$ electron in a p_x orbital, and there are thus a total of four p_x electrons of oxygen and nitrogen. In addition, each oxygen has two unshared pairs of electrons lying in the plane of the nitro group. One of these pairs may be assigned to the s orbital or to some sp hybrid. The other pair may be assigned to a p orbital, which will be designated as n. The four p_x electrons are used for π bonding and belong to the three p_x atomic orbitals, one from nitrogen and one from each oxygen atom. These AO's combine into three MO's, one of which is bonding, π_1 (see Fig. 9.4a), one antibonding π_3^* (Fig. 9.4c), and the third nonbonding, π_2 (Fig. 9.4b). The resulting energy-level diagram is shown in Fig. 9.5.

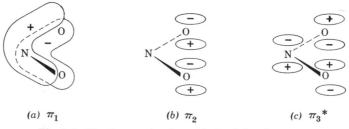

(a) π_1 (b) π_2 (c) π_3^*

Fig. 9.4   The three molecular orbitals of the nitro group.

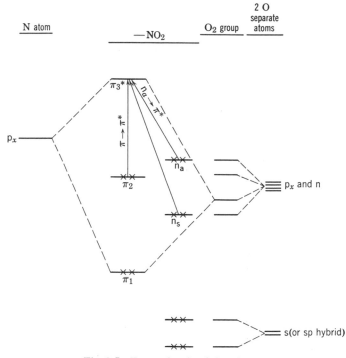

Fig. 9.5   Energy levels of the nitro group.

This diagram also includes the lone-pair orbitals; at the bottom of the diagram at quite low energy are the two s (or sp hybrid) orbitals of the two oxygen atoms, slightly split in the NO_2 group because of interaction between the two atoms. The two n orbitals in the isolated oxygen atoms are degenerate with the p_x orbitals. In the NO_2 group, the proximity of the two oxygen atoms requires interaction of these n orbitals, leading to symmetric and antisymmetric combinations, n_s and n_a, respectively, again occurring at slightly different energies because of nonbonded interaction. Possible low-energy promotions observable in the ultraviolet would then consist of a $V \leftarrow N$ transition from the highest occupied π molecular orbital, π_2, to an antibonding, unoccupied level, π_3^*, and also various possible promotions of an electron from any unshared pairs of the oxygen atoms to the π_3^* level (e.g., $n_a \rightarrow \pi_3^*$).

Nitromethane has a spectrum consisting of two broad bands: a high-intensity band at $\lambda_{max} = 210\ m\mu$ (log $\epsilon = 4.2$) and a weak band at $\lambda_{max} = 270\ m\mu$ (log $\epsilon = 1.3$), which probably arise from the $\pi_2 \rightarrow \pi_3^*$ and $n_a \rightarrow \pi_3^*$ transitions shown in Fig. 9.5, respectively. In addition, another $n \rightarrow \pi^*$ transition, $n_s \rightarrow \pi_3^*$, should occur at shorter wavelength, probably in the vacuum ultraviolet, and with low intensity. The $n_a \rightarrow \pi_3{}^*$ $Q \leftarrow N$ transition is similar to the carbonyl $n \rightarrow \pi^*$ transition and in fact occurs at approximately the same wavelength with a similar intensity.

It is interesting to note that the carboxylate anion $-C\!\!\begin{array}{c} \nearrow O \\ \searrow O^- \end{array}$ is iso-electronic with the nitro group and that the enolate ion $\begin{array}{c} C\!\!-\!\! \\ -C\!\!\nearrow \\ \searrow O^- \end{array}$ is also isoelectronic with these two, with the exception that there is a single n level in place of n_s and n_a.

It is instructive to consider the relation between the nitro group and the ethylene substituted by a lone-pair-bearing substituent B, the energy-level diagrams for which are given in Figs. 9.2 and 9.5, respectively. Both groups contain the same number (4) of π electrons accommodated in the ground state by the lower two of three π molecular orbitals. The number of lone pairs varies, and, as seen above, cases with intermediate numbers of lone pairs can readily be found. The main differences between the two groups come from the degeneracies of the AO's (an inherent difference) and from the order in which the combinations into MO's is performed (an arbitrary difference of treat-ment). The relation can perhaps best be demonstrated by considering a whole series of compounds (groups), all of the form $-X\!\!\begin{array}{c} \nearrow Y \\ \searrow Z \end{array}$, having four π electrons in three π molecular orbitals and various numbers of lone pairs.

For the $-NO_2$ group, $X = N$, $Y = Z = O$, there are two lone pairs for each O, as discussed above; the same is true for the carboxylato group, $-CO_2{}^-$. In the anion derived from an amide, $-C\!\!\begin{array}{c} \nearrow O \\ \searrow N^-\text{-R} \end{array}$, one of the s (or sp hybrid) lone pairs is used to form the N-R bond, but this is spectroscopically unimportant. Of more concern is that now the p_x orbitals, and the n orbitals of N and O are no longer degenerate, leading to a much more complex level diagram; cf. Fig. 9.6a. The molecular orbital π_2 (cf. Fig. 9.4b) is no longer restricted to atoms Y and Z. The relation between the orbitals and their spacing can no longer be qualitatively fixed. In the amide molecule, $-C\!\!\begin{array}{c} \nearrow O \\ \searrow NHR \end{array}$, the n-electron pair of N also is used in σ bonding and disappears from the level scheme; the reduction of the charge on N also rearranges the levels. Isoelectronic with this molecule is the

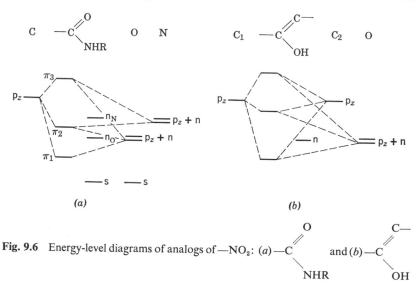

Fig. 9.6 Energy-level diagrams of analogs of —NO₂: (a) —C (with O and NHR) and (b) —C (with C— and OH)

enolate ion, —C (with O⁻ and C—) . In this group, the p_π orbital of Z, of course, becomes degenerate with that of X, since both are carbon atoms, and the resulting diagram begins to resemble that of —C=C—B. Finally, the enol, or enol ether, —C (with OR and C—), loses the s (or sp-hybrid) pair of O also and, in the present terms, becomes as shown in Fig. 9.6b. This diagram is exactly equivalent to Fig. 9.2, except for the presence of the n level, which was ignored at the time that Fig. 9.2 was developed, since attention was focused exclusively on the π-electron pair of B.

The *azo group* ＼N=N˙ is structurally very similar to the vinyl group, and the two groups are iso-π-electronic. In place of two of the σ bonds of the ethylene group, the azo group has two lone pairs of electrons which, like the σ-bonding orbitals of ethylene, are probably approximately sp² hybrids. The energy-level diagram of the azo group is shown in Fig. 9.7; its similarity to the ethylene diagram (Fig. 9.1) should be noted. The $V \leftarrow N$ transition in azomethane, similar to the ethylene transition, occurs at short wavelengths. An n → π* (or $Q \leftarrow N$) transition occurs at 347 mμ, and the band has the expected low intensity.

N $-\overset{..}{N}=\overset{..}{N}-$ N

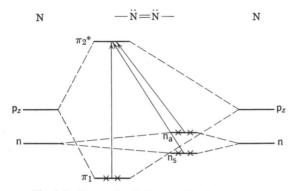

Fig. 9.7   Energy-level diagram for the azo group.

The energy-level diagram (Fig. 9.7) suggests that there should be two $n \to \pi^*$ transitions ($n_a \to \pi^*$ and $n_s \to \pi^*$); only one has been observed, presumably because the interaction between the two n levels and hence the splitting of n_a and n_s are very small. This is not surprising, since in azomethane, which undoubtedly has a *trans* configuration, the two nitrogen lone-pair orbitals are geometrically far separated, overlap very little, and consequently interact only weakly.

9.7   Solvent Effects

One of the earliest thorough and systematic investigations of the effect of solvents on absorption spectra was due to Burawoy,[10] who examined the spectra of azo compounds, aldehydes, ketones, and thioketones in various solvents. In all these compounds Burawoy noted the presence of a low-intensity long-wavelength band that moved to *shorter* wavelengths in changing the solvent from hexane to ethanol. With the same solvent change, the other band in the spectra of these compounds, the high-intensity, shorter-wavelength band, moved to *longer* wavelengths; with increasing solvent polarity, the two bands approached one another. Burawoy designated the weak bands which shift toward shorter wavelength with change in solvent from hexane to ethanol as R bands [from the German *radikalartig* (radical-like)] and the generally strong bands which shift toward longer wavelength as K bands [from the German *konjugierte* (conjugated)]. These designations refer to the supposed type of electronic origin of the respective bands; and, although it is now known that the assignments were inaccurate, the nomenclature has persisted. It is now commonly accepted that some of Burawoy's R bands in the compounds listed above correspond to $n \to \pi^*$ transitions and that his K bands

[10] A. Burawoy, *Ber.*, **63**, 3155 (1930); *J. Chem. Soc.*, 1177 (1939); 20 (1941).

correspond to $V \leftarrow N$ or $\pi \rightarrow \pi^*$ transitions. It is instructive to consider in particular the solvent effect on the spectrum of a simple carbonyl group.

In the presence of hydroxylic solvents, the lone pair of electrons on the carbonyl oxygen acts as an electron donor to the hydrogen of the solvent to form a hydrogen bond. The formation of this hydrogen bond lowers the energy of the n orbital by an amount approximately equal to the energy of the hydrogen bond.[11a] Now in the n $\rightarrow \pi^*$ transition, which is responsible for the long-wavelength low-intensity band, one of the electrons is removed from the n orbital and promoted to an empty antibonding or π^* orbital. The one n electron remaining on oxygen is not adequate to sustain the hydrogen bond. Hence the hydrogen bond must be broken in the process of promotion, and the polar solvent should not affect the energy of the excited state.[11b] The difference in the position of the wavelength maximum when the solvent is changed from hexane to ethanol or water should, accordingly, be a measure of the strength of the hydrogen bond in the latter solvents. The shift is a hypsochromic or blue shift, and the extent of the blue shift of the n $\rightarrow \pi^*$ band has indeed been correlated with hydrogen-bond strengths.[11] The effects of solvents on the n $\rightarrow \pi^*$ transition in acetone are shown in Table 9.3. The effects should be in the

TABLE 9.3
The Effects of Solvents on the n $\rightarrow \pi^*$ Transition in Acetone

Solvent:	water	methanol	ethanol	chloroform	hexane
λ_{max}, mμ:	264.5	270	272	277	279

order of the hydrogen-bonding ability of the solvents, water > methanol > ethanol > chloroform > hexane, and the observed effects are in precisely this order. The energy associated with absorption in water at 264.5 mμ is approximately 126 kcal/mole, and in hexane at 279 mμ corresponds to approximately 121 kcal/mole. Thus the blue shift of 14.5 mμ in going from hexane to water corresponds to an energy change of approximately 5 kcal/mole, which is in quite good agreement with the known energy associated with a hydrogen bond.

An even more dramatic example of the effect of solvent on an n $\rightarrow \pi^*$ band is encountered in N-nitrosodimethylamine, shown in Fig. 9.8; the n $\rightarrow \pi^*$ transition occurs at 362 mμ in cyclohexane and at 332 mμ in water, and the shift of 30 mμ corresponds to a hydrogen-bond energy of 7.2

[11] (a) G. J. Brealey and M. Kasha, *J. Am. Chem. Soc.*, **77**, 4462 (1955); cf. also H. McConnell, *J. Chem. Phys.*, **20**, 700 (1952). (b) V. G. Krishna and L. Goodman, *J. Am. Chem. Soc.*, **83**, 2042 (1961), have definitely shown that hydrogen bonds are broken, or are at least extremely weak, in excited states of pyrimidine.

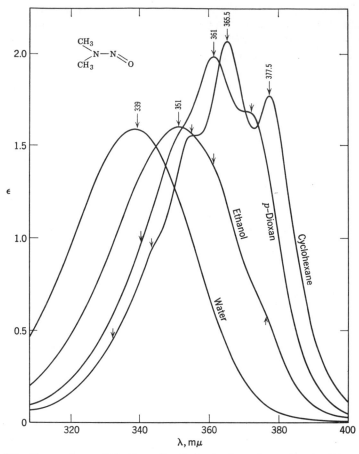

Fig. 9.8 The spectrum of N-nitrosodimethylamine in various solvents. [From unpublished work of W. L. Layne, by permission.]

kcal/mole.[12] It is further worth noting that the very pronounced vibrational structure of the n $\rightarrow$ π^* level of the nitroso compound in cyclohexane completely disappears in polar solvents.

The red shifts of the $V \leftarrow N$ transitions (K bands) noted by Burawoy are not nearly as readily explained, and are best treated in terms of a more general discussion of solvent effects, to be given now. Such effects are of considerable interest, since the vast majority of absorption spectra are measured in solution. In the vapor phase, the spectrum observed is due to

---

[12] W. L. Layne, unpublished results; see also R. N. Haszeldine, *J. Chem. Soc.*, 691 (1954).

isolated molecules; with sufficient resolution, the vibrational and rotational structure can be resolved. In solution, molecules are not isolated but are in some manner associated with, or solvated by, solvent molecules. Solvent and solute molecules are generally so crowded together that no free rotation is possible. Consequently all rotational structure is obliterated, as in spectra of vapors at fairly high pressure, where the disappearance of rotational structure is referred to as pressure broadening. Furthermore, in solution, the vibrations may be partially modified by solvation; because of the largely random arrangement in the liquid state, the solvent environment of no two molecules is identical, and hence spectra in solution generally appear as broad bands, with or without a certain amount of vibrational structure. In the solid state, either pure or in dilute solid solution, the environment of different molecules is much more uniform, and consequently spectra of solids and solid solutions generally show much better defined vibrational structure. An example of the kind of resolution possible in solid solution is shown in Fig. 6.5.

The effect of solvent is directly related to the degree of interaction of solvent and solute, which is the greater, the more polar the solvent. Nonpolar solutes can interact with nonpolar solvents (having no dipole moment) only through temporary dipole-induced dipole forces, i.e., London dispersion forces. With polar solvents, solute-solvent interaction depends on permanent dipole-induced dipole forces, which are, in general, stronger than London dispersion forces. With polar solutes, the solute-solvent interaction with a nonpolar solvent depends on the same dipole-induced dipole forces, but interaction with a polar solvent depends on the stronger dipole-dipole forces. Consequently, solutions in the least polar solvents, with the lowest solvating power, have the least effect on spectra (i.e., give spectra most nearly resembling vapor spectra) and are least effective in inhibiting vibrational structure. As a consequence, spectroscopists prefer such nonpolar liquids as hydrocarbons (hexane, heptane, isooctane, cyclohexane) as solvents in spite of the considerable work necessary to obtain them in spectroscopic purity. At the same time, the most convenient solvents (water, alcohols) are the least desirable from a spectroscopic point of view because they tend to obliterate vibrational structure in the spectra.

A rather general and comprehensive treatment of solvent effects on spectra has been given by Bayliss and McRae.[13] These authors point out that, because of the Franck-Condon effect, excitation from a solvated ground state leads, not to the energetically most stable solvated conformation of the excited state, but to a conformation [which they call the Franck-Condon (F-C) state] geometrically identical to the solvated ground state

[13] N. S. Bayliss and E. G. McRae, *J. Phys. Chem.*, **58**, 1002, 1006 (1954).

and necessarily having an energy higher than the equilibrium conformation of the solvated excited state. A number of factors are involved in the solvation of the ground and excited states, some of which occur in all systems, others only in some. The most general interaction is that due to polarization forces (London dispersion forces), which is present even when both solvent and solute are nonpolar, and accordingly occurs in all systems. Since polarization forces, however, are the weakest intermolecular forces, interactions arising from them are likely to be overshadowed when either solvent or solute, or both, are polar. Bayliss[14] has treated these interactions in detail, both by classical electromagnetic theory and by the quantum-mechanical method. By the latter technique he obtains an expression for the frequency shift, $\Delta\nu$, relative to the vapor spectrum:

$$\Delta\nu = (e^2 Q^2/a^3 hc)[(\epsilon - 1)/(2\epsilon + 1)]$$

where e is the charge on the electron, Q the transition moment, a the radius of the cavity in the solvent (assumed spherical) in which the solute molecule is located, h Planck's constant, c the velocity of light, and ϵ the dielectric constant of the medium. The relation obtained classically is similar:

$$\Delta\nu = 10.71 \times 10^9 \frac{f}{\nu a^3} \frac{n^2 - 1}{2n^2 + 1}$$

where f is the oscillator strength, ν the frequency, and n the refractive index of the solvent. Bayliss' relations should be best applicable on allowed transitions of nonpolar molecules in nonpolar systems. This effect *always* leads to a red shift due to solvation, the larger the more polar the solvent. The equations have been tested on a few systems[15] and have been found to represent solvent effects in a qualitative and even semiquantitative manner, as shown in Table 9.4.

A second effect considered by Bayliss and McRae,[13] likely to be present in all systems but frequently unimportant, arises from the fact that the excited state usually has a different geometry; in particular, most excited states have longer bond lengths than ground states, and consequently the excited molecule is compressed in the F-C state by the solvent cavity, which has the size determined by the smaller ground state. This effect is called *packing strain.*

When the solvent, but not the solute, is polar, dipole-induced dipole forces, in general larger than dispersion forces, contribute to solvent effects. In this case again, relations similar to those given by Bayliss obtain, and red shifts are anticipated. When, however, the solute is polar, the solvent nonpolar, the dipole-induced dipole forces differ between the ground and

---

[14] N. S. Bayliss, *J. Chem. Phys.*, **18**, 292 (1950).
[15] N. D. Coggeshall and A. Pozefsky, *J. Chem. Phys.*, **19**, 980 (1957).

the excited state in different directions, depending on whether the dipole moment increases or decreases on excitation. When the dipole moment decreases a blue shift is expected; when it increases, as is usually the case, a red shift. When both solute and solvent are polar, the situation is most complicated, since then the solvent is oriented around the solute molecule, leading to *orientation strain*. Hydrogen bonding, as described above, is just a special and extreme example of this situation. In the case of polar solvent and solute, the predominant interaction is of the dipole-dipole type, and again the change of the dipole moment on excitation is important. When

TABLE 9.4
Average Frequency Shifts between Aliphatic Solvent and Benzene Solvent

Compound	$\Delta\nu$, cm^{-1}		
	^1L_a	^1L_b	^1B_b
Phenanthrene	295	118	310
Anthracene	275	. . .	. . .
1,2-Benzanthracene	312	155	570
9,10-Dimethylanthracene	313	. . .	470
1,2,5,6-Dibenzanthracene	297	150	440
Methylcholanthrene	340	210	470
Naphthacene	323	120	. . .

the dipole moment decreases (in the extreme case to zero), the solute is in an oriented solvent cage, and the orientation strain actually produces a solvation energy for the F-C state which is negative,[16] and hence results in a blue shift. On the other hand, when the solute dipole moment increases on excitation, a red shift is again expected. A quantitative treatment of these effects has been given by Lippert.[17]

In addition to these frequency shifts, the same considerations lead to predictions concerning vibrational structure. The F-C state is very short lived, since the solvent rearranges to an equilibrium configuration during a time of the order of a few molecular vibrations. When the solute is non-polar, the solvent, whether polar or nonpolar, is substantially unoriented, and vibrational structure is observed. When the solute and the solvent are polar, however, the rapid relaxation of the solvent cage prevents establishment of vibrational quantization of the solvent cage, and leads to the

[16] L. Pauling, *Phys. Rev.*, **34**, 954 (1929).
[17] E. Lippert, *Z. Elektrochem.*, **61**, 962 (1957); cf. also E. G. McRae, *J. Phys. Chem.*, **61**, 562 (1957).

blurring of vibrational structure of the spectra of polar solutes by polar solvents. Thus, vibrational structure is frequently observed for nonpolar molecules (e.g., benzene) in all solvents, but the strong vibrational structure of the spectra of polar molecules (e.g., of the n $\rightarrow \pi$ transitions; cf. Fig. 9.8) is generally completely blurred in polar solvents.

An alternative, but substantially similar, treatment of solvent effects, particularly of $V \leftarrow N$ transitions in polar molecules, has often been given. In general, the excited (V) state receives predominant contributions from highly polar structures, like R_2C^+—O^- in ketones, and is consequently more polar than the ground state. Such structures with separated charges are stabilized by solvent polarity[18] in accord with simple electrostatic theory. Hence the polar solvent facilitates excitation and results in a red or bathochromic shift, as compared to the nonpolar solvent. In the $V \leftarrow N$ transition of compounds like ketones in hydroxylated solvents, the hydrogen bond persists in both the ground and the excited states, and stabilization of the more polar excited state leads to a red shift by polar solvents. Only when the ground state is very highly polar, the excited state less polar, can we expect to find a blue shift with increasing polar nature of the solvent.

On the basis of solvent effects on ultraviolet spectra, Kosower[19] has established a scale of solvent polarity, which he calls Z values. This scale is based on a particularly solvent-dependent absorption band, the charge-transfer band of the 1-alkylpyridinium iodides. The high solvent dependence of this band is understandable in terms of the foregoing arguments, since the transition, as a charge-transfer transition, involves a large change in polarity. The scale of Z values obtained by Kosower is parallel, as far as comparable data are available, to Grunwald and Winstein's Y values, a kinetic scale of solvent polarity.[20]

In the solvent effects considered thus far the chemical species in solution was not appreciably altered. Altogether different types of solvent effects occur when there is a change of the chemical species (or predominant chemical species) present in the solution. Three types of situations should probably be distinguished: (*a*) acid-base equilibria, (*b*) tautomeric equilibria, and (*c*) complex formation.

Whenever the chemical species under investigation are acids and bases, special attention must be paid to the possible acid-base equilibria, particularly when dealing with solvents which themselves can act as acids or bases (H_2O, EtOH, etc.). A common technique of empirical investigation

[18] R. W. Taft, Jr., R. E. Glick, I. C. Lewis, I. Fox, and S. Ehrenson, *J. Am. Chem. Soc.*, **82**, 756 (1960).

[19] E. M. Kosower, *J. Am. Chem. Soc.*, **80**, 3253, 3261, 3267 (1958); E. M. Kosower and B. G. Ramsey, *ibid.*, **81**, 856 (1959).

[20] E. Grunwald and S. Winstein, *J. Am. Chem. Soc.*, **70**, 846 (1948).

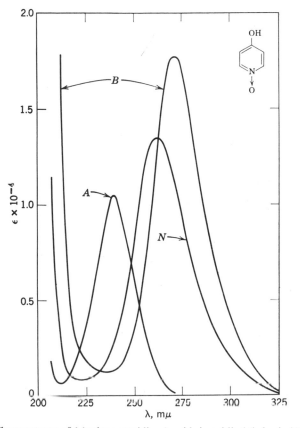

Fig. 9.9 The spectrum of 4-hydroxypyridine 1-oxide in acidic (*A*), basic (*B*), and neutral (*N*) solution. [Reprinted by permission from H. H. Jaffé, *J. Am. Chem. Soc.*, **77**, 4445 (1955).]

of organic compounds by spectrophotometry is to observe the spectra in neutral, acidic, and basic aqueous or alcoholic solutions. When an acidic or basic center is present and is either part of the chromophore or directly attached to it (i.e., is an auxochrome), occurrence of acid-base reactions can be expected to produce considerable spectroscopic changes, because the spectra of the various species are not likely to be identical. A typical situation is illustrated in Fig. 9.9, which shows the spectrum of 4-hydroxy-pyridine 1-oxide in neutral, acidic, and basic aqueous solution. Curve *N* (neutral solution) shows the spectrum of the neutral species, *A* (acidic solution) that of the conjugate acid, and *B* (basic solution) that of the conjugate base. The use of these spectral differences in the determination of acidic and basic dissociation constants is discussed in Chapter 20.

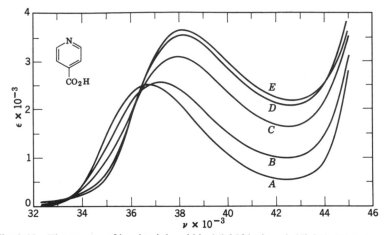

Fig. 9.10   The spectra of isonicotinic acid in (A) 95 % ethanol, (B) 3:1, (C) 1:1, (D) 1:3 95 % ethanol-water mixtures, and (E) water. [Reprinted by permission from H. P. Stephenson and H. Sponer, *J. Am. Chem. Soc.*, **79**, 2050 (1957).]

Determination of the spectrum in acidic, basic, and neutral solution alone is not necessarily sufficient to ensure recognition of the presence of acidic or basic groups. Thus, benzenesulfonic acid exists predominantly ionized even in quite strongly acidic solutions, and the spectrum observed is that of the ion, the same as in the neutral or alkaline solution.

Tautomeric equilibria may also be affected by solvent composition, and such effects are particularly important in the equilibria between a zwitterions and neutral molecules. Such a case is illustrated in Fig. 9.10, where the spectrum of isonicotinic acid in a series of water-ethanol mixtures is shown. In aqueous solution, the compound exists predominantly as the zwitterion;[21] less polar solvents, however, favor the neutral form with respect to the dipolar zwitterion, and the equilibrium shifts to the neutral form.[22]

A third type of equilibrium potentially affected by solvent is AB $\rightleftharpoons$ A + B. In determining the spectrum of a compound AB, dissociation may prevent observation of the spectrum of the pure species AB and always lead to the spectrum of the equilibrium mixture $(1 - \alpha)AB + \alpha(A + B)$, where α is the degree of dissociation. The equilibrium constant for such dissociation, and hence α, depend on the solvent and on temperature, and consequently the apparent spectrum of AB will appear solvent and temperature dependent. The use of such information in the determination of equilibrium constants is discussed also in Chapter 20.

[21] H. H. Jaffé, *J. Am. Chem. Soc.*, **77**, 4445 (1955).
[22] H. P. Stephenson and H. Sponer, *J. Am. Chem. Soc.*, **79**, 2050 (1957).

The problem of complex formation is actually quite complicated. Since, in solution, molecules are constantly in contact, or virtually in contact, with other molecules, it becomes difficult to determine accurately what is meant by a complex. The problem has been considered in some detail by Orgel and Mulliken.[23] These authors attempt to answer the question of the spectroscopic behavior of two molecules capable of complex formation in collision or in immediate proximity of each other, and the effects of the relative orientation, i.e., deviations from the geometric relation to form the stable compound.

[23] L. E. Orgel and R. S. Mulliken, *J. Am. Chem. Soc.*, **79**, 4839 (1958).

10 Conjugated dienes and α,β-unsaturated carbonyl compounds

The spectra of substituted butadienes and conjugated polyenes, both acyclic and cyclic, will be considered in this chapter. α,β-Unsaturated carbonyl compounds will also be discussed, but the systems in which an aromatic nucleus is conjugated to a carbonyl or vinyl group will not be explicitly considered. Attention will be focused almost exclusively on the long-wavelength $\pi \rightarrow \pi^*$ or $V \leftarrow N$ transition.

Most of the compounds discussed in this chapter are very closely related. The *ab initio* theoretical methods, and even most semiempirical methods, are generally not able to account more than qualitatively for differences between closely related compounds, and consequently most of the discussion in this chapter will be concerned with a series of empirical rules which help to systematize the available data and to predict spectra of new compounds.

10.1 Alkyl-Substituted Dienes

The spectrum of butadiene has already been discussed in considerable detail. The energies of the MO's of this compound are shown in Fig. 10.1, which indicates the combination of atomic C orbitals to form ethylene and the combination (center) of the two ethylene units to form butadiene.

In the ground state, the electronic configuration of the four π electrons is $\pi_1^2 \pi_2^2$. The lowest unoccupied MO is the antibonding π_3^* orbital, and hence the longest-wavelength band at 217 mμ is due to the $V \leftarrow N$ transition, $\pi_1^2 \pi_2^2 \rightarrow \pi_1^2 \pi_2 \pi_3$. The bathochromic effect of alkyl substitution on ethylene has already been discussed. This red shift and intensification are due to the raising of the energy level of the highest occupied MO by the resonance effect. Similar effects are to be expected in substituted butadienes. The shifts produced appear to be rather uniform, and empirical rules have been developed which correlate the known absorption data of substituted dienes. One rule, due to Woodward,[1] states that λ_{max} for a diene can be

[1] R. B. Woodward, *J. Am. Chem. Soc.*, **64**, 72 (1942).

C=C   C=C—C=C   C=C

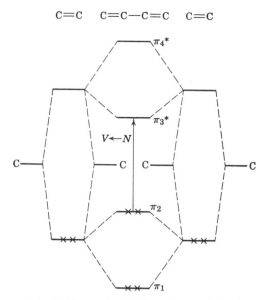

Fig. 10.1   Energy levels of ethylene and butadiene.

determined by adding to 217 mμ (λ_{max} for butadiene) 5 mμ for each alkyl substituent on the diene. If the double bond which is part of the conjugated system is exocyclic to a six-membered ring, a further 5 mμ is added. The data of Table 10.1 illustrate the utility of these rules. The 5 mμ shift for the exocyclic double bond was justified on the basis that the introduction of strain in a given chromophore labilizes the electronic system (by raising the ground-state energy) with a consequent bathochromic shift. A double bond exocyclic to a six-membered ring is unstable by about 3.5 kcal with respect to the corresponding endocyclic compound. In the 220–250 mμ region of the spectrum an energy difference of this magnitude corresponds to about 5 mμ, and so the increment for an exocyclic double bond seems reasonable on theoretical grounds. Substantial evidence has now accumulated that an endocyclic double bond in the cyclohexane series is more stable than an exocyclic one. An exocyclic double bond distorts the strainless staggered conformation of the chair form of cyclohexane more than does an endocyclic one, and this accounts for the difference in stability. The phenomenon is further illustrated by the reactivity of cyclohexanone in addition reactions and by equilibrium data[2] for the system cyclohexenylacetic acid-cyclohexenylideneacetic acid, which indicate that the endo form is the favored structure.

[2] R. P. Linstead, *J. Chem. Soc.*, 1603 (1930).

TABLE 10.1

Spectra of Conjugated Dienes in Ethanol[1]

Compound	λ_{max}, mμ	
	Calculated	Observed
C=C—C=C	. . .	217
C=C—C=C with C C substituents below the central carbons	227	226
C—C=C—C=C—C	227	227
C=C—C=C with C substituent	222	220.0
C—C=C—C=C	222	223.5
(cyclohexylidene)=C—C=C	232	236.5
(cyclohexenyl)—C=C with C substituent	232	235
C, C—C—(cyclohexene ring)=C	232	232
(cyclohexenyl)—(cyclohexenyl)	237	236
HO—(cyclohexenyl)=C—C=(cyclohexyl)	247	248
(cyclohexene)=C	232	231[a]

[a] W. J. Bailey and J. C. Goossens, *J. Am. Chem. Soc.*, **78**, 2804 (1956).

The spectra of hydrocarbons are relatively unaffected by solvent polarity; within the limits of error and applicability of empirical rules, the same results are obtained, for example, with isooctane and ethanol as solvents. Hence no correction need be applied for interconversion of solvent systems when dealing with hydrocarbon dienes and polyenes if attention is focused on the position of maximum absorption to within 1 or 2 mμ.

Ultraviolet spectrophotometry has been a particularly powerful tool in structure determinations in the steroid field. The steroids are a group of naturally occurring compounds containing a carbon skeleton of four fused rings arranged as in cyclopentanoperhydrophenanthrene, and possessing an almost endless variety of substituents, centers of unsaturation, and stereochemical configurations. A typical and particularly important steroid is cholesterol, I. Frequently the steroids contain a conjugated diene system. If the two double bonds are in different rings, so-called heteroannular dienes, Woodward's rule is generally satisfactory. However, if the double bonds are in the same ring (i.e., homoannular dienes),

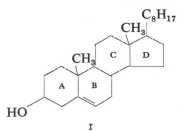

I

absorption occurs at considerably longer wavelengths (260–280 mμ) than predicted from the rule. An enormous number of steroids have been examined spectroscopically, and the results are reported in at least four important[3,4,5,6] publications. A careful analysis of the many data led Fieser and Fieser[6] to propose the rules shown in Table 10.2; examples[6] of the application of these rules are shown in Table 10.3. When both homoannular- and heteroannular-diene systems are present, as in compounds (4), (5), (6), and (7), the calculation is based on the longer-wavelength-absorbing homoannular chromophore.

It is tempting to speculate on the striking spectral difference between homoannular and heteroannular dienes. The homoannular dienes are necessarily constrained in the *s-cis* form, whereas most heteroannular dienes exist predominantly in the *s-trans* form. Not only do the homoannular

[3] H. Dannenberg, *Abhandl. preuss. Akad. Wiss.*, **21**, 3 (1939).
[4] L. Dorfman, *Chem. Revs.*, **53**, 47 (1953).
[5] H. Booker, L. K. Evans, and A. E. Gillam, *J. Chem. Soc.*, 1453 (1940).
[6] L. F. Fieser and M. Fieser, *Steroids*, Reinhold Publishing Corp., New York, 1959.

TABLE 10.2

Steroid Dienes and Polyenes[6]

Group	Increment, $m\mu$
Parent heteroannular diene	214
Parent homoannular diene	253
Double bond extending conjugation	30
Alkyl substituent or ring residue	5
Exocyclic double bond	5
Groups OAc or OR on diene system	0

TABLE 10.3

Spectra of Steroid Dienes and Trienes[6]

		Observed		Calculated
Compound		λ_{max}, $m\mu$	ϵ_{max}	λ_{max}, $m\mu$
(1)		282	11,900	$253 + 4(5) + 2(5) = 283$
(2)		234	20,000	$214 + 3(5) + 5 = 234$
(3)[a]		245	. . .	$214 + 4(5) + 2(5) = 244$
(4)		324	11,800	$253 + 30 + 5(5) + 3(5) = 323$
(5)	AcO	306	14,500	$253 + 30 + 3(5) + 5 = 303$
(6)		315	19,800	$253 + 30 + 4(5) + 2(5) = 313$
(7)	AcO	355	19,700	$253 + 2(30) + 5(5) + 3(5) = 353$

[a] For this example and others of spectra of heteroannular compounds see Woodward (footnote 1).

dienes absorb at considerably longer wavelengths than their hetero counterparts, but also the ϵ values are usually smaller and the band somewhat broader in the homo series. The suggestion has been made[1] that in the homoannular diene the σ electrons in the carbon-carbon bond are labilized and interact with the four $p\pi$ electrons to form a six-electron system. This appears quite unlikely because the carbon-carbon σ electrons do not possess the proper symmetry for interaction. A more attractive possibility is the hyperconjugative interaction of the two $\diagdown C{=}H_2$ groups at the ends of the *cis* diene system, the extensive interaction leading to the observed bathochromic displacements.[7] In any case it will be obvious that the ends of the chromophore in an *s-cis* system are much closer together than in an *s-trans* system, and hence the transition moment and the intensity of the absorption band of the homoannular system should be less than those of the heteroannular system. This generalization has been amply verified.[8]

The homoannular-diene systems of Table 10.3 are in a ring which is part of a polycyclic system. Data for a group of terpene compounds[9] in which the homoannular-diene system is in an isolated ring are listed in Table 10.4. All the dienes absorb in the 260–265 mμ region, which is again at much longer wavelength than would be predicted on the basis of Woodward's rule. The similarity in the λ_{max} positions of all these compounds is unexpected; the position of absorption appears to be quite independent of the number of alkyl substituents attached to the diene system. However, the bands are relatively broad, and the purity of many of the compounds is uncertain.

The ϵ values of these compounds are considerably lower than those of other conjugated diene systems. Heteroannular and acyclic dienes frequently have ϵ values of 15,000–25,000. The relatively low intensity is characteristic of the homoannular *s-cis* diene system; the bathochromic displacement may again be a consequence of the extensive C—H or C—C hyperconjugation.

Almost in a class by itself is the conjugated diene, 1,2-dimethylenecyclohexane, II,[10],[11] which has λ_{max} at 220 mμ and $\epsilon_{max} = 10,050$. Apparently none of the empirical rules developed thus far accounts for the spectrum of this interesting diene. The unexpected hypsochromic effect may be

[7] R. S. Mulliken, *J. Chem. Phys.*, **7**, 121, 339, 353 (1939).

[8] H. P. Koch, *Chem. & Ind.*, **20**, 273 (1942).

[9] R. T. O'Connor and L. A. Goldblatt, *Anal. Chem.*, **26**, 1726 (1954), and private communication.

[10] W. J. Bailey and H. R. Golden, *J. Am. Chem. Soc.*, **75**, 4780 (1953).

[11] W. J. Bailey and W. B. Lawson *J. Am. Chem. Soc.*, **79**, 1444 (1957).

TABLE 10.4
Spectra of Homoannular Dienes in Isooctane[9]

Name	Compound	λ_{max}, mμ	ϵ_{max}
α-Terpinene		265	6400
α-Pyronene		263	5800
β-Pyronene		264	5700
1-Ethyl-5,5-dimethyl-1,3-cyclohexadiene		260	6100
2-Ethyl-6,6-dimethyl-1,3-cyclohexadiene		261	6100
1,2,4,6-Tetramethyl-1,3-cyclohexadiene		265	6100
1,2,3,5-Tetramethyl-1,3-cyclohexadiene		265	6100

related to the lack of planarity of the two double bonds and hence their reduced interaction, or the ring may be bent away from the plane of the diene system in a way which does not permit the hyperconjugation normally expected in a disubstituted butadiene. The presence of methyl

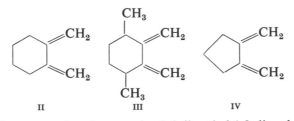

II   III   IV

groups adjacent to the ring, as in 3,6-dimethyl-1,2-dimethylenecyclohexane, III, causes an even further restriction to planarity, and this compound absorbs[12] below 220 mμ. In 1,2-dimethylenecyclopentane, IV, the smaller five-membered ring constrains the system, and the diene system is considerably more planar. This compound[11] has a spectrum with λ_{max} at 243 mμ, a wavelength which is not greatly different from the one expected, if it is assumed that a double bond exocyclic to a five-membered ring warrants an increment of 5 mμ, i.e., $217 + (2 \times 5) + (2 \times 5) = 237$ mμ. Perhaps because of its rigidity, this system appears to have some of the properties of a homoannular diene.

If a part of the chromophore system is included in a bicyclo[3.1.1]heptyl system, a further 15 mμ increment must be added to the value calculated from Woodward's rule. The introduction of strain in the ground state and its partial relief in the excited state may explain this interesting observation.[13] Thus the calculated absorption for verbenene, 7,7-dimethylbicyclo-[3.1.1]hepta-2,4(8)-diene, V, without a correction for strain would be $217 + (3 \times 5) = 232$ mμ. In fact the observed λ_{max} occurs at 245.5 mμ. Similarly, in nopadiene, VI, the value calculated without allowance for strain would be 227 mμ, whereas the observed value is 243 mμ. It may very well be that the bathochromic effect of 15 mμ can be accounted for by the rigidity of the bicyclic system and the raising of the ground-state energy by about 9 kcal.

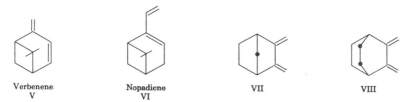

Verbenene   Nopadiene   VII   VIII
V   VI

[12] W. J. Bailey and R. L. Hudson, *J. Am. Chem. Soc.*, **78**, 2806 (1956).
[13] R. N. Moore and G. S. Fisher, *J. Am. Chem. Soc.*, **78**, 4362 (1956).

Although 1,2-dimethylenecyclohexane has an anomalous spectrum based on Woodward's rule, 2,3-dimethylenebicyclo[2.2.1]heptane, VII, can be assumed to be normal, since the calculated maximum is $217 + (2 \times 5) + (2 \times 5) + 15 = 252$ mμ and the observed value[14] is 248 mμ ($\epsilon = 10,800$). 2,3-Dimethylenebicyclo[2.2.2]octane, VIII, has a spectrum[10] with λ_{max} at 247 mμ, and $\epsilon_{max} = 8280$. If the bicyclo increment of 15 mμ is applied here, the calculated λ_{max} again would be at 252, as with VII. It may very well be that with [2.2.1] and [2.2.2] bicyclo systems the empirical increment of 15 mμ assigned to the [3.1.1] system is too large, since the five- and six-membered rings are not as restrictive in the ground state as the four-membered ring in the [3.1.1] system.

Finally, special consideration must be given to the difference in treatment of cross-conjugated and linear-conjugated systems. Cross-conjugated systems must be resolved into the various possible partial linear-conjugated systems, and the empirical rules require that calculations be based on that partial linear-conjugated system which absorbs at longer wavelength. Thus, for the linear-conjugated tetraene, IX, the rules predict $\lambda_{max} = 353$ mμ (Table 10.2), in excellent agreement with the observed value[6] of 355 mμ ($\epsilon = 19,700$). The triene, X, contains a cross-conjugated system. Two partial linear-conjugated systems are possible, one heteroannular with one double bond each in rings B and C, the other homoannular in ring C; the latter is expected to absorb at longer wavelength, and hence should be considered as the parent, with the double bond in ring B neglected. Accordingly, the calculated value is $253 + (5 \times 5) + (2 \times 5) = 288$ mμ, again in excellent agreement with the observed value of λ_{max} of 285 mμ ($\epsilon = 9100$).[6]

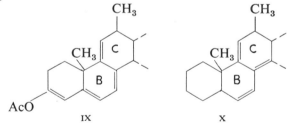

IX   X

10.2   α,β-Unsaturated Ketones

The spectra of unsaturated carbonyl compounds in which the double bond and the carbonyl groups are not conjugated are simple summations of the absorption of the ethylene and carbonyl chromophores. In ethylene, the absorption occurs in the far ultraviolet and is due to a $\pi \to \pi^*$ transition which, being a $V \leftarrow N$ transition, is very intense. The spectrum was

[14] W. J. Bailey and W. B. Lawson, *J. Am. Chem. Soc.*, **77**, 1606 (1955).

discussed more fully in Chapter 5. The simple isolated carbonyl group gives rise to two bands. The energy-level diagram and a full discussion of the spectrum were given in section 9.5. The short-wavelength band is in the far ultraviolet and is not generally observed. It involves the promotion

of one of the bonding π electrons in the $\ce{C=O}$ group to an antibonding

or π^* orbital and is an intense $V \leftarrow N$ transition. The second, long-wavelength band is due to the promotion of one of the nonbonding pair of electrons on the oxygen atom to the π^* level. This $Q \leftarrow N$ transition is forbidden by symmetry, since the nonbonding electrons are in a p orbital of oxygen which is at approximately right angles to the π^* orbital. Accordingly, this is a low-intensity band. In the case of acetone (in ethanol), this band is at 270.6 mμ and has an ϵ value of 15.2. The effect of solvent on this band was discussed in section 9.7.

When the ethylenic grouping and the carbonyl group are conjugated, the $Q \leftarrow N$ band of the carbonyl group is displaced to longer wavelength, and an intense $V \leftarrow N$ band occurs at longer wavelength than the corresponding band in either isolated chromophore. The energy-level diagram of the conjugated system is illustrated by Fig. 10.2.

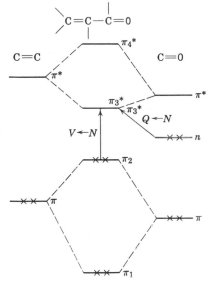

Fig. 10.2   Energy-level diagram of α,β-unsaturated carbonyl compounds.

The system described by Fig. 10.2 is somewhat similar to butadiene in that each of the four atoms is contributing one electron to the π-electron system, and the lowest energy level involves a bonding orbital encompassing all four atoms. This level is of course lower, and the next level (π_2) higher, than either π level of the separate chromophores; the lowest unoccupied level, π_3^*, is lower than the π^* level of ethylene or the carbonyl group. Hence the $V \leftarrow N$ transition of the conjugated system is shifted toward the red, compared to the $V \leftarrow N$ transition of either separate chromophore. Since π_3^* is lower than π^* of the isolated carbonyl, the promotion of one of the lone-pair oxygen electrons n to π_3^* requires less energy than the similar promotion in the isolated carbonyl group, and hence the $Q \leftarrow N$ (or n $\rightarrow \pi^*$) transition is also shifted to the red in the conjugated system. The $V \leftarrow N$ transition may be designated $\pi_1^2\pi_2^2 n^2 \rightarrow \pi_1^2\pi_2 n^2\pi_3^*$. This high-intensity transition is also frequently called the K band in accordance with Burawoy's suggestion. The low-intensity $Q \leftarrow N$ transition, indicated by $\pi_1^2\pi_2^2 n^2 \rightarrow \pi_1^2\pi_2^2 n\pi_3^*$, is frequently called the R band, also following Burawoy.

The energy-level diagram (Fig. 10.2) permits a ready visualization of the resonance energy of the conjugated system. This quantity is defined as the difference $\Delta\mathscr{E}$ in total π-electron energy between the actual molecule and its most stable resonance structure. The energy $\mathscr{E}_R$ of the latter is the sum of the energies of the two π electrons in the vinyl group and the two π electrons in the carbonyl group, $\mathscr{E}_R = 2\varepsilon(\pi_{C=C}) + 2\varepsilon(\pi_{C=O})$. The π-electron energy of the molecule ($\mathscr{E}$) is the sum of the energies of the four π electrons, $\mathscr{E} = 2\varepsilon(\pi_1) + 2\varepsilon(\pi_2)$. The difference, the resonance energy RE, is

$$RE = \mathscr{E} - \mathscr{E}_R = 2\varepsilon(\pi_1) + 2\varepsilon(\pi_2) - 2\varepsilon(\pi_{C=C}) - 2\varepsilon(\pi_{C=O})$$

and thus is twice the lowering of π_1 below π of C=O minus twice the raising of π_2 above π of C=C.

TABLE 10.5

$$\text{CH}_3$$
$$|$$

Effect of Solvent on Spectrum of CH_3—C=CH—$COCH_3$[15]

	$V \leftarrow N$		$Q \leftarrow N$	
Solvent	λ_{max}, mμ	ϵ_{max}	λ_{max}, mμ	ϵ_{max}
Hexane	229.5	12,600	327	97.5
Ether	230	12,600	326	96
Ethanol	237	12,600	315	78
Methanol	238	10,700	312	74
Water	244.5	10,000	305	60

The locations of the $V \leftarrow N$ and the $Q \leftarrow N$ bands are strongly affected by solvents; and when a displacement occurs in passing from one solvent to another, the $V \leftarrow N$ band is always displaced in a direction opposite to that of the $Q \leftarrow N$ carbonyl band. The effect of solvent on the spectrum of mesityl oxide[15] is shown in Table 10.5. The explanation of the solvent shifts was discussed in section 9.7.

A set of empirical rules for determining the spectra of α,β-unsaturated

[15] G. Scheibe, *Ber.*, **58**, 586 (1925).

carbonyl compounds analogous to those formulated for dienes has been suggested by Woodward and by the Fiesers.[6] These rules correlate an enormous number of data in the literature and have resulted in many instances in a reassignment of structures which had been incorrectly assigned in the published literature. The rules permit not only predictions of the spectra of unknown compounds but also decisions between alternate probable structures of compounds on the basis of their observed spectra.

In order to correlate the mass of data in the literature it is necessary to know the solvent in which spectra have been determined and to correct

TABLE 10.6

Solvent Corrections of the $V \leftarrow N$ Band in
α,β-Unsaturated Ketones

Correction to Ethanol, mμ

From Solvent	Woodward[16]	Fieser and Fieser[6]
Methanol	−1	0
Chloroform	0	+1
Ether	+6	+7
Hexane	+7	+11
Water	...	−8
Dioxan	...	+5

the observed wavelengths of the bands to a standard solvent. In order to convert literature data obtained with various solvents for spectra in the standard solvent, ethanol, Woodward[16] applied the corrections shown in Table 10.6. On the basis of reported solvent effects on testosterone, a steroid enone, Fieser and Fieser[6] proposed slightly different corrections, also shown in Table 10.6. In methyl vinyl ketone, the unsubstituted compound of formula XI, R = CH_3, α = β = β = H, the $V \leftarrow N$ transi-

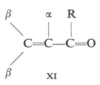

tion is observed at 215 mμ. Woodward proposed an increment of 11 mμ for each alkyl substituent at the α or β positions, starting with a value of 215 mμ for methyl vinyl ketone. It is interesting to note that this increment is about twice the corresponding increment in dienes. If the conjugated

[16] R. B. Woodward, *J. Am. Chem. Soc.*, **63**, 1123 (1942).

system includes a double bond exocyclic to a six-membered ring, an additional increment of 5 mμ is used, which is identical with that for an exocyclic double bond in dienes. The most probable locations of the $V \leftarrow N$ band in carbonyl compounds with various alkyl substitutions are given in Table 10.7.

TABLE 10.7
Location of the $V \leftarrow N$ Band in Unsaturated Ketones, XI

Alkyl Substitution		Most Probable λ_{max}, mμ
None		215
α or β		225
α,β or β,β	No exocyclic bond	235
	One exocyclic bond	240
α,β,β	No exocyclic bond	247
	One exocyclic bond	252

Application of these rules to a few selected unsaturated ketones is shown in Table 10.8. An interesting example of the value of these generalizations is cited by Woodward.[16] The sesquiterpene ketone, α-cyperone, was assigned[17] structure XII. Its ultraviolet absorption spectrum showed an intense band (log ϵ = 4.28) with λ_{max} at 251 mμ. These data are inconsistent with structure XII, for which 225 mμ is predicted, but consistent with the alternate structure, XIII, which was proposed by Woodward and subsequently was found to be correct.[18]

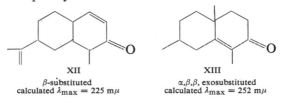

XII
β-substituted
calculated λ_{max} = 225 mμ

XIII
α,β,β, exosubstituted
calculated λ_{max} = 252 mμ

In two of the compounds listed in Table 10.8, the double bond is exocyclic to a five-membered ring. Although the rules in Table 10.7 refer to double bonds exocyclic to six-membered, not to five-membered, rings, the increment of 5 mμ appears to apply to both types of exocyclic double bonds. The same increment was shown earlier to give good results with 1,2-dimethylenecyclopentane.

[17] A. E. Bradfield, B. J. Hegde, B. S. Rao, J. L. Simonsen, and A. E. Gillam, *J. Chem. Soc.*, 667 (1936).
[18] A. E. Bradfield, R. R. Pritchard, and J. L. Simonsen, *J. Chem. Soc.*, 760 (1937).

Endocyclic double bonds in five- and six-membered rings, however, appear to require separate treatment. The two compounds listed in Table 10.8 involving a double bond endocyclic in a five-membered ring absorb at longer wavelength than their homologs involving six-membered rings. The bathochromic effect of the endocyclic double bond in the five-membered ring has been attributed[19] to probable strain of this olefinic system, whereas such strain is absent in the ground state of the cyclohexene system. In the excited state, which can be represented largely by ionic structures with the double bond moved out of the ring, there is considerable relief of this strain in the five-membered system.

Cyclopentenone absorbs at 218 mμ and cyclohexenone at 224.5 mμ; in general, cyclopentenone derivatives absorb at shorter wavelength than their six-membered-ring analogs.[20] It is difficult to rationalize this difference,[19] but perhaps the single-bond character of the C-O bond in the excited state is more favorable for the six-carbon ring system, and the energy is somewhat lower for the excited state in this system than in the five-carbon ring system.

The discussion thus far in this chapter has been concerned with the position of the $V \leftarrow N$ transition and the empirical rules for calculating the location of this band. Not much discussion has been devoted to the effect of substitution on the n → π* transition. Since substitution on the ethylenic linkage raises the π* levels, and since the n level is practically unaffected, the effect of substitution in an α,β-unsaturated ketone is to cause a hypsochromic shift. Such systematic work as is reported in the literature[21] confirms this prediction. In the case of cyclohexenones, one α or β substituent causes a shift of 6 mμ to shorter wavelength, and two alkyl substituents cause a shift of 20 mμ in the same direction.

In a compound such as 1-acetylcyclohexene and its derivatives, *s-cis* and *s-trans* configurations (or *cisoid* and *transoid*, as they are sometimes called) are possible. The energy difference between *s-cis-* and *s-trans-*butadiene has been shown[22] to be about 2.3 kcal. A similar energy difference

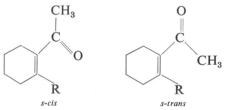

s-cis   *s-trans*

[19] W. M. Schubert and W. A. Sweeney, *J. Am. Chem. Soc.*, **77**, 2297 (1955).

[20] H. S. French, *J. Am. Chem. Soc.*, **74**, 514 (1952).

[21] R. C. Cookson and S. H. Dandegaonker, *J. Chem. Soc.*, 1651 (1955).

[22] J. G. Aston, G. Szasz, H. W. Woolley, and F. G. Brickwedde, *J. Chem. Phys.*, **14**, 67 (1946); A. D. Walsh, *Nature*, **157**, 768 (1946).

TABLE 10.8

Location of $V \leftarrow N$ Band of Some Ketones in Ethanol

Compound	Substituents	λ_{max}, mμ Calc.	λ_{max}, mμ Obs.	ϵ_{max}
$CH_2{=}\overset{\displaystyle C_2H_5}{\underset{\textstyle \|}{C}}{-}COCH_3$	α	225	221	6,450
$CH_2{=}\overset{\displaystyle CH_3}{\underset{\textstyle \|}{C}}{-}COC_2H_5$	α	225	220	7,900
$CH_3{-}CH{=}CH{-}CO{-}CH_3$	β	225	224	9,750
$(CH_3)_2C{=}CHCOCH_3$	β,β	235	235	14,000
(cyclohexenyl)$-COCH_3$	α,β	235	233.5	...
$(CH_3)_2C{=}C(CH_3)COCH_3$	α,β,β	247	249	...
(octalone structure)	β,β, exo	240	240	...
(bicyclohexylidene ketone structure)	α,β,β, exo, exo	257	257.5	...
(octalone structure)	α,β, exo	240	241	4,700
(cyclobutylidene–cyclopentanone structure)	α,β,β, exo, exo	257	259	10,790

TABLE 10.8 (continued)

Compound	Substituents	λ_{max}, mμ Calc.	Obs.	ϵ_{max}
	α,β,β, exo	252	254	9,550
	α,β	235[a]	239	13,000
	α,β	235	233	13,000
	α,β,β	247	253	10,010
	α,β,β	247	249	6,890

[a] Better agreement with the observed value is obtained if 5 mμ is added for the endocyclic double bond in the five-membered ring; see the following discussion and Schubert and Sweeney (footnote 19).

may be assumed to exist between the corresponding forms of the α,β-carbonyl system:

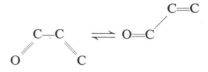

1-Acetylcyclohexene should exist predominantly as the *s-trans* form, and the high ϵ value (which among other things is related approximately to the square of the distance separating the ends of the chromophore)[23] is indicative of the *s-trans* conformation. However, when a substituent is introduced at the 2 position, there is more interference to a planar ground state in the *s-trans* than in the *s-cis* form. The observed spectral effect of such substitution, as can be seen from Table 10.8, is hypochromic. The various theories proposed to explain these phenomena will be discussed in detail in Chapter 15.

In the consideration of the spectra of conjugated dienes in section 10.1, attention was directed to the increment of 15 mμ to the band maximum when a strained ring was part of the diene system.[13] The increment of 15 mμ also applies to the similar situation in unsaturated ketones. Thus pinocarvone, XIV, would be expected to have λ_{max} at 245 mμ, since it has an α substituent and an exocyclic bond in addition to the [3.1.1] system. The observed[13] λ_{max} is at 247 mμ. Verbenone, XV, with β,β substitution, would be expected to absorb at 250 mμ; the observed absorption[13] is at 253 mμ.

XIV   XV

10.3   α,β-Unsaturated Aldehydes and Acids

The empirical rules for the location of the $V \leftarrow N$ band in an α,β-unsaturated aldehyde[24] are very similar to those applying to the ketones and are summarized in Table 10.9, where several examples are given. All these bands are about 5 mμ displaced toward shorter wavelength from those of the corresponding unsaturated ketones given in Table 10.7, as may be expected in the absence of the bathochromic effect of the alkyl group.

[23] R. B. Turner and D. M. Voitle, *J. Am. Chem. Soc.*, **73**, 1403 (1951).
[24] L. K. Evans and A. E. Gillam, *J. Chem. Soc.*, 565 (1943).

TABLE 10.9

Rules and Examples of Spectra of α,β-Unsaturated Aldehydes

$$\begin{matrix} \beta & & H \\ \diagdown & & \diagup \\ & C{=}C{-}C & \\ \diagup & | & \diagdown \\ \beta & \alpha & O \end{matrix}$$

Substituent	$\lambda_{max} \pm 5\ m\mu$	Compound	Obs. λ_{max}
Parent	208	$CH_2{=}CH{-}CHO$	208
Mono-(α or β)	220	$CH_3CH{=}CHCHO$	217
Di-(α,β or β,β)	230	$(CH_3)_2C{=}CCHO$	235
Tri-(α,β,β)	242	. . .	. . .

The only absorption band shown by saturated carboxylic acids is the $n \rightarrow \pi^*$ transition, which occurs at 204 mμ, $\epsilon = 60$, in acetic acid, considerably hypsochromically shifted from its position in acetaldehyde, λ_{max} at 293 mμ, $\epsilon = 12$, by the cooperation of resonance and inductive effects described in section 9.5. Similarly, it may be expected that the $n \rightarrow \pi^*$ transitions of α,β-unsaturated acids occur at shorter wavelength than in the corresponding aldehydes and ketones.

Conjugation with a vinyl group shifts the $V \leftarrow N$ transition of carboxylic acids into the quartz ultraviolet region. Rules for empirical prediction of α,β-unsaturated acids and esters, as proposed by Nielsen,[25] are given in Table 10.10 and show fair agreement with the representative data in Table 10.11.

TABLE 10.10

Location of $V \leftarrow N$ Transition in Acyclic and Alicyclic α,β-Unsaturated Acids and Esters

Substitution	$\lambda_{max} \mp 5\ m\mu$
α	208
α,β or β,β	217[a]
α,β,β	225[a]

[a] Add 5 mμ for an exocyclic double bond or for an endocyclic double bond in a five- or seven-membered ring compound.

10.4 Dienones

The chromophoric dienone unit, $C{=}C{-}C{=}C{-}C{=}O$, may be expected to have the $V \leftarrow N$ transition at longer wavelength than either dienes or

[25] A. T. Nielsen, *J. Org. Chem.*, **22**, 1539 (1957).

TABLE 10.11

Spectra of Selected α,β-Unsaturated Acids in 95 Per Cent Ethanol

Compound	λ_{max}, mμ
$CH_2{=}CMeCO_2CH_3$	208
$CH_2{=}C(C_2H_5)CO_2H$	208 (water)
trans-$MeCH{=}CHCO_2H$	208 (water)
cis-$HO_2CCH{=}CHCO_2H$	210 (water)
trans-$MeCH{=}CMeCO_2H$	213
cis-$MeCH{=}CMeCO_2H$	216
$MeCH{=}CMeCO_2Me$	215
$Me_2C{=}CHCO_2H$	216
$Me_2C{=}CMeCO_2H$	221
	222
	217
	222
	231
	224
	220
	235

enones. The addition of the ethylenic linkage to the enone brings into the system two more $p\pi$ electrons and two more AO's. Although the lowest occupied MO is lowered by the increased conjugation, the highest occupied MO is now at a higher level than the corresponding MO in the simpler system, and the lowest unoccupied MO is lowered. Accordingly, the energy required for promotion is considerably less in the longer conjugated system, thus accounting for the known bathochromic shift in the dienones.

The application and extension of Woodward's rules to dienones in the area of steroid chemistry was initiated by the Fiesers and their collaborators.[26] The general rules[6] proposed for the position of the $V \leftarrow N$ transition in such compounds are given in Table 10.12. It will be noted from these rules that the parent absorbs at 245 mμ, or 30 mμ higher than the simple enone (Table 10.7). In general, extending the conjugation with an additional double bond results in a 30 mμ bathochromic shift, and substituents on such additional double bonds require increments of 18 mμ each. The rules in Table 10.7 and Table 10.10 could be combined, but the dienones are encountered in so many steroids and the generalizations are based on so many examples that it is advantageous to treat the dienones and related compounds separately. The solvent corrections that should be applied, based on the observed solvent effects[6] on testosterone, were shown in Table 10.6. Several examples of observed and calculated maxima in the

TABLE 10.12

Absorption Maxima for Dienones in Ethanol[6]

Parent, 245 mμ

$$\overset{\displaystyle \delta \qquad\;\; \beta \qquad\;\; R}{\underset{\displaystyle \gamma \qquad\;\; \alpha}{\delta-C=C-C=C-C=O}}$$

R (alkyl or ring residue, OR, $OCOCH_3$)	Increment, mμ
α	10
β	12
γ, δ, and $\delta+$	18
α-Hydroxyl (enolic)	35
α-Cl	15
α-Br	23
Exocyclic double bond	5
Homoannular diene component	39
Double bond extending conjugation (extd)	30

TABLE 10.13

Spectra of Some Dienones and Related Compounds, Corrected to Ethanol as Solvent

Compound	Substitution	λ_{max}, mμ		ϵ_{max}
		Calc.	Obs.	
	β,δ, exo	280	284	28,000
	β,δ, exo	280	279	26,400
	γ,δ, exo	286	290	12,600
	β,γ,δ, exo, exo	303	292	13,100
	α,γ, exo, homo	317	315	7,000
	$\beta,\delta+_1$, exo, extd, homo	349	348	11,000
	$\beta,\delta+_1,\delta+_1,\delta+_1$, exo, extd, homo	385	388	12,300
	$\beta,\delta+_1,\delta+_1,\delta+_1$, exo, exo, extd	351	348	26,500

steroid series are shown in Table 10.13. Structures in which there is cross conjugation, such as C=C—CO—C=C—C=C, or enedione structures, —CO—C=C—CO—, cannot be handled readily by empirical rules.

The acyclic dienoic acid, sorbic acid,

$$CH_3—CH=CH—CH=CH—CO_2H,$$

has λ_{max} at 254 mμ in ethanol. This value compares favorably with that which might be expected from the application of Fieser's rules for dienones.[26] To the basic value of the unsaturated acids of 208, 30 mμ is added for the extended conjugation and 18 mμ for substitution in the δ position, giving $208 + 30 + 18 = 256$ mμ.

10.5   Summary of Empirical Rules

The empirical rules discussed in this chapter are combined in Table 10.14. (pp. 218–219).

[26] L. F. Fieser, M. Fieser, and S. Rajagopalan, *J. Org. Chem.*, **13**, 800 (1948); L. F. Fieser and M. Fieser, *Natural Products Related to Phenanthrene*, Reinhold Publishing Corp., New York, 1949.

TABLE 10.14

Empirical Rules for Calculating Absorption Maxima of Dienes and α,β-Unsaturated Carbonyl Systems in Ethanol

Table	System[a]	Structure	λ_{max}, mμ	Increment for Each Substituent, mμ						
				$\alpha =$				$\beta =$		$\gamma, \delta =$
				R^b	OH	Cl	Br	R^b	OH	R^b
10.1, 10.2, 10.3	Diene[c,d]		217^e	5	…	17	17	…	…	…
10.7, 10.8	α,β-Unsaturated ketones[c,f]		215	10	35	…	23	10	35	…
10.9	α,β-Unsaturated aldehyde[c,f]		209	11	…	…	…	11	…	…

10.10, 10.11	α,β-Unsaturated esters or acids[c,f]	197	10	...	...	10	35	...
10.12, 10.13	Dienone[c,f]	245	10	35	15	23	12	...	18

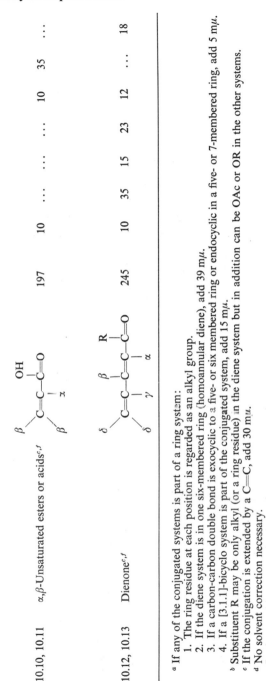

[a] If any of the conjugated systems is part of a ring system:
  1. The ring residue at each position is regarded as an alkyl group.
  2. If the diene system is in one six-membered ring (homoannular diene), add 39 mμ.
  3. If a carbon-carbon double bond is exocyclic to a five- or six-membered ring or endocyclic in a five- or 7-membered ring, add 5 mμ.
  4. If a [3.1.1]-bicyclo system is part of the conjugated system, add 15 mμ.
[b] Substituent R may be only alkyl (or a ring residue) in the diene system but in addition can be OAc or OR in the other systems.
[c] If the conjugation is extended by a C=C, add 30 mμ.
[d] No solvent correction necessary.
[e] In the steroid compounds, the preferred value is 214 mμ.
[f] For solvent corrections see Table 10.6.

11 Spectra of polyenes and related compounds; the free-electron model

Compounds with series of alternating single and double (or single and triple) bonds are reasonably common, and their spectra involve some rather interesting features. A special quantum-mechanical method,[1] the free-electron model, has been devised for use with such compounds. In the first section of this chapter this method will be developed, and then in later sections will be used as a basis of discussion of various types of compounds.

11.1 The Free-Electron Model

All the quantum-mechanical methods used in previous chapters were based on expression of the molecular wave functions in terms of atomic functions in one form or another. The method to be discussed here makes no reference whatever to individual atomic functions; it is related, however, to MO theory in that the molecular wave function is expressed as a product (or rather a determinant of products) of one-electron functions.

The free-electron method (FEM) is applicable essentially only to sets of electrons with very analogous properties. In practice its usefulness has been almost completely restricted to π-electron systems in conjugated organic compounds. In such systems, chemists have long considered the electrons as being especially *mobile*, and little restricted to specific nuclei. The FEM makes use of this property by assuming that there is a region in which the electron is free to move without restriction, and that this region extends over the entire π-electron system. In other words, the FEM assumes that there is a region in space in which the potential energy of the electron is finite (and constant), and that outside this region it is infinite.

---

[1] (a) N. S. Bayliss, *J. Chem. Phys.*, **16**, 287 (1948). (b) H. Kuhn, *J. Chem. Phys.*, **16**, 840 (1948); *Helv. Chim. Acta*, **31**, 1441 (1948), **32**, 2247 (1949); **34**, 1308, 2371 (1951); W. Huber, H. Kuhn, and W. Huber, *Helv. Chim. Acta*, **36**, 1597 (1953). (c) W. T. Simpson, *J. Chem. Phys.*, **16**, 1124 (1948). (d) J. R. Platt, *J. Chem. Phys.*, **17**, 484 (1949); S. Nikitine, *J. Chim. Phys.*, **50**, 282 (1953).

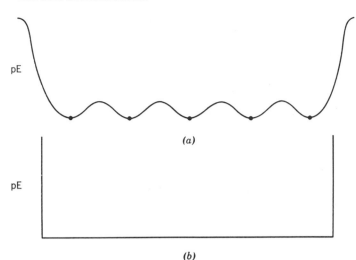

Fig. 11.1   Potential energy: (*a*) as a function of distance along the conjugated chain and (*b*) the approximate potential commonly assumed.

With this assumption the problem of the behavior of the electrons becomes the well-known problem of the particle or electron in a box.[2]

Some discussion of this box or, better, this potential well is indicated. Logically the potential well should be three dimensional. However, from the molecular point of view the only freedom of motion of the electrons of interest is the motion along the conjugated system. Motion away from it is probably not, or at best little, affected by conjugation, and hence is ignored. With this restriction, the problem becomes one dimensional, the dimension being the "electron path" along the conjugated system. The problem to be considered is the form of the potential-energy function along this path. The potential energy should be lowest near the nuclei and higher between them; furthermore, some distance *beyond* the end nuclei the potential energy should rise steeply, but not discontinuously, to a high value, but not to infinity. Such a potential-energy function is given by Fig. 11.1*a*. In most applications of the FEM, this potential-energy function is approximated by the one shown in Fig. 11.1*b*, in which the periodic potential is replaced by a constant one, and the steep rise to a high value by a discontinuous rise to infinity. The point at which this rise to infinity occurs must be decided arbitrarily. Apparently the most satisfactory convention is to place this wall of the energy well one bond distance beyond the end atoms of the conjugated system.

[2] W. Kauzman, *Quantum Chemistry*, Academic Press, New York, 1957, pp. 183 ff.

In the region within the one-dimensional box, it is therefore assumed, according to Fig. 11.1b, that the potential energy is constant and equal to zero. The wave equation[2] is:

$$-\frac{h^2}{8\pi^2 m}\frac{d^2\psi}{dx^2} = E\psi \quad (0 \le x \le a)$$

the solution for which is

$$\psi_n = \sqrt{2/a}\,\sin\left[\frac{\pi n}{a}\right]x \quad (0 \le x \le a)$$

where a is the length of the potential well or box, x is the distance along the well, and the quantum number n is a positive whole number, $1, 2, 3, \ldots$. To each ψ_n there corresponds an energy:

$$E_n = \frac{n^2 h^2}{8ma^2} \tag{11.1}$$

where n and a have the meanings defined above, h is Planck's constant, and m is the mass of the electron. In a conjugated hydrocarbon containing k double bonds there are $2k$ π electrons. In the ground state of the molecule each of the k orbitals is doubly occupied, Fig. 11.2. The first electronically excited state of the conjugated molecule is derived from the corresponding ground state by the promotion of one electron from the highest occupied level ($n = k$) to the lowest unoccupied level ($n = k + 1$). The energy of excitation, ΔE, is therefore

$$\Delta E = E_{k+1} - E_k = \frac{(k+1)^2 h^2}{8ma^2} - \frac{k^2(h^2)}{8ma^2}$$

$$= \frac{(2k+1)h^2}{8ma^2} \tag{11.2}$$

Since $E = h\nu = hc/\lambda$, where c is the velocity of light,

$$\lambda = \frac{hc}{\Delta E} = \frac{8ma^2 c}{(2k+1)h} \tag{11.3}$$

The only variables in equation (11.3) are a and k, and it is helpful to evaluate the constants in the equation: $m = 9.1 \times 10^{-28}$ g, $c = 3.0 \times 10^{10}$ cm, and $h = 6.6 \times 10^{-27}$ g cm^2 sec^{-1}, whereupon $8mc/h = 3.3 \times 10^{10}$ cm^{-1}, and

$$\lambda = \frac{33a^2}{(2k+1)}\,m\mu \tag{11.4}$$

when a is in angstrom units. In applying equation (11.4) to any system, the choice of a proper value for a, the length of the potential well, poses some problems. In the case of a conjugated polyene, the average distance between carbon atoms is approximately 1.4 A. If, for example, it is desired to calculate λ for octatetraene,

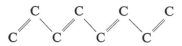

the distance along the conjugated path is 7 bond lengths, or 9.8 A, and, if a bond length is added at each end, $a = 12.6$ A. The value for k, the number of orbitals occupied by the π electrons, is 4, and substitution into equation (11.4) gives

$$\lambda = 33 \times (12.6)^2/9 = 582\,m\mu$$

The observed value[1a] for octatetraene is 286 $m\mu$. Although the order of magnitude is correct, the calculated value is not in very good agreement with the observed one. The lack of agreement with experiment may be due in part to the uncertainty in a, to the assumption of a uniform potential, and to many other assumptions and approximations.

It will be apparent from equation (11.3) that λ varies as a^2, and so any errors or assumptions regarding the value of a are magnified in λ. From the variation of a with the number of double bonds in the system, $a \propto (k + 1)$, and from equation (11.3),

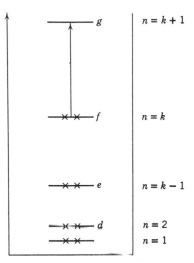

Fig. 11.2   The FEM energy levels in octatetraene.

$$\lambda \propto (k + 1)^2/(2k + 1)$$

Accordingly, λ should increase with increasing k, and substantial experience indicates that increasing the length of a conjugated chain increases the wavelength of absorption. At large k, $k + 1$ is approximately equal to k and hence λ is proportional to k, which suggests that λ should increase linearly with k. This conclusion appears to be incorrect, since, as will be shown below, the longest wavelength of absorption of linear polyenes approaches a constant value.

In addition to its ability to make fair predictions of the spectra of certain restricted classes of dyes (the polymethines and related compounds; see the following sections), and to provide information on the spectra of polyenes, polyynes, and aromatic fused rings (see Chapter 13), the FEM has two further important applications.

The first is of a qualitative nature. It is well known that, the longer a conjugated system, the longer the wavelength at which it absorbs. Molecular-orbital theory is well able to reflect this fact, but the simple relation of equation (11.4) provides an at least semiquantitative explicit relation between length of conjugated system and wavelength of absorption. No other theory is able to do so. Free-electron method theory gives insight into the reasons for this relation, not readily apparent from other theories, and provides justification for the frequently used concept of the "longest conjugated path."

The wavelengths of further bands are also readily predicted by the FEM. In order to provide a uniform notation, Platt[3] has suggested designating the highest occupied orbital as f and succeeding lower-lying orbitals as e, d, etc., and, similarly, the lowest unoccupied orbital as g and succeeding higher ones as h, i, etc. In this notation, the longest-wavelength transition, for which $\Delta n = 1$, is $f \rightarrow g$, and Platt has proposed to designate the singlet-singlet component of this transition as $^1B \leftarrow {}^1A$, where A refers to the ground state and B to the first excited state. For $\Delta n = 2$, there are two possible one-electron promotions, $e \rightarrow g$ and $f \rightarrow h$, which are designated as $^1C \leftarrow {}^1A$ and $^1C_2 \leftarrow {}^1A$, respectively. For $\Delta n = 3$, three excitations are possible, $d \rightarrow g$, $e \rightarrow h$, and $f \rightarrow i$, designated as $^1D \leftarrow {}^1A$, $^1D_2 \leftarrow {}^1A$, and $^1D_3 \leftarrow {}^1A$, respectively. Evaluation of the associated energy follows directly from equation (11.3); for ^1C and $^1C_2$,

$$\Delta E = \frac{(k+1)^2h^2}{8ma^2} - \frac{(k-1)^2h^2}{8ma^2} = \frac{kh^2}{2ma^2} \quad (e \rightarrow g)$$

$$\Delta E = \frac{(k+2)^2h^2}{8ma^2} - \frac{k^2h^2}{8ma^2} = \frac{(k+1)h^2}{2ma^2} \quad (f \rightarrow h)$$

And for ^1D, $^1D_2$, and $^1D_3$:

$$\Delta E = \frac{(k+1)^2h^2}{8ma^2} - \frac{(k-2)^2h^2}{8ma^2} = \frac{3(2k-1)h^2}{8ma^2} \quad (d \rightarrow g)$$

$$\Delta E = \frac{(k+2)^2h^2}{8ma^2} - \frac{(k-1)^2h^2}{8ma^2} = \frac{3(2k+1)h^2}{8ma^2} \quad (e \rightarrow h)$$

$$\Delta E = \frac{(k+3)^2h^2}{8ma^2} - \frac{k^2h^2}{8ma^2} = \frac{3(2k+3)h^2}{8ma^2} \quad (f \rightarrow i)$$

It is readily seen that the ratio of the energies of the two C bands is $k:(k+1)$, and of the three D bands is $(2k-1):(2k+1):(2k+3)$, so

[3] J. R. Platt, *J. Opt. Soc. Am.*, **43**, 252 (1953).

that, in each type, excitation from the lowest orbital permitting the given Δn is at the longest wavelength; the other transitions seem to be considered only rarely.

A second utility of the FEM is that it provides a graphic method of representing MO wave functions. It has been shown that the values of free-electron method ψ's at the positions of the nuclei are exactly equal to the coefficients c_{jr} occurring in the molecular orbital ψ_j obtained by the lowest approximation in Hückel theory.[4] It has accordingly been suggested that free-electron method ψ's provide a graphic representation of the corresponding MO's; the representations of the five MO's for the pentadienyl (cation, radical, anion) are shown in Fig. 11.3. The FEM functions further, of necessity, possess the same symmetry properties as the MO's and will resemble them closely, even when the MO's are obtained in higher approximations. Considerable work has been done along the lines of providing a complete FEM methodology, analogous to the MO methodology;[5] since few spectroscopic applications, other than those discussed in this chapter and Chapter 13, have been published, the results of these investigations will not be discussed further.

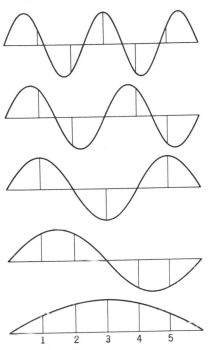

Fig. 11.3   The correspondence of FEM and MO wave functions for pentadienyl. [Reprinted by permission from H. H. Jaffé, *J. Chem. Phys.*, **20**, 1646 (1952).]

11.2   Cyanine Dyes, Polymethines, and Related Compounds

The application of equation (11.3) to the calculation of the long-wavelength transition in a conjugated system requires only a knowledge of a, since all the other quantities are known; indeed frequently the process is reversed and the computation of a proceeds from the experimental λ's of known compounds. In a carbon chain of conjugated double bonds, the

[4] H. H. Jaffé, *J. Chem. Phys.*, **20**, 1646 (1952); **21**, 1287 (1953).
[5] Cf. K. Rüdenberg, *J. Chem. Phys.*, **22**, 1878 (1954); N. S. Ham and K. Rüdenberg, *J. Chem. Phys.*, **29**, 1199 (1958), and references cited there.

C—C distance is certainly different between the double- and the single-bonded C atoms. From the resonance point of view this is immediately obvious from a consideration of the structures which make the principal contributions to the ground state:

$$CH_2\!\!=\!\!CH\!\!-\!\!CH\!\!=\!\!CH\!\!-\!\!CH\!\!=\!\!CH_2 \leftrightarrow \overset{+}{C}H_2\!\!-\!\!CH\!\!=\!\!CH\!\!-\!\!\overset{-}{C}H\!\!-\!\!CH\!\!=\!\!CH_2$$

The structure on the left makes the principal contribution; the distance between the vinyl groups is longer than the distance between the atoms connected by the double bond. A class of compounds in which this complication of alternating bond lengths is avoided is the cyanine dyes of the type:

$$R_2\overset{\oplus}{N}\!\!=\!\!CH\!\!-\!\!(CH\!\!=\!\!CH)_j\!\!-\!\!NR_2$$

which have been extensively studied by Kuhn.[1b] If we consider two of the principal resonance structures of a particular cyanine dye, for example,

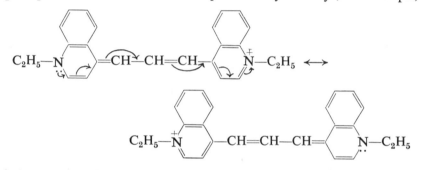

it is apparent that both structures are equivalent and therefore make equal contributions to the resonance hybrid; hence all C-C bond distances in the chain are equal. But this cyanine-dye system gives rise to two new difficulties. First, the fact that nitrogen is more electronegative than carbon conflicts with the simplifying assumption of the particle-in-the-box treatment, namely, that the potential energy in the well is a constant. Second, the calculation of a is complicated by the end benzenoid rings, which ought to be taken into account. Kuhn[1b] has made calculations, based on reasonable assumptions concerning the length of a, which agree rather well with observed values. However, the complications caused by the end benzenoid rings can be avoided by employing acyclic analogs of the cyanine dyes. Thus Simpson[1c] considered the following three compounds:

$$(Me)_2\overset{+}{N}\!\!=\!\!CH\!\!-\!\!(CH\!\!=\!\!CH)_r\!\!-\!\!\overset{..}{N}(Me)_2, \quad \text{where } r = 1, 2, \text{ and } 3$$

In applying equation (11.1) to this system it must be realized that the number of double bonds in the repeating unit is r but that the total number of π electrons is $2r + 4$, and hence in the ground state there are $r + 2$ occupied levels and in the excited state one electron each is in the $r + 2$ and $r + 3$ levels. Substitution in equation (11.1) gives:

$$\Delta E = \frac{(r + 3)^2 h^2}{8ma^2} - \frac{(r + 2)^2 h^2}{8ma^2} = \frac{(2r + 5)h^2}{8ma^2}$$

and from equation (11.3)

$$\lambda = \frac{8ma^2 c}{(2r + 5)h} \tag{11.5}$$

The appropriate value of a must still be chosen in order to make the calculations. The average length of the chromophore —(CH=CH)— is considered to be 2.48 A, and the additive term to allow for the lengths of

TABLE 11.1

Absorption Spectra of Cyanine Analogs[1c]

$$\overset{+}{Me_2N}{=}CH{-}(CH{=}CH)_r{-}NMe_2$$

	Wavelength, $m\mu$	
r	Calc.	Obs.
1	309	309
2	409	409
3	509	511

the bonds outside this group is 5.04 A. Accordingly, the value $(2.48r + 5.04)$ A is substituted for a in equation (11.5). The excellent agreement[1c] between observed and calculated wavelengths is shown in Table 11.1.

A monumental amount of work has been done by L. G. S. Brooker and his colleagues[6] on the synthesis of cyanine dyes and the study of the relationship between their colors and constitutions. A wide variety of heterocyclic nuclei have been employed as end groups in the cyanine dyes. The structures of some of these groups are:

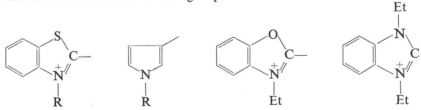

[6] For example, L. G. S. Brooker and coworkers, *J. Am. Chem. Soc.*, **67**, 1869, 1875, 1889 (1945); *Chem. Revs.*, **41**, 325 (1947).

and further variety is afforded by having the two end groups equal or different. In this general class of compounds, λ_{max} varies linearly with r, the number of vinyl groups interposed between the end N atoms.

11.3 Hydrocarbon Polyenes and Polyynes

Not a great deal of systematic spectral work has been done on the acyclic vinylogs of butadiene because until very recently these compounds were unavailable. However, the discovery that 1,5-enynes can be rearranged to conjugated polyenes[7] has provided the desired series, $H(CH=CH)_nH$, and ultraviolet data are now available for compounds up to and including

TABLE 11.2
Spectra of Conjugated Polyenes, $H(CH=CH)_nH$, in 2,2,4-Trimethylpentane

n	λ_{max}, mμ	ϵ_{max}
2^a	217	21,000
3	268	34,600
4^b	304	...
5	334	121,000
6	364	138,000
7	390	...
8	410	...
10	447	...

[a] In hexane.

[b] In cyclohexane; G. F. Woods and L. H. Schwartzman, *J. Am. Chem. Soc.*, **71**, 1396 (1949).

eicosadicaene ($n = 10$), with the exception of the compound where $n = 9$. The data for the long-wavelength band for known members of the series are given in Table 11.2.

As expected, the wavelength of absorption becomes progressively greater as the length of the conjugated chain is increased and the intensity also increases. The compounds in Table 11.2 were not stereochemically pure although the all-*trans* configuration probably predominates.

The most intense absorption would be expected from a polyene with *trans* configuration around each double bond and *s-trans* configuration around each single bond. The very intensive work of Zechmeister and his

[7] F. Sondheimer, D. A. Ben-Efraim, and R. Wolovsky, *J. Am. Chem. Soc.*, **83**, 1675 (1961).

colleagues in the carotenoid field has shown[8] that the intensity is very dependent on the stereochemical configuration. This phenomenon will be elaborated upon in Chapter 15, but at this point strict comparisons cannot be made without detailed knowledge of the exact stereochemistry of the polyenes.

It is apparent from Table 11.2 that the longest-wavelength absorption of linear polyenes does not continuously increase, as predicted by free-electron theory, but rather appears to approach a single maximum value. Calculations taking account of the known alternation of bond lengths in an infinite linear polyene,[9] by a periodic variation of the potential in the box of the FEM,[10] or by assignment of alternating slightly different resonance integrals in MO theory,[11] are capable of predicting this behavior.

11.31 PHENYLPOLYENES.   In contrast to the lack of a series of strictly comparable compounds in the acyclic polyenes, there are extensive series

TABLE 11.3

Spectra of α,ω-Diphenylpolyenes,
Ph(—CH=CH —)$_n$Ph, in Benzene

		λ_{max}, mμ			$\epsilon_{max} \times 10^{-3}$
n	$\lambda^2 \times 10^{-4}$	Obs.[12]	Calc.[15]	Calc.[14]	Obs.[12]
1	9	306	305	310	24
2	10.9	334	335	334	40
3	12.6	358	360	358	75
4	14.8	384	382.5	380	86
5	16.1	403	402	400	94
6	17.6	420	420	420	113
7	18.9	435	435.5	438	135

of conjugated polyenes terminated by phenyl groups in which configuration is known. One of the earliest complete series for which data became available[12] was the all-*trans*-α,ω-diphenylpolyenes shown in Table 11.3. In this series of substituted polyenes it is expected that λ_{max} and ϵ_{max} increase with increased length of the conjugated chain. From a comparison of the values of λ_{max} in Tables 11.2 and 11.3, it appears that each phenyl

    [8] L. Zechmeister, *Chem. Revs.*, **34**, 267 (1944); *Fortsch. Chem. org. Naturstoffe*, **18**, 221 (1960).
    [9] H. C. Longuet-Higgins and L. Salem, *Proc. Roy. Soc.* (*London*), **A251**, 172 (1959).
    [10] H. Kuhn, *J. Chem. Phys.*, **17**, 1198 (1949).
    [11] M. J. S. Dewar, *J. Chem. Soc.*, 3544 (1952).
    [12] K. W. Hausser, R. Kuhn, and A. Smakula, *Z. physik. chem.*, **B29**, 384 (1935).

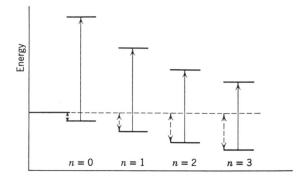

Fig. 11.4 The energy of ground and excited states of α,ω-diphenylpolyenes as a function of the number of vinyl groups. [Reprinted by permission from A. Maccoll, *Quart. Revs. (London)*, **1**, 16 (1947).]

group of the diphenylpolyene is equivalent to about $1\frac{1}{2}$ double bonds with respect to λ_{max}. From the resonance point of view, the many more charged structures that are possible as conjugation increases contribute toward stabilization of the excited state more than such structures contribute toward stabilization of the ground state. Accordingly, the energy difference between states decreases with increasing conjugation, although the decrease (Fig. 11.4) is not as rapid as it is in the case of the cyanine dyes.[13]

In the α,ω-diphenylpolyenes the variation of λ_{max} with increasing number of vinyl groups, n, is expressed by the linear relation:[14]

$$(\lambda_{max})^2 = A + Bn \tag{11.6}$$

A plot of this relation is shown in Fig. 11.5. Values of λ calculated from equation (11.6) are compared with observed values in Table 11.3. Agreement can be improved slightly by a modification[15] of the equation to the form

$$(\lambda_{max})^2 = A - BC^n$$

where, in benzene solution, the appropriate constants are

$$(\lambda_{max})^2 = (38.08 - 30.81 \times 0.934^n) \times 10^4 \text{ m}\mu^2$$

Good correlation between molar absorptivity and the number of double bonds in the diphenylpolyene series has been observed.[12] When all the bonds in the phenylpolyene are *trans*, a plot of ϵ against n, the number of double bonds in the system, gives a straight line, Fig. 11.6a.

[13] A. Maccoll, *Quart. Revs. (London)*, **1**, 16 (1947).
[14] G. N. Lewis and M. Calvin, *Chem. Revs.*, **25**, 273 (1939).
[15] K. Hirayama, *J. Am. Chem. Soc.*, **77**, 373, 379, 383 (1955).

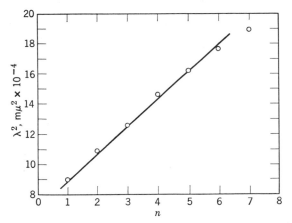

Fig. 11.5 The relation of λ^2 to the number of vinyl groups in α,ω-diphenylpolyenes, Ph(CH=CH)-Ph.

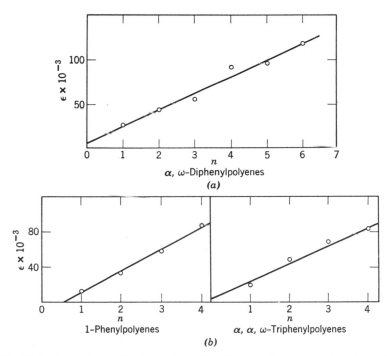

Fig. 11.6 Intensity as a function of number of double bonds in various *trans*-phenyl-polyene series. [Reprinted by permission from: (*a*) K. W. Hausser, R. Kuhn, and A. Smakula, *Z. physik. chem.*, **B29,** 384 (1935); (*b*) H. M. Walborsky and J. F. Pendleton, *J. Am. Chem. Soc.*, **82,** 1405 (1960).]

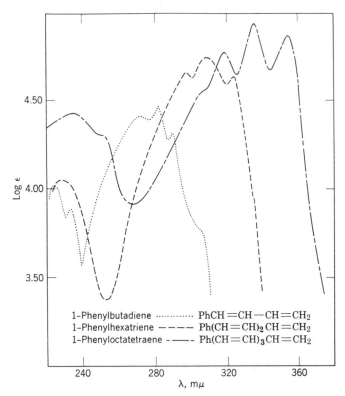

Fig. 11.7 The spectra of three 1-phenylpolyenes. [Reprinted by permission from H. M. Walborsky and J. F. Pendleton, *J. Am. Chem. Soc.*, **82**, 1405 (1960).]

A series of α-phenyl- and α,α,ω-triphenylpolyenes has become available by a novel synthetic procedure.[16] The compounds belong to the all-*trans* series. The spectra of three of the α-phenylpolyenes, shown in Fig. 11.7, have three well-defined peaks which are considered characteristic of the all-*trans* configuration, and ϵ_{max}, as well as λ_{max}, increases with length of conjugation. A plot of ϵ_{max} against the number of double bonds again gives a straight-line relationship; a similar straight-line relationship exists in the α,α,ω-triphenylpolyene series,[16] Fig. 11.6b.

The preceding discussion has focused only on the longest-wavelength band, to be identified with the $^{1}B \leftarrow {}^{1}A$ transition. All polyenes have additional bands at shorter wavelength. In butadiene, these occur in the vacuum ultraviolet, but they shift to longer wavelengths with increasing chain length, as predicted by the FEM. According to the theory developed

[16] H. M. Walborsky and J. F. Pendleton, *J. Am. Chem. Soc.*, **82**, 1405 (1960).

in section 11.1, a series of bands $^1C \leftarrow {}^1A$, $^1D \leftarrow {}^1A$, etc., should occur. However, the all-*trans* compounds have a center of symmetry, and the A, C, etc., states are gerade, the B, D, etc., states ungerade. Since $g \rightarrow g$ transitions are forbidden, $g \rightarrow u$ transitions allowed, the ^1C bands should be of low intensity, the ^1D bands of higher intensity, and this intensity alternation is observed. Furthermore, the center of symmetry is destroyed when one bond becomes *cis*, and consequently the ^1C band should increase in intensity; at the same time, the allowed ^1B and ^1D bands should decrease in intensity.[17] These predictions have been well established by Zechmeister and coworkers.[18] The intensification of the ^1C band has led to the name *cis* band, suggested by Zechmeister.[8]

A beautiful illustration of the development of the *cis* band is shown in Fig. 11.8, where the spectra of three stereoisomeric β-carotenes are compared. When all eleven double bonds are in the *trans* relationship, the

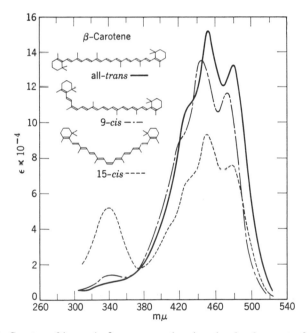

Fig. 11.8 Spectra of isomeric β-carotenes, showing the development of the *cis* band.

[17] N. S. Bayliss, *J. Chem. Phys.*, **16**, 287 (1948); *Quart. Revs. (London)*, **6**, 319 (1952); H. Kuhn, *J. Chem. Phys.*, **16**, 840 (1948); W. T. Simpson, *J. Chem. Phys.*, **16**, 1124 (1948).

[18] (*a*) L. Zechmeister and A. Polgar, *J. Am. Chem. Soc.*, **65**, 1522 (1943); A. Sandoval and L. Zechmeister, *J. Am. Chem. Soc.*, **69**, 553 (1947). (*b*) J. H. Pinckard, B. Wille, and H. Zechmeister, *J. Am. Chem. Soc.*, **70**, 1938 (1948).

$^1B \leftarrow {}^1A$ band is very intense. When the penultimate double bond is *cis*, as in the 9-*cis* isomer, the intensity of the $^1B \leftarrow {}^1A$ band decreases, and a weak *cis* band $^1C \leftarrow {}^1A$, appears at 340 mμ. The isomer containing a *cis* double bond in the middle of the molecule, resulting in a maximum bending of the molecule, shows a spectrum with a well-developed *cis* band and the lowest-intensity $^1B \leftarrow {}^1A$ band. The intensity of the *cis* peaks is related to the location of the *cis* bond; the more centrally located the *cis* bond, the more intense the *cis* band. When two appropriately placed bonds have *cis* conformation, the center of symmetry may be restored, and the ^1C band again has low intensity.

An alternate distinction between *cis-trans* isomers in the diphenylpoly-enes is found in the structure of the $^1B \leftarrow {}^1A$ transition. In the all-*trans* compounds, this band shows vibrational structure, with three separate

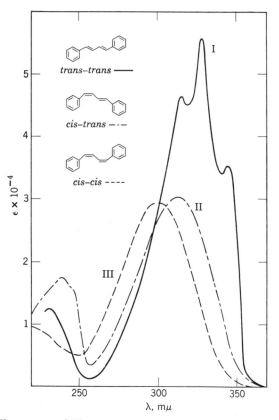

Fig. 11.9 The spectra of (*I*) *trans-trans*-, (*II*) *cis-trans*, and (*III*) *cis-cis*-1,4-diphenyl butadiene. [Reprinted by permission from J. H. Pinckard, B. Willie, and H. Zechmeister, *J. Am. Chem. Soc.*, **70**, 1938 (1948).]

maxima in evidence (see Fig. 11.7). That this vibrational structure is characteristic of the all-*trans* compound is seen from Fig. 11.9, where the spectra of the three isomers of 1,4-diphenylbutadiene, the *trans-trans*, I, *trans-cis*, II, and *cis-cis*, III, are compared.[18b] The all-*trans* compound is characterized by the highest ϵ value. The ϵ values are frequently used as a criterion of stereochemical configuration.

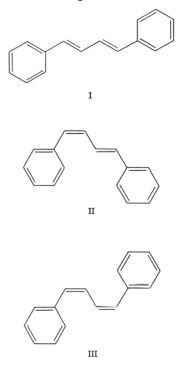

I

II

III

11.4   Polyene Aldehydes, $R—(CH{=}CH)_n—CHO$, Acids, and Ketones

Several studies of a series of compounds of the general formula

$R—(CH{=}CH)_n—CHO$, where $R = Me,$ ⌐⌐⌐—, and $C_6H_5—$ and $n = 1–7$,

have been made. In the aliphatic series, data are available[19] for Me and $n = 1–7$. The spectra of these compounds are characterized by a single intense absorption band. In the lowest member of the series, crotonaldehyde, there is the low-intensity, long-wavelength $n \rightarrow \pi^*$ band, but with

[19] (*a*) For $n = 1–3$, see K. W. Hausser, R. Kuhn, A. Smakula, and M. Hoffer, *Z. physik. Chem.*, **29B**, 371 (1935); K. W. Hausser, R. Kuhn, A. Smakula, and A. Deutsch, *Z. physik. Chem.*, **29B**, 378 (1935). (*b*) For $n = 1–7$ see E. R. Blout and M. Fields, *J. Am. Chem. Soc.*, **70**, 189 (1948).

increasing length of the conjugated system this band is overrun and swamped by the high-intensity band. In the higher members of the series, a second strong band, less intense than the main high-intensity band, develops at shorter wavelengths. The highest-intensity band is shifted to longer wavelengths, and its intensity decreases somewhat on passing from hexane to alcohol as solvent. No evidence of the fine structure typical of the polyene hydrocarbons that have the *trans* configuration appears in the spectra of the polyene aldehydes. Data for the long-wavelength, high-intensity band are given in Table 11.4.

TABLE 11.4

Spectra of Polyene Aldehydes, Me—(CH=CH)$_n$—CHO (Dioxan),[19b] and Acids, Me—(CH=CH)$_n$—CO$_2$H (Alcohol)[19a]

	Aldehydes		Acids	
n	λ_{max}, mμ	ϵ_{max}	λ_{max}, mμ	ϵ_{max}
1	220^a	15,000	204	11,700
2	270	27,000	254	24,800
3	312	40,000	294	36,500
4	343	40,000	327	48,700
5	370	57,000	. . .	. . .
6	393	65,000	. . .	. . .
7	415	63,000	. . .	. . .

^{a} Ethanol as solvent.

The data for the polyene acids with $n = 1$–4 are also shown in Table 11.4. The absorption spectra again consist of a single absorption band, having high intensity and showing no fine structure, which moves toward the red with increasing chain length. For corresponding values of n, the acids absorb at shorter wavelength than the aldehydes. The simple α,β-unsaturated acids also absorb at shorter wavelength than the corresponding aldehydes (cf. section 10.5) because the aldehyde group conjugates with the double bond much more effectively than does the carboxyl group.

Extensive spectral data are also available for the 2-furylpolyene aldehydes,[19b] ⟨furan⟩—(CH=CH)$_n$CHO, and the corresponding acids.[20] These data, given in Table 11.5, show the expected difference between aldehydes

[20] R. W. Hausser and A. Smakula, *Angew. Chem.*, **47**, 657 (1934); **48**, 152 (1935).

and acids. They indicate that the furyl group may be considered as equivalent to two double bonds. This is indicated by the fact that the wavelengths of the furylpolyene aldehydes are virtually identical with those of the ω-methylpolyene aldehydes with two more vinyl groups; this relation is shown in the last column of Table 11.5. The relation is not as good for the carboxylic acids. However, as might have been anticipated

TABLE 11.5

Spectra of 2-Furylpolyene Aldehydes and Acids

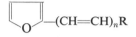

λ_{max}, mμ

n	$R = CO_2H^a$	$Me(CH\!=\!CH)_{n+2}CO_2H^b$	$R = CHO^c$	$Me(CH\!=\!CH)_{n+2}CHO^b$
0	254	254	270	270
1	306	294	312	312
2	337	327	346	343
3	357	...	366	370
4	...	...	389	393
5	...	...	412	415
6	...	...	429	...

[a] Solvent: hexane, reference in footnote 20.
[b] Solvent: alcohol, references in footnote 19a.
[c] Solvent: dioxan, reference in footnote 19b.

(cf. section 10.1), ϵ_{max} is much less for the cyclic compound (15,000 for 2-furanecarboxaldehyde) than for the corresponding acyclic one (27,000 for 2,4-hexadienal), in agreement with the above generalization that the all-*trans* compound has the highest intensity.

Equation (11.6) holds for the polyene and furylpolyene aldehydes and acids,[21] and plots of λ^2 versus n for these series are shown in Fig. 11.10. It is particularly interesting to note that all the lines are virtually parallel.

The final polyene series of compounds to be discussed is vinylogous aldehydes and ketones of the general formula $Ph(CH\!=\!CH)_nCHO$ and $Ph(CH\!=\!CH)_nCOPh$. Spectral data for these compounds[22] are given in Table 11.6.

[21] L. N. Ferguson, *Electron Structure of Organic Molecules*, Prentice-Hall, Englewood Cliffs, N.J., 1952, p. 284.
[22] J. F. Thomas and G. Branch, *J. Am. Chem. Soc.*, **75**, 4793 (1953).

The aldehyde series from $n = 0$ to $n = 5$ gives excellent agreement with the relationship

$$(\lambda_{max})^2 = 5.94 \times 10^4 + (2.18 \times 10^4)n \ m\mu^2$$

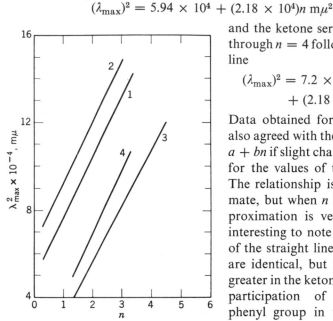

Fig. 11.10   Plot of λ^2_{max} versus the number of ethylenic bonds, n, for some polyenes.

1. ![cyclic structure]—$(CH{=}CH)_n CO_2 H$.

2. ![cyclic structure]—$(CH{=}CH)_n CHO$.

3. $Me(CH{=}CH)_n CO_2 H$.
4. $Me(CH{=}CH)_n CHO$. (Reprinted by permission from L. N. Ferguson, *Electronic Structure of Organic Molecules*, Prentice-Hall, Englewood Cliffs, N.J., 1959.)

and the ketone series from $n = 1$ through $n = 4$ follows the straight line

$$(\lambda_{max})^2 = 7.2 \times 10^4$$
$$+ (2.18 \times 10^4)n \ m\mu^2$$

Data obtained for other solvents also agreed with the equation $\lambda^2 = a + bn$ if slight changes were made for the values of the constant a. The relationship is only approximate, but when n is small the approximation is very good. It is interesting to note that the slopes of the straight lines in each series are identical, but the intercept is greater in the ketones, showing the participation of the terminal phenyl group in the conjugated system.

It was pointed out in section 5.3 that the theoretical interpretation of the spectrum of acetylene is quite complicated and has not been completely and satisfactorily resolved. Acetylene has a strong absorption band below 150 mμ in the far ultraviolet, which is probably due only in part to Rydberg transitions. A well-defined band occurs at λ_{max} of 172.5 mμ, which is of quite low intensity. In the conjugated polyynes, there are two main series of bands: a long-wavelength, rather low-intensity band and a shorter-wavelength band of extremely high intensity and considerable vibrational structure. The latter band is characteristic of all polyynes and, as expected, moves to the red with increasing chain length. Spectral data for a series of acyclic conjugated polyynes are shown in Table 11.7, where only the position and ϵ value of the highest vibrational peak of each band are given. In the lower-intensity bands there are usually four sharp vibrational

TABLE 11.6

Absorption Maxima of $Ph(CH{=}CH)_nR$ Series in Methanol[21]

	R = CHO		R = COPh	
n	λ_{max}, mμ	$\epsilon \times 10^{-4}$	λ_{max}, mμ	$\epsilon \times 10^{-4}$
0	244	1.2	254	2.0
1	285	2.5	305	2.5
2	323	4.3	342	3.9
3	355	5.4	373	4.6
4	382	5.1	400	6.0
5	408	...	418	6.6
6	425	...	430	...

subbands; in the high-intensity bands, after $n = 4$, there are also four sharp subbands. The spectra of the polyacetylenes are characterized by remarkably high intensity.

The spectra of a series of diphenylpolyynes have also been determined.[23] These spectra are much more complex than those of the corresponding

TABLE 11.7

Spectra of Conjugated Polyynes, $Me{-}(C{\equiv}C)_n{-}Me$, in Ethanol

	High Intensity		Low Intensity	
n	λ, mμ	$\epsilon \times 10^{-3}$	λ_{max}, mμ	ϵ
1^a	177.5	107	222.5	160
2^b	...	...	226.5	360
3^c	207	135	268.0	200
4^d	234.0	281	306.0	180
5^e	260.5	352	324.5	230
6^e	284.0	445	340.0	1000

^{a} In heptane.
^{b} J. B. Armitage, C. L. Cook, N. Entwistle, E. R. H. Jones, and M. C. Whiting, *J. Chem. Soc.*, 1998 (1952).
^{c} J. B. Armitage, C. L., Cook, E. R. H. Jones, and M. C. Whiting, *J. Chem. Soc.* 2010 (1952).
^{d} J. B. Armitage, E. R. H. Jones, and M. C. Whiting, *J. Chem. Soc.*, 2014 (1952).
^{e} C. L. Cook, E. R. H. Jones, and M. C. Whiting, *J. Chem. Soc.*, 2883 (1952).

[23] H. H. Schlubach and V. Franzen, *Ann.*, **573**, 110 (1951).

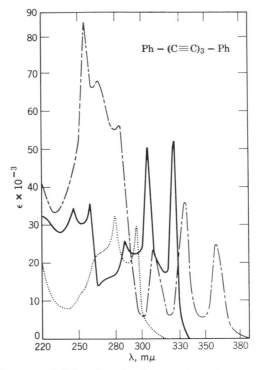

Fig. 11.11 Spectrum of diphenylacetylenes; $n = 1$ ($\cdots$), $n = 2$ (——), $n = 3$ (—·—).
[Reprinted by permission from F. Bohlmann, *Chem. Ber.*, **84**, 545, 785 (1951).]

α,ω-diphenylpolyenes, especially because of the vibrational structure of the very high-intensity, short-wavelength bands in the acetylene series. The spectrum of diphenyltriacetylene[24] is shown in Fig. 11.11. Intensity calculations on the basis of the molecular dimensions[25] of the polyacetylenes agree quite well with observed values.

11.5   Cumulenes

The cumulenes are the compounds belonging to the allene series, i.e., compounds in which all the carbon atoms are attached to each other by double bonds. The first member of the series is allene, $CH_2{=}C{=}CH_2$. The spectra of the compounds in this series change with cumulation in a manner similar to the lengthening of diene chains, but data for the cumulene series are not very extensive. The general resemblance to dienes may

[24] F. Bohlmann, *Chem. Ber.*, **84**, 545, 785 (1951).
[25] E. A. Braude, *J. Chem. Soc.*, 379 (1950); R. Kuhn and K. Wallenfels, *Ber.*, **71**, 783, 1510 (1938).

be due to the similarity in resonance structures which stabilize both ground and excited states of cumulenes, e.g.,

$$CH_2{=}C{=}C{=}C{=}CH_2 \leftrightarrow$$

$$\overset{\cdot\cdot}{C}H_2{-}C{\equiv}C{-}\overset{\overline{}}{C}{=}CH_2 \leftrightarrow \overset{\overline{}}{C}H_2{-}C{\equiv}C{-}\overset{+}{C}{=}CH_2, \text{ etc.}$$

The spectrum of butatriene,[26] $CH_2{=}C{=}C{=}CH_2$, has λ_{max} at 241 mμ and $\epsilon_{max} = 20,300$; whereas the comparable values for butadiene, which might be assumed to have the same chromophore length, are 217 mμ and 21,000, and for 1,3,5-hexatriene[27] with the same number of double bonds, λ_{max} is 256 mμ, $\epsilon = 22,400$. Data for the phenylcumulenes[28] also can be compared with those for the phenylpolyenes. In general, values for λ_{max} and ϵ_{max} are higher in the cumulenes than in the dienes.

[26] W. M. Schubert, T. H. Liddicoet, and W. A. Lanka, *J. Am. Chem. Soc.*, **74**, 569 (1952).

[27] D. R. Howton, *J. Org. Chem.*, **14**, 1 (1949).

[28] R. Kuhn and G. Platzer, *Ber.*, **73B**, 1410 (1940); R. Kuhn and J. Jahn, *Ber.*, **86B**, 759 (1953).

12 Benzene and its derivatives

12.1 Benzene and Spectral-Band Nomenclature

In benzene, each carbon atom is joined by two other carbon atoms and a hydrogen atom by σ bonds involving the three sp^2 hybrid orbitals of trigonal carbon. Each carbon atom has a $p\pi$ orbital available for MO formation; and, since a total of six $p\pi$ orbitals is available, six MO's are possible. The energy-level diagram of these MO's is shown in Fig. 12.1a. The dotted lines on the hexagons indicate the nodal planes of the MO's; these MO's were depicted in Fig. 5.5. The orbitals π_2 and π_3 are degenerate. Each wave function of a degenerate pair is distinct and independent, but both have the same energy and the same number of nodal planes, although the orientation of these planes is different. Since six $p\pi$

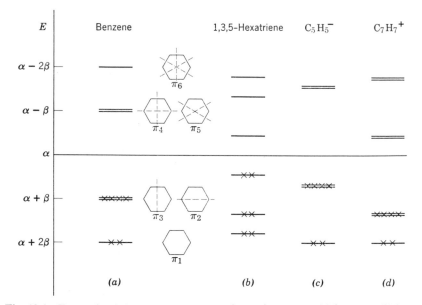

Fig. 12.1 Energy levels in the 6π electron conjugated systems: (a) benzene, (b) hexatriene, (c) cyclopentadienide ion, and (d) tropylium ion.

electrons are available, the configuration of the ground state of benzene is $\pi_1^2\pi_2^2\pi_3^2$ or $a_{2u}^2 e_{1g}^4$. Figure 12.1*a* shows that the two next higher (unoccupied) orbitals are also a degenerate pair. Each has one more nodal plane than the highest occupied orbitals, and they are antibonding. The electronic configurations and the symmetry types of the excited states were discussed fully in section 5.5. The three principal transitions are the symmetry-forbidden $^1B_{2u} \leftarrow ^1A_{1g}$ transition, giving rise to the long-wavelength band centered around 256 mμ; the forbidden $^1B_{1u} \leftarrow ^1A_{1g}$ transition, which is thought to be responsible for the band at about 200 mμ; and the allowed $^1E_{1u} \leftarrow ^1A_{1g}$ transition, associated with the far ultraviolet band at 180 mμ. The term diagram is given in Fig. 12.2, and the solution spectrum is shown in Fig. 12.3*a*; the vapor spectrum in 12.3*b*.

The group of medium-intensity bands between 230 and 260 mμ with maximum intensity at 256 mμ cannot be classified as either a K or an R band in the nomenclature scheme of Buroway (cf. section 9.7), and has been called the benzenoid fine-structure band, or B band. The Buroway notation can then be employed to describe the spectral characteristics of benzene and its derivatives, in which band assignments are made in accordance with the characteristic intensities:

$$R \text{ bands,} \quad \epsilon = 10\text{--}100$$

$$B \text{ bands,} \quad \epsilon = 250\text{--}3000$$

$$K \text{ bands,} \quad \epsilon = >10{,}000$$

This nomenclature is largely of historical value; although encountered frequently in the literature, it has little theoretical justification and will not in general be employed in the discussions which follow.

An extensive correlation of the spectra of benzene derivatives has been made by Doub and Vandenbelt.[1] In their thorough and valuable series of papers, these authors proposed a nomenclature which has gained considerable acceptance. The short-wavelength, high-intensity band of benzene at 200 mμ, resulting from the $^1B_{1u} \leftarrow ^1A_{1g}$ transition, is called the *primary band*, and the long-wavelength, lower-intensity band (B band) is called the *secondary band*. Appropriately substituted benzenes give rise to spectra in which displacement of all the benzene bands occurs, and frequently the 180 mμ band arising from the $^1E_{1u} \leftarrow ^1A_{1g}$ transition is shifted to the quartz ultraviolet, in which case this high-intensity band is called the *second primary band*.

[1] (*a*) L. Doub and J. M. Vandenbelt, *J. Am. Chem. Soc.*, **69**, 2714 (1947). (*b*) L. Doub and J. M. Vandenbelt, *J. Am. Chem. Soc.*, **71**, 2414 (1949).

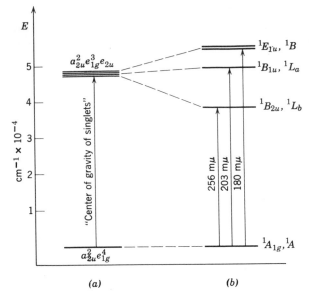

Fig. 12.2 Term-level diagram for benzene (a) neglecting and (b) including electron correlation.

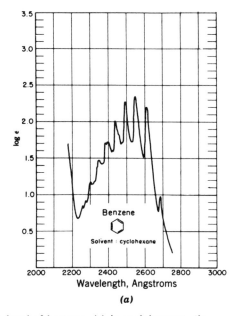

Fig. 12.3 The ^1L_b band of benzene, (a) in cyclohexane; (b) as vapor. (Reprinted by permission from R. A. Friedel and M. Orchin, *Ultraviolet Spectra of Aromatic Compounds*, John Wiley and Sons, New York, 1951.)

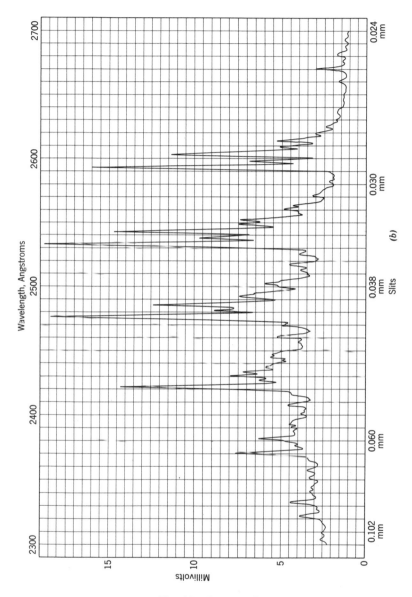

Fig. 12.3 (*continued*)

A method of systematic nomenclature for the various states[2] and transitions of benzene and of polycyclic aromatic compounds has been designed by Platt.[3] This system, which is based on the free-electron model (see sections 11.1 and 14.1), will be discussed in detail in connection with polycyclic compounds in section 13.2. Since it is applicable to benzene and serves to relate the benzene spectrum to the spectra of the other aromatic hydrocarbons, it should be noted here that the $^1B_{2u} \leftarrow {}^1A_{1g}$ transition at 256 mμ is denoted by $^1L_b \leftarrow {}^1A$ in this system, the $^1B_{1u} \leftarrow {}^1A_{1g}$ transition at 203 mμ by $^1L_a \leftarrow {}^1A$, and the $^1E_{1u} \leftarrow {}^1A_{1g}$ transition by $^1B \leftarrow {}^1A$; in the last, no subscript a or b is appropriate, since the two B states (cf. section 13.2) are degenerate and together constitute the E_{1u} state.

It is of considerable interest to compare the spectrum of benzene with that of its acyclic iso-π-electronic analog, 1,3,5-hexatriene. According to the MO method of pooling electrons and feeding them into MO's in accordance with the Aufbau principle, the six π electrons in each system are fed into MO's extending over the whole carbon skeleton. The relative energies of the hexatriene MO's are shown in Fig. 12.1b. Although valuable conclusions may be drawn from the MO representation, the essential difference between benzene and hexatriene in the ground state is more conveniently illustrated in terms of the valence-bond method. In this scheme, benzene can best be represented in the ground state by the two equivalent Kekulé structures, which contribute most to the resonance hybrid. In hexatriene, however, only one covalent resonance structure without long bonds can be written. In benzene, all the bonds and bond distances are equal. On the other hand, conjugation between acyclic double bonds is very much less than between conjugated double bonds in a ring.[4] The resonance energy of hexatriene is thus considerably less than that of benzene, and the physical and chemical properties of the two compounds are vastly different.

The six π electrons in a ring are recognized as conferring special "aromatic" properties on the ring; not only do they give this aromatic

---

[2] Although in much of this book, one-electron functions are used and consequently transitions are frequently described as occurring between configurations, this practice is not practical for benzene and its derivatives. Because of its high symmetry, a particular configuration in benzene usually gives rise to several states; hence state notation is essential. Actually, the three main bands of benzene, with upper states $^1B_{1u}$, $^1B_{2u}$, and $^1E_{1u}$, all arise out of a transition between the same configurations:

$$(a_{1u})^2(e_{1g})^4 \rightarrow (a_{1u})^2(e_{1g})^3 e_{2u}$$

[3] J. R. Platt, *J. Chem. Phys.*, **17**, 484 (1949).

[4] For a recent discussion of this topic, see C. A. Coulson, *Chemical Society Symposia, Bristol* 1950, *Special Publication* 12, *Developments in Aromatic Chemistry*; M. J. S. Dewar and H. N. Schmeising, *Tetrahedron*, **5**, 166 (1959).

stability to benzene and certain of its isosteres, such as pyridine, but also the unusual properties and stability of the cyclopentadienyl anion, $C_5H_5^-$, and the cycloheptatrienyl (tropylium) cation, $C_7H_7^+$, are attributed to their benzene iso-π-electronic structure. The MO energy levels for these systems are shown in Figs. 12.1c and d. The relationship between $C_5H_5^-$, $C_7H_7^+$, and C_6H_6 is apparent. The general pattern consists of a low-level MO which accommodates two electrons, followed by a higher-energy degenerate pair which accommodates four electrons. This pattern is characteristic of all aromatic systems, the homologous series differing by the number of pairs of degenerate levels. The stable number of electrons for all aromatic systems is thus $4n + 2$, where n is an integer; in the three aromatic systems in Fig. 12.1, $n = 1$. Although all aromatic systems have $4n + 2$ electrons, the Hückel rule, this number of electrons is not the sole criterion for aromatic character. The notation of Platt referred to above and discussed in detail in section 13.2 is based in part on this $4n + 2$ sequence.

12.2   Monosubstituted Benzenes

12.21 GENERAL.   Benzene is a highly symmetrical compound, of point group D_{6h}. Of all the substituted benzenes, only those hexasubstituted with six identical, highly symmetrical substituents belong to the same point group. However, for spectroscopic purposes we are interested not so much in the whole molecule and its point group, but rather in the symmetry properties of the wave functions involved in the spectra. Thus, although hexamethyl- or hexaethylbenzene may, depending on the relative orientations of the alkyl groups, belong to any one of a number of point groups, the π-electron system does, to a very good approximation, retain the D_{6h} symmetry. 1,3,5-Trisubstituted derivatives, $C_6H_3R_3$, also have quite high symmetry, D_{3h} if the R are again taken as atoms or pseudoatoms. para-Disubstituted derivatives $C_6H_4R_2$ belong to D_{2h}, while most other substituted derivatives of benzene belong to the relatively lower point groups C_s and C_{2v}.

In spite of these large changes in symmetry the spectroscopic behavior of substituted benzenes is largely uniform and greatly resembles that of the parent compound. Thus in benzenes substituted by auxochromes, we can usually find the 256 mμ band ($^1B_{2u} \leftarrow {}^1A_{1g}$, $^1L_b \leftarrow {}^1A$) of the parent compound with its characteristic vibrational structure (cf. Fig. 6.6), and the two shorter-wavelength bands (at 203.5 and 185 mμ in benzene). These bands are of course shifted by the substitution.

Thus substitution in benzene does not usually produce great changes or new bands in the spectra, but only modifies the spectrum of the parent compound. It is thus convenient to describe the effect of substitution as a perturbation. The spectrum of benzene is said to be perturbed by the introduction of substituents, the more so the greater the resonance interaction.

One complication arises when comparisons are made between the spectrum of benzene and the spectra of some of its derivatives, particularly when such comparisons are made in terms of λ_{max} values, as is the custom. Since the $^1B_{2u} \leftarrow {}^1A_{1g}$, $^1L_b \leftarrow {}^1A$ transition in benzene is forbidden and is observed only because of vibrational interaction, the $0 \rightarrow 0$ transition is not observed. In the case of substituted compounds the corresponding band is no longer strictly forbidden, and a rather different distribution of intensity among the vibrational levels may be expected; e.g., the $0 \rightarrow 0$ transitions will be observed. Such changed distribution may shift the relative position of λ_{max} within the band system; however, these effects do not appear to be serious.

12.22 SUBSTITUENTS WITH LONE-PAIR ELECTRONS. When a group is attached to benzene through an atom having a lone pair of electrons, such as N, O, or S, the substituent perturbs the ring by both the resonance and the inductive effects. The inductive effect, just as in the case of ethylene (cf. section 9.3 and Fig. 9.2), affects the ground and excited states about equally and in the same direction, and so the inductive effect of the substituent produces little change in the position or intensity of the benzene bands. This is best illustrated by the fact that anilinium salts have spectra virtually superimposable on the benzene spectrum. However, an atom with a lone pair of electrons can donate these electrons to the ring, and this delocalization (resonance) does shift the position of the benzene bands. As will be shown later, the 203 mμ high-intensity or primary band, $^1L_a \leftarrow {}^1A$, as well as the low-intensity, secondary band $^1L_b \leftarrow {}^1A$, is shifted to the red, both by about equal amounts. Much of the quantitative work has been concerned with the shift produced in the secondary band centered at about 260 mμ, which not only is shifted to longer wavelength by substitution but also is intensified.

The lone-pair electrons on the substituent atom interact most effectively with the π electrons of benzene when the orbital containing the lone pair is parallel to the π orbitals of benzene. This condition is always fulfilled with substituents such as the halogens, which are monatomic. With larger substituents contributing a single lone pair, such as NR_2 and OR, however, coplanarity of the substituent group with the benzene ring is required for this purpose. If for any (steric) reason the substituent group is twisted out of the plane of the ring, the interaction of the lone-pair π orbital with the π orbitals of benzene is reduced, and the spectrum is affected accordingly. Such situations will be discussed in detail in Chapter 15.

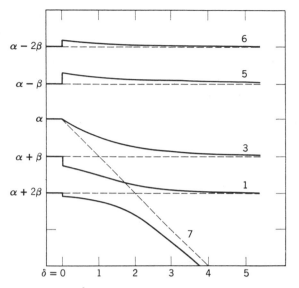

Fig. 12.4 Energy levels of a monosubstituted benzene as a function of δ. (Reprinted by permission from F. A. Matsen, in Vol. IX of *Technique of Organic Chemistry*, edited by A. Weissberger, Interscience Publishers, New York, 1956.)

When the lone-pair electrons of a substituent participate in ring conjugation, these electrons, added to the aromatic sextet, give a total of eight electrons and seven MO's in the substituted benzene. The new (occupied) MO which is established through participation of the AO of the lone-pair atom may be referred to as π_7. The ground-state configuration is then $\pi_7{}^2\pi_1{}^2\pi_2{}^2\pi_3{}^2$. Reference to the shape of the MO's of benzene (Fig. 5.5) shows that π_2 and π_4 have nodal planes through carbon atoms 1 and 4, and hence substitution at position 1 does not affect the energy of either of these orbitals. The remaining five orbitals are affected by the nature of the substituent and in particular by its electronegativity, which is commonly expressed[5] by a parameter δ and measured using the resonance integral β between two ring carbon atoms as the unit of energy. The effect[6] on the energy levels of the five affected MO's as a function of δ is shown in Fig. 12.4. The dotted lines indicate the energies of the original benzene and substituent orbitals, and the solid lines show these levels after the resonance interaction.

The identification of the longest-wavelength absorption in terms of

[5] G. W. Wheland and L. Pauling, *J. Am. Chem. Soc.*, **57**, 2086 (1935).

[6] (a) F. A. Matsen, *J. Am. Chem. Soc.*, **72**, 5243 (1950). (b) F. A. Matsen, in *Chemical Applications of Spectroscopy*, Vol. IX of *Technique of Organic Chemistry*, edited by A. Weissberger, Interscience Publishers, New York, 1956, pp. 672–673.

one-electron energy levels is not straightforward. For benzene, we can write four possible transitions, $\pi_2 \rightarrow \pi_4{}^*$, $\pi_2 \rightarrow \pi_5{}^*$, $\pi_3 \rightarrow \pi_4{}^*$, and $\pi_3 \rightarrow \pi_5{}^*$, all of which should occur at the same wavelength, but are split owing to electron correlation (cf. Fig. 12.2). In the substituted benzene, the degeneracy is removed, and we might expect the transition $\pi_3 \rightarrow \pi_4{}^*$ to be the one of lowest energy (cf. Fig. 12.4). However, as long as we are dealing with a relatively small perturbation, electron correlation and configuration interaction (the four excited states belong, in pairs, to two symmetry species, and since they have comparable energy, configuration interaction probably is quite important) will appreciably affect the states. Fortunately, it is immaterial for the qualitative result whether we consider the transition $\pi_3 \rightarrow \pi_5{}^*$ or $\pi_3 \rightarrow \pi_4{}^*$, or an average of all four transitions.

Let us assume the long-wavelength (lowest-energy) transition to be due to the promotion $\pi_3 \rightarrow \pi_5{}^*$. The substituent raises substantially the energy of the highest occupied orbital (π_3) and affects the lowest unoccupied orbital to only a minor extent ($\pi_5{}^*$) or not at all ($\pi_4{}^*$); the greatest effect in each case is caused by the atom with the smallest δ, i.e., the atom which allows the greatest interaction of the lone pair with the ring. The larger the value of δ, the electronegativity, the more difficult it is to remove an electron, and the electronegativity is directly related to the ionization potential, the energy required to remove the electron. The order in which the wavelength of absorption is affected is thus related to the ionization energy of the substituent. Figure 12.5 shows this relationship.[6] The frequency shift is greatest for the substituent $NHCH_3$, in which the lone-pair participation is enhanced by the low nuclear charge on nitrogen and the electron-release effect of the methyl group; and the shift is least for fluorine, since there is relatively little tendency for its nonbonding $p\pi$ electrons to migrate into the ring because of the very strong attraction of fluorine for electrons, which also gives rise to the observed high ionization potential.

The above discussion was concerned with the effect on wavelength displacement caused by the resonance effect of the substituent; resonance also affects the intensity. The long-wavelength (benzenoid) band associated with the spectrum of benzene has low intensity as a consequence of the forbiddenness of the $^1B_{2u} \leftarrow {}^1A_{1g}$ transition arising out of the hexagonal symmetry. The migration of charge distorts this symmetry, removes some of the forbiddenness, and intensifies the absorption. The greater the migration of charge, the greater the intensification. The spectrum of aniline is about ten times as intense as that of benzene.[7]

It has frequently been generalized that the resonance but not the inductive effects of substituents affects the spectrum of benzene, but this is probably a considerable oversimplification. It seems quite definitely

[7] A. L. Sklar, *J. Chem. Phys.*, **7**, 984 (1939).

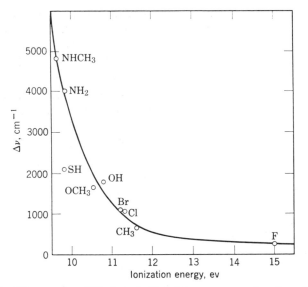

Fig. 12.5 Wavenumber shifts for substituted benzenes as a function of the ionization potential of the substituent. (Reprinted by permission from F. A. Matsen, in Vol. IX of *Technique of Organic Chemistry*, edited by A. Weissberger, Interscience Publishers, New York, 1956.)

established that the inductive effect, in the absence of resonance effects, does not appreciably modify spectra, since introduction of an NR_4^+ group into almost any aromatic parent compound (benzene, substituted benzenes, polycyclic aromatics) does not affect the spectrum of the parent. On the other hand, it does not follow that an inductive effect when accompanying a resonance effect must be equally ineffective. Sponer[8] has suggested, from a consideration of the spectra of various fluoro- and trifluoromethyl-substituted benzenes, that the net effect of the substituents on the spectrum is a balance of opposing inductive and resonance effects. In confirmation of this conclusion, Goodman and Shull[9] have found that the inductive effect cannot be neglected when the resonance effect is large. The interaction between conjugative and inductive effects has been carefully considered by these investigators,[10] but the details of their treatment are too complex to be reproduced here.

The interpretation of the spectrum of iodobenzene is somewhat more complicated than that of the other halobenzenes. It was generally assumed that the 226 mμ (log ϵ = 4.12) band is the shifted first primary band of

[8] H. Sponer, *J. Chem. Phys.*, **22**, 234 (1954); cf. also H. B. Klevens, J. R. Platt, and L. E. Jacobs, *J. Am. Chem. Soc.*, **70**, 3526 (1948).

[9] L. Goodman and H. Shull, *J. Chem. Phys.*, **23**, 33 (1955).

[10] L. Goodman and H. Shull, *J. Chem. Phys.*, **27**, 1388 (1957).

benzene. However, it has been shown[11] that iodobenzene has another high-intensity short-wavelength band at 207 mμ (log $\epsilon = 3.86$). The band at 226 mμ may be due to iodine absorption ($\lambda_{max} = 219$ mμ, log $\epsilon = 4.25$ for iodide ion), and hence the spectrum of iodobenzene consists of the superposition of iodide absorption on that of a slightly perturbed benzene. The higher intensity of the long-wavelength band of iodobenzene (254 mμ; $\epsilon = 660$), as compared to that of the other halobenzenes, may be explained by the superposition of the alkyl iodide absorption.[12] There is good reason to believe that this interpretation of the iodobenzene spectrum is correct because the band assignments are more consistent with the $\lambda_{primary}/\lambda_{secondary}$ ratios and the $\Delta\lambda$ versus $\Delta\sigma$ relationship of other substituted benzenes (see section 12.25). The excited state of the 226 mμ band, however, must involve a π-electron level, since the band undergoes considerable shifts upon further substitution. Thus the band occurs at 235 mμ (log $\epsilon = 4.19$) in p-chloroiodobenzene, and at 248 mμ (log $\epsilon = 4.22$) in p-iodoaniline. The high intensity of this band suggests that the upper π level must be largely localized on iodine. This may well be a π level arising out of the interaction of a dπ orbital of iodine and the π orbitals of the ring (cf. section 17.3).

12.23 ALKYL SUBSTITUTION. Alkyl substitution intensifies and shifts the benzene spectrum to longer wavelength, and in this respect alkyl groups are similar to groups with lone-pair electrons, such as NH_2 and OR, a fact which has been cited as good evidence for hyperconjugation (e.g., $-C\equiv H_3$ $\leftrightarrow =C=H_3^+$). Of all the alkyl groups, methyl causes the greatest wavelength shift and intensification; this behavior accords with the prevailing opinion that methyl is the most effective hyperconjugating substituent. As the hydrogens in the methyl group are replaced by alkyl groups, the bathochromic effect decreases;[13] this is illustrated in Table 12.1, which shows the wavelength of the $0 \rightarrow 0$ band resulting from electron promotion from the lowest vibrational level of the ground state to the lowest vibrational level of the excited state.

As the substituent becomes more complex, the spectra lose structure and become more diffuse. This is thought to be due to greater possibility for conversion of the electronic energy of the ring to vibrational energy in the substituent. The result is broadening of the band, since the width of an energy state is inversely proportional to the lifetime of the state; the shorter the lifetime, the wider the band.

[11] F. M. Beringer and I. Lillien, *J. Am. Chem. Soc.*, **82**, 5141 (1960).

[12] T. M. Dunn and T. Iredale, *J. Chem. Soc.*, 1592 (1952); R. A. Durie, T. Iredale, and J. M. S. Jarvie, *J. Chem. Soc.*, 1181 (1950).

[13] F. A. Matsen, W. W. Robertson, and R. L. Chuoke, *Chem. Revs.*, **41**, 273 (1947); W. W. Robertson, J. F. Music, and F. A. Matsen, *J. Am. Chem. Soc.*, **72**, 5260 (1950).

Alkyl substitution reduces the ionization energy of benzene through resonance and inductive effects, since both operate to release electrons to

TABLE 12.1

Wavelengths of the $0 \rightarrow 0$ Bands of $R_1R_2R_3CC_6H_5$[13]

Substituent			Wavelength,
R_1	R_2	R_3	$m\mu$
H	H	H	266.75
CH_3	H	H	266.43
C_2H_5	H	H	266.52
CH_3	CH_3	H	265.87
C_3H_7	H	H	266.63
C_2H_5	CH_3	H	266.10
CH_3	CH_3	CH_3	266.52
$-(CH_2)_4-$		H	267.05
$-(CH_2)_5-$		H	265.95

the ring. The ionization energy of *tert*-butylbenzene is 8.5 ev and of toluene is 8.9 ev indicating that, in the ground state, the inductive effect of *tert*-butyl outweighs the resonance effect of methyl.

The spectra of a series of chloroalkylbenzenes have been reported by Hamner and Matsen,[14] and some of their data are reproduced in Table 12.2.

TABLE 12.2

Wavelengths and Relative Intensities of the $0 \rightarrow 0$ Bands of Some Monosubstituted Benzenes in the Vapor Phase[14]

Compound	λ, $m\mu$	Relative Intensity[a]
$PhCH_2Cl$	269.4	MS
$PhCHCl_2$	270.1	VS
$PhCCl_3$	272.1	VS
$PhCH_2CH_2Cl$	266.2	W
$PhCH_2CH_2CH_2Cl$	266.4	MS

[a] MS = medium strong; VS = very strong; W = weak.

This series of spectra is particularly instructive, since it shows that either donation or withdrawal of electrons by a substituent leads to bathochromic and hyperchromic effects in the spectrum of benzene. The alkyl groups undoubtedly donate electrons; the Cl_3C group, because of the

[14] W. F. Hamner and F. A. Matsen, *J. Am. Chem. Soc.*, **70**, 2482 (1948).

higher electronegativity of chlorine, surely withdraws electrons from the ring, presumably by an inverse hyperconjugative effect.[15] Somewhere between these extremes, donation and withdrawal should be balanced, resulting in no effect on the spectrum; in the series reported in Table 12.2, this point appears to be reached between CH_2CH_2Cl and CH_2Cl.

12.24 OTHER MONOSUBSTITUTED BENZENES.   Most of the previous discussion has been concerned with the effect of electron-releasing (i.e., *ortho-para*-directing) substituents on the spectrum of benzene. It may be anticipated, and is actually found, that electron-withdrawing (*meta*-directing) substituents also perturb the π-electron cloud of benzene and

TABLE 12.3

The Effect of the Degree of Conjugation on the 0 → 0 Band
of Benzene[16]

Compound	cm^{-1}
(Benzene)	(38,089)
Isopropylbenzene	37,601
Cyclohexylbenzene	37,590
Cyclopentylbenzene	37,435
Cyclopropylbenzene	36,861
Phenylacetylene	36,370
Styrene	34,761

thus affect the spectra. The case of chloroalkyl groups was dealt with at the end of section 12.23. Another interesting series[16] is shown in Table 12.3. Typical alkyl groups, by resonance interaction, presumably of a hyperconjugative type, shift the 0 → 0 band of the $^1B_{2u} \leftarrow {}^1A_{1g}$ transition to longer wavelength. The effect of the cyclohexyl group is interpreted as an example of this type of interaction, and the fact that it is slightly greater than the effect of isopropyl is ascribed to the larger mass of the cyclohexyl group. Cyclopentyl, however, has an even greater effect, in spite of its smaller mass, and is believed to have delocalizable electrons resembling π electrons, because of the geometry and strain in the ring.

This effect is further increased in the cyclopropyl group, which is well known to exert conjugative effects intermediate between the hyperconjugation of alkyl groups and the true (first-order) conjugation of the vinyl group. This resonance effect has been ascribed to two nonlocalized MO's of the ring which have relatively low binding energy; these orbitals lie in the plane of the cyclopropyl ring but have π symmetry with respect to the

[15] F. H. Seubold, *J. Org. Chem.*, **21**, 156 (1956).

[16] W. W. Robertson, J. F. Music, and F. A. Matsen, *J. Am. Chem. Soc.*, **72**, 5260 (1950).

nonring bonds of cyclopropane, and hence the correct symmetry for conjugation with the benzene ring[17] (it should be noted that the cyclopropyl ring is not coplanar with the benzene ring in cyclopropylbenzene).

In phenylacetylene, first-order conjugation with the ring appears. This conjugation is not particularly effective, since the short bond distance in the triple bond leads to a relatively high resonance integral for this bond, and hence the π electrons are quite tightly held in it. Finally, in styrene, with a lower resonance integral, the π electrons are not as tightly held and are more readily and extensively delocalized, leading to the largest bathochromic effect in the whole series.

Similar effects are observed in benzene substituted by a carbonyl group, e.g., benzaldehyde, acetophenone, and benzoic acid. Again the main bands ($^1B_{2u} \leftarrow {}^1A_{1g}$ and $^1B_{1u} \leftarrow {}^1A_{1g}$) are shifted to longer wavelength, in the order $C_6H_5COOH < C_6H_5COCH_3 < C_6H_5CHO$ (cf. Table 12.4). Although n $\rightarrow \pi^*$ transitions might be expected for these compounds, they have not been observed, presumably because they occur in the same region as the more intense absorption bands. A wide variety of other compounds (e.g., benzonitrile and nitrosobenzene) could be discussed, but all show qualitatively similar behavior, with varying degrees of bathochromic and hyperchromic effects.

A special case is nitrobenzene, which shows the greatest red shift of all the common monosubstituted benzenes. This compound has $\lambda_{max} = 268.5$ mμ, with $\epsilon_{max} = 7800$, which has been interpreted to indicate that this band is the "first primary" band, i.e., that the excited state is derived from the $^1B_{1u}$ (^1L_a) state of benzene. This interpretation is not unreasonable, since the nitro group is known, from a massive volume of independent chemical evidence, to have a larger effect than any other common substituent, particularly a very strong resonance effect. This effect is possibly best illustrated by indicating the main resonance forms of nitrobenzene:

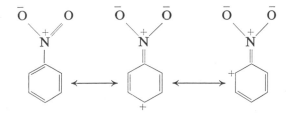

where the quinoid structures make a substantial contribution to the ground state, but the predominant contribution to the excited state. Again, the n $\rightarrow \pi^*$ transition is not observed, presumably because it is submerged

[17] H. H. Jaffé, Z. Elektrochem., **59**, 823 (1955).

under the high-intensity band; even the transition corresponding to the $^1B_{2u} \leftarrow {}^1A_{1g}$ ($^1L_b \leftarrow {}^1A$) transition appears to be submerged under the more intense band.

A different approach to an understanding of the spectra of nitro- and carbonyl-substituted benzenes has been suggested.[18] In this approach attention is focused on the transfer of charge accompanying excitation. Except in the $V \leftarrow N$ transitions in highly symmetrical compounds, excitation is generally accompanied by a redistribution of electrons (i.e., of charges), since the excited-state wave functions represent a different charge distribution from the ground-state function. Nagakura makes use of, and focuses attention on, this particular aspect of the excitation process by considering in detail the highest occupied orbital (H_x) of one part of the molecule (the phenyl ring) acting as electron donor in the excitation, and the lowest unoccupied orbital (V_A) of the other part (the nitro or carbonyl group), the electron acceptor. He shows that H_x is higher than the highest occupied orbital of the acceptor group, and that V_A is lower than the lowest unoccupied orbital of the donor group. H_x and V_A are allowed to interact, forming two new orbitals extending over both the acceptor and donor groups, and excitation is believed to occur by promotion of an electron from the lower orbital of this pair to the higher one, and is accompanied by a considerable transfer of charge from the donor to the acceptor group.

On the basis of this transfer of charge, and in analogy with the inter-molecular charge-transfer spectra to be discussed in section 12.6, Nagakura refers to the spectra of nitrobenzene and the carbonyl-substituted benzenes (as well as certain other nitro and carbonyl compounds) as *intramolecular charge-transfer spectra*. It should be noted that this interpretation of the spectra of these compounds is not a basically different theory from standard MO theory, but is only an abbreviation of the complete theory with special emphasis on the charge-transfer process. It is encouraging, however, that this simplified treatment has permitted calculation of excitation energies and intensities in very satisfactory approximation.[18]

12.25 CORRELATIONS IN THE SPECTRA OF THE MONOSUBSTITUTED BENZENES. In the first part of their exhaustive and now classic study of the benzene spectra, Doub and Vandenbelt[1a] showed that, in the monosubstituted benzenes, there is a regularity in the amount of displacement of both the primary 203.5 mμ ($^1B_{1u} \leftarrow {}^1A_{1g}$, $^1L_a \leftarrow {}^1A$), band and the secondary ($^1B_{2u} \leftarrow {}^1A_{1g}$, $^1L_b \leftarrow {}^1A$) band. This was shown by the near constancy of the ratio, $\lambda_{sec}/\lambda_{pri}$, as can be seen from the data in Table 12.4.

[18] S. Nagakura and J. Tanaka, *J. Chem. Phys.*, **22**, 236 (1954); S. Nagakura, *J. Chem. Phys.*, **23**, 1441 (1955).

Doub and Vandenbelt proposed that the primary band was the most typical of the benzene bands and was most readily correlated with substituent properties. If the substituent groups listed in Table 12.4 are

TABLE 12.4

Spectra of Monosubstituted Benzenes[a, 1a]

R	Primary Band (^1L_a)		Secondary Band (^1L_b)		$\lambda_{sec}/\lambda_{pri}$
	λ_{max}, mμ	ϵ_{max}	λ_{max}, mμ	ϵ_{max}	
H	203.5	7,400	254	204	1.25
NH_3^+	203	7,500	254	160	1.25
CH_3	206.5	7,000	261	225	1.25
I	207[b]	7,000	257	700	1.24
Cl	209.5	7,400	263.5	190	1.25
Br	210	7,900	261	192	1.24
OH	210.5	6,200	270	1450	1.28
OCH_3	217	6,400	269	1480	1.24
SO_2NH_2	217.5	9,700	264.5	740	1.22
CN	224	13,000	271	1000	1.21
CO_2^-	224	8,700	268	560	1.20
CO_2H	230	11,600	273	970	1.19
NH_2	230	8,600	280	1430	1.22
O^-	235	9,400	287	2600	1.22
$NHCOCH_3$[c]	238	10,500	...	...	...
$COCH_3$	245.5	9,800	...	...	...
CHO	249.5	11,400	...	...	...
NO_2	268.5	7,800	...	...	...

[a] Water as solvent, trace of MeOH added for solubility where necessary.
[b] Reference in footnote 11; see section 12.21.
[c] H. E. Ungnade, *J. Am. Chem. Soc.*, **75**, 432 (1953).

divided into *ortho-para*-directing and *meta*-directing types and arranged in order of increasing $\Delta\lambda$ values of the primary band, the following series are obtained:

$$CH_3 < Cl < Br < OH < OCH_3 < NH_2 < O^- < NHCOCH_3 < N(CH_3)_2$$

$$NO_2 > CHO > COCH_3 > CO_2H > CO_2^- = CN > SO_2NH_2 > NH_3^+$$

This order of the displacement of the primary band suggests a relationship to other established orders of electronic interaction of a substituent with the ring. The most useful quantitative expression relating structure and reactivity in the aromatic series is the Hammett equation.

Hammett[19] found that the rate, or equilibrium, constant associated with a reaction occurring at R of *meta*- or *para*-substituted benzene derivatives of the formula Y—C_6H_4—R may be determined from the corresponding constant for the parent compound (Y = H) if two parameters are known. The first parameter, σ, is characteristic only of the nature and the position of the substituent Y and represents the ability of the group to attract or repel electrons. The σ values are characteristic of the particular substituent and differ according to whether the substituent Y is located *meta* or *para* to R.

The second parameter, ρ, is related to the particular reaction under consideration and is a measure of the sensitivity of the reaction to ring substitution. If k_Y and k_H are the rate constants for reaction of the substituted and unsubstituted compound, respectively, the Hammett equation may be written as log $(k_Y/k_H) = \rho\sigma$. A positive σ value of a substituent indicates that the substituent attracts electrons more than hydrogen, whereas a negative σ value indicates that the substituent is an electron repeller or donor. Each substituent has a characteristic σ_m value and σ_p value which, in the first approximation, are independent of the reaction at R. The difference, $\sigma_p - \sigma_m$, is $\Delta\sigma$, which should be an approximate measure of the resonance effect of the substituent, Y. Doub and Vandenbelt showed that $\Delta\sigma$ correlates quite well with the primary-band displacement of the different substituents on benzene, in consistency with the concept that this displacement also depends on the electron withdrawal or repelling nature of the substituent. Their data are plotted in Fig. 12.6, using the $\Delta\sigma$ values given by Price.[20] As is frequently the case in σ plots, improvements are possible by adjusting values and by variations in the treatment. There appears to be little question that there is indeed a relationship between the location of the primary band in the substituted benzenes and the ability of the substituent to attract or repel electrons. In the monosubstituted benzenes the interaction between the ring and the substituent is large if the substituent is either a strong electron donor or a strong electron acceptor. The secondary bands are affected in the same way as the primary bands, but the primary bands are somewhat more sensitive to substitution and are sharper and more intense.

The ability of a substituent to undergo resonance interaction with the ring, measured in Doub and Vandenbelt's correlation by $\Delta\sigma$, is supposed to be better expressed by Taft's[21] resonance parameter, σ_R. Consequently

[19] L. P. Hammett, *Physical Organic Chemistry*, McGraw-Hill Book Co., New York, 1940; cf. H. H. Jaffé, *Chem. Revs.*, **53**, 191 (1953).

[20] C. C. Price, *Mechanism of Reactions at Carbon-Carbon Double Bonds*, Interscience Publishers, New York, 1946, p. 26.

[21] R. W. Taft, in *Steric Effects in Organic Chemistry*, edited by M. S. Newman, John Wiley and Sons, New York, 1956, p. 556; R. W. Taft and I. C. Lewis, *J. Am. Chem. Soc.*, **81**, 5343 (1949).

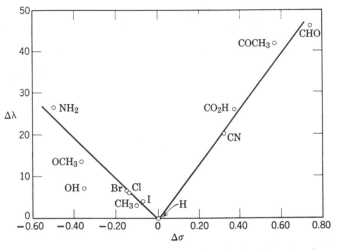

Fig. 12.6 Displacement of primary bands plotted against $\Delta\sigma$.

it is not surprising that Rao[22] finds fair correlations of $\Delta\lambda$ values with σ_R. The fact that there seems to be no really good relation between $\Delta\lambda$ (or $\Delta\nu$) and any parameter measuring the resonance effect of a substituent further confirms the observation that some interaction of inductive and resonance effects seems to be important. Attempts to treat intensities in terms of similar chemical parameters[23] (σ, σ_R, etc.) have met with much less success.

12.3 Polysubstituted Benzenes

When benzene is *disubstituted* by a *meta*-directing (electron-withdrawing) group and an *ortho-para*-directing (electron-releasing) group in *para* positions to each other, the effects of the separate groups are enhanced. This is strikingly illustrated by the dipole moment of *p*-nitroaniline. The dipole moments of nitrobenzene and aniline are 3.95 D and 1.35 D, respectively, but the moment of *p*-nitroaniline is 6.1 D, 0.8 D larger than the sum of the moments in the two compounds. This enhancement has been ascribed to interaction resonance.[24] Such an effect is also manifest in the ultraviolet absorption spectra of *para*-disubstituted benzenes; the shift in the position of the 203 mμ (primary) band of benzene is greater than would be expected from the separate groups when these groups are of

[22] C. N. R. Rao, *Chem. & Ind.*, 1239 (1957); *J. Sci. Industr. Res. (India)*, **17B**, 56 (1958).
[23] C. N. R. Rao and G. B. Silverman, *J. Sci. Industr. Res. (India)*, **17B**, 131 (1958).
[24] See L. N. Ferguson, *Electron Structures of Organic Molecules*, Prentice-Hall, Englewood Cliffs, N.J., 1952, p. 278.

opposite type. Some illustrative data from the articles[1b] by Doub and Vandenbelt are shown in Table 12.5. The excited ^1L_a state must receive substantial contributions from quinoid structures such as $A^+ = \langle \rangle = B^-$.

Doub and Vandenbelt observed that when two groups of the same type are opposed, there is very little displacement over that caused by the most

TABLE 12.5

Effect of *para* Disubstitution A—C$_6$H$_4$—B on the ^1L_a Band of Benzene in Water[1b]

A	Shift, mμ, for A	B	Shift, mμ, for B	Shift for p-A—C$_6$H$_4$—B Calc. Sum, A + B	Obs.
Cl	6	CO$_2$H	26.5	32.5	38
Br	6.5	CO$_2$H	26.5	33	42
OH	7	CO$_2$H	26.5	33.5	52
NH$_2$	26.5	CN	20.5	47	67
OH	7	COCH$_3$	42	47	72
Br	6.5	COCH$_3$	42	48.5	55
OH	7	CHO	46	53	80
OCH$_3$	13.5	COCH$_3$	42	55.5	73
NH$_2$	26.5	COCH$_3$	42	68.5	108
O$^-$	31.5	COCH$_3$	42	73.5	121
Cl	6	NO$_2$	65	71	77
OH	7	NO$_2$	65	71	114
O$^-$	31.5	CHO	46	77.5	127
NH$_2$	26.5	NO$_2$	65	91.5	178
O$^-$	31.5	NO$_2$	65	96.5	199

displaced monosubstituted compound.[1b] Thus, in p-nitrobenzoic acid [$\Delta\lambda(CO_2H) = 26.5$, $\Delta\lambda(NO_2) = 65.0$] the primary (203 m$\mu$) band is displaced 61 m$\mu$. When groups of opposite character are substituted *ortho* or *meta* to each other, the effects of the displacements on the ^1L_b and ^1B bands of benzene are the same as those caused by similar *para* substitution. The effect of *para* disubstitution has been studied in detail in the acetanilide series.[25] Pertinent data are shown in Table 12.6. First it is of interest to note that the bathochromic shift of the ^1L_a band is greater for —NHCOCH$_3$ than for —NH$_2$. The π electrons on the carbonyl group can apparently participate in the conjugated system, which now involves the ring, the N-atom p electrons, and the π electrons of the carbonyl group. As

[25] H. E. Ungnade, *J. Am. Chem. Soc.*, **76**, 5133 (1954).

compared to benzene, the rise in the energy of the highest occupied MO is greater, relative to the ground state in acetanilide, than the corresponding rise in aniline. However, the differences between found and calculated shifts are greater for the *para*-substituted anilines than for their amides.

TABLE 12.6

Bathochromic Shift of the ^1L_a Benzene Band in *para*-Disubstituted Benzenes A—C_6H_4—B in Ethanol[25]

A	Displacement, $m\mu$, for A	B	Displacement, $m\mu$, for B	A—C_6H_4—B Shift Calc. Sum	Obs. Displacement
NHCOCH₃	38.5	SO₂NH₂	14.5	53.0	55.5
NH₂	30.5	SO₂NH₂	14.5	45.0	58.5
NHCOCH₃	38.5	CO₂H	24.5	63.0	66.5
NH₂	30.5	CO₂H	24.5	55.0	84.5
NHCOCH₃	38.5	NO₂	56.5	95.0	112.5
NH₂	30.5	NO₂	56.5	87.0	171.5

The incremental shift over that produced by each substituent separately is again a measure of group interaction. The data show that the substitution of —$COCH_3$ for H on aniline inhibits the electron-release tendency. This is, of course, the explanation for the much greater base strength of a free amine than of an amide.

Some of the above generalizations appear to be open to question.[25a] When the analyses are made in terms of frequency, rather than wavelength, it is found that the effects of a series of substituents (2) on the L_a band of a monosubstituted benzene (substituent 1), given by $(\nu_1 - \nu_{12})/\nu_1$, are nearly proportional to the effects which the same substituents have on unsubstituted benzene, $(\nu_H - \nu_2)/\nu_H$:

$$(\nu_1 - \nu_{12})/\nu_1 = m_1(\nu_H - \nu_2)/\nu_H$$

m itself is approximately linear in the substituent 1:

$$m_1 = C(\nu_H - \nu_1)/\nu_H$$

giving

$$\nu_{12} = \frac{\nu_1\nu_2}{\nu_H} + \frac{C}{\nu_H}[\nu_H(\nu_1 + \nu_2) - (\nu_H^2 + \nu_1\nu_2)]$$

with $C = 5.1$ for *para*-, $C = -1.3$ for *meta*-disubstituted compounds, always with water as solvent. No segregation of *o*-, *p*-, and *m*-directing

[25a] B. G. Gowenlock and K. J Morgan, *Spectrochim. Acta*, **17**, 310 (1961).

groups was observed, since the simple relation holds for all combination of substituents. A few compounds in which both substituents interact strongly with the ring failed to obey the relations given.

There has been a great deal of interest in the effect of halogen substitution on the spectra of benzene and some of its derivatives. The interest has centered around the relative importance of the inductive and resonance effects of the halogens. The inductive effect is one of electron withdrawal and coincides with the decreasing order of electronegativities, $F > Cl > Br > I$. The resonance effect, which allows migration of the lone-pair electrons into the ring, is also presumed to be in the order $F > Cl > Br > I$. The two effects, as is usually the case, oppose each other, but apparently the net effect with all halogens is electron withdrawing, as reflected in the positive σ values. In an attempt to shed light on this problem, Schubert, Craven, and Steadly[26] studied the vapor spectra of various halosubstituted compounds. With p-halonitrobenzenes the ultraviolet absorption may be represented by transitions such as the following:

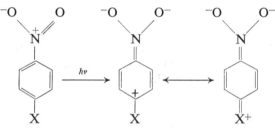

The formulas convey the idea that the transition involves an electron demand from the halogen. On the other hand, the transition in the p-haloanisoles requires electron acceptance by the halogen:

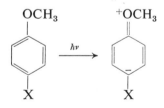

In both series of compounds, as well as in the p-haloacetophenones, the authors[26] found that the wavelength shift was in the order $I > Br > Cl > F$. The fact that the order of net electron acceptance in the anisoles corresponds to the order of net electron release in the nitrobenzenes suggests that the polarizability of the substituent was the controlling factor.

[26] W. M. Schubert, J. M. Craven, and H. Steadly, *J. Am. Chem. Soc.*, **81**, 2695 (1959).

Buroway and Thompson[27] have come to substantially the same conclusion. Molar refraction is a property which depends on the polarizability of the electrons, and an excellent correlation between the frequency shift and the molar refraction of the halo compounds was observed.[26] The substituent effects would have been difficult to rationalize on the basis of either an inductive or electromeric order of $F > Cl > Br > I$, or both orders.

If nitrobenzene is substituted by alkyl groups in the *para* position, the excitation requirements are similar to those of the *p*-halonitrobenzenes. The ability of various alkyl groups to furnish electrons and thus facilitate the excitation was examined by comparing the vapor spectra of a series of *p*-alkylnitrobenzenes,[28] and the data are given in Table 12.7. It is known

TABLE 12.7
The Wavelength of the ^1L_a Band of p-$RC_6H_4NO_2$[28]

R	Gas Phase λ_{max}, mμ	Heptane λ_{max}, mμ
H	239.1	252.3
CH_3	250.2	264.1
CH_3CH_2	251.0	265.0
$CH_3CH_2CH_2$	251.6	265.5
$(CH_3)_2CHCH_2$	252.5	266.3
$(CH_3)_3CCH_2$	253.2	267.4

from many rate studies (e.g., of hydrolysis of $RC_6H_4CH_2X$) that the transition state is electron demanding, and the order of rate constants with change in R is Et > *n*-Pr > iso-Bu > neopentyl. The same order has been observed in $RCH_2C_6H_4CH_2X$, and the retarding effect of an increase in the size of R has been ascribed to various factors, chiefly steric inhibition to hyperconjugation[29] of the methylene hydrogens, even though it has been shown[30] that hyperconjugation is relatively insensitive to the conformation of the alkyl group. However, the spectra of the *p*-alkylnitrobenzenes show that neopentyl is the most effective electron-releasing alkyl group. It is suggested[28] that the enhancement of electron release by neopentyl may be due to its greater polarizability, or to the relief of strain on excitation. In rate studies the inhibiting effect of neopentyl in solution, despite its greater inherent electron-release properties, is then ascribed to steric inhibition of solvation by the bulky group.

[27] A. Burawoy and A. R. Thompson, *J. Chem. Soc.*, 4314 (1956).
[28] W. M. Schubert and J. Robins, *J. Am. Chem. Soc.*, **80**, 559 (1958).
[29] R. T. Arnold and W. L. Truett, *J. Am. Chem. Soc.*, **73**, 5508 (1951); G. Baddeley and M. Gordon, *J. Chem. Soc.*, 2190 (1952).
[30] H. H. Jaffé and J. L. Roberts, *J. Am. Chem. Soc.*, **79**, 391 (1957).

The spectra of substituted benzoic acids have been the subject of several studies. The two main benzenoid bands are present, and a third band, the second primary band (^1B), appears at about 205 mμ. Electron-repelling substituents in the *para* position cause the expected red shift in the first primary band, and the extent of the shift is in the order OH > OCH$_3$ > Br > Me > Cl.[31] There is a good correlation between $\Delta\lambda$ and σ.[32] In aqueous alcoholic solution the secondary bands are submerged in the shifted primary band, but the vibrational structure can be brought out in hydrocarbon solvents. When the substituents are in the *ortho* position, the primary band is not shifted nearly as much as in the *para* compounds; undoubtedly steric factors play a role in such spectra.

A different interpretation and band assignment for substituted benzoic acids (and acetophenones) has been made.[33] The longest-wavelength, low-intensity band of *para*-substituted acetophenones ($\sim$320 mμ in heptane) is assigned to an n → π^* transition, since this band shows the typical n → π^* solvent shifts. In the benzoic acid series this band is fused with the high-intensity adjacent band and hence cannot be analyzed carefully.

For disubstituted benzenes in general, Rao[22] finds that a total resonance effect, measured by the absolute value of the difference of the σ_R values of Taft,[21] correlates well with the wavelength shifts:

$$\Delta\lambda = A \, |\sigma_R(1) - \sigma_R(2)| + C$$

where $\sigma_R(1)$ and $\sigma_R(2)$ are the σ_R values appropriate to the two substituents. The constants A and C are, approximately, 6.5 and 20 mμ, except that in substituted nitrobenzenes special values, 90 and 43 mμ, apply.

The *trisubstituted benzene* spectra are reported in the third of the massive studies of benzene derivatives by Doub and Vandenbelt,[34] who determined the spectra of substituted benzenes of type I,

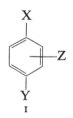

I

[31] C. M. Moser and A. I. Kohlenberg, *J. Chem. Soc.*, **804** (1951).

[32] C. N. R. Rao, *Chem. & Ind.*, 666 (1956); 1239 (1957).

[33] (*a*) J. Tanaka, S. Nagakura, and M. Kobayashi, *J. Chem. Phys.*, **24**, 311 (1956); (*b*) A. I. Scott, *Experientia*, **17**, 68 (1961), gives empirical rules for calculating the spectra of such compounds.

[34] L. Doub and J. M. Vandenbelt, *J. Am. Chem. Soc.*, **77**, 4535 (1955).

where only one of the groups X, Y, and Z was electron attracting (i.e., *meta* directing). The spectra are best understood in terms of the constituent disubstituted compounds. Thus, for example, the spectrum of 2,4-dihydroxybenzoic acid (*β*-resorcylic acid) is best discussed in terms of 2-hydroxybenzoic acid (salicylic acid), 1,3-dihydroxybenzene (resorcinol), and 4-hydroxybenzoic acid. The spectra of these four compounds[34] are shown in Fig. 12.7. In salicylic acid, the secondary band of benzene is displaced from 256 to 303 mμ, while the 203 mμ band is displaced to 237 mμ. In the *para* isomer, the secondary band is only an inflection at about 273 mμ, but the primary band is shifted to 255 mμ. The spectrum of the trisubstituted compound contains the most shifted bands of the constituent disubstituted compounds, i.e., the secondary band of the *ortho* isomer and the primary band of the *para* isomer. In this case the weak bands of resorcinol, if they make any contribution, are masked by the contributions from the carboxy constituent compounds. This pattern of displacements in the trisubstituted benzene derivatives of formula I was found to be quite general, and Doub and Vandenbelt proposed the following empirical rule.[34] Each of the secondary or first primary bands of the trisubstituted benzenes, I, can be related to that band which is the most displaced among the corresponding bands of the constituent compounds.

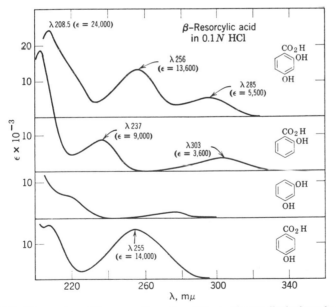

Fig. 12.7 The spectra of *β*-resorcylic acid and its constituent disubstituted compounds. [Reprinted by permission from L. Doub and J. M. Vandenbelt, *J. Am. Chem. Soc.*, **77**, 4535 (1955).]

These bands are often similar, not only in wavelength, but also in shape and intensity.

Very interesting correlations have been observed in the spectra of some aromatic compounds able to undergo acid-base reactions.[35] The differences between the frequencies ($\Delta\nu$) in neutral and alkaline solutions of the long-wavelength bands of a series of 2,4-dinitrophenylhydrazones of aldehydes and ketones were correlated[35a] with parameters presumably describing charge migration into the phenylhydrazone group; these parameters were Hammett substituent constants[19] for the aromatic carbonyl derivatives, and Taft inductive substituent constants[21] for the aliphatic. In an even more striking relation,[35b] the frequencies of the long-wavelength bands of a series of 4-substituted 2-nitrophenols and of the corresponding phenolate ions each were correlated with Brown and Okamoto's σ^+ constants.[36] This is the more surprising, since the constants for the equilibria between the phenols and the phenolate ions are correlated with σ-constants. The separate correlations of frequencies of phenols and phenolate ions imply, of course, that a similar relation exists for the difference, $\Delta\nu$, between the frequencies, just like the one found in the 2,4-dinitrophenylhydrazones. Reasons for the existence of these correlations are not well understood.

12.4   Solvent Effects

Many of the data on benzenoid compounds have been obtained from aqueous or alcoholic solutions. This is perhaps unfortunate because such hydroxylic solvents often obscure vibrational structure which can be brought out by vapor spectra or by solution spectra in nonpolar, non-

TABLE 12.8

The ^1L_a Band of Nitrobenzene[37]

Solvent:	water	ethanol	heptane	vapor
λ_{max}, mμ:	265.5	259.5	251.8	239.1

hydrogen-bonding solvents. Furthermore, band position is affected by relative stabilization of the ground and excited states by solvation. The effect of solvent on the spectra of nitrobenzene is apparent from the data in Table 12.8. The difference of 26.4 mμ in the location of the ^1L_a band of nitrobenzene in changing from water to no solvent (vapor) corresponds to a facilitation of the transition in aqueous solution corresponding to

[35] (a) L. A. Jones and C. K. Hancock, J. Org. Chem., 25, 226 (1960); L. E. Scoggins and C. K. Hancock, J. Org. Chem., 26, 3490 (1961); (b) M. Rapoport, C. K. Hancock, and E. A. Meyers, private communication.

[36] H. C. Brown and Y. Okamoto, J. Am. Chem. Soc., 80, 4979 (1958).

12 kcal/mole. The increased ease of excitation is no doubt due to the stabilization of the excited state by solvation. The effect is even greater, as might be expected, in *para*-substituted nitrobenzenes, since the excitation may be identified with the transition to a dipolar, quinoid structure:

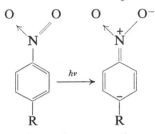

The spectrum of *p*-nitrotoluene in water shows the ^1L_a band, λ_{max} at 285 mμ, compared to 250.2 mμ for the vapor spectrum; the difference of 34.8 mμ is equivalent to about 15 kcal/mole. The facilitation of excitation must again be due to stabilization of the more polar excited state by solvent.

It was shown in section 9.7 that excitation leads not to the equilibrium conformation of the excited state, but to a conformation (the F-C state) in which the solvent cage is the same as it is in the ground state. The more polar the ground state, the more highly solvated it is, and the larger will be the solvation energy in the F-C state, since the excited state is more polar than the ground state.

TABLE 12.9

Solvent Effects on the ^1L_a Band in Substituted Benzenes, C_6H_5R[37]

R	$\lambda_{max}(H_2O)$, mμ	$\lambda_{max}(EtOH)$, mμ	$\Delta\lambda(H_2O\text{-}EtOH)$, m$\mu$	$\Delta\lambda$,[a] mμ
CO_2H	230	228	2	26.5
$COCH_3$	245.5	241	4.5	42.0
CHO	249.5	243	6.5	46.0
NO_2	268.5	260	8.5	65.0

[a] Wavelength shift of the 203.5 mμ benzene band caused by the substituent (water as solvent).

Large solvent shifts in substituted benzenes are observed primarily when the substituent is an electron acceptor, and water causes the greatest shift. The wavelength shift between two solvents (e.g., water and ethanol) appears to be roughly proportional to the shift induced by the same substituent on the corresponding band of benzene.[37] This relation is illustrated in Table 12.9. With electron-donor substituents, such as OH,

[37] H. E. Ungnade, *J. Am. Chem. Soc.*, **75**, 432 (1953).

OCH_3, SH, and NH_2, solvent shifts are negligible, but some loss of structure generally occurs in polar solvents. Certain compounds, such as benzoic acid, can associate in solution, and the mixture of species present in solution depends on the degree of association.[38] Hence, the observed spectrum is a superposition of the spectra of the various species and will vary with concentration. Benzoic acid is almost completely dimeric in 0.5 molal solution in benzene, and hence the spectrum in this solution is the spectrum of the dimer. In water, benzoic acid is partially ionized, and the spectrum of the anion as well as of the undissociated species appears. Again, the spectrum will vary with concentration, since ionization increases with increasing dilution. The degree of ionization can readily be calculated from spectrophotometric measurements.

Acidity changes in the solvent ought to affect the spectra of aromatic compounds because it is reasonable to suppose that solvation or complexing of the weakly basic aromatic will vary with the acidity of the solvent. In order to test this concept, the effect of solvent acidity on the spectrum of benzene and some methylbenzenes has been studied.[39] The solvent systems employed were formic acid, trifluoroacetic acid, sulfuric acid - trifluoroacetic acid, and aqueous sulfuric acid of varying concentrations. With mesitylene in strong acid, the vibrational structure of the ^1L_b band is lost and the intensity is increased. It was suggested that the changes are due to the charge-transfer spectra of a weak acid-base complex.

12.5 Intensities

A quantitative approach to the intensities of the ^1L_b band in polysubstituted benzenes has been summarized by Matsen.[6] The intensity is proportional to the square of the transition moment, which is a vector parallel to the electric vector of the light being absorbed. In monosubstituted benzenes, the direction of the transition moment is parallel to the plane of the ring and perpendicular to the two-fold axis of the compound (i.e., the axis through the substituent and bisecting the ring), and its magnitude, m, is a measure of the extent of resonance interaction between the substituent and the ring. The transition moment in a polysubstituted benzene is the vector sum of the transition moments of the corresponding monosubstituted benzenes, provided no substituent interacts too strongly with the ring. The intensity, then, is proportional to the square of the vector sum of the individual transition moments; for two substituents

$$I \sim m_i^2 + m_j^2 + m_i m_j \cos \theta_{ij}$$

[38] H. E. Ungnade and R. W. Lamb, *J. Am. Chem. Soc.*, **74**, 3789 (1952).
[39] M. Kilpatrick and H. H. Hyman, *J. Am. Chem. Soc.*, **80**, 77 (1958).

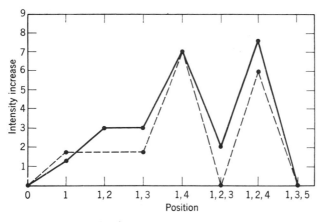

Fig. 12.8 Intensities of the ^1L_b band in the polymethylbenzenes. Solid line = experimental values; dashed line, from Table 12.10. (Reprinted by permission from A. Matsen, in Vol. IX of *Technique of Organic Chemistry*, edited by A. Weissberger, Interscience Publishers, New York, 1956.)

where θ_{ij} is the angle between the axes through each substituent and bisecting the ring. The ^1L_b band represents the $^1B_{2u} \leftarrow {}^1A_{1g}$ transition in benzene. The $^1B_{2u}$ state has three nodal planes in addition to the one in the plane of the molecule, as indicated by the broken lines:

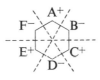

m is negative if the substituent is in the B, D, or F position, since the wave function is negative at these positions, and m is positive at A, C, and E. By convention, the first substitution is made at A. Since the intensity is proportional to the square of the transition moment, the relative intensities of the various substituted benzenes with identical substituents may be calculated readily. The results are shown in Table 12.10 and agree quite well with experimental results,[40] as shown in Fig. 12.8.

When the substituents are not identical, the vectors are not equal in length but are added vectorially in the same way. Furthermore, the vectors will differ in sign according to whether the substituent is electron releasing or electron attracting. Platt has assigned[41] to each group a quantity called the spectroscopic moment, m, which has units of (centimeter moles/liter)$^{1/2}$ and from which the increase in the maximum extinction, ϵ,

[40] A. L. Sklar, *Revs. Modern Phys.*, **14**, 232 (1942).
[41] J. R. Platt, *J. Chem. Phys.*, **19**, 263 (1951).

TABLE 12.10

Relative Intensities of the ^1L_b Band of Polysubstituted Benzenes
with Identical Substituents

Position of Substituent	Relative Intensity
1	1
1,2	1
1,3	1
1,4	4
1,3,5	0
1,2,3	0
1,2,4	3

may be calculated by the vector-addition formula. Some of the assigned
spectroscopic moments are shown in Table 12.11; the same values apply
to substituted pyridines and naphthalenes.

TABLE 12.11

Spectroscopic Moments[41]

Group	Spectroscopic Moment, $(cm\ mole/l)^{1/2}$	Group	Spectroscopic Moment, $(cm\ mole/l)^{1/2}$
OH	34	CH_2Cl	-3
OCH_3	31	NC	-6
F	21	CHF_2	-11
CH_3	7	$CHCl_2$	-11
Cl	6	CF_3	-15
C_2H_5	5	SO_2NH_2	-15
Br	4	CCl_3	-17
$i\text{-}C_3H_7$	35	CN	-19
$tert\text{-}C_4H_9$	2	$CHBr_2$	-25
H	0	CO_2H	-28
CH_2F	-2	SO_3H	-42

These rules for calculating intensity do not apply to groups which
interact very strongly with the benzene rings, e.g., the NH_2 and NO_2 groups.

12.6 Intermolecular Charge-Transfer Spectra; the Benzene-Iodine Complex

Benzene and substituted benzenes form a large group of complexes,
which are usually relatively unstable (e.g., with iodine and silver salts).

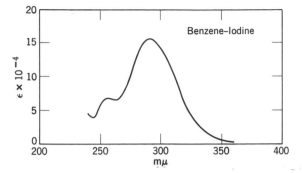

Fig. 12.9 The spectrum of the benzene-iodine complex in CCl_4. [Reprinted by permission from N. S. Ham, J. R. Platt, and H. McConnell, *J. Chem. Phys.*, **19**, 1301 (1951).]

This large class of compounds (complexes) is believed to be characterized by the fact that the bonding arises from the interpenetration of the π-electron cloud of the benzene ring and the electron cloud of the other partner, and they are often referred to as π complexes. The most extensively investigated of these complexes is probably the benzene-iodine complex,[42] $C_6H_6 \cdot I_2$. Although this complex is quite weak, so that it cannot be isolated as a solid, and is always partially dissociated in solution, it has an absorption spectrum of its own,[42b] shown in Fig. 12.9, with a maximum at 290 mμ. This spectrum is obtained by subtraction of the benzene and iodine spectra from the spectrum of the equilibrium mixture.

Mulliken[43] has proposed that these complexes may be considered formed by an acid-base reaction of a Lewis acid (A, I_2 in this case) and a Lewis base (B, benzene). The complex may then be described as a resonance hybrid between two states, one nonbonded (AB, Ψ_{NB}) and the other dative (A^-B^+, Ψ_D). In the ground state, Ψ_D makes a relatively small contribution, but an excited state exists in which Ψ_D makes the major contribution. The characteristic absorption band of the complex corresponds to the transition from the ground state to this excited state; and, since this transition involves the transfer of almost a complete electronic charge from B to A, the band has been called a *charge-transfer band*.

The energy of this charge-transfer band can be approximately evaluated in a relatively simple manner. The energy required to transfer an electron from B to A may be pictured as equivalent to removing an electron from B, involving an expenditure of energy equal to I_B, the ionization potential

[42] (a) H. A. Benesi and J. H. Hildebrand, *J. Am. Chem. Soc.*, **71**, 2703 (1949); L. J. Andrews, *Chem. Revs.*, **51**, 713 (1954). (b) N. S. Ham, J. R. Platt, and H. McConnell, *J. Chem. Phys.*, **19**, 1301 (1951).
[43] R. S. Mulliken, *J. Am. Chem. Soc.*, **74**, 811 (1952).

of B, followed by placing the electron on A, thus liberating the amount of energy E_A, the electron affinity of A. Since now A^- and B^+ are oppositely charged ions, in addition the Coulombic attraction of the two ions, e^2/r, where r is the distance from A^- to B^+, is obtained. Hence, the energy difference $(W_{NB} - W_D)$ between the structures Ψ'_{NB} and Ψ'_D is given by

$$W_{NB} - W_D = I_B - E_A - \frac{e^2}{r} + \phi \qquad (12.1)$$

where ϕ is an undetermined quantity absorbing all other energy differences. Now, the two structures Ψ'_{NB} and Ψ'_D interact, the resonance integral $\int \Psi'_{NB} H \Psi'_D \, d\tau$ is called β, and the energies of the ground and excited states, respectively, become

$$E_G = \frac{W_{NB} + \beta^2}{W_D - W_{NB}}$$

$$E_E = \frac{W_D - \beta^2}{W_D - W_{NB}}$$

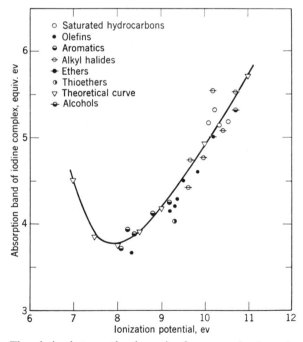

Fig. 12.10   The relation between the absorption frequency of a charge-transfer complex and the ionization potential of the basic component. (Reprinted by permission from F. A. Matsen, in Vol. IX of *Technique of Organic Chemistry*, edited by A. Weissberger, Interscience Publishers, New York, 1956.)

The binding energy of the complex (i.e., the energy of the complex below that of the nonbonded structure) is $\beta^2/(W_D - W_{NB})$, and the frequency of the charge-transfer band is:

$$\nu = \frac{W_D - W_{NB} + 2\beta^2/(W_D - W_{NB})}{h}$$

and, substituting from equation (12.1) and neglecting ϕ,

$$\nu = \frac{[E_A + (e^2/r) - I_B + 2\beta^2]/[E_A + (e^2/r) - I_B]}{h} \tag{12.2}$$

If, for a series of complexes of a single acid with various bases, E_A, e^2/r and β are considered constant, equation (12.2) defines a curve which is shown as the solid curve in Fig. 12.10, with $E_A + e^2/r = 6$ ev, $\beta = 1.3$ ev. It is seen that this curve gives quite good agreement with a wide range of experimental data.

As is obvious from the foregoing treatment, the concept of the charge-transfer complex can be satisfactory only for quite loose complexes, because only in these can the ground state involve Ψ_D to merely a minor extent, and hence can excitation involve transfer of substantially an integral charge. However, the concept of the charge-transfer complex has been extremely fruitful in the consideration of a wide variety of loose complexes. A relation between the intensity of the charge-transfer absorption band and the stability of the complex has been proposed.[44]

12.7 Biphenyl and Polyphenyls

Biphenyl, II, displays only a single absorption band in the readily accessible ultraviolet,[45] a structureless band at 251.5 mμ with $\epsilon = 18,300$. The fact that the intensity is so much greater than that for the benzene band in the same wavelength region strongly suggest that this is not the $^1L_b \leftarrow {}^1A$ but rather the $^1L_a \leftarrow {}^1A$, transition, or possibly one of the allowed $^1B \leftarrow {}^1A$ transitions. If this is so, the $^1L_b \leftarrow {}^1A$ transition is apparently hidden below the long-wavelength tail of the 251.5 mμ band. This assignment is consistent with the expectation that conjugation of the two phenyl rings results in a bathochromic shift. It is interesting to note that fluorene, III,

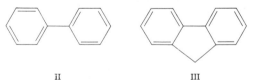

II   III

[44] J. N. Murrell, *J. Am. Chem. Soc.*, **81**, 5037 (1959); *Quart. Revs.*, **15**, 2 (1961).
[45] A. E. Gillam and D. H. Hey, *J. Chem. Soc.*, 1170 (1939); A. Wenzel, *J. Chem. Phys.*, **21**, 403 (1953).

which may be considered as an o-, o'-disubstituted biphenyl, has another band[46] at about 300 mμ, which presumably may represent the $^1L_b \leftarrow {}^1A$ transition. The notation used here (^1L_a and ^1L_b) is not strictly applicable to biphenyl, but is chosen for purposes of comparison with benzene. A notation more appropriate for biphenyl will be introduced in the next section.

Theoretical calculations by the MO method for biphenyl have been reported by London,[47] but the results are not in sufficiently close agreement with the experimental findings to be very helpful in the assignments.

When more than two phenyl groups are directly joined together, the various possible isomers show some rather striking spectroscopic differences. In the all-*meta* polyphenyls, conjugation between any two adjacent rings is possible and effective (cf. structures IV and V), but conjugation

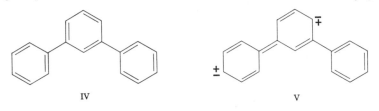

| IV | V |

between more than two rings would involve structures with long bonds, such as VI, and is accordingly unimportant. Consequently it is not

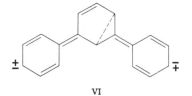

VI

surprising that all the m-polyphenyls absorb at substantially the same wavelength, 253 $\pm$ 2 mμ, and with an intensity[45] which is approximately proportional to the maximum number of separate biphenyl groupings possible. This is demonstrated by the near constancy of $\epsilon/(n-1)$ observed in Table 12.12. In the p-polyphenyl series, however, the wavelength of the absorption band increases with increasing number of rings, although a maximum value is approached asymptotically in a manner similar to the polyenes. This relationship has been discussed by a number of workers. Thus Davydov[48] derived the following equation from quantum-mechanical considerations:

$$\Delta E = A - 2\,|M|\,|\cos\,[\pi/(n+1)]|$$

[46] R. N. Jones, *J. Am. Chem. Soc.*, **67**, 2021 (1945).

[47] A. London *J. Chem. Phys.*, **13**, 396 (1945).

[48] A. S. Davydov, *Zhur. Eksptl. i Teort. Fiz.*, **18**, 515 (1948).

where ΔE is the transition energy corresponding to the $^1L_a \leftarrow {}^1A$ band, and M is the matrix element of the interaction between neighboring benzene rings, a constant independent of n, the number of benzene rings in the polyphenyl. Thus, with increasing n, ΔE decreases and a bathochromic shift results, but the magnitude of the shift also decreases with

TABLE 12.12

The Spectra of the Polyphenyls, $H(C_6H_4)_nH$[45]

n^a	para Series			meta Series		
	λ, mμ	ϵ	ϵ/n	λ, mμ	ϵ	$\epsilon/(n - 1)$
2	251.5	18,300	9,150	251.5	18,300	18,300
3	280	25,000	8,300	251.5	44,000	22,000
4	300	39,000	9,850	...	...	...
5	310	62,500	12,500	...	...	...
6	317.5	56,000	...	...	...	...
9	...	...	...	253	184,000	23,000
10	...	...	...	253	213,000	22,500
11	...	...	...	253	215,000	21,500
12	...	...	...	253	233,000	21,200
13	...	...	...	253	252,000	21,000
14	...	...	...	253	283,000	21,800
15	...	...	...	254	309,000	22,700
16	...	...	...	255	320,000	21,300

^{a} n is the number of rings.

increasing n. Using the experimental data[38] for biphenyl and p-sexiphenyl, the values of A and of M have been estimated as 50,060 cm^{-1} and 10,300 cm^{-1}, respectively, in chloroform. Accordingly, when n is infinity, the asymptotic value is at 339 mμ.[49] An equation somewhat similar to the above theoretical one has been derived experimentally.[50] Unfortunately, no data appear to exist for compounds with more than six rings. The continuing increase is consistent with the picture that, in this series, conjugation can extend over all phenyl rings, as shown by structure VII.

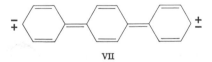

VII

The fact that the intensity is larger in the m-polyphenyl series than in the $para$-series is consistent with the proposed assignment. The $^1L_a \leftarrow {}^1A$

[49] H. Suzuki, Bull. Chem. Soc. Japan, 33, 109 (1960).
[50] K. Hirayama, J. Chem. Soc. Japan, Pure Chem. Sect., 75, 682 (1954).

transitions are polarized along the short molecular axis, and inspection of structures IV and VII shows that the extension of the *meta* compounds in this direction is slightly over twice that of the *para* analogs.

12.8   Stilbene and Related Compounds

In the preceding sections, a wide variety of benzene derivatives was discussed, and ethylene and its derivatives were discussed in sections 9.2–9.4. The simplest combination of the ethylene (i.e., double-bond) and phenyl chromophore, styrene, VIII, was discussed in section 12.24. This section will be devoted to the combination of the ethylene with two phenyl chromophores in stilbene, and a series of compounds isoelectronic or virtually isoelectronic with stilbene. These compounds may be considered derived from stilbene by replacement of one or both of the —CH groups by —N=, —N⁺H=, —N⁺O=, or —N⁺OH= (i.e., benzalaniline, IX; azobenzene, X, and its conjugate acid, XI, azoxybenzene, XII, and its conjugate acid, XIII, and phenylnitrone, XIV). Attention will be predominantly focused on the *trans* isomers because they are largely free of steric effects.

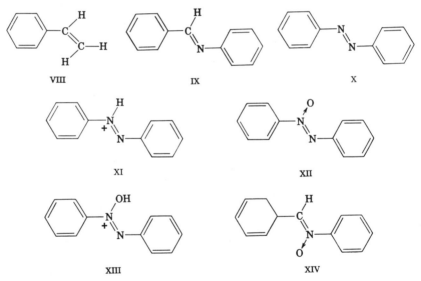

The parent compounds for this discussion are the hydrocarbons *trans-*, XV, and *cis*-stilbene, XVI, the spectra[51] of which are shown in Fig. 12.11. Although the spectra of the *trans* isomer are surprisingly different in heptane and in benzene, there are three major bands in each. The long-wavelength band, frequently denoted as the A band,[52] consists of four

[51] H. Suzuki, *Bull. Chem. Soc. Japan*, **33**, 381 (1960).

vibrational peaks, at 283, 294.1, 306.9, and 320.5 mμ with ϵ_{max} of 27,950 at 294.1 mμ. In benzene these peaks are at 289, 298.8, 311.2, and 324.5, respectively, with ϵ_{max} of 25,600 at 311.2 mμ. The bathochromic and hyperchromic effects of benzene (as well as of carbon tetrachloride) are greater than would be expected on the basis of the greater refractivity of these solvents (cf. section 9.7) as compared to heptane[51]; this phenomenon is not understood and warrants further investigation. The two other bands in the spectrum of *trans*-stilbene are centered (in heptane) at 228.5 mμ, $\epsilon = 16,200$ (called the B band) and at 201.5 mμ, $\epsilon = 23,800$ (called the C band). The spectrum of *cis*-stilbene (Fig. 12.11) has a structureless long-wavelength band at considerably shorter wavelength and of lower intensity than that of its isomer. These features are related to the steric crowding in *cis*-stilbene, a subject that will be discussed in Chapter 15.

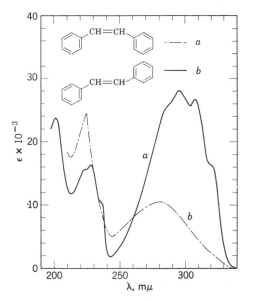

Fig. 12.11 Spectra of (*a*) *trans*- and (*b*) *cis*-stilbene in heptane and ethanol, respectively. [Reprinted by permission from H. Suzuki, *Bull. Chem. Soc. Japan*, **33**, 381 (1960).]

[52] R. N. Beale and E. M. F. Roe, *J. Chem. Soc.*, 2755 (1953).

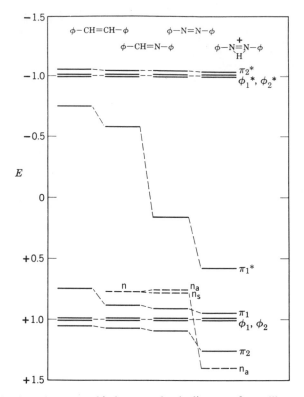

Fig. 12.12 One-electron orbital energy-level diagram for stilbene, benzalaniline, azobenzene, and its conjugate acid. [Reprinted by permission from H. H. Jaffé, S.-J. Yeh, and R. W. Gardner, *J. Mol. Spectroscopy*, **2**, 120 (1958).]

Before proceeding to discuss the spectra, it is profitable to consider the energy-level diagram of *trans*-stilbene. This compound belongs to the point group C_{2h}, and *cis*-stilbene to C_{2v}; however, any MO treatment neglecting interaction between nonneighboring atoms is equivalent to consideration of the linear structure, XVII, for both compounds, which

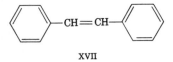

XVII

belongs to the point group D_{2h}. An orbital diagram[53] for this linear molecule is given in Fig. 12.12. Of spectroscopic interest are, possibly, the

[53] H. H. Jaffé, S.-J. Yeh, and R. W. Gardner, *J. Mol. Spectroscopy*, **2**, 120 (1958); cf. also P. P. Birnbaum, J. H. Linford, and D. W. G. Style, *Trans. Faraday Soc.*, **49**, 735 (1953); W. Maier, A. Saupe, and A. Englert, *Z. physik. Chem. N.F.*, **10**, 273 (1957).

four highest occupied orbitals and the four lowest unoccupied orbitals. These orbitals fall into two classes: those antisymmetric with respect to *rotation* about the lengthwise (z) axis of the molecule, and those symmetric with respect to this axis. Following a suggestion by Platt,[54] the unoccupied antisymmetric orbitals are called g (b_{2g}) and h (b_{3u}) in order of increasing energy, and the occupied antisymmetric ones, f (b_{3u}) and e (b_{2g}) in order of decreasing energy. The two occupied symmetric orbitals are called v_g (b_{1g}) and v_u (a_u), respectively, depending on their gerade or ungerade character,

TABLE 12.13

The Excited States in Stilbene

Configuration	Symmetry	Platt	Polarization	Forbiddenness[a]	C$_{2h}$	C$_{2v}$
(1) $e_g^2 v_g^2 v_u^2 f_u g_g$	$^1B_{1u}$	^1B	∥	A	B_u	B_2
(2) $e_g^2 v_g^2 v_u f_u g_g^2$	$^1B_{2u}$			A	B_u	A_1
(3) $e_g^2 v_g v_u^2 f_u^2 g_g$	$^1B_{3g}$	^1G	⊥	F	A_g	B_2
(4) $e_g^2 v_g^2 v_u^2 f_u w_g$	$^1B_{2u}$			A	B_u	A_1
(5) $e_g^2 v_g^2 v_u^2 f_u w_u$	$^1B_{3g}$			F	A_g	B_2
(6) $e_g^2 v_g^2 v_u f_u^2 w_g$	$^1B_{1u}$			A	B_u	B_2
(7) $e_g^2 v_g^2 v_u f_u^2 w_u$	^1A_g	^1H	∥	F	A_g	A_1
(8) $e_g^2 v_g v_u^2 f_u^2 w_g$	^1A_g			F	A_g	A_1
(9) $e_g^2 v_g v_u^2 f_u^2 w_u$	$^1B_{1u}$			A	B_u	A_1
(10) $e_g^2 v_g^2 v_u^2 f_u h_u$	^1A_g	^1C	∥	F	A_g	A_1
(11) $e_g v_g^2 v_u^2 f_u^2 g_g$	^1A_g	^1C	∥	F	A_g	A_1
Etc.						

[a] A = allowed; F = forbidden.

and the corresponding unoccupied ones, w_g (b_{1g}) and w_u (a_u). The ground state has the configuration $e_u^2 v_g^2 v_u^2 f_u^2$, species ^1A_g, and the possible excited configurations, with the appropriate state designations, both in symmetry and in Platt notation, are given in Table 12.13.[55] This table shows five allowed transitions, three polarized parallel, two polarized perpendicular, to the lengthwise axis, and six forbidden transitions. Any further transitions are doubtlessly of too high an energy to be of interest, except in the far ultraviolet.

[54] J. R. Platt, in A. Hollaender, *Radiation Biology*, McGraw-Hill Book Co., New York, 1956, pp. 93–96.

[55] See T. E. Peacock, *Proc. Phys. Soc.* (*London*), **70A**, 654 (1957).

The spectra of all the compounds, IX–XV, under discussion are quite similar; they consist of a very intense band at relatively long wavelength, varying from about 300 mμ in stilbene, to about 420 mμ in the conjugate acid of azobenzene. A second band occurs with lower intensity at about 230 mμ in all the compounds. In addition, some of the compounds have an additional low-intensity band at longer wavelength. The assignment of the high-intensity long-wavelength band to the $^1B \leftarrow {}^1A$ transition appears immediately obvious. Its great intensity identifies it as a $V \leftarrow N$ transition, and of course $^1B \leftarrow {}^1A$ should occur at the longest wavelength.

A clue to the assignment of the shorter-wavelength transition comes from its insensitivity to the nature of the bridge bonding the phenyl groups, which indicates either that both upper and lower levels are equally displaced, or that neither is displaced at all by modification of the bridge. Energy-level diagrams using some reasonable assumptions for Coulomb and resonance integrals for the various bridge atoms are shown in Fig. 12.12, where it is seen that there are no orbital pairs undergoing approximately equal shifts, but that the orbitals v and w are independent of the nature of the bridge. This fact is due to their symmetry, which restricts them to a linear combination of the AO's of atoms not lying on the lengthwise axis. Accordingly, the short-wavelength band must be assigned to a $^1H \leftarrow {}^1A$ transition.

Inspection of Fig. 12.12 shows that the transitions $^1G \leftarrow {}^1A$ ($v \to g$ and $f \to w$) should occur at longer wavelength than $^1H \leftarrow {}^1A$, but, as noted above, no unassigned absorption region is available. Since these two transitions belong to the same symmetry species, undoubtedly configuration interaction lowers one ($^1G \leftarrow {}^1A$) ($v \to g$) transition and raises the energy of the other ($f \to w$). Also, calculations including overlap, which always compress all bonding levels and spread out the antibonding ones, further increase this spread, and thus it is not unlikely that the $f \to w$ transition falls into the 230 mμ region, or even below it. But, certainly, one allowed transition is missing.

The missing transition may be found by a careful examination of the spectra. The long-wavelength, intense band is observed to be rather unsymmetrical and quite broad. Although there is no theoretical reason why spectral bands should be symmetrical, experience shows that they usually are. A rather interesting analysis of the spectra is obtained if we assume the bands to have a symmetrical shape, and subtract from the over-all spectrum a symmetrical band,[53] as shown for azobenzene in Fig. 12.13. By such an analysis, a band of moderate intensity is revealed on the short-wavelength side of the $^1B \leftarrow {}^1A$ transition, which may be assigned to the $^1G \leftarrow {}^1A$ ($^1B_{2u} \leftarrow {}^1A_g$) transition. This assignment is further confirmed by more elaborate theoretical calculations.[55]

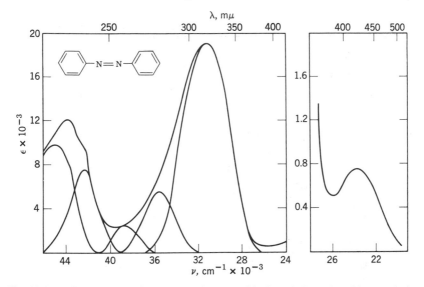

Fig. 12.13 The spectrum of azobenzene in 15 wt. % ethanol. [Reprinted by permission from H. H. Jaffé, S.-J. Yeh, and R. W. Gardner, *J. Mol. Spectroscopy*, **2**, 120 (1958).]

Repetition of the reflection and subtraction reveals a third band, at about 258 mμ in azobenzene. Of course, since the validity of this procedure can be questioned in the first place, and since the band arises as a matter of second differences, its reality is open to considerable question. However, such a band is found in all compounds for which these analyses have been made. The assignment of this band is not obvious. It might be the second allowed $^1B_{2u} \leftarrow {}^1A_g$ ($f_u \rightarrow w_g$) transition; however, its intensity ($\epsilon \sim 2400$) seems somewhat low for this assignment. It might also be the forbidden component of the $^1G \leftarrow {}^1A$ ($^1B_{3g} \leftarrow {}^1A_g$) transition, although the intensity seems too high for a $g \rightarrow g$ transition.

The short-wavelength band also appears to consist of several components; at least in some compounds this band appears clearly split into at least two bands. It is unknown whether these represent the two components of the $^1H \leftarrow {}^1A$ transitions, split by configuration interaction and different electron correlation, or whether the second band is a $^1C \leftarrow {}^1A$ transition.

The situation in benzalaniline, IX, is slightly different. The analysis of the compound spectrum into its presumed component bands is shown in Fig. 12.14. Again, the long-wavelength band appears to consist of three separate bands, but the intensity relations are considerably different. Here, the central band is the most intense. It is fairly obvious that in the less symmetrical benzalaniline the $^1B \leftarrow {}^1A$ transition should be less intense

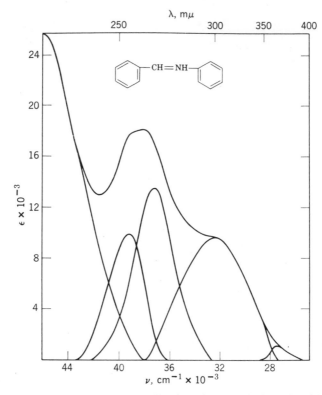

Fig. 12.14   The spectrum of benzalaniline in 95% ethanol. [Reprinted by permission from H. H. Jaffé, S.-J. Yeh, and R. W. Gardner, *J. Mol. Spectroscopy*, **2**, 120 (1958).]

than in stilbene and azobenzene. The identification of the three bands is probably the same as in the other compounds, but the exact correspondence between the bands of the symmetrical compounds and of benzalaniline is unknown.

The spectra of azoxybenzene, XII, and of its conjugate acid, XIII, are similar to those just discussed.[56] These molecules are not quite isoelectronic with the others, even with respect to the π-electron system. However, rough MO calculations indicate that introduction of the oxygen atom, which contributes one π molecular orbital and two electrons to the conjugated system, does not greatly affect the orbitals of spectroscopic interest. This is undoubtedly due to the electronegativity of the oxygen atom, which places the new orbital relatively low.

trans-Azoxybenzene has the intense $^1B \leftarrow {}^1A$ band at 322 mμ ($\epsilon = 15,400$), and the $^1H \leftarrow {}^1A$ band is, as usual, split into two (or possibly

---

[56] C. S. Hahn, Ph.D. thesis, University of Cincinnati, Cincinnati, Ohio, 1961.

three) components at 238, 231 (and possibly 227) mμ. The $^1G \leftarrow {}^1A$ transition now is clearly separated, at 260 mμ ($\epsilon = 7800$), and careful analysis suggests that an additional band occurs at about 282 mμ with ϵ about 5000. It is interesting to note that the intensity relation of the two bands identified as $^1G \leftarrow {}^1A$ is the reverse of that in azobenzene.

The spectrum of the conjugate acid of azoxybenzene is quite similar to that of the free base. The $^1B \leftarrow {}^1A$ transition is shifted to 383 mμ, a somewhat smaller shift than the corresponding one between azobenzene and its conjugate acid. The $^1H \leftarrow {}^1A$ transition is very broad, not resolved into separate bands. The $^1G \leftarrow {}^1A$ transition appears only as a shoulder, not as well resolved as in the free base, at 298 mμ with ϵ_{max} of 4600, and the reflection and subtraction procedure shows a weak band, at about 337 mμ, presumably the usual third band in this group.

The various assignments made in this way are summarized in Table 12.14. The assignments discussed receive considerable further support from vapor[57] and solid[58] spectra. In the vapor spectra of azobenzene, benzalaniline, and stilbene, bands have been observed in the regions of the $^1H \leftarrow {}^1A$ and $^1B \leftarrow {}^1A$ transitions; the two bands, ($^1G \leftarrow {}^1A$), apparently isolated in the solution spectra in the high-intensity absorption, have not been specifically observed in the vapor, but no vibrational frequencies of the order of magnitude necessary to explain these bands in terms of vibrational structure have been reported. In solid stilbene,[58] very weak transitions observed at 387 and 367 mμ are presumably $^3B \leftarrow {}^1A$ and $^3G \leftarrow {}^1A$; these are apparently of different polarization as expected for this assignment. A third band at slightly shorter wavelength also appears to be present.

The assignments discussed in the preceding paragraphs were based on the assumption of D_{2h} symmetry. The actual symmetry of the *trans* compounds, however, is C_{2h}. Table 12.13 also lists the symmetry species of the excited states in this point group, and it is readily verified that the same bands are allowed and forbidden, and that the polarizations are the same. The unsymmetrical compounds, benzalaniline, azoxybenzene, and phenylnitrone, of course, belong to the even lower point group C_s, but their π-electron systems may be considered as slightly perturbed C_{2h}, and the foregoing analysis remains valid.

The discussion thus far has neglected the low-intensity long-wavelength band of azobenzene at about 420 mμ (cf. Fig. 12.13), and a very low-intensity band appearing in the analysis of the spectrum of benzalaniline

[57] S. Imanishi and T. Tachi, *J. Chem. Soc. Japan*, **64**, 521 (1943); *Chem. Abstr.*, **41**, 3367 (1947); Y. Kanda, *Mem. Fac. Sci. Kyushu Univ.*, Ser. C., Chem., **1**, 189 (1950); *Chem. Abstr.*, **46**, 9982 (1951).
[58] P. Pesteil, *Compt. rend.*, **233**, 924 (1951).

TABLE 12.14
The Spectra of Stilbene and Analogs
(All wavelengths in millimicrons)

Transition	Stilbene		Benzalaniline		Azobenzene		Azobenzene Conj. Acid		Azoxybenzene		Azoxybenzene Conj. Acid		Phenylnitrone	
	λ	ϵ	λ	ϵ	λ	ϵ	λ	ϵ	λ	ϵ	λ	ϵ	λ	ϵ
$^1W \leftarrow {}^1A$	...	...	~360	100	420	760	300	3,000	...	...	...	...	...	...
$^1B \leftarrow {}^1A$	297	27,000	312[a]	10,000	314	19,200	418	26,900	322	15,400	383	14,500	315	14,000
$^1G \leftarrow {}^1A$	~275	...	~270[a]	13,500	281	5,500	382	14,800	282[a]	5,000	(377)[a]	2,000	~285	...
$^1G \leftarrow {}^1A$	~260	...	253	10,000	258	2,400	352	4,800	260[a]	7,800	298[a]	4,600	~265	...
$^1H \leftarrow {}^1A$	226	15,000	~218	14,400	236	7,400	236	8,000	238	8,200	~232	2,900	227	9,850
$^1H \leftarrow {}^1A$ or $^1C \leftarrow {}^1A$	...	...	...	...	223	9,800	~220	~5,000	231	9,400	...	...	236	9,060

[a] The assignments in these pairs may be reversed.

as a tail of the high-intensity band (cf. Fig. 12.14). These bands are $n \rightarrow \pi^*$ transitions. Since the n orbitals of the nitrogen atoms are approximately sp^2 hybridized, the transitions are allowed by *local* symmetry and are designated as $^1W \leftarrow {}^1A$ in the Platt notation.

Azobenzene, with two nitrogen atoms, has two n orbitals; in nonlocalized MO terminology, these should be represented as n_a and n_s, the antisymmetric and symmetric combinations of the lone-pair orbitals of the nitrogen atoms, respectively. The symmetry species of the excited states of the $n_a \rightarrow \pi^*$ and $n_s \rightarrow \pi^*$ transitions then are A_u and B_g, respectively, and one is allowed, the other forbidden, by *molecular* symmetry. However, it appears likely that *local* symmetry is more important, and that both occur with low intensity. The interaction between the two sp^2 hybrid orbitals of the nitrogens is likely to be small, and the width of the 420 mμ band has been interpreted as indicating a superposition of the two bands. In benzalaniline, only one such transition is possible, and the analysis in Fig. 12.14 suggests that it occurs at the long-wavelength tail of the high-intensity band. The relation between the $n \rightarrow \pi^*$ bands in these two compounds is reasonable, since the n levels in both should be about equal energetically, but the g level lies considerably higher in benzalaniline, as shown in Fig. 12.14.

In azoxybenzene and the conjugate acids of azo- and azoxybenzene, there should be only one n level; this should be, because of the positive charge in the —N+=N— group, considerably depressed relative to azobenzene. Analysis of the spectrum of the conjugate acid of azobenzene (Fig. 12.15) shows, in addition to the bands previously discussed, a broad band at about 300 mμ, which has been ascribed to the $^1W \leftarrow {}^1A$ transition.

$n \rightarrow \pi^*$ transitions ($^1W \leftarrow {}^1A$) are not apparent in either azoxybenzene or its conjugate acid. It is possible that these transitions appear in the long-wavelength tails of both compounds.

In the *cis* compounds, the situation is considerably more complicated. These compounds, when symmetrical, belong to the point group C_{2v}, and the symmetry species of all transitions are given in Table 12.13. All of them are allowed. Examination of the structure also suggests that the distinction between the normal MO's (e, f, g, h) and the special type (v, w) disappears. An additional complication lies in the fact that these molecules, because of steric interference, are probably not completely planar, a problem which will be dealt with in detail in Chapter 15. No really satisfactory interpretation of the spectra of these compounds which are shown in Figs. 15.15 and 15.16, seems to have been proposed.

Considerable work has been done on the spectra of substituted stilbenes and related compounds, mostly with emphasis on the long-wavelength absorption. These results will not be discussed here in detail except to

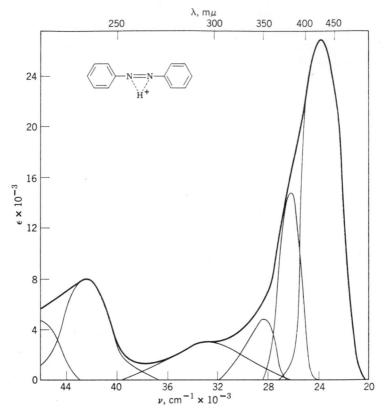

Fig. 12.15   The spectrum of the conjugate acid of azobenzene. [Reprinted by permission from H. H. Jaffé, S.-J. Yeh, and R. W. Gardner, *J. Mol. Spectroscopy*, **2**, 120 (1958).]

point out that they tend to confirm the proposed assignments. The $^1B \leftarrow {}^1A$ transitions show the usual sensitivity to substituents, particularly in the *p* and *p'* positions, where they lie on the axis of polarization. The $^1H \leftarrow {}^1A$ transitions are relatively insensitive to *p* and *p'* substituents, which are attached to atoms making no contributions to the *v* or *w* orbital.

In conclusion, it may be worth noting that the n $\rightarrow$ π^* ($^1W \leftarrow {}^1A$) transition of azobenzene is suprisingly insensitive to solvent effects, in contrast to the usual behavior of such bands.

13 Polycyclic hydrocarbons

Extensive reviews, surveys, compilations, and interpretations of the spectra of polynuclear hydrocarbons and their derivatives are available. The most systematic and successful schemes for correlating these extensive data are those of E. Clar,[1] contained in his book, *Aromatische Kohlenwasserstoffe*, and of John R. Platt and collaborators, detailed in a series of articles in *Journal of Chemical Physics*.

13.1 Clar's Generalizations

Before discussing the spectra of the polycyclic hydrocarbons, some basic nomenclature practices need to be discussed. The polycyclic aromatics have been grouped, especially for purposes of discussion of spectra, into two large classes: the *"cata-*condensed" and the *"peri-*condensed" aromatics.[1] The *cata*-condensed aromatics consists of those compounds of empirical formula $C_{4n+2}H_{2n+4}$ which have no carbon atom belonging to more than two rings, thus implying that every carbon atom is on the periphery of the conjugated system. The *cata*-condensed aromatic hydrocarbons can be further classified into the "acenes" and the "phenes." The acenes are polycyclic systems in which all the rings are linear. The first member of the series is anthracene, I, followed by naphthacene (or tetracene), II, pentacene, III, etc. The phenes are the *cata*-condensed polycyclic aromatics containing an angular or bent system of rings. The first member

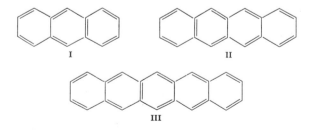

I   II

III

[1] E. Clar, *Aromatische Kohlenwasserstoffe*, Julius Springer, Berlin, 1952, 2nd Ed.

of the series is phenanthrene or triphene, IV. It will be noted that the middle ring of phenanthrene has benzene rings fused on neighboring sides. The phenes are built up by linear extension of the ring system on each side of the middle ring. In naming the phenes, a prefix is added to indicate the total number of rings in the system. If the number of rings on each side of the middle phenanthrene ring, A, is equal or differs by only one ring, nothing further is added to the name, e.g.:

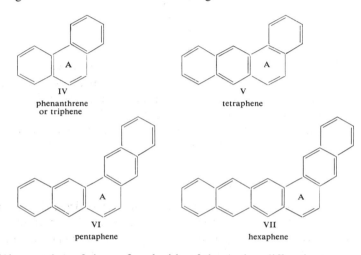

If the number of rings of each side of the A ring differs by two or more, Roman numerals are added in parentheses after the phene to indicate the number of rings on each side of A, e.g.:

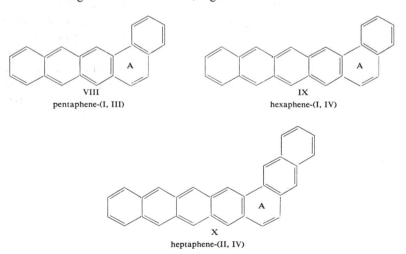

There are other *cata*-condensed aromatics which belong to neither the acene or the phene series, e.g.:

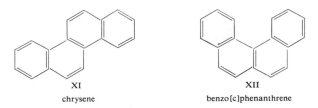

XI   XII
chrysene   benzo[c]phenanthrene

No special names for classes outside of the acenes or phenes have been suggested, probably because no systematic, unambiguous Aufbau principle can be utilized.

The other large classification of polycyclic aromatics is the *peri*-condensed compounds, in which some carbon atoms belong to three or more rings, e.g.:

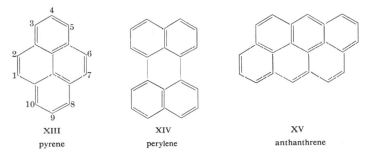

XIII   XIV   XV
pyrene   perylene   anthanthrene

Most of the aromatic hydrocarbons have three rather well-defined band systems in the ultraviolet or visible regions. The longest-wavelength band has the lowest intensity, and the shorter-wavelength bands have successively higher intensity. The first group of bands (shortest-wavelength) has $\log \epsilon_{max}$ 4.5–5.2; the second, 3.6–4.1; the third band is a region of low-intensity absorption, $\log \epsilon_{max}$ 2.3–3.2. Clar[1] calls these band systems β, *para*, and α and suggests that they are related to the three band systems of benzene. In the polyacenes, all the absorption bands are progressively displaced toward longer wavelengths as the number of rings increases. One of the most striking features of the spectral behavior of this group of compounds is the rapid shift in the wavelength of the *para* band. This shift is so rapid that in the linear tricyclic compound, anthracene, the α band, which is the low-intensity, long-wavelength band in benzene and naphthalene, already is swamped by the *para* band. This effect is illustrated by Fig. 13.1, which shows the complete spectra of

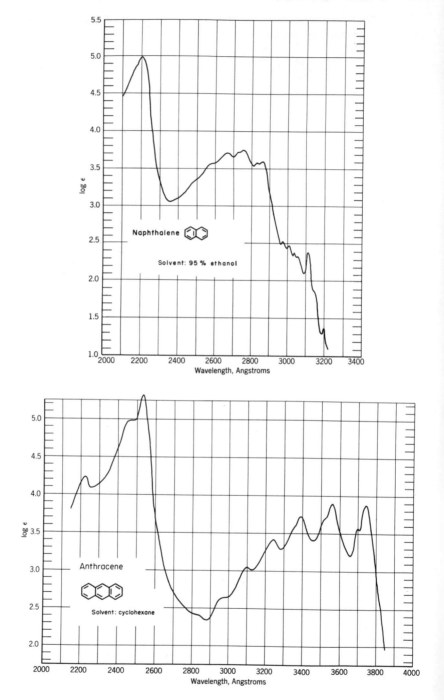

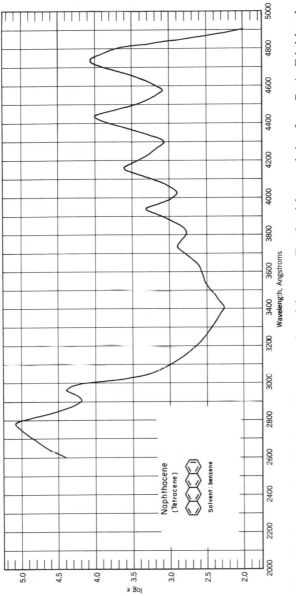

Fig. 13.1 Spectra of naphthalene, anthracene, and naphthacene. (Reprinted by permission from R. A. Friedel and M. Orchin, *Ultraviolet Spectra of Aromatic Compounds*, John Wiley and Sons, New York, 1951.)

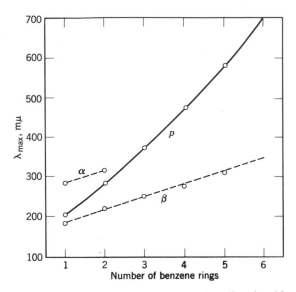

Fig. 13.2 The α, β, and *para* bands in the acene series. (Reprinted by permission from G. M. Badger, *The Structure and Reactions of Aromatic Compounds*, Cambridge University Press, 1954.)

naphthalene, anthracene, and naphthacene,[2] and by Fig. 13.2, which gives a plot[3] of the first (longest-wavelength) absorption band of the α, *para*, and β bands as a function of the length of the polyacene.

In the angular polycyclic compounds, the phenes, the three band systems again shift to longer wavelengths with increasing number of benzene rings, but the *para*-band system does not shift as rapidly as it does in the acene series. The spectra of phenanthrene and 1,2-benzanthracene[2] are shown in Fig. 13.3, and the change in band location with number of rings is shown[3] in Fig. 13.4.

For both linear and angular compounds the positions of the longest-wavelength component of the absorption bands are given by expressions of the form

$$\lambda = \frac{K^2}{R}$$

where K is the "order number," the value of which depends on the number of π electrons in the aromatic system, and R is a constant which differs for the α, β, and *para* bands.

[2] R. A. Friedel and M. Orchin, *Ultraviolet Spectra of Aromatic Compounds*, John Wiley and Sons, New York, 1951.

[3] G. M. Badger, *The Structures and Reactions of the Aromatic Compounds*, Cambridge University Press, 1954, pp. 392 f.

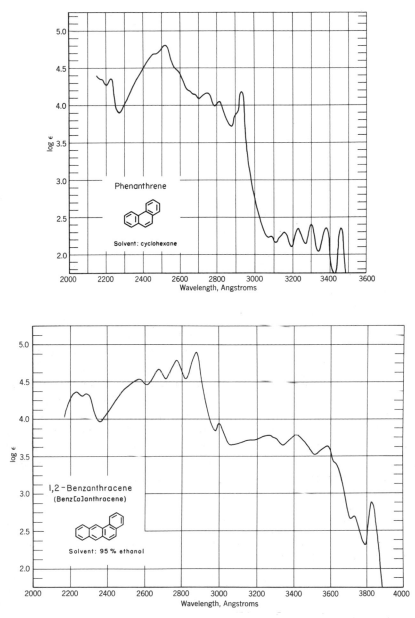

Fig. 13.3 Spectra of phenanthrene and 1,2-benzanthracene. (Reprinted by permission from R. A. Friedel and M. Orchin, *Ultraviolet Spectra of Aromatic Compounds*, John Wiley and Sons, New York, 1951.)

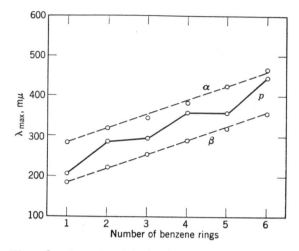

Fig. 13.4 The α, β, and *para* bands in the phene series. (Reprinted by permission from G. M. Badger, *The Structure and Reactions of Aromatic Compounds*, Cambridge University Press, 1954.)

13.2   The Platt Classification

The free-electron model discussed in connection with the spectra of the conjugated dienes and polyenes in section 11.1 has been applied to the classification of the spectra of *cata*-condensed aromatic systems by Platt.[4] His treatment is based on the assumption that, to a crude approximation, one-electron orbitals in *cata*-condensed aromatic hydrocarbons may be treated as analogous to the wave functions of an electron rotating around the periphery of the molecule. This periphery is further considered distorted into a circle; and, in analogy with the FEM treatment of linear systems, the potential energy is assumed constant all around the periphery. With these assumptions the problem of finding the one-electron orbitals reduces to the well-known problem of the plane rotator,[5] leading to the wave functions

$$\psi = e^{im_q \varphi} \tag{13.1}$$

where $m_q = 0, \pm 1, \pm 2$, etc., and φ is the polar angle about the center of the circle. Associated with these ψ are the energy values

$$E = \frac{q^2 h^2}{2ml^2} = \frac{1{,}210{,}000 q^2}{l^2} \text{ cm}^{-1} \tag{13.2}$$

if l, the length around the perimeter, is given in angstrom units, and where q is a quantum number having integral values $0, 1, 2, \ldots$, and measuring

---

[4] J. R. Platt, *J. Chem. Phys.*, **17**, 484 (1949).

[5] W. Kauzman, *Quantum Chemistry*, Academic Press, New York, 1957, pp. 198 f.

the units of angular momentum about the axis of rotation possessed by the rotator. As usual, h is Planck's constant and m the mass of the electron. Since E depends on q^2, the energy levels are quadratically spaced (cf. Fig. 13.5), just like the levels of the electron in a linear box. All levels except the lowest ($q = 0$) are doubly degenerate, because the angular momentum, if different from 0, may point along either direction of the rotational axis, i.e., its z component m_q may be equal to $+q$ or $-q$; by a classical analogy we may say that the electron, if rotating ($q \neq 0$), may be moving in a clockwise or counterclockwise direction.

In the Platt scheme, the molecular state is characterized by the *total* angular momentum Q of all the electrons. A state of total angular momentum Q is also doubly degenerate (unless $Q = 0$) with z components of Q, $M_Q = \pm Q$. These components M_Q are obtained by addition of the m_q for all the individual electrons.[6] This simple recipe permits calculation of M_Q and hence Q for any state of a *cata*-condensed hydrocarbon.

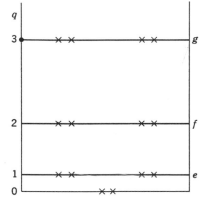

Fig. 13.5 Energy levels of the plane rotator.

In a *cata*-condensed system of n rings, there are $2(2n + 1)$ carbon atoms and an equal number of π electrons which fill successive orbitals, as shown in Fig. 13.5. Since the first (lowest) level is nondegenerate, all others doubly degenerate, the $2(2n + 1)$ π electrons, in the ground state, just completely fill the first $n + 1$ levels, so that the highest filled level has $q = n$; the four electrons (or any electrons) occupying this level are called f electrons. In accord with usual notation, electrons in shells below this are called, successively, by the next preceding letters of the alphabet (e for $q = n - 1$, etc.). The first vacant level is $q = n + 1$, and electrons in the higher levels are referred to by the next following letters of the alphabet, g for $q = n + 1$, etc. The notation starting with f and g for the last filled and first unfilled levels of the ground state has the advantage that the transition of longest wavelength, in one-electron notation $f \rightarrow g$, has the same symbol independently of the molecule and its size.

As long as all levels are filled, the nondegenerate level $q = 0$ with two electrons, all others with four, the m_q always occur in pairs of equal magnitude but opposite sign, so that their sum, M_Q, is 0 and hence $Q = 0$.

[6] This is quite analogous to the treatment of angular momenta of linear molecules, detailed for acetylene in section 5.3.

This situation occurs for the ground state of all *cata*-condensed hydro-carbons. Since there appears to be left no sequence of letters which does not lead to some conflict, Platt has arbitrarily assigned A to states with $Q = 0$, and successive letters of the alphabet to successive values of Q: for $Q = 1$, B; for $Q = 2$, C; etc.[7]

The longest-wavelength excitation is described in one-electron notation by $f \rightarrow g$. For the f electron q is n; for the g electron, $n + 1$. Then m_q for the f electron is $+n$ or $-n$; for the g electron, $+(n + 1)$ or $-(n + 1)$. If an f electron with $m_q = +n$ is promoted to $m_q = +(n + 1)$, or one with $m_q = -n$ to $m_q = -(n + 1)$, M_Q changes by $+1$ or -1 from 0, so that Q for the final state becomes 1, and the excited state a B state. On the other hand, if an f electron with $m_q = +n$ is promoted to $m_q = -(n + 1)$, or $-n$ to $+(n + 1)$, M_Q changes by $\pm(2n + 1)$ and Q of the final state is $2n + 1$. Such states are called L states. Thus the transitions which, in one-electron notation are $f \rightarrow g$, in conformational notation $f^4 \rightarrow f^3 g$, give rise to two transitions in notation of molecular states: $B \leftarrow A$ and $L \leftarrow A$. Excitation of an e electron to the g level, $e \rightarrow g$, or $e^4 f^4 \rightarrow e^3 f^4 g$, gives rise to $C \leftarrow A$ and $K \leftarrow A$ transitions, where K stands for $Q = 2n$ [arrived at by promotion of an e electron with $m_q = n - 1$ to $m_q = -(n + 1)$]. Similarly, M stands for states with $Q = 2n + 2$, arising in $f \rightarrow h$ promotion, etc.

As can be readily seen from inspection of the M_Q values, all states, $B, C, \ldots, K, L, \ldots$, are doubly degenerate except the A states, for which $M_Q = 0$, and which therefore are single (nondegenerate) and, since all electrons are paired, necessarily singlets. The other states may occur as singlets or triplets (any possible higher multiplets are of no spectroscopic interest). The degeneracies of the states with $Q \neq 0$ are split in actual molecules because the periphery is not spherical, because the cross links in molecules exert an effect, and because the potential is not constant around the periphery.

To characterize better the splitting of these degeneracies, it is convenient to perform a linear transformation on the complex wave functions of equation (13.1). The two degenerate functions for a given value of q are

$$\psi_+ = e^{iq\varphi} \quad \text{and} \quad \psi_- = e^{-iq\varphi}$$

Because of the occurrence of $i \, (= \sqrt{-1})$ in the exponent, these functions are complex; they can, however, be transformed into real functions by a simple expedient. It was shown in section 4.4 that any linear combination of a pair of degenerate wave functions is also a satisfactory wave function, and that any such pair may be replaced by any other orthonormal pair of linear combinations. Taking the following linear combinations:

$$\psi_b = \frac{e^{iq\varphi} + ie^{-iq\varphi}}{2} = \frac{1}{\sqrt{2\pi}} \cos(q\varphi)$$

$$\psi_a = \frac{e^{iq\varphi} - ie^{-iq\varphi}}{2i} = \frac{1}{\sqrt{2\pi}} \sin(q\varphi)$$

(13.3)

[7] The letters A and B used here have no relation to the group-theory symbols A and B.

gives two real functions which are very convenient. For $q = 0$, $\psi_a = (1/\sqrt{2\pi}) \sin 0 = 0$ is not a satisfactory wave function, so that $\psi_b = (1/\sqrt{2\pi}) \cos 0 = 1/\sqrt{2\pi}$ is the only function, and hence ψ for $q = 0$ is nondegenerate. For all other values of q, the two functions are degenerate, with the energy given by equation (13.2). In the case of a more realistic molecule, as stated above, the degeneracy is split. Then it is convenient to measure φ from some axis, say the short symmetry axis (transverse axis) of the molecule, which will be arbitrarily taken as the z axis, as indicated in Fig. 13.6 for a few typical examples. The wave functions ψ_a and ψ_b then have q nodes, and the nodal planes of ψ_a and ψ_b are turned by an angle of π/q with respect to each other. For the special case of $n = 2$ (naphthalene), the symmetry of the functions for $q = 0, 1, 2$, and 3 (i.e., d, e, f, and g orbitals) is shown in Fig. 13.7.

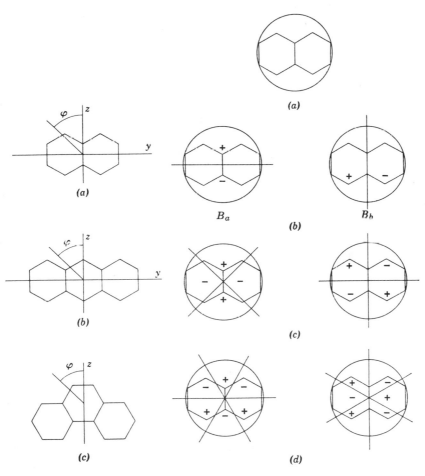

Fig. 13.6 The symmetry properties of (a) naphthalene, (b) anthracene, and (c) phenanthrene.

Fig. 13.7 The symmetry properties of the wave function for ψ_a and ψ_b for (a) $q = 0$, (b) $q = 1$, (c) $q = 2$, and (d) $q = 3$.

The symmetry properties of these functions can be used to derive the selection rules for the various transitions. From the discussion in section 6.5 it is apparent that the three components of the intensity integral are given by $\int \Psi'_i x \Psi'_f \, d\tau$, $\int \Psi'_i y \Psi'_f \, d\tau$, and $\int \Psi'_i z \Psi'_f \, d\tau$. Since each of the ψ is antisymmetric with respect to the molecular plane, which is taken perpendicular to the x axis, and since there is always an even number of ψ functions in Ψ', both Ψ'_i and Ψ'_f are symmetric with respect to reflection on the molecular plane, while x is antisymmetric, so that the integrand in the first of the above integrals is odd and the integral vanishes. For all transitions $\Psi'_i = A$, and is totally symmetric. For the $B_a \leftarrow A$ and $B_b \leftarrow A$ transitions, $\Psi'_f = B_a$ and B_b, respectively, and these have the same symmetry as y and z, respectively; accordingly, the second and the third integrals, respectively, are different from 0. Therefore, both $B \leftarrow A$ transitions are allowed, $B_a \leftarrow A$ is polarized in the z direction (i.e., transverse to the long axis), and $B_b \leftarrow A$ is polarized in the y direction (i.e., longitudinally polarized).

Whenever the molecule has three planes of symmetry, and therefore a center of symmetry, all other transitions are forbidden. However, upon distortion of the symmetry, the functions subscripted a are seen to be still transversely polarized, and those subscripted b, longitudinally polarized. In the absence of a center of symmetry, the $C \leftarrow A$ transitions are also allowed, but the $L \leftarrow A$ transitions are always forbidden, and hence have a low intensity and considerable vibrational structure.

The lower configurations, and the states to which they give rise, according to the Platt scheme, are given in Table 13.1, in which they are grouped

TABLE 13.1

Configurations and States for *cata*-Condensed Hydrocarbons

Δq from Ground State	Configuration	ΔQ	State
2	f^3h	$\begin{cases} 2 \\ 2n + 2 \end{cases}$	$^{1,3}C_{a,b}{}^a$ $^{1,3}M_{a,b}{}^a$
2	e^3f^4g	$\begin{cases} 2 \\ 2n \end{cases}$	$^{1,3}C_{a,b}$ $^{1,3}K_{a,b}{}^a$
1	f^3g	$\begin{cases} 1 \\ 2n + 1 \end{cases}$	$^{1,3}B_{a,b}$ $^{1,3}L_{a,b}$
0	f^4	0	^1A

[a] Latest theoretical information suggests that the two C states of equal multiplicity, and possibly also the two K states and the two M states, pair up to form two combinations, "+" and "−," one of which is highly forbidden, the other quasi-allowed.

in order of the change of quantum number of the excited electron, Δq.

The two allowed transitions $^1B_a \leftarrow {}^1A$ and $^1B_b \leftarrow {}^1A$, which are polarized along mutually perpendicular axes of the molecule, correspond to the classical fundamental electrical oscillations in a flat metal-plate model suggested by Lewis, Calvin, and Bigeleisen.[8] The longitudinal transition $^1B_b \leftarrow {}^1A$ lies at the longer wavelength. The $^1C \leftarrow {}^1A$ bands are forbidden if the molecule has a center of symmetry, e.g., anthracene. If the molecule has no center of symmetry, the transitions are allowed and the $^1C_b \leftarrow {}^1A$ transition is assigned to the one involving polarization along the long dimension, and the $^1C_a \leftarrow {}^1A$ transition will be transverse, polarized. The $^1L \leftarrow {}^1A$ bands are intrinsically weak bands of low intensity.

TABLE 13.2

Nomenclature of Benzene Band Spectra

λ_{max}, mμ	ϵ_{max}	Braude[a]	Clar[b]	D and V[c]	K and P[d]	Group Theory[e]
183	46,000	Group I	β	Second primary	^1B	$^1E_{1u}$
198⎫ 203⎬ 207⎭	7,400	Group II	*para*	Primary	^1L_a	$^1B_{1u}$
229⎫ 234 238 244⎬ 249 255 261 289⎭	220	Group III	α	Secondary	^1L_b	$^1B_{2u}$

[a] E. A. Braude, *Ann. Rept. Chem. Soc.*, **42**, 105 (1945).
[b] E. Clar (see footnote 1).
[c] L. Doub and J. M. Vandenbelt, *J. Am. Chem. Soc.*, **69**, 2714 (1947).
[d] H. B. Klevens and J. R. Platt, *J. Chem. Phys.*, **17**, 470 (1949).
[e] The assignments are those proposed by M. G. Mayer and A. L. Sklar, *J. Chem. Phys.*, **6**, 645 (1938) and are generally accepted.

The various nomenclature systems that have been proposed for the classification of aromatic band spectra are summarized in Table 13.2, using benzene as an example. The ^1B_a and ^1B_b states are degenerate in benzene because of the high symmetry. As pointed out earlier, Clar[1]. was able to make important generalizations relating to the spectra of the acenes and the phenes. The Platt classification encompasses both kinds of compounds in a general scheme but leads to correlations in the acene series which are extremely useful and will now be examined.

[8] G. N. Lewis and M. Calvin, *Chem. Revs.*, **25**, 273 (1939); G. N. Lewis and J. Bigeleisen, *J. Am. Chem. Soc.*, **65**, 520, 2102, 2107 (1943).

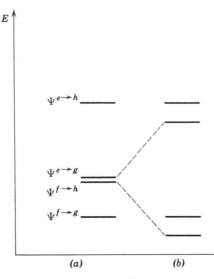

Fig. 13.7A The term values of an alternant hydrocarbon (*a*) before and (*b*) after configuration interaction.

An alternative interpretation of the spectra of polycyclic hydrocarbons, and actually any alternant hydrocarbon, has been given.[8a] Considering only the two highest occupied orbitals, *e* and *f*, and the two lowest unoccupied ones, *g* and *h*, as shown in Fig. 13.7A*a*, one may anticipate four transitions, $f \rightarrow g$, $e \rightarrow g$, $f \rightarrow h$, and $e \rightarrow h$. But, according to MO theory, $e \rightarrow g$ and $f \rightarrow h$ are degenerate, and since they are generally of the same symmetry type, may undergo important configuration interaction, in such a way that the degenerate pair splits into two components, Fig. 13.7A*b*. It has been suggested that the lower energy component, in polycyclics, lies below the $f \rightarrow g$ transition, and that thus the longest wavelength transition is not the $f \rightarrow g$ transition but one of the components of the $e \rightarrow g$, $f \rightarrow h$ pair.

Table 13.3 gives data[9] on the main features of the spectra of the acenes, and Fig. 13.8 shows the energy levels of the various bands[9] and their correlation. The bands are discussed separately below.

The ^1L_b band is the 256 mμ (39,000 cm^{-1}) band in benzene and in this compound is associated with the $^1B_{2u} \leftarrow {}^1A_{1g}$ transition. There is a similar band in the spectrum of all aromatic compounds, though it may be hidden sometimes by a stronger band. This band nearly always has similar

[8a] M. J. S. Dewar and H. C. Longuet-Higgins, *Proc. Phys. Soc.* (*London*), **A67**, 795 (1954).

[9] H. B. Klevens and J. R. Platt, *J. Chem. Phys.*, **17**, 470 (1949).

intensity, $\log \epsilon \sim 2.5$, and the same kind of vibrational structure of about six sharp bands as in benzene. Figure 13.8 shows that the ^1L_b band moves slowest with increasing chain length. This state has nodal planes *through* the atoms, and hence the ^1L_b band is little affected in position or intensity by substitution. The direction of polarization is longitudinal in the polyacenes.

TABLE 13.3

Data from the Spectra of Some Acenes[9]

Compound	$^1L_b \leftarrow {}^1A$	$^1L_a \leftarrow {}^1A$	$^1B_b \leftarrow {}^1A$	$^1C_b \leftarrow {}^1A$	$^1B_a \leftarrow {}^1A$	
Benzene						
onset, λ, mμ	263	208	...	...	...	
λ_{max}, mμ	...	...	183	...	...	
ϵ_{max}	220	6900	46,000	...	...	
f	0.002	0.10	0.69	...	...	
Naphthalene						
onset, λ, mμ	312	289	...	...	...	
λ_{max}, mμ	...	...	220	190	$\sim$167	
ϵ_{max}	280	9300	133,000	10,000	$\sim$30,000	
f	0.002	0.18?	1.70	0.20	$\sim$0.6?	
Anthracene						
onset, λ, mμ	...	379	...	...	...	
λ_{max}, mμ	...	...	256	221	186	
ϵ_{max}	...	9000	180,000	14,500	32,000	
f	...	0.1	2.28	0.28	0.65	
Naphthacene[a]						
onset, λ, mμ	...	474	...	230	...	...
λ_{max}, mμ	...	...	272	...	211	187
ϵ_{max}	...	12,500	180,000	17,000	44,000	16,000
f	...	0.08	1.85	0.20	0.45	0.27

[a] Also has a $^1C_a \leftarrow {}^1A$ band and some unassigned transitions.

The ^1L_a band is the 203 mμ band in benzene and is associated with the $^1B_{1u}$ state, which has nodes *between* the atoms. Reference to Fig. 13.8 shows that this band moves fastest to the red with increasing length. It is assumed to be polarized in a transverse direction. A smooth curve connects this state in the acene series, and all transitions to these levels have five or six diffuse bands with $\log \epsilon \sim 3.8$.

The ^1B_b band increases in *intensity* almost linearly with length of the acene in the manner analogous to increasing ϵ with increasing chain length in the polyene series. Accordingly, these bands are associated with

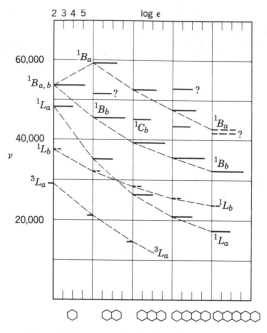

Fig. 13.8 Correlation of the energy levels for the states in the acenes. [Reprinted by permission from H. B. Klevens and J. R. Platt, *J. Chem. Phys.*, **17**, 470 (1949).]

longitudinal polarization. The wavelength of absorption of this band increases with length of the chain. In naphthalene and anthracene these transitions occur at approximately the same wavelength as the strong bands of polyenes of the same molecular length.[9] The ^1B_b and ^1B_a states together form a degenerate pair in benzene which is the $^1E_{1u}$ state. The $^1E_{1u} \leftarrow ^1A_{1g}$ transition in benzene at 183 mμ is the strongest transition.

The ^1B_a band has almost constant intensity in the polyacenes and is thus assumed to be due to an allowed transition, polarized transversely to the long axis of the molecule.

The ^1C_a and ^1C_b bands appear weakly in most polyacenes, although the ^1C_b band is rather strong in anthracene. The intensity of these bands increases when the central symmetry is lost, and hence is stronger in the phenes than in the acenes.

The spacing of the vibrational subbands is different in each transition and can further serve to identify the transition. Table 13.4 gives the $(\Delta\nu)_{avg}$ for the various transitions in seven different compounds, i.e., the average frequency separation between individual bands for any transition.[10]

[10] N. D. Coggeshall and A. Pozefsky, *J. Chem. Phys.*, **19**, 980 (1951).

From the table it is apparent that $(\Delta\nu)_{\text{avg}}$ is of the order of 1300 cm^{-1} for either the ^1L_a or ^1B_a transition but is only about 700 cm^{-1} for the ^1L_b transition. The spacings observed can be identified with some of the vibrational frequencies of the hydrocarbons known from infrared and Raman spectra. Since these frequencies are presumably the motions which

TABLE 13.4

Average Vibrational Frequencies Associated with Several Transitions in Aromatics (2,2,4-Trimethylpentane)

Compound	$(\Delta\nu)_{\text{avg}}$, cm^{-1}		
	^1L_a	^1L_b	^1B_b
Phenanthrene	1320	705	1460
Anthracene	1430	...	...
1,2-Benzanthracene	1350	690	1400
9,10-Dimethyl-1,2-benzanthracene	1325	...	1300
1,2,5,6-Dibenzanthracene	1250	697	1360
Methylcholanthrene	1410	725	1380
Naphthacene	1430	...	...

distort the molecule from ground-state to excited-state geometry, they provide important information about the geometry of the excited state. Furthermore, since the symmetry species of these frequencies are known, they assist in elucidation of the symmetry of the electronic excited state.

The qualitative model proposed by Platt[4] for the *classification* of the spectra of *cata*-condensed hydrocarbons has received wide acceptance; it has also been considerably refined by many authors[11] and used as a basis for quantitative calculations of absorption frequencies and intensities. Although the results of such calculations do not agree closely with observed data, they lie within the right order of magnitude and excellently reflect the observed trends.

Having discussed the various bands in the series of polyacenes, and with the background of assignments in general, it is appropriate to consider now some of the individual aromatic systems in more detail.

13.3   The Spectra of Naphthalene and Its Derivatives

Naphthalene has three main bands in the accessible ultraviolet (Fig. 13.1) and at least one in the far ultraviolet. These bands and their assignments[12] are given in Table 13.5. The location of the bands has been

[11] K. Rüdenburg and R. G. Parr, *J. Chem. Phys.*, **19**, 1268 (1951); G. Araki and T. Murai, *J. Chem. Phys.*, **22**, 954 (1954); W. Moffitt, *J. Chem. Phys.*, **22**, 320 (1954).

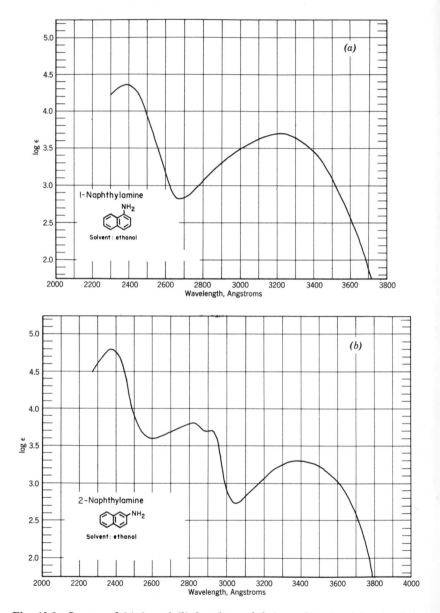

Fig. 13.9 Spectra of (*a*) 1- and (*b*) 2-aminonaphthalene. [Reprinted by permission from Y. Hirshberg and R. N. Jones, *Can. J. Research*, **27B**, 437 (1949).]

calculated by LCAO methods, allowing for configuration interaction, with surprisingly good results.[12]

The most impressive corroborative evidence for the correct assignment of the bands and their polarization comes from the study of spectra of

TABLE 13.5

Absorption Bands of Naphthalene

Transition[a]	Polarization[b]	λ_{max}, mμ[c]	log ϵ_{max}[c]
$^1L_b \leftarrow {}^1A$	Longit.	312	2.40
$^1L_a \leftarrow {}^1A$	Trans.	286	3.62
$^1B_b \leftarrow {}^1A$	Longit.	221	4.98
$^1B_a \leftarrow {}^1A$	Trans.	169[a]	. . .
$^1C_b \leftarrow {}^1A$		190[a]	. . .

[a] Reference in footnote 9.
[b] Longit. is longitudinal or parallel to the long axis of the molecule; trans. is transverse or perpendicular to the long axis of the molecule.
[c] Reference in footnote 2. The wavelength is the location of the first (longest-wavelength) maximum in the band if the band has vibrational structure.

naphthalene derivatives substituted in various positions in the nucleus. The effects on the various bands of extending conjugation by substitution are readily predictable. Extension in a given direction will primarily affect a band polarized in that direction. Thus, 1-substitution extends conjugation in the transverse direction, as seen from structure XVI, and hence should cause bathochromic and hyperchromic effects, predominantly in the transverse-polarized ^1L_a and ^1B_a bands. 2-Substitution (see structure XVII) extends conjugation primarily in the longitudinal direction

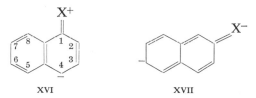

XVI   XVII

and hence should primarily red-shift and intensify the longitudinally polarized ^1L_b band. Figure 13.9 shows the spectra of 1- and 2-naphthylamine.[13] The 1-amino group causes a broadening of the ^1B_a band, and the ^1L_a and ^1L_b bands fuse, probably because of the large bathochromic displacement on the ^1L_a band. The 2-amino group also causes a red shift

[12] J. R. Platt, *J. Chem. Phys.*, **18**, 1168 (1950).
[13] Y. Hirshberg and R. N. Jones, *Can. J. Research*, **27B**, 437 (1949).

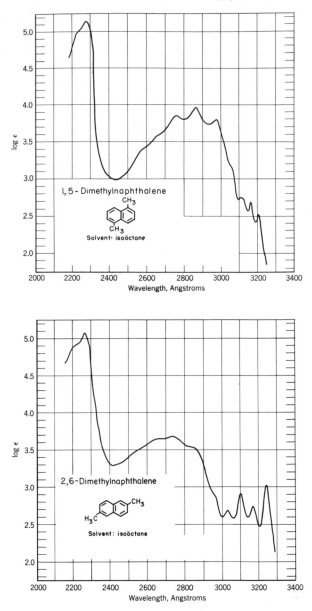

Fig. 13.10   Spectra of 1,5- and 2,6-dimethylnaphthane. (Reprinted by permission from R. A. Friedel and M. Orchin, *Ultraviolet Spectra of Aromatic Compounds*, John Wiley and Sons, New York, 1951.)

and broadening of the ^1B_a band, but the ^1L_a band is hardly affected whereas the ^1L_b is red-shifted and intensified. Comparison of the spectra[2] of 1,5- and 2,6-dimethylnaphthalene (Fig. 13.10) shows similar results and further increases the confidence of the assignments of polarization to the ^1L_a and ^1L_b bands. In the 1,5 derivative the transverse band, ^1L_a, is red-shifted and intensified, while in the 2,6 derivative the longitudinally polarized band undergoes these effects. The spectrum of 2,3,6,7-tetramethylnaphthalene[14] has relatively intense long-wavelength peaks, which also can be ascribed to augmentation by hyperconjugation of the longitudinally polarized ^1L_b band. The spectra of all the possible dimethylnaphthalenes,[15] thirteen of the fourteen possible trimethylnaphthalenes,[16] four tetramethylnaphthalenes,[14] two pentamethylnaphthalenes,[14,17] four hexamethylnaphthalenes,[14,17] a heptamethylnaphthalene,[17] and, finally, octamethylnaphthalene[17] have been reported. All these compounds have the characteristic naphthalene spectra with the expected bathochromic displacements. Some small deviations[14] from expected spectra are due to steric interactions in the more highly substituted compounds.

Acenaphthene, XVIII, may be considered as a disubstituted naphthalene,

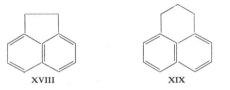

XVIII   XIX

and indeed its spectrum is similar to that of 1,8-dimethylnaphthalene (Fig. 13.11) except that its deviation from naphthalene is somewhat greater than might have been expected.[18] In perinaphthane, XIX (Fig. 13.11), the long-wavelength $^1L_b \leftarrow {}^1A$ transition has disappeared, and the spectrum shows much less vibrational structure than that of the *nor*-homolog, acenaphthene. The difference in spectra is interesting and may be due to the greater strain in the five-membered ring.

13.31 PHENYLNAPHTHALENES AND RELATED COMPOUNDS. Interesting differences occur in the spectra[2] of 1- and 2-phenylnaphthalene (Fig. 13.12), and some of these differences are preserved in compounds such as the benzfluorenes, which may be viewed as being derived from, or at least related to, the phenylnaphthalenes.

[14] W. L. Mosby, *J. Am. Chem. Soc.*, **75**, 3348 (1953).

[15] A. S. Bailey, K. C. Bryant, R. A. Hancock, S. H. Morrell, and J. C. Smith, *J. Inst. Petrol.*, **33**, 503 (1947).

[16] E. Heilbronner, U. Frolicher, and P. A. Plattner, *Helv. Chim. Acta*, **32**, 2479 (1949); R. A. Morton and A. J. A. de Gouveia, *J. Chem. Soc.*, 916 (1934).

[17] B. J. Abadir, J. W. Cook, and D. T. Gibson, *J. Chem. Soc.*, 8 (1953).

[18] J. R. Platt, *J. Chem. Phys.*, **19**, 263 (1951).

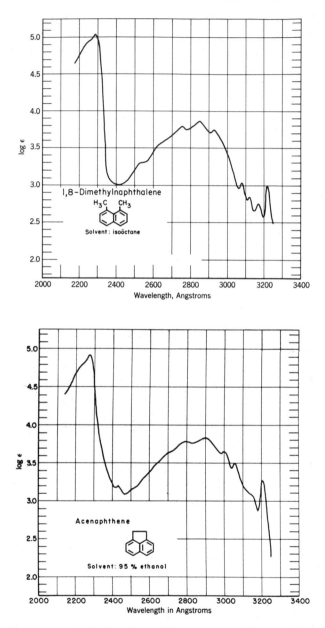

Fig. 13.11 Spectra of 1,8-dimethylnaphthalene, acenaphthene, and perinaphthane. (Reprinted by permission from R. A. Friedel and M. Orchin, *Ultraviolet Spectra of Aromatic Compounds*, John Wiley and Sons, New York, 1951.)

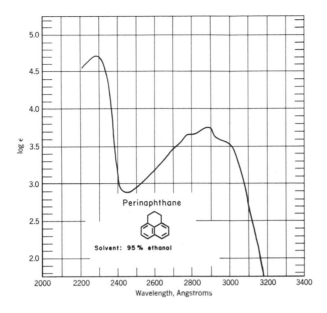

A phenyl group in the 1 position red-shifts and intensifies the ^1L_a band of naphthalene, as expected from the transverse polarization of the band. The shift is sufficient to obscure and submerge the ^1L_b band and is accompanied by considerable loss of vibrational structure. The alteration in the spectrum, however, is not as great as might have been expected, probably because of interference between hydrogen atoms of the phenyl and naphthyl groups;[19] some similarity between the spectrum of 1-phenylnaphthalene and a spectrum calculated by addition of separate benzene and naphthalene chromophores has been pointed out.[20] Consistent with these observations and their interpretation is the spectrum of 1,1'-binaphthyl[2] (Fig. 13.12), which is very similar to that of 1-phenylnaphthalene.

The ^1L_b band in 2-phenylnaphthalene, although not well resolved, appears red-shifted, and all vibrational structure has disappeared. The phenyl group in the 2 position obviously interacts strongly with the naphthalene nucleus, much more strongly than the group in the 1 position, because there is no hindrance to planarity. The ^1L_a band is not appreciably shifted, but the ^1B_b band occurs at about 250 mμ. All these facts (Fig. 13.12) are consistent with the extension of the conjugated system in the longitudinal direction.

[19] R. A. Friedel, M. Orchin, and L. Reggel, *J. Am. Chem. Soc.*, **70**, 199 (1948).
[20] R. N. Jones, *Chem. Revs.*, **32**, 1 (1943).

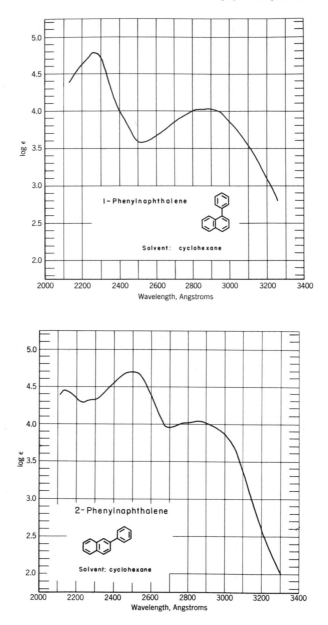

Fig. 13.12 Spectra of 1- and 2-phenylnaphthalenes and the three isomeric binaphthyls. (Reprinted by permission from R. A. Friedel and M. Orchin, *Ultraviolet Spectra of Aromatic Compounds*, John Wiley and Sons, New York, 1951.)

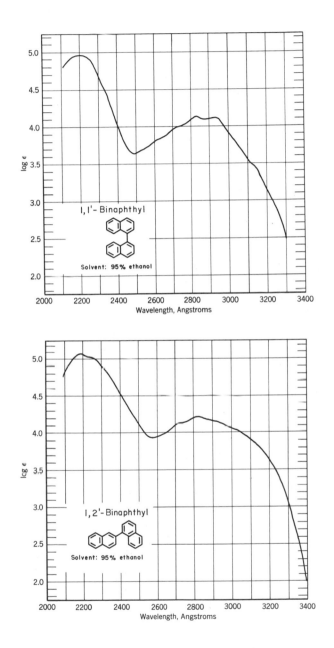

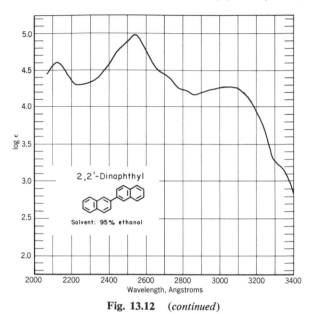

Fig. 13.12 (*continued*)

In 2,2'-binaphthyl the ^1L_b band is resolved at about 335 mμ, and all bands are intensified. Transverse extension is also increased, as shown by the ^1L_a band at 305 mμ. A fourth band, possibly the ^1C_b band, appears at about 212 mμ. The spectrum of 1,2'-binaphthyl (Fig. 13.12) shows characteristics of both its isomers; it has two very broad bands, one of which is probably formed by coalescence of the ^1L_a and ^1L_b bands.

The spectra of the three isomeric benzfluorenes (Fig. 13.13) bear some relationship to those of the phenylnaphthalenes.[21] 1,2-, XX, and 2,3-benzfluorene, XXI, may be considered to be 2-phenylnaphthalene with a methylene bridge between the phenyl and naphthyl rings. The spectra of these two isomers resemble each other, and both have the three bands characteristic of the 2-phenylnaphthalene spectrum. The fact that there is considerably more structure in the fluorene spectrum may be due to what Jones[22] has termed the "fine structure, or Fs, effect." Vibrational structure is observed in certain compounds when a methylene bridge is introduced, thereby increasing the rigidity and strain, and hindering the dissipation of the energy of the excited molecule. In this respect the Fs effect is opposed to that produced by alkyl groups or other auxochromes, which tend to obscure structure and facilitate dissipation of energy among the vibrational levels of the excited state.

[21] M. Orchin and R. A. Friedel, *J. Am. Chem. Soc.*, **71**, 3002 (1949); W. A. Jacobs, L. C. Craig, and G. I. Lavin, *J. Biol. Chem.*, **141**, 51 (1941).
[22] R. N. Jones, *J. Am. Chem. Soc.*, **67**, 2127 (1945).

The spectrum of 3,4-benzfluorene, XXII (Fig. 13.13), has some resemblance to that of 1-phenylnaphthalene (Fig. 13.12). There are two main bands in the spectra of both compounds. The phenyl group, which might be out of the plane of the naphthalene ring in the ground state of 1-phenylnaphthalene, is certainly more nearly in plane in 3,4-benzfluorene. The long-wavelength band in the spectrum of 1-phenylnaphthalene is shifted and develops considerable structure in the fluorene.

Clemo and Felton[23] have attributed the difference in spectra in the benzfluorene series to the extended p-quinoid system possible in the 1,2- and 2,3-benzfluorenes, XX and XXI, compared to the less extended system in the 3,4 isomer, XXII.

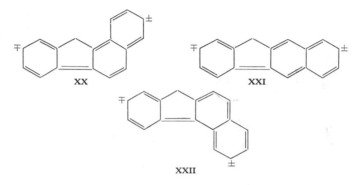

Just as the spectrum of 3,4-benzfluorene was related to that of its parent chromophore, 1-phenylnaphthalene, so benzanthrene, XXIII, may be visualized as a 1-phenylnaphthalene[24] in which the 1-phenyl group is further joined to the naphthalene nucleus at the 8 position through a methylene bridge. There is a strong resemblance between the spectra of 3,4-benzfluorene (Fig. 13.13) and benzanthrene (Fig. 13.14), and both have some resemblance to the spectrum of 1-phenylnaphthalene. The possibilities for p-quinoid polarizations in benzanthrene, XXIV, are similar to the forms that are possible with 3,4-benzfluorene, XXII, and such forms are not as extended as those derived from 2-phenylnaphthalene. The spectrum of XXIII has somewhat less structure than that of 3,4-benzfluorene, an

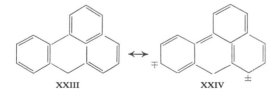

[23] G. R. Clemo and D. G. I. Felton, *J. Chem. Soc.*, 305 (1952).
[24] R. A. Friedel, *Appl. Spectroscopy*, **2**, 13 (1957).

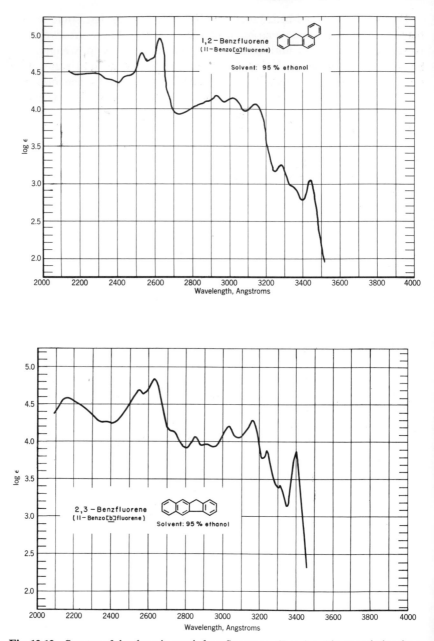

Fig. 13.13 Spectra of the three isomeric benzfluorenes. (Reprinted by permission from R. A. Friedel and M. Orchin, *Ultraviolet Spectra of Aromatic Compounds*, John Wiley and Sons, New York, 1951.)

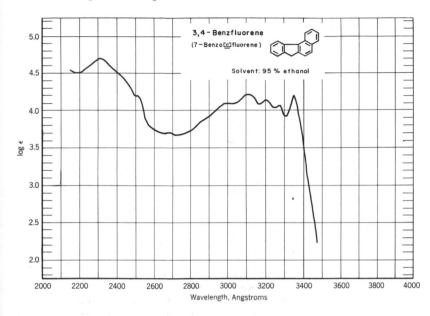

effect which may be related to the fusion of the chromophores by a six-membered ring, as compared to fusion by a five-membered ring in the fluorene derivative.

Whereas, with the benzfluorene hydrocarbons, the 1,2- and 2,3- benz-fluorenes have similar spectra but the 3,4 isomer is different, the benz-fluorenones show a different grouping. Thus, in the ketone series, the 3,4- and 2,3-benz isomers have somewhat similar spectra, and the 1,2 isomer (Fig. 13.15) is different.[19] The *p*-quinoid polarizations may again be responsible for the similarities and differences;[23] the 3,4-, XXV, and 2,3-benzfluorenones, XXVI, have extended quinoid forms, whereas such forms in the 1,2 isomer, XXVII, are much less extended. It is also possible that strong hydrogen bonding between the 1' position and the carbonyl oxygen in the 1,2-benzfluorenone affects the spectrum.

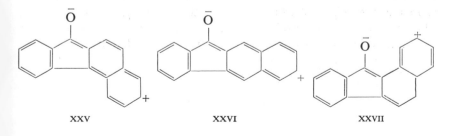

XXV   XXVI   XXVII

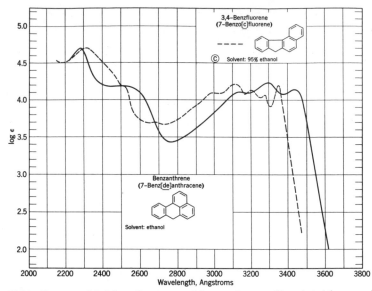

Fig. 13.14 Spectra of 3,4-benzfluorene and benzanthrene. (Reprinted by permission from R. A. Friedel and M. Orchin, *Ultraviolet Spectra of Aromatic Compounds*, John Wiley and Sons, New York, 1951.)

13.4 Anthracene and Derivatives

The spectrum of anthracene (Fig. 13.1) shows some resemblance to that of naphthalene except for a considerable red shift. The weak ^1L_b (α) band at long wavelength in the spectrum of naphthalene has disappeared. The most intense peak is at 254 mμ (39,000 cm^{-1}), with an ϵ value of 180,000, and is the β band, due to the $^1B_b \leftarrow {}^1A$ transition. The nodal plane in the ^1B_b state bisects the *meso* carbon atoms. Polarization in this state is longitudinal and can be represented by resonance structures such as **XXVIII** and **XXIX**. The other major band in the spectrum of anthracene

is due to the $^1L_a \leftarrow {}^1A$ transition, and consists of a series of five vibrational subbands, the longest of which occurs at about 378 mμ with $\epsilon = \sim$9000. This transition is transversely polarized and associated with excitation to a state to which polarized forms such as **XXX–XXXII** contribute.

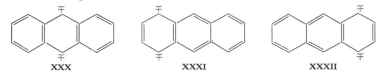

The ^1L_b band is not observed but is probably submerged under the ^1L_a band; this behavior is characteristic of the acenes. Anthracene has three planes of symmetry and hence a center of symmetry; as pointed out earlier in this chapter, the transitions $C \leftarrow A$ are therefore forbidden. The ^1C_b band in anthracene occurs at about 220 mμ, $\epsilon = \sim$14,500, which is surprisingly intense for a forbidden transition. The spectrum of anthracene has been determined[25] in alcohol solution at $-170°$ C, and a great deal more vibrational structure appears, as expected. The five peaks observed in the ^1L_a band at room temperature are resolved into eleven peaks at $-170°$ C, and the virtually structureless ^1B_b band is resolved into five peaks at the lower temperature; all the peaks undergo a bathochromic and hyperchromic shift.

The transverse polarization of the long-wavelength ^1L_a band of anthracene and the longitudinal polarization of the ^1B_b band are clearly shown by the spectra of substituted anthracenes[22] and further confirmed by calculation.[26] Thus, the spectra of 9-methylanthracene and 9,10-dimethylanthracene show little change in the ^1B_b band of anthracene, but marked (Fig. 13.16) bathochromic shifts and some intensification the ^1L_a band.

The addition of an amino group to the anthracene nucleus has a profound effect on the spectrum, independent of the position of substitution, although the spectra of the various aminoanthracenes also differ significantly among themselves. Thus the spectrum of 9-aminoanthracene (Fig. 13.17) at first glance appears to bear no resemblance to that of anthracene. However, the ^1B_b band is only slightly shifted relative to anthracene or 9,10-dimethylanthracene. However, all the vibrational structure associated with the ^1L_a band in anthracene has disappeared, and there is an enormous red shift into the visible. Although no analysis of the spectrum has been published, it is possible that the ^1L_b band which was submerged in anthracene makes a more substantial and independent contribution to the spectrum of the 9-amino derivative. There is a considerable loss in symmetry in going from anthracene in point group D_{2h}, to the 9-amino compound, which belongs to point group C_{2v}. Furthermore, the amino group is quite a powerful chromophore and strongly conjugates with the aromatic π electrons in the absence of steric effects. In 2-aminoanthracene (Fig. 13.17) the longitudinally polarized ^1B_b band is very broad. Although the spectrum in Fig. 13.17 does not extend below 240 mμ, it appears that a new band is appearing in this region which may be the forbidden ^1C_b band. 2-Aminoanthracene has only a single plane of symmetry, and hence bands which are symmetry forbidden in anthracene may be observed with higher intensity. The series of peaks in the 310–360

[25] E. Clar, *Spectrochim. Acta*, **4**, 116 (1950).
[26] C. A. Coulson, *Proc. Phys. Soc.*, **60**, 257 (1948).

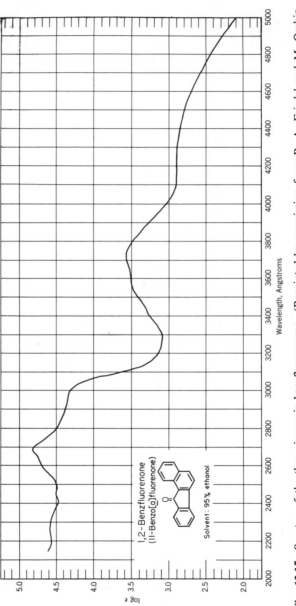

Fig. 13.15 Spectra of the three isomeric benzfluorenones. (Reprinted by permission from R. A. Friedel and M. Orchin, *Ultraviolet Spectra of Aromatic Compounds*, John Wiley and Sons, New York, 1951.)

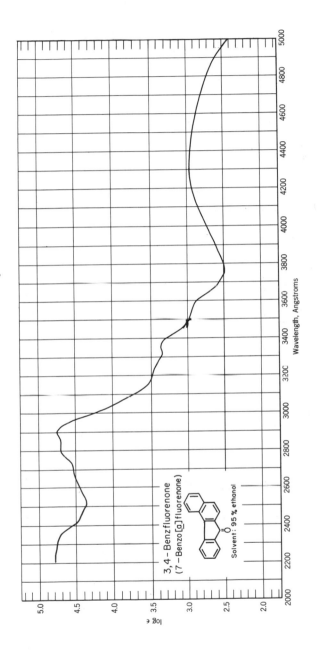

3, 4 – Benzfluorenone
(7 –Benzo [a] fluorenone)

Solvent : 95 % ethanol

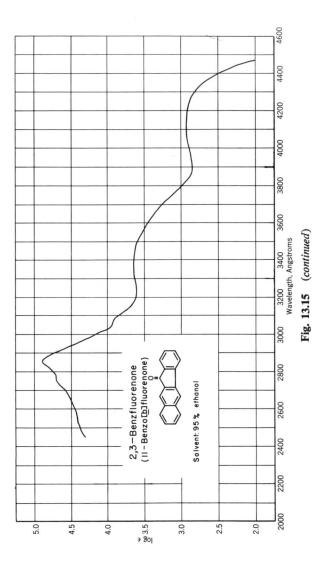

2,3–Benzfluorenone
(11 – Benzo[b]fluorenone)

Solvent: 95 % ethanol

Wavelength, Angstroms

log ε

Fig. 13.15 *(continued)*

$m\mu$ region may be associated with the ^1L_b band; but, in view of the fundamental differences of the spectrum from that of the parent, it is dangerous to make such an assignment.

It is perhaps surprising that the addition of phenyl chromophores to the 9 and 10 positions in anthracene produces very little change in the spectrum of the parent anthracene; the spectrum of 9,10-diphenylanthracene (Fig. 13.18) is very similar to that of 9,10-dimethylanthracene. This failure of the phenyl groups to conjugate effectively with the anthracene is due to steric overlap of the phenyl *ortho*-hydrogen atoms with the hydrogens in the 1,4,5, and 8 positions, which keeps the phenyl group out of the plane of the anthracene ring.[22]

13.5 Naphthacene and Higher Acenes

The most intense band in the spectrum of tetracene or naphthacene (Fig. 13.1) is the longitudinally polarized ^1B_b band with a peak at about 274 mμ ($\epsilon = 180,000$). Not only does the position of this band increase linearly with the number of benzene rings in the acenes (Fig. 13.2, β band), but also its intensity increases linearly with increase in the length of the acene, just like the corresponding strong transition in the polyenes. This behavior is strong evidence for the longitudinal polarization assigned to the band. Pentacene, the linear five-ring system, has the maximum of the ^1B_b band at about 310 mμ, $\epsilon = 300,000$. The analogous transition in hexacene has not been reported, although the compound is known.[1] It is a deep-green, almost black, crystalline material that decomposes before it melts; its very low solubility in ordinary solvents probably accounts for the lack of data concerning the ^1B_b band.

The longest-wavelength band of naphthacene is the ^1L_a band, which has considerable structure, consisting of five well-defined peaks; the longest one occurs at about 471 mμ, and hence the compound has an orange color. The ^1L_a (or *para*) band is the band which shifts most rapidly with increasing length of the acene. In pentacene, the longest-wavelength peak is at about 575 mμ; in hexacene, using methylnaphthalene as a solvent, the analogous peak is at about 693 mμ.[1] The ^1L_b peak, which in anthracene already was masked by the ^1L_a band, is masked also in naphthacene, but a weak peak at about 417 mμ in the spectrum of pentacene has been assigned to this transition.[9]

The short-wavelength band in naphthacene, with peaks at about 187 mμ ($\epsilon = 16,000$) and 211 mμ ($\epsilon = 44,000$), is assigned to the ^1B_a transition.[9] Since this transition is associated with transverse polarization and the width of the acenes remains constant in the homologous series, the observed constancy in the intensity of the ^1B_a transition in the series is consistent with the assignment.

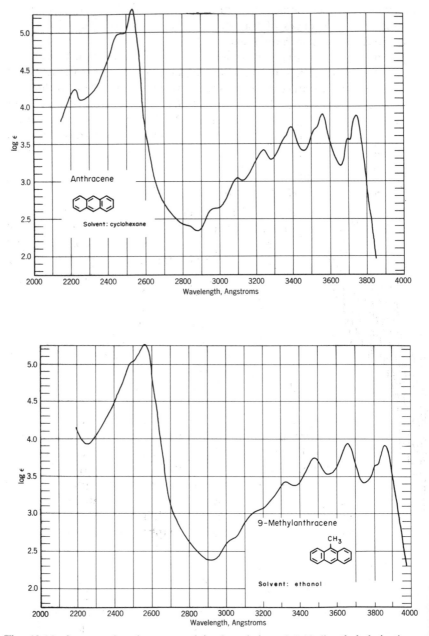

Fig. 13.16 Spectra of anthracene and its 9-methyl- and 9,10-dimethyl derivatives. (Reprinted by permission from R. A. Friedel and M. Orchin, *Ultraviolet Spectra of Aromatic Compounds*, John Wiley and Sons, New York, 1951.)

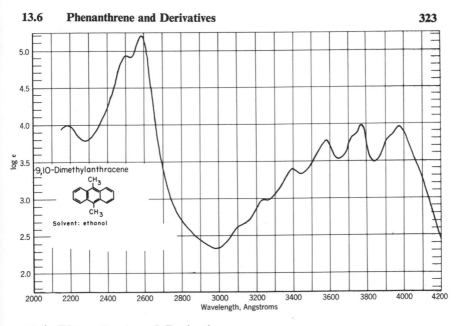

13.6   Phenanthrene and Derivatives

The spectrum of phenanthrene (Fig. 13.19) indicates that some of the bands are in the same position as in anthracene, but that the intensity of the phenanthrene bands is much smaller. The band associated with longitudinal polarization, the ^1B_b band, with the major peak at about 251 mμ ($\epsilon = 65,000$), is weaker than it is in anthracene (254 mμ, $\epsilon = 180,000$) because of reduction of the effective length caused by the angular ring. The ^1L_b band, which was submerged in anthracene under the ^1L_a band, appears in phenanthrene, probably because the ^1L_a band appears at shorter wavelength. The ^1L_b band (α band) has a great deal of vibrational structure with six distinct peaks; the longest-wavelength component is at about 350 mμ ($\epsilon = 350$).

In the acene series, the ^1L_a band (*para* band) shows the greatest sensitivity to increase in length, and the intensity of this band is increased by substitution which increases the width of the molecule. This behavior is consistent with the transverse polarization assigned to the band. Phenanthrene belongs to point group C_{2v}. Transverse polarization is polarization perpendicular to the symmetry axis. The longest-wavelength component of the ^1L_a band in phenanthrene has a peak at about 293 mμ ($\epsilon = \sim16,000$). As was pointed out earlier, this band is at considerably longer wavelength in the anthracene spectrum.

The acenes all have three planes of symmetry and a center of symmetry and belong to point group D_{2h}; hence the ^1C_b band is forbidden in these

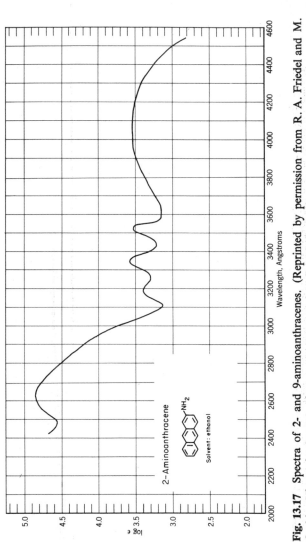
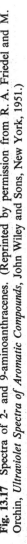

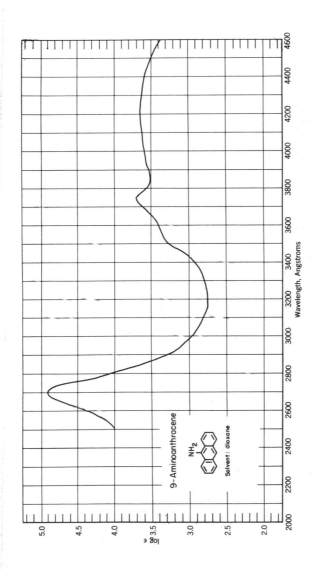

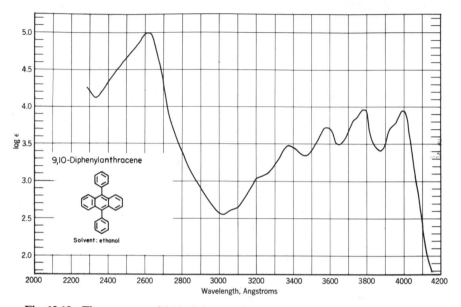

Fig. 13.18 The spectrum of 9,10-diphenylanthracene. (Reprinted by permission from R. A. Friedel and M. Orchin, *Ultraviolet Spectra of Aromatic Compounds*, John Wiley and Sons, New York, 1951.)

compounds. Phenanthrene, however, does not have a center of symmetry, and the band at about 212 mμ ($\epsilon = 33,000$) arises from the $^1C_b \leftarrow {}^1A$ transition.[9]

The spectra of the alkylphenanthrenes closely resemble the spectrum of the parent compound. There is the usual loss of structure, especially in the long-wavelength ^1L_b band. Substitution of hydrogen by a chromophore such as OH or Ph has a more profound effect; spectra of variously 2-substituted phenanthrenes are shown in Fig. 13.19.

13.7   Tetracyclic Hydrocarbons

Thus far the only tetracyclic system discussed has been naphthacene; the spectra of the other four possible *cata*-condensed aromatics, 3,4-benzphenanthrene, triphenylene, 1,2-benzanthracene, and chrysene, are shown in Fig. 13.20. A thorough discussion of these spectra and the spectral resemblance of *cata*-condensed hydrocarbons is given by Klevens and Platt, and the reader is referred to this now-classical article for particulars.[9] The energy levels for the tetracyclic compounds[9] are shown in Fig. 13.21. The energies for similar transitions are quite alike in all the isomers. The ^1L_a position moves toward shorter wavelength (higher frequency) with increased bending of the molecule.

The intensities (as logs of the f value) of the ^1L_b, ^1L_a, and ^1B_b bands for all *cata*-condensed systems of four rings or less are shown in Fig. 13.22. The greatest variation in intensity occurs in the ^1L_b bands, but these intensities are well segregated from the other bands. The ^1L_b bands have sharp vibrational structure with five or six peaks. The ^1L_a bands are more diffuse. The ^1B_b band is the strongest band in each spectrum, and vibrational structure is completely absent.

A rather extensive study of the spectra of 1,2-benzanthracene derivatives has been made by Jones.[22] This study, which was made possible by the availability of numerous 1,2-benzanthracenes prepared in connection with an investigation of their carcinogenic properties, has proved valuable in suggesting and confirming the assignment of bands. Thus, for example, Jones found that in the spectrum of the hydrochloride 10-amino-1,2-benzanthracene, XXXIII · HCl, a group of bands at 320–370 mμ was shifted to 380–420 mμ in the free amine, XXXIII, with considerable loss of structure. The corresponding series of bands in the spectrum of 3-amino-1,2-benzanthracene, XXXIV, is comparatively unaffected in the

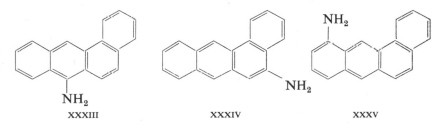

XXXIII   XXXIV   XXXV

hydrochloride (see Fig. 13.23). It is reasonable to associate this group of bands with transverse polarization, i.e., the ^1L_a band. Further confirmation for this assignment is found in the spectrum (Fig. 13.23) of 8-amino-1,2-benzanthracene, XXXV, where this band is again shifted considerably toward the red.

The magnitude of the bathochromic effect due to the introduction of methyl groups into various positions of 1,2-benzanthracene has been studied by Pullman and Berthier.[27] The effect was correlated with the difference in the ground and the excited states of the so-called[28] "free valence number" (see section 8.8) of the peripheral carbon to which the methyl group was attached. The difference in free valence number in the two states is a measure of the ability of the methyl group to conjugate with the ring; the greater this difference, the larger the bathochromic effect.

[27] B. Pullman and G. Berthier, *J. chim. phys.*, **52,** 114 (1955).

[28] G. Berthier, C. A. Coulson, H. N. Greenwood, and A. Pullman, *Compt. rend.*, **226,** 1906 (1948).

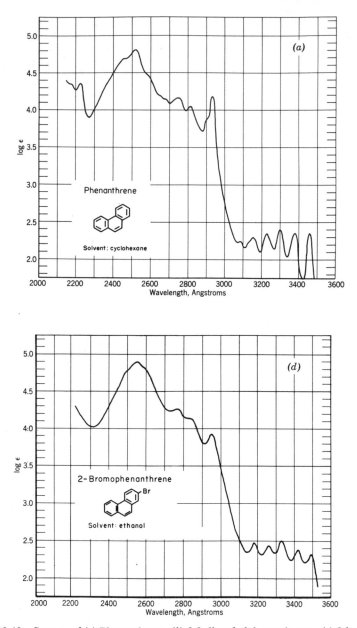

Fig. 13.19 Spectra of (*a*) Phenanthrene, (*b*) 2,3-dimethylphenanthrene; (*c*) 2-hydroxy-phenanthrene, and (*d*) 2-bromophenanthrene. (Reprinted by permission from R. A. Friedel and M. Orchin, *Ultraviolet Spectra of Aromatic Compounds*, John Wiley and Sons, New York, 1951.)

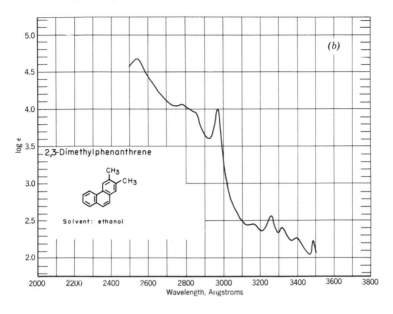

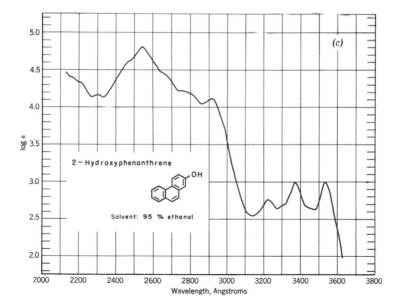

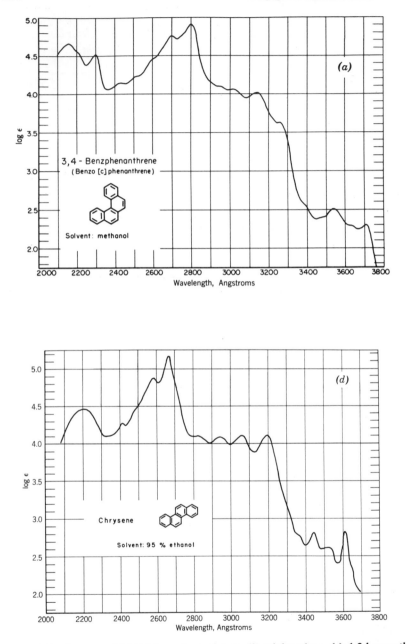

Fig. 13.20 Spectra of (*a*) 3,4-benzphenanthrene, (*b*) triphenylene, (*c*) 1,2-benzanthracene, and (*d*) chrysene. (Reprinted by permission from R. A. Friedel and M. Orchin, *Ultraviolet Spectra of Aromatic Compounds*, John Wiley and Sons, New York, 1951.)

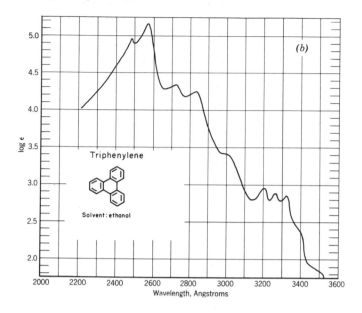

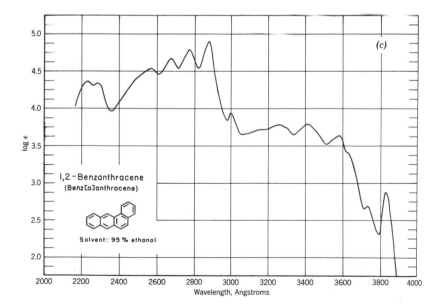

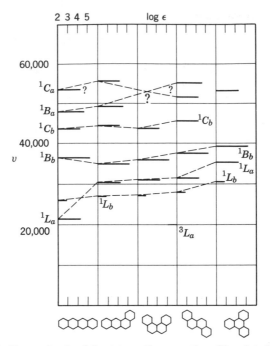

Fig. 13.21 Energy levels of the tetracyclic aromatics. [Reprinted by permission from H. B. Klevens and J. R. Platt, *J. Chem. Phys.*, **17**, 470 (1949).]

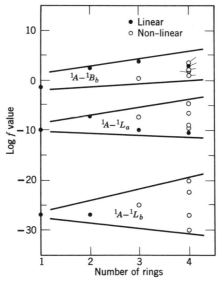

Fig. 13.22 Intensities of the ^1L_a, ^1L_b, and ^1B_b bands for all *cata*-condensed systems through four rings. [Reprinted by permission from H. B. Klevens and J. R. Platt, *J. Chem. Phys.*, **17**, 470 (1949).]

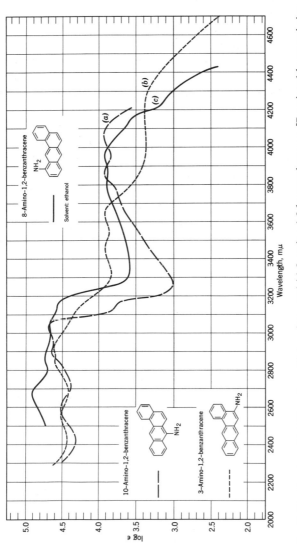
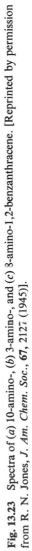

Fig. 13.23   Spectra of (*a*) 10-amino-, (*b*) 3-amino-, and (*c*) 3-amino-1,2-benzanthracene. [Reprinted by permission from R. N. Jones, *J. Am. Chem. Soc.*, **67**, 2127 (1945)].

13.8 *Peri*-condensed Aromatic Hydrocarbons: Pyrene

The free-electron model, as discussed by Platt and presented in section 13.2, assumes that the π electrons are moving around the periphery of the aromatic molecule, which in the first approximation is taken to be a circle. The *cata*-condensed aromatics are quite successfully treated by this model, since all the carbon atoms lie on the periphery. The *peri*-condensed aromatics, such as pyrene, XIII, and perylene, XIV, contain internal carbon atoms, and hence the treatment of such hydrocarbons by the FEM is less straightforward and less successful than that of the *cata*-condensed aromatics.

The correlation between band structure and direction of polarization is rather readily made in terms of the effects of substitution. In the spectrum of pyrene (Fig. 13.24) there are three strong bands of slightly decreasing intensity with increasing wavelength, and a fourth, long-wavelength, low-intensity band in the 350–375 mμ region. All four bands have considerable structure. In the spectrum of 4-aminopyrene (Fig. 13.24) the two short-wavelength bands have merged into a single broad band extending from 240 to 290 mμ, somewhat reminiscent of the spectrum of biphenyl, while the third band in the range 290–340 mμ has hardly been

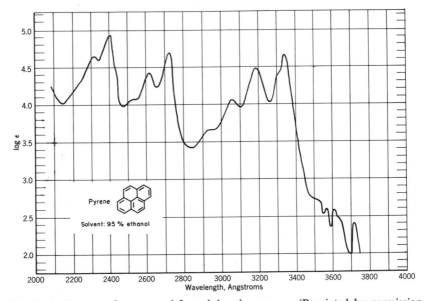

Fig. 13.24 Spectra of pyrene and 3- and 4-aminopyrene. (Reprinted by permission from R. A. Friedel and M. Orchin, *Ultraviolet Spectra of Aromatic Compounds*, John Wiley and Sons, New York, 1951.)

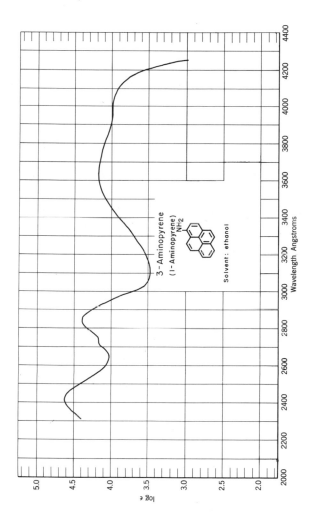

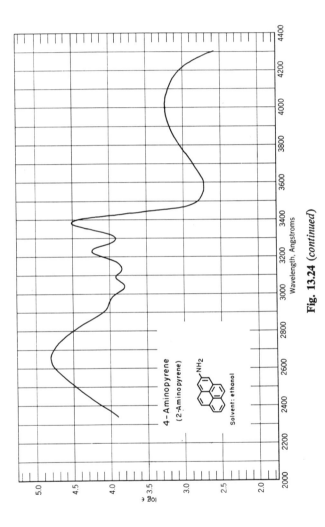

Fig. 13.24 (*continued*)

affected. The longest-wavelength, low-intensity band in the spectrum of the parent has been intensified and red shifted in the 4-amino derivative. It is, accordingly, reasonable to assign the bands in the 230–250 mμ and 250–280 mμ regions in the pyrene spectrum to transitions involving vertical polarizations, as in XXXVI. Further confidence in this assignment[22] derives from a study of the spectrum of 3-aminopyrene, XXXVII

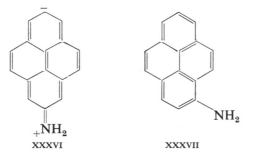

XXXVI   XXXVII

(Fig. 13.24). This spectrum shows that the 3-amino group red-shifts the 290–340 mμ band, which was unchanged in the 4-amino derivative. In the 3-amino compound, the 290–340 mμ band is shifted and merged with the shifted and intensified longest-wavelength band. It is accordingly reasonable to associate the 290–340 mμ band in pyrene with horizontal polarization.

13.9   Nonalternant Hydrocarbons: Azulene, Fulvene, Fluoranthrene

An alternant[29] molecule is one in which the carbon atoms may be divided into two groups, the starred and the unstarred, such that no member of either group is adjacent to a member of the same group. One particular way of starring naphthalene is shown in XXXVIII; each starred atom is flanked only by unstarred ones, and vice versa. In a nonalternant hydrocarbon, such as azulene, XXXIX, such a division is

XXXVIII   XXXIX

not possible. All molecules containing odd-membered rings are non-alternants, and all nonalternants contain odd-membered rings. In the alternant aromatic hydrocarbons the π electrons are distributed almost equally on all the carbon atoms, leading to low reactivities and small if any

[29] C. A. Coulson and G. S. Rushbrooke, *Proc. Cambridge Phil. Soc.*, **36**, 193 (1940); C. A. Coulson and H. C. Longuet-Higgins, *Proc. Roy. Soc.* (*London*), **191A**, 39 (1947).

dipole moments. This is not necessarily the case in nonalternant hydrocarbons. Thus, azulene, XXXIX, has a dipole moment of 1.0 D. This is
qualitatively explained as follows. The drive for a cyclopentadienyl radical
to take up a sixth π electron to give a pseudoaromatic cyclopentadienyl
anion, and the drive for a cycloheptatrienyl radical to give up an electron
and convert to the pseudoaromatic tropylium cation, $C_7H_7^+$, result in the
partial transfer of charge from the seven-membered to the five-membered
ring, and the development of the observed dipole moment. This statement,
which is equivalent to saying that resonance structures XL and XLI make

XL   XLI   XLII

more important contributions to the ground state of azulene than other
ionic structures, is often graphically summarized by writing structure XLII.
The charge distribution obtained for azulene by simple MO theory is also
in agreement with this explanation, and the direction of the dipole has
been ascertained to conform to this interpretation. Another important
difference between alternant and nonalternant hydrocarbons lies in some
special relations between certain orbitals and their energies. In alternant
hydrocarbons, all orbitals occur in pairs, one bonding with energy $\alpha + k\beta$,
the other antibonding with energy $\alpha - k\beta$, except for nonbonding orbitals,
of energy α, which need not occur as pairs. The wave functions of the
pairs of orbitals also are closely related: the coefficients c_{jr} in each pair of
orbitals are equal if r is an unstarred atom, equal in magnitude but of
opposite sign if r is a starred atom (see the orbitals of butadiene in section
3.8 and of benzene, Table 5.3, as examples). This correspondence of
energies and wave functions between corresponding bonding and antibonding orbitals does not hold with the nonalternant hydrocarbons, and
this fact is important for spectral interpretations.

The ten π electrons of azulene are delocalized around the periphery,
and in many respects the molecule may be regarded as cyclodecapentaene
with a transannular valence bridge. Neither of the Kekulé-type structures
which can be written involves a double bond common to the two rings.
The perimeter model is thus perhaps very appropriate for azulene. The
energy levels for the ten MO's of azulene[30] are shown in Fig. 13.25, with
the MO's numbered in ascending order and classified as belonging to the
species b_1 or a_2 of the point group C_{2v}. The ground state is $(\psi_3^2\psi_4^2\psi_5^2)\,^1A_1$;
the transition, the direction of polarization, the band assignment,[31] and

[30] C. A. Coulson, *Proc. Phys. Soc.* (*London*), **65**, 933 (1952).
[31] D. E. Mann, J. R. Platt, and H. B. Klevens, *J. Chem. Phys.*, **17**, 481 (1949).

the region of absorption and intensity are given in Table 13.6. The system of five absorption bands found in azulene (Fig. 13.26) corresponds with respect to vibrational structure, intensity, and sequence to the five found in naphthalene, except that in azulene all the bands are shifted to much longer wavelengths. It will be noted from Fig. 13.27 that the shifts in the bands are quite uniform, except for the ^1L_b transition in azulene, which is shifted much farther than the other bands; this band is responsible for the blue color of azulene.

The behavior of the azulene bands in the *ultraviolet* region on substitution of various groups in the nucleus has been investigated by Plattner and Heilbronner.[32] The introduction of a methyl group always results in a bathochromic shift, which is larger for substitution on the five-membered ring than for similar substitution in the seven-membered ring. Furthermore, not all the bands are affected to the same extent. On the other hand, in the *visible* region, the introduction of alkyl substituents may cause either hypsochromic or bathochromic effects, depending on the position of substitution. Substitution in the 1, 3, 5, or 7 position gives a shift to longer wavelength, and substitution in the 2, 4, 6, or 8 position has the opposite effect.[33] The wavelength shifts (in millimicrons) of the longest-wavelength band as a function of position of methyl substitution are shown in structure XLIII. Among the monomethyl derivatives the

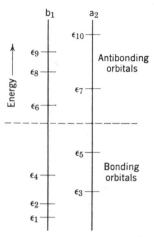

Fig. 13.25 Energy levels for azulene. [Reprinted by permission from C. A. Coulson, *Proc. Phys. Soc. (London)*, **65**, 937 (1952).]

TABLE 13.6

Characteristics of the Azulene Spectrum

Configuration	Transition	Polarization	Band Assignment	λ_{max}, mμ	ϵ_{max}
$\psi_3^2\psi_4^2\psi_5\psi_6$	$\psi_5 \rightarrow \psi_6$	$\perp$	^1L_b	700	300
$\psi_3^2\psi_4\psi_5^2\psi_6$	$\psi_4 \rightarrow \psi_6$	$\parallel$	^1L_a	357	4,000
$\psi_3^2\psi_4^2\psi_5\psi_7$	$\psi_5 \rightarrow \psi_7$	$\parallel$	^1B_b	269	47,000
$\psi_3\psi_4^2\psi_5^2\psi_6$	$\psi_3 \rightarrow \psi_6$	$\perp$	^1K_b or ^1C_b	236	22,000
$\psi_3^2\psi_4\psi_5^2\psi_7$	$\psi_4 \rightarrow \psi_7(?)$	$\perp$	$^1B_a(?)$	193	18,000

[32] P. A. Plattner and E. Heilbronner, *Helv. Chim. Acta*, **31**, 804 (1948).

[33] P. A. Plattner, *Helv. Chim. Acta*, **24**, 283 (1941); P. A. Plattner and E. Heilbronner, *Helv. Chim. Acta*, **30**, 910 (1947).

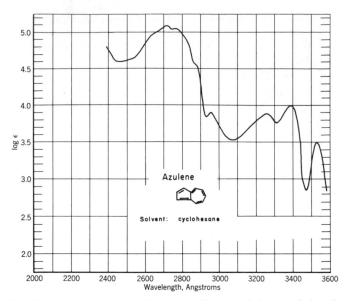

Fig. 13.26 Ultraviolet spectrum of azulene. (Reprinted by permission from R. A. Friedel and M. Orchin, *Ultraviolet Spectra of Aromatic Compounds*, John Wiley and Sons, New York, 1951.)

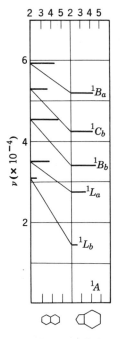

Fig. 13.27 Shifts in azulene compared to naphthalene. [Reprinted by permission from H. B. Klevens, *J. Chem. Phys.*, **18**, 1063 (1950).]

1 and 5 isomers are blue, whereas azulene itself is blue-violet. The 2-, 4-,

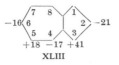

XLIII

and 6-methyl derivatives are violet. For di- and polysubstitution, the shifts are approximately additive, and it is possible to predict both the position of the absorption band of longest wavelength and the color of the compound. The wavenumber shifts and colors of some of the dimethylazulenes are shown in Table 13.7.

TABLE 13.7

Observed Shifts for Visible Band of Azulenes

λ, mμ	Compound	Frequency, cm^{-1}	Shift, cm^{-1}	Color
696	Azulene	14,350	...	Blue-violet
...	1,2-Dimethyl	13,950	−400	Blue
...	1,3-Dimethyl	12,990	−1360	Blue-green
...	1,4-Dimethyl	13,870	−480	Blue
...	4,8-Dimethyl	15,010	+660	Violet

Coulson[30] analyzed the effect of methyl groups into the usual two components, the inductive and resonance effects. If a substituent Y is attached to a conjugated system at an atom r of the system, the inductive effect arises from the fact that, because of the electronegativity difference of the carbon atom r and the substituent atom Y (which may also be a carbon atom, but as a result of different hybridization or different surroundings has an electronegativity different from r), Y either pushes electrons toward r or withdraws them from r. In MO theory this effect may be treated by assigning r a Coulomb integral α_r different from the Coulomb integral of a normal atom in the conjugated system by an amount $\delta\alpha_r$. The value of this quantity has been discussed extensively, and various workers use values of $\delta\alpha_r$ between one-tenth and one-third of $\delta\alpha_Y$, the difference between the Coulomb integrals of Y and a normal atom of the conjugated system. Anyway, $\delta\alpha_r$ has the same sign as $\delta\alpha_Y$; and hence for an atom Y more electronegative than an aromatic carbon atom (i.e., an electron-withdrawing substituent) $\delta\alpha_r < 0$; for an electron-donating substituent (a less electronegative Y) $\delta\alpha_r > 0$. An approximate MO treatment[30] then gives

$$\delta\nu = (c_{r2}{}^2 - c_{r1}{}^2)\,\delta\alpha_r/h \qquad (13.4)$$

where $\delta\nu$ is the frequency shift caused by the inductive effect of the substituent, and c_{r1} and c_{r2} are, respectively, the coefficients of the AO's of atom r in the highest occupied and lowest unoccupied MO's. In alternant hydrocarbons, because of the MO correspondence rule discussed above, $c_{r1}{}^2 = c_{r2}{}^2$, and no inductive effect is observed, as pointed out in Chapter 12; and the observed effects of alkyl groups are due to resonance interaction, i.e., hyperconjugation. Since, according to equation (13.4), $\delta\nu$ is proportional to $\delta\alpha_r$, the effect of substitution can be expected to be either hypsochromic or bathochromic, depending on the sign of $\delta\alpha_r$. The effect of carboxyl substitution on the long-wavelength band of azulene is opposite to the effect of methyl,[32] as expected if the displacement is dominated by the phenomenon represented by equation (13.4), i.e., the inductive effect.

The effects caused by the same substituent introduced at different positions of the molecule depend on the value and sign of the expression $(c_{r2}{}^2 - c_{r1}{}^2)$. This expression will be positive for certain atoms r and negative for others, according to the character of the wave function involving these atoms in the ground and excited states. Thus, a single substituent can cause either a hypsochromic or a bathochromic effect,[34] depending on the position of substitution.

The effect of substitution in azulene on its visible spectrum has been treated on a theoretical basis by several groups of workers.[30,35] This theoretical treatment of the effects of alkyl groups on a conjugated system leads to the following conclusions:

(1) In nonalternant hydrocarbons the inductive effects of alkyl groups predominate over the resonance effects. In the longest-wavelength band of alternants, the inductive effect vanishes because of the correspondence of bonding and antibonding orbitals; hence the resonance effect alone is operative and always produces a bathochromic shift.

(2) The inductive effect in the nonalternant depends on the electronegativity of the substituent, through the Coulomb term $\delta\alpha_r$, and on the position of substitution through $c_{r2}{}^2 - c_{r1}{}^2$, the difference between the squares of the coefficients of the AO of the substituent-bearing atom in the excited and ground MO's. The over-all effect is proportional to the product of these two quantities; the first depends *only* on the substituent, and the second *only* on the ring position. Consequently, ratios of $c_{r2}{}^2 - c_{r1}{}^2$ for different ring positions give relative shifts for these positions which are applicable to any substituent not having a large resonance effect.

(3) The resonance effect, predominant in alternants but of subsidiary importance in nonalternants, depends on the square of c_{r1}, the coefficient of the AO of the substituent-bearing atom in the highest occupied MO.

Theoretical oscillator-strength calculations for the bands in azulene have been made by Moffitt,[36] who also discusses the variable alkyl shifts on the visible band of azulene.

Fulvene, XLIV, one of the simplest of the nonalternant aromatic hydrocarbons, has six π electrons which are delocalized over the six carbon atoms. Although this compound has never been prepared, some

---

[34] R. D. Brown, *Nature*, **169,** 287 (1952).

[35] B. Pullman, M. Mayot, and G. Berthier, *J. Chem. Phys.*, **18,** 257 (1950); H. C. Longuet-Higgins and R. G. Sowden, *J. Chem. Soc.*, 1404 (1952).

[36] W. Moffitt, *J. Chem. Phys.*, **22,** 320 (1954).

of its derivatives are well known. Dimethylfulvene, XLV, has a dipole

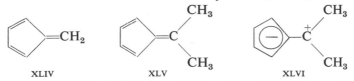

moment of 1.44 D, which may be explained by contributions from resonance structure XLVI; as in the case of azulene, such structures are stabilized by formation of the cyclopentadienyl anion. Contributions from a cyclopentadienyl system are also responsible for the stability of the red, liquid diazocyclopentadiene, XLVII.[37] The dialkylfulvenes have weak absorption at long wavelength,[38] $\lambda_{max} = 364$, $\epsilon_{max} = 200$, which trails into the visible region, and a strong band at 270 mμ, with $\epsilon_{max} =$

16,000. The substitution of phenyl for hydrogen on fulvene results in the expected bathochromic shifts, but anomalous results[39] are obtained when benzene rings are fused on the fulvene structure, e.g., benzhydrylidene-fluorene, XLVIII. Derivatives of this compound have interesting thermo-

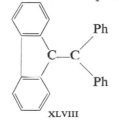

chromic properties.[40]

Still another nonalternant hydrocarbon is fluoranthene, XLIX, which may be considered as having a phenylene system attached to the *peri*

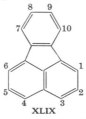

[37] W. von E. Doering and C. H. DePuy, *J. Am. Chem. Soc.*, **75**, 5955 (1953).

[38] E. D. Bergmann and Y. Hirshberg, *Bull. soc. chim.*, 1091 (1950).

[39] B. Pullman, G. Berthier, and J. Baudet, *J. chim. phys.*, **50**, 69 (1953).

[40] E. D. Bergmann, E. Fischer, Y. Hirshberg, and D. Lavie, *Bull. Soc. Chem.*, 709 (1952), and related papers.

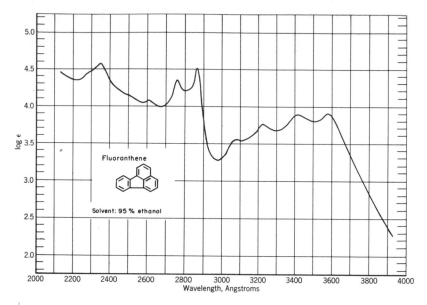

Fig. 13.28 The spectrum of fluoranthene. (Reprinted by permission from R. A. Friedel and M. Orchin, *Ultraviolet Spectra of Aromatic Compounds*, John Wiley and Sons, New York, 1951.)

positions of naphthalene. The spectrum of fluoranthene (Fig. 13.28) shows three main bands. The long-wavelength band with λ_{max} at 358 mμ is the *para*-band of the Clar classification. It has been suggested[41] that this band is associated with the naphthalene portion of fluoranthene. The spectra of 1-methoxy-, 3-methoxy-, and 3-phenylfluoranthene are all similar[42] and are considerably different in the long-wavelength region from the spectrum of fluoranthene. On the other hand, substituents on the phenyl ring of fluoranthene have only a minor spectral influence; the spectra of 7- and 8-methoxyfluoranthene are very similar to the spectrum of the parent.

[41] E. Clar, H. W. D. Stubbs, and S. H. Tucker, *Nature*, **166**, 1075 (1950).
[42] H. W. D. Stubbs and S. H. Tucker, *J. Chem. Soc.*, 227 (1954).

14 Heterocycles

14.1 Saturated Heterocyclic Compounds

Like ethers and amines, saturated cyclic compounds containing an oxygen or nitrogen atom have no absorption maxima in the near or middle ultraviolet region (above 200 mμ). With one exception the vapor spectra in the vacuum ultraviolet[1] (Table 14.1) of saturated oxygen heterocycles show two bands slightly below 200 mμ. In 1,4-dioxan only one band is observed. The absence of a second band may result from strong overlap of the two bands, or perhaps one band is absent because the transition is forbidden by the $g \nleftrightarrow g$ selection rule. This selection rule may operate here, but not in the other compounds because dioxan belongs to point group C_{2h} and hence has a center of symmetry which is lacking in the other compounds. The transitions are considered as first members of a Rydberg series involving excitation of oxygen 2p electrons ($^1R \leftarrow {}^1A$), and are quite similar to the corresponding transitions in saturated acyclic ethers.

The spectrum of ethylene oxide in the vacuum ultraviolet[2] contains two bands at relatively long wavelength which are quite likely to be similar in origin to the corresponding bands in the five- and six-membered rings. Ethylene oxide also shows two Rydberg series, starting at 143.5 and 138.2 mμ, and converging to a common ionization potential at 10.81 ev.

The saturated nitrogen heterocycles[3] absorb at somewhat longer wavelengths than their oxygen analogs (Table 14.1). The six-membered ring compounds have only one absorption band, although this may possibly be a superposition of two bands; pyrrolidine, however, has two bands, with possibly a third, very weak band near 233 mμ (ϵ about 300). The spectra of the nitrogen heterocycles have much less resolved vibrational structure than those of their oxygen analogs. The bands again are probably Rydberg bands corresponding to excitation of the nitrogen lone-pair

[1] L. W. Pickett, N. J. Hoeflich, and T.-C. Liu, *J. Am. Chem. Soc.*, **73**, 4865 (1951).

[2] T.-K. Liu and A. B. F. Duncan, *J. Chem. Phys.*, **17**, 241 (1949).

[3] L. W. Pickett, M. E. Corning, G. M. Wieder, D. A. Semenow, and J. M. Buckley, *J. Am. Chem. Soc.*, **75**, 1618 (1953).

TABLE 14.1

**Vacuum Ultraviolet Absorption Spectra of Some
Saturated Heterocycles**

Compound		Absorption Region		f Value
		cm^{-1}	mμ	
Ethylene oxide,		63,597	157.2	...
		69,684	143.5	...
Tetrahydrofuran,		50,000–55,500	180–200	0.012
		55,500–61,800	162–180	0.041
Tetrahydropyran,		54,300–57,500	174–184	0.008
		57,500–60,500	165–174	0.085
Dioxan,		52,200–60,510	165–192	0.11
Piperidine,		40,000–56,700	176–250	0.11
Pyrrolidine,		40,000–53,500	187–250	0.05
		53,500–61,700	162–187	0.08
Piperazine,		47,000–57,100	175–213	0.20

electrons, although they may also be $Q \leftarrow N$ (n $\rightarrow \sigma^*$, $^1W \leftarrow {}^1A$) transitions. All bands in the spectra of the nitrogen heterocycles are displaced to shorter wavelength in solution; the shift is small in isooctane and larger in polar solvents. The absorption seems to disappear in acid solution. These observations suggest that the bands are due to excitation of lone-pair electrons.

14.2   Conjugated Five-Membered Heterocycles

14.21 FIVE-MEMBERED CYCLIC DIENES WITH ONE HETEROATOM.   Considerable work has been done on the measurement (Table 14.2) and interpretation of spectra of five-membered heterocyclic dienes, but no agreement
seems to have been reached on the nature of these spectra.

TABLE 14.2
Spectra of Five-Membered Heterocyclic Dienes

Compound	λ_{max}, mμ	λ_{max}, mμ	$\log \epsilon_{max}$
Cyclopentadiene,	...	200, 238	3.4
Furan,	191	205	3.8 (vapor)
Pyrrole,	172, 183	211	4.5 (vapor)
Thiophene,	204–220	221–245, 221–260	(2 band systems) (vapor)
		235	3.65 (hexane)
		231	3.85 (isooctane)
Selenophene,	197–209, 186.5, 182.8, 172.1	266–269, 242–252	... (vapor)

The vapor spectrum of furan[1,4] shows a virtually structureless band
about 205 mμ with log ϵ about 3.8. Overlapping this band, beginning at
about 200 mμ and having a maximum at about 191 mμ, is a band of
considerable vibrational structure, which is possibly of origin similar to
that of the corresponding one in the saturated compounds, but has
considerably greater intensity. A third band system, certainly a Rydberg
series, begins about 167 mμ and converges to an ionization potential at
9.01 ev.

[4] W. C. Price and A. D. Walsh, *Proc. Roy. Soc.* (*London*), **A179,** 201 (1941).

Pyrrole[3,5,6] has an absorption band at about 211 mμ, with some resolved vibrational structure. Further bands occur at about 183 mμ, similar in vibrational structure to the 191 mμ band of furan, and at 172 mμ with much higher intensity. All bands are more intense than their analogs in furan.

Thiophene and selenophene absorb at considerably longer wavelength than the oxygen and nitrogen compounds. In solution in hexane,[7] thiophene has λ_{max} at 235 mμ with ϵ_{max} about 4500, and in isooctane[8] λ_{max} is at 231 mμ with ϵ_{max} of 7100. In the vapor, Price and Walsh[4] have observed a long-wavelength band system extending from 210 to 240 mμ, and a Rydberg series extending from 188 to 140 mμ and converging to an ionization potential of 8.91 ev. Milazzo,[5] however, has observed two overlapping band systems, one between 221 and 260 mμ, the second between 221 and 245 mμ, with the 0-0 bands at 41,595 and 42,992 cm^{-1}, respectively, and a third band system between 204 and 220 mμ, with a 0-0 transition at 45,378 cm^{-1}. In selenophene, Milazzo and coworkers[9,6] observed band systems at 266–268 mμ, 242–252 mμ, 197–209 mμ, and, overlaid on a continuous absorption, probably three distinct bands at 186.5, 182.8 and 172.1 mμ. The existence of the three separate band systems in selenophene above 200 mμ seems to confirm Milazzo's assignment of two band systems in the 220–260 mμ range in thiophene.

The theoretical interpretation of the data for furan, pyrrole, and thiophene, coupled with information on cyclopentadiene, cyclohexadiene, and the cyclopentadienide anion, $C_5H_5^-$, has been attempted by many workers, and no consensus of opinion has been reached.

Mulliken[10] has suggested treating these molecules by one of three models which really represent two extremes and an intermediate. One extreme is represented by a simple diene, having the properties of s-cis-butadiene, plus an isolated lone-pair orbital on the heteroatom. In the intermediate case, this lone-pair orbital interacts with the diene orbitals, in particular lowering the lowest unoccupied orbital. Finally, the other extreme is represented by the $C_5H_5^-$ ion, in which all carbon pπ orbitals are equivalent (the energy-level diagram for this ion was given in Fig. 12.1c). Mulliken further points out that the large bathochromic effect in cyclopentadiene

[5] G. Milazzo, *Spectrochimica Acta*, **2**, 245 (1944); *Gazz. chim. ital.*, **78**, 835 (1948), **83**, 392 (1953).

[6] G. Milazzo, *Gazz. chim. ital.*, **83**, 787 (1953).

[7] G. Leandri, A. Mangini, F. Montanari, and R. Passerini, *Gazz. chim. ital.*, **85**, 769 (1955).

[8] F. S. Boig, G. W. Costa, and I. Osvar, *J. Org. Chem.*, **18**, 775 (1953).

[9] G. Milazzo and L. Paoloni, *Gazz. chim. ital.*, **82**, 576 (1952); G. Milazzo and E. Miescher, *Gazz. chim. ital.*, **83**, 782 (1953).

[10] R. S. Mulliken, *J. Chem. Phys.*, **7**, 342 (1939).

(and cyclohexadiene), compared to the absorption expected for an *s-cis* compound, is due to hyperconjugation, i.e., to a doubly occupied orbital of quasi-π symmetry forming part of the two bonds between C and H_2. The CH_2 group further has an antibonding quasi-π orbital, which Mulliken also considers as interacting with the diene orbitals. Thiophene has also an added vacant d orbital on the sulfur atom.

Price and Walsh[4] disagree with some of the details of Mulliken's treatment. They point out, in particular, that the effect of the heteroatom is not, as implied by Mulliken, a lowering of the excited state, but a raising of the ground state, since all absorption bands, compared with those of an acyclic diene, undergo a bathochromic shift, and, in particular, because the ionization potential is lowered.

Longuet-Higgins[11] has suggested an alternate treatment of thiophene, particularly to bring out the similarity to benzene. His treatment consists of hybridizing the two $3d\pi$ orbitals of sulfur with the $3p\pi$ orbital, forming two nonorthogonal hybrid π orbitals, each so oriented as to strongly overlap the $p\pi$ orbital of one of the adjacent carbon atoms. The third $d\pi$-$p\pi$ hybrid of sulfur is assumed to remain vacant and is directed away from the ring. The assumption is then made that the Coulomb integrals of the two hybrid orbitals along the C-S bonds, the resonance integral between them, and the resonance integral for their interaction with the $p\pi$ orbitals of the adjacent carbon atoms are all about equal to the corresponding quantities involving carbon atoms in benzene. This simple assumption, which is not justified *a priori*, leads to an electronic structure which is quite analogous to that of benzene, and hence is capable of explaining the similarity of the physical, chemical, and spectroscopic properties of the two compounds. Thus, the long-wavelength band in thiophene is supposed to be the equivalent of the $^1B_{2u} \leftarrow {}^1A_{1g}$ ($^1L_b \leftarrow {}^1A$) transition of benzene at 256 mμ, and the much greater intensity in thiophene again must depend on the lower symmetry (point group C_{2v}) of this compound.

Neither Mulliken's nor Longuet-Higgins' treatment of thiophene appears completely satisfactory. Objections to Longuet-Higgins' treatment are the use of nonorthogonal hybrid orbitals, and the fact that he fails to account for the rather close spectroscopic analogy between thiophene and pyrrole, and the even closer analogy of these five-membered heterocycles in fused-ring systems (see below). Mulliken's treatment seems somewhat inadequate, since it takes into account one of the $d\pi$ orbitals (of species b_1 in the point group C_{2v} of thiophene), but fails to consider the other $d\pi$ orbital of species a_2.

[11] H. C. Longuet-Higgins, *Trans. Faraday Soc.*, **45**, 173 (1949); cf. also J. Metzger and F. Ruffler, *J. chim. phys.*, **51**, 52 (1954); J. De Heer, *J. Am. Chem. Soc.*, **76**, 4802 (1954); K. Maeda, *Bull. Chem. Soc. Japan*, **33**, 303 (1960).

TABLE 14.3
Spectra of Some Substituted Pyrroles and Furans

		Substituents in Position			Band I		Band II	
N	1	2	3	4	λ, mμ	ϵ	λ, mμ	ϵ
				Pyrroles				
H	H	H	H	H	183	...	211	15,000
H	H	Et	Me	H	203	5,670	...	...
H	Me	Et	Me	H	200	7,450	...	...
H	COOEt	Me	H	Me	(240)	5,000	276	19,300
H	COOEt	Me	Et	Me	250	5,900	283.5	18,900
H	Ac	Me	Et	Me	(266)	4,700	308	19,600
H	H	COOEt	Me	Me	231.5	9,980	263.5	3,740
H	Me	COOEt	Me	H	232	8,480	259	5,030
H	Me	Ac	Me	H				
H	COOEt	COOEt	H	Me	243	5,640	290	10,570
					210	12,400		
H	COOEt	Me	COOEt	Me	221	25,300	273	16,100
H	COOEt	Me	Et	COOMe	221	17,700	280	21,900
H	Me	COOEt	COOEt	Me	215	11,200	267.5	8,450
H	COOEt	Me	Ac	Me	235	22,800	283	11,800
					(255)	12,000		
H	COOEt	Me	Et	CHO	231	14,200	303	21,100
Ac	H	H	H	H	238.5	10,800	288	760
H	CHO	H	H	H	252	5,000	289.5	16,600
H	Ac	H	H	H	250	4,400	287	15,900
H	COOH	H	H	H	228	4,500	258	12,600
H	COOEt	H	H	H	233	4,500	265	15,900
H	CONH$_2$	H	H	H	228	3,700	263	14,500
Me	CHO	H	H	H	255	5,300	288.5	12,600
Me	Ac	H	H	H	245	4,900	270	10,500
Me	COOH	H	H	H	236	6,300	260.5	12,300
Me	COOEt	H	H	H	240	6,000	260	14,500
				Furans				
	H	H	H	H	205	6,400	...	...
	CHO	H	H	H	227	3,000	272	13,200
	Ac	H	H	H	225.5	2,300	270	12,900
	COOH	H	H	H	214	3,800	242.5	10,700
	COOEt	H	H	H	220	2,900	250.5	13,500
	CONH$_2$	H	H	H	214	5,400	248	11,500
	NO$_2$	H	H	H	225	3,400	315	8,100
	CHO	H	H	NO$_2$	225	8,250	310	11,600
	CH(Ac)$_2$	H	H	NO$_2$	...	...	298	13,200
	Br	H	H	NO$_2$	...	...	315	9,600
	Me	H	H	NO$_2$	...	...	340	1,100

Despite the lack of agreement on the theoretical interpretation of the spectra of the five-membered heterocyclics, there is agreement that the resemblance of their spectra to that of benzene increases in the order furan, pyrrole, and thiophene. This is the order expected on the basis of the relative electronegativity of the heteroatoms and hence of participation or delocalization of the lone pair, predominantly p electrons. Delocalization of the oxygen lone pair is least, because of the higher nuclear charge of oxygen as compared to nitrogen. The sulfur atom has approximately the same electronegativity as carbon, and hence conjugation of the sulfur electrons with the four π electrons of the butadiene system is more complete than in the oxygen or nitrogen analog. In addition the low-lying d orbitals of sulfur undoubtedly play some role in the conjugation.

14.22 SUBSTITUENT EFFECTS.   Considerable information is available concerning the effects of substituents on the heterocyclic dienes. The spectrum of N-methylpyrrole is almost identical with that of the parent compound; 0-0 vibrations for the band about 219 mμ are, in the vapor state, at 46,568 and 47,320 cm^{-1}, respectively.[6,9]

Cookson[12] has studied the spectra of a variety of substituted pyrroles (Table 14.3). Alkyl substituents, particularly in the α position, appear to produce a slight hypsochromic effect. Carbonyl groups, however, produce a new absorption band in the 260–300 mμ range, and a second band in the 220–250 mμ range. Both bands occur at longer wavelength when the carbonyl group is aldehydic or ketonic than when it is in a carboxy or a carbalkoxy group. Also, the carbonyl group in an α position gives rise to longer-wavelength bands than such a group in the β position. The long-wavelength band of a carbonyl group in the α position has an intensity ϵ above 10,000; the shorter band is weaker and usually has ϵ below 10,000. In β-carbonyl derivatives, the relation is reversed; the long-wavelength band, with an intensity of about 5000, is weaker than the short-wavelength band. N-methyl substitution does not appreciably affect the spectra of α-carbonyl pyrroles, but N-acetyl substitution gives rise to a spectrum[13] with an intense band at 238.5 mμ, and a weak one, possibly an n → π band, at 288 mμ (log ϵ, 2.88). The α-carbonyl derivatives of furan have spectra similar to those of the pyrrole derivatives.[13] Furfural and α-furyl ketones have an intense band (log ϵ, 4.1) at 272 mμ; furoic acid, amide, and esters have the band at about 250 mμ. The α-carbonyl derivatives all have a short-wavelength weaker band (log $\epsilon \sim 3.5$) which occurs at about 226 mμ for aldehyde and ketone, at 214 mμ for the acid and amide, and at 220 mμ for the esters. Most of the 2-substituted 5-nitrofurans which have been studied[14]

[12] G. H. Cookson, *J. Chem. Soc.*, 2789 (1953).
[13] R. Andrisano and G. Pappalardo, *Gazz. chim. ital.*, **85**, 1430 (1955).
[14] S. A. Hiller and N. O. Soldabols, *Doklady Akad. Nauk S.S.S.R.*, **17**, 708 (1953).

have the longer-wavelength band shifted to about 310 mμ. This band usually is slightly less intense than the corresponding one in furfural. The spectra of these carbonyl derivatives of pyrrole and furan can probably best be interpreted as butadiene derivatives (see sections 10.5 and 11.4).

Data relating to substituent effects in thiophene are given in Table 14.4.

TABLE 14.4

Spectra of Substituted Thiophenes in Isooctane

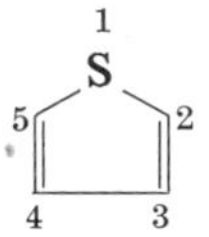

Substituent	λ_{max}, mμ	ϵ_{max}
None	231	7,100
2-Br	235.5	9,100
2-Cl	236	8,700
2-CN	243	9,300
2-I	243 / 300	9,300 / 320
2-NO$_2$	268–272 / 294–298	6,300 / 6,000
2,5-Br$_2$	252	9,100
2,5-Cl$_2$	252	7,400
2,5-I$_2$	266 / 315	14,000 / 270
2-COOH	249 / 268.5	(11,500) / 8,200
2-Ac	252 / 273	10,500 / 7,200
2-CHO	265 / 278.5	10,500 / 6,500
2-Br-5-COOH	260 / 281	9,800 / 12,400
2-Br-5-Ac	265 / 288.5	8,200 / 12,400
2-Br-5-CHO	265 / 291	8,200 / 12,400

Halogens in the 2 position[8] produce a bathochromic effect of a few millimicrons, with iodine (12 mμ) producing the largest effect, equal to that of a cyano group.[8] Disubstitution in the 2,5 positions more than doubles the bathochromic shift. The intensities are also increased by the substitutions. The spectrum of 2-iodothiophene shows a weak, unexplained band at 300 mμ (ϵ, 2.5), which appears at 315 mμ (ϵ, 270) in 2,5-diiodothiophene.

A methyl group[15] in either the 2 or 3 position also causes a bathochromic shift of some 10–15 mμ. In the acetyl thiophenes[15] weak transitions, presumably n $\rightarrow$ π*, are observed at 310–330 mμ. An acetyl group in the 3 position causes a moderate bathochromic effect of some 12–15 mμ, but the 2-propionyl compound has bands at 255 and 280 mμ. The spectra of 2-nitro- and 2,5-dinitrothiophene[8] are considerably different from those of other substituted compounds, probably because of stronger interaction between the two chromophores and the appearance of charge-transfer absorption (see section 12.24).

In thiophenes bearing a carbonyl substituent in the 2 position,[16] a new band appears; both bands have intensities about 10^4 and are separated by some 20 mμ; the shorter-wavelength band is generally slightly more intense. Introduction, in addition, of a bromine atom in the 5 position produces an additional small bathochromic shift, of the order of 10 mμ, and a reversal of the intensity relation.

In an extensive study of thirty-four thiophene derivatives,[17] the positions of the longest-wavelength band of 2-substituted thiophenes and of the ^1L_a band of monosubstituted benzenes were found to be linearly related, but no similar relation for the 3-substituted analogs was detected. In general, the effect of a substituent in the 2 position was greater than the effect of the same substituent in the 3 position. No generalizations in polysubstituted compounds were found.[17]

14.23 COMPOUNDS WITH SEVERAL HETEROATOMS.   Little information is available on the spectra of the five-membered heterocycles having more than one heteroatom, but some examples are given in Table 14.5. No striking effects are observed in imidazole, pyrazole, or isoxazole,[7] all of which have a single absorption band at about 210 mμ with $\epsilon = 4000$–5000. Methyl substitution in all three compounds[7] causes a considerable bathochromic effect. In thiazole, the 235 mμ (in ethanol) band of thiophene[7] is shifted slightly to the red, to 240 mμ, or to the blue,[18] to 232–233 mμ (ethanol), depending upon the authors. Substituents in thiazole appear to give the usual red shifts.

14.24 FIVE-MEMBERED HETEROCYCLES FUSED TO BENZENE RINGS.   A great deal of work has been done by organic chemists on the synthesis and reactions of compounds containing one or more benzene rings fused to a five-membered heterocyclic system, and the spectra of many such

[15] P. Ramart-Lucas, *Bull. soc. chim. France*, 1017 (1954), unfortunately gives only reproductions of curves, from which accurate information cannot be obtained.

[16] G. Pappalardo, *Gazz. chim. ital.*, **89**, 540 (1959).

[17] N. Sugimoto, S. Nishimura, and E. Imoto, *Bull. Univ. Osaka Prefecture*, **A8**, No. 1, 71 (1959).

[18] U. N. Shejnker, V. V. Kushkin, and I. Ya. Postovski, *Zhur. Fiz. Khim.*, **31**, 214 (1957).

compounds have been reported. The interpretation and correlation of
these spectra are rendered difficult, not only by their inherently complicated
nature, but also by the problem of even distinguishing between vibrational

TABLE 14.5

Spectra of Five-Membered Ring Compounds having Two Heteroatoms, in Ethanol[7]

Compound		λ_{max}, mμ	log ϵ_{max}
Imidazole,		207	3.70
N-Me		212	3.63
4-Me		215	3.67
2-Ph		271	4.20
Pyrazole,		210	3.50
4-Me		219	3.51
Isoxazole,		211	3.60
3-Me		217	3.74
4-Me		222	3.50
5-Me		213	3.19
Thiazole,		240	3.60
4-Me		243	...
2-Br		247	...

structure and separate electronic transitions. Few vapor spectra are available for even the simple compounds, and the low vapor pressure of many
of the compounds adds to the experimental difficulty of securing such
spectra.

Perhaps the outstanding feature of the spectra of the heterocyclics is their general resemblance to the spectra of the corresponding fused-ring hydrocarbons with the same number and disposition of rings, all six-membered and aromatic. Thus the spectra of benzfuran, I, indole, II, and thionaphthene, III, have been compared[19] and found to have some features in

benzfuran, I, X = O
indole, II, X = NH
thianaphthene, III, X = S

IV

common with each other; all three have some resemblance to naphthalene. Even benzimidazole, IV, with two heteroatoms, has considerable resemblance to naphthalene.[7]

It is important to emphasize that comparison of the heterocyclic compound must be made with the corresponding system in which all rings are aromatic; the heteroatom is equivalent to a —CH=CH— group and

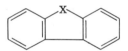

fluorene, V, X = CH₂
dibenzfuran, XIII, X = O
carbazole, VI, X = NH
dibenzthiophene, XIV, X = S
phenanthrene, X = —CH=CH

not a methylene group. In order to demonstrate the noncorrespondence of the methylene group and the heteroatom, a discussion of the properties and spectra of fluorene, V, and carbazole, VI, is instructive.

In fluorene the methylene carbon uses sp^3 orbitals, and the C=H_2 electrons on this tetrahedral carbon atom are not delocalized except through hyperconjugation. On the other hand, in the nitrogen analog, carbazole, VI, the lone-pair electrons on the nitrogen atom are largely p in character and hence of the proper symmetry to coalesce with the π cloud on the adjacent benzenoid rings. The electron distributions in these two molecules are, accordingly, quite different. This difference is reflected not only in the relatively different spectra (Fig. 14.1) but also in the chemical reactivity, e.g., in the position at which electrophilic substitution occurs. Thus mono-, di-, and trinitration of fluorene leads to the 2-nitro, 2,7-dinitro, and 2,4,7-trinitro derivatives, respectively, consistent with the

[19] G. M. Badger and B. J. Christie, *J. Chem. Soc.*, 3438 (1956).

polarization indicated in VII (or VIII), which emphasizes the relation between fluorene and biphenyl. However, mono-, di- and trinitration of carbazole leads to 3-, 3,6-, and 1,3,6- substitution, respectively, consistent

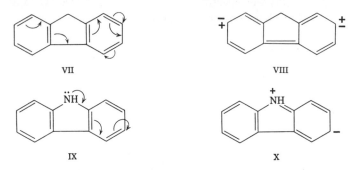

with the polarization indicated in IX (or X), which rationalizes electrophilic substitution at positions on the benzenoid nuclei *para* to the imino group.[20] Structures of carbazole, XI, analogous to those in fluorene, VIII,

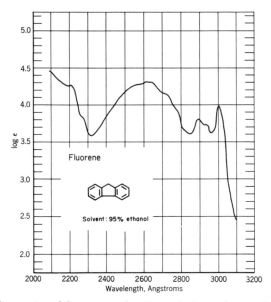

Fig. 14.1 The spectra of fluorene, carbazole, and phenanthrene. (Reprinted by permission from R. A. Friedel and M. Orchin, *Ultraviolet Spectra of Aromatic Compounds*, John Wiley and Sons, New York, 1951.)

[20] Further evidence for the predominence of polarizations of structure IX is found in a study of the difference in base strengths of various aminoacridines as a function of the position of the amino group: A. Albert, R. Goldacre, and J. Phillips, *J. Chem. Soc.*, 2240 (1948).

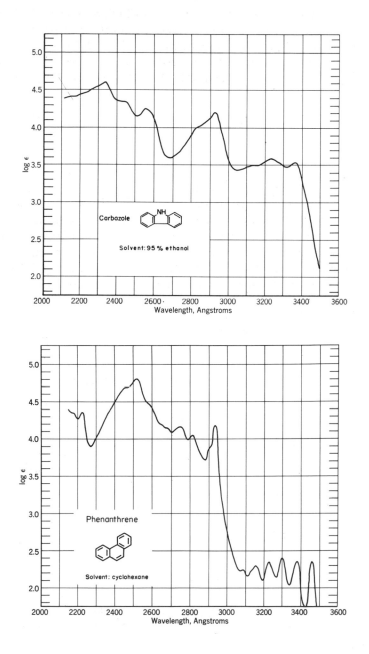

are possible and probably do make some contribution to the excited state. A comparison of the spectra of fluorene, carbazole, and phenanthrene (Fig. 14.1) does indicate some resemblance in the 270–300 mμ region in each. That similar polarizations are possible is perhaps best illustrated by comparing structures VIII, XI, and XII. Over-all, however, the spectrum of

XI   XII

carbazole resembles that of phenanthrene much more closely than that of fluorene. That the intensity of the long-wavelength band is higher in carbazole than in phenanthrene is expected on the basis of the lower symmetry of the heterocyclic compound. The resemblance of the spectra of dibenzfuran (or diphenylene oxide), XIII, and dibenzthiophene, XIV, to carbazole has been reported,[19] and of the three heterocycles, VI, XIII, and XIV, the oxygen compound is least like phenanthrene. (For XIII and XIV, see structure on p. 355.)

The similarity between the spectra of the heterocyclic compound and of its carbocyclic aromatic analog has been pointed out in other tricyclic systems. Thus 4,5-, XV, and 6,7-benzthionaphthene, XVI, have three well-defined groups of bands quite similar to those of phenanthrene; and thiophanthrene, XVII, has a spectrum very similar to that of anthracene except for a bathochromic shift of the long-wavelength band.[21]

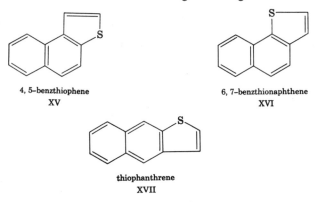

4, 5–benzthiophene   6, 7–benzthionaphthene
XV   XVI

thiophanthrene
XVII

It was pointed out in section 13.31 that in the benzfluorene series 1,2- and 2,3-benzfluorene have spectra which resemble each other, whereas 3,4-benzfluorene has a rather different spectrum. In the benzcarbazole

[21] W. Carruthers and J. R. Crowder, *J. Chem. Soc.*, 1932 (1957).

series the situation is more like it is in the benzfluorenones (section 13.31), and it is the spectrum of the 1,2-benz compound which appears to be different, whereas the spectra of 2,3- and 3,4-benzcarbazole share certain similarities. In an analysis of these spectra[22] it was suggested that in the paired isomers, 2,3- and 3,4-benzcarbazole, just as in the benzfluorenones, extended *p*-quinoid polarizations are facilitated by the availability of the lone-pair nitrogen electrons, giving rise, respectively, to structures XVIII and XIX. However, in 1,2-benzcarbazole, participation in conjugation of the nitrogen lone pair gives rise to the much less extended system, XX and XXI. It is assumed that structures in which the benzene portion of the molecule conjugates with the naphthalene portion, such as XXII, do not make as significant contributions as structures XX and XXI. Just as in

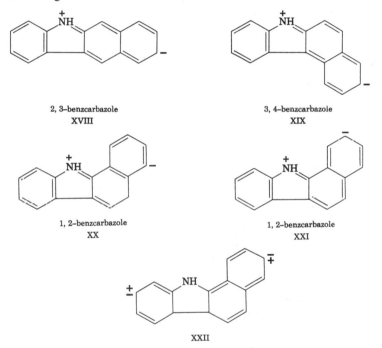

carbazole, the diphenyl-type structures are assumed to be of less importance than structures in which nitrogen participates. The spectra of the three benzcarbazoles are shown in Fig. 14.2. The resemblance between the related pair of 2,3- and 3,4-benzcarbazoles is not as great as that between the related pair of hydrocarbons, 1,2- and 2,3-benzfluorene, presumably because of minor contributions from polarizations in the benzcarbazole series related to structure XXII.

[22] G. R. Clemo and D. G. I. Felton, *J. Chem. Soc.*, 1658 (1952).

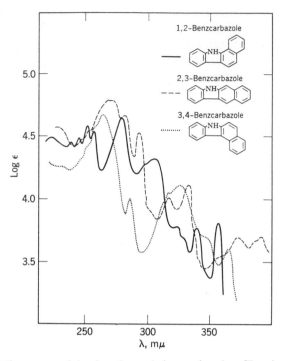

Fig. 14.2 The spectra of the three isomeric benzcarbazoles. [Reprinted by permission from G. R. Clemo and D. G. I. Felton, *J. Chem. Soc.*, 1658 (1952).]

The explanation for the similarities and differences in the spectra of the benzcarbazoles has been shown to apply to the dibenzcarbazoles.[23] Of the three angular dibenzcarbazoles, dibenzo[c,g]carbazole, XXIII, with

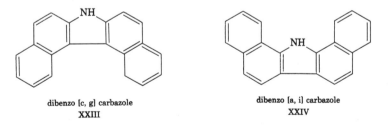

dibenzo [c, g] carbazole
XXIII

dibenzo [a, i] carbazole
XXIV

two possible sets of extended quinoid structures related to XIX, absorbs at the longest wavelength. Furthermore, dibenzo[a,i]carbazole, XXIV, which can give rise to only relatively short polarized systems related to

[23] D. G. I. Felton, *J. Chem. Soc.*, 1668 (1952).

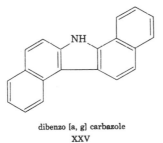

dibenzo [a, g] carbazole
XXV

XX and XXI, absorbs at shorter wavelength than either XXIII or XXV. The spectrum of dibenzo[a,g]carbazole, XXV, can be considered to arise from a mixture of the isomers XXIII and XXIV.

14.3   Pyridine and Other Aza Aromatics

14.31 PYRIDINE.   The outstanding feature of the absorption spectra of aza aromatic hydrocarbons in which the —N= groups replaces a methine group, —CH=, is their similarity to those of the parent homocyclic compounds. Thus, the spectrum of pyridine closely resembles that of benzene, with which it is compared in Fig. 14.3. This observation is not unexpected, since the compounds are π-isoelectronic. The most striking difference between the two lies in the greater intensity and loss of vibrational structure of the long-wavelength band of pyridine. Both these facts find a ready explanation in the reduced symmetry of pyridine (point group C_{2v}) compared with benzene (D_{6h}). Whereas the longest-wavelength band, $^1B_{2u} \leftarrow {}^1A_{1g}$ ($^1L_b \leftarrow {}^1A$), in benzene is forbidden, and hence is weak and shows prominently the vibronic interaction making it partially allowed (section 6.6), the corresponding ^1L_b transition in pyridine is $^1B_1 \leftarrow {}^1A_1$ and is allowed. The intensity of this band, however, still is not large ($\epsilon \sim$ 2000), considerably less than that of a typical $V \leftarrow N$ transition, indicating that the distortion of the π-electron cloud from D_{6h} symmetry is not great. Some of the vibrational structure typical of the forbidden benzene band persists in the allowed pyridine transition, but is much less prominent.

The shorter-wavelength bands in pyridine, although somewhat shifted, both in wavelength and intensity, are readily recognizable, and undoubtedly should be assigned to transitions analogous to those observed in benzene.

One basically new feature is to be expected in the spectrum of pyridine. The nitrogen atom has a lone pair of electrons; and it should be possible to excite one of these to the unoccupied, antibonding π^* orbitals. No band corresponding to such transitions is readily observable in the solution

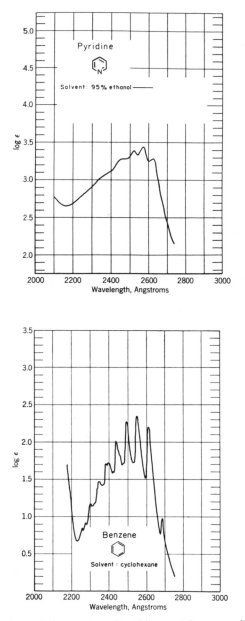

Fig. 14.3 Comparison of the spectra of pyridine and benzene. (Reprinted by permission from R. A. Friedel and M. Orchin, *Ultraviolet Spectra of Aromatic Compounds*, John Wiley and Sons, New York, 1951.)

spectra of pyridine. Careful analysis of vapor spectra,[24] however, has shown that the expected n $\rightarrow \pi^*$ transition ($^1B_2 \leftarrow {}^1A_1$, $^1W \leftarrow {}^1A$) is indeed observed, although partially submerged under the $\pi \rightarrow \pi^*$ ($^1B_1 \leftarrow {}^1A_1$, $^1L_b \leftarrow {}^1A$) transition, and, in nonpolar solvents, produces a long-wavelength tail[25] of the latter transition. These band assignments are consistent with the solvent effects observed in the pyridine spectrum. The spectrum of benzene is relatively insensitive to a change from a nonpolar solvent, such as hexane, to a polar one, such as ethanol, although the $^1L_b \leftarrow {}^1A$ transition undergoes a slight bathochromic shift and some loss

TABLE 14.6

Solvent Effects in the Spectra of Pyridine and Some Derivatives[a]

Solvent	Pyridine		2-Picoline		4-Picoline	
	λ_{max}, mμ	ϵ_{max}	λ_{max}, mμ	ϵ_{max}	λ_{max}, mμ	ϵ_{max}
Hexane	252	2090	260	2000	261.5	2000
Chloroform	...	...	263	4500	262	4100
Ethanol	253	3600	260	4000	262	3200
Water	253	3600	260	4000	260	3200
EtOH:HCl(1:1)	254.5	5200	262	5200	261.5	5200
98% H_2SO_4	252.5	5200	260.5	5200	260.5	5200

[a] V. I. Bliznynkov and V. M. Reznikov, *Zhur. Obshchei Khim.*, **25**, 401 (1955); *Chem. Abstr.*, **49**, 9384d (1955).

of structure. The $^1L_b \leftarrow {}^1A$ transition in pyridine shows no wavelength shift, or a minute bathochromic shift with a similar solvent change (Table 14.6). Although in benzene the intensity of this band is also insensitive to solvent, in pyridine a polar solvent produces a considerable hyperchromic effect.

As shown in Table 14.6, similar effects are noted in the spectra of the methylpyridines or picolines. The hyperchromic effect noted with polar solvents has been ascribed to hydrogen bonding of solvent molecules to the nitrogen lone pair. This interpretation is corroborated by the spectrum of pyridine in acid solution. Here a proton is directly bonded to the nitrogen atom through the lone pair, and the intensity is further increased over the value in a polar solvent without appreciable shift in wavelength.

[24] M. Kasha, *Discussions Faraday Soc.*, **9**, 14 (1950); J. H. Rush and H. Sponer, *J. Chem. Phys.*, **20**, 1847 (1952).
[25] H. P. Stephenson, *J. Chem. Phys.*, **22**, 1077 (1954).

The long-wavelength tails ascribed to the n → π* transition disappear completely in polar solvents (and in acidic solution), as expected, because of the stabilization of the lone pair by the hydrogen bond, and presumably become completely submerged under the π → π* transition.

Some interesting observations on pyridinium compounds have been reported by Kosower and coworkers. The spectrum of 1-methylpyridinium perchlorate[26] is substantially the same as that of pyridinium ion. The iodide, however, shows an additional shoulder at long wavelength, which is interpreted as a charge-transfer absorption of a complex between the pyridinium cation and the iodide ion. A second charge-transfer band has been observed.[27] In chloroform, these bands occur at 294.5 and 379.6 mμ, respectively, with ε of 1550 and 1210. The energy difference of 21.8 kcal/mole is interpreted as that between two states, $^2P_{3/2}$ and $^2P_{1/2}$, of the iodine atom formed in the transfer of charge from the iodide ion.[28]

14.32 THE DIAZINES. The spectra of the three diazines[29] substantiate the assignments made for pyridine. The electronegativity of nitrogen is greater than that of carbon, and hence all π- and π*-electron levels may be expected to be lowered in comparison with those of pyridine; the exact lowering depends on the contribution each atom makes to the particular wave function. Hence we may expect the diazines to absorb at approximately the same wavelength as pyridine, and this expectation is borne out, since the first π → π* ($^1L_b ← {}^1A$) transitions of pyridazine, XXVI, and pyrimidine, XXVII, occur at slightly shorter wavelength than those of

| pyridazine | pyrimidine | pyrazine |
| XXVI | XXVII | XXVIII |

pyridine and benzene, and that of pyrazine, XXVIII, at somewhat longer wavelength. The lone-pair level of each of the nitrogen atoms in the diazines should, however, lie at about the same energy as that of pyridine, and excitation of n electrons to the lowered π* levels should, accordingly, occur at longer wavelength. In accord with this expectation, absorption bands assigned to n → π* ($^1W ← {}^1A$) transitions are observed at 375 mμ in pyridazine, 321.7 mμ in pyrimidine, and 323.8 mμ in pyrazine; the wavelengths given are those ascribed to 0-0 transitions in the vapor

[26] E. M. Kosower and P. E. Klinedinst, Jr., *J. Am. Chem. Soc.*, **78**, 3493 (1956).

[27] E. M. Kosower, *J. Am. Chem. Soc.*, **80**, 3253 (1958).

[28] E. M. Kosower, J. A. Skorcz, W. M. Schwarz, Jr., and J. W. Patton, *J. Am. Chem. Soc.*, **82**, 2188 (1960).

[29] F. Halverson and R. C. Hirt, *J. Chem. Phys.*, **17**, 1165 (1949).

spectra. These long-wavelength transitions show the strong hypsochromic effect in polar solvents characteristic of $n \to \pi^*$ transitions, and disappear in solution in concentrated sulfuric acid, where the lone-electron pairs are tied up by protonation.

Actually, two $n \to \pi^*$ transitions should occur in the diazines because of the presence of two lone-electron pairs and the consequent existence of two lone-pair levels. Although these levels belong to different symmetry classes, they should be very nearly degenerate because of the small overlap and consequent small interaction between the appropriate AO's of the two nitrogen atoms. In accord with this picture, careful analysis of the near ultraviolet spectrum of pyrazine[30] has revealed the presence of two band systems in the long-wavelength region, one allowed and one forbidden, as predicted by theory.

A more careful analysis of the differences between the spectra of the diazines has been made by Mason,[31] by considering the perturbation introduced into the benzene MO's by introduction of the nitrogen atoms. On the basis of the orbitals described in Table 5.3, the nitrogen atom in pyridine must be assumed in position 1 and those in pyrazine, XXVIII, in positions 1 and 4, whereas those in pyridazine, XXVI, must be placed in positions 2 and 3 and those in pyrimidine, XXVII, in positions 2 and 6. These assignments are necessary in order to have orbitals ψ_2 to ψ_5 of Table 5.3 reflect the symmetry properties of the point groups C_{2v} (for pyridine, pyridazine, and pyrimidine) and D_{2h} (for pyrazine). Since nitrogen is more electronegative than carbon, nitrogen substitution lowers all energy levels; this lowering depends on two factors: (1) the $2p\pi$ orbitals of the nitrogen atom have lower energy and hence lower each orbital according to the extent of their contribution, i.e., according to the weighting factors c given in Table 5.3; (2) by the inductive effect, the nitrogen atoms lower the $2p\pi$ energy levels of the carbon atoms, particularly the vicinal ones, and thus produce a smaller, more uniform, lowering of all levels. Since the nitrogen atoms contribute differently to ψ_2 and ψ_3, and to ψ_4 and ψ_5, the degeneracy of these pairs of levels is split. ψ_2 and ψ_4 do not receive any contributions from atoms 1 and 4 and hence are not directly affected by the nitrogen atoms in pyridine and pyrazine through the first of the above mechanisms. Consideration of the c's in the various orbitals leads to the schematic energy-level diagram shown in Fig. 14.4, which is constructed assuming that each nitrogen atom lowers each level proportional to the appropriate c^2, and neglecting the inductive effect.

[30] See L. Orgel, *J. Chem. Soc.*, 121 (1955); M. Ito, R. Shimada, T. Kuraishi, and W. Mizushima, *J. Chem. Phys.*, **26**, 1508 (1957).
[31] S. F. Mason, *J. Chem. Soc.*, 1240 (1959).

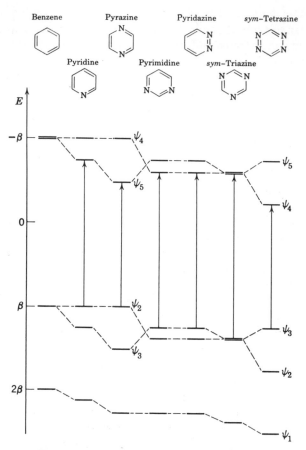

Fig. 14.4 Energy-level diagram in aza benzenes.

This diagram should permit correlation with the observed transition frequencies. Comparison with the benzene spectrum is complicated by the fact that the one-electron levels suggest four degenerate transitions which are, however, split by electron correlation. But Fig. 14.4 clearly suggests that the ^1L_b transition of pyridine (251 mμ) should be shifted to a longer wavelength in pyrazine (260 mμ) and to a shorter wavelength in pyridazine (240 mμ) and pyrimidine (243 mμ);[32] the slight difference between the two latter compounds, which is not predicted in Fig. 14.4, may well arise out of the inductive effect just discussed under (2).

The relations between the n $\rightarrow$ π^* ($^1W \leftarrow {}^1A$) transitions are not quite

---

[32] The data given in parentheses are from measurements in cyclohexane by S. F. Mason, *J. Chem. Soc.*, 1247 (1959).

as readily explained. The shift from pyridine ($\nu_{0\text{-}0}$, 34,770) to pyrazine ($\nu_{0\text{-}0}$, 30,870)[33] is larger than the corresponding shift of the $\pi \rightarrow \pi^*$ band, although Fig. 14.4 suggests that the shifts should be equal. The discrepancy may be explained by the inductive lowering of all π levels. The n $\rightarrow \pi^*$ transition in pyrimidine occurs at an intermediate frequency ($\nu_{0\text{-}0}$, 31,060) as suggested by the figure. The transition in pyridazine occurs at a substantially lower frequency ($\nu_{0\text{-}0}$, 27,390), possibly because interaction between the lone-pair orbitals of the original nitrogen atoms leads to a substantial splitting of their degeneracy.[34]

Finally, Fig. 14.4 also has a schematic diagram for *sym*-triazine and *sym*-tetrazine. The n $\rightarrow \pi^*$ transition in the former ($\nu_{0\text{-}0}$, 31,520) occurs at approximately the same frequency as in pyrimidine, as suggested by the figure. In *sym*-tetrazine, Mason has assigned two n $\rightarrow \pi^*$ transitions, with $\nu_{0\text{-}0}$ for the first at 18,135, and with $\nu_{\max}$ for the second at 31,250 in cyclohexane. Figure 14.4 does indicate that the first n $\rightarrow \pi$ transition should occur at quite long wavelength, but the observed shift seems even larger than anticipated. Of course, the same splitting suggested in pyridazine, and further inductive lowering, may play important roles here. Finally, the $\pi \rightarrow \pi^*$ transition in *sym*-tetrazine ($\lambda_{\max} = 255$ mμ in cyclohexane) appears to occur at a wavelength lower than expected.

The problem of the n $\rightarrow \pi^*$ transitions of the azines has recently been very carefully considered by Goodman,[35] who concludes that the intensities are well described by a simple model involving sp^2 hybridization for the lone-pair electrons, but that no satisfactory treatment for the transition energies has been given. In consideration of singlet-triplet separations, however, he concludes that the simple model is inadequate, and proposes that a rehybridization occurs on excitation, and that the lone electron in the excited state occupies an orbital having no more than about 10 per cent s character. The same author has also shown[36] that the hydrogen bond between azines and a polar solvent is broken in the excited state.

14.33 AZANAPHTHALENES (QUINOLINE AND ISOQUINOLINE). Substitution of nitrogen for methine in naphthalene, just as in benzene, produces only relatively small spectroscopic changes, which, moreover, have not been investigated nearly as thoroughly. Figure 14.5 shows a comparison of the ultraviolet absorption spectra of naphthalene, quinoline, and isoquinoline. Some wavelength shifts are discernible in the aza compounds,

---

[33] The frequencies for the $0 \rightarrow 0$ transitions in the vapor are given, since they are available; see footnote 29.

[34] L. Goodman and R. W. Harrel, *J. Chem. Phys.*, **30**, 1131 (1959).

[35] L. Goodman, *J. Mol. Spectroscopy*, **6**, 109 (1961).

[36] V. G. Krishna and L. Goodman, *J. Am. Chem. Soc.*, **83**, 2042 (1961).

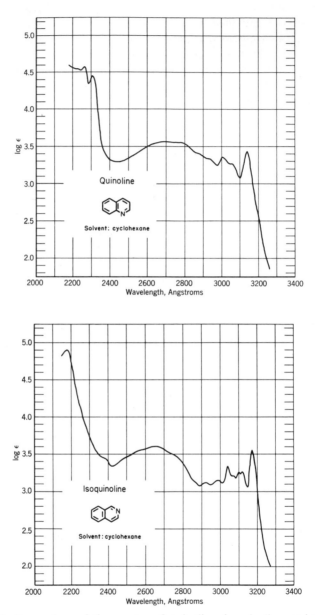

Fig. 14.5 Comparison of the spectra of quinoline, isoquinoline, and naphthalene. (Reprinted by permission from R. A. Friedel and M. Orchin, *Ultraviolet Spectra of Aromatic Compounds*, John Wiley and Sons, New York, 1951.)

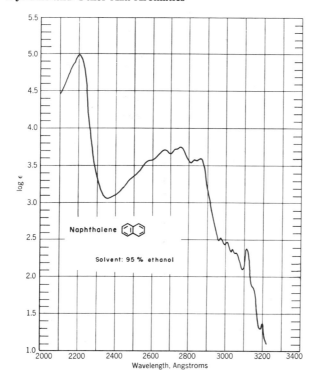

but a detailed analysis of the spectra is difficult because of their complexity and the variability of the vibrational structure. Attempts have been made to relate the bands in the aza compounds to those of naphthalene. Thus the long-wavelength band of quinoline at 313 mμ has been assigned[37] to the transition to the ^1L_b state; this assignment is supported by noting that this band is most affected by substitution in the 2, 3, 6, or 7 position. The relatively high intensity of the long-wavelength bands in the aza compounds is to be expected on the basis of the reduced symmetry.

It is noteworthy that several of the bands of intermediate wavelength appear to be missing in the spectra of the conjugate acids of quinoline and isoquinoline (Table 14.7). In a study of the effect of pH on the spectra of the methylquinolines it was found[38] that the 278 mμ band of the methylquinolines (quinaldines) became less intense and shifted to the red with decreasing pH, finally disappearing under the long-wavelength transition. It seems likely that in the less resolved spectra in acidic solution the missing bands are hidden behind the more prominent transitions.

[37] V. Zanker, *Z. physik. Chem.*, **2**, 52 (1954).

[38] (*a*) S. B. Knight, R. H. Wallick, and J. Bowen, *J. Am. Chem. Soc.*, **76**, 3780 (1954). (*b*) S. B. Knight, R. H. Wallick, and C. Balch, *J. Am. Chem. Soc.*, **77**, 2577 (1955).

The conversion of the aza compounds to methiodides results in a bathochromic shift of the long-wavelength band, a result not unexpected in view of the similar effect brought about by protonation. Complete tying up of the nitrogen lone pair by methylation or by protonation also

TABLE 14.7

The Spectra of Azanaphthalenes[a]

| | | Transition | | | | | | | |
| | | I | | II | | III | | IV | |
Compound	Solvent	λ, mμ	ϵ	λ, mμ	ϵ	λ, mμ	ϵ	λ, mμ	ϵ
Quinoline	95% EtOH	314	3000	300	2600	278	3500	225	35,000
Quinolinium ion	0.01N HCl	315	7000	...	...	...	...	235	35,000
						271			
Isoquinoline	95% EtOH	320	2700	308	2500	267	3700	...	...
						260			
						273			
Isoquinolinium ion	0.01N HCl	335	4000	...	...	267	2000	230	40,000

[a] J. M. Hearn, R. A. Morton, and J. C. E. Simpson, *J. Chem. Soc.*, 3318 (1951); cf. also G. W. Ewing and E. A. Steck, *J. Am. Chem. Soc.*, **68**, 2181 (1946).

results in a hyperchromic effect. The methiodides are colored, but the color probably arises from charge transfer from the anion to the base.[39]

The spectra of various diazanaphthalenes resemble the spectrum of naphthalene to varying degrees (Table 14.8). Phthalazine (2,3-diazanaphthalene) is quite similar to naphthalene, and this diaza compound is the most symmetrical of those whose spectra are shown in the table. Cinnoline (1,2-diazanaphthalene) is perhaps least like naphthalene. Its spectrum has three rather strong bands in the 310–320 mμ region, whereas the other compounds have no bands in this region.[40] The interpretation of these complex spectra has been attempted[41] but cannot be said to have been satisfactorily resolved. It is to be expected, as discussed in the case of the diazabenzenes, that the π^* levels are appreciably lowered in the diazanaphthalenes and that the n $\rightarrow$ π^* transitions are shifted far enough to the red to make them discernible. They are observed in cinnoline and to a lesser degree in phthalazine, both of which contain vicinal nitrogen atoms; interaction of the lone-pair orbitals of vicinal nitrogen atoms and consequent splitting of the degeneracy may again play an important role.

[39] See footnotes 24–26.
[40] E. D. Amstutz, *J. Org. Chem.*, **17**, 1508 (1952).
[41] A rather complete summary of the spectra of cinnoline and quinoxaline (1,4-diazanaphthalene) derivatives is given by J. C. E. Simpson, *Condensed Pyridazine and Pyrazine Rings*, Interscience Publishers, New York, 1953, Appendix I.

14.34 POLYCYCLIC AZA COMPOUNDS.   It is obviously beyond the scope of this section to discuss all the nitrogen analogs of the polycyclic hydrocarbons; indeed, a thorough consideration of these compounds alone could well be the topic of an entire book. Accordingly, the discussion here will be restricted to a few examples.

TABLE 14.8

Spectra of Naphthalene and Some Diazanaphthalenes

Naphthalene[a,b]		1,2-Diazanaphth.[b,c] (cinnoline)		2,3-Diazanaphth.[b,d] (phthalazine)		1,3-Diazanaphth.[c,e] (quinazoline)	
λ, mμ	log ϵ	λ, mμ	log ϵ	λ, mμ	log ϵ	λ, mμ	log ϵ
221	4.98	275.5	3.45	252	3.63	220	4.60
286	3.62	286	3.42	259	3.69	270	3.50
...	...	308.5	3.29	267	3.59	308	3.48
...	...	317	3.25	290	1.11	...	...
312	2.40	322.5	3.32	296.5	1.06	...	...
...	...	390	2.43	...	...	...	...

[a] H. B. Klevens and J. R. Platt, *J. Chem. Phys.*, **17**, 470 (1949).
[b] In hydrocarbon solvent.
[c] J. M. Hearn, R. A. Morton, and J. C. E. Simpson, *J. Chem. Soc.*, 3318 (1951).
[d] Footnote 40.
[e] In ethanol.

As has been pointed out for the simpler aza compounds and as is probably even truer in the polycyclic series, the replacement of a methine group by a nitrogen atom results in relatively little change in the spectrum of the hydrocarbon. This is especially true when the replacement of N for CH occurs at positions where it does not seriously affect the symmetry of the molecule, e.g., in the series anthracene, XXIX, acridine, XXX, and phenazine, XXXI. Indeed, structural assignments of heterocyclic isomers

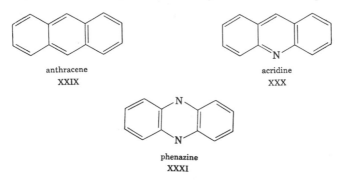

anthracene
XXIX

acridine
XXX

phenazine
XXXI

have been corroborated by relating the spectra of the aza compounds to those of their carbocyclic analogs. Thus the two different benzoquinolines prepared from 2-naphthylamine were shown to be a benzo[f]quinoline, XXXII, and a benzo[g]quinoline, XXXIII, by (among other evidence)

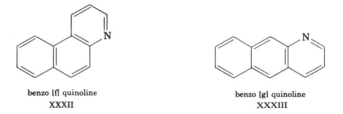

benzo [f] quinoline
XXXII

benzo [g] quinoline
XXXIII

relating the spectra of the isomers to the carbocyclic analogs, phenanthrene and anthracene, respectively.[42] The similarity between the linear analogs XXXIII and XXIX was greater than that between the angular analogs, benzo[f]quinoline and phenanthrene.

The similarity in spectra of the naphthoquinolines and their corresponding analogs has also been reported.[43] Thus spectra of substituted naphtho-[2,1-g]quinoline, XXXIV, and naphtho[1,2-g]quinoline, XXXV, resemble

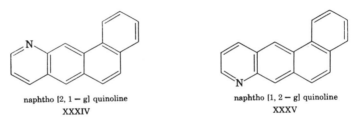

naphtho [2, 1 – g] quinoline
XXXIV

naphtho [1, 2 – g] quinoline
XXXV

each other, and both have spectral resemblance to 1,2-benzanthracene, XXXVI. Similarly, naphtho[2,1-f]quinoline, XXXVII, has a spectrum

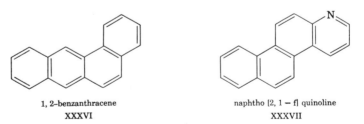

1, 2–benzanthracene
XXXVI

naphtho [2, 1 – f] quinoline
XXXVII

resembling that of chrysene, XXXVIII, and naphtho[1,2-f]quinoline, XXXIX, has spectral resemblance to 3,4-benzphenanthrene, XL. In all

[42] W. S. Johnson and F. J. Mathews, *J. Am. Chem. Soc.*, **66**, 210 (1944).
[43] W. S. Johnson, E. Woroch, and F. J. Mathews, *J. Am. Chem. Soc.*, **69**, 566 (1947).

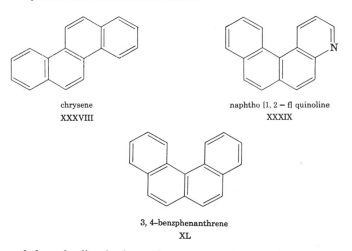

chrysene
XXXVIII

naphtho [1, 2 – f] quinoline
XXXIX

3, 4–benzphenanthrene
XL

the naphthoquinoline-hydrocarbon comparisons, the aza compounds absorb more strongly at the longer wavelengths than do the carbocyclic analogs; again this is probably attributable to the lower symmetry resulting from nitrogen-carbon substitution.

It apparently matters relatively little which methine group in the carbocyclic compound is replaced by nitrogen. The isomers XXXIV and XXXV have quite similar spectra, and the spectra of, for example, benzo-[f]quinoline, XXXII, and benzo[h]quinoline, XLI, are alike and, in the

benzo [h] quinoline
XLI

long-wavelength region, practically superimposable. Similarly, the spectra of indolo[2,3-f]quinoline, XLII, and indolo[3,2-h]quinoline, XLIII, are also very similar.[44]

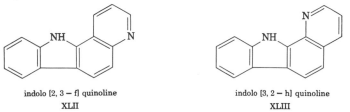

indolo [2, 3 – f] quinoline
XLII

indolo [3, 2 – h] quinoline
XLIII

[44] G. R. Clemo and D. G. I. Felton, *J. Chem. Soc.*, 671 (1951).

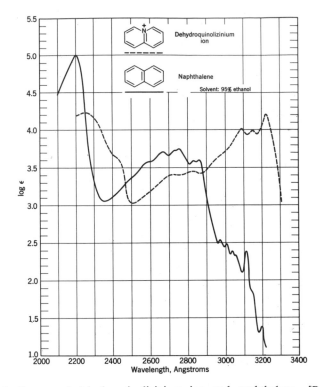

Fig. 14.6 Spectra of dehydroquinolizinium ion and naphthalene. [Reprinted by permission from V. Boekelheide and W. G. Gall, *J. Am. Chem. Soc.*, **76**, 1832 (1954).]

An interesting class of heterocyclic compounds is derived from de-hydroquinolizinium ion, XLIV, which contains a quaternary nitrogen

XLIV

atom completely within a conjugated system. This ion[45] may be con-sidered derived from naphthalene by replacement of $\geqslant C-$ by $\geqslant N^+-$, and the spectra of the two compounds are compared in Fig. 14.6. Although the spectra appear considerably different at first glance, careful examina-tion shows that there is a close correspondence of bands. The most striking differences are a moderate bathochromic shift of all bands in the heterocyclic ion, of about 10–20 mμ, and a strong intensification of the long-wavelength forbidden bands, presumably because of the lowered

[45] V. Boekelheide and W. G. Gall, *J. Am. Chem. Soc.*, **76**, 1832 (1954).

symmetry. Benzo derivatives of XLIV also are known;[46] their spectra show the same similarities to those of the parent hydrocarbons. The vibrational structure in the heterocyclic ions is less pronounced than in the hydrocarbons, presumably because of stronger solvent interaction in the ions, but also because the ion spectra are of necessity obtained in more polar solvents.

14.4   Substituent Effects in Aza Aromatics

Considerable information is available on the effect of substituents on the ^1L_b transition of pyridine;[47] some of it is given in Table 14.9. Just as

TABLE 14.9

The Wavelengths and Intensities of the $^1L_b \leftarrow {}^1A$ Transition in Monosubstituted Pyridines[47]

R	Solvent[a]	2-R λ, mμ	ϵ	3-R λ, mμ	ϵ	4-R λ, mμ	ϵ
H[b]	C	...	...	251	2000	...	...
H	W	...	...	253	3600	...	...
CN[b]	C	265	2730	265	2230	271	2840
OMe	W	269	3230	276	2960	235	2000
Me	I	262	2420	258	2260	256	1600
Me	W	262	3560	263	3110	255	2090
Et	W	262	3690	263	3210	255	2150
CHMe$_2$	W	262	3780	262	3250	255	2100
CMe$_3$	W	261	3400	261	3230	255	2120
F	A	258	3200	262	2990	...	...
Cl	I	265	2920	268	2400	...	...
Br	I	266	2950	258	2270	...	...
NH$_2$	H	290	3800	294	3500	...	...

[a] A = alcohol; C = cyclohexane; H = heptane; I = isooctane; W = water.
[b] The $^1W \leftarrow {}^1A$ transition is determined to lie at 270 mμ (ϵ, 450) in pyridine, and at 278 mμ (ϵ, 340), 279 mμ (ϵ, 430) and 290 mμ (ϵ, 500) in 2-, 3-, and 4-cyanopyridine, respectively.

[46] C. K. Bradsher and L. E. Beavers, *J. Am. Chem. Soc.*, **77**, 453, 4812 (1955); C. K. Bradsher, L. E. Beavers, and J. H. Jones, *J. Org. Chem.*, **22**, 1740 (1957).

[47] (a) H. C. Brown and X. R. Mihm, *J. Am. Chem. Soc.*, **77**, 1723 (1955). (b) R. L. J. Andon, J. D. Cox, and E. F. G. Herington, *Trans. Faraday Soc.*, **50**, 1918 (1954). (c) V. I. Bliznynkov and V. M. Reznikov, *Zhur. Obshchei Khim.*, **25**, 401 (1955); *Chem. Abstr.*, **49**, 9384d (1955). (d) C. W. F. Spiers and J. P. Wibaut, *Rec. trav. chim.*, **56**, 573 (1937). (e) S. F. Mason, *J. Chem. Soc.*, 1253 (1959). (f) See also references cited in footnotes 25 and 32.

in benzene, almost every substituent produces a bathochromic effect, and the effects in benzene and pyridine are of comparable order of magnitude. In pyridine, however, a substituent can be introduced in any one of three distinguishable positions and, as might be expected, produces somewhat different effects, depending on the position of substitution. The methyl group produces a red shift in all three positions, and the methoxy group in the 4 position causes a considerable blue shift. The intensity of the ^1L_b band appears to be higher in the 4-substituted derivatives than in the 2 and 3 analogs. Unfortunately, many 4-substituted compounds are quite unstable; hence only a few of them are available, and most of these are so reactive that some doubt may exist concerning the identity of the chemical species on which measurements are reported. Interestingly, in 4-methoxy pyridine, bearing the only mesomerically electron-withdrawing substituent in Table 14.9, the hypsochromic effect is largest, whereas with mesomerically electron-repelling substituents the effect of 4 substitution is small or is actually bathochromic. It has been suggested that the base strength, and hence the hydrogen-bonding power of the nitrogen atom, play a major role in determining the spectrum.

Unfortunately, the n $\rightarrow$ π* ($^1W \leftarrow {}^1A$) transition in pyridine and substituted derivatives cannot directly be observed in solution spectra. It must either be determined by analysis of vapor spectra or be isolated from the overlapping ^1L_b band in the solution spectra by a complicated and rather unreliable differencing method.[25,32] However, there appears little doubt that the n $\rightarrow$ π* transition undergoes a hypsochromic effect upon substitution of hydrogen in pyridine by halogen. The effect of halogen is particularly noticeable in the 2-substituted derivatives, where the n $\rightarrow$ π* transition completely disappears under the ^1L_b transition. This fact suggests that an inductive effect may play a major role in this shift.[32] Mesomerically electron-withdrawing substituents such as cyano appear to produce a bathochromic shift in this band.

Both acid-base and tautomeric equilibria cause considerable difficulties in the interpretation of the spectra of substituted nitrogen heterocycles. Whenever the substituent is either an acidic or a basic group, such as OH, SH, NH_2, or COOH, such equilibria are likely to occur in dilute solution, particularly in polar solvents. In nicotinic acid (pyridine-3-carboxylic acid), for instance, in neutral solution, an equilibrium exists between the neutral form (BH) and the zwitterion form (B′H) (Fig. 14.7), and interpretation of the spectra of such solutions without prior knowledge of the equilibrium position is complicated. In moderately acidic solution both species are ionized to give the anion B$^-$, and in slightly basic solution they form the conjugate base $BH_2{}^+$. Again, without prior knowledge of the acid-base equilibrium constants (i.e., the pK), interpretation of the spectra is difficult.

Furthermore, the tautomeric equilibria are frequently very solvent depend-ent, particularly when polar (zwitterionic) and nonpolar species are in equilibrium (cf. Fig. 9.10).

A slightly different situation is encountered in 4-hydroxypyridine, where the tautomeric equilibrium BH $\rightleftharpoons$ B'H occurs between two nonpolar forms, one aromatic and the other quinoid:

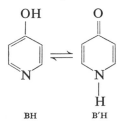

In such cases, much less solvent dependence is to be expected.

Extensive investigations of such acid-base and tautomeric equilibria have been reported; the detailed results are not pertinent to the present discus-sion except to focus attention on the existence of these equilibria, and the great importance of careful control of solvent and pH in the determination of spectra in which they occur. Unless equilibrium constants are known, and pH and solvent are appropriately chosen, the chemical species for

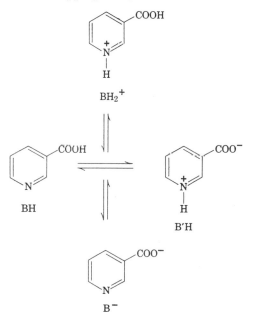

Fig. 14.7   Acid-base equilibria in solutions of nicotinic acid.

which the spectrum is determined in any given experiment cannot be known. The problem of determination of such equilibrium constants by spectrophotometric methods will be discussed in detail in Chapter 20.

In heterocyclic compounds containing several nitrogen atoms, the problem is even more acute and further complicated. Here the number of possible equilibria is increased, because of the behavior of each nitrogen atom as a basic center.

Substituent effects in the diazines XLV-XLVII have been investigated by Mason,[32] and his results are summarized in Table 14.10. All substituents

| pyrazine | pyridazine | pyrimidine |
| XLV | XLVI | XLVII |

investigated, alkyl, alkoxyl, and carboxyl, produce bathochromic effects in the ^1L_b ($\pi \to \pi^*$) transition. The electron-donating substituents produce the expected hypsochromic effects on the n $\to \pi^*$ transitions in all three diazines; the expected bathochromic shifts in the carboxy and carbomethoxy compounds, however, are not uniformly and directly apparent.

A careful analysis of these shifts, however, suggests that the deviations from the predicted regularities are only apparent[32] and are due to the use of λ_{max} values. Thus, Mason points out that in pyrazine the $0 \to 0$ transition is the most intense and hence gives correctly the energy of the electronic transition; in the 2-methyl and 2,5-dimethyl derivatives, the the $0 \to 1$ and $0 \to 2$ transitions, respectively, are most intense and hence give a value of λ_{max} lower than is applicable to the true transition. In ethanol, the vibrational structure is completely blurred, and comparisons in this solvent are probably better. Mason[32] further gives an analysis of the shifts based on a semiquantitative MO treatment similar to that given for the diazines.

Substituent effects in quinolines have been studied extensively[38, 48] (Table 14.11), with special emphasis on the two main bands, at 313 and 276 mμ in quinoline, which have been referred to as B and E_2 bands, following Braude, and which correspond to the ^1L_b and ^1L_a bands. With the exception of the 2-fluoro substituent, which produces a slight hypsochromic effect, and the 4-methyl and 8-fluoro substituents, which produce no effect, methyl, chloro, bromo, and fluoro groups in all ring positions[49]

[48] W. K. Miller, S. B. Knight, and A. Roe, *J. Am. Chem. Soc.*, **72**, 1629 (1950).
[49] Except 4-fluoro, 4-bromo, and 5-methyl, which are not reported.

TABLE 14.10

The Spectra of Substituted Diazines

Diazine	Solvent[a]	$^1W \leftarrow {}^1A$		$^1L_b \leftarrow {}^1A$	
		λ, mμ	ϵ	λ, mμ	ϵ
Pyrazine⎱	C	328	1040	260	5600
XLV ⎰	A	310	860	261	6000
2-Me	C	320	830	266	5700
2,5-Me$_2$	C	314	908	271	5700
2,3-(COOMe)$_2$	C	319	660	268	6820
		311	700	268	6950
2,3-(COOH)$_2$	A	314	269	269	6200
2-MeO	C	...	...	277	5760
Pyridazine⎱	C	340	315	246	1300
XLVI ⎰	A	313	303	246	1160
3-Me	A	310	400	251	1300
4-Me	C	331	375	252	1296
		303	350	250	1370
3-OMe	C	327	326	272, 214	1990, 3140
4-OMe	C	307	258	259, 216	1560, 5970
3,6(OMe)$_2$	C	325	312	292	2500
4,5(COOH)$_2$	A	345	274	266	3020
Pyrimidine⎱	C	298	326	243	2030
XLVII ⎰	A	280	373	243	2930
2-OMe	C	295	400	264, 210	4180, 7500
4-OMe	C	270	274	248, 215	3100, 6000
2-COOMe	C	290	370	247	1840
2-COOH	A	277	374	246	2120
4-COOH	A	303	295	256	3820
5-COOH	A	280	561	247	1870

[a] A = alcohol; C = cyclohexane.

produce bathochromic effects ranging up to 10 mμ in the longest-wavelength (313 mμ) B band. The 2-, 6-, and 7-fluoro and 6-bromo substituents produce a hypsochromic effect on the E$_2$ band, 6-chloro produces no effect, and all other substituents produce bathochromic effects up to 17 mμ. The effect of 6 and 7 substituents on the wavelength of the B band is slightly larger than that of 5 and 8 substituents, whereas the effect of 5- and 8-halogen substituents on the E$_2$ band is considerably larger than that of the 6- and 7-halogen atoms. These facts are consistent with polarization of the B band approximately along the long axis of the molecule and of the E$_2$

TABLE 14.11

The Spectra of Substituted Quinolines in 10 Per Cent Ethanol[38,48]

Substituent	B Band ($^1L_b \leftarrow {}^1A$)		Band II		E$_2$ Band ($^1L_a \leftarrow {}^1A$)	
	λ, mμ	$\epsilon \times 10^{-3}$	λ, mμ	$\epsilon \times 10^{-3}$	λ, mμ	$\epsilon \times 10^{-3}$
None	313	3.41	300	3.26	276	3.59
2-Me	315	3.86			279	3.20
3-Me	318	3.12			286	3.35
4-Me	313	2.73			283	4.53
6-Me	317	2.33			285	2.34
7-Me	318	2.40			292	2.17
8-Me	314	2.65			292	3.75
2-Cl	318	4.61			282	3.32
3-Cl	323	3.56			283	3.06
4-Cl	316	2.85			289	4.90
5-Cl	317	3.17			292	4.64
6-Cl	319	3.50			276	3.65
7-Cl	319	3.67			279	3.56
8-Cl	315	2.99			292	4.50
2-F	312	2.88	299	2.70	270	3.81
3-F	319	3.52	306	3.33	284	3.18
5-F	314	1.85	300	2.80	285	3.18
6-F	316	3.74	302	3.04	270	3.82
7-F	316	3.80	303	3.31	270	3.15
8-F	313	1.67	299.5	2.78	284	3.30
2-Br	319	4.16			277	3.42
3-Br	323	3.22			279	3.38
5-Br	317	2.89			293	4.96
6-Br	320	3.38			273	3.18
7-Br	320	3.81			269	4.04
8-Br	315	2.90			291	4.96

band approximately along the short axis, and hence with identification as ^1L_b and ^1L_a, respectively. These assignments are in agreement with the assignments of corresponding bands in naphthalene. The intensities of the B bands of 5-, 6-, 7-, and 8-haloquinoline and of the E$_2$ bands of the 5-, 6-, 7-, and 8-bromo- and chloroquinolines also seem to be in agreement with these assignments. The band labeled II in Table 14.11 also seems to be lengthwise polarized but is of unknown origin.

A few isolated data on substituted isoquinolines and their conjugate acids are given in Table 14.12 but do not lend themselves to any immediate interpretation.

Another interesting class of substituted aza aromatics are the N-oxides. In nonpolar solvents, introduction of the oxygen atom at the nitrogen in pyridine, quinoline, and isoquinoline produces a considerable red shift[50] and hyperchromic effect, presumably because of lengthening of the

TABLE 14.12

Spectra of Substituted Isoquinolines and Their Conjugate Acids[a]

	Free Bases				Conjugate Acids			
	Band I		Band II		Band I		Band II	
Substituent	λ, mμ	$\epsilon \times 10^{-3}$	λ	ϵ	λ	ϵ	λ	ϵ
None	319	2.79	268	3.29	329	3.86	275	1.94
1-F	318	3.00	265	3.92	[b]	...	[b]	...
3-F	325	3.12	270	2.61	[c]	...	[c]	...
4-F	321	3.09	270	3.90	333	4.80	274	2.39

[a] S. B. Knight, W. K. Miller, and A. Roe, *J. Am. Chem. Soc.*, **74**, 1599 (1952).
[b] The compound hydrolyzes in acid solution.
[c] The spectrum in 0.01 *M* HCl is unchanged from 10 per cent EtOH, and presumably the compound is too weakly basic to have formed the conjugate acid.

conjugated system. When hydrogen bonding of the oxygen atom occurs in hydroxylic solvents, the bands of the N-oxide are shifted back to the blue, and practically coincide with those of the parent heterocycle,[50,51] but with considerably greater intensity. The ground state of pyridine N-oxide is presumably a resonance hybrid of three structures, XLVIII–L, which

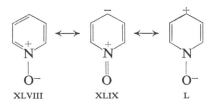

| XLVIII | XLIX | L |

are claimed[51] to make about equal contributions. The ground state of a compound involving such highly polar structures is undoubtedly considerably stabilized by polar solvents and by general electrostatic effects, as well as by specific hydrogen bonds to the oxygen atom. The bathochromic shift of the $\pi \rightarrow \pi^*$ transition indicates that the π^* level is considerably

[50] T. Kubota, *Yakugaku Zasshi* (*Bull. Pharm. Soc. Japan*), **77**, 785 (1957).
[51] H. H. Jaffé, *J. Am. Chem. Soc.*, **76**, 3527 (1954).

TABLE 14.13

Spectra of N-Oxides and Their Conjugate Acids[51]

Compound	Free Base				Conjugate Acid			
	λ, mμ	$\epsilon \times 10^{-4}$	λ, mμ	$\epsilon \times 10^{-4}$	λ, mμ	$\epsilon \times 10^{-4}$	λ, mμ	$\epsilon \times 10^{-4}$
Pyridine 1-oxide	(205	1.7)	254	1.19	217	0.49	257	0.29
3-Me	209	1.98	254	1.17	220	0.42	263	0.35
4-Me	206	1.87	256	1.43	226	0.83	254	0.27
3-COOH	220	2.24	260	1.02	(218	(0.69)	265	0.21
4-COOH	216	1.12	280	1.71	232	0.96	272	0.35
3-NH$_2$	234	2.28	(252 314	(1.15) 0.27	...	...	...	...
4-NH$_2$	...	...	276	1.90	...	...	268	1.61
4-NO$_2$	226	0.80	313	1.25	244	0.82	(280)	0.38)
Isoquinoline 2-oxide	(218	2.33	...	...	212	2.05	280	0.27)
	250)	3.10	294	0.86	234	4.74	330	0.36)

less stabilized by polar solvents; and, since the excited state must also receive its predominant contributions from structures XLVIII–L (and other similar polar structures), almost certainly the difference between the ground and excited states must lie predominantly in hydrogen bonding. But greatly reduced hydrogen bonding in the excited state would imply that structure XLIX (and related structures) are most important and that the oxygen atom has lost much or most of its charge. In this sense, then, the spectrum of pyridine N-oxide may be classed as an intramolecular charge-transfer spectrum.

In pyridine N-oxide, furthermore, a long-wavelength $n \rightarrow \pi^*$ ($^1B_2 \leftarrow {}^1A_1$, $^1U \leftarrow {}^1A$) transition, presumably due to excitation of oxygen 2p electrons, has been identified at 330 mμ.[52] In strongly acidic solution, pyridine N-oxide forms a conjugate acid, and the long-wavelength absorption, although not appreciably shifted, loses greatly in intensity. Some of the data are summarized in Table 14.13.

Introduction of substituents in pyridine N-oxide and its conjugate acid produces effects not greatly different from those in pyridine.[51] Substituents in the 3 position cause small bathochromic effects on the 254 mμ, ^1L_b, band of the free base; substituents in the 4 position increase the intensity, up to almost two-fold, and lead to red shifts of up to 26 mμ. The short-wavelength, ^1L_a, band, at about 205 mμ in the free base, is considerably more susceptible to substituent effects. Shifts in the conjugate acids are of similar magnitude, although there is no direct correlation. The spectra of 4-nitropyridine N-oxide and of its conjugate acid appear rather different from those of the other compounds. Selected data are presented in Table 14.13.

[52] M. Ito and W. Mizushima, *J. Chem. Phys.*, **24**, 495 (1956).

15 Steric effects

15.1 General

Steric effects on electronic absorption spectra must, like all other factors affecting such spectra, be evaluated in terms of the effect on transition probability (intensity) and the energy difference between ground and excited states (wavelength or frequency). In general, as the length l of a conjugated system increases, the wavelength and the intensity of the band associated with polarization along the lengthwise axis of the chromophore system both increase. In the simplest models the relationship can be expressed by $\lambda^2 \propto l$ and $\epsilon \propto l^2$, indicating that λ is a much less sensitive function of l than ϵ, but that both λ and ϵ increase with increasing elongation of the conjugated system. In order for the conjugated system[1] to be an effective chromophore, it must be planar or nearly planar because maximum interaction between the chromophoric groups occurs in the planar arrangement. If chromophores, which are conjugated in a hypothetical planar model, are unable for steric reasons to assume coplanar positions, then spectral properties arise which differ from those expected on the basis of the planar model. The degree of deviation from the spectrum which would be expected on the basis of a planar model increases with the degree of steric crowding. Three basic types of behavior of the longest-wavelength band have frequently been distinguished on the basis of the steric crowding:[2]

(1) Slight crowding; the spectroscopic result is a hypochromic effect alone.

(2) Moderate crowding; this results in both a hypochromic effect and a hypsochromic shift relative to the spectrum of a planar model.

(3) Severe crowding; this results in complete steric inhibition of

---

[1] These generalizations apply to conjugation involving first-row elements. It will be shown in Chapter 17 that conjugation involving atoms with d electrons may be affected in a different manner.

[2] L. L. Ingraham in *Steric Effects in Organic Chemistry*, edited by M. S. Newman, John Wiley and Sons, New York, 1956, p. 484.

resonance and isolates the separate chromophores in the molecule. The spectrum thus is the sum of the individual spectra of the isolated chromophores.

In an analysis of the spectral effects of steric crowding, attention must be focused on the geometry of the excited state as well as that of the ground state. In the ground state, the sterically crowded molecule will assume a geometry of minimum potential energy. Groups may be twisted, or bonds bent or stretched, or a combination of twisting, bending, or stretching may most effectively relieve the steric strain. It is helpful in discussing steric strain in conjugated systems to recall the definition of "essential" single and double bonds.[3] A single bond is called essential if it is single in all principal resonance structures which do not involve long bonds or formal charges. Similarly, a double bond is essential if it is double in all principal resonance structures. Thus the bond between the two rings of biphenyl is an essential single bond, but the bonds in the aromatic rings of this compound are neither essential single nor essential double bonds because two Kekulé structures of each ring may be written by interchanging the single and double bonds in the ring. On the other hand, the central bond in stilbene (1,2-diphenylethylene) is an essential double bond, and the bonds between the double bond and the ring are essential single bonds.

15.2   Twisting Around an Essential Double Bond: Ethylene and Fulvene

In the case of a double bond flanked by bulky groups, steric strain can be relieved either by stretching of the double bond, by in-plane deformation, or more effectively, by twisting around the double bond. The situation in the olefin series will be considered first.

The ground state of *ethylene* is planar because of the stabilization resulting from the two $p\pi$ electrons occupying the π molecular orbital, π_u (cf. section 7.2). The potential-energy curve for the lowest excited state of ethylene, shown in Fig. 15.1a, however, has a minimum in the right-angle conformation, and every other conformation has higher energy. In other words, the lowest excited state of ethylene is twisted, with the CH_2 groups at right angles, as indicated by the following end-on projection formula:

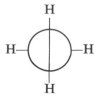

[3] H. C. Longuet-Higgins, *J. Chem. Phys.*, **18**, 265 (1950).

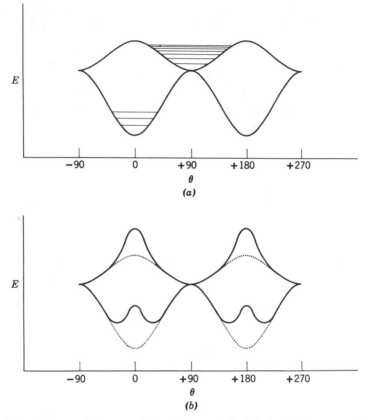

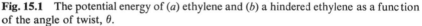

Fig. 15.1 The potential energy of (*a*) ethylene and (*b*) a hindered ethylene as a function of the angle of twist, θ.

Three factors contribute to this potential-energy minimum:

(1) The electron configuration of this state is $\pi_u\pi_g^*$ (cf. section 5.3). Although π_u, the bonding MO, is considerably more stable than the isolated $2p\pi$ atomic orbitals of carbon, π_g^*, the antibonding MO is considerably less stable. As pointed out in Chapter 3, the destabilizing contribution of π_g^* is greater than the stabilizing contribution of π_u, and consequently the most stable geometric conformation of this excited state results when the $2p\pi$ orbitals of the two carbon atoms interact least, which is the case when the CH_2 groups are at right angles to each other.[4]

(2) Electron correlation, i.e., the mutual repulsion of the two $p\pi$ electrons, is at a minimum when the molecule is twisted, because then the average distance between the electrons is largest.

[4] R. S. Mulliken and C. C. J. Roothaan, *Chem. Revs.*, **41**, 219 (1947).

(3) Least important, but possibly also significant is the fact that in the twisted conformation the hydrogen atoms of one CH_2 group are farthest removed from those of the other, and hence their repulsions also are at a minimum.

When bulky groups replace some of the hydrogen atoms in ethylene, especially if such bulky groups are *cis* to each other, the energy of the ground state is raised relative to that of a substituted ethylene in which steric strain is absent. The strain can be relieved by a deformation involving either stretching of the double bond or twisting around the double bond. Twisting about the double bond is the energetically less expensive way of relieving the strain because even a small twist serves to separate the interfering atoms by a considerable amount, and because the force constants for twisting are generally much smaller than those for stretching. As a result of such twisting, the spectrum of the unhindered olefin shows a bathochromic and hyperchromic effect relative to the unhindered olefin. These effects can be more readily understood by reference to the potential curves shown in Fig. 15.1.

The bathochromic effect will be considered first. The figure shows schematically the variation of the potential energy of the ground and excited states as a function of the angle of twist θ around the essential double bond (*a*) in an unhindered and (*b*) in a hindered olefin. The lower curve in each case represents the ground state, and the upper curve the excited state. The ground-state curve in the unhindered ethylene indicates the minimum energy at $\theta = 0°$ and the maximum at $\theta = 90°$, while the excited-state curve shows the minimum energy at $\theta = 90°$ and the maximum at $0°$. At $90°$, the energies of both states are essentially identical. Since the bond order p in the ground state is 2 and in the excited state 1, the potential-energy curve is steeper in the ground state; i.e., a small twist is energetically more expensive in the ground than in the excited state. It will also be obvious from Fig. 15.1*a* that, if the molecules in the ground state are in conformations on either side of $\theta = 0°$, the energy required for the transition to the excited state will decrease as the deviation increases. It can therefore be predicted that twisting around the double bond, i.e., steric interference to coplanarity, will result in a bathochromic shift.

Figure 15.1*a* is also useful for understanding the effect of twisting around an essential double bond on the intensity of absorption. In the unhindered ethylene, most of the molecules are nearly planar with $\theta = \sim 0°$. According to the Franck-Condon principle, excitation occurs vertically, and excitation of molecules with $\theta \sim 0°$, leads to the relatively high vibrational levels near the maximum of the excited-state potential-energy curve. In this region, the density of vibrational levels is high, and the total intensity is made up of a large number of individual contributions from individual lines. Now, with the introduction of bulk around the double bond, steric interference results in a high population in the ground state of molecules with values of θ appreciably different from 0°. Because of the operation of the Franck-Condon principle, the angle θ does not change during the excitation process. It was shown in section 6.7 that the total integrated intensity, or the oscillator strength, is unaffected by the operation of the Franck-Condon principle. In the hindered molecule, where larger values of θ predominate, excitation leads to a region of the potential-energy curve where the density of vibrational energy levels is low relative to the situation with small θ, and accordingly the same total intensity is made up of a much smaller number of lines, which then individually must have higher intensity and hence a higher ϵ_{max}. Accordingly, it is expected from an analysis of Fig. 15.1a that steric hindrance will have both a bathochromic and a hyperchromic effect. Figure 15.1b shows the change in the potential-energy curves which results from steric hindrance. The hump in the ground-state curve at $\theta = 0°$ and 180° ensures a high population of molecules with θ different from these values and leads to the bathochromic and hyperchromic effects on the spectrum. Although the steric interference raises the potential energy of both the ground and the excited states in the neighborhood of $\theta = 0°$, this effect is probably larger in the ground than in the excited state because of the larger p of the ground state. Furthermore, raising the ground-state energy makes the potential-energy minima considerably more shallow, and this fact serves to augment further the population of molecules with large twist.

I

An interesting series of compounds in which steric effects can be relieved by twisting around an essential double bond consist of the derivatives of *fulvene*, I. Although fulvene itself has never been prepared, derivatives are known; one such is dibiphenylene-ethylene, II. This compound has been

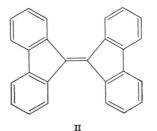

II

shown[5] to absorb at unexpectedly long wavelengths, a fact which has been attributed to steric overlap with resultant twisting around the double bond.

15.3   Twisting Around an Essential Single Bond

Many of the studies dealing with steric effects on ultraviolet absorption spectra have been concerned with chromophores connected by essential single bonds. Introduction of substituents around the single bond results in more or less interference and steric inhibition of coplanarity of the chromophores. The reduced interaction of the chromophores in the non-planar compound is responsible for the deviations in the absorption spectrum of the hindered compound from that expected for the planar model. Reduction of ϵ_{max} with little or no hypsochromic shift of λ_{max} is usually associated with small interference to planarity; and, if both hypochromic and hypsochromic effects are observed, as they are with the introduction of large or more numerous interfering groups, appreciable interference to coplanarity is assumed. In some cases (e.g., with bimesityl) the observed spectrum appears to be a summation of the spectra of the separate chromophores; then it may be concluded that there is essentially no interaction between the two chromophores (i.e., the π-electron systems of the chromophores are at right angles to each other and do not interact).
The extent of interaction between orbitals in adjacent carbon atoms r and s may be measured by the overlap integral, defined as

$$S = \int \phi_r \phi_s \, d\tau$$

which can have an absolute value between zero and unity. If atoms r and s are the atoms at which two chromophores R and S are connected, as, e.g., atoms 1 and 1' of biphenyl, III, the overlap integral of the pπ orbitals

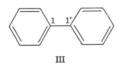

III

on r and s varies from a maximum value, S_{rs}^0, at 0° twist [i.e., when the chromophores (the two rings) are coplanar] to a value of zero when the angle of twist, θ, is 90°. In particular the overlap integral, S_{rs}, is proportional to $\cos\theta$:

$$S_{rs}^\theta = S_{rs}^0 \cos\theta$$

[5] E. D. Bergmann, G. Berthier, A. Pullman, and M. B. Pullman, *Bull. soc. chim. France*, **17**, 1079 (1950).

The resonance integral, β_{rs}, is approximately proportional to the overlap integral,[6] and accordingly,

$$\beta_{rs}{}^\theta \cong \beta_{rs}{}^0 \cos \theta$$

The resonance energy of a molecule is, to the organic chemist, a familiar criterion of the extent of interaction of π orbitals; and, if R and S are separate chromophores connected by a single bond, the resonance energy of RS relative to the isolated chromophores R + S is a measure of the interaction across the bond between R and S. The change in energy of the system, $\delta\mathscr{E}$, due to the interaction is related to the resonance integral, β.

Unfortunately it is not possible to give an analytical expression for the resonance energy as a function of the angle of twist. A crude approximation to such an expression can be obtained from one of the most powerful approximation methods of quantum mechanics, the *perturbation theory*. This method is based on the concept, which is always valid, that any quantity of interest, here the change, $\delta\mathscr{E}$, in the total energy $\mathscr{E}$, can be expressed as an infinite power series in $\delta\beta$:

$$\delta\mathscr{E} = \alpha_1 \, \delta\beta + \alpha_2 \, (\delta\beta)^2 + \alpha_3 \, (\delta\beta)^3 + \cdots \tag{15.1}$$

As long as $\delta\beta$ is small, $(\delta\beta)^2$ and terms involving higher powers are negligible, provided all the α's are of the same order of magnitude; hence *first-order perturbation theory* neglects all terms but the first. Thus, for small angles of twist, β is proportional to $\cos \theta$, and so is the total energy. This relation is shown in Fig. 15.2. However, as soon as θ is appreciable, the second term cannot be ignored, and the simple cosine dependence breaks down. The proportionality constant, α_1, has been identified with the bond order p_{rs} of the bond about which the twist occurs,[7] so that

$$\delta\mathscr{E} = p_{rs} \, \delta\beta_{rs} \tag{15.2}$$

The problem can also be approached from the other extreme. Consider the two chromophores R and S separately (i.e., $\beta = 0$) because they are twisted by 90°. Now let the angle θ decrease slightly, leading to some resonance interaction between R and S. In this extreme, $p_{rs} = 0$; hence $\alpha_1 = 0$, and the *first-order* perturbation theory gives[8] a vanishing energy change.

The reasons for the zero value of the first term can be illustrated by using the simple example of two ethylene chromophores joined by a single bond in the conjugated system of butadiene. The combination of the two ethylene chromophores gives four MO's. In the first approximation the energy split of the ethylene MO's will be equal; i.e., the

[6] R. S. Mulliken, C. A. Rieke, and W. G. Brown, *J. Am. Chem. Soc.*, **63**, 41 (1941).
[7] C. A. Coulson and H. C. Longuet-Higgins, *Proc. Roy. Soc.* (*London*), **A191**, 39 (1947).
[8] M. J. S. Dewar, *J. Am. Chem. Soc.*, **74**, 3345 (1952).

lowest-energy MO in butadiene will be as much below the bonding MO of ethylene as the second MO of butadiene is above the bonding MO of ethylene. The four π electrons of butadiene occupy the two lowest-energy MO's, but the total energy of the molecule will be identical with the sum of the energies of the two ethylene chromophores. Since the lowering $(-\delta\beta)$ is equal to the raising $(+\delta\beta)$ of the level and since each level is doubly occupied, these changes cancel; and in this first approximation the excess energy of butadiene over the two isolated chromophores, the resonance energy, is zero. This argument, however, has ignored the existence of the antibonding orbitals of ethylene. If their presence is taken into account in the second approximation, the splitting of the levels is not equal, and the energy of the lowest level in butadiene, π_1, is a greater distance below the π level of ethylene than π_2, the next level in butadiene, is above this level. The energy-level diagram is shown in Fig. 10.1, and the resonance energy is the difference in splitting of the two ethylene levels. The same situation applies to the combination of any two chromophores in both of which all levels are completely filled, as, e.g., the resonance energy of an α,β-unsaturated carbonyl system shown in Fig. 10.2 and discussed in section 10.2.

In the above case we resort to *second-order perturbation*, i.e., use the second term of equation (15.1). This then gives a $\cos^2\theta$ dependence,[8] as illustrated in Fig. 15.2. The behavior between the two extremes, the $\cos\theta$ dependence at small θ and the $\cos^2\theta$ dependence near $\theta = 90°$, is not easily obtained, but we may expect the $\mathscr{E}$ versus θ curve to be continuous and monotonous from 0 to 90°, as shown by the dotted line of Fig. 15.2. But the cosine of a small angle is not much different from 1, and hence not much different from its square. Consequently the $\mathscr{E}$ versus θ curve does not deviate from the $\cos^2\theta$ curve by much over the whole range, as shown in Fig. 15.2, and $\mathscr{E} \approx \cos^2\theta$ is a fair approximation. This discussion shows

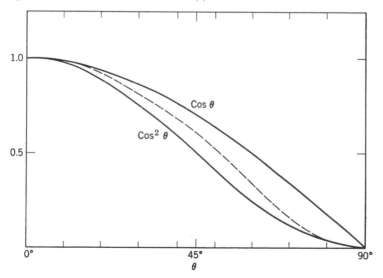

Fig. 15.2   The resonance energy of the system RS as a function of the angle of twist, θ.

that the extra resonance energy in the system RS relative to R + S varies approximately as $\cos^2 \theta$, where θ is the angle of twist. Appreciable deviation from coplanarity is required before the resonance energy is reduced by a significant amount, since $\cos \theta$ (and $\cos^2 \theta$) are slowly changing functions near $\theta = 0°$. Thus, $\cos^2 20°$ is 0.88, and accordingly the extra resonance energy of the coplanar system RS is reduced only 12 per cent by a twist of 20°; then reduction is only 50 per cent by a twist as large as 45° (Fig. 15.2).

In the preceding paragraphs it was shown that the excess *resonance energy* due to the interaction of two chromophores R and S follows a $\cos^2 \theta$ law when the R-S bond is an essential single bond. A similar $\cos^2 \theta$ law has been postulated by several groups of workers for the relation between intensity and angle of twist. Thus, the oscillator strengths[9] of *ortho*-substituted dimethylanilines were found to be proportional to $\cos^2 \theta$, and Braude and Sondheimer[10] suggested that, in general, in cases in which ϵ_{max} is reduced without a concurrent hypsochromic shift,

$$\epsilon^\theta / \epsilon^0 = \cos^2 \theta$$

where ϵ^0 applies to a planar reference compound. These suggestions were empirical in nature, in that the authors sought a function of θ which would behave in the expected manner. Obviously, the function should decrease from 1 to 0 in going from 0° to 90°, but on further increase to 180° the function should again increase. If the twist occurs about a bond which lies on a rotational axis of the molecule, the function *must* be symmetric about 90°. The function $\cos^2 \theta$ has these properties.

It is well to consider at this point the theoretical basis for the reduction of ϵ_{max} in the $V \leftarrow N$ transition of a coplanar system RS when the introduction of bulk results in slight twisting of the single bond. If no concomitant hypsochromic effect (less than about 5 mμ) is caused by the twist, it may be assumed that the transition energy and the vibrational levels of the ground and excited states do not differ significantly from those of the unhindered compound, and that the transition moment associated with any particular absorption also is unchanged. The details of this effect can best be considered in terms of the potential-energy diagrams of the relevant ground and excited states as a function of the angle of twist shown schematically in Fig. 15.3a.

In the system RS, the bond between R and S is an essential single bond, and the highest occupied orbital of the ground state (π) has a node between R and S. The lowest unoccupied orbital π^* has no such node, and hence excitation of an electron from π to π^* *increases* the bond order of the bond

[9] H. B. Klevens and J. R. Platt, *J. Am. Chem. Soc.*, **71**, 1714 (1949).
[10] E. A. Braude and F. Sondheimer, *J. Chem. Soc.*, 3754 (1955).

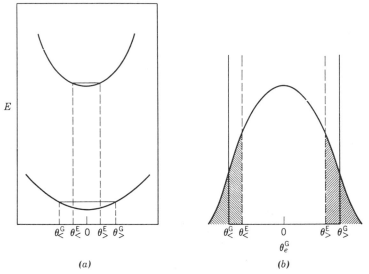

(a)   (b)

Fig. 15.3 (a) The potential energy of an unhindered system RS in the ground and excited states as a function of θ. (b) The probability distribution function. [Reprinted by permission from H. H. Jaffe and M. Orchin, *J. Chem. Soc.*, 1078 (1960).]

between R and S. In resonance notation, this is equivalent to representing the ground state by structures such as R—S and the excited state by structures[11] $^\pm$R$=$S$^\mp$. As discussed above, a change in total energy $\delta\mathscr{E}$ is proportional to both the bond order p_{rs} and the change in resonance integral $\delta\beta_{rs}$, which, in turn, is proportional to cos θ. Consequently, near $\theta = 0°$, the potential-energy curve will behave as p_{rs} cos θ. Both potential-energy curves have a minimum at $\theta = 0°$, but the curve of the excited state, because of the larger value of p_{rs}, is steeper than that of the ground state. The two curves are shown schematically in Fig. 15.3a.

The horizontal lines in Fig. 15.3a represent schematically the lowest vibrational level of the two electronic states. The values $\theta_<{}^G$ and $\theta_>{}^G$ are the minimum and maximum angles, respectively, of twist θ classically permitted in a given vibrational level (e.g., the lowest) of the ground state. The values of $\theta_<{}^E$ and $\theta_>{}^E$ are the permitted values of θ in the same vibrational level of the excited state. Since the absolute values of $\theta_<{}^G$ and $\theta_>{}^G$ are larger than $\theta_<{}^E$ and $\theta_>{}^E$, and since excitation must occur vertically, there is no possibility of excitation of a molecule from the lowest vibrational level of the ground state to the lowest vibrational level of the excited state (i.e., of a $0 \rightarrow 0$ transition) if, at the moment of excitation,

---

[11] A better statement might be that structures such as R—S make a predominant contribution to the ground state, whereas structures such as $^\pm$R$=$S$^\mp$ make the most important contribution to the excited state.

$|\theta| > |\theta_<^{\mathrm{E}}|$. In other words, when the molecule during its vibration is in a position in which the value of θ lies outside the limits allowed classically in the 0 vibrational level of the excited state, excitation can occur only to higher vibrational levels; i.e., the excitation must correspond to the $0 \rightarrow 1$, $0 \rightarrow 2$, or higher bands.

This point is further emphasized by a consideration of Fig. 15.3b, which shows the (quantum-mechanical) distributions of molecules in the lowest vibrational level among different values of the angle θ.

It is interesting to note that this distribution function has finite, although small, values outside the region $\theta_<^{\mathrm{G}} < \theta < \theta_>^{\mathrm{G}}$, which is classically allowed. Molecules represented by these outside "tails" of the distribution function appear to have negative kinetic energy, an apparent paradox.

The dashed vertical lines in Fig. 15.3b represent the classical limits of θ in the lowest level of the excited state, and by mixing classical and quantum-mechanical arguments we arrive at the conclusion that molecules represented by the part of the area under the distribution function which is shaded cannot undergo a $0 \rightarrow 0$ transition.

The potential-energy curves of unhindered and slightly hindered molecules should become identical for values of θ exceeding zero by a few degrees. Near $\theta = 0°$, however, a steric repulsion energy (E_s) raises the curves for the hindered molecule above those for the unhindered one. The minima no longer occur at $\theta = 0°$; instead, there is a maximum there, and shallow minima occur a few degrees displaced from $0°$. These relationships are illustrated in Fig. 15.4a. It appears possible, or even likely, that even the zero-point vibrational level lies above the central minimum, although this assumption is not necessary for the subsequent argument.

In order to describe the quantitative difference between effects on ground and excited states, the following quantities are conveniently defined. The equilibrium value of θ in the ground state is denoted by $\theta_e^{\mathrm{G}'}$ and in the excited state by $\theta_e^{\mathrm{E}'}$, where the prime identifies the slightly hindered molecule. The corresponding quantities in the unhindered molecule, $_e^{\mathrm{G}}\theta$ and θ_e^{E}, are, of course, zero. Energy differences also are required; and the energies at the potential minima in the ground and excited states, respectively, of the unhindered molecule are denoted by E^{G} and E^{E}, of the hindered one by $E^{\mathrm{G}'}$ and $E^{\mathrm{E}'}$. In Fig. 15.4a the broken lines represent the curves for the unhindered molecule, corresponding to the curves in Fig. 15.3a.

In considering Fig. 15.4a it should again be remembered that the bond order of the essential single bond in RS increases on excitation, and the resulting greater resistance to twist leads to $\theta_e^{\mathrm{G}'} > \theta_e^{\mathrm{E}'}$. However, since $\cos \theta$ is a slowly changing function of θ near $\theta = 0$, and since the steric repulsion energy also is small, $E^{\mathrm{G}'} - E^{\mathrm{G}} \approx E^{\mathrm{E}'} - E^{\mathrm{E}}$; i.e., E is the same

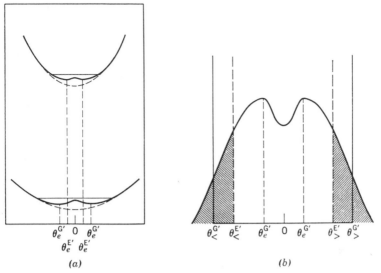

Fig. 15.4 The potential energy (*a*) and distribution (*b*) functions in slightly hindered RS. [Reprinted by permission from H. H. Jaffé and M. Orchin, *J. Chem. Soc.*, 1078 (1960).]

in the two states. The excitation energy of the slightly hindered molecule is then essentially the same as that of the unhindered molecule; no hypsochromic effect should be noted.

The effect of slight hindrance on the intensity (as measured by ϵ_{max}) of an absorption band is conveniently considered in terms of the distribution function of the hindered molecule, schematically shown in Fig. 15.4*b*, which should be compared with the corresponding function for the unhindered case (Fig. 15.3*b*). Comparison of these figures shows that hindrance increases $\theta_>^{E}$ (and decreases $\theta_<^{E}$) considerably less than $\theta_>^{G}$ (and $\theta_<^{E}$), because the excited-state potential function is much steeper than the ground-state one, and hence the steric repulsion energy E_s becomes unimportant at much lower values of θ. Consequently, a much larger fraction of the molecules will be represented by the shaded area in the hindered molecule than in the unhindered one (as shown by the larger shaded area in Fig. 15.4*b*), and hence will be unable to be excited to the lowest vibrational level of the excited state. Consequently, the hypochromic effect in slightly hindered molecules may be explained as a Franck-Condon effect resulting from the twist around the single bond in RS.

The case of moderate steric hindrance is somewhat more complicated than that of slight hindrance. The potential-energy curve for the ground state (Fig. 15.5*a* solid line), must have a fairly high and reasonably steep maximum at $\theta = 0°$. The equilibrium value $\theta_e^{G''}$ (double primes identify

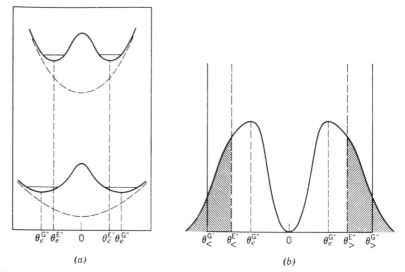

Fig. 15.5 The potential energy (a) and distribution (b) functions in moderately hindered RS. [Reprinted by permission from H. H. Jaffé and M. Orchin, *J. Chem. Soc.*, 1078 (1960).]

the moderately hindered molecule) for θ occurs at considerably larger values of θ than in the slightly hindered case. The potential-energy curve asymptotically approaches that of the unhindered case (broken line), but only at relatively large values of θ—unless the hindering groups are so bulky that even the completely twisted conformation is hindered, so that the chromophores are isolated. The steric repulsion energies $E_s^{G''}$ and $E_s^{E''}$ (i.e., the height of the maximum above the minimum at $\theta = 0°$, for the unhindered molecule should also be considered.

Just as in the slightly hindered case, the equilibrium value of θ is increased more in the ground than in the excited state, $\theta_e^{G''} > \theta_e^{E''}$, and both quantities are considerably larger than they were in the slightly hindered molecule, $\theta_e^{G''} > \theta_o^{G'}$ and $\theta_e^{E''} > \theta_e^{E'}$. But in the moderately hindered case, the distortion in θ is considerable, and hence $\cos\theta$ is less than 1 by an appreciable amount. This information, together with the knowledge that the bond order in the excited state (p^E) is greater than in the ground state (p^G), $p^E > p^G$, leads to the inequality

$$\mathscr{E}^{G''} - \mathscr{E}^{G} < \mathscr{E}^{E''} - \mathscr{E}^{E} \tag{15.3}$$

Further, the higher bond order in the excited states indicates a smaller bond distance, and consequently $E_s^{E''}$ is slightly larger than $E_s^{G''}$; this difference, however, is probably small enough to be neglected. Figure 15.5a is drawn to reflect these considerations. Inequality (15.3) is the explanation for the hypsochromic effect observed in these cases.

The hypochromic effect is probably due to a combination of two factors.

First, there is the redistribution of the total intensity between various vibrational levels, analogous to the one discussed for the slightly hindered case. This is illustrated by the distribution function shown in Fig. 15.5*b*, in which the shaded area representing the fraction of molecules unavailable for excitation to the lowest vibrational level of the excited state is seen to be further increased. Second, it can be shown that the transition moment also decreases with increasing θ, so that the total (integrated) intensity, or the oscillator strength, may also be expected to decrease. The relative importance of these two factors is difficult to evaluate.

The above considerations explain the effects observed when the system RS of two chromophores R and S is subjected to steric interference by introducing groups which prevent the ground state of RS from assuming coplanarity. In the case of slight hindrance, a Franck-Condon effect, manifested by a hypochromic effect relative to the unhindered model, is expected; where moderate hindrance occurs, both a hypsochromic and a hypochromic effect should be observed. Naturally there is no sharp demarcation between slight and moderate hindrance, and each case must be considered on the evidence. Several examples of the effects discussed will now be examined in some detail; the first are the various mono- and poly-*ortho*-substituted biphenyls.

15.31 BIPHENYL AND ITS DERIVATIVES. The solution spectrum of biphenyl (Fig. 15.6) shows a single structureless band with λ_{max} at 252 mμ

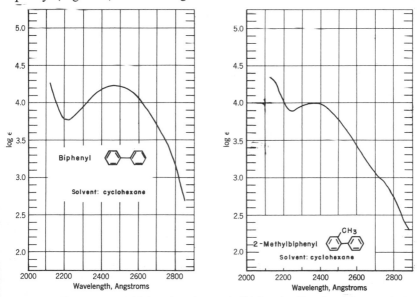

Fig. 15.6 The spectra of biphenyl and 2-methylbiphenyl. (Reprinted by permission from R. A. Friedel and M. Orchin, *Ultraviolet Spectra of Aromatic Compounds*, John Wiley and Sons, New York, 1951.)

Species

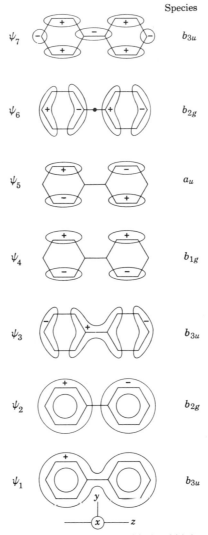

Fig. 15.7 The molecular orbitals of biphenyl.

and ϵ_{max} of 18,300. Presumably this band represents the $^1L_a \leftarrow {}^1A$ transition corresponding to the 208 mμ band in benzene, which is shifted by conjugation with the chromophoric phenyl substituent. The $^1L_b \leftarrow {}^1A$ transition of benzene, the forbidden transition at 256 mμ, is probably hidden below the 252 mμ band of biphenyl (cf. section 12.6).

The planar model of biphenyl belongs to point group D_{2h}. The shapes of the six occupied orbitals and of the lowest unoccupied orbital are shown in Fig. 15.7. These MO's belong to the symmetry species indicated next to the orbital. The z axis is placed along the long axis of the molecule, the y axis is also in the plane of the molecule, and the x axis is perpendicular to the molecule. With this set of axes, $\psi_6(f_g)$ belongs to symmetry species b_{2g} and $\psi_7(g_u)$ to b_{3u}, and the promotion $\psi_6 \to \psi_7$ ($f_g \to g_u$) is not parity forbidden.[2] ψ_4 and ψ_5 (v_g and v_u) are a degenerate pair localized on the benzene rings and hence are nonbonding with respect to the 1,1' bond.[12] These orbitals will not be affected by any kind of deformation around the central bond. The amplitudes and nodes of f and g are shown graphically in Fig. 15.8, where it is seen that f has a node but g lacks one through the central 1,1' bond. Accordingly, f makes a negative and g a positive contribution to the bond order $p_{1,1'}$. These changes in bond order are consistent with the usual resonance description of the two states, in which the high-intensity $V \leftarrow N$ transition is associated with a decrease in the importance of structure IV and an increase in the importance of structure V:

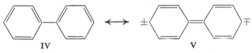

The bond order of the 1,1' bond increases in the excited state, and the potential-energy curve of this bond as a function of the angle of twist is steeper than the similar curve for the ground state.

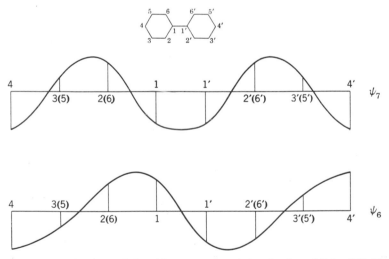

Fig. 15.8 The highest occupied and lowest unoccupied molecular orbitals of biphenyl.

[12] The orbital notation in parentheses is that of J. R. Platt in A. Holländer, *Radiation Biology*, McGraw-Hill Book Co., New York, 1956, pp. 193–196.

Examination of scale models of biphenyl indicates that the completely planar conformation is sterically somewhat hindered. This steric hindrance is relieved principally by twisting about the central $(1,1')$ bond and, to a lesser extent, by stretching of this bond. Suzuki[13] has carefully analyzed the spectroscopic consequences of this steric crowding and has developed a method permitting estimation of the angle θ between the two planes. For this purpose he expresses the resonance integral $\beta_{1,1'}$ of the central bond as $\beta_{1,1'} = \mu\beta$, where β is the resonance integral between two π orbitals of adjacent carbon atoms in a benzene ring, and μ is a variable parameter. Because of the proportionality between β and the overlap integral S, and because of the proportionality of S to $\cos\theta$,

$$\mu = \cos\theta \times S(R, 0°)/S(1.39 \text{ A}, 0°) \tag{15.4}$$

Here, $S(1.39 \text{ A}, 0°)$ represents the $\pi - \pi$ overlap integral for the C-C bond in benzene, the length of which is 1.39 A, and $S(R, 0°)$ is the corresponding integral for the $1,1'$ bond of length R. A table of overlap integrals[14] indicates that S is proportional to R in the region of R values of interest. Assuming the geometry determined[15] by x-ray analysis of crystalline biphenyl, giving $R = 1.48$ A and $\theta = 0°$, the value μ for the planar form is evaluated as 0.858. The value of R is further assumed to vary from 1.48 A in the planar model to the normal C—C single-bond value of 1.54 A in the right-angle model of biphenyl,[16] and at the same time μ varies from 0.858 to 0 [cf. equation (15.4)]. The variation of μ in this interval is then expressed as

$$\mu = 0.77\cos\theta + 1.45\,(1.54 - 1.48)\cos^2\theta$$

$$= 0.77\cos\theta + 0.09\cos^2\theta$$

Here, the $\cos^2\theta$ term arises from the variation of R and is seen to be practically negligible.

Energies for the various MO's have been evaluated from the secular equation by the LCAO method for μ values from 0 to 1.1 at intervals of 0.1. The resonance energy is found to be roughly proportional to μ^2, and the bond order $p_{1,1'}$ to μ. A further discussion of the spectra now requires consideration of the orbitals and their variation with θ. The fully twisted model ($\theta = 90°$) belongs to the point group D_{2d}, and the highest occupied

[13] H. Suzuki, *Bull. Chem. Soc. Japan*, **32**, 1340 (1959).

[14] R. S. Mulliken, C. A. Rieke, D. Orloff, and H. Orloff, *J. Chem. Phys.*, **17**, 1248 (1949).

[15] J. Dahr, *Indian J. Phys.*, **7**, 43 (1932); *Proc. Natl. Inst. Sci. India*, **15**, 11 (1949).

[16] This assumption may be questioned on the basis of the recent postulation that the sp^2-sp^2 single bond is 1.48 A long (see footnote 17, p. 60); however, the results are not sensitive to this assumption.

and lowest unoccupied orbitals will each be quadruply degenerate. In this model, because of $\beta_{1,1'} = 0$, the two benzene rings are not conjugated, and in each the highest occupied and lowest unoccupied orbitals are doubly degenerate. The energies of these orbitals are β and $-\beta$, respectively. As the angle θ is decreased from 90°, the quadruply degenerate highest occupied orbital splits, as shown in Fig. 15.9, into a doubly degenerate pair (v_g and v_u), and higher and lower orbitals, e and f; the lowest unoccupied quadruply degenerate orbital similarly splits into w_u, w_g, g, and h. The quantity of spectroscopic interest is the energy difference ΔE_A between the MO's f and g, corresponding to the longest-wavelength transition $f \rightarrow g$. This energy quantity can be evaluated from Suzuki's energy values for the orbitals, but no simple relation between ΔE_A and μ is found.

In order to evaluate the angle of twist θ, Suzuki[13] now has proposed a relatively simple correlation of observed frequencies ν with calculated energies ΔE. The two extreme configurations with $\theta = 0°$ and $\theta = 90°$ are chosen as reference compounds, and ΔE and ν are assumed to be

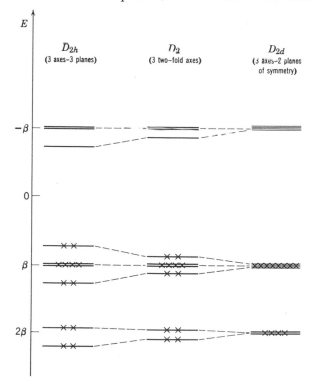

Fig. 15.9 A correlation diagram for the energy levels of planar and twisted biphenyl.

linearly related between these two extreme fixed points. Since crystalline biphenyl is known to be planar, its absorption maximum ν_L (corrected for solid-state effects) is chosen as the *l*onger-wavelength (*l*ower-frequency) reference, and the ΔE calculated for this compound is denoted as ΔE_L. The other reference compound, the D_{2d} 90° model, absorbs at *s*horter wavelength of frequency ν_S, and the corresponding energy difference is denoted by ΔE_S. The energy difference ΔE_A for a partially twisted form, as presumably exists in solution and in the vapor, is designated by ΔE_A and is obtained from the observed frequency ν_A by the linear interpolation formula:

$$\Delta E_A = \Delta E_S - (\Delta E_S - \Delta E_L)\frac{\nu_S - \nu_A}{\nu_S - \nu_L}$$

$$= \frac{\Delta E_L \nu_S - \Delta E_S \nu_L}{\nu_S - \nu_L} + \frac{\Delta E_S - \Delta E_L}{\nu_S - \nu_L}\nu_A \qquad (15.5)$$

This is the equation for a straight line of slope $(\Delta E_S - \Delta E_L)/(\nu_S - \nu_L)$ and intercept $(\Delta E_L \nu_S - \Delta E_S \nu_L)/(\nu_S - \nu_L)$, expressing ΔE_A as a function of ν_A. From the value of ΔE_A obtained from equation (15.5), the value of μ can be obtained by reference to Suzuki's tables. From such values of μ, θ, R, and RE (resonance energy) can, in turn, readily be interpolated. The choice of numerical values for ΔE_L, ν_L, ΔE_S, and ν_S for the reference compounds remains the only difficult problem.

Crystalline biphenyl is chosen as the long-wavelength reference compound, and μ and ΔE_L are computed to be 0.858 and -1.482β, respectively. As the short-wavelength reference compound, benzene is chosen, and the values of μ and ΔE_S are 0 and -2β, respectively. However, the values of the frequencies ν_L and ν_S are not so readily selected. In solution spectra of benzene, there are presumably three singlet-singlet transitions[17] (cf. section 12.1):

$$^1L_b \leftarrow {}^1A \quad \text{or} \quad {}^1B_{2u} \leftarrow {}^1A_{1g} \quad \text{at 38,200 cm}^{-1} \quad \text{or 261.8 m}\mu$$

$$^1L_a \leftarrow {}^1A \quad \text{or} \quad {}^1B_{1u} \leftarrow {}^1A_{1g} \quad \text{at 48,000 cm}^{-1} \quad \text{or 208.3 m}\mu$$

$$^1B \leftarrow {}^1A \quad \text{or} \quad {}^1E_{1u} \leftarrow {}^1A_{1g} \quad \text{at 53,000 cm}^{-1} \quad \text{or 188.7 m}\mu$$

and the weighted mean of the energies of these transitions or the "center of gravity of singlets"[18] (see Fig. 12.2) corresponding to the transition energy -2β is 48,000 cm^{-1}, which value is then taken as ν_S.

The selection of the long-wavelength band ν_L, corresponding to ΔE_L of planar biphenyl, is complicated by a number of factors. Thus, it is almost

---

[17] H. B. Klevens and J. R. Platt, *J. Chem. Phys.*, **17**, 470 (1949).

[18] J. R. Platt, *J. Chem. Phys.*, **18**, 1168 (1950).

certain that biphenyl in solution does not have the same geometry as crystalline biphenyl, and there is no agreement as to the true interpretation of the spectrum of biphenyl. Wenzel[19] has proposed that the 250 mμ intense band is a superposition of a strong and a weak transition corresponding to the 210 mμ and 260 mμ bands of benzene, respectively. The existence of the hidden transition in biphenyl has been corroborated by Dale,[20] who measured the absorption spectrum of biphenyl in the crystalline state and found a weak band at about 275 mμ. This band may be assigned to a transversely polarized transition. The intense band was found at 39,526 cm^{-1} or 253 mμ, and Suzuki assumes this to be ν_L corresponding to the transition energy ΔE_L of -1.482β. However, the maximum observed in the spectrum of a sample prepared by the disc technique always occurs at longer wavelength than that found in solution spectra. This red shift is supposed to be due to the effect of interactions between molecules in the crystal and is thought to amount to 2.0–3.5 mμ in the biphenyl case. Solvent effects are of course eliminated if the spectrum can be determined in the vapor phase, and such studies have been made of biphenyl.[21] The absorption maximum in the vapor occurs at considerably shorter wavelength than in the disc, presumably indicating that the deviation from coplanarity is larger in the vapor than in the solid state. Solution spectra can be compared to vapor spectra by subtracting out the solvent effect according to the equation of Bayliss,[22] which was discussed in section 9.7, and which relates the frequency displacement to the refractivity of the solvent.

Because of the uncertainty in the correction that should be applied to the disc spectra, Suzuki has based calculations[13] on two values of ν_L, 40,080 cm^{-1} (249.5 mμ) and 39,841 cm^{-1} (251 mμ) for the planar model of biphenyl. Using the 251 mμ value and $\Delta E_L = -1.523\beta$, he found, for solution in heptane, $\theta = 23°$, while in the vapor state at 20°, $\theta = 43°$.

The steric interference of the phenyl groups in biphenyl is greatly increased when some or all of the hydrogen atoms in the 2, 2′, 6, and 6′ positions of biphenyl are replaced by other atoms or groups. Suzuki has extended the method for biphenyl [i.e., the use of equation (15.5)] to such compounds[23] and has attempted to calculate the angle of twist θ in 2-alkyl- and 2,2′-dialkylbiphenyls. Again, it is necessary to choose ΔE and ν for two reference compounds. For 2-methylbiphenyl new MO calculations are avoided by assuming that the relation between μ and ΔE

[19] A. Wenzel, *J. Chem. Phys.*, **21**, 403 (1953).
[20] J. Dale, *Acta Chem. Scand.*, **11**, 650 (1957).
[21] F. Almasy and H. Laemmel, *Helv. Chim. Acta*, **33**, 2092 (1950).
[22] N. S. Bayliss, *J. Chem. Phys.*, **18**, 292 (1950).
[23] H. Suzuki, *Bull. Chem. Soc. Japan*, **32**, 1350 (1959).

is the same as in biphenyl. In order to account for the bathochromic effect of the 2-methyl group in the absence of steric effects, it is assumed that this is equivalent to the effect of a 4-methyl group, and from $\lambda_{max} = 253$ mμ of 4-methylbiphenyl, $\nu_L = 39,526$ cm^{-1} is obtained. Similarly, the center of gravity of singlets for toluene, $\nu_S = 46,882$ cm^{-1}, is chosen. Since the observed spectrum for 4-methylbiphenyl is a solution spectrum in hexane, ΔE_L must also be the value empirically found applicable to biphenyl in solution (heptane), i.e., 1.523β with $\mu = 0.780$. It is then possible to calculate ΔE_A, μ, θ, and R for 2-methylbiphenyl. Similar treatment allows calculations for other *ortho*-substituted biphenyls of interest, and the results are shown in Table 15.1.[23] The values for 2-*n*-propyl-, 2-isopropyl-,

TABLE 15.1
Characteristics of Hindered Biphenyl Compounds

Substituent	λ_{max}, mμ	ν_A, cm^{-1}	ΔE_A, $-\beta$	μ	θ, deg	R, A
2-Methyl	235	42,553	1.719	0.438	58	1.508
2-Ethyl	233	42,918	1.743	0.399	60.7	1.5105
2,2'-Dimethyl	227	44,053	1.826	0.267	70	1.5193
2,2'-Diethyl	227	44,053	1.829	0.262	70.3	1.5195
2-Phenyl	252	39,680	1.504	0.611	43	1.496
None (vapor)	238	41,966	1.617	0.611	43	1.496
None (solution)	247	40,486	1.523	0.780	23	1.485

and 2-*n*-butylbiphenyl are identical with those of 2-ethylbiphenyl. This would indicate that methylene groups attached to the carbon atom which is attached to the 2 position can adopt conformations which cause little or no additional interference over the one carbon atom.[24]

The next compound to be considered in the biphenyl series is 2-phenylbiphenyl or *o*-terphenyl, VI. The planar model of this compound belongs

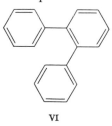

VI

to point group C_{2v}, but the nonplanar model, in which the end phenyls are equally twisted by an angle different from 90°, belongs to point group C_2.

[24] E. A. Braude and W. F. Forbes, *J. Chem. Soc.*, 3776 (1955).

The resonance integral for the single bonds between rings is $\mu\beta$, where μ is again the parameter which incorporates the allowance for the change in β associated with changes in interplanar angle and bond length. The transition energy ΔE_A, corresponding to the transition between the highest occupied and lowest unoccupied orbitals, has been evaluated as a function of μ by the LCAO method.[25] As the value of μ decreases from unity to zero, ΔE_A increases from 1.2206β to 2β, indicating that the $\pi \rightarrow \pi^*$ band should be shifted toward shorter wavelength with increasing hindrance to coplanarity (decreasing μ). The reference long-wavelength compound necessary for the application of equation (15.5) is p-terphenyl in the crystalline state, and the short-wavelength reference compound is benzene. Then, from the observed position of the o-terphenyl $\pi \rightarrow \pi^*$ band (252 mμ), ΔE_A is obtained, from which μ is estimated from Table 15.1 relating μ to ΔE_A. From the value of μ, θ and R are calculated. The results of this calculation indicate that the most probable configuration of o-terphenyl is one in which the end rings are twisted about $43°$ out of the plane of the parent ring. This result is in quite good agreement with the value of $50°$ obtained[26] by x-ray analysis of crystalline o-terphenyl.

Before leaving the biphenyl system, it is of value to point out the possibility of evaluating the height of the potential-energy barrier to coplanarity in a system in which there is hindrance to the planarity of the conjugated system RS, e.g., Fig. 15.5, $\theta = 0°$. In order for an optically active biphenyl to racemize, it must pass through the planar or symmetrical conformation (activated state), and hence theoretically it should be possible to gain information on the height of this barrier from data on the energy of activation of the racemization of optically active biphenyls. Westheimer[27] has investigated 2,2'-dibromobiphenyl and has shown that the lowest-energy planar conformation involves a *trans* structure, considerable bending of the C-Br bonds, lesser bending of the C-H bonds, and an in-plane deformation of the $C_4C_1C_1'C_4'$ axis. The sum of these deformations decreases the two H-Br interactions by increasing the distances between these two atoms. Bond bending is much more important than bond stretching. Westheimer's general theory of the quantitative evaluation of steric strain involves setting up an energy function of the molecule on the basis of particular arrangements of the atoms in space and then minimizing the van der Waals energy of repulsion. Calculations based on the mathematical treatment agree quite well with energies of activation found for the racemization.

The spectra of a variety of compounds related to biphenyl have been reported and interpreted in terms of steric effects. Some such compounds are 1-phenyl- and 1-o-tolylnaphthalene, 9-phenyl- and 9,10-diphenyl-anthracene, 1,1'- and 1,2'-binaphthyl. Few quantitative data are available for these systems, but the qualitative steric effects were discussed in sections

[25] H. Suzuki, *Bull. Chem. Soc. Japan*, **33**, 109 (1960).

[26] C. J. B. Clews and K. Lonsdale, *Proc. Roy. Soc.* (*London*), **A161**, 493 (1957).

[27] F. Westheimer in *Steric Effects in Organic Chemistry*, edited by M. S. Newman, John Wiley and Sons, New York, 1956, Chapter 12.

TABLE 15.2

The Effect of o,o'-Ring Closure on the Spectrum of Biphenyl

	Compound	λ_{max}, mμ	θ, deg
(1)		251[a]	23[a]
(2)		261.5[b]	0[b]
(3)		263.5[c]	20[c]
(4)		272[d]	0[b]
(5)		250[c]	44.5[b]
(6)		249[e]	46.7[b]
(7)		248[c]	47.3[b]
(8)		239.5[f]	58.0[b]
(9)		236.5[f]	61.5[b]

[a] H. Suzuki, *Bull. Chem. Soc. Japan*, **32**, 1340 (1959).
[b] H. Suzuki, *Bull. Chem. Soc. Japan*, **32**, 1357 (1959).
[c] G. H. Beavan, D. M. Hall, M. S. Lesslie, and E. E. Turner, *J. Chem. Soc.*, 854 (1952).
[d] R. N. Jones, *J. Am. Chem. Soc.*, **63**, 1658 (1941).
[e] D. C. Iffland and H. Siegel, *J. Am. Chem. Soc.*, **80**, 1947 (1958).
[f] G. H. Beavan, G. R. Bird, D. M. Hall, E. A. Johnson, J. E. Ladbury, M. S. Lesslie, and E. E. Turner, *J. Chem. Soc.*, **2708** (1955).

13.31 and 13.4). Analysis of the spectra of these compounds in the manner just described is complicated by the fact that comparison must be made with the unhindered isomer in each case. The compound which must be considered as such an unhindered reference compound must have the phenyl substituent attached to the polycyclic aromatic chromophore at some other position, which should, however, be electronically equivalent to the position of attachment in the hindered compound. Unfortunately, the spectra are generally so complicated that correlation of bands between reference compound and hindered compound is not practicable. In addition, frequently no electronically equivalent positions are available.

The biphenyl compounds in which the o,o' positions are tied together by rings of various sizes are of considerable interest. The first member of the series, fluorene, in which the rings are joined through one methylene group, has a spectrum very similar to that of the second member of the series, 9,10-dihydrophenanthrene, although the spectrum of fluorene has much more vibrational structure, presumably because of its strained, near-planar geometry. Although the interplanar angle in 9,10-dihydrophenanthrene [compound (3), Table 15.2] is about the same as in biphenyl, the two methylene groups in the tricyclic compound produce the bathochromic shift noted. In compound (4), which contains both a one- and a two-carbon bridge, the combined steric requirements of the two bridges probably result in a near-planar structure, and the three methylene groups produce the bathochromic shift.

The spectra of the compounds in which the o,o'-biphenyl is bridged by three atoms [compounds (5), (6), (7), Table 15.2] show the $\pi \rightarrow \pi^*$ band at considerably shorter wavelengths than do the spectra of fluorene and 9,10-dihydrophenanthrene; and, when the bridging is by four atoms [compounds (8), (9)], there is a further shift to shorter wavelengths. The hypsochromic displacements are probably due to the nonplanarity of these molecules, and Suzuki has calculated the biphenyl interplanar angle in these compounds by his general method; the results are shown in Table 15.2. The nonplanar structure of compound (6) has been confirmed by its recent resolution (footnote e, Table 15.2).

15.32 ANILINE AND ITS DERIVATIVES. Extensive studies on the effect of bulky groups around the nitrogen atom on the absorption spectra of aniline and its derivatives have been published. Before proceeding to a consideration of the spectral evidence, it is necessary to examine the geometry of the anilines and especially the configuration of atoms around nitrogen.

In ammonia, NH_3, the nitrogen atom, in the first approximation, uses p orbitals for bonding. In this configuration, the ammonia molecule is a pyramid with an apical angle of 90° and with nitrogen at one of the corners,

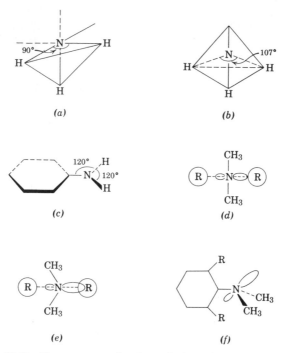

Fig. 15.10 The geometry of various trivalent nitrogen compounds.

as shown in Fig. 15.10*a*. As a matter of experimental fact[28] the HNH angle is not 90° but about 107°, and so the pyramid is flattened somewhat toward the planar configuration and the nitrogen p orbitals apparently are hybridized with some s character, approaching sp^3, which requires an angle of 109.5°. Such a pyramidal NH_3 molecule is shown in Fig. 15.10*b*, where the lone-pair electrons, instead of being in an s orbital, are in an orbital approaching sp^3 in character, and point toward the unoccupied corner of a tetrahedron with the nitrogen at the center. In aniline, the maximum overlap of the nitrogen lone pair with the carbon pπ electrons of the phenyl group occurs if all the atoms of the $\diagdown C{-}NH_2$ group are in the same plane.

This is the configuration in which nitrogen uses sp^2 orbitals, the HNH angle is 120° (Fig. 15.10*c*), and the lone pair occupies a pure p orbital. Overlap between the lone-pair electrons and the ring π electrons is larger, the more p character the lone pair has. Consequently resonance tends to open the HNH angle toward 120° at the expense of the promotion energy

[28] W. Gordy, W. V. Smith, and R. F. Trambarulo, *Microwave Spectroscopy*, John Wiley and Sons, 1953, Table A.9.

required to raise the lone pair from an sp^3 hybrid orbital to a pure p orbital. Accordingly, it is expected that the HNH bond angles of aromatic amines should lie between 109° and 120°, the angles expected for sp^3 and sp^2 hybridization, respectively.[28a]

In unsubstituted N,N-dimethylaniline, the nitrogen valences are probably nearly planar at about 120° to each other.[28a] Substitution at the *ortho* positions causes the —$N(CH_3)_2$ group to twist out of the plane of the phenyl ring, and the nitrogen valences become increasingly more pyramidal as the —$N(CH_3)_2$ is twisted; at the same time the lone-pair electrons gain s character. In order to avoid steric repulsions, less twist is probably required in the pyramidal than in the planar configuration. Distortion to the pyramidal configuration is favored by a lowered promotion energy (less sp^3 to p promotion required); however, overlap with the ring is better with a p orbital than with an sp^3 orbital, so some conjugation energy is lost by conversion of p to sp^3. It is difficult to evaluate these opposing factors quantitatively. Finally, when the $N(CH_3)_2$ plane is perpendicular to the ring, the nitrogen valences are pyramidal as in ammonia or alkyl amines.

The relation of the various groups can be illustrated by means of projection formulas looking down at the N atom with the projection carried out on a plane at right angles to the NC_1C_4 line (Figs. 15.10d and 15.10e). The plane of the benzene ring is denoted by a horizontal broken line, the R's denote the bulky *ortho* substituents, and the dumbbell shapes indicate the lone-pair orbitals. In Figs. 15.10d and 10.15e the C—N—C plane is perpendicular to the benzene ring as a result of *ortho* disubstitution by bulky R groups. In the hypothetical structure Fig. 15.10d the three groups around N are coplanar, with sp^2 hybridization, and the axis of symmetry of the lone-pair orbital is in the plane of the benzene ring corresponding to no overlap (orthogonality) and complete elimination of conjugation. Instead of the hypothetical structure of Fig. 15.10d, the actual structure of a hindered dimethyl aniline is given by Fig. 15.10e, which illustrates pyramidal nitrogen with sp^3 hybridization. The side view of 15.10e is shown in Fig. 15.10f, in which the plane of the ring and the sp^3 lone-pair orbital are in the plane of the paper. In neither configuration 15.10d or 15.10e is resonance interaction between the lone-pair orbital and the ring possible; Fig. 15.10e then represents the more stable structure because it avoids promotion of lone-pair electrons from sp^3 to p.

It might be thought that a decision between planar and pyramidal nitrogen in amines could be reached from optical-activity studies. Thus pyramidal nitrogen in which three different groups are attached to nitrogen

---

[28a] Some recent evidence [M. Van Meerssche and A. Crucq, *Bull. soc. chim. Belges*, **68**, 599 (1959); M. Van Meerssche and G. Leroy, *ibid.*, **69**, 204 (1960)] even indicates that, in some α-cyano-4′-dimethylaminostilbenes, the dimethylamino group is planar.

should give a resolvable compound, whereas the planar model of such a compound would not be resolvable. However, no example has been found to date of an optically active compound of structure NABC, where A, B, C are different groups none of which is itself dissymmetric. Although this fact would argue for a planar nitrogen, a variety of physical measurements have unequivocally demonstrated the pyramidal structure around nitrogen. Geometric considerations of the structure of molecules such as quinuclidine and hexamethylenetetramine, as well as x-ray analysis of the latter, also definitely indicate the pyramidal structure. The failure to

TABLE 15.3

Absorption Spectra of Hindered Anilines in Isooctane[29]

Compound	λ_{max}, mμ	ϵ_{max}
Aniline	234	9,130
2-Me	234	8,800
2,4,6-Me$_3$	237	8,600
2-t-Bu	237	7,800
2-Me-4,6-(t-Bu)$_2$	239	10,100
2,4,6-(t-Bu)$_3$	242	8,750
2,6-(t-Bu)$_2$	240	6,900
N-Methylaniline	243	13,200
2,4,6-(t-Bu)$_3$	247	4,900
N,N-Dimethylaniline	251	15,500
2-Me	248	6,360
2,4,6-Me$_3$	257	2,500
2-t-Bu	250 (no max)	630

isolate optically active NABC compounds is ascribed to the ready inversion of the pyramidal nitrogen; such inversion results in spontaneous racemization.

Turning now to spectral considerations, the introduction of methyl, or even *tert*-butyl groups, at the *ortho* positions of the parent aniline results in only small alteration of the spectrum. The slight reduction in intensity indicates some steric hindrance. Although the base strength of nuclear alkylated anilines decreases with increasing bulk around the amino group, the similarity in spectra, as well as scale models of these compounds and their conjugate acids, argues against the steric resistance to protonation being responsible for the decreased base strength. Instead, it is more likely that the relatively diminished stability of the ion is due to steric hindrance of solvation.[29]

[29] B. M. Wepster, *Symposium on Steric Effects in Conjugated Systems*, The University, Hull, July 15–17, 1958; see also *Steric Effects in Conjugated Systems*, edited by G. W. Gray, Butterworth, London, 1958.

In contrast to the anilines with an unsubstituted amino group the spectrum of N-methylaniline is affected, although to only a small extent, by *tert*-butyl groups in the *ortho* position, and there is extensive alteration in the spectrum of N,N-dimethylaniline, VII, caused by introduction of bulky groups. Data for the main absorption band[29] are given in Table 15.3 for a few members of the series.

Full participation of the lone-pair electrons on nitrogen in the π-electron system of the phenyl group requires that the axis of symmetry of the p orbital of the lone pair be normal to the plane of the phenyl ring, so that all $p\pi$ orbitals on the six carbons and the nitrogen may most effectively overlap. To the extent that steric crowding prevents the —N(CH$_3$)$_2$ group from being coplanar with the phenyl ring, there will be steric inhibition of resonance. In conventional valence-bond notation, this concept may be

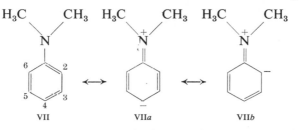

$$\text{VII} \qquad\qquad \text{VII}a \qquad\qquad \text{VII}b$$

expressed by stating that the contributions to the ground state from structures VII*a* and VII*b* are reduced by twisting the —N(CH$_3$)$_2$ group out of the plane of the phenyl group.

The spectrum of N,N-dimethylaniline, as well as scale models of the compound, is consistent with full conjugation of the nitrogen atom with the ring. When groups of progressively larger size are added at the 2 and 6 positions, the —N(CH$_3$)$_2$ group is twisted out of the plane with progressive loss of double-bond character of the N-Ph bond. With a 90° twist, the bond is completely a single bond; the axis of symmetry of the nitrogen p orbital is at right angles to the $p\pi$ orbitals of the ring carbons. The phenyl group is thus insulated from the chromophore, and the spectrum of such a highly hindered dimethylaniline resembles that of an alkylbenzene.[30] With intermediate angles of twist, the changes in the spectrum have been shown to be quantitatively related to the angle of twist.[31]

Dimethylaniline and its substituted derivatives show four characteristic regions of absorption. These bands are centered around 180, 210, 250, and 300 mμ and have been designated as the A, B, C, and D band, respectively. The longest-wavelength or D band has no counterpart in the

[30] W. R. Remington, *J. Am. Chem. Soc.*, **67,** 1838 (1945).
[31] H. B. Klevens and J. R. Platt, *J. Am. Chem. Soc.*, **71,** 1714 (1949).

TABLE 15.4
Spectra of Dimethylanilines

Absorption Bands

Substituent	A λ_{max}, mμ	A f	B λ_{max}, mμ	B f	C λ_{max}, mμ	C f	D λ_{max}, mμ	D f	Total f	Van der Waals Radius, A	Eff. Spec. Angle, deg
H	176.1	0.79	199.6	0.54	250.0	0.28	295.9	0.04	1.65	1.2	0
4-Me	183.3	0.40	203.3	0.46	253.8	0.32	304.0	0.03	1.21	...	...
2-F	175.7	0.80	201.2	0.43	250.0	0.21	283.3	0.03	1.47	1.4	33
2-Cl	185.5	0.72	212.3	0.39	255.8	0.14	...	0.03	1.28	1.8	44
2-Br	188.0	0.74	216.0	0.30	254.5	0.12	...	0.03	1.19	1.9	54
2-Me	185.2	0.69	207.0	0.23	247.5	0.12	...	0.02	1.06	2.0	60
2,6-Me$_2$	193.8	0.66	209.1	0.15	259.1	0.05	...	...	0.86	...	90

benzene spectrum. The A band may be associated with the allowed $^1B \leftarrow {}^1A$ transition, and the B and C bands with the forbidden $^1L_a \leftarrow {}^1A$ and the $^1L_b \leftarrow {}^1A$ transitions, in benzene. The most highly hindered derivatives do not show the D band, and their spectra resemble the alkylbenzenes. In moving from the unsubstituted compound through the series of compounds with increasing steric bulk around the $-N(CH_3)_2$ group, three features of the spectra show progressive change: (a) the A and B bands undergo red shifts, causing reduction of the total spread of the bands; (b) the total oscillator strength of the bands decreases; and (c) the intensity of B, C, and D bands undergo decreases, both absolute and relative to the A band, which remains fairly constant. Some of these effects are shown in Table 15.4. The total f (i.e., the sum of the f values for the A, B, C, and D bands) decreases linearly with the van der Waals radii of the crowding group, the *ortho* substituents. If the minimum angle of twist of the $-N(CH_3)_2$ group with respect to the ring, as estimated from the van der Waals radii, is plotted separately against the oscillator strength of bands A, B, C, the resulting points lie on a $\cos^2 \theta$ curve, which at $0°$ passes through the dimethylaniline f value and at $90°$ through the f value for the o,o'-dimethyl derivative. It is also possible to use f values and the $\cos^2 \theta$ curve to compute an "effective spectroscopic angle of twist." Such values are included in Table 15.4 and are derived from averaging the B- and C-band data. A more comprehensive set of data[32] for the C band of alkylated dimethylanilines is shown in Table 15.5.

TABLE 15.5

Absorption Spectra of N,N-Dimethylanilines[a] in 2,2,4-Trimethylpentane

Substituent(s)	λ_{max}, mμ	ϵ_{max}	ϵ/ϵ^0	θ, deg
H	251	15,500	(1)	(0)
2-Me	248	6,360	0.41	50
2-Et	249	4,950	0.32	56
2-i-Pr	248	4,300	0.28	58
2-t-Bu	250*	630*	0.04	78
2,6-Me$_2$	262	2,240	0.14	68
2,4,6-Me$_3$	257	2,500	0.16	66
2,3,5,6-Me$_4$	(256)	2,090	0.13	68
2,4,6-(i-Pr)$_3$	250*	1,540*	0.099	72
2,4-Me$_2$-6-t-Bu	250*	800*	0.052	77
2-Me-4,6-(t-Bu)$_2$	250*	840*	0.054	77

[a] Starred values of λ_{max} and ϵ_{max} refer to spectra without a maximum.

[32] J. Burgers, M. A. Hoefnagel, P. E. Verkade, H. Visser, and B. M. Wepster, *Rec. trav. chim.*, **77**, 491 (1958).

The $\cos^2 \theta$ relationship has been widely used to calculate angles of twist. The common procedure is to employ the main band in the accessible ultraviolet and to calculate the angle of twist θ from the expression

$$\epsilon/\epsilon^0 = \cos^2 \theta \qquad (15.6)$$

where ϵ is the molar extinction coefficient of the partially twisted compound under study, and ϵ^0 is the corresponding value for the homolog having no *ortho* substituent and hence assumed to be planar ($\theta = 0°$).

The application of this relation to a series of *p*-nitroanilines is shown in Table 15.6. The data present a number of new and some surprising

TABLE 15.6

Absorption Spectra of 4-Nitroanilines in Ethanol

Substituents	λ_{max}, mμ	ϵ_{max}	ϵ/ϵ^0	θ, deg*	f
H[a]	376	15,500	(1)	(0)	0.376
2,3-Trimethylene[c,f]	376	13,900	0.90	19	...
2,5-Me$_2$[d]	378	13,600	0.88	21	0.347
3-Me[e]	374	13,200	0.85	23	...
2,3-Tetramethylene[d]	383	11,200	0.72	32	0.306
2,3-Me$_2$[d]	382	9,750	0.63	38	0.286
3,5-Me$_2$[1]	385	4,840	0.31	56	0.126
2,3,5,6-Me$_4$[a]	396	1,560	0.10	72	0.039
3,5-(t-Bu)$_2$[b]	401	540	0.03	79	0.015

* The angles of rotation, θ, have been calculated from $\cos^2 \theta = \epsilon/\epsilon° = \epsilon/15,500.$
[a] B. M. Wepster, *Rec. trav. chim.*, **76**, 335 (1957).
[b] J. Burgers, M. A. Hoefnagel, P. E. Verkade, H. Visser, and B. M. Wepster, *Rec. trav. chim.*, **77**, 491 (1958).
[c] R. T. Arnold and J. Richter, *J. Am. Chem. Soc.*, **70**, 3505 (1948).
[d] R. Van Helden, P. E. Verkade, and B. M. Wepster, *Rec. trav. chim.*, **73**, 39 (1954).
[e] R. A. Morton and A. McGookin, *J. Chem. Soc.*, 901 (1934).
[f] B. M. Wepster, *Rec. trav. chim.*, **75**, 1473 (1956).

features. A substituent in the 2 or 6 position may interfere with coplanarity of the amino group with the ring, whereas a substituent in the 3 or 5 position similarly interferes with coplanarity of the nitro group and the ring. It is immediately apparent that bulky substituents decrease the intensity greatly. On the other hand, contrary to the previous findings, steric hindrance is accompanied in this series by a bathochromic shift. As in the aniline series, methyl groups do not appear to interfere seriously with the coplanarity of the amino group, as may be seen from a comparison of the 3-methyl- and 2,5-dimethyl compounds. A single methyl group does not greatly hinder coplanarity of the nitro group: the intensity of the 3-methyl compound is only moderately lower than that of the parent. The 2,3-dimethyl compound reveals the chemically well-known but spectroscopically rarely observed *buttressing* effect: the intensity in this compound is reduced by more than twice the amount observed in the electronically equivalent 2,5-dimethyl analog. The ring compounds, 2,3-tri- and tetramethylene-4-nitroanilines, in which the interfering alkyl groups are tied back, produce smaller effects, decreasing with decreasing ring size; and in the five-membered ring compound, the effect is even smaller than in the 2,5-dimethyl compound. As usual, *ortho* disubstitution greatly enhances steric hindrance, so that the intensity falls to about one-third of the value of the parent by 3,5-dimethyl substitution, and to one-thirtieth (i.e., probably complete inhibition of resonance of the nitro group) in 3,5-di-*t*-butyl-4-nitroaniline. Introduction of methyl groups in the 2 and 6 positions, which may be assumed to be virtually without effect in the parent compound, reduces the intensity of the 3,5-dimethyl compound by a further factor of 3, indicating again the tremendous importance of the buttressing effect.

The spectra of benzocyclamines, VIII, as a function of ring size have been studied by several groups of workers[30,33]. The spectra of N-methylindole, VIII ($n = 2$), and N-methyltetrahydroquinoline, VIII

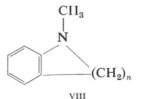

VIII

($n = 3$), are quite similar to each other and to the spectrum of N,N-dimethylaniline except for slight bathochromic shifts in the C and D bands, which may be considered normal for the introduction of an additional alkyl substituent into the benzenoid ring. Undoubtedly the saturated rings are constrained to the near-planar configuration. However, the spectrum of compound VIII with $n = 4$ shows a considerable difference from the spectra of the two lower homologs, and this difference is almost certainly due to the nonplanarity of the seven-membered ring. This general subject will be discussed further in connection with the benzocyclanones.

15.33 BENZALDEHYDE, ACETOPHENONE, AND RELATED COMPOUNDS. The spectra of simple molecules containing a carbonyl group conjugated to a

[33] G. Baddeley, J. Chadwick, and S. B. Rawlinson, *Nature*, **164**, 833 (1949).

phenyl ring were discussed in section 12.24. The benzoyl chromophore gives rise to three band systems in the generally accessible ultraviolet: a weak ($\epsilon \sim$ 5–100) n $\to \pi^*$ band (^1W) at about 320 mμ; a moderately intense ($\epsilon \sim$ 1000–2000) band between 270–290 mμ corresponding to the benzene-forbidden $^1B_{2u} \leftarrow {}^1A_{1g}$ ($^1L_b \leftarrow {}^1A$) transition, also called the secondary band; and finally the high-intensity or first primary band associated with the $^1B_{1u} \leftarrow {}^1A_{1g}$ ($^1L_a \leftarrow {}^1A$) transition (variously denoted as the conjugation, K, or C band). This band has also been called the intramolecular charge-transfer band (section 12.24) and is the band of reference in most studies of substituent effects. The substitution of methyl for hydrogen in the *ortho* positions of benzaldehyde produces a bathochromic effect.[34] This is the expected effect in the absence of any appreciable steric hindrance to the coplanarity of the Ph—C=O grouping. However, an *o*-methyl substituent does not produce as large a bathochromic shift as a methyl in the *meta* position, and a *p*-methyl produces the largest effect. Furthermore, an *o*-methyl substituent causes a small but definite decrease in ϵ compared to the parent compound; a second *o*-methyl produces a further small decrease. The interplanar angles of *o*-methylbenzaldehyde and 2,6-dimethylbenzaldehyde, calculated from $\epsilon/\epsilon^0 = \cos^2 \theta$, are 21° and 28°, respectively, where ϵ^0 refers to ϵ_{max} of benzaldehyde.[35] The spectral data indicate that *ortho* substitution in benzaldehyde does not lead to large deviations from coplanarity; the deviation is about equal to that in biphenyl in solution.

It is to be expected that in general the steric effects around the Ph—C=O chromophore would bear some resemblance to those already discussed for $PhNH_2$, since in both cases conjugation requires coplanarity of the auxochrome with the ring. Such resemblance has been shown to exist, but the analogy is not exact because of the difference in size, shape, and electronic configuration of the auxochrome.

It would be anticipated that steric effects are more important in substituted acetophenones than in analogously substituted benzaldehydes. The data of Braude and Sondheimer,[34] Table 15.7, support this thesis; the $\cos^2 \theta$ relationship was used to estimate the angle of twist. The *ortho* effects have been demonstrated in a slightly different manner,[34] using again the high-intensity band. In this treatment, the oscillator strength, f, for the $^1L_a \leftarrow {}^1A$ transition is represented by

$$f = f^0 + f_p - f_o$$

where f^0 is the observed value for acetophenone (0.22), f_p is the normal intensifying increment of *p*-methyl, and f_o is the decrement of a methyl

[34] E. A. Braude and F. Sondheimer, *J. Chem. Soc.*, 3754 (1955).
[35] E. A. Braude, F. Sondheimer, and W. F. Forbes, *Nature*, **173**, 117 (1954).

group in the *ortho* position. With the assumption that an *m*-methyl group is without appreciable effect, good correlation is obtained by assigning f_p the numerical value 0.04 and f_o the value 0.07. In addition to the 2-alkylacetophenones, many other 2-substituted derivatives have been studied, and their spectra confirm the steric interference to coplanarity.[36]

TABLE 15.7

Steric Effects in *ortho*-Substituted Acetophenones and Benzaldehydes

Substituent	Acetophenones		Benzaldehydes	
	ϵ/ϵ^0	θ, deg	ϵ/ϵ^0	θ, deg
None	1.00	0	1.00	0
2-Me	0.58	40	0.86	21
2,4-Me$_2$	0.85	24	...	...
2,5-Me$_2$	0.66	35	...	...
2,6-Me$_2$	0.34	55	0.78	28
2,4,6-Me$_3$	0.20	63	0.85	22

On the basis of analogies between the pairs styrene–benzaldehyde and α-methylstyrene–acetophenone, Suzuki suggests that acetophenone itself is slightly hindered.[37] The carbonyl derivatives of acetophenone, such as the semicarbazones and 2,4-dinitrophenylhydrazones, show much greater sensitivity to substitution in the *ortho* position than do the corresponding derivatives of the benzaldehydes.[35]

The spectra of the benzocyclanones, IX, provide considerable information on the coplanarity of the carbonyl group with the phenyl ring as a

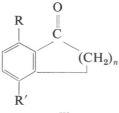

IX

[36] D. D. Clarke and F. F. Nord, *J. Am. Chem. Soc.*, **77**, 6618 (1955); R. A. Morton and A. L. Stubbs, *J. Chem. Soc.*, 1347 (1940); N. A. Valyaske and Y. S. Rozum, *J. Gen. Chem. U.S.S.R.*, **16**, 593 (1946); **17**, 755 (1947); H. Dannenberg, *Z. Naturforsch.*, **4b**, 327 (1949), K. Bowden, E. A. Braude, and E. R. H. Jones, *J. Chem. Soc.*, 948 (1946); W. J. Horton and J. T. Spence, *J. Am. Chem. Soc.*, **80**, 2453 (1958); W. J. Horton and D. E. Robertson *J. Org. Chem.*, **25**, 1016 (1960); D. J. Cram and F. W. Cranz, *J. Am. Chem. Soc.*, **72**, 595 (1950).

[37] H. Suzuki, *Bull. Chem. Soc. Japan*, **33**, 613 (1960).

TABLE 15.8

Steric Effects in Benzocyclanones, IX

Substituents				Primary Band			Secondary Band			
n	R	R′	No.	λ_{max}, mμ	ϵ_{max}	f	λ_{max}	ϵ_{max}	f	θ, deg
2	H	H	(1)	239	12,720	0.208	284	2,650	0.031	...
3	H	H	(2)	244	10,550	...	291.5	2,550	...	...
				243	11,450	0.196	285.5	1,550	0.024	...
4	H	H	(3)	240	9,000	0.153	296	1,430	...	...
5	H	H	(4)	243	6,500	0.115	281	1,200	0.019	37
2	CH$_3$	H	(5)	238	12,800	0.208	285.5	1,100	0.016	45
				243	10,500	...	284	2,600	0.031	...
2	CH$_3$	CH$_3$	(6)	244.5	12,300	0.179	291.5	2,550	...	...
				251	11,950	...	302	2,500	0.035	...
3	CH$_3$	CH$_3$	(7)	246.5	10,390	0.169	292.5	2,500	...	...
				250	10,090	...	300	2,310	0.036	...
4	CH$_3$	CH$_3$	(8)	244.5	4,950	0.088	288	1,290	0.024	51

function of the ring size of the cyclanone portion and of *ortho* substitution on the phenyl ring.[38] Pertinent data are given in Table 15.8. In the unsubstituted compounds, IX, with $n = 2$ and 3, the observed f values are high, as expected, indicating ring constraint and coplanarity of the phenyl and carbonyl groups. However, when $n = 4$ and 5, there are hypsochromic shifts concomitant with reduced f values. A similar phenomenon, but with a more abrupt decrease at $n = 4$, appears in the series of the methyl-substituted cyclic ketones listed in Table 15.8. These results are consistent with the view that the carbonyl group is fixed in the plane of the benzene ring for $n = 2$ and 3 and is twisted out of the plane for $n \geq 4$; the degree of twist, assuming the usual $\cos^2 \theta$ relationship, is indicated in Table 15.8.

The spectra of compounds containing two carbonyl groups adjacent to each other present certain new problems. The dicarbonyl system may be considered as related to the butadiene system and can also exist in the *s-cis* and *s-trans* conformations:

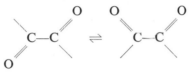

Both conformations tend to be planar in order to achieve maximum pπ overlap. It is expected, however, the *s-trans* would be favored, for in this conformation the negative oxygen atoms are farthest removed from each other and intramolecular Coulombic repulsions are at a minimum. In the simplest dicarbonyl system, glyoxal $(CHO)_2$, there is strong evidence that the carbonyl groups are *trans* and coplanar.[39] Two n → π transitions are expected in these dicarbonyl components. The longest-wavelength absorption band is the n → π_3^* transition, where π_3^* is the lowest-energy unoccupied MO formed from the interaction of the four pπ AO's of the two conjugated carbonyl groups. Glyoxal, which is yellow, has a long-wavelength absorption band[40] at 450 mμ, $\epsilon = \sim 5$. If the 1,2-dicarbonyl system is part of a small ring system, the two carbonyl systems are held in a coplanar *s-cis* conformation. A series of alicyclic 1,2-diketones of structure X have been studied[41] to ascertain the effect of ring size on their ultraviolet spectra. The α positions were fully substituted in order to avoid complications due to enolization. When $n = 1$, the system is coplanar and the n → π* transition occurs at the longest wavelength in the series of

[38] G. D. Hedden and W. G. Brown, *J. Am. Chem. Soc.*, **75**, 3744 (1953).

[39] J. E. Lu Valle and V. Schomaker, *J. Am. Chem. Soc.*, **61**, 3520 (1939).

[40] A. Luthy, *Z. physik. Chem.*, **107**, 285 (1923).

[41] N. J. Leonard and P. M. Mader, *J. Am. Chem. Soc.*, **72**, 5388 (1950).

homologs studied. As the ring size is increased, the angle between the carbonyl groups increases and the n → π* band undergoes a hypsochromic

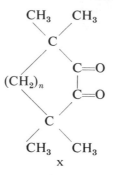

shift. The location of the n → π* band and the interplanar carbonyl angles deduced from models are given in Table 15.9.

TABLE 15.9

Spectra of 1,2-Dicarbonyls, X

n	λ_{max}, mμ (n → π*)	θ, deg
1[a]	466	0–10
2	380	0–60
3	337	90–110
4	343	110–140
14	384	100–180

[a] Camphorquinone, a trialkyl-substituted diketone.

The spectra of benzil, XIa, and related compounds, although 1,2-dicarbonyl compounds, are more complicated than those of the cycloalkanediones.[42] Each carbonyl group is strongly conjugated and coplanar with the phenyl group to which it is attached. This strong conjugation of the carbonyl with phenyl apparently minimizes the conjugation of the two benzoyls with each other, for a variety of evidence indicates that the two groups are twisted with respect to each other, perhaps as much as 90°, and benzil has a skew structure. Thus, the long-wavelength band of benzil is not at 450 mμ as in glyoxal but at 370 mμ, $\epsilon = \sim 75$, and benzil and certain of its derivatives have spectra which resemble those of benzaldehyde and its derivatives. When benzil is substituted in the *ortho* positions as in

[42] N. J. Leonard, R. T. Rapala, H. L. Herzog, and E. R. Blout, *J. Am. Chem. Soc.*, **71**, 2997 (1949); N. J. Leonard and E. R. Blout, *J. Am. Chem. Soc.*, **72**, 484 (1950). See also N. J. Leonard, A. J. Kresge, and M. Oki, *J. Am. Chem. Soc.*, **77**, 5078 (1955) for further corroboration using "fixed" benzils.

XIb and XIc, the 370 mμ band is successively shifted to longer wavelengths ($\lambda_{\text{XI}a} < \lambda_{\text{XI}b} < \lambda_{\text{XI}c}$). Presumably, with increasing hindrance at the *ortho* positions, each phenyl ring is twisted out of the plane of the carbonyl group to which it is attached, and the two carbonyl groups are forced into the coplanar *s-trans* conformation (90° → 180°).

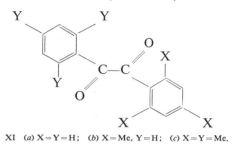

XI (*a*) X=Y=H;   (*b*) X=Me, Y=H;   (*c*) X=Y=Me.

15.34 CYCLOALKENYL KETONES.   Acetylcyclohexene, XII, has an absorption maximum at a wavelength which agrees with the empirical rules for absorption for α,β-unsaturated ketones discussed in section 10.2.   If a methyl group is substituted at the 2 position (2-methyl-1-acetylcyclohexene, XIII), the spectrum shows the expected bathochromic shift (Table 15.10) but there is also a considerable hypochromic effect. The rationalization of this (steric) effect has elicited much discussion in the literature.

In the absence of steric effects, it is generally agreed that α,β-unsaturated ketones possess the *s-trans* conformation, XII. The introduction of a methyl group at the 2 position of acetylcyclohexene causes less steric crowding in the *s-cis*, XIIIb than in the *s-trans* XIIIa conformation, and

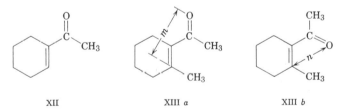

XII   XIII a XIII b

in view of the relatively small difference in energy of the two conformations (about 2.5 kcal in butadiene), Turner and Voitle[43] proposed that this compound exists in the *s-cis* conformation. They further assumed that the compound was planar because conjugation is most effective in the planar arrangement and $\lambda_{\max}$ was at the expected position for the fully conjugated chromophore. The hypochromic effect was explained as due to the shorter distance separating the ends of the chromophore in the *s-cis* than in the *s-trans* conformation. The f value of an absorption band

[43] R. B. Turner and D. M. Voitle, *J. Am. Chem. Soc.*, **73**, 1403 (1951).

is a function of the dipole strength of the chromophore and is accordingly proportional to the square of the distance between the ends of the absorbing system responsible for the band.[44] The ratio f/f^0 was 0.65, where f is the integrated intensity of the long-wavelength band of 2-methylacetylcyclohexene and f^0 the similar value of the unsubstituted homolog, whereas the ratio of the squares of the respective chromophore lengths $(n^2 : m^2)$ was determined to be 0.68 from scale models. Similar calculations for some of the carotenoids of known stereochemistry showed good correlation between the ratio of integrated intensities and the chromophore lengths.[43]

The difference in the steric crowding between s-cis, XIIIb, and s-trans, XIIIa, as determined from scale models, depends on an assumed value for van der Waals radii. These radii are usually based on the equilibrium distance between nonbonded atoms in crystals. However, considerable evidence indicates that smaller values should be applied when dealing with solution phenomena, since, for example, spectral effects expected on the basis of these radii are frequently not observed. Radii assigned values about half-way between van der Waals and covalent radii give better agreement with observed spectral effects;[45] thus, for hydrogen interference, a radius of 0.6 A, rather than either the covalent radius of 0.3 A or the van der Waals radius of 1.2 A, appears to be the most reasonable value. Even with these reduced values, the s-trans conformation drawn to scale shows some steric crowding in the planar conformation. However, Braude and Timmons[46a] proposed that such crowding can be relieved from the favored s-trans conformation by out-of-plane twisting of the carbonyl group. Small twists do not affect the resonance energy appreciably but are effective in relieving steric crowding, since steric repulsion is a highly sensitive function of interatomic distances. The reduced intensity of the hindered compound, XIII, can then be ascribed to the situation previously discussed and expressed by Fig. 15.4. The barrier to planarity in the ground state increases the population of molecules at angles on both sides of $\theta = 0°$. Since the potential-energy curve of the excited state is steeper than that of the ground state, vertical promotions required by the Franck-Condon principle lead to high vibrational levels in the excited state, and hence are less probable than $0 \rightarrow 0$ excitations in the unhindered planar

---

[44] N. Q. Chako, *J. Chem. Phys.*, **2**, 644 (1934); R. S. Mulliken, *J. Chem. Phys.*, **7**, 14 (1939); L. Pauling, *Fortschr. Chem. org. Naturstoffe*, **3**, 203, (1939); *Helv. Chim. Acta*, **32**, 2241 (1949).

[45] E. A. Braude and E. S. Waight in *Progress in Stereochemistry*, edited by W. Klyne, Academic Press, New York, 1954, p. 142.

[46] (a) E. A. Braude and C. J. Timmons, *J. Chem. Soc.*, 3766 (1955). (b) R. L. Erskine and E. S. Waight, *J. Chem. Soc.*, 3425 (1960); E. S. Waight and R. L. Erskine in *Steric Effects in Conjugated Systems*, edited by G. W. Gray, Butterworth, London, 1958.

compound. If the angle of twist in the ground state is calculated for some hindered acetyl-cyclohexenes according to the formula $\epsilon/\epsilon^0 = \cos^2 \theta$, the results shown in Table 15.10 are obtained.[43,46a] The question of

TABLE 15.10

Steric Effects in the Spectra of Acetylcyclohexenes[43,46a]

Compound	λ_{max}, mμ	ϵ	ϵ/ϵ^0	θ, deg
cyclohexene–C(=O)Me	232.0	12,500	1.0	0
methyl-cyclohexene–C(=O)Me	245.0	6,500	0.52	44
methyl-cyclohexene–C(=O)CMe$_3$	239.0	1,300	0.10	71
dimethyl(Me, Me)-cyclohexene–C(=O)Me (Me)	243.0	1,400	0.11	71

whether XIII is a planar s-cis compound or a twisted s-trans compound is now rather firmly resolved in favor of the s-cis form.[46b]

It has been claimed[46b] that the ratio of the integrated band intensities of the C=O and C=C stretching frequencies is much higher in fixed s-trans structures than in fixed s-cis structures. On this basis it has been concluded again that compound XIII exists predominantly in the s-cis conformation.

15.4   Systems Containing Essential Single and Essential Double Bonds: Stilbene and Related Compounds

The *cis* and *trans* isomers of stilbene and their isosteres such as *cis*- and *trans*-azobenzene are systems that contain essential single and double bonds. When substituents are added to these molecules in positions which cause steric crowding, there are (at least theoretically) a variety of ways in which the steric hindrance can be relieved or minimized. The experimental spectra of these hindered molecules, as well as theoretical considerations, are useful in deciding on the geometry that such molecules assume. *trans*-Stilbene and its derivatives will be considered first.

The spectra of *trans*-stilbene, XIV, and some of its hindered derivatives[47]

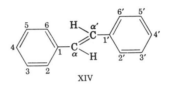

XIV

are compared in Fig. 15.11. The *f* value calculated[47] from the shape of the long-wavelength band in *trans*-stilbene is 0.745. Substitution of a methyl group in the 4 (or 4′) position increases the *f* value by about 0.050, whereas in the 3 (or 3′) position the increment is 0.005. A single methyl group in the hindering 2 (or 2′) position causes a decrement of 0.04; if a second hindering methyl is added to the same ring, the total decrement of the long-wavelength band is 0.100. If the second hindering methyl is in the other ring, the decrement is 0.075; and when four hindering methyls (2, 2′, 6, 6′) are present, the decrement is 0.135.

The spectrum of *trans*-stilbene was discussed in detail in section 12.8. The long-wavelength band is the $^1B \leftarrow {}^1A$ transition, polarized along the long axis of the molecule. Increasing hindrance to planarity, caused by methyl substitution at the *ortho* positions, results in the expected hypsochromic and hypochromic effects. An analysis[48] of the possible deformations of planar stilbene that are caused by steric crowding of substituents led to the conclusion that the principal deformation consists of twisting around the 1,α and 1′,α′ bonds, XIV. These bonds are essential single bonds, and the effect of twisting around such a bond was discussed earlier in this chapter. Such effects are readily visualized in terms of the potential-energy diagrams as a function of the angle of twist expressed by Figs. 15.4*a* and 15.5*a* and by the distribution (population) functions given in Figs. 15.4*b* and 15.5*b*. The figures show that the hypochromic effect

[47] R. N. Beale and E. M. F. Roe, *J. Am. Chem. Soc.*, **74**, 2302 (1952).
[48] H. H. Jaffé and M. Orchin, *J. Chem. Soc.*, 1078 (1960).

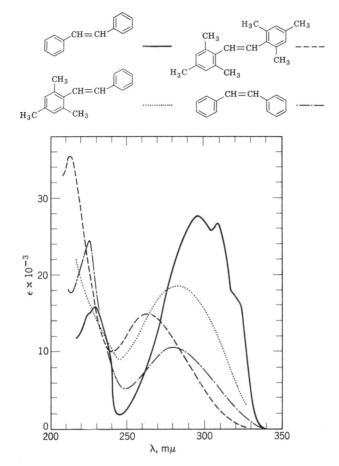

Fig. 15.11 Spectra of *trans*-stilbene and some hindered derivatives, all in ethanol. [Reprinted by permission from E. A. Braude and E. S. Waight in *Progress in Stereochemistry*, edited by W. Klyne, Academic Press, New York, 1954; R. N. Beale and E. M. F. Roe, *J. Am. Chem. Soc.*, **74**, 2302 (1952); cf. H. Suzuki, *Bull. Chem. Soc. Japan*, **33**, 381 (1960).]

produced by substituents inhibiting coplanarity may be explained as a Franck-Condon effect resulting from the angle of twist, $\theta_{\alpha,1}$. An analysis of the effect on potential energy as a function of angle of twist $\theta_{\alpha,\alpha'}$ around the essential double bond shows that such twist would not explain the observed hypochromic effect.

The relevant curves leading to this conclusion are shown in Fig. 15.12. The bond order of the α,α' bond decreases on excitation, and the equilibrium angle $\theta_e^{G'}$ in the ground state of a hindered stilbene is less than the equilibrium angle $\theta_e^{E'}$ in the excited state. Accordingly, the experimental hypochromic effect in the hindered stilbenes cannot be due to twisting around the essential double bond, since such twisting would not lead to a

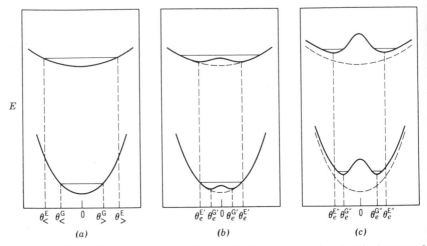

Fig. 15.12   Potential energy as a function of θ_{aa}, for the ground and excited states of (a) unhindered, (b) slightly hindered, and (c) moderately hindered stilbene. [Reprinted by permission from H. H. Jaffé and M. Orchin, *J. Chem. Soc.*, 1078 (1960).]

Franck-Condon restriction. An analysis of the effect of relieving steric strain by stretching the α,α' bond shows that stretching this bond cannot give rise to the observed spectral effect of hindrance.[48] Because the bond order of the α,α' bond is smaller in the excited than in the ground state, the steric repulsion energy caused by *ortho* substitution will be less in the excited than in the ground state, i.e., $E^{E'} - E^{E} < E^{G'} - E^{G}$, where the superscripts refer to states and the primes denote the hindered case. Also, because the bond order decreases on excitation, the difference in equilibrium distance of the α,α' bond between the hindered and the unhindered models is less in the excited than in the ground state, i.e., $r_e^{E'} - r_e^{E} > r_e^{G'} - r_e^{G}$. These inequalities predict that operation of the Franck-Condon principle can only lead to a bathochromic and a hyperchromic effect in contradiction to the experimental facts. A similar analysis of the effects of stretching the $\alpha,1$ or $\alpha',1$ bond indicates that again the stretching mode can not be an important way of relieving strain.

The hypsochromic effect of steric crowding can be explained by comparison of the π-electron energies of the ground and excited states in the twisted stilbene model and in the planar nonhindered model. Twisting the $\alpha,1$ bond reduces the resonance integral $\beta_{\alpha,1}$ in the unhindered or planar model to $\beta'_{\alpha,1}$ in the twisted model: $\beta'_{\alpha,1} = \beta_{\alpha,1} \cos \theta_{\alpha,1}$. Crude semi-empirical LCAO-MO calculations based on assumed values for the β's are shown in Table 15.11. The π-electron energies given in Table 15.11 are shown in the energy-level diagrams of Fig. 15.13a. This figure shows that the bonding and the antibonding energy levels are compressed in the hindered compound and that the highest occupied and lowest unoccupied levels are spread apart. This spread explains the observed hypsochromic shift. Addition of the energy values for the various MO's correctly

TABLE 15.11
Results of MO Calculations for the Stilbene System[48]

	Planar Stilbene	Hindered Stilbene	Isolated Chromophores[a]
$\beta_{\alpha,1}^b$	0.6	0.5	0
$\beta_{\alpha,\alpha}^b$	1.2	1.1	1.2
E^b of ψ_8*	-0.754	-0.768	-1.000
ψ_7	0.754	0.768	1.000
$\psi_{6,5}$	1.000	1.000	1.000
ψ_4	1.054	1.039	1.000
ψ_3	1.436	1.335	1.200
ψ_2	2.020	2.012	2.000
ψ_1	2.083	2.050	2.000

	Planar Stilbene	Hindered Stilbene	Isolated Chromophores[a]
$\mathscr{E}^{e,b}$	18.694	18.412	18.400
$\Delta\nu^{a,b}$	1.508	1.537	2.000
$RE^{e,b,a}$	0.294	0.012	0
TM^f	0.899	0.842	...
$p_{\alpha1}^{Gg}$	1.244	1.212	1.000
$p_{\alpha1}^E$	1.48	1.462	1.000
$p_{\alpha\alpha'}^G$	2.000	2.000	2.000
$p_{\alpha\alpha'}^E$	1.680	1.640	1.000

[a] Referred to two benzene rings and an ethylene molecule.
[b] In units of β_{CC} in the ring.
[c] The total π-electron energy.
[d] The energy of the $V \leftarrow N$ transition.
[e] The resonance energy.
[f] The transition moment, in arbitrary units.
[g] The bond order; J. Jacobs and C. A. Coulson, J. Chem. Soc., 1983 (1949), give somewhat different bond orders. The superscript G refers to the ground state, E to the excited state; the subscript identifies the bond.

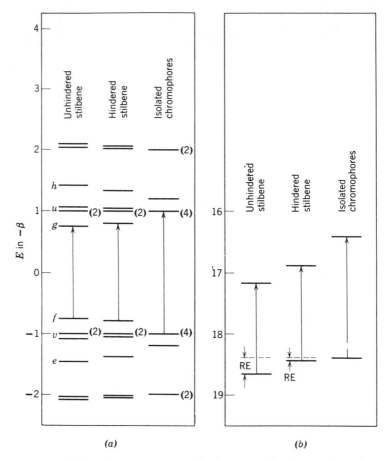

Fig. 15.13 (a) One-electron energy and (b) term-level diagrams for stilbenes. The numbers in parentheses indicate degeneracy. [Reprinted by permission from H. H. Jaffé and M. Orchin, *J. Chem. Soc.*, 1078 (1960).]

indicates the decrease in stability in the hindered stilbene, as shown in the term diagram, Fig. 15.13*b*. In both parts of Fig. 15.13, the column at the far right represents the completely twisted stilbene in which the chromophores are isolated. It is assumed for the sake of simplicity that the α,α' bond is not twisted at all, although this is probably not quite true.

Oscillator strengths or transition moments have also been estimated (Table 15.11) for the unhindered and hindered stilbenes, using the β's shown in the table. These moments are for the $\psi_7 \rightarrow \psi_8^*$ ($f \rightarrow g$) promotion, which is assumed to be responsible for the $^1B \leftarrow {}^1A$ transition. The graphical representation of these two orbitals is shown in Fig. 15.14 for planar stilbene. The transition moment is calculated from the amplitude of the wave functions according to the usual procedure (cf. section 6.4). The calculations for hindered stilbene are in agreement with the observed hypochromic effect.

The spectrum of *cis*-stilbene (Fig. 15.11) differs considerably from that of the *trans* isomer. The long-wavelength band is a structureless, broad band occurring at considerably shorter wavelength than the corresponding band in the *trans* isomer. The shorter-wavelength (B) band, presumably polarized perpendicular to the long axis, is a much more intense band in the *cis* isomer and occurs at shorter wavelength than the corresponding band in *trans*-stilbene. The difference in spectra between the two isomers is due, at least in part, to the nonplanarity of the *cis* form. It is

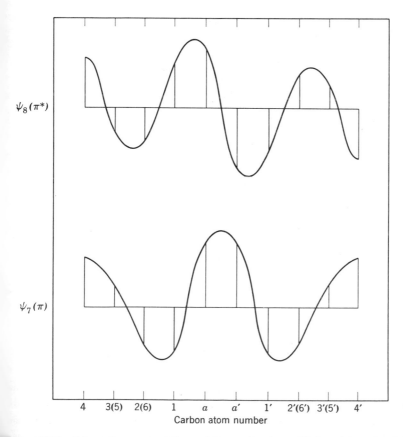

Fig. 15.14 Schematic representation of the molecular orbitals $\psi_7(\pi)$ and $\psi_8(\pi^*)$ of stilbene. [Reprinted by permission from H. H. Jaffé and M. Orchin, *J. Chem. Soc.*, 1078 (1960).]

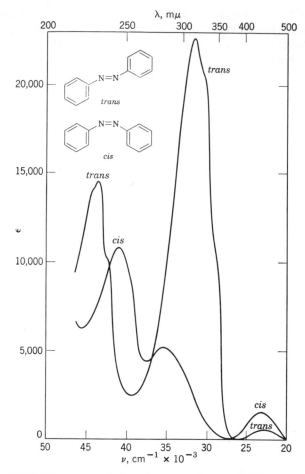

Fig. 15.15 The spectra of *cis*- and *trans*-azobenzene in 95 per cent ethanol.

of interest to note that the spectra of 2,4,6-trimethyl- and 2,4,6,2′,4′,6′-hexamethyl-*trans*-stilbene are quite similar to the spectrum of *cis*-stilbene (Fig. 15.11).

It should also be pointed out that in *cis*-stilbene the length of the chromophore along the long axis of the molecule is less than in the *trans* isomer, and hence the longest-wavelength, lengthwise-polarized absorption should be less intense, as it is. The width of the chromophore, however, is greater in the *cis* isomer, and hence the shorter-wavelength, perpendicularly polarized band should be more intense. Because of the difference in symmetry between the two isomers, it is difficult to relate corresponding states, and the associated transitions and hence correlation of the spectra are not attempted. The relations between the spectra of *trans-* and *cis*-stilbene are almost exactly repeated in the *trans* and *cis* forms of azobenzene (Fig. 15.15) and azoxybenzene (Fig. 15.16).

Suzuki has applied the treatment described in connection with the spectrum of biphenyl and its derivatives, section 15.31, to the problem of the stilbenes.[49] The values of ΔE_A, the transition energy for the long-wavelength band, is calculated from equation (15.5), where ΔE_L, 1.1423β, refers to the long-wavelength reference model when $\theta = 0°$, ν_L is the frequency of the long-wavelength maximum of *trans*-stilbene (34,002 cm^{-1} or 294.1 mμ), ΔE_S is 2β, and the corresponding value of the frequency, ν_S, is assumed to be 48,000 cm^{-1} (208 mμ), the center of gravity of singlets of benzene. The method is then applied to *cis* stilbene. The results are

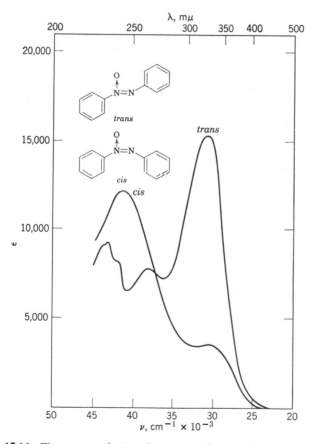

Fig. 15.16   The spectra of *cis-* and *trans*-azoxybenzene in 95 per cent ethanol.

[49] H. Suzuki, *Bull. Chem. Soc. Japan*, **33**, 379 (1960).

summarized in Table 15.12; the value of 28° for the interplanar angles in *cis*-stilbene is in good agreement with the value of 25° estimated from the scale model.[50] Suzuki estimates that the difference in resonance energy between the two isomers is about 3.5 kcal/mole, in good agreement with the experimental value of the energy difference between the isomers of 3 kcal/mole, estimated from the equilibrium of the thermal isomerization.[51]

TABLE 15.12

Calculated Properties of the Stilbenes[49]

Stilbene	λ_A, mμ	ν_A, cm^{-1}	ΔE_A, β	μ	θ, deg	$R_{\alpha,1}$, A	RE, $-\beta$	$p_{\alpha,1}$	$p_{\alpha,\alpha'}$
trans-	294.1	34002	1.142	0.908	0	1.445	0.704	1.384	1.855
cis-	280	35714	1.247	0.787	28	1.456	0.530	1.333	1.890

The spectra of a series of α-alkyl and α,α'-dialkyl derivatives of *cis*- and *trans*-stilbene have been determined,[52] and the following generalizations deduced: (1) with increasing number and size of substituents in *cis*- and *trans*-stilbene the long-wavelength band undergoes both increasing hypso- chromic and hypochromic shifts; (2) the longest-wavelength band of the *trans* isomer is usually more intense than that of the corresponding *cis* isomer; (3) the long-wavelength band of the α-methyl derivative occurs at longer wavelength in the *trans* than in the *cis* compound, but the reverse is true with α,α'-dimethyl- and α,α'-diethylstilbenes; (4) all the hindered *trans*-stilbenes lose the vibrational structure characteristic of the long-wavelength band of the parent. The data and results of calculations for these compounds are shown in Table 15.13. The calculated interplanar angle θ becomes larger with the increasing size and number of substituents. The fact that *cis*-α,α'-dimethylstilbene absorbs at longer wavelength than the *trans* isomer appears to indicate that there is less conjugation in the *trans* isomer, and the calculated interplanar angle is consistent with this view. The spectra of 4,4'α,α'-*cis*- and *trans*-tetramethylstilbene have also been analyzed, [53] the *cis* isomer absorbs at longer wavelength and θ has been calculated as 51.7°, compared to 54.3° for the corresponding *trans* isomer. A series of 2-substituted *cis*- and *trans*-stilbenes with identical substituents has been reported,[54] but no detailed analysis of these data has been made.

[50] H. Suzuki, *Bull. Chem. Soc. Japan*, **25**, 145 (1952).

[51] G. B. Kistiakowsky and W. R. Smith, *J. Am. Chem. Soc.*, **56**, 638 (1934); T. W. J. Taylor and A. R. Murray, *J. Chem. Soc.*, 2078 (1938). It is probable that the equilibrium concentration of the *trans* isomer is greater than has been reported.

[52] H. Suzuki, *Bull. Chem. Soc. Japan*, **33**, 396 (1960).

[53] H. Suzuki, *Bull. Chem. Soc. Japan*, **33**, 406 (1960).

[54] D. F. DeTar and L. Carpino, *J. Am. Chem. Soc.*, **78**, 475 (1956).

The spectra of α-cyanostilbene and some of its derivatives with and without 2-substituents have been reported and used to calculate angles of twist.[54a] The results are consistent with the above generalizations. Some pairs of 4,4'-disubstituted *cis*- and *trans*-stilbenes have also been examined,[54b] and careful MO calculations have confirmed that rotation about the a-1 bond should be most effective in relieving strain in *cis*-stilbenes.

TABLE 15.13

Calculated Properties of α-Substituted Stilbenes

Stilbene	Solvent[a]	λ_A, mμ	ΔE_A, β	μ	θ, deg	$R_{1,\alpha}$, A	RE, β
trans-α-Methyl-	H	273.5	1.299	0.730	34.5	1.462	0.457
cis-α-Methyl-	E	267	1.354	0.671	40	1.467	0.387
trans-α,α'-Dimethyl-	H	243.3	1.577	0.446	58	1.490	0.173
cis-α,α'-Dimethyl-	H	252.0	1.490	0.531	51.5	1.481	0.243
trans-α-Methyl-α'-ethyl-	E	240	1.612	0.412	60.5	1.493	0.146
trans-α,α'-Diethyl-	H	236.6	1.649	0.378	63	1.497	0.124
cis-α,α'-Diethyl-	E	244	1.570	0.453	57.5	1.489	0.178
trans-α,α'-Dichloro-	H	268.0	1.345	0.680	39	1.467	0.397
trans-α,α'-Dibromo-	H	248.5	1.525	0.497	54.5	1.485	0.212
trans-α,α'-Diiodo-	H	220.5	1.838	0.200	75.7	1.517	0.034

[a] H = heptane; E = ethanol.

The spectra of triphenylethylene (or α-phenylstilbene) and tetraphenylethylene are compared[55] with the spectrum of *trans*-stilbene in Fig. 15.17. Unlike the parent compound, the phenylstilbene spectra show no vibrational structure in the long-wavelength band. Comparison of the long-wavelength, structureless bands in this series shows a progressive bathochromic shift with increase in the number of phenyl groups (for the purpose of this comparison the highest-intensity component of the stilbene band is chosen). The $^1G \leftarrow {}^1A$ (or B) band is similarly shifted. On the other hand, ϵ_{max} of the long-wavelength band decreases with increasing number of phenyls, while the intensity of the two shorter-wavelength bands increases. The increased intensity of these short-wavelength bands is probably associated with the greater number of phenyl groups, since the

[54a] A. Bruylants, G. Leroy, and M. Van Meerssche, *Bull. soc. chim. Belges*, **69**, 5 (1960).

[54b] W. H. Leerhoven, R. J. F. Nivard, and E. Havinga, *Rec. trav. chim.*, **79**, 1153 (1960); G. Riezebos and E. Havinga, *ibid.*, **80**, 446 (1961).

[55] (a) H. Suzuki, *Bull. Chem. Soc. Japan*, **33**, 389 (1960). (b) See also R. N. Jones, *J. Am. Chem. Soc.*, **65**, 1818 (1943).

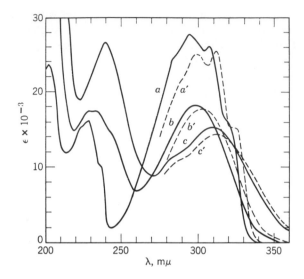

Fig. 15.17   The spectra of (*a*) *trans*-stilbene and (*b*) tri- and (*c*) tetraphenylethylene in heptane and (primed) in benzene. [Reprinted by permission from H. Suzuki, *Bull. Chem. Soc. Japan*, **33**, 379 (1960).]

transitions probably involve the degenerate benzene orbitals and there are a greater number in the more highly phenylated derivatives. Suzuki concludes, from his analysis of the spectra, that in triphenyl- and tetraphenylethylene each of the rings is rotated along its 1,4 axis, rather than having an intact *trans*-stilbene structure with only one (or two) of the rings twisted completely out of the plane.

Other diarylethylenes have been studied with interesting results, but essentially the same effects are to be expected. Recent extensive MO calculations will facilitate such studies.[56]

15.5   Nonalternant Compounds

All the compounds discussed previously in this chapter belong to the class called alternants, i.e., these compounds do not possess any odd-membered conjugated rings. Biphenyl and stilbene, for example, are alternant hydrocarbons; compounds like the anilines and acetophenones are alternants and can be treated as perturbed alternant hydrocarbons or as ions derived from the hydrocarbons. For alternant hydrocarbons, the bond order of every essential double bond decreases and of every essential single bond increases when an electron is excited from the highest occupied

---

[56] G. Drefahl and G. Rasch, *Z. phys. Chem.*, **213**, 352 (1960).

to the lowest unoccupied orbital. This rule depends upon the correspondence or complementary character of the bonding and antibonding orbitals of the alternants.[57] Thus, the highest occupied orbital of an alternant with energy of $\alpha + k\beta$ is matched by the lowest unoccupied orbital of energy $\alpha - k\beta$. The change in bond order on excitation of essential single and double bonds is generally similar for perturbed alternant hydrocarbons and thus may be considered valid for all alternants. It was shown earlier in this chapter that, if steric strain is introduced into a molecule containing two chromophores joined by an essential single bond, relief of strain is usually achieved by twisting around this bond. Since the bond order of this essential single bond increases on excitation, the excitation of the nonplanar ground-state molecule to the excited state requires more energy than is required in the nonhindered molecule, and hence the observed hypsochromic shift.

The Coulson-Rushbrooke theorem does not apply to nonalternant molecules, i.e., those molecules containing odd-membered conjugated rings (fulvene, azulene, etc.). Steric strain in such molecules does not produce the predictable and uniform results observed with alternants. In particular, in some compounds the bond order of an essential single bond in the ground state decreases on excitation. If steric strain in such a molecule is relieved by twisting around this essential single bond, then the sterically hindered molecule will show a bathochromic effect relative to the unhindered molecule. Such compounds have been prepared, and their spectra do indeed show bathochromic shifts. An excellent example has been reported in the azulene series by Heilbronner and Gerdil.[58]

1-Acetylazulene probably has structure XV, in which the carbonyl

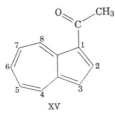

XV

group is pointed toward the seven-membered ring, since scale models show that the alternate conformation would lead to interference between the methyl group and the hydrogen at the 8 position. The long-wavelength band in the spectrum of this compound results from the $^1L_b \leftarrow {}^1A$

[57] The Coulson-Rushbrooke theorem: C. A. Coulson and G. S. Rushbrooke, *Proc. Cambridge Phil. Soc.*, **36**, 193 (1940); C. A. Coulson and H. C. Longuet-Higgins, *Proc. Roy. Soc.* (*London*), **A191**, 39 (1947).

[58] E. Heilbronner and R. Gerdil, *Helv. Chim. Acta*, **39**, 1996 (1956).

TABLE 15.14

Spectra of Some Azulenes in Cyclohexane

(λ_{max} of $^1L_b \leftarrow {}^1A$ Band)

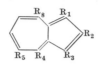

If no substituent is indicated, hydrogen is understood.

Compound No.	R_1	R_2	R_3	R_5	R_8	λ_{max}, mμ	ϵ_{max}
(1)	Ac	...	...	...	...	546	440
(2)	Ac	Me	Me	...	...	577	436
(3)	Ac	Me	...	...	...	548	322
(4)	Ac	...	Me	i-Pr	Me	584	481
(5)	Bz	...	Me	i-Pr	Me	586	478
(6)	Ac	...	Ac	...	...	516	574
(7)	Ac	Me	Ac	...	...	526	433
(8)	...	...	...	...	...	580	329
(9)	...	...	Me	...	...	608	294
(10)	...	Me	...	...	...	566	325
(11)	...	...	Me	i-Pr	Me	605	425

TABLE 15.15

Spectral Effect of Acetyl Groups at Various Positions in
Azulene[a]

Azulene	Ketone	$\Delta\lambda$, mμ	$\Delta\epsilon_{max}$
(8)	(1)	-34	111
(9)	(2)	-31	142
(10)	(3)	-18	62
(11)	(4)	-21	56
(11)	(5)	-19	53
(8)	(6)	$-64 = 2 \cdot -32$	$245 = 2 \cdot 123$
(10)	(7)	$-40 = 2 \cdot -20$	$173 = 2 \cdot 87$

[a] Compound numbers refer to corresponding numbers in Table 15.14.

transition. This band has considerable vibrational structure showing about six vibrational subbands. The subbands with the largest ϵ of 1-acetyl-azulene and some related compounds are indicated in Table 15.14.[58] It should be recalled (section 13.9) that alkyl substitution in azulene can produce either a bathochromic or a hypsochromic shift of the visible $^1L_b \leftarrow {}^1A$ band, depending upon the position of substitution. Accordingly, in evaluating the steric effect of acetyl groups in various alkylated azulenes, any acylated alkylazulene should be compared to the parent alkylazulene; such comparisons[58] are shown in Table 15.15. These data indicate that,

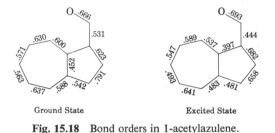

Ground State   Excited State

Fig. 15.18   Bond orders in 1-acetylazulene.

with increasing steric hindrance to the conjugation between the acetyl (or benzoyl) group and the ring, there is an increasing bathochromic shift. Thus, for example, the introduction of an acetyl group in the 3 position of 1-methylazulene [compounds (9) and (2) of Table 15.14] results in a shift of -31 mμ, whereas the introduction of an acetyl group in the 1 position of 2-methylazulene, where considerable steric overlap occurs, results [compounds (10) and (3)] in a shift of only -18 mμ; hence the introduction of strain has resulted in a net bathochromic shift. It should be noted, however, that there is the usual decrease in intensity with increasing hindrance. The bond orders of the ground and excited states of 1-acetylazulene are shown in Fig. 15.18.

15.6 Interacting Nonconjugated Chromophores

The discussion in this chapter has been concerned almost exclusively with conjugated chromophores and the spectral effects of restrictions to the interaction of these chromophores. This section will be concerned with chromophores which are not conjugated but which, by virtue of their arrangement in space, do interact with each other, in either the ground or the excited state or both. Such interaction results in spectral effects which correspond neither to the simple addition of the spectra of the two insulated chromophores, nor to the spectra of the completely conjugated system.

15.61 TRANSANNULAR NITROGEN-CARBONYL INTERACTIONS.   If a nitrogen atom possessing a lone pair of electrons is located in a molecule at a position suitable for interaction with a carbonyl group in the same molecule, nitrogen-carbonyl interaction may occur as follows:

$$R—N: \quad C=O \longleftrightarrow R—N^{+\delta}—C—O^{-\delta}$$

The interaction may consist of the generation of a true $— \overset{+}{\underset{|}{>N}}—\overset{|}{\underset{|}{C}}—$ bond;

in this case, the interaction is best described as a "reaction" between the amino and the carbonyl groups. On the other hand, the interaction may result from only a partial orbital overlap of the lone pair on nitrogen with the pπ electrons of the carbonyl group. Actually, no definite dividing line between interaction and reaction can be drawn. In compounds which, on treatment with a strong acid such as perchloric, form the conjugate acid, $R—\overset{+}{N}—C—OH$, the N—C bond is probably largely preformed, even in neutral solution.

The correlation between ring size and nitrogen-carbonyl interaction has been extensively studied by Leonard and coworkers,[59] both in the series of aza acyloins, such as XVI, and amino ketones, such as XVII. The

XVI   XVII

interaction apparently occurs for eight-, nine-, and ten-membered rings in which a five- or six-membered ring (i.e., a [3.3.1], [3.4.1], or [4.4.1] bicyclo system) is created within the larger ring. In other words, the tertiary nitrogen atom and the carbonyl group common to one ring must be separated by at least three carbon atoms. The degree of interaction is most effectively deduced from the infrared spectra, although some ultraviolet-spectra correlations have been made.[60] The spectrum of the carbocyclic ketone, cyclononanone, has the n → π^* band at 264 mμ (log ϵ = 2.13), but 1-methyl-1-azacyclononan-5-ol-6-one (XVI, R = Me, $n = m = 3$) has a band at 228 mμ (log ϵ = 3.77) and only weak absorption at 264 mμ. The band at 228 mμ is due to some type of nitrogen-carbonyl interaction, the nature of which has not been determined; almost

[59] N. J. Leonard, *Record Chem. Progr.*, **17**, 243 (1956).
[60] N. J. Leonard and M. Oki, *J. Am. Chem. Soc.*, **77**, 6241 (1955).

certainly, however, the n electrons on nitrogen are involved. The new band is possibly a charge-transfer band resulting from promotion of an occupied MO involving the lone-pair nitrogen and the $p\pi$ electrons of the carbonyl group into a π^* level. The spectra of the compound with structure XVII (R = Me, $n = m = 3$) also shows a band at 225 mμ (log $\epsilon = 3.80$) and again only a weak band at 264 mμ.

If the carbonyl group is not part of the ring containing a nitrogen atom, interesting possibilities of interaction exist.[61] The benzoylpiperidine, XVIII, has essentially the spectrum expected, with a strong band at about 242 mμ ($\epsilon = 10,300$ in methylene chloride) and the carbonyl band at 352 mμ ($\epsilon = 252$). However, the bicyclic compound XIX, in which the piperidine

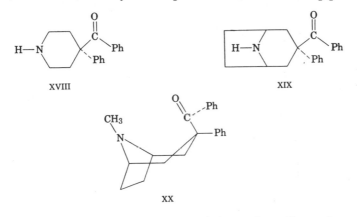

XVIII   XIX

XX

ring is part of a bicyclic system, has general absorption of lower intensity in the 240–250 mμ region with no definite maximum; when the solvent is changed from methylene chloride to methanol, the intensity is appreciably lowered. It has been proposed that compound XIX exists in a boat conformation XX, with resultant nitrogen-carbonyl interaction. The spectrum of the hydrochloride of XVIII is very similar to that of the free base and completely different from that of the hydrochloride of XIX, which shows only weak general absorption in the whole ultraviolet range, with none of the characteristics of the benzoyl group. The spectrum of the secondary amine analogous to XX, where CH$_3$ is replaced by H, is completely different from that of XX, indicating complete nitrogen carbonyl interaction with the development of an almost complete σ N-C bond. The large solvent effect on the spectrum of XX probably results from the stabilization of the dipolar species $-\overset{+}{\text{N}}-\text{C}-\text{O}^-$ in the polar, hydrogen-bonding solvent.

[61] M. R. Bell and S. Archer, *J. Am. Chem. Soc.*, **82**, 151 (1960).

15.62 TRANSANNULAR DOUBLE BOND–CARBONYL INTERACTIONS. Although the infrared spectrum of 5-cyclodecen-1-one, XXI, shows no abnormality, the ultraviolet spectrum of this compound is vastly different from that expected on the basis of noninteracting chromophores.[62a] Furthermore, there is a striking difference between solvent effect in the spectrum of XXI and in the spectra of the model compounds, cyclodecanone, XXII, and *trans*-cyclodecene, XXIII, which might be considered to be the component parts of XXI. Scale models show that the $\begin{smallmatrix} \diagdown & & \diagup \\ & C{=}C & \\ \diagup & & \diagdown \end{smallmatrix}$

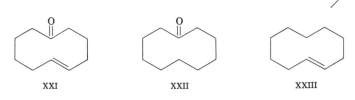

XXI   XXII   XXIII

and $>C{=}O$ chromophores can readily approach each other in parallel planes. The simple ketone, XXII, has the $n \to \pi^*$ band at 288 mμ ($\epsilon = 16$) in cyclohexane. The corresponding $n \to \pi^*$ band in the unsaturated ketone, XXI, occurs at 302 mμ ($\epsilon = 73$). The $n \to \pi^*$ band of the simple ketone gave the expected blue shift of 5 mμ on changing from cyclohexane to ethanol as solvent, but the solvent change had no effect on the 302 mμ band in XXI. No explanation has been advanced for this lack of solvent effect.[62b] If the 302 mμ band is indeed the $n \to \pi^*$ transition (and there is no reason to doubt it), either the ground and excited states are raised exactly the same amount by the change from cyclohexane to ethanol, or neither state is affected at all. Perhaps the folded structure makes the lone-pair electrons inaccessible to solvent, and thus solvation in the polar solvent is hindered. The bathochromic shift of the $n \to \pi^*$ band relative to a cyclic α,β-unsaturated ketone conceivably could be due to interactions of a $p\pi$ orbital on the olefinic carbon atoms with the n level of the oxygen in the carbonyl with resultant raising of the n level, but this has not been established.

An even more unusual aspect of the spectrum of the enone, XXI, is a band at 260 mμ ($\epsilon = 423$ in cyclohexane). A monosubstituted α,β-unsaturated ketone would be expected to absorb at about 227 mμ

[62] (*a*) N. J. Leonard and F. H. Owens, *J. Am. Chem. Soc.*, **80**, 6039 (1958). (*b*) For the use of solvent effects to identify transannular interactions see E. M. Kosower, W. D. Closson, H. L. Goering, and J. C. Gross, *J. Am. Chem. Soc.*, **83**, 2013 (1961). (*c*) The appearance of moderately intense bands in the 230 mμ region of the spectra of 1,4-enones in boat cyclohexane derivatives has been ascribed to charge-transfer $\pi_0 \to \pi_0^*$ transitions: S. Winstein, L. de Vries, and R. Orloski, *J. Am. Chem. Soc.*, **83**, 2021 (1961); R. C. Cookson, R. R. Hill, and J. Hudec, *Chem. Ind.*, 589 (1961).

(log $\epsilon > 3$). Obviously the band at 260 mμ in XXI is not analogous to the $V \leftarrow N$ transition in a conjugated ketone. The infrared spectrum and the dipole moment of XXI indicate little if any interaction between the olefinic and carbonyl groups in the ground state. Leonard and Owens[62] suggested that the interaction occurs principally in the excited state. The low intensity and wavelength of the band also suggest the possibility of a weak charge-transfer band[62c] as a result of the incipient formation of a transannular bond with polarization which may be represented as $\overset{+}{—C}—C—C—O^-$. Such interaction has also been suggested[63] for dehydro-norcamphor, XXIV, and for some cyclic dienones,[64,65] all of which show anomalous spectral effects.

15.63 TRANSANNULAR DOUBLE BOND–DOUBLE BOND INTERACTIONS. The spectrum of the bicycloheptadiene, XXV, in ethanol has weak peaks at

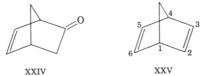

XXIV   XXV

205 mμ ($\epsilon = 2100$), 214 mμ ($\epsilon = 1480$), and 220 mμ ($\epsilon = 870$), and a shoulder at 230 mμ ($\epsilon = 200$). The vapor spectrum shows considerable vibrational structure with at least seventeen sharp bands, the strongest absorption occurring at 211 mμ. This system has been treated theoreti-cally,[66] using three of the common semiempirical wave-mechanical methods, the simple LCAO model, and two more refined models which included electron-repulsion and configuration-interaction terms.

The calculations show that the delocalization or resonance energy of the ground state of the bicycloheptadiene is exactly zero. There are no contributions from bonding interactions between the double bonds.

The conclusion that the ground state of this compound involves no resonance energy may be demonstrated, at least in the first approximation, in the following way. The compound may be treated as a modified cyclobutadiene, in which resonance integrals between atom pairs 1 and 2, 1 and 3, and 1 and 4, and between corresponding pairs, are all considered, but are different. Compound XXVI belongs to point group D_{2h}, and hence the π molecular orbitals $\psi = c_1\phi_1 + c_2\phi_2 + c_3\phi_3 + c_4\phi_4$ belong to the species b_{1u} ($c_1 = c_2 = c_3 = c_4$), b_{2g} ($c_1 = c_2 = -c_3 = -c_4$), b_{3g} ($c_1 = -c_2 = -c_3 = c_4$), and a_u ($c_1 = -c_2 = c_3 = -c_4$). Only one equation is needed to evaluate the energies,

$$-c_1\varepsilon + c_2\beta_{12} + c_3\beta_{13} + c_4\beta_{14} = 0$$

[63] P. D. Bartlett and B. E. Tate, *J. Am. Chem. Soc.*, **78**, 2473 (1956).

[64] J. Meinwald, S. L. Emerman, N. C. Yang, and G. Buchi, *J. Am. Chem. Soc.*, **77**, 4402 (1955).

[65] C. H. DePuy and P. R. Story, *J. Am. Chem. Soc*, **82**, 627 (1960).

[66] C. F. Wilcox, S. Winstein, and W. G. McMillan, *J. Am. Chem. Soc.*, **82**, 5450 (1960).

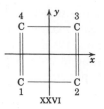

and the other secular equations are equivalent to this one. Substituting the relations between the various c's yields

$$\varepsilon(b_{1u}) = \beta_{14} + \beta_{12} + \beta_{13}$$

$$\varepsilon(b_{2g}) = \beta_{14} - \beta_{12} - \beta_{13}$$

$$\varepsilon(b_{3g}) = -\beta_{14} + \beta_{12} - \beta_{13}$$

$$\varepsilon(a_{u}) = -\beta_{14} - \beta_{12} + \beta_{13}$$

Since $\beta_{14} > \beta_{12} > \beta_{13}$ in absolute value (though each is a negative quantity), the energies decrease in the order given. These energy levels are represented schematically in Fig. 15.19. In the ground state, two electrons are assigned to b_{1u} and two to b_{2g}, and the total energy is $2(\beta_{14} + \beta_{12} + \beta_{13}) + 2(\beta_{14} - \beta_{12} - \beta_{13}) = 4\beta_{14}$, which is equal to the energy of two isolated double bonds and indicates no resonance energy. The first excited state belongs to the configuration $b_{1u}{}^2 b_{2g} b_{3g}$ and is a B_{1g} state. The energy of this configuration is $2(\beta_{14} + \beta_{12} + \beta_{13}) + (\beta_{14} - \beta_{12} - \beta_{13}) + (-\beta_{14} + \beta_{12} - \beta_{13}) = 2(\beta_{14} + \beta_{12})$. The energy of a singly excited system of two double bonds is $2\beta_{14}$, and hence the B_{1g} state has a resonance energy of $2\beta_{12}$. The transition $^1B_{1g} \leftarrow {}^1A_g$, however, is forbidden by the $g \nleftrightarrow g$ rule. The difference is pointed out by the inequality in length of the arrows shown in Fig. 15.19. It must be recognized, however, that this treatment neglects all interaction between the "π" electrons and the "σ" electrons of the single bond skeleton, even though separation of electrons into these two types cannot be made on the basis of symmetry.

This result is not dependent on inclusion of β_{13}, which is commonly neglected in MO theory, since examination of the equations shows that none of the conclusions is changed when β_{13} is equated to zero. In cyclobutadiene itself, $\beta_{12} = \beta_{14}$, but even in this case,

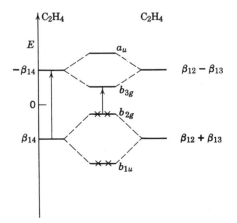

Fig. 15.19 The energy levels of a distorted cyclobutadiene.

according to the present approximation of MO theory, no resonance energy results in the ground state. It is interesting to note that this is one case in which MO and VB theory give different results, since the latter leads to considerable resonance energy.

The diene, XXV, belongs to point group C_{2v}. The lowest-energy wave function belongs to species a_1; the next lowest, also occupied, belongs to species b_1. The lowest unoccupied orbital belongs to species b_2, and the highest unoccupied orbital to species a_2. The lowest energy band involving excitation from b_1 to b_2 is forbidden, since the total change in π-electron symmetry is a_2, i.e., $b_1 \times b_2 = A_2$. The next higher-energy transition involving promotion from b_1 to a_2 orbitals is allowed. Calculations for the energy of transition for the forbidden band using the refined models gave a value of 5.78 ev or 214 mμ, as compared to the observed value of 211 mμ. The excited state may be represented by structure XXVII, in

XXVII

which, from the refined calculations, the bond order between atoms 2 and 3 is 1.50 and that between 2 and 6 is 0.12.

15.64 INTERACTION OF NONCONJUGATED AROMATIC RINGS. One of the earliest suggestions regarding the possibility of interacting nonconjugated aromatic rings arose in connection with the examination of the ultraviolet absorption spectrum of triptycene,[67] XXVIII [9,10-(*o*-phenylene)-9,10-

XXVIII   XXIX

dihydroanthracene]. The spectrum somewhat resembles that of triphenyl-methane with both bathochromic and hyperchromic shifts. The bridgehead hydrogen cannot readily participate in hyperconjugation, but the rings are suitably situated for aromatic π overlap, which, in VB notation, may be represented by structure XXIX, one of 108 possible equivalent structures.

An interesting example of transannular interaction of nonconjugated aromatic rings is found in the series of cyclophanes, XXX, prepared and studied by Cram and coworkers. The ultraviolet spectra[68] of a series of

[67] P. D. Bartlett and E. S. Lewis, *J. Am. Chem. Soc.*, **72**, 1005 (1950).

[68] (a) D. J. Cram, N. L. Allinger, and H. Steinberg, *J. Am. Chem. Soc.*, **76**, 6132 (1954). (b) D. J. Cram and H. Steinberg, *J. Am. Chem. Soc.*, **73**, 5691 (1951). (c) K. C. Dewhirst and D. J. Cram, *J. Am. Chem. Soc.*, **80**, 3115 (1958). (d) D. J. Cram and K. C. Dewhirst, *J. Am. Chem. Soc.*, **81**, 5963 (1959).

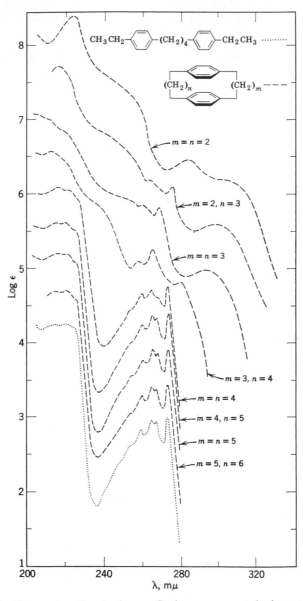

Fig. 15.20 The spectra of cyclophanes. Each curve, except the lowest one, has been displaced upward by a 0.5 log ε unit increment from the one immediately below it. [Reprinted by permission from D. J. Cram, N. L. Allinger, and H. Steinberg, *J. Am. Chem. Soc.*, **76**, 6132 (1954).]

these compounds are shown in Fig. 15.20. It is apparent from these curves that cyclophanes with four or more methylene groups, XXX ($n = m \geq 4$),

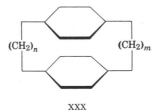

XXX

have spectra almost identical with that of the open-chain analog; p-EtC$_6$H$_4$(CH$_2$)$_4$C$_6$H$_4$Et-p. However, there is a sharp discontinuity with a smaller number of methylene groups. The short-wavelength band around 215 mμ undergoes a bathochromic and a hypochromic effect, and the

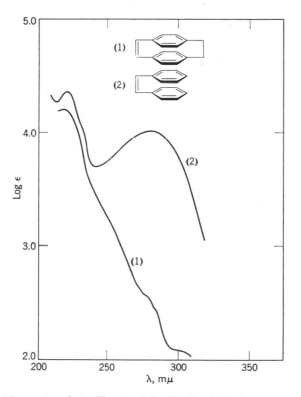

Fig. 15.21   The spectra of *cis*-stilbene and the dihydro derivative of XXXI. [Reprinted by permission from K. C. Dewhirst and D. J. Cram, *J. Am. Chem. Soc.*, **80**, 3115 (1958).]

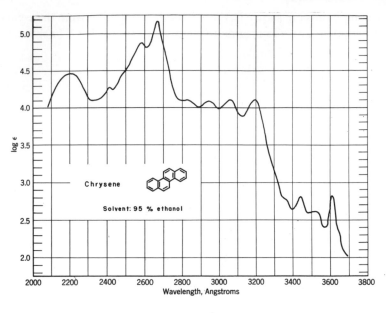

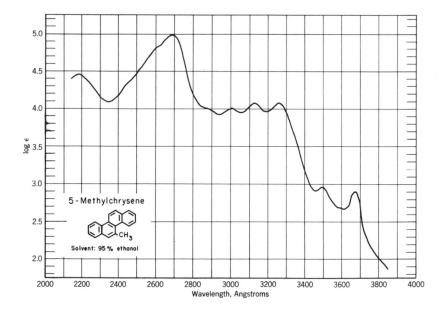

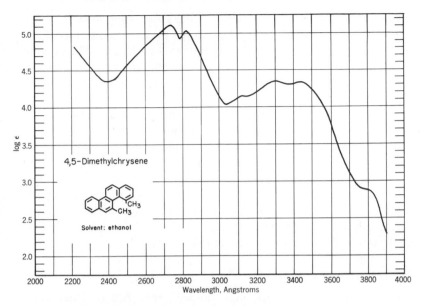

Fig. 15.22   The effect of ring strain on the ultraviolet spectrum of chrysenes. (Reprinted by permission from R, A. Friedel and M. Orchin, *Ultraviolet Spectra of Aromatic Compounds*, John Wiley and Sons, New York, 1951.]

long wavelength band around 270 mμ undergoes similar shifts accompanied by loss of the vibrational structure. The spectral effects arise from a combination of trans-annular interactions and nonplanarity of the rings.

The brilliant synthetic work in this series has been extended[68c] to cyclophanes in which the two benzene rings are joined in the *para* positions by ethylenic linkages, XXXI. This may be considered as an extreme

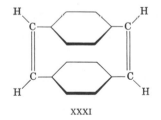

XXXI

example of steric inhibition of resonance in a classically conjugated hydrocarbon, since the benzene rings and the ethylenic linkages must be at right angles to each other. The spectrum of XXXI is very similar to that shown by the dihydro derivative of XXXI, in which one of the ethylenic linkages is saturated. The spectrum of the latter compound,[68c] compared with that of cis-stilbene in Fig. 15.21, shows the expected results of further hindering conjugation in an already hindered molecule. The cyclophane studies have been extended[68d] to molecules containing more than two linked benzene rings and to compounds containing multiple olefinic bonds between rings.

Theoretical calculations have been made[69] in the cyclophane, di-p-xylylene, XXX ($n = m = 2$). The LCAO model indicated no stabilization of the ground state with respect to two completely separated benzene rings. The situation is similar to that discussed earlier for two double bonds in the cyclobutadiene model. Again as a first approximation, the combination of the two benzene rings gives energy levels in both states, equally spaced above and below the levels of the isolated benzene rings. The long-wavelength shift is then to be expected on the same basis as that described for the interacting nonconjugated double bonds.

15.7   Overcrowded Molecules

X-ray diffraction analysis has shown[70] that benzo[c]phenanthrene, XXXII, is nonplanar, presumably because of overlap of hydrogen atoms. Substitution of methyl groups at the 1 and 12 positions increases out of

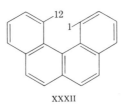

XXXII

plane distortion. This type of intramolecular crowding actually leads to molecular dissymmetry and optical activity, as has been demonstrated by resolution of some simple 4,5-dimethylphenanthrene derivatives.[71] It may be anticipated that the ultraviolet spectra of aromatic compounds subject to such intramolecular overcrowding differ considerably from those of analogous compounds free of such interference.

There has been no theoretical treatment of the ultraviolet spectra of overcrowded molecules. Unquestionably the entire aromatic nucleus is

---

[69] L. L. Ingraham, *J. Chem. Phys.*, **18**, 988 (1950), and also in *Steric Effects in Organic Chemistry*, edited by M. S. Newman, John Wiley and Sons, New York, 1956, p. 498.

[70] F. H. Herbstein and G. M. J. Schmidt, *J. Chem. Soc.*, 3302 (1954).

[71] M. S. Newman and A. S. Hussey, *J. Am. Chem. Soc.*, **62**, 3023 (1947); also M. S. Newman, *Steric Effects in Organic Chemistry*, John Wiley and Sons, New York, 1956, p. 476.

distorted in these cases. Usually the spectroscopic result of such distortion consists of loss of vibrational structure, bathochromic shifts, and, frequently, increased intensities. A typical example[72] is shown in Fig. 15.22, in which the spectra of chrysene, 5-methylchrysene, and 4,5-dimethyl-chrysene are shown.

[72] R. A. Friedel, *Appl. Spectroscopy*, **2**, 13 (1956).

GENERAL REFERENCE

G. W. Gray (ed.), *Steric Effects in Conjugated Systems*, Butterworth, London, 1958.

16 Organic ions and free radicals

16.1 Tri- and Tetra-atomic Radicals

The previous chapters have dealt with the spectroscopic properties of a wide variety of stable organic molecules. In recent years considerable information with regard to certain quite unstable species has become available. This chapter will deal with some of these, the organic free radicals and ions.

Emission spectra of quite a large number of *diatomic* radicals have been known for some time. Thus spectra of the radicals OH, NH, CH, C_2, and CN can be observed in the light emitted in flames, explosions, and electric discharges. The same spectra are also observed as absorption spectra in high-temperature gases. Identification of the emitting or absorbing species is not easily made; however, since they are observed as gases, the spectra are band spectra, and it is often possible to observe the individual vibrational bands and sometimes the separate rotational lines within these bands. Vibrational and rotational analysis, coupled with information of the source of the spectra, often has permitted an unequivocal assignment of the species responsible for the spectra. The spectra of these diatomic radicals, which are of little chemical interest, will not be discussed further.[1]

Emission spectra of more complicated, polyatomic radicals have also been observed in similar experiments. However, the chemical nature of the mixture appearing in flames and discharges, for instance, is so complex and so little understood that rarely had such spectra been interpreted successfully until the advent of new techniques, which permitted observation of absorption spectra under more readily controlled conditions. These methods have included production of reasonable concentrations of the species by flash photolysis (i.e., by light pulses of very high intensity and short duration) and the techniques of trapping the radicals at low temperatures in solid matrices, often frozen rare gases.

---

[1] The reader is referred to the excellent book of G. Herzberg, *Spectra of Diatomic Molecules*, D. Van Nostrand and Co., Princeton, N.J., 1950. Herzberg treats the theory and reviews the literature on these compounds.

One of the first species to be observed[2] by such techniques was NH_2. This radical is now known to absorb over the entire visible range, 400–830 mμ in the vapor phase,[2a] or 340–790 mμ in a matrix of frozen argon, or dissolved in liquid helium.[2b] Vibrational analyses of the spectra have been made, and lead to the conclusion that the ground state is nonlinear, with an HNH angle of about 103°, whereas the excited state is linear. The spectrum is ascribed[3] to the $^2\Pi_u \leftarrow {}^2B_1$ transition,[4] where the ground state is believed to have the configuration $(K\,a_1{}^2b_2{}^2a_1{}^2b_1)\,{}^2B_1$, and the excited state $(K\,a_1{}^2b_2{}^2a_1b_1{}^2)\,{}^2\Pi_u$; results of theoretical calculations are in reasonable agreement with the observed spectrum.

The results discussed in the preceding paragraph serve to illustrate some of the reasons for the tremendous importance of the measurements of such spectra. Although chemists have long postulated the existence of such free radicals, and have written mechanisms invoking them as intermediates, the evidence for their existence has been indirect. Their direct spectroscopic observation and the consequent determination of some of their physical properties have placed all chemical argument based on such radicals on a much sounder basis. In addition, the spectroscopic method is, to date, the only one capable of giving important information concerning their geometry (through rotational constants) and force constants (through vibrational analysis), and such data are of tremendous importance in problems in chemical kinetics and reaction mechanisms.

Closely related to NH_2 is PH_2, which absorbs in the range 360–550 mμ.[5] From the decrease of absorption intensity with time it has been estimated that PH_2 has a half-life of the order of 50 μsec at 5 mm Hg pressure. The spectrum of PD_2, except for vibrational structure, is similar to that of PH_2.

Other triatomic radicals with a single unpaired electron which have been identified are HCO and DCO, which absorb at 479–756 mμ and 462–739 mμ, respectively.[6] The ground state is nonlinear, the excited state linear, and the transition is $^2\Sigma^+ \leftarrow {}^2A''$. NCO, produced by flash photolysis of HNCO or C_2H_5NCO, has two regions of absorption, 360–450 mμ and

[2] (a) G. Herzberg and D. A. Ramsay, *Discussions Faraday Soc.*, **14**, 11 (1953); D. A. Ramsay, *J. Phys. Chem.*, **57**, 415 (1953); *J. Chem. Phys.*, **25**, 188 (1956). (b) G. W. Robinson and M. McCarty, Jr., *J. Chem. Phys.*, **30**, 999 (1959). (c) K. Dressler and D. A. Ramsay, *Proc. Roy. Soc.* (*London*), **A251**, 69 (1959).

[3] J. Higuchi, *J. Chem. Phys.*, **22**, 1467 (1954).

[4] The symmetry symbols used here are those applicable to the point groups of the ground and excited states, C_{2v} and $D_{\infty h}$, respectively. In describing the configuration of the excited state, however, the orbitals are given in terms of the symmetry species of the ground state to facilitate comparison.

[5] D. A. Ramsay, *Nature*, **178**, 374 (1956).

[6] G. Herzberg and D. A. Ramsay, *Proc. Roy. Soc.* (*London*), **A233** (1955).

262–316 mμ, assigned,[7] respectively, to $^2\Sigma \leftarrow {}^2\Pi$ and $^2\Pi \leftarrow {}^2\Pi$. In NCS, only the $^2\Pi \leftarrow {}^2\Pi$ transition is observed, at 335–400 mμ.

A particularly interesting species from the chemical point of view is CF_2, since it is the prototype of the carbene intermediates, CR_2, believed to be involved in many chemical reactions. Its absorption spectrum extends from 234 to 266 mμ.[8] It is a linear molecule, and the ground state appears to be a triplet, so that CF_2 may be described as a diradical. The decay of the absorption indicates a half-life of the order of 1 sec. In emission, CF_2 covers the range from 234 to 500 mμ.[8,9] Vibrational analysis[10] of the spectrum showed prominent appearance of the bending frequency, which indicates that the FCF angle changes drastically during excitation. The stretching frequencies were not observed in the spectra, strongly indicating that the bond lengths are almost identical in the ground and excited states.

Methylene, CH_2, also finally has been observed,[11] after an intensive search extending over many years. When diazomethane, H_2CN_2, is photolyzed by flash photolysis, the products show absorption in the 1400 A region, with the main band at 1414.5 A. In the products from D_2CN_2 the band occurs at 1415.8 A, and in partially deuterated diazomethane *one* additional band appears at 1415.5 A. These findings indicate that the spectrum is due to a molecule containing two hydrogen atoms, presumably CH_2. Rotational and vibrational analysis of the bands indicates that CH_2 is either linear or bent with an HCH angle not less than 140°. The lower state of the spectrum is probably $^3\Sigma_g^-$, which is consistent with the predicted ground state for CH_2. The lifetime of CH_2 is estimated as 15 μsec. If this information is correct, the lifetime of CH_2 is about 1/100,000 that of CF_2.

One of the most important free radicals from the chemical point of view is undoubtedly the methyl free radical, CH_3. This radical and its homologs have been postulated as intermediates in a tremendous number and variety of chemical reactions. Its existence was demonstrated[12] rather conclusively in 1929, but observation of its spectrum by Herzberg and Shoosmith[13] in 1956 was a tremendously important achievement.

As a culmination of a long search for a spectrum ascribable to the methyl radical, a series of bands was observed in the vacuum ultraviolet, between 130 and 151 mμ, following the flash photolysis of dimethyl

[7] R. Holland, D. W. G. Style, R. N. Dixon, and D. A. Ramsay, *Nature*, **182**, 336 (1958).

[8] R. K. Laird, E. B. Andrews, and R. F. Barrow, *Trans. Faraday Soc.*, **46**, 803 (1950).

[9] P. Venkateswarlu, *Phys. Rev.*, **77**, 676 (1950).

[10] D. E. Mann and B. A. Thrush, *J. Chem. Phys.*, **33**, 1732 (1960).

[11] G. Herzberg and J. Shoosmith, *Nature*, **183**, 1801 (1959).

[12] F. Paneth and W. Hofeditz, *Ber.*, **62B**, 1335 (1929).

[13] G. Herzberg and J. Shoosmith, *Can. J. Phys.*, **34**, 523 (1956).

mercury and its perdeuterated derivative.[13] The bands disappeared after about 250 μsec, indicating that the species was very short lived. Once the spectrum of the methyl radical had been observed, conditions of production of the radical were varied until maximum concentrations were obtained. Under such optimum conditions, bands were also observed at 216 mμ in $Hg(CH_3)_2$ and at 214 mμ in $Hg(CD_3)_2$. Similar bands were observed in the photolysis of acetaldehyde, diazomethane, acetone, methyl iodide, and methyl bromide. Since all these compounds are believed to yield methyl radicals upon photolysis, identification of these spectra as belonging to this radical seems convincing. All these bands appear to belong to a Rydberg series, and in agreement with this assignment the frequencies are given by the formula

$$\nu = I - R/(n - 0.077)^2$$

where I is 79,380 cm^{-1} (9.840 $\pm$ 0.002 ev) for CH_3 and 79,305 cm^{-1} (9.832 ev) for CD_3, and identified with the ionization potential of these radicals. These values are in excellent agreement with ionization potentials obtained from electron-impact measurements of about 9.9 ev. All the bands are broad, and devoid of vibrational structure, presumably because of predissociation, and hence are unable to provide detailed information about the structure of the radical. The absence of strong bands at longer wavelength is consistent with the MO prediction that the radical is planar, or nearly so, because then the longer-wavelength bands are forbidden. However, ability to detect the radical increases the hope of finding conditions under which sufficient concentrations are present to observe the forbidden transition. This transition, which is expected near 260 mμ, should not involve predissociation and hence should permit vibrational and possible rotational analysis, and, accordingly, determination of the structure. Photolysis of acetone containing 25, 50, and 75 per cent deuterium, respectively, leads to observation of *two* additional bands between 214 and 216 mμ, presumably due to the radicals CH_2D and CHD_2, thus further confirming the assignment of the spectrum to the methyl radical.

16.2   Aromatic Radicals and Ions

The simplest aromatic ions are the nonalternants, cyclopentadienyl anion, $C_5H_5^-$, and tropylium cation, $C_7H_7^+$, both of which possess the aromatic sextet of pπ electrons and are iso-π-electronic with benzene (see section 12.1). The tropylium ion has a spectrum with λ_{max} at 275 mμ (ϵ = 4400). The yellow color is due to a long tailing rather than to a sharp discrete band.[14] The spectrum of a substituted cyclopentadienide ion,

[14] W. von E. Doering and L. H. Knox, *J. Am. Chem. Soc.*, **76**, 3204 (1954).

1-methyl-2,3,4,5-tetracarbomethoxycyclopentadienide, which is stable in water, has been reported[15] to have bands at 270 mμ (ϵ = 34,100) and 308 mμ (ϵ = 13,570).

The concept of radical and ion intermediates has been one of the most fruitful developments in organic chemistry. The methyl radical, the methyl cation, and the methyl anion have all been postulated as intermediates in many chemical reactions occurring in solution. Because of the short-lived nature of these intermediates, however, their existence *in solution* has not been unequivocally demonstrated.

It has been reported, however, that the spectra of a variety of substituted methyl cations and alicyclic carbonium ions have been observed.[16] Thus, a solution of any of the butyl alcohols, isobutylene, or *tert*-butyl halides in 98 per cent sulfuric acid gives rise to essentially the same spectrum, showing a band at about 292 mμ, ϵ = $\sim$6000.[17] The absorbing species has been presumed to be the *tert*-butylcarbonium ion, $(CH_3)_3C^+$. Furthermore, solution of either 1-methylcyclohexanol or methylcyclohexane in sulfuric acid gives essentially identical spectra, with a band again at 293 mμ, ϵ = $\sim$5000. However, the sulfuric acid solution of the hydrocarbon is claimed to contain 1 mole of SO_2, presumably generated by the oxidation of the hydrocarbon to the carbonium ion:

$$-\overset{|}{\underset{|}{C}}-H + 4H_2SO_4 \rightarrow -\overset{|}{\underset{|}{C}}{}^+ + SO_2 + 2H_3{}^+O + 2HSO_4{}^-$$

Contrary to this work, strong evidence has been advanced[17] to indicate that the species absorbing at about 293 mμ is probably not a simple saturated carbonium ion but is, rather, the butenyl (or isobutenyl) cation, $[CH_2{=\!\!=}CH{=\!\!=}CH—CH_3]^+$. By adsorbing 1-butene on a silica alumina catalyst and examining the catalyst specimen in both the ultraviolet and the infrared regions, Leftin[17] has shown that the species giving rise to the band at about 300 mμ has C-H stretching frequencies with intensities consistent with the presence of one CH_3, one CH_2, and two CH groups; these are just the numbers and kinds of groups present in the butenyl cation. Furthermore, solution of the saturated hydrocarbon, *n*-hexane, in 98 per cent H_2SO_4 was shown to generate 2 moles of SO_2 per mole of hexane, and the solution gives a spectrum with the 300 mμ band. These

[15] R. C. Cookson, J. Hudee, and B. Whitear, *Proc. Roy. Soc.*, 117 (1961).

[16] J. Rosenbaum and M. C. R. Symons, *J. Mol. Phys.*, **3**, 205 (1960).

[17] (a) H. P. Leftin in a private communication suggests that the high extinction coefficient may be due to contributions from the cyclohexyl ion generated from the cyclohexane solutions used in the experiments. (b) Private correspondence with H. P. Leftin.

facts are consistent with the generation of a substituted allyl cation:

$$R—CH_2CH_2CH_3 \xrightarrow{[O]} R—CH_2\overset{+}{C}HCH_3 \rightleftarrows R—CH_2—CH{=}CH_2 \xrightarrow{[O]}$$

$$[R—CH{\cdots}CH{\cdots}CH_2]^+$$

A 300 mμ band has also been observed in the spectrum of the ion obtained by dissolving 1-octene in sulfuric acid, but simultaneous oxidation of the hydrocarbon was inferred, since the solution contained SO_2.[18] The butenyl cation, developed from a variety of precursors by solution in 98 per cent sulfuric acid,[19] gives rise to a band at 290 mμ, $\epsilon = \sim 3000$. It appears likely that the band at 290–300 mμ represents a substituted allyl and not a saturated hydrocarbon cation, although the problem cannot be considered as completely resolved. The possible assignment of the 300 mμ band to the *tert*-butylcarbonium ion is further rendered unlikely[13] by comparison with the isoelectronic compound, trimethylboron $(CH_3)_3B$, which absorbs at about 220 mμ.

The nomenclature of carbonium ions presents certain difficulties, and no uniformity exists in the literature. One system consists of naming these ions on a derived basis analogous to the carbinol nomenclature. According to this scheme, CH_3^+ is carbonium ion, $CH_3CH_2^+$ is methylcarbonium ion, Ph_3C^+ is triphenylcarbonium ion, etc. An alternate naming system consists of employing the systematic group or radical name and adding the word "cation," e.g., the above species are methyl cation, ethyl cation, triphenylmethyl cation, respectively. A third system involves the use of common names where applicable, thus Ph_3C^+, Ph_2CH^+ and $PhC^+(CH_3)_2$ may be called trityl, benzhydryl, and cumyl cations, respectively. The possibly most popular nomenclature, methyl carbonium ion (in three separate words) for CH_3^+, is not systematic, leads to ambiguities, and hence should be avoided.

The probable existence and spectra of the cations of this series have been discussed in the preceding paragraphs. There is a tremendous body of experimental evidence to show the presence of relatively stable carbonium ions and radicals and, to a lesser extent, carbanions. In the systems

$$—C^+, \quad —C\cdot, \quad \text{and} \quad —C{:}^-,$$

the carbon atom has a largely unhybridized p orbital which can form π molecular orbitals with pπ orbitals of unsaturated systems. Such systems are resonance stabilized and hence are reasonably stable. The replacement of hydrogen in methyl by a vinyl group to give the allyl species leads to some such stabilization, by hyperconjugation.

[18] J. Gonzales-Vidal, E. Kohn, and F. A. Matsen, *J. Chem. Phys.*, **25**, 181 (1956).

[19] J. Rosenbaum and M. C. R. Symons, *J. Chem. Soc.*, **1**, (1961). In this article, the spectrum of Me$_3$B previously reported by these authors [*Proc. Chem. Soc.*, **92** (1959)] was redetermined in the absence of air and the 260 mμ ($\epsilon = 6000$) band corrected to 220–230 mμ, thus confirming the results of A. G. Davies, D. G. Hare, and L. F. Larkworthy, *Chem. Ind.*, 1519 (1959).

Replacement of hydrogen in methyl by one, two, or three phenyl groups leads to the increasingly stable $PhCH_2$, Ph_2CH, and Ph_3C cations, radicals, and anions.

The benzyl, diphenyl-, and triphenylmethyl radicals and ions are odd alternant hydrocarbons. A theoretical treatment[20] of these species has led to certain important predictions regarding their ultraviolet spectra. In accordance with the starring procedure described previously, the benzyl species may be represented as I, having $2m - 1$ conjugated atoms of which m are "starred" and $m - 1$ "unstarred," each starred atom being linked *only* to unstarred atoms and vice versa. In any odd alternant

I

hydrocarbon there exists at least one nonbonding orbital, which receives contributions only from the starred atoms. The remaining orbitals in the system occur in pairs, with energies symmetrically distributed above and below this nonbonding orbital. The nonbonding orbital is vacant in the cation, singly occupied in the radical, and doubly occupied in the anion. In the first approximation[21] the lowest excited configurations of the cation, radical, and anion lie above their ground states by an equal amount, as shown in Fig. 16.1. These configurations represent a singlet and a triplet level for the two ions and two doublets for the radical. In addition, the radical has an excited quartet state and two further doublets, arising out of the configuration *efg*, in which an electron is raised from the lowest to the highest of the three orbitals shown in Fig. 16.1. This treatment neglects electron interaction, due to which the two lower doublet levels are split,[22] and this splitting has been treated for both even alternant[23] and odd alternant[20] radicals and ions.

Singly charged, odd alternant ions generally have closed-shell ground states, and it is to be expected that there are strong similarities between the cation and the anion. The excitation energy to the lowest excited singlet and triplet states should be the same for corresponding positive and negative ions.[20] However, the energy levels for the radical are different from those of the charged species. The doublet levels are split by an amount roughly equal to the singlet-triplet separation in the ions; the

[20] H. C. Longuet-Higgins and J. A. Pople, *Proc. Phys. Soc.*, **68**, 591 (1955).
[21] H. C. Longuet-Higgins, *J. Chem. Phys.*, **18**, 265 (1950).
[22] M. J. S. Dewar and H. C. Longuet-Higgins, *Proc. Phys. Soc.*, **67**, 795 (1954).
[23] J. A. Pople, *Proc. Phys. Soc.*, **68**, 81 (1955).

center of gravity of the two doublets of the radical lies generally higher than the center of gravity of the singlet and triplet of the ions. On the basis of simple orbital theory, the quartet of the radical of configuration *efg* is expected to lie twice as high as the degenerate doublets, but more refined calculations show that its excitation energy will be less than twice that of the *lower* doublet; the higher of the doublets should lie *above* the quartet. The absorption spectrum of the radical should contain two long-wavelength bands which arise jointly from excitation of electrons into and out of the singly occupied orbital, $e \rightarrow f$ and $f \rightarrow g$, and, in addition, possibly the weak doublet-quartet band. The spectrum of the ions should contain the one strong, long-wavelength band due to the singlet-singlet transition. The calculated[20] excitation energies for the

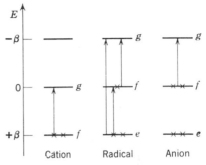

Fig. 16.1 Electronic energy levels and possible excitations in odd alternants.

allyl and benzyl species are given in Table 16.1. Moffitt[24] has also calculated the spectrum of the allyl radical with approximately the same results; both calculations predict the singlet-singlet transition at about 250 mμ.

Diphenylmethyl and triphenylmethyl cations, Ph_2CH^+ and Ph_3C^+, are readily obtained by dissolving the respective carbinols in 100 per cent sulfuric acid. With triphenylcarbinol, the reaction has been shown[25] to

TABLE 16.1

Calculated Excitation Energies of Odd Alternants[20]

(Energies in electron volts)

Group	Ion		Radical			
	State: Triplet	Singlet	Doublets			Quartet
			First (weak)	Second (strong)	Third	
Allyl	2.39	4.94	2.74	5.29	7.74	4.51
Benzyl	1.96	2.68	3.46	4.18	6.23	3.97

[24] W. Moffitt, *Proc. Roy. Soc.* (*London*), 218, 486 (1953).

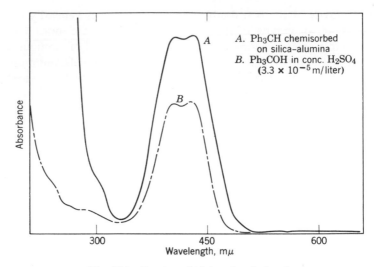

Fig. 16.2 Spectra of triphenylmethyl cation.

proceed as follows:

$$Ph_3COH + 2H_2SO_4 \rightarrow Ph_3C^+ + 2HSO_4^- + H_3O^-$$

A great many substituted benzhydrols and triphenylcarbinols have been converted to the corresponding carbonium ions by this simple procedure, the spectra of such solutions have been intensively investigated, and the ions have been well characterized.

The diphenylmethyl cation has a sharp, strong band at 442 mμ (ϵ = 53,000) and a weak band at 300 mμ (ϵ = 3000). The triphenylcarbonium ion gives a spectrum with a double band at 409 mμ and 428 mμ with ϵ of 38,000 at each maximum.[26]

It is of interest to note that the ion Ph_2CH^+ absorbs at longer wavelength than Ph_3C^+. This is almost certainly due to steric strain in the Ph_3C^+; the three phenyl groups cannot possibly lie in the same plane and very likely each phenyl group is partially twisted out of plane. The Ph_2CH^+ can be more nearly planar, and hence the bathochromic and hyperchromic shift noted in the spectrum. Substitution of alkyl groups in the *ortho* positions of benzhydrol and triphenylcarbinol brings about the results expected from steric inhibition to planarity[25a] discussed in Chapter 15.

Triphenylcarbonium ion can also be generated from the hydrocarbon,

[25] (a) M. S. Newman and N. C. Deno, *J. Am. Chem. Soc.*, **73**, 3644 (1951); (b) L. P. Hammett and A. Deyrup, *J. Am. Chem. Soc.*, **55**, 1900 (1933).

[26] G. Branch and H. Walba, *J. Am. Chem. Soc.*, **76**, 1564 (1954); A. Hantzsch, *Z. physik. Chem.*, **61**, 257 (1908).

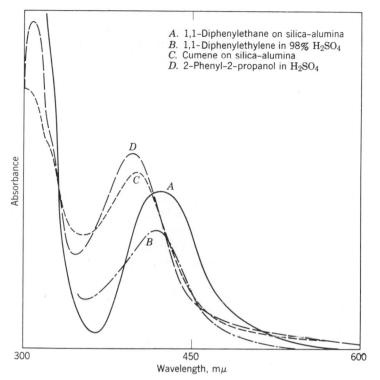

Fig. 16.3 Spectra of methyldiphenylmethyl and cumyl cations.

triphenylmethane,[27] by adsorbing triphenylmethane at 50° on a thin slice
of a silica-alumina cracking catalyst. The spectrum of this sample is
compared with that of triphenylcarbinol in concentrated sulfuric acid in
Fig. 16.2, where the two are seen to be almost identical. These spectra
show conclusively that Ph_3C^+ is formed on the catalyst surface and strongly
suggests that the silica-alumina functions as a Lewis acid and is able to
rupture the C-H bond of a tertiary carbon atom. Further demonstration
that silica-alumina produces surface carbonium ions was obtained by a
comparison of the spectrum of 2-phenyl-2-propanol in concentrated
sulfuric acid with that obtained by adsorbing cumene (isopropylbenzene)
on silica-alumina; these spectra are shown in Fig. 16.3 and are also almost
identical.

Carbonium ions can be formed not only from saturated compounds
such as tertiary carbinols, halides, and hydrocarbons, but also from
olefins. Thus, for example, 1,1-diphenylethylene is readily protonated by

[27] H. P. Leftin, *J. Phys. Chem.*, **64**, 1714 (1960).

concentrated sulfuric acid, and such a solution gives a strong band at 423 mμ ($\epsilon = 30,000$), which is certainly due to the methyldiphenyl-carbonium ion, $Ph_2C^+CH_3$.[28] The same ion (Fig. 16.3) has been obtained by adsorbing 1,1-diphenylethane on silica-alumina.[29]

The most general method of generating carbonium ions from aromatic hydrocarbons takes advantage of their basic properties and consists of protonation with strong acids:

$$Ar + H^+ \rightleftharpoons ArH^+$$

The acids most frequently used for bringing out this base or acceptor property of aromatic hydrocarbons are sulfuric and hydrofluoric. Equilibrium studies in the methylated benzene series with HF showed equilibrium constants varying from 10^{-8} for the least basic compound, benzene, to 10^{-2} for the most basic one, hexamethylbenzene.[30] The protonated species ArH^+ may be considered as an intermediate in electrophilic attack on the aromatic nucleus by a proton. Analogous attack by electrophilic reagents, E (e.g., NO_2^+, Br^+, and R^+), leads to analogous cations, ArE^+, so that the properties of such ions are of considerable general interest.

Extensive calculations have been carried out[31] for the species $C_6H_7^+$, resulting from proton addition to benzene. This cation has been called the benzenium ion, and its structure may be represented by II:

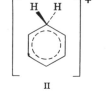

II

The six carbon atoms form a ring in a plane which also contains five of the hydrogen atoms; the other two hydrogens are located symmetrically in front of and behind this plane so that the ion has C_{2v} symmetry. Strong hyperconjugation is assumed to exist between the CH_2 group and the four π electrons of the ring, and the ion is treated as if it had six π electrons in orbitals made by combining the six $p\pi$ atomic orbitals of the ring carbons

[28] V. Gold and F. L. Tye, *J. Chem. Soc.*, 2172 (1952).

[29] H. P. Leftin and W. K. Hall, *Paper* 65, Second International Congress on Catalysis, Paris, July, 1960. The NMR spectrum of the ion has been reported by D. E. O'Reilly and H. P. Leftin, *J. Phys. Chem.*, **64**, 1555 (1960).

[30] M. Kilpatrick and F. E. Luborsky, *J. Am. Chem. Soc.*, **75**, 577 (1953).

[31] N. Muller, L. W. Pickett, and R. S. Mulliken, *J. Am. Chem. Soc.*, **76**, 4770 (1954).

and a quasi-π orbital on the H_2 atoms of the $\diagdown$C$=$H$_2$ group. The seven AO's give seven MO's, the energies of which are shown schematically in Fig. 16.4; the orbitals belong to the symmetry species indicated.

The two lowest energy excitations consist of the promotions: $1a_2 \rightarrow 3b_1$ and $2b_1 \rightarrow 3b_1$. The first of these transitions is polarized parallel to the symmetry axis, and the latter perpendicular to it and to the plane of the ring. The calculations[31] indicate excitation energies leading to wavelengths of 600 mμ and 430 mμ for the two transitions. These wavelengths correspond to the center of gravity of corresponding singlets and triplets. Assuming a reasonable value (2.0 ev) for the singlet-triplet separation, the predicted values of the two singlet transitions are 400 mμ and 320 mμ, respectively. The intensities of these transitions have also been calculated,[31] and the results indicate that the 320 mμ band should be about twice as intense as the longer-wavelength band. The experimental[30] spectrum of benzene dissolved in HF-BF$_3$ shows a long-wavelength band at 420 mμ and a short-wavelength

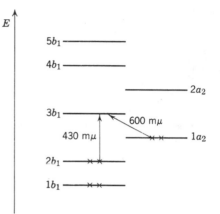

Fig. 16.4   The energies and symmetry species of the molecular orbitals of benzenium ion, $C_6H_7{}^+$.

band about twice as intense somewhat below 300 mμ, in good agreement with the calculations.

Spectra of a series of aromatic hydrocarbons were determined in the same solvent system (HF-BF$_3$).[32] Toluene, mesitylene, hexaethylbenzene, naphthalene, and anthracene all gave ions with very similar spectra and with a long-wavelength band at about 400 mμ. Phenanthrene, naphthacene, pyrene, and fluoranthene gave ions with spectra which showed the long-wavelength band at around 480–500 mμ. There appears to be no obvious relationship between the structure of the parent molecule and the position of the absorption maximum in the spectrum of the carbonium ion formed by solution of the hydrocarbon in HF-BF$_3$. It has been suggested that, in the group of ions having the 400 mμ band, the charge of the carbonium ion is delocalized over only one ring, whereas in ions with the 480–500 mμ band delocalization occurs over more than one ring. The close resemblance between the spectra of acid solutions of benzene and of

[32] C. Reid, J. Am. Chem. Soc., 76, 3264 (1954).

anthracene can be explained on this basis. The anthracenium ion very likely has structure III:

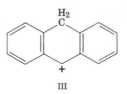

III

It is assumed that the probability of the positive charge migrating into the terminal rings is low, and that the positive charge is largely confined to the middle ring.

The spectra of radicals and anions have not been investigated nearly as extensively as those of cations because of the greater experimental difficulties in preparing stable solutions. The spectrum of triphenylmethyl radical[33] shows a band at about 340 mμ which is at somewhat shorter wavelength than in the corresponding cation. A similar hypsochromic shift has been calculated for the benzyl radical relative to the carbonium ion (Table 16.1). The spectrum of triphenylmethyl anion has been reported[33] and shows absorption in the same range as the corresponding cation, but no detailed analysis of the spectrum has been made.

16.3 Radical Ions and Polyvalent Ions

When a tetrahydrofuran solution of an aromatic hydrocarbon such as naphthalene or anthracene is treated with sodium, 1 mole of sodium is consumed per mole of hydrocarbon with the formation of a deeply colored solution. The species responsible for these colors are unquestionably radical anions, for the solutions show paramagnetic resonance absorption as well as electrical conductivity. The spectra of the resulting solutions have been determined.[34] At relatively short wavelengths in the ultraviolet, the absorption bands of the radical anion are similar to those of the parent hydrocarbon. However, additional long-wavelength bands appear. These facts may be rationalized by reference to Fig. 16.5. The odd electron occupies the first vacant hydrocarbon orbital (g), and the high-energy transitions of the hydrocarbon are still possible in the radical, while excitation of the odd electron can give rise to new low-energy transitions.

When lithium, sodium, potassium, or calcium reacts with an excess of 1,1-diphenylethylene in tetrahydrofuran,[35] a dark blue solution results,

[33] L. C. Anderson, *J. Am. Chem. Soc.*, **57**, 1673 (1935).
[34] D. E. Paul, D. Lipkin, and S. I. Weissman, *J. Am. Chem. Soc.*, **78**, 116 (1956).
[35] H. P. Leftin and W. K. Hall, *J. Phys. Chem.*, **64**, 382 (1960).

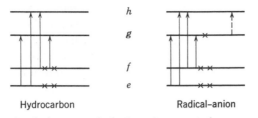

Fig. 16.5   Energy levels in aromatic hydrocarbons and the corresponding radical anions.

which has an intense band near 600 mμ. The metal presumably transfers an electron to the olefinic substrate in a manner analogous to electron transfer from the same metals to aromatic hydrocarbons. The species produced is presumably the radical anion: [Ph$_2$C—CH$_2$]$^{\cdot-}$.

A similar visible band at about 600 mμ can be observed in another radical ion formed from 1,1-diphenylethylene. Solutions of this compound in concentrated sulfuric acid show λ_{max} at 423 mμ ($\epsilon = 31,000$), as expected for the methyldiphenylcarbonium ion. However, in weakly acidic media an additional, intense band at 600 mμ ($\epsilon \geq 20,000$) appears. Rather convincing evidence has been advanced[35] to show that this band is due to a radical ion, produced by oxidation of (or electron removal from) the hydrocarbon. Kinetic studies were performed on a solution of 1,1-diphenylethylene in a solvent system composed of sulfuric acid diluted with acetic and monochloracetic acids. The formation of the 600 mμ absorbing species involved an induction period, autocatalysis, and a competing decomposition process. Most significantly, the rate of formation of the radical ion could be increased over 100-fold by addition of trace amounts of an oxidizing agent such as selenic acid, H$_2$SeO$_4$, persulfuric acid, H$_2$S$_2$O$_8$, or potassium ferricyanide, K$_3$Fe(CN)$_6$. Although the structure for the absorbing species has not been established, it is at present best formulated as a radical-cation, [Ph$_2$—C—CH$_2$].$^{\cdot+}$ When 1,1-diphenylethylene is absorbed on a silica-alumina cracking catalyst and the ultraviolet absorption spectrum of the catalyst is examined, bands at 423 mμ and 600 mμ are again observed.[35] These bands obviously correspond to the carbonium ion and radical-cation observed in the acid-solution spectrum. The oxidation on the surface of the catalyst is not understood; conceivably an electron is transferred to an electron-deficient (Lewis acid) acceptor site of the silica-alumina. As has been pointed out earlier, negative and positive ions of the same odd alternant hydrocarbon should show similar ultraviolet spectra. This expectation is realized in the similar spectra of the positive and negative radical ions of 1,1-diphenylethylene.

Perhaps the best-known[36] examples of organic radical ions are the so-called Wurster's salts, which are univalent oxidation products of aromatic p-diamines, a simple example of which is the radical ion, IV, derived from the one-electron oxidation of p-phenylenediamine. These salts may be prepared by the oxidation of the diamine by a very small

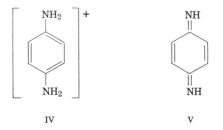

IV   V

amount of bromine and have appreciable half-life (in some suitably substituted derivatives, as long as 7 days) in methanol solutions of pH about 3. Further oxidation of the Wurster's salts leads to loss of hydrogen and formation of the diimine, V. The formation, stability, and absorption spectra of some of these salts have been described[36b], and the absorption spectra have been calculated theoretically.[37]

The radical ion derived from p-phenylenediamine has nine $p\pi$ electrons, six from the carbon atoms, and three from the two nitrogen atoms. These nine electrons are accommodated in the five lowest MO's formed by the linear combination of the two nitrogen atoms and the three lowest orbitals of the benzene ring. The lowest unoccupied orbital corresponds to the lowest unoccupied orbital of benzene. The molecule belongs to point group D_{2h}; the ground state of the radical ion belongs to species B_{3g}, and the lowest excited state to B_{1u}, and hence the transition $^2B_{1u} \leftarrow {}^2B_{3g}$, the long-wavelength transition, is allowed. The calculations predict absorption at 407 mμ for the ion in the gas phase. The observed spectrum of the radical ion, $[p\text{-}NH_2C_6H_4\dot{N}H_2]^+$, has a strong band in the visible region with two peaks, one at 462 mμ ($\epsilon = 7200$) and the other at 479 mμ ($\epsilon = 6500$). The rather short distance between the two peaks and the existence of a carbon vibration in benzene of the correct symmetry and frequency indicate that the peaks result from vibrational structure of a single electronic transition.

Successive substitution of methyl for the hydrogens in nitrogen results in bathochromic and hyperchromic shifts. In the tetramethyl derivative, $[p\text{-}Me_2NC_6H_4\dot{N}Me_2]^+$, the two peaks occur at 560 mμ ($\epsilon = 11,500$) and 610 mμ ($\epsilon = 11,000$).

[36] (a) R. Willstatter and J. Piccard, Ber., **41**, 1458 (1908). (b) L. Michaelis, M. P. Schubert, and S. Granick, J. Am. Chem. Soc., **61**, 1981 (1939).
[37] M. G. Mayer and K. J. McCallum, Revs. Modern Phys., **14**, 248 (1942).

The first polyvalent carbonium ion which has been demonstrated conclusively is VI, prepared by dissolving trichloromethylpentamethyl-benzene, VII, in 100 per cent sulfuric acid.[38] The spectrum of the solution

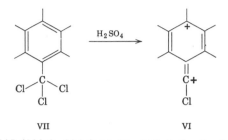

has maxima at 545 (1031), 394 (16,160), 382 (inflection), 265 (3860), and 235 mμ (5120), with the ϵ values given in parentheses. No theoretical analysis of this spectrum has been attempted.

Dicarbanions have been demonstrated to be present in solution. When a solution of stilbene in tetrahydrofuran is treated with 1 mole of sodium, a dark green color due to [PhCH=CHPh]⁻ is observed. Addition of another mole of sodium changes this color to deep red,[39] and it has been postulated that this color is due to a divalent carbanion [PhCHCHPh]²⁻. Addition of an excess of stilbene to the red solution reverses the color to the deep green of the monocarbanion. Similar behavior is noted with tri- and tetraphenylethylene and tetraphenylbutadiene.[35] Treatment of 1,1-diphenylethylene with potassium produces a red solution of the dianion which gives a spectrum[40] with a band at 500 mμ.

[38] H. Hart and R. W. Fish, *J. Am. Chem. Soc.*, **80**, 5894 (1958).

[39] A. G. Brook, H. L. Cohen, and G. F. Wright, *J. Org. Chem.*, **18**, 447 (1953). For a summary of such reactions see G. E. Coates, *Organo-metallic Compounds*, Methuen and Co., 1956, pp. 15 f.

[40] G. J. Hoijtink and P. H. van der Meij, *Z. Phys. Chem.*, **20**, 1 (1959).

17 Spectra of sulfur and phosphorus compounds; the expansion of the valence shell

Previous chapters have been concerned primarily with the spectra of conjugated systems of carbon atoms and other first-row elements, and consequently, the discussion has been restricted to consideration of s and p electrons. In this and the following chapter, the effect of d electrons will be investigated.

In transition metals the shell with principal quantum number one less than the s and p valence electron shell, the penultimate d electron shell, is only partially filled, and these d electrons and orbitals are involved in chemical and spectroscopic phenomena. The problems involved will be discussed in the next chapter.

In the elements on the right of the periodic system, in all rows but the first, but particularly for silicon, phosphorus, and sulfur in the second row, the d orbitals with quantum number equal to the valence shell s, and p orbitals, although unoccupied in the free atoms, are energetically not too far above the valence shell and hence may be of considerable chemical interest. Since G. N. Lewis proposed the octet rule and defined the valence shell as a shell capable of accommodating an octet of electrons (i.e., a shell made up of one s and three p orbitals), involvement of d orbitals has often been referred to as expansion of the valence shell.

Expansion of the valence shell may be involved in the formation of single (σ) bonds or multiple bonds. The use of d orbitals in σ bonds, such as must occur in PCl_5 and SF_6, has been discussed theoretically by many authors;[1] however, it is of little spectroscopic interest and will not be considered further. Involvement of d orbitals in π bonds, however, is of considerable spectroscopic interest and has been discussed theoretically in

[1] For example, D. P. Craig, A. Maccoll, R. S. Nyholm, L. E. Orgel, and L. E. Sutton, *J. Chem. Soc.*, 332 (1954).

a general manner,[1,2] and with special reference to sulfur[3] and to phosphorus.[4]

The formation of double bonds by expansion of the valence shell (i.e., by involvement of $d\pi$ orbitals) may be divided into two separate classes: (*a*) the formation of such double bonds between a central atom, say silicon, phosphorus, or sulfur, and another atom or group, say oxygen, halogen, or an unsaturated or aromatic group, and (*b*) the conjugation of two chromophoric groups through such a central atom. Failure to make this distinction has led many authors into apparent contradictions. These two types of phenomena will now be discussed in general, and the principles developed will then be applied to the interpretation of the vast variety of experimental spectroscopic data available.

17.1   The Theory of the Expansion of the Valence Shell

The problem of the structure of many compounds of second-row elements is an old one and has had quite a stormy history. For instance, many years ago chemists considered sulfur as hexavalent, and wrote the structure of sulfuric acid as I, which appeared to do justice to all classical

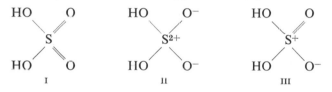

ideas about valence. With the advent of electronic interpretations of valence, Lewis' octet rule, and the concept of the coordinate covalent bond, the structure of sulfuric acid was written as II. This preference for structure II reflected the belief that the valence shell of second-row elements consists of the 3s and 3p electrons, and the Pauli principle permits no more than eight electrons in this shell. In the 1930's chemical and physical evidence was adduced to show that structures such as II also were inadequate, and resonance between I, II, and additional structures like III was postulated.[5] Structures I and III were believed to involve *expansion of the valence shell* of the sulfur atom to include two and one d orbitals, respectively.

[2] H. H. Jaffé, *J. Phys. Chem.*, **58**, 185 (1954).

[3] W. Moffitt, *Proc. Roy. Soc.* (*London*), **A200**, 409 (1950); H. P. Koch and W. Moffitt, *Trans. Faraday Soc.*, **47**, 7 (1951); G. Cilento, *Chem. Revs.*, **60**, 147 (1960).

[4] J. R. Van Wazer, *J. Am. Chem. Soc.*, **78**, 5709 (1956); H. H. Jaffé, *J. Inorg. & Nuclear Chem.*, **4**, 372 (1957).

[5] See L. Pauling, *The Nature of the Chemical Bond*, Cornell University Press, Ithaca, Third Edition, N.Y., 1960.

Ever since the suggestion was made that second-row elements can expand their valence shells to form multiple bonds, the problem of whether this expansion occurs, and if so, under what conditions, has occupied chemists. Complete agreement has not been reached to date, but evidence appears to show that expansion does occur *when, and only when, the second-row atom, without multiple bonds, would be positively charged.* This conclusion rests on a rather firm theoretical foundation.[1,2]

In a molecule in which a central atom M from the second row of the periodic system, Si, P, S, or Cl, is bonded to a series of other atoms or groups, i.e., ligands L, which have filled orbitals having π symmetry with respect to the M-L bond (e.g., O, Cl, or an unsaturated group), the electrons may be divided, at least roughly, into three types: inner-shell, σ, and π electrons. The inner-shell electrons are of no interest in compound formation and hence are ignored in what follows. The σ electrons (i.e., the electrons which form the σ bonds in structures such as II) are believed to make the predominant contribution to the binding energy of the molecule and hence determine its geometry. The π electrons are those which have π symmetry with respect to the σ bonds and are of spectroscopic interest. The central atom M has no π electrons, but the atoms or groups L do. M, however, has d orbitals which have π symmetry with respect to some or all of the σ bonds. Accordingly, the formation of a π bond between M and L and thus valence-shell expansion of M can occur only by donation of π electrons by L to M.

Two conditions must be met for the formation of a chemical bond: (*a*) the orbitals involved in forming the bond must overlap appreciably, and (*b*) the energies of the orbitals (i.e., the energy required to remove electrons from the orbitals) must be of similar magnitude. These two criteria appear to be the clue to the question of expansion of the valence shell; they are not, however, independent.

Consider first a compound such as SiL_4, PL_3, or SL_2 in which the M-L bonds are pure covalent bonds, i.e., where M and L have equal electronegativities. Then, in the single-bonded structures, the central atom is neutral—in other words, carries no formal charge. The energy of the d orbital (i.e., the energy required to remove a d electron added to M) is then the ionization potential of M^- or the electron affinity of M. But the electron affinity of these atoms is certainly quite small. On the other hand, the ionization potential of the π electrons from L is usually of the order of 10–15 ev; consequently requirement (*b*) is not fulfilled.

At the same time, a high-energy orbital, such as the 3d orbital of M, is very diffuse; an electron in such an orbital is distributed over a large volume, with a low density in any one element of volume. Consequently, the overlap with any of the π orbitals of L is small. If the overlap integral

S for a Slater orbital, using Slater's recipe for the wave function,[6] is calculated, it is found to be identically equal to zero because the effective nuclear charge of the *neutral* central atom for the 3d electron is zero. Although Slater's recipe is undoubtedly not sufficiently accurate for this calculation, it can be safely assumed that S will be quite small, and, accordingly, the other condition for bond formation also is not met.

The situation changes drastically if M is not neutral but instead carries a formal positive charge. Such a positive charge may appear on M by either of two mechanisms. If the number of bonds n in ML_n exceeds the number of holes remaining in the valence shell of M, as in SL_4, some of the ML bonds are coordinate covalent bonds and leave M with one or more positive charges, as in structure II. Alternatively, if L is more electronegative than M, the σ bonds are polarized toward L, and leave M with a partial positive charge.

In the case of positive M, the energy released by placing an electron into one of the 3d orbitals is no longer the electron affinity of the neutral atom, but the electron affinity (for a d electron) of the positive ion. This is equivalent to the ionization potential of the neutral atom (or even a positive ion) in an excited configuration. Thus, for a single positive charge this is the ionization potential of the configuration $3s3p^23d$ of Si (5.0 ev),[7] $3s3p^33d$ of P (6.4 ev), and $3s3p^43d$ of S (6.7 ev), and for a doubly positive S, $3s3p^33d$ of S^+ (19.9 ev). Since these quantities are now of the same order of magnitude as the ionization potentials of the π electrons of L, condition (*b*) of bond formation is fulfilled.

The same factors which increase the orbital energy also increase the overlap integral. The positive charge of the nucleus contracts the d orbital; it pulls an electron in this orbital closer to it and, consequently, leads to an appreciable density of such electrons in the region of high electron density of the π electron of L. This results in appreciable overlap integrals. If we look at the problem in a different way, the effective nuclear charge for the d orbital, as calculated by Slater's recipe, is considerably larger than zero (for unipositive M, it is 1); consequently, the overlap integral has a non-vanishing value. Calculations of such overlap integrals for some typical cases involving second-row elements[2] give values in the range of 0.15–0.30, which are of the same order of magnitude as those encountered in the typical double bonds of organic chemistry (0.27 in ethylene, 0.25 in benzene).

[6] J. C. Slater, *Phys. Rev.*, **36**, 57 (1930).

[7] These ionization potentials are crude approximations following H. H. Jaffé, *J. Chem. Educ.*, **33**, 25 (1956) from data given by C. E. Moore, "Tables of Atomic Energy Levels," *Nat. Bur. Standards Circ.* 467, U.S. Government Printing Office, Washington, D.C., 1952.

An additional factor may be considered. Although all d electrons in a free atom are degenerate, in the field of the molecule this degeneracy is split; the particular manner in which this splitting occurs depends on the molecular symmetry, as will be discussed in Chapter 18, It follows from the arguments presented there that, the more nearly the d orbitals of M coincide with the M-L bonds in space, the higher the energy of these d orbitals is raised. Accordingly, whatever the molecular geometry, the d orbitals having π symmetry with respect to the σ bonds are the lowest d orbitals in energy, and the ones most likely, from energetic considerations, to accept electrons. At the same time these orbitals, of course, overlap the π orbitals of the ligands, from which electrons can be withdrawn most easily. Consequently a $p\pi$-$d\pi$ resonance is the most likely interaction by which the formal charge of M can be neutralized, as required by Pauling's electroneutrality principle.[5]

Thus it is seen that theoretical considerations predict that a central atom may expand its valence shell when it bears, in the single-bonded structure, an appreciable positive charge, whether this is derived from coordinate covalent bonds or from inductive effects. This is substantially the same conclusion reached by Pauling on the basis of the principle of electroneutrality.

Although it was seen that double-bond formation, or conjugation, using d orbitals, can occur only if the central atom is positive, compounds like PL_3 and SL_2 have lone pairs of p (or sp hybrid) electrons, and should consequently be able to conjugate using these electrons. This is the case, and these groups will be seen to behave in many respects very much like NL_3 and OL_2. Such conjugation may be important and lead to a considerable delocalization of charge from M when L is an unsaturated organic group which can act as an electron acceptor, but not when L is oxygen or halogen. In this case some positive charge may be built up on M and lead to a contraction of the d orbital and hence of its ability to accept electrons in return. Such charge is, however, generally not large, and these effects are rarely observed. An especially favorable case appears to be thiophene. In this compound, the σ-bond framework leaves the S atom neutral. But π bonding, using the $p\pi$ orbitals of S with the carbon π electrons of the ring, is sure to occur, and can lead only to delocalization of $p\pi$ electrons away from the sulfur atom. This imparts to the sulfur atom the positive charge necessary to contract the d orbital and permit its involvement in the conjugated system generally accepted in this molecule (see section 14.21).

Having thus discussed multiple-bond formation and conjugation by second-row atoms, let us examine the possibilities of conjugation of several chromophores attached to one of these atoms. When dealing with first-row elements only, it has been seen that the condition for interaction between two chromophores was complete coplanarity or at least approximate coplanarity, since such interaction is dependent on overlap of $2p\pi$ orbitals, which is at a maximum when the orbitals have a common nodal plane (cf. Chapter 15). The situation is quite analogous in compounds in which the second-row element is neutral, since, as we have seen, conjugation then again involves a $p\pi$ orbital. Consequently the behavior of groups such as SiR_3, PR_2, and SR, as long as R is not strongly electronegative, is quite analogous to that of CR_3, NR_2, and OR. The fact that a small positive charge is induced on the central atom by delocalization of the π electrons does not appear to lead to any detectable effects except in rare cases.

However, when the central atom acquires positive charge in the single-bonded structure, the situation is considerably more complex, since five d orbitals are available to accept donation of electrons, and since the geometric shape (cf. Fig. 2.10) of these orbitals is considerably more complicated than that of p orbitals. Most of the types of compounds to be considered have an at least roughly tetrahedral arrangement of σ bonds about the central atom. These are almost surely made up of the four tetrahedrally hybridized $3sp^3$ orbitals, although some minor admixture of 3d orbital is not impossible. Although the molecular symmetry is usually lower, it is probably best to consider these compounds as having T_d *local* symmetry about the central atom, and hence to classify three of the d orbitals as belonging to the symmetry species t_2 and the other two to e.

In order to visualize the π overlap in a tetrahedral compound, it is well to consider carefully the orbitals and their orientation in space. If we identify the three C_2 axes with the Cartesian coordinate axes x, y, and z, and place two of the ligands in the xz plane and two in the yz plane, two of the σ-bonding orbitals lie in each of these planes (cf. Fig. 17.1). One of these σ-bonding orbitals belongs to the symmetry species a_1, the other three to t_2. The three d orbitals of species t_2 thus belong to the same symmetry species as three of the σ-bonding orbitals and might be hybridized with them, but are not of appropriate symmetry for π bonding with the ligand atoms. The nodes of the e-species orbitals on the other hand, accurately, or at least approximately, include the σ bonds and consequently may form π bonds with the ligands. This is illustrated in Fig. 17.1a for the d_{z^2} orbital, where the top two ligands lie in the plane of the paper (the xz plane), and the lower two ligands, which are not shown, in a plane normal to the paper, the yz plane. Figure 17.1b shows a similar relation for the orbital $d_{x^2-y^2}$, where it is to be noted that two of the ligands, opposite one another, lie above the plane of the paper, the xy plane, and the other two, below.

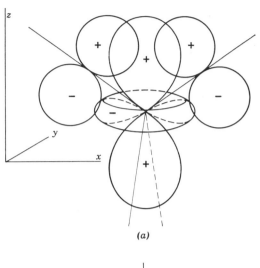

(a)

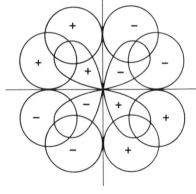

(b)

Fig. 17.1   The overlap of e-type orbitals in a tetrahedral molecule. (a) A cut through the d_{z^2} orbital of M and the "in-plane" orbitals of the ligands. (b) The $d_{x^2-y^2}$ orbital of M and the "out-of-plane" orbital of the ligands.

The simplest case is that of a compound of true T_d symmetry, such as $SiCl_4$ or ClO_4^-. This case has been treated in some detail.[8] The various oxygen orbitals in ClO_4^- are combined into group orbitals by the usual linear combinations. The most interesting orbitals so formed are a pair of species e; one of these is formed by using the π orbital lying in the same plane as the O atoms (Fig. 17.1a), the other from the π orbital at right angles

[8] M. Wolfsberg and L. Helmholz, *J. Chem. Phys.*, **20**, 837 (1952).

to this plane (Fig. 17.1*b*). The figure shows that each of the two equivalent sets of π orbitals of the four tetrahedrally bonded ligands interacts with one of the *e* orbitals of the central atom, and consequently the two sets may be expected to interact with each other.

Unfortunately, however, this simple type of situation is rarely if ever encountered in nature when the ligands are chromophores; it applies to such compounds as $SiCl_4$ and ClO_4^-, which do not have spectra in the quartz ultraviolet, and compounds like $Si(C\equiv CH)_4$, which has not been studied. Two complications arise in most molecules: (*a*) most of the compounds studied do not have four identical ligands: the more symmetric types are R_3PO, $R_2PO_2^-$, RPO_3^{2-}, R_2SO_2, etc., which belong to point group C_{3v} or C_{2v}; (*b*) most chromophoric ligands are nonlinear, though usually planar. Consequently, the π orbitals lie only in one plane, not, as with O, Cl, or —C≡CH, in two perpendicular ones, and the relative orientation of the ligands with respect to each other and to the molecular symmetry axes is of considerable importance. This orientation is generally determined by steric effects, but is usually unknown. For these reasons a complete and simple general analysis is not possible, and only some generalizations can be made.

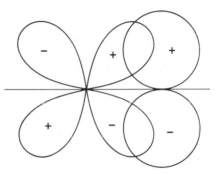

Fig. 17.2 pπ-dπ overlap. [Reprinted by permission from H. H. Jaffé, *J. Phys. Chem.*, **58**, 185 (1954).]

One of these is closely connected with the inequality of the ligands. In most cases one or more of these are oxygen atoms or, better, O^- groups, as in the single-bonded structures like II; since O^- is a more powerful electron donor than most organic chromophores, considerable electron donation from O^- occurs, and interaction with the other groups is less important. In addition, the orientation of the d orbitals will be affected so as to give optimum overlap with the oxygens, since this interaction is energetically most profitable.

In the lower symmetry of point group C_{3v} the orbital orientation of Fig. 17.1 is not demanded. The d orbitals may be considered as rotated in any desired manner. Thus, the O atom may be considered as lying on the z axis, and its two π orbitals then interact with d_{xz} and d_{yz}, forming what might be considered a partial triple bond. This type of overlap is illustrated by Fig. 17.2, but occurs in two mutually perpendicular planes. Once the axes of the d orbitals are thus fixed by overlap with the oxygen atom, the

π orbitals of the three chromophoric R groups do not optimally overlap with any of the remaining d orbitals of the phosphorus atom, or with the triple-bonding PO group orbitals. Furthermore, none of the d orbitals simultaneously interacts well with the π orbitals of all three R groups, whatever their orientation. On the other hand, some interaction is possible whatever the orientation of the chromophore plane with respect to the rest of the molecule, and hence a steric limitation on possible orientations is not a limiting factor on conjugation between the central atom and the chromophoric group.

The problems barely focused in this section have been carefully and extensively considered for at least one case, the sulfones, by Koch and Moffitt,[3] and their treatment will be discussed below with the sulfone spectra. The general application of the principles developed will be discussed and illustrated in the following sections with a variety of compounds.

17.2   Sulfur Compounds

17.21 SULFIDES.   The spectra of organic sulfides, R_2S, have been extensively studied; although most of the work is concerned with aromatic compounds,[9,10] considerable information is available on aliphatic and olefinic sulfides.[10] *Dialkyl sulfides* have a low-intensity absorption band, usually observed only as an inflection near 230 mμ,[10a,b] with log ϵ about 2.14. In addition a band occurs at shorter wavelength,[10a] about 210 mμ, with ϵ between 1000 and 2500. This band appears to shift to slightly longer wavelength and higher intensities with increasing branching of the alkyl groups. It undergoes a further bathochromic displacement in β,γ-unsaturated sulfides (allyl propyl sulfide[10b] and diallyl sulfide[10a,b]) to about 221 mμ, and in dibenzyl sulfide and ethyl benzyl sulfide. That some interaction between the unsaturated system and the sulfur atom occurs is apparent; the nature of the interaction, however, is unknown. These interactions are strongly reminiscent of the so-called homoallylic interactions frequently invoked in nonclassical carbonium ions and the transannular interactions discussed in section 15.6. Koch[10b] proposed that some hyperconjugation-like interaction, IV $\longleftrightarrow$ V, might be involved.

$$R\text{—}S\text{—}CH_2\text{—}CH\text{=}CH_2 \quad \longleftrightarrow \quad RS^{\pm}\text{—}CH\text{=}CH\text{—}CH_2^{\mp}$$
$$\qquad\quad \text{IV} \qquad\qquad\qquad\qquad\qquad \text{V}$$

[9] A. Mangini, *J. chim. phys.*, 240 (1959); *Ricerca sci., Suppl.*, "Contributi teorici e sperimentali di polarografia," **5**, 101 (1960), and references cited there; A. Mangini and R. Passerini, *J. Chem., Soc.* 1168 (1952).

[10] (a) E. A. Fehnel and M. Carmack, *J. Am. Chem. Soc.*, **71**, 84, 2889 (1949). (b) H. P. Koch, *J. Chem. Soc.*, 387 (1949). (c) H. H. Szmant and J. J. McIntosh, *J. Am. Chem. Soc.*, **73**, 4356 (1951).

An alternative possibility would be a conjugation through the sulfur 3d orbitals, which, as pointed out above, are very diffuse, and thus may well extend far enough to overlap considerably the β,γ-conjugated system. When the unsaturated system is two atoms removed from the sulfur, as in ethyl phenethyl sulfide,[10a] the spectrum appears as the sum of that of the sulfide and that of the conjugated system.

A similar interaction is observed in *β-keto sulfides*.[10a] Thus, n-butyl-mercaptoacetone, n-$C_4H_9SCH_2COCH_3$, absorbs at 243 and 299 mμ, with log ϵ of 2.56 and 2.41, respectively, representing a considerable bathochromic and hyperchromic effect over the separate chromophores (acetone, n-butyl methyl sulfide).

Especially interesting effects are observed in *mercaptals*; thus, bis-(methylmercapto)- and bis(n-butylmercapto)methane and 2,2-bis(n-butyl-mercapto)propane have an absorption band at 235 mμ with $\epsilon \sim 700$.[10a] The presence of this band is definite evidence of interaction of the *gem*-sulfur atoms, and it is interesting to speculate about the nature of this interaction. Considering the relatively large size of the sulfur atoms and the diffuseness of their 3d orbitals, it is not difficult to envisage a consider-able interaction of the 3d orbitals of the two S atoms leading to an MO(g) of lower energy than either of the separate 3d orbitals, into which an electron could be promoted from one of the lone pairs of the S atom with less expenditure of energy. This is schematically suggested in Fig. 17.3a. The occupied lone-pair orbitals of the S atoms presumably would also interact, although to a lesser extend because of their lower extension in space, and the highest occupied one (f) in the *gem* compound would be raised over that in the simple sulfide.

The picture might be even further refined by allowing some hybridization of the lone pairs with d orbitals. Admixture of appropriate d orbitals to the two lone-pair orbitals might improve overlap of the lower one (e), and reduce overlap of the higher one (f), thus lowering both. The concomitant admixture of s and p character to the two upper, unoccupied orbitals of Fig. 17.3b would also increase overlap of the lower one (g) and

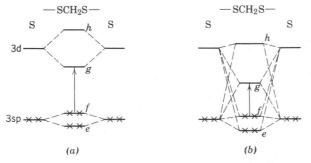

Fig. 17.3   A schematic energy-level diagram of *gem*-dimethylthio compounds.

decrease it for the higher one (h), thus again lowering both. But the limiting factor to such hybridization would be the promotion energy of the lone-pair electrons required. This would counteract the lowering of the lower, occupied pair (e and f), but the accompanying admixture of s and p character to the two unoccupied orbitals (g and h) would further drop them.

This interpretation is quite similar to that postulated above for the β,γ-unsaturated- and β-keto sulfides, and is consistent with the failure to observe a band at relatively longer wavelength in compounds such as n-butylmercaptomethyl ethyl ether, bis(methoxymethyl) sulfide, and 1,2-bis(alkylmercapto)ethanes.[10a]

Thus the long-wavelength absorption in the mercaptals may be explained without appreciable interaction of the sulfur atoms in the ground state, although some interaction involving d hybridization seems possible. The band appears to involve excitation of lone-pair electrons into the d shell of the S atoms. It seems likely, then, that the 210 mμ band in the simple alkyl sulfides also corresponds to such excitation of a lone-pair electron to a d orbital, and thus may be described as the first member of a Rydberg series, $R \leftarrow N$.

Some long-range sulfur-to-sulfur interaction, presumably of a similar nature but to a smaller extent, also appears to occur in 1,4-dithiane (1,4-dithiacyclohexane, $\lambda_{max} = 225$, log $\epsilon_{max} = 2.54$).

In α,β-*unsaturated sulfides*, true, first-order conjugation appears. Olefinic sulfides have been studied relatively little because of their low stability and high reactivity, but the spectrum of divinyl sulfide is known,[11] and includes a band at 255 mμ with $\epsilon = 5000$. This undoubtedly is a $\pi \rightarrow \pi^*$ transition, presumably $^1B \leftarrow {}^1A$ in Platt notation. 2-Chlorovinyl vinyl sulfide[12] absorbs at 228 mμ with $\epsilon = 7000$. More readily available are alkyl acyl sulfides (thiol acid esters); acetyl cyclohexyl sulfide (cyclohexyl thiolacetate) absorbs[10b] at 231.5 mμ with $\epsilon = 4500$.

Successive replacement of the H atoms in the acetyl group by Cl atoms produces bathochromic shifts to 238, 249.5, and 254.5 mμ, respectively, in the mono-, di-, and tri-chloroacetyl cyclohexyl sulfides,[10b] although the intensity remains almost unaffected. Effects in the thiolacetic (RCOSH) acids are similar. All these spectra must undoubtedly be ascribed to $\pi \rightarrow \pi^*$ transitions of the three-atom conjugated system C=C—S or O=C—S, and presumably the S atom is involved through its 3p electron pair. This is indicated, for example, by the fact that the effects observed are quite similar to those reported for the chloroacetic acids. Benzoyl cyclohexyl sulfide (cyclohexyl thiolbenzoate) shows two sharp bands at 268 and 235 mμ, with $\epsilon = 7300$ and 12,000, respectively, which have been

[11] M. Mohler and J. Sorge, *Helv. Chim. Acta*, **23**, 1200 (1940).

[12] K. Bowden, E. A. Braude, and E. R. H. Jones, *J. Chem. Soc.*, 948 (1946).

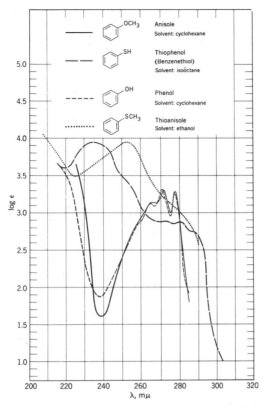

Fig. 17.4 Spectra of phenol, thiophenol, anisole, and thioanisole. (Reprinted by permission from R. A. Friedel and M. Orchin, *Ultraviolet Spectra of Aromatic Compounds*, John Wiley and Sons, New York, 1951.)

interpreted as due to the separate parts of the cross-conjugated system.[10b] The longer-wavelength band is supposed to be due to the O=C—S group and to correspond to the 231.5 mμ band of the thiolacetate, whereas the 235 mμ band is ascribed to the benzoyl group, corresponding to the $^1L_a \leftarrow ^1A$ band of a substituted benzene.

The spectra of *thiophenol* and *thioanisole* are compared with those of their oxygen analogs in Fig. 17.4. These spectra are not too readily interpreted. The spectrum of thiophenol in the 260–295 mμ region shows considerable vibrational structure and has been assigned to the ^1L_b band of benzene, bathochromically shifted by the substituent.[10b] The shorter-wavelength absorption, about 236 mμ, then ought to be the ^1L_a band. Careful examination of the spectrum, however, seems to permit an alternate explanation: on the long wavelength side of the 236 mμ band there

TABLE 17.1
The Absorption Spectra of Some Aryl Alkyl Sulfides, ArSR

Ar	R	λ, mμ	log ϵ	λ, mμ	log ϵ	λ, mμ	log ϵ	Ref. in Footnote
Ph	Me	(275)	3.15	254	3.98	...	...	9, 10a
Ph	Et	(270)	3.40	256	3.90	210	3.94	10a
Ph	iso-Pr	...	...	258	3.75	215	3.94	10a
Ph	t-Bu	...	...	266	3.19	218	4.08	10a
Ph	Cyclohexyl	(270)	3.60	260	3.76	...	...	10b
Ph	2-Mecyclohexyl	(273)	3.34	262	3.82	...	...	10b
Ph	1-Mecyclohexyl	...	...	~270	3.20	...	...	10b
Ph	$PhCH_2$	...	...	255	3.83	...	...	10a
$p\text{-MeC}_6\text{H}_4$	Me	(282)	3.01	256	4.00	...	...	10a
$2,4,6\text{-Me}_3\text{C}_6\text{H}_4$	Me	286	3.11	265	3.36	223	4.03	10a
$p\text{-HOC}_6\text{H}_4$	Me	(292)	(3.42)	256	3.89	229	3.84	10a
$p\text{-}^{-}\text{OC}_6\text{H}_4$	Me	289	3.51	263	4.14	...	...	10a
$o\text{-HOC}_6\text{H}_4$	Me	(294)	(3.22)	252	3.76	212	4.21	10a
$p\text{-NH}_2\text{C}_6\text{H}_4$	Me	(281)	(3.13)	264	4.14	(240)	3.80	9, 10a
$p\text{-NH}_3^+\text{C}_6\text{H}_4$	Me	...	...	254	4.03	~215	3.81	10a
$p\text{-NO}_2\text{C}_6\text{H}_4$	Me	...	...	338	4.12	...	...	10a
$o\text{-NO}_2\text{C}_6\text{H}_4$	Me	(266)	3.71	372	3.55	244	4.27	10a
$p\text{-NMe}_2\text{C}_6\text{H}_4$	Me	(303)	3.39	271	4.31	...	...	...

appears a shoulder; this may be interpreted as the partially submerged ^1L_b band occurring here between 250 and 260 mμ with ϵ about 2–3 × 10³. In this case the long-wavelength band at about 260–295 mμ must be assigned to some new type of transition. Sulfur is considerably less electronegative than oxygen, and hence its lone pairs are considerably less tightly bound. Excitation of these electrons, presumably to d orbitals, has been discussed. Excitation of the lone-pair electrons to π orbitals should occur at considerably longer wavelength. Thus, an interpretation of the long-wavelength band with an intensity $\epsilon < 10^3$ as an n → π transition seems a possible assignment.

In contrast to the similarity of the oxygenated pair, the spectrum of thioanisole is surprisingly different from that of thiophenol (cf. Fig. 17.4). A main band appears at 254 mμ with ϵ about 10,000; partially submerged at the long-wavelength side of this band is another band at about 275 mμ with an apparent ϵ of about 1.5 × 10³. A third band appears to be present shortly below 210 mμ, which is shifted to higher wavelength in the higher alkyl phenyl sulfides (cf. Table 17.1). This spectrum is unexpectedly different not only from that of thiophenol but also from that of anisole. Two alternative interpretations seem possible. The 254 mμ band might be ascribed to the ^1L_b band of benzene, although the wavelength seems somewhat too short and the intensity too high. If this assignment is correct the band below 210 mμ must be the ^1L_a band, and the long-wavelength absorption presumably an n → π ($^1W \leftarrow {}^1A$) transition. Alternatively, the 254 mμ band, judging from its intensity, may correspond to the ^1L_a band, albeit at surprisingly long wavelength, the 275 mμ band to the ^1L_b band, and the short-wavelength band to the $^1B \leftarrow {}^1A$ transition of benzene. The large difference between thiophenol and thioanisole may be due to the relatively strong hydrogen-bonding ability of the mercapto group, which possibly causes thiophenol to exist predominantly as dimers and polymers in solution. The bathochromic shifts in thioanisole, as compared with anisole, if we accept the assignment of the 254 mμ band to the ^1L_a band, may be ascribed to the fact that sulfur, having considerably lower electronegativity than oxygen, is a more effective electron donor. This would mean that in thioanisole we deal with the case, discussed in section 12.22, of small δ and consequently a large bathochromic effect.

Selected data for other *alkyl phenyl sulfides* and *methyl aryl sulfides* are given in Table 17.1. These compounds, in general, have the same three regions of absorption as thioanisole. The main band in the 254–270 mμ region undergoes bathochromic shifts and hypochromic effects with increasing branching of the alkyl group, and is shifted to longer wavelengths by nuclear substitution. The long-wavelength absorption frequently disappears when the 254 mμ band is bathochromically shifted, presumably because it becomes completely submerged. The short-wavelength absorption undergoes a bathochromic shift with branching of the alkyl group, although its intensity remains relatively constant at about 10,000.

The spectrum of mesityl methyl sulfide, $\lambda_{max} = 265$ and 223 mμ, with log $\epsilon = 3.36$ and 4.00, respectively, has been interpreted[10a] as indicating considerable steric effects due to the o-methyl groups, and this interpretation confirms the fact that the S atom conjugates only by use of its p orbital.

Very revealing is an examination of the data given for p-amino- and p-nitrophenyl methyl sulfide. The spectrum of the p-amino (and the p-hydroxy) compound shows no striking red shift over the parent, rather, if anything, a lesser effect is observed for the p-amino group than for benzene. In the p-nitro compound, on the other hand, the bathochromic shift is

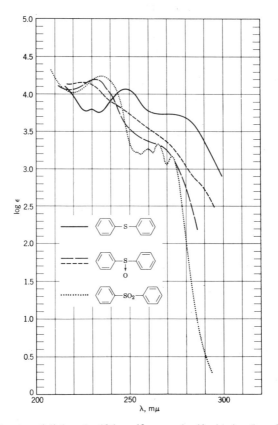

Fig. 17.5 Spectra of diphenyl sulfide, sulfone, and sulfoxide in ethanol and the last also in cyclohexane (- - - -). [Reprinted by permission from E. A. Fehnel and M. Carmack, *J. Am. Chem. Soc.*, **71**, 84, 231 (1949); G. Leandri, A. Mangini, and R. Passerini, *J. Chem. Soc.*, 1386 (1957).]

tremendous, larger than in nitrobenzene. These facts strongly indicate that the atom acts as an electron donor using its lone-pair electrons, but not as an electron acceptor involving the vacant 3d orbitals.

Diphenyl sulfide (cf. Fig. 17.5) shows two absorption bands in the ultraviolet, one at 274 mμ ($\epsilon = 5700$) and one at 250 mμ ($\epsilon = 11,800$).[9,10] It appears attractive to assign the first of these to the ^1L_a, the second to the ^1B band, since such an assignment is most consistent with the arguments presented in the preceding paragraphs, and would tend to confirm the assignment of the 254 mμ band of thioanisole to the ^1L_a band. Substituent effects on these bands are illustrated in Table 17.2. The insensitivity to substituents which generally cause only moderate perturbations (Me, Cl) is remarkable. Just as in the alkyl aryl sulfides, the amino group has only a small effect, the nitro group a very large one, confirming that the S atom acts as an electron donor. Little, if any, conjugation of the two phenyl groups through the S atom is apparent, since introduction of an amino group into the 4' position of 4-nitrophenyl phenyl sulfide produces little further effect. This has been interpreted[9] as indicating that the two benzene rings, because of steric interference of the *ortho*-hydrogen atoms, are not coplanar. The spectra of *ortho*-substituted diphenyl sulfides further indicate the characteristic hypso- and hypochromic effects ascribed to steric inhibition of resonance, although the effects are of quite small magnitude. These effects again confirm that the S atom conjugates through a p orbital and consequently acts as an electron donor.

17.22 SULFONES AND OTHER "HEXAVALENT" SULFUR COMPOUNDS. The spectroscopic properties of a wide variety of sulfones[10c,13] have been investigated, and some of the data are summarized in Table 17.3. In contrast to the sulfides, *dialkyl sulfones* are transparent throughout the quartz ultraviolet (down to at least 210 mμ and probably beyond). This is not surprising, since the S atom has no lone-pair electrons in sulfones and the oxygen electrons are quite tightly bound.

In sulfides, a rather surprising resonance interaction was apparent between the sulfide S atom and a chromophoric group insulated from it by *one* methylene group. No similar effect is observed in the sulfone series, although relatively few compounds have been investigated. Thus, the spectra of benzyl methyl sulfone and of dibenzyl sulfone[13a] (Table 17.3) do not suggest any special effects.

In α,β-*unsaturated sulfones*, however, resonance interaction is apparent. Thus the absorption band at about 210 mμ of ethyl vinyl sulfone occurs at considerably longer wavelength than is expected from either an isolated

[13] (a) E. A. Fehnel and M. Carmack, *J. Am. Chem. Soc.*, **71**, 231 (1949); **72**, 1292 (1950). (b) H. P. Koch, *J. Chem. Soc.*, 408 (1949). (c) G. Leandri, A. Mangini, and R. Passerini, *Gazz. chim. ital.*, **84**, 73 (1954); *J. Chem Soc.*, 1386 (1957).

TABLE 17.2
The Spectra of Diaryl Sulfides, ArSAr'

Ar	Ar'	λ, mμ	log ϵ	λ, mμ	log ϵ	λ, mμ	log ϵ	Ref. in Footnote
Ph	Ph	277	3.76	250	4.08	...	...	9, 10a, 10b
Ph	p-MeC$_6$H$_4$	274	3.76	250	4.09	230	3.92	9
Ph	m-MeC$_6$H$_4$	275	3.74	250	4.06	232	3.90	9
p-MeC$_6$H$_4$	p-MeC$_6$H$_4$	276	3.83	252	4.16	...	...	9
Ph	p-ClC$_6$H$_4$	275	3.76	250.5	4.08	...	...	9
Ph	m-ClC$_6$H$_4$	273	3.73	250	4.05	(234)	3.98	9
Ph	p-NH$_2$C$_6$H$_4$	...	...	256	4.28	...	...	9
Ph	p-NHAcC$_6$H$_4$	280	4.17	258	4.30	...	...	9
p-NH$_2$C$_6$H$_4$	p-NH$_2$C$_6$H$_4$	...	...	264	4.39	...	...	9
Ph	p-NO$_2$C$_6$H$_4$	337	4.13	260	3.70	...	...	9
Ph	m-NO$_2$C$_6$H$_4$	336–342	3.02	250	4.28	...	...	9
p-NH$_2$C$_6$H$_4$	p-NO$_2$C$_6$H$_4$	345	4.12	265	4.21	245	4.12	9
p-NO$_2$C$_6$H$_4$	p-NO$_2$C$_6$H$_4$	341	4.18	250	4.08	235	...	10c
Ph	o-MeC$_6$H$_4$	272	3.67	248	4.08	232	3.93	9
o-MeC$_6$H$_4$	o-MeC$_6$H$_4$	274	3.70	248	4.11	...	...	9
Ph	o-ClC$_6$H$_4$	275	3.69	249	4.09	234	3.96	9
Ph	o-NHAcC$_6$H$_4$	276	3.76	246	4.25	...	...	9
p-HOC$_6$H$_4$	p-HOC$_6$H$_4$	292.5	3.83	250.7	4.20	...	...	22

—SO_2— group or a vinyl group, and consequently must be ascribed to a resonance interaction between the two,[13a] which must involve expansion of the valence shell of sulfur.

A similar resonance effect is apparent in the spectrum of phenyl methyl sulfone, shown in Fig. 17.6;[13a] the larger number of bands, however, permits a better analysis. The long-wavelength band has the characteristic vibrational structure of the ^1L_b bands of benzene and substituted benzenes.

TABLE 17.3

The Ultraviolet Spectra of Some Sulfones, RSO_2R'

Compound	λ_1, mμ	$\log \epsilon_1$	λ_2, mμ	$\log \epsilon_2$
Et_2SO_2	. . .	. . .	. . .	. . .
$CH_2{=}CHSO_2Et$	. . .	. . .	210	2.45
$PhSO_2Me$	264[a]	2.99	217	3.83
$PhSO_2CMe_3$	265[a]	3.02	216	3.94
Ph_2SO_2	266[a]	3.33	235	4.24
$PhCH_2SO_2Et$	265[a]	2.26	. . .	. . .
$(PhCH_2)_2SO_2$	265[a]	2.61	219	4.32
$PhCH_2SO_2Ph$	265[a]	3.08	219	4.10
$(PhCH_2CH_2)_2SO_2$	264[a]	2.47	. . .	. . .
$(MeSO_2)_2CH_2$	[b]	. . .	. . .	. . .
$[(MeSO_2)_2CH]^-$	256[c]	1.33	210	3.20
$(PhSO_2)_2CH_2$	267[a]	3.35	221	4.29
$[(PhSO_2)_2CH]^-$	267	3.85	. . .	. . .

[a] Typical ^1L_b band with vibrational structure.
[b] Transparent to <210 mμ.
[c] Assignment doubtful.

The bathochromic shift of some 10 mμ, relative to unsubstituted benzene, is indicative of a moderate resonance interaction, which is confirmed by the five-fold hyperchromic effect. The bathochromic effect of the methanesulfonyl group on the ^1L_a band is also consistent with this interpretation. Still, these effects are of relatively small magnitudes, of the same order as those of halogen or alkyl substituents, and considerably smaller than those of amino, hydroxy, or carbonyl groups (cf. Table 12.4). The alkanesulfonyl group unquestionably undergoes resonance interaction with the benzene ring, but this interaction is of a relatively weak nature and produces only a mild perturbation of the π-electron system.

The same conclusions are apparent from an examination of the spectrum of diphenyl sulfone (Fig. 17.5). This spectrum shows the ^1L_b band at

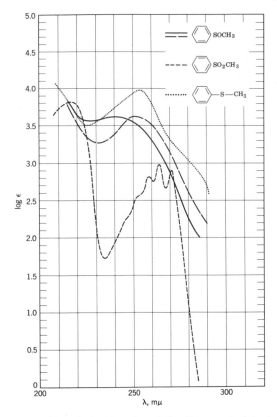

Fig. 17.6 Spectra of thioanisole, phenyl methyl sulfone, and phenyl methyl sulfoxide, in ethanol, and the last also in cyclohexane (———). [Reprinted by permission from E. A. Fehnel and M. Carmack, *J. Am. Chem. Soc.*, **71**, 84 (1949); **71**, 231 (1949); G. Leandri, A. Mangini, and R. Passerini, *J. Chem Soc.*, 1386 (1957).]

about the same wavelengths as in the monoaromatic analog. Again, the spectra of benzenesulfonamide (Table 12.4) and of sulfonic acids and their esters are in agreement with these conclusions.

The effects of substituents on the absorption of phenyl sulfones shed further light on their electronic structure. Selected data from the tremendous body of experimental information, collected principally by Mangini and coworkers,[13c] are shown in Table 17.4a. Moderately perturbing and electron-donating substituents, like *p*-methyl and *p*-chloro, produce small bathochromic and hyperchromic effects, as is expected from the addition of a mesomerically electron-donating substituent to a benzene already bearing an electron-withdrawing substituent. The ammonio ($-NH_3^+$) group, as expected, has no effect. The behavior of *p*-methanesulfonylaniline and -phenolate ion is probably best examined by considering

TABLE 17.4

Substituent Effects in the Spectra of Aryl Methyl Sulfones, $ArSO_2Me$, and Diaryl Sulfones, $ArSO_2Ar'$

(References in footnotes 13a, 13c, and 10c)

(a) Aryl Methyl Sulfones

Ar	$^1L_b{}^a$		^1L_a		^1B	
	λ, mμ	log ε	λ, mμ	log ε	λ, mμ	log ε
Ph	264	2.99	217	3.83		
p-MeC6H4	267	2.73	225	4.07		
p-ClC6H4	266	3.3	228	4.18		
2,4,6-Me3C6H2	280	3.21	230	3.95		
p-HOC6H4	268	3.22	239	4.20		
p-⁻OC6H4			269	4.31		
p-H2NC6H4			269	4.30	213	4.01
p-H3N⁺C6H4	263	3.03	216	3.97		
p-NO2C6H4	330^b	3.79	282	3.36	248	4.05

(b) Diaryl Sulfones

Ar	Ar'	$^1L_b{}^a$		^1L_a		^1B	
		λ, mμ	log ε	λ, mμ	log ε	λ, mμ	log ε
Ph	Ph	266^a	3.33	235	4.24		
p-MeC6H4	Ph	266	3.37	241	4.26		
Mesityl	Ph	277	3.29	241.5	4.24		
p-ClC6H4	Ph	273	3.19	239	4.21		
p-O2NC6H4	Ph			262	4.16		
p-H2NC6H4	Ph			291	4.26		
p-AcHNC6H4	Ph			276	4.36		
p-Me2NC6H4	Ph^c			307	4.40	220	4.17
p-HOC6H4	Ph	295	3.23	255	4.17		
p-⁻OC6H4	Ph			290	4.26		
p-MeC6H4	p-MeC6H4			245	4.32	222	4.04
Mesityl	Mesityl	286	3.46	242	4.28		
p-ClC6H4	p-ClC6H4			248	4.39		
p-NO2C6H4	p-NO2C6H4			270	4.27		
p-NO2C6H4	p-NH2C6H4			338^b	3.82	266.5^b	4.29
p-NH2C6H4	p-NH2C6H4			295	4.47	260	4.26

^{a} Typical ^1L_b band with vibrational structure.
^{b} Assignment doubtful.
^{c} 251 mμ, 3.63.

the effect of the p-methanesulfonyl group on the spectra of aniline and phenolate ion. Strong bathochromic shifts of 39 and 34 mμ, respectively, are observed, accompanied by a hyperchromic effect of a factor of about 2 (0.3 in log ϵ). This is, of course, consistent with the interpretation of resonance interaction involving, in the excited state, considerable contributions from structure VI.

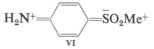

$$H_2N^+=\!\!\!\left\langle\begin{array}{c}\\\end{array}\right\rangle\!\!\!=\bar{S}O_2Me^+$$

VI

The spectrum of p-nitrophenyl methyl sulfone is difficult to interpret. Fehnel and Carmack[13a] assume that the 248 mμ band is the ^1L_a band (the first primary band) shifted toward shorter wavelength by the interaction of the two electron-withdrawing substituents. With this assignment, however, the two longer-wavelength bands are not readily understood; neither appears to have the characteristic structure of a ^1L_b band, and accordingly this spectrum is not yet adequately resolved.

The effects of substituents in the spectrum of diphenyl sulfone closely resemble those in the spectrum of phenyl methyl sulfone. p-Alkyls and -halogens in one ring produce the same moderate types of effects. The strongly electron-donating p-NH$_2$ and O$^-$ groups in one ring again shift the ^1L_a band sufficiently to obliterate the ^1L_b, and in some cases also shift the ^1B (second primary) band enough to make it readily observable in the quartz ultraviolet. p-Nitrophenyl phenyl sulfone has a considerably simpler spectrum than p-nitrophenyl methyl sulfone, with a strong band at 262 mμ, which may be tentatively assigned to the ^1L_a band and hence seems to be unchanged from its position in nitrobenzene.

Symmetrical disubstitution in both rings does not appear to lead to any substantially new effects. In general, the bathochromic shifts and hyperchromic effects appear moderately enhanced. Obliteration of the ^1L_b band seems more common, although by no means uniform. In bis(p-aminophenyl) sulfone the ^1L_a band seems to have inordinately high intensity, and the ^1B band at 260 mμ appears to have undergone a greater than expected bathochromic shift. Little information is available on unsymmetrically disubstituted compounds, but fortunately one of the most important ones, p-nitrophenyl p-aminophenyl sulfone, has been investigated. Its spectrum shows two absorption bands, one at 338 mμ with log $\epsilon = 3.82$, the other at 266.5 mμ with log $\epsilon = 4.29$. The interpretation of these bands is not very clear. The first one has intensity rather low for the ^1L_a band, and the second appears at somewhat too short a wavelength for this assignment. These bands will be discussed again later.

The problem of conjugation of several chromophoric groups bonded to the sulfonyl group is an inherently difficult one for several reasons. First,

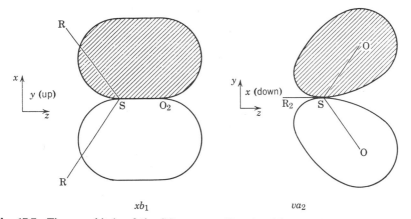

xb_1 va_2

Fig. 17.7   The a_2 orbitals of the SO_2 group. [Reprinted by permission from H. P. Koch and W. E. Moffitt, *Trans. Faraday Soc.*, **47**, 7 (1951).]

the nature of the S-O bonds remains open to discussion. Second, the usual organic chromophoric π-electron systems are planar; the orientation of the chromophore plane relative to the SO_2 plane, and to the plane of the other chromophore attached to the sulfonyl group, is important, but generally not well known. The problem has been discussed extensively by Koch and Moffitt,[14] but many questions remain unanswered.

By taking the symmetry of R_2SO_2 as belonging to the point group C_{2v}, MO's can be set up for the electrons of the SO_2 group which are not involved in σ-bond formation. Choosing coordinate axes so that the C_2 axis is the z axis, and the SO_2 group lies in the yz plane, Moffitt finds the π electrons of the SO_2 group occupying two MO's, xb_1 and va_2, where xb_1 is strongly bonding and involves an approximately equal distribution of charge between S and O. The second MO, va_2, is much less strongly bonding and is largely localized on the O atoms. These orbitals are schematically shown in Fig. 17.7.

When the R groups of a sulfone R_2SO_2 are unsaturated (chromophores), each having a π orbital on the α-carbon atom, two extreme cases may be visualized; in case I, the π orbitals of both R groups have a common nodal plane, the xz plane; in case II, the groups are so oriented that the nodal planes are normal to the xz plane, i.e., the maximum intensity of the π orbitals lies *in* that plane. The two cases need separate consideration.

In case I, the π orbitals of the α-carbon atoms, and hence the MO's of the chromophores, are combined into symmetric and antisymmetric linear

[14](a) H. P. Koch and W. E. Moffitt, *Trans. Faraday Soc.*, **47**, 7 (1951). (b) W. E. Moffitt, *Proc. Roy. Soc. (London)*, **200A**, 409 (1950); cf. also Gy. Varsanyi and J. Ladik, *Acta Chim. Acad. Sci. Hung.*, **3**, 243 (1953).

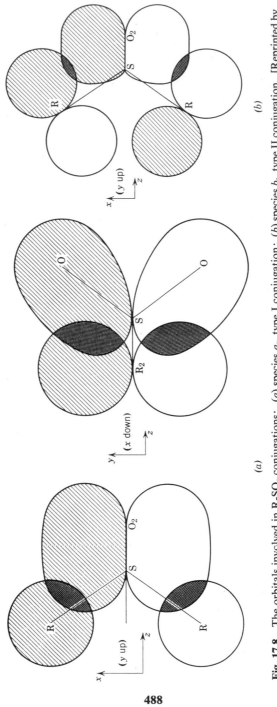

Fig. 17.8 The orbitals involved in R-SO₂ conjugations: (a) species a_2, type I conjugation; (b) species b_1, type II conjugation. [Reprinted by permission from H. P. Koch and W. E. Moffitt, *Trans. Faraday Soc.*, **47**, 7 (1951).]

combinations of species b_2 and a_2, respectively. These GO's can interact with sulfur AO's or SO_2-group MO's of the same symmetry. In the case of the b_2 group orbital only a vacant sulfur 3d orbital of species b_2 is available; hence conjugation using b_2 would have to occur by donation of electrons to sulfur. The GO of species a_2, however, may interact with the filled, weakly bonding SO_2-group MO called va_2 above, and hence may accept electrons from the S atom (or the SO_2 group). The form of such an MO of species a_2 involving R—SO_2 conjugation is shown schematically in Fig. 17.8a; overlap in the a_2 case is quite favorable to relatively strong interaction, and overlap in the b_2 case, although somewhat less, is sufficient to be potentially of importance.[14] Conjugation appears most likely to involve both mechanisms simultaneously, since use of the a_2 mechanism, by increasing the effective charge on S and hence contracting the b_2 orbital, helps conjugation using b_2; such conjugation in turn, by further destabilization of va_2, assists in a_2 conjugation. Use of b_2 orbitals does not directly affect the SO bonds, but use of a_2 orbitals does, so that their properties may be a barometer of the importance of a_2 conjugation alone.

In case II combination of the chromophore orbitals again leads to two GO's, of species a_1 and b_1. The SO_2 group has an MO of species b_1 potentially capable of interaction with the b_1 group orbital; the combination is shown in Fig. 17.8b, where it is seen that the overlap is not at all favorable for interaction. In addition, the b_1 orbital of the SO_2 group is strongly bonding, so that delocalization of its electrons is quite unlikely, and hence the b_1 orbitals probably are of no importance. There is, however, a vacant sulfur orbital of a_1 symmetry available, overlap with which is likely to be favorable, and case II may be assumed to involve some conjugation, though probably weak, of this type.

Actually, of course, cases I and II are extremes, and in any one compound the actual situation is likely to lie somewhere between. In diphenyl sulfone and its derivatives, case I (i.e., coplanarity of the phenyl groups) is undoubtedly sterically unfavorable, and it appears to be generally agreed that diaryl sulfones belong to case II. The spectrum of diphenyl sulfone and particularly the strong bathochromic shifts due to electron-donating substituents (NR_2, OH), are consistent with this picture. Conjugation between the two phenyl groups is also indicated by a comparison of the spectra of methyl phenyl sulfone and diphenyl sulfone; in the absence of conjugation of the two groups, the diphenyl compound might be expected to have the same maxima with double the intensity, whereas the observed spectra show a small bathochromic shift and a somewhat more than two-fold hyperchromic effect. The same effects are observed, to a somewhat greater degree, in compounds with electron-repelling substituents. The lack of effective conjugation in p-nitrophenyl phenyl sulfone and bis(*p*-nitrophenyl) sulfone in excees of that in nitro-benzene is also consistent with this picture. Conjugation through the sulfone group from one phenyl group to the other seems to be demonstrated by the *p*-nitrophenyl *p*-aminophenyl sulfone, although assignment of the observed bands at 338 and 266 mμ is not straightforward. The interpretation given is also consistent with the absence of steric effects on the resonance of the sulfonyl group, as demonstrated by the relations between *p*-tolyl phenyl and mesityl phenyl sulfone, and between di-*p*-tolyl and dimesityl sulfone (cf. Table 17.4).

The properties of the semiquinone[15] radical-anion, VII, and particularly its visible spectrum, have been interpreted[14] as indicating that this

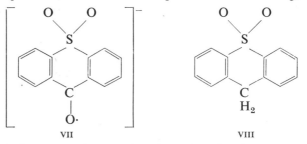

compound belongs to class I. On the other hand, examination[16] of thiaxanthene 9,9-dioxide, VIII, has failed to reveal any evidence that this compound shows class I conjugation, as might have been expected.

The differences between case I and case II conjugation on *ground states* have been examined[16a] using a series of cyclic and analogous open-chain sulfones.

The above interpretation is also consistent with the demonstration[17] that the conjugation is sterically inhibited in N-acetyl-4-methanesulfonyl-2,6-xylidene, IX; it should be noted, however, that resonance of the

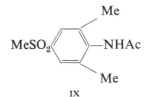

acetylamino group, and *not* of the methane sulfonyl group, is sterically inhibited.

[15] H. Heymann, *J. Am. Chem. Soc.*, **71**, 260 (1949); E. A. Fehnel, *J. Am. Chem. Soc.*, 1063.
[16] E. S. Waight, *J. Chem. Soc.*, 2440 (1952).
[16a] R. Breslow and E. Mohassi, *J. Am. Chem. Soc.*, **83**, 4100 (1961); **84**, 684 (1962).
[17] H. Kloosterziel and H. J. Backer, *Rec. trav. chim.*, **72**, 655 (1953).

17.23 SULFOXIDES.   The sulfoxides, although a particularly interesting group of compounds since they have both a lone pair of electrons and a positive S atom, have not been investigated nearly as extensively as either the sulfides or the sulfones. Some of the experimental material on these compounds[10c,18] is summarized in Table 17.5.

The first notable observation is that even *saturated sulfoxides* have an absorption band in the quartz ultraviolet, near 220 mμ in ethanol, with a relatively low intensity of about 1500. The same band occurs in methyl 2-methylallyl sulfoxide and in diallyl sulfoxide, although with somewhat increased intensity.[18a] In the first of these compounds this band is strongly solvent dependent; it shifts from about 230 mμ in cyclohexane to 210–215 mμ in ethanol, and even slightly further in water. These shifts identify the transition as involving promotion of one of the sulfur lone-pair electrons, presumably to an antibonding π orbital of the sulfoxide group. The enhanced intensity of this band in the β,γ-unsaturated compounds over that in the dialkyl analogs has been interpreted[18a] as due to an interaction similar to that in the β,γ-unsaturated sulfides.

The two allyl sulfoxides display an additional absorption band near 300 mμ with low intensity ($\epsilon \sim 10$) which has solvent dependence of the opposite sense, i.e., shifts bathochromically with increasing solvent polarity. This band has been interpreted as due to an enolic form,

$$CH_2{=}CMeCH{=}S(OH)Me.^{18a}$$

In dibenzyl sulfoxide,[18b] the characteristic ^1L_b band of the phenyl chromophore is observed with typical vibrational structure at 260 mμ in ethanol. The ^1L_a band occurs at 222 mμ ($\epsilon_{max} \sim 20,000$), and the n $\rightarrow$ π transition of the dialkyl sulfoxides apparently is hidden below the ^1L_a band, or may be responsible for a shoulder at 215 mμ. In cyclohexane solution the ^1L_a band is almost unaffected, but the absorption does not drop nearly as rapidly toward the longer-wavelength side, and the ^1L_b only appears as a shoulder at 265 mμ. This broadness of the ^1L_a band may well be due to the n $\rightarrow$ π, ^1W band, occurring at longer wavelength in the less polar solvent, somewhere in the 230–240 mμ region, and being poorly resolved.

The spectra of the *aryl alkyl sulfoxides* and *diaryl sulfoxides* are a good deal more complicated, particularly since considerable solvent effects appear. Methyl phenyl sulfoxide (Fig. 17.6) in cyclohexane shows a single strong band, devoid of vibrational structure, at 253 mμ, which may possibly

[18] (a) H. P. Koch, *J. Chem. Soc.*, 2892 (1950). (b) G. Leandri, A. Mangini, and R. Passerini, *J. Chem. Soc.*, 1386 (1957). (c) S. Oae and C. Zalut, *J. Am. Chem. Soc.*, **82**, 5359 (1960). (d) F. G. Bordwell and P. J. Boutan, *J. Am. Chem. Soc.*, **79**, 717 (1957).

TABLE 17.5
Spectra of Sulfoxides, RSOR′

R	R′	Solvent[a]	^1L_b λ, mμ	^1L_b log ε	$n \to \pi(^1W)$ λ, mμ	$n \to \pi(^1W)$ log ε	^1L_a λ, mμ	^1L_a log ε
Me	Cyclohexyl	E	260	2.68	~210–215	~3.2		
Me	2-Methallyl	E	265	2.55	~210–215	~3.5		
Allyl	Allyl[c]	E	265	2.90	~210–215	~3.5		
PhCH₂	PhCH₂	E	253	3.60			222	4.29
Ph	Me	C	256	3.45	238	3.61	222	4.26
Ph	Me	E	280[d]	3.50				
Ph	PhCH₂	C	267	3.42	261[d]	3.71	226	4.13
Ph	PhCH₂	E	265	3.32			233	4.15
Ph	Ph	C	280	3.17	248[d]	3.76	228	4.07
Ph	Ph	E	265	3.38			235	4.14
Ph	o-Tolyl	C	278	3.30			230	4.07
Ph	o-Tolyl	E	270	3.29			233	4.16
Ph	m-Tolyl	C	270	3.28			233	4.05
Ph	m-Tolyl	E	270	3.28			237	4.20
Ph	p-Tolyl	C	280	3.28			227	4.05
Ph	p-Tolyl	E	270	3.28			237	4.16
o-Tolyl	o-Tolyl	E	282	3.30	245	3.85	230	4.07
o-Tolyl	o-Tolyl	C	274	3.43			235	4.21
o-Tolyl			278	3.28				
m-Tolyl	m-Tolyl	C	270	3.42			237	4.20
m-Tolyl			280	3.49			240	4.27
m-Tolyl		E	270	3.61				
p-Tolyl	p-Tolyl	C	275	3.35			230	4.13
p-Tolyl		E	275	3.35				
Ph	o-ClC₆H₄	C	265	3.45			235	4.17
Ph	o-ClC₆H₄	E	265	3.35				

R₁	R₂	Solvent	λ (mμ)	log ε	λ (mμ)	log ε	λ (mμ)	log ε
Ph	m-ClC₆H₄	C	281	3.35			232	4.11
Ph	p-ClC₆H₄	E	273	3.12			234	4.20
		C	268	3.30			239	4.26
p-ClC₆H₄	p-ClC₆H₄	E	280	3.16			240	4.29
		C[e]	275	3.20			244	4.34
p-BrC₆H₄	p-BrC₆H₄	E	280	3.40			244	4.34
		C	260	3.78			248[c]	4.34
			268	3.75			226[c]	4.19
							248[c]	4.42
Ph	p-H₂NC₆H₄	E	268	3.75			227[c]	4.20
p-H₂NC₆H₄	p-H₂NC₆H₄	C	290	3.57			259	4.21
		E					278	4.21
p-H₂NC₆H₄	p-O₂NC₆H₄	E	300[c]	4.25			264[c]	4.17
Me		C	296	3.75			244	3.94
Ph	o-O₂NC₆H₄	E	284	3.78			248	3.88
		C	300	3.40			244	4.05
o-O₂NC₆H₄	o-O₂NC₆H₄	E	315[c]	3.34	270[c]	3.80	225	4.23
		C	295	3.45			248	4.14
m-O₂NC₆H₄	m-O₂NC₆H₄	E					230	4.20
Ph		C	295	3.02	258[c]	4.00	225[c]	4.29
		E					245[c]	4.12
p-O₂NC₆H₄	p-O₂NC₆H₄	E	295	3.15	262[c]	3.96	229[c]	4.30
		C	345[c]	2.90			250[c]	4.03
Ph	p-O₂NC₆H₄	E	295	3.65	273[c]	4.20	257[c]	4.28
		C	290	3.86			271	4.27
		E	330[c]	2.95			260	4.08
p-O₂NC₆H₄	p-H₂NC₆H₄	E					265	4.06
							276	4.30

[a] E = ethanol; C = cyclohexane.
[b] Also 295 mμ, 1.0.
[c] Also 285 mμ, 0.9.
[d] Assignment unknown.
[e] Also 221 mμ, 4.18.

be interpreted as arising out of the ^1L_b band of benzene, with, however, very considerable perturbation due to two-fold resonance interaction with the sulfoxide group. One of these interactions involves donation of electrons from the lone pair of the S atom into an unoccupied orbital of the benzene ring; the other, donation of electrons from an occupied orbital into a vacant $d\pi$ orbital of the S atom. The first is similar to the resonance in the sulfides, except that the lone pair in sulfoxides must occupy a hybrid orbital involving considerable s character, as demonstrated by the pyramidal geometry of sulfoxides, and only the p part of the hybrid can interact with the π orbital of the ring. The other type of resonance interaction is more similar to that in the aryl sulfones (case II of section 17.22). For lack of a better name, this band will still be called the ^1L_b band, although its actual relation to this band is largely obscured. In ethanol, the spectrum of phenyl methyl sulfoxide consists of two bands,[18b] one essentially unchanged, the other at shorter wavelength, 238 mμ. It then seems likely that the band in cyclohexane is a superposition of the ^1L_b band and the n → π transition, and that, because of hydrogen bonding, the latter is hypsochromically shifted in the more polar solvent. This is consistent with the above suggestion of an n → π^* transition in dialkyl sulfoxides about 230 and 210 mμ, in nonpolar and polar solvents respectively, since the π^* level, because of resonance interaction, is considerably lowered in the aromatic compound.

Some substituted aryl methyl sulfoxides have been examined,[18d] and both electron-withdrawing and electron-donating substituents produce considerable bathochromic effects.

Diphenyl sulfoxide[18b] (Fig. 17.5) has been reported to have two absorption bands at 226 and 267 mμ in cyclohexane, and at 233 and 265 mμ in ethanol. Intensities of corresponding bands are comparable in the two solvents, log ϵ about 4.13 and 3.40 for the shorter- and longer-wavelength bands, respectively: it is suggested that these be identified as strongly perturbed ^1L_a and ^1L_b transitions, respectively. Close examination of the spectra again reveals much less clean separation of the two bands in cyclohexane than in ethanol, suggesting that the n → π transition occurs between the ^1L_a and ^1L_b bands, at about 250 mμ in cyclohexane, and is shifted to underlie the ^1L_a band in ethanol.

The bathochromic shift of 3–5 mμ observed with the ^1L_a band of diphenyl sulfoxide in going from cyclohexane to ethanol is also observed with a series of p- and p,p'-substituted diphenyl sulfoxides when the substituents cause relatively small perturbation. Thus, the ^1L_a band occurs in cyclohexane and ethanol, respectively, at 233 and 237 mμ for the p-methyl-, at 237 and 240 mμ for p,p'-dimethyl-, at 234 and 239 mμ for p-chloro-, at 240 and 244 mμ for p,p'-dichloro-, and at 260 and 265 mμ

for p-nitrodiphenyl sulfoxides. This bathochromic shift is of course well known from the $\pi \rightarrow \pi^*$ transitions of the conjugated carbonyl compounds (Chapter 10). In most of these compounds, the ^1L_b band, the position of which is not as clearly defined because it is observed as a shoulder or point of inflection, appears to remain substantially unchanged. Similar relations also appear to hold in *meta*-substituted compounds as far as identification of bands is possible.

The spectra of bis(4-hydroxy-) and bis(4-methoxyphenyl) sulfoxides in 6 per cent aqueous ethanol and in dioxan have been reported.[18c] Both compounds have a single band, at 250 and 251.3 mμ, respectively, presumably the ^1L_a band, which, however, splits in dioxan into two components, 254.1 and 248.9 mμ in the methoxy compound, and 253.5 and 248 mμ in the hydroxy. It is impossible to say at this time whether this is vibrational structure, or a splitting of accidentally degenerate ^1L_a and ^1W bands. In the spectra of the 2- and 3-methyl- and 2,6-dimethyl substituted hydroxy compounds no steric effects are observed, although the ^1L_b bands are now apparent, at 285, 286, and 292 mμ, respectively.[18c]

In other members of the aryl alkyl and diaryl sulfoxide series, however, the spectra and solvent effects are more complicated and less readily understood. Thus, benzyl phenyl sulfoxide in cyclohexane has a band at 261 mμ, with some structure suggested near 280 mμ; in ethanol, this compound is reported to absorb[18b] at 248 mμ with substantially the same extinction. The hypsochromic shift is what might be expected from the n $\rightarrow \pi$ transition, but where is the ^1L_b band in ethanol? Again, phenyl m-tolyl sulfoxide absorbs at 230 (^1L_a) and 278 (^1L_b) mμ in cyclohexane, but at 233 (the expected bathochromic shift) and at 270 mμ in ethanol, with log $\epsilon_{max} = 4.14$ and 3.30, respectively, approximately the same in both solvents. The wavelengths of the ^1L_b band seem longer than expected! The situation is worse in m-chlorophenyl phenyl sulfoxide; the ^1L_b band is split (273 and 280 mμ), the ^1L_a band absent, in cyclohexane, but the ^1L_b band is unsplit at 268, the ^1L_a band present, at 232 mμ in ethanol. A similarly complicated situation exists in p-aminophenyl phenyl sulfoxide with absorption at 259 (^1L_a) and 290 (^1L_b) mμ in cyclohexane, but only at 278 mμ (^1L_a) in ethanol. In bis(p-bromophenyl) sulfoxide a new band appears: in cyclohexane, at 268 (^1L_b), 248, and 226 mμ, and in ethanol at 268, 248, 227 mμ. None of these is readily identified as the n $\rightarrow \pi$ transition, since no solvent shifts occur. Further examples are found in Table 17.5.

The *ortho*-substituted compounds have been less extensively investigated, but largely appear to follow the pattern found above. No clear-cut steric effects seem evident. Phenyl o-tolyl sulfoxide absorbs at 228 (^1L_a) and 280 (^1L_b) mμ in cyclohexane, at 235 (^1L_b, with typical bathochromic shift) and 265 (^1L_b, with unusual hypsochromic shift) mμ in ethanol. In bis-(o-tolyl) sulfoxide, the ^1L_b band is split: 270 and 280 mμ in cyclohexane, 274 and 282 in ethanol; the ^1L_a band (227 and 237 mμ, respectively) undergoes a rather larger bathochromic shift than usual, probably because a band at 245 mμ in cyclohexane, most likely the n $\rightarrow$ π^* transition, has disappeared, and presumably merged with the ^1L_a transition in ethanol. o-Chlorophenyl phenyl sulfoxide behaves normally. o-Nitrophenyl phenyl and bis(o-nitrophenyl) sulfoxides, however, behave so differently in the two solvents, and so differently from each other (cf. Table 17.5), that no interpretation will be attempted.

In view of the extreme complexity of these spectra, most of the available experimental material is reproduced in Table 17.5.

17.24 SULFONIUM SALTS. Very little information appears to be available on the spectroscopic behavior of sulfonium salts. Rothstein and co-workers[19] have investigated the spectra of 1,3-bis(methylbutylsulfonio)-propane dichloride,

$$n\text{-BuMeS}^+(CH_2)_3S^+Me \cdot Bu\text{-}n \cdot 2Cl^-$$

and of

$$\text{BuMeS}^+CH_2\text{—}CH\text{=}CHS^+MeBu \cdot 2Cl^-$$

Unfortunately, accurate spectra were not obtained. The most important finding is that Beer's law is not obeyed by these compounds, which has led these authors to postulate formation of dimers or higher polymers. The saturated compound absorbs at about 208–210 mμ, with a log ϵ_{max} in the range 1.73–2.76 as the concentration decreases from 126 $\times$ 10^{-4} to 0.9 $\times$ 10^{-4} mole per liter. The unsaturated compound absorbs at slightly longer wavelength, 208–214 mμ, with log ϵ varying from 2.05 to 2.50 in the concentration range 182 $\times$ 10^{-4} to 7.3 $\times$ 10^{-4} mole per liter. Nothing is known regarding the origin of these spectra. The authors interpret them as indicating lack of expansion of the valence shell of the S atom in the sulfonium salts, in agreement with Rothstein's empirical conclusion.[20] However, in the absence of more knowledge of the spectra and the nature of the absorbing species, this conclusion is not convincing.

Contrary to Rothstein's conclusion, Bordwell and Boutan[21] find that the dimethylsulfonio group conjugates strongly with the benzene ring. These authors observe the ^1L_b transition of phenyl dimethyl sulfonium perchlorate at 265 mμ with log ϵ = 3.04, and the ^1L_a band at 220 mμ with log ϵ = 3.94.

[19] D. C. Nicholson, E. Rothstein, R. W. Saville, and R. Whiteley, *J. Chem. Soc.*, 4019 (1953).

[20] E. Rothstein, *J. Chem. Soc.*, 3991 (1953).

[21] F. G. Bordwell and P. J. Boutan, *J. Am. Chem. Soc.*, **78**, 87 (1956).

Both bands thus show a bathochromic effect, and the ^1L_b band a considerable hyperchromic effect, clearly indicating conjugation which can occur only by an expansion of the valence shell of the S atom, and is consistent with the above prediction that such conjugation is to be expected whenever the S is positive. The results for some substituted dimethyl phenyl

TABLE 17.6

Spectra of Some Dimethyl Phenyl Sulfonium Salts
$Me_2SC_6H_4R \cdot X^-$

| R | X | ^1L_a | | ^1L_b | | Solvent |
		λ, mμ	log ϵ	λ, mμ	log ϵ	
H	ClO_4	220	3.94	265	3.04	H_2O
m-HO	Cl	215	4.17	283	3.56	H_2O
m-O$^-$	Cl	217	4.35	304	3.62	0.01N NaOH
p-HO	SO_4Me	242^a	4.08	262	3.6	H_2O
p-O$_2$N	SO_4Me	252	4.28	...	...	H_2O
p-O$^-$	SO_4Me	269	4.29	...	...	0.01N NaOH

^{a} Also $\lambda = 214$ mμ, log $\epsilon = 3.68$.

sulfonium salts[21,22] (cf. Table 17.6) are also consistent with this interpretation. Of particular interest is the observation[22] that, in 2-methyl-, 2,6-dichloro- and -dibromo-4-hydroxyphenyl dimethyl sulfonium salts, the substituents *ortho* to the dimethyl sulfonic group have no effect on the conjugation between the hydroxy group and the sulfonic group. Even in the much more strongly hindered tris(4-hydroxyphenyl) sulfonium salts and their 2,2′,2″-trimethyl derivatives no steric effects are observed. This observation is in perfect agreement with the concept that conjugation involving d orbitals is not subject to steric effects.

17.3   Compounds of Phosphorus, Silicon, and Iodine

Although a tremendous amount of work has been done on a wide variety of sulfur compounds, the compounds of other second-row elements have been little investigated. Nevertheless enough information seems to be available to conclude that the generalizations made in section 17.1 seem to be valid.

Thus, in general, a central atom with an unshared electron pair, when bound to one or more phenyl groups, is responsible for a considerable

[22] S. Oae and C. C. Price, *J. Am. Chem. Soc.*, **80**, 3427, 4938 (1958); S. Oae and C. Zalut, *J. Am. Chem. Soc.*, **82**, 5359 (1960).

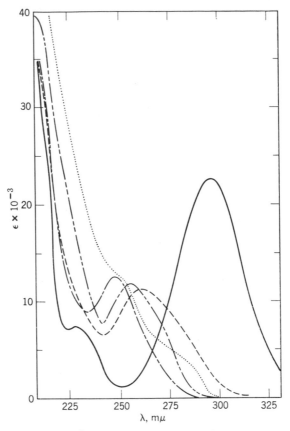

Fig. 17.9 The spectra of Ph$_3$N(———), Ph$_3$P(- - -), Ph$_3$As(— · — ·), Ph$_3$Sb(— · · —), and Ph$_3$Bi(· · · ·) in ethanol. [Reprinted by permission from H. H. Jaffé, *J. Chem. Phys.*, **22**, 1430 (1954).]

perturbation of the benzene spectrum.[23] The spectra of the triphenyl derivatives of the group V elements all show a single major band (Fig. 17.9); this band cannot be clearly identified with either the ^1L_b or ^1L_a band of benzene, since the perturbation is too large. Examination of Fig. 17.9 focuses on the similarity and regularity of these spectra. As might have been anticipated from the generally known greater conjugating ability of first-row elements, triphenylamine absorbs at the longest wavelength and has the highest intensity. The bands for the next three members of the series occur quite close together. The extra, short-wavelength band of triphenylamine at 228 mμ disappears below end absorption in the higher members of the series. Triphenylbismuthine apparently presents a special case, but it

[23] H. H. Jaffé, *J. Chem. Phys.*, **22**, 1430 (1954).

seems safe to assume that the shoulder at 248 mμ represents the same transition as that observed in the other compounds, and that the additional shoulder at 280 mμ represents an n$\rightarrow \pi$ transition which occurs at relatively long wavelength, since, in the whole group of compounds, the lone pair in the bismuth compound is least tightly bound. The spectrum of triphenylantimony also seems to suggest a slight shoulder at the long-wavelength side of the main band, which might represent the n $\rightarrow \pi$ transition.

The spectra of phenyl derivatives in which the central atom has no lone pair of electrons are completely different. The benzenoid spectra are only mildly perturbed, and it is always possible to recognize the ^1L_b band by its characteristic vibrational structure, just as it was in the sulfones. The conjugation, which must involve expansion of the valence shell, is readily recognized by the bathochromic and hyperchromic effects on the ^1L_b band, and particularly by the bathochromic effect on the ^1L_a band. Typical examples are the spectra of triphenylphosphine oxide, triphenylarsine oxide hydrate, and triphenylstibine dichloride, which are shown in Fig. 17.10, and of the various mono-, di-, and triphenyl derivatives of phosphorus(V),[24] shown in Fig. 17.11.

Substituent effects in the arylphosphonic and diarylphosphinic acids appear to be in reasonable agreement with this interpretation, although unfortunately data on the most critical compounds, the amino and hydroxy compounds, are not available. However, in p-nitrophenyl phosphonic, p-nitrophenyl phenyl-, and bis(p-nitrophenyl) phosphinic acids, the resonance of the nitrophenyl group is only slightly enhanced by the phosphorus grouping; the observed $\Delta\lambda$ values (cf. section 12.3) are somewhat less than the additive values. In the p-chloro compounds, on the other hand, with the electron-repelling chloro group, $\Delta\lambda$ values slightly exceed the additive values.

Possibly the most striking observation to be made from these spectra is the additivity of the effects of several phenyl groups bound to the phosphorus atom, indicating the lack of interaction between them. This is illustrated by Fig. 17.12, where the observed spectrum of m-chlorophenyl phenyl phosphinic acid is compared with an average of the spectra of diphenyl phosphinic and bis(m-chlorophenyl) phosphinic acids. This relation was found to be general for all the acids. Similarly the intensities of the mono-, di-, and triphenyl derivatives (Fig. 17.11) are in the ratio of 524 : 1200 : 1967, quite close to 1 : 2 : 3.

In a quite analogous manner, the phosphono group modifies the spectrum of biphenyl to only a minor extent. The main band, presumably

[24] H. H. Jaffé and L. D. Freedman, *J. Am. Chem. Soc.*, **74**, 1069, 2930 (1952).

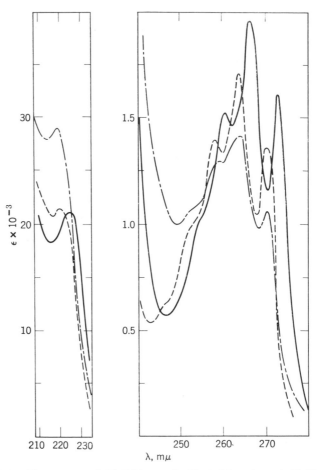

Fig. 17.10   The spectra of Ph₃PO(————), Ph₃AsO(- - -), and Ph₃SbCl₂(— · — ·), in ethanol.   [Reprinted by permission from H. H. Jaffé, *J. Chem. Phys.*, **22**, 1430 (1954).]

related to the ^1L_a band of benzene, occurs at 248 mμ with $\epsilon = 16{,}600$ in biphenyl.[25] Substitution by a single phosphono group in the 4 position produces a bathochromic shift of 7 mμ and an intensification by about one-third. Substitution by two phosphono groups in the 3 and 3′ positions causes an even smaller bathochromic effect of only 2.5 mμ, and actually a slight decrease in ϵ, and 4,4′ substitution by phosphono groups gives a maximum at 262.5 mμ, with $\epsilon = 23{,}300$. Substitution of a phosphono group in the 2 position of biphenyl, however, leads to steric hindrance, with

[25] L. D. Freedman, *J. Am. Chem. Soc.*, **77**, 6223 (1955).

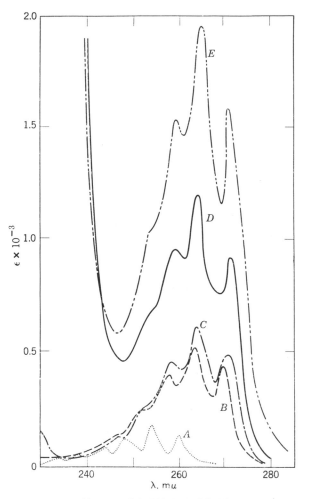

Fig. 17.11   The spectra of benzene (A), $PhPO_3H_2$ (B), $PhPO_2H_2$ (C), Ph_2PO_2H (D), and Ph_3PO (E). [Reprinted by permission from H. H. Jaffé and L. D. Freedman, *J. Am. Chem. Soc.*, **74**, 1069, 2930 (1952).]

a ^1L_a band of the phenyl chromophores at 237 mμ, $\epsilon = 8220$, and a ^1L_b band at 274.5 mμ, $\epsilon = 2030$.

The spectra of the tetraphenyl derivatives of the group IV elements have been examined;[26] all closely resemble one another, and all show the typical ^1L_b band with its vibrational structure. A bathochromic shift, moderate compared to that in benzene, may be due to a minor resonance

[26] G. Milazzo, *Gazz. chim. ital.*, **71**, 73 (1941).

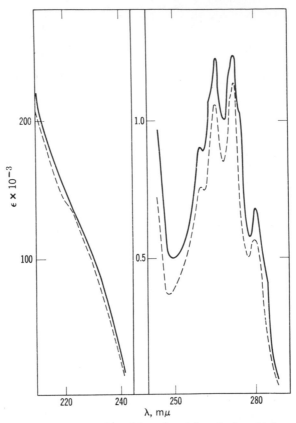

Fig. 17.12 The spectrum of *m*-chlorophenylphenyl phosphinic acid: ——found, – – –calculated. [Reprinted by permission from H. H. Jaffé and L. D. Freedman, *J. Am. Chem. Soc.*, **74**, 1069, 2930 (1952).]

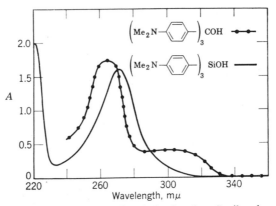

Fig. 17.13 The spectra of tris-(*p*-dimethylaminophenyl) silanol and carbinol. [Reprinted by permission from Gilman and Dunn, *J. Am. Chem. Soc.*, **72**, 2178 (1950).]

interaction. Triphenylsilane and triphenylsilanol have been compared to the corresponding carbon compounds.[27] No bathochromic shifts exceeding the experimental error were observed. In mono- and tri-p-dimethylamino-substituted triphenylsilanols, however, a considerable bathochromic shift of the main absorption band is apparent (Fig. 17.13), which may be ascribed to resonance involving quinoid structures using silicon d orbitals. Oddly enough, a long-wavelength, low-intensity band of the carbon compounds is missing in the silicon analogs.

TABLE 17.7

The Absorption Spectra of Alkyl Iodides[28]

Compound	In Heptane		In Water
	λ, mμ	ϵ	λ, mμ
MeI	257.5	378	249.4
EtI	258.2	444	250.9
PrI	257.6	481	250.5
Me$_2$CHI	262.5	531	255.8
BuI	257.2	486	250.0
Me$_3$CI	268.8	575	. . .
CH$_2$I$_2$	$\begin{cases} 212 \\ 240 \\ 290 \end{cases}$	1580 600 1300	. . . 240 285
CHI$_3$	$\begin{cases} 274 \\ 207 \\ 349 \end{cases}$	1300 1860 2170	. . . .

The situation is more complicated in iodine compounds. Because Russell-Saunders coupling is breaking down in the heavy iodine atom, the distinction between p and d orbitals becomes less valid; the d levels are also lower than in lighter atoms.

All organic iodides have absorption bands in the ultraviolet region. The spectra of a series of alkyl iodides have been carefully analyzed,[28] and some of the data are collected in Table 17.7. The bands are interpreted as arising from n → σ* transitions in which one of the lone-pair electrons on iodine is promoted into the antibonding σ* orbital. The fact that these bands undergo a hypsochromic shift when the solvent is changed from heptane to water is consistent with this assignment. The data also show that substitution on the carbon bearing the iodine causes a red shift. The

[27] H. Gilman and G. E. Dunn, *J. Am Chem. Soc.*, **72**, 2178 (1950).
[28] K. Kimura and S. Nagakura, *Spectrochim. Acta*, **17**, 166 (1961).

analogous bromine compounds also have an absorption band, just above 200 mμ, which is believed to be of similar origin.[28] Some special and striking effects are observed in compounds having two or three iodine atoms bonded to the same carbon atom. Thus, methylene iodide and iodoform have three bands each, at 212, 240, and 290, and at 274, 307, and 349 mμ, respectively, in heptane. These are interpreted as n $\rightarrow$ σ* bands, related to the 258 mμ band of methyl iodide, but with both lower and upper orbitals split by iodine-iodine interaction.[28] This interaction is reminiscent of the effects discussed above for the bis(methylmercapto) compounds, $R_2C(SCH_3)_2$, but in the large iodine atom the splitting is much larger. In the bromine analogs, CH_3Br: 202 mμ, CH_2Br_2: 220 mμ, $CHBr_3$: 205 and 224 mμ, all in heptane, the effects are also observed, although they are much smaller.

A final series of compounds to be discussed here, in which expansion of the valence shell is likely to play an important role according to the principles of section 17.1, is the diaryliodonium cations, which have been studied carefully by Beringer and Lillien[29] and contrasted to the aryl iodides. Unfortunately, the interpretation of the spectra of both series of compounds is anything but straightforward. The diaryliodonium salts, like the sulfoxides, have both lone-pair electrons and, because of the positively charged iodine atom, low-lying d orbitals, so that conjugation may involve either normal pπ resonance involving electron donating or dπ resonance involving acceptance into an unoccupied d orbital. Because of the special difficulties arising with iodine, any interpretations suggested here must be considered tentative and speculative.

Iodobenzene shows three absorption bands, at 257 mμ (log ϵ 2.85) and at 226 and 207 mμ (log ϵ, 4.12 and 3.86 respectively). The 257 mμ band, although obviously a typical ^1L_b band from its shape, may well be a superposition of this and the n $\rightarrow$ σ* transition of the alkyl iodides. Although the 226 mμ band had long been ascribed to the $^1L_a \leftarrow {}^1A$ transition, Beringer and Lillien suggest, probably correctly, that this band is related to the bands shown by all iodine compounds in this region (cf. also section 12.22) and that the 207 mμ band must be ascribed to the $^1L_a \leftarrow {}^1A$ transition. If this assignment is accepted, the 226 mμ band must involve excitation of one of the iodine lone-pair electrons. Although in unconjugated iodine compounds (including the iodide ion) the upper state very likely involves a d orbital, and hence is substantially the first member of a Rydberg series, in the aromatic compounds the upper level is most likely an MO of π symmetry; this assignment is mandatory, since this

[29] (a) F. M. Beringer and I. Lillien, *J. Am. Chem. Soc.*, **82**, 5135 (1960). (b) See also H. Irving, G. P. A. Turner, and R. W. Reid, *J. Chem. Soc.*, 2082 (1960).

band is the most strongly substituent dependent of all the bands in the iodobenzene spectrum. Its high intensity (log $\epsilon = 4.12$), however, makes it rather unique as an n $\rightarrow \pi$ band; if this interpretation is to be accepted, we must, at least, assume that the excited MO receives a major contribution from an orbital of the iodine atom. This band will be referred to as ^1W.

The spectrum of diphenyl iodonium salts is surprisingly similar to that of iodobenzene; the most striking difference is the apparent absence of the ^1L_b band, although this band may just be obscured under the long-wavelength tail of the ^1W band. The ^1L_a band is present at 209 mμ, with about twice the intensity, presumably because of the presence of two benzene rings, whereas the ^1W band occurs at precisely the same wavelength in both compounds, with essentially the same intensity. The unchanged intensity is consistent with the assignment of ^1W, since doubling the aryl radical does not change the availability of iodine electrons. The unchanged wavelength may be rationalized by assuming that, although the energy of the lone-pair electrons must be lowered by the introduction of the positive charge on iodine, the energy of the excited π orbitals is equally lowered, particularly if, as suggested above, it receives a predominant contribution from an iodine AO. It is also worth noting that the spectra of diaryliodonium salts are independent of the nature of the anion, provided this has no spectrum of its own, or are the simple sums of cation and anion spectra.[29b] This observation permits the simple explanation of the spectra as belonging to the cation alone, and elimination of the possibility of charge-transfer spectra of ion pairs.

Substituent effects in the diaryliodonium ions and in the aryl iodides are very revealing. Some typical data are summarized in Table 17.8. The ^1L_b band in the aryl iodides undergoes large bathochromic shifts when electron-donating substituents are introduced in the ring, and also upon m-nitro substitution; but since this band is observed only in o- and m-substituted cations and apparently is obscured by the ^1W band in other ions, comparison is difficult. The ^1L_a band in both series is relatively insensitive to substituent effects, but the ^1W band is very susceptible. This may be rationalized by the argument that the ground level, an iodine lone-pair orbital, is affected little, but the upper level, since it is a π molecular orbital is affected more strongly. It is particularly interesting to note that electron-donating substituents produce large bathochromic effects in this band in the cations, much smaller ones in the aryl iodides. If it is assumed that the 294 mμ band of p-nitroiodobenzene is the ^1W band, which appears reasonable, electron-withdrawing substituents also have large bathochromic effects on the spectra of both series of compounds, but now the effect is much larger in the aryl iodides than in the diaryliodonium ions. This relation seems highly reasonable. In the iodonium

TABLE 17.8

Spectra of Aryl Iodides and Diaryliodonium Ions[29a]

X	XC$_6$H$_4$I						XC$_6$H$_4$I$^+$Ph				(XC$_6$H$_4$)$_2$I$^+$			
	^1L_a		^1W		^1L_b		^1L_a		^1W		^1L_a		^1W	
	λ, mμ	log ε	λ, mμ	log ε	λ, mμ	log ε	λ, mμ	log ε	λ, mμ	log ε	λ, mμ	log ε	λ, mμ	log ε
H	207	3.86	226	4.12	257	2.85	209	4.05	226	4.19	209	4.05	226	4.19
p-Me	...	...	228	4.21	258	3.84	...	...	...	...	209	4.23	234	4.24
p-Cl	207	3.96	235	4.19	265^a	2.94	...	...	...	...	209	4.25	239	4.28
p-MeO	209	3.89	233	4.30	280	3.15	210	4.28	245	4.16	209	4.32	252	4.29
p-H$_2$N	211	4.04	248	4.22	298	3.24	211	3.79	285	4.03	...	...	288	4.21
p-O$^-$	220	3.78	250	4.46	~298	3.38	222	4.19	292	4.21	218	4.70	292	4.27
p-O$_2$N^b	...	...	294	4.07	...	...	209	4.05	251	4.14	220	4.06	260	3.83
m-MeO^c	...	...	...	...	...	...	210	4.39	218	4.38	...	...	...	...
m-H$_2$N^d	217	4.31	243	3.86	...	...	211	4.02	226	4.37	...	...	...	...
m-O$_2$N^b	...	...	260	3.81	315	3.18	217	4.05	248	4.02	...	...	...	...

^{a} The more intense of two component bands.
^{b} The assignment of these bands is uncertain.
^{c} For p-MeOC$_6$H$_4$I$^+$Ph, ^1L_b at 298 mμ, 3.34.
^{d} For m-NH$_2$C$_6$H$_4$I$^+$Ph, ^1L_b at ~313 mμ, 3.26.

ions, the d orbital should play a major role; hence electron-donating substituents are effective in lowering the energy levels (including the unoccupied ones), and have the largest effects. In the iodides, however, the d orbitals, although apparently still involved, play a less important role than the p orbitals, and hence electron-withdrawing substituents have the more pronounced effects.

Measurements are also available on 4-nitro-4'-aminodiphenyliodonium ion, with bands at 210 mμ (log ϵ, 4.44), 248 mμ (log ϵ, 4.30), and 295 mμ (log ϵ, 4.12). The longest-wavelength absorption is tentatively assigned the ^1W band, and the short-wavelength absorption the relatively constant ^1L_a band, but the intermediate band remains unidentified. Comparison

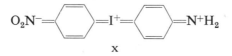

X

with the 3-nitro-4'-amino isomer ($\lambda = 210$, 240, 286, and log $\epsilon = 4.43$, 4.20, 4.06, respectively) indicates a certain degree of conjugation through the iodine atom, according to X, but of a relatively weak nature.

18 The ligand-field theory; the spectra of inorganic complexes

18.1 General Introduction

Most of the discussion of preceding chapters has dealt with organic compounds and has been simplified by the fact that the vast majority of spectra observable in these compounds in the visible and near ultraviolet region (above 220 mμ) are due to π-electron systems. In Chapter 17 the effects due to the availability of outer d orbitals were discussed. This chapter will introduce the spectra of transition-metal compounds and complexes, where the presence of d electrons produces completely new and vastly more complicated problems. The spectra of the complexes of most transition metals and of the lanthanides and actinides are characterized by one or more absorption bands in the near infrared and visible region, often extending into the ultraviolet; they have strikingly low intensity and are responsible for the pale color of these complexes. The problems in the rare earths are similar to those in the transition elements and will not be discussed further. In addition to these weak bands, most transition-metal complexes have considerably stronger bands in the ultraviolet, which are called *charge-transfer bands* and will be briefly discussed in section 18.8. The weak bands have long been believed to be in some way connected with the presence of a partially filled shell of d electrons in these complexes.

Little progress had been made in classifying and systematizing these spectra until a few years ago, when crystal-field theory, first discussed by Bethe,[1] was applied to the spectroscopic properties of complexes.[2a] In

[1] H. A. Bethe, *Ann. physik.* [5], **3**, 133 (1929). See also W. G. Penney and R. Schlapp, *Phys. Rev.*, **41**, 194 (1932), **42**, 666 (1932); J. H. Van Vleck, *Phys. Rev.*, **41**, 208 (1932); *J. Chem. Phys.*, **3**, 803, 807 (1935), **8**, 787, 790 (1940).

[2] (a) F. E. Ilse and H. Hartmann, *Z. physik. Chem.* (*Leipzig*), **197**, 239 (1951); *Z. Naturforsch.* **6a**, 751 (1951). (b) L. E. Orgel, *J. Chem. Phys.*, **23**, 1004, 1819, 1824 (1955). (c) V. Tanabe and S. Sugano, *J. Phys. Chem.* (*Japan*), **9**, 753, 766 (1954). (d) C. K. Jørgensen, *Kgl. Danske Videnskab. Selskab, Mat.-fys. Medd.*, **29**, #7 (1955), **30**, #22 (1956). (e) C. J. Ballhausen, *Kgl. Danske Videnskab. Selskab, Mat.-fys. Medd.*, **29**, #4 (1954), **29**, #8 (1955). (f) J. Owen, *Proc. Roy. Soc.* (*London*), A**227**, 183 (1955).

the manner in which this theory will be used here, the term *ligand-field theory*, due to Orgel,[2b] seems preferable; the transitions are often called *ligand-field transitions.*

Ligand-field theory (LFT) considers the complex as made up of a central positive ion, surrounded by a number of ligands which are either anions (e.g., Cl^-, OH^-, CN^-,) or dipoles (e.g. H_2O, NH_3) with the negative end oriented toward the central positive ion. The subsequent treatment will be entirely in terms of negative ions, but it must be remembered that dipoles, with the negative end oriented toward the central ion, could be substituted throughout. Alternately, the central ion may be introduced into a field by substituting it into the crystal lattice of a compound having a lattice of appropriate symmetry. Considerable work on such solids has been done in the last few years; the theoretical treatment is substantially the same as that of an isolated complex, since the predominant contribution to the field comes from the nearest neighbors only. The field of the ionic ligands has a symmetry characteristic of the complex; only octahedral, tetrahedral, and square planar complexes will be considered here, but the methods can be extended to other types of complexes, although the treatment becomes progressively more difficult and cumbersome the lower the symmetry, and the results become less useful.

According to atomic theory, the five d orbitals of a transition metal are strictly degenerate in the centrosymmetric force field applicable to the isolated atom. However, the atom in a molecule is not isolated but has the symmetry of the molecule. When the electrostatic field due to the ligands is superimposed on the centrosymmetric field of the central atom, the degeneracy of the five d orbitals is split. If all ligands are assumed identical, the manner of this splitting is readily derived. In an octahedral complex with six ligands, equidistant from the central ion, one on each of the positive and negative Cartesian coordinates, the lobes of the d_{z^2} and $d_{x^2-y^2}$ orbitals point directly at the various ligands (cf. Fig. 18.1a). Any electron in one of these orbitals is strongly repelled by the negative charge of the ligands. The d_{xz}, d_{yz}, and d_{xy} orbitals (Fig. 18.1b), however, point in directions each halfway between a pair of ligands, and consequently any electron occupying such an orbital is repelled to a much lesser extent. The difference in repulsion then leads to a splitting of the degeneracy of the orbitals. It can be shown by the methods of group theory that the repulsions of the first two orbitals, of symmetry species e_g of the point group O_h of the octahedral complex, are equal, and similarly that the repulsions are equal for the latter three orbitals, which belong to the species t_{2g}. Thus, the five d orbitals split into two groups, e_g of higher energy and t_{2g} of lower energy, as shown schematically in Fig. 18.2b. The amount of splitting depends on the magnitude of the ligand charge q and the

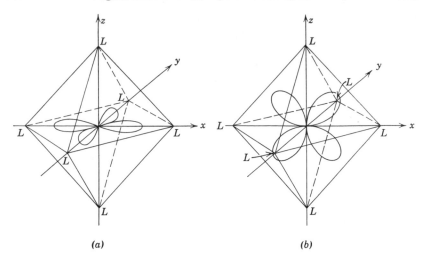

Fig. 18.1 The relation of d orbitals and ligands, (a) $d_{x^2-y^2}$ and (b) d_{xz}.

susceptibility—analogous to a polarizability—of the central ion, D, and is generally denoted by $10Dq$. If LFT did not involve some rather drastic assumptions, we might hope to evaluate a quantity q for each ligand and a susceptibility D for each ion; unfortunately, however, this is not possible, as will be shown later, and we must be satisfied with treating Dq as a single empirical, adjustable parameter.

Since considerable use is made in this chapter of the symmetry species of the point group O_h of octahedral complexes, it is desirable to review the previous discussion of symmetry species and extend it to this point group. The symmetry elements applicable to the point group O_h, represented by the octahedron, are three four-fold axes (C_4), passing through pairs of opposite corners, and coincident with them three two-fold axes (C_2'') and three four-fold rotation-reflection axes (S_4); four three-fold axes (C_3), through the centers of opposite faces, and coincident with them four six-fold rotation-reflection

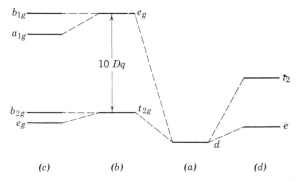

Fig. 18.2 Ligand-field splitting of the five degenerate d orbitals: (a) the isolated atom, (b) the octahedral, (c) square planar (tetragonal), and (d) tetrahedral fields.

axes (S_6); six two-fold axes (C_2) passing through the midpoints of opposite edges; a center of inversion (i); three planes of symmetry (σ_h), each the plane defined by four corners; and six planes (σ_d), each defined by two corners and the midpoints of two edges. The symmetry species appropriate to this point group are of types A_1, A_2, E, T_1, and T_2, each subdivided into a g and a u class because of the center of symmetry; these are shown in Table A3.22, together with the corresponding characters.

The s orbital is totally symmetric and obviously belongs to species a_{1g}. The three p orbitals are degenerate, and their characters will now be derived. Under a symmetry operation each orbital ϕ is transformed into another orbital ϕ'; in the nondegenerate species ϕ' is either $+\phi$ or $-\phi$, and the character is $+1$ or -1. In the triply degenerate species each orbital ϕ' is a linear combination of the three degenerate orbitals of the same species:

$$\phi_1' = d_{11}\phi_1 + d_{12}\phi_2 + d_{13}\phi_3$$
$$\phi_2' = d_{21}\phi_1 + d_{22}\phi_2 + d_{23}\phi_3$$
$$\phi_3' = d_{31}\phi_1 + d_{32}\phi_2 + d_{33}\phi_3$$

The character is defined as the sum of the diagonal elements of the transformation matrix (d_{ii}). Thus, under the identity operation, each p orbital transforms into itself, so that $\phi_1' = \phi_1$, $\phi_2' = \phi_2$, and $\phi_3' = \phi_3$, $d_{11} = d_{22} = d_{33} = 1$, $d_{12} = d_{13} = d_{21} = d_{23} = d_{31} = d_{32} = 0$, and the character, $d_{11} + d_{22} + d_{33} = +3$. Under the operation C_4, p_x transforms into p_y, p_y into $-p_x$, and p_z into itself, so that $\phi_1' = \phi_2$, $\phi_2' = -\phi_1$, and $\phi_3' = \phi_3$; $d_{11} = d_{22} = d_{13} = d_{31} = d_{23} = d_{32} = 0$, $d_{12} = d_{33} = 1$, $d_{21} = -1$; the character $d_{11} + d_{22} + d_{33} = 0 + 0 + 1 = +1$. Application of the same argument to the other two C_4 axes shows the equivalence of p_x and p_z (C_4^y) and p_y and p_z (C_4^x). Under the operation C_3^{xyz}, representing an axis through the corner (x,y,z) of the cube circumscribed about the octahedron, p_x is transformed into p_z, p_z into p_y, and p_y into p_x, so that $d_{11} = d_{22} = d_{33} = d_{12} = d_{23} = d_{31} = 0$, $d_{21} = d_{32} = d_{13} = 1$, and the character $d_{11} + d_{22} + d_{33} = 0$. The fact that none of the orbitals transforms into itself but that each one of them transforms into another one of the group indicates that they must jointly belong to a t species. The character of $+1$ with respect to the C_4 axes identifies the p orbitals as belonging to a t_1 species, and the well-known ungerade character of all p orbitals completes the identification as t_{1u}. The characters with respect to the other symmetry elements can be worked out in the same way.

Application of the same arguments shows that the three orbitals d_{xy}, d_{xz}, and d_{yz} transform into one another under the operation C_3 and hence must belong to a t species. Under the C_4 operations, however, they have a character of -1, and, since they are gerade, they belong to species t_{2g}. Similarly the orbitals $d_{x^2-y^2}$ and d_{z^2} can be shown to belong to species e_g.

In square planar coordination, further splits occur. Choosing the plane of the square of ligands as the xy plane, all four lobes of $d_{x^2-y^2}$ (belonging to the species b_{1g} of the point group D_{4h} to which these complexes belong) point toward ligands, whereas the lobes along the z axis of d_{z^2} (a_{1g}) do not, and consequently the repulsions involving the latter orbital are less than those involving b_{1g}, and the orbitals split as shown in Fig. 18.2c. Furthermore, although none of the other three orbitals points toward any ligands, each of the lobes of d_{xy} (b_{2g}) lies halfway between a pair of them, but each lobe of d_{xz} and d_{yz} (together e_g) comes near only one ligand, and hence the e_g orbitals (or the electrons occupying them) are repelled less than b_{2g}, leading to the splitting of t_{2g} shown in Fig. 18.2c. The splittings can again be expressed in terms of the parameter Dq.

In tetrahedral coordination, the ligands must be assumed to lie at the corners of a tetrahedron having the Cartesian coordinates as two-fold rotational axes. Consequently, d_{z^2} and $d_{x^2-y^2}$ (e), pointing between ligands, are least (cf. Fig. 18.3a), but equally repelled, as may be shown by group theory; d_{xz}, d_{yz}, and d_{xy} (t_2) (Fig. 18.3b) are also equally, and more strongly, repelled, leading to the pattern shown in Fig. 18.2d. The splitting in the tetrahedral field is smaller, $10 \cdot \frac{4}{9} Dq$.

Although the simple theory given predicts two levels each for octahedral and tetrahedral coordination, and four levels for square planar coordination, the situation is complicated by electron repulsions. Thus, in octahedral complexes, up to three d electrons are readily accommodated by the three lower energy levels, and, according to Hund's rule, occupy separate orbitals. But, as is well known, electronic repulsions are minimized when electrons occupy different orbitals. Consequently, when a fourth electron is to be accommodated by an octahedral complex, two possibilities need to be considered. The splitting of the energy levels shown in Fig. 18.2a is proportional to the strength of the field of the ligands, q. If this field is strong, the so-called *strong-field* case, the splitting is large compared to the extra electronic repulsion arising from double occupancy of one of the energy levels, and the electron configuration shown in the top half of Fig. 18.4b results; this configuration has two unpaired electrons. If the field is weak (low q) (the *weak-field* case), the configuration shown in the bottom part of the Fig. 18.4b results, and gives rise to four unpaired electrons. Five d electrons lead to the configurations shown in Fig. 18.4c with five and one unpaired electron in the weak- and the strong-field case, respectively. The configurations for six and seven unpaired electrons are given in Figs.

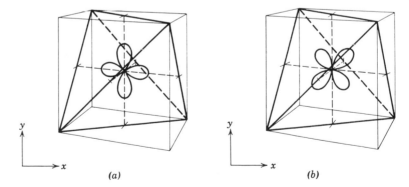

y   *x*
(a)

y   *x*
(b)

Fig. 18.3 The orientation of d orbitals in tetrahedral complexes: (a) $d_{x^2-y^2}$, e; (b) d_{xy}, t_1. [Reprinted by permission from D. S. McClure, *Solid State Phys.*, **9**, 399 (1959).]

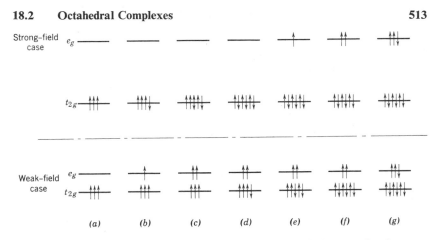

Fig. 18.4   The strong- and weak-field cases in LFT, octahedral coordination.

18.4d and 18.4e and involve four and none, and three and one, unpaired electrons, respectively, for the two cases. With eight or more d electrons, just as with three or fewer, the two cases are not distinct, as shown in Figs. 18.4a and 18.4f.

The strong- and weak-field cases correspond to the two types of complexes differentiated by the magnetic criterion; these have previously been called *ionic* and *covalent*, respectively, by Pauling, and *outer* and *inner* orbital complexes by Nyholm and Taube. The terminology *strong* and *weak field* also may not be completely satisfactory, since it is based on the assumption of a purely electrostatic interaction of ligand and central ion, which undoubtedly is a drastic oversimplification. Nevertheless, the results obtained are consistent with what may be obtained by an MO treatment, and help to shed considerable light on the nature of complexes.

In tetrahedral complexes, similar situations are likely to occur, but differentiation between the two cases would be expected to appear for central ions involving three to six d electrons, and ions with less than seven d electrons do not usually form tetrahedral complexes. In square planar complexes the situation is obviously considerably more complicated because of the more extensive splitting, and will not be discussed further.

18.2   Octahedral Complexes

The treatment so far has been kept in terms of the one-electron orbital approximation, and has given rise, in the case of octahedral complexes, to only two energy levels, separated by an amount $10Dq$ of energy. Consequently, theory at this level predicts a single transition, $t_{2g} \rightarrow e_g$. Since this is a $g \rightarrow g$ transition, it is quite strictly forbidden. A number of factors contribute to removal of this forbiddenness, but even so the transition is very weak. Most transition-metal complexes, including ones known to be octahedral, have at least one such transition in the visible region, but in very many cases more than one is observed. It remains to see whether ligand-field theory can account for the multiplicity of bands and the relation between their wavelengths.

It was shown in Chapter 5, that description of configurations in terms of one-electron orbitals is frequently inadequate and that a single electronic configuration can give rise to a variety of states. This multiplicity of states becomes particularly important when the configuration involves degenerate orbitals, as do the d^n configurations under consideration.

When a single d electron is involved, no problems arise. The configuration is simply t_{2g}, which gives rise to only one state, $^2T_{2g}$. Excitation of the single electron to an e_g orbital leads to the configuration e_g and the single state ^2E_g. The spectrum should contain a single $g \to g$ forbidden band at an excitation energy of $10Dq$. This prediction has been verified for Ti^{3+} complexes.[2b]

The case of two d electrons is more complicated. The configuration t_{2g}^2 can be written in six ways: d_{xz}^2, d_{yz}^2, d_{xy}^2, $d_{xy}d_{xz}$, $d_{xy}d_{yz}$, and $d_{xz}d_{yz}$. The first three of these, by the Pauli principle, must have paired spins and hence singlet states only. The other three can give rise to singlet and triplet states. It can be shown by group theory that the resulting states are $^3T_{1g}$, $^1T_{2g}$, $^1A_{1g}$, and ^1E_g. According to Hund's rule, the lowest state, the ground state, must be a triplet, hence $^3T_{1g}$. Excitation of one electron leads to the configuration $t_{2g}e_g$, which gives rise to two triplets, $^3T_{1g}$ and $^3T_{2g}$; singlets $^1T_{1g}$ and $^1T_{2g}$ also arise but are of relatively little interest, since transitions to them are forbidden by both the $g \leftrightarrow g$ and the multiplicity change selection rules, and hence they are extremely weak, occurring only because of spin-orbit coupling. Excitation of both electrons leads to the configuration e_g^2, with the states $^3A_{2g}$, ^1E_g, and $^1A_{1g}$. Thus, three triplet-triplet transitions $^3T_{2g} \leftarrow {}^3T_{1g}$, $^3T_{1g} \leftarrow {}^3T_{1g}$, and $^3A_{2g} \leftarrow {}^3T_{1g}$, are possible.

The energies corresponding to these transitions can be evaluated rather readily. In the first approximation, the configurations $t_{2g}e_g$ and e_g^2 lie $10Dq$ and $20Dq$, respectively, above the ground-state configuration, t_{2g}^2. Since the electrons of interest are assumed to occupy pure atomic d orbitals, the splitting of the different states of any configuration can be treated just as the splitting of the various states, so-called multiplets, in atoms. The theory of multiplet splittings has been well worked out,[3] and the actual splitting energies are expressed in terms of certain integrals, the so-called Slater-Condon parameters; in the case where only d electrons

---

[3] (a) E. U. Condon and G. H. Shortley, *The Theory of Atomic Spectra*, Cambridge University Press, London, 1951. (b) G. Racah, *Phys. Rev.*, **62**, 438 (1942).

are involved, only two such parameters are needed, F_{dd}^2 and F_{dd}^4, abbreviated F_2 and F_4, or, in the notation of Racah,[3b] expressed in terms of two other parameters, B and C. These parameters can be evaluated theoretically, if the atomic wave functions are known, as integrals over certain expressions involving these functions, but are most commonly evaluated empirically from the splittings of multiplets observed in the atomic spectra. Where they have not previously been tabulated,[2] they can be obtained from the spectroscopic data so carefully assembled by Moore.[4]

The parameters F_2 and F_4 in the molecule, in keeping with the assumption of purely electrostatic interaction, are normally assumed to be the same as in the free ions. Alternately, when this assumption seems undesirable and a fairly large number of transitions are observed, F_2 and F_4 are sometimes treated as additional empirical parameters of the complex. Thus the various transition energies can be expressed in terms of three parameters, Dq, F_2, and F_4, two of which are usually considered known.

As an example the ground state $^3T_{2g}$ has an energy $W = -8F_2 + 40F_4$, and the excited $^3A_{2g}$ state has $W = 10Dq - 8F_2 + 40F_4$, so that in this particular case the transition energy ΔW is just $10Dq$. In the first approximation, neglecting configuration interaction, the two $^3T_{1g}$ states have energies $4F_2 - 20F_4$ and $10Dq + 5F_2 - 25F_4$, leading to transition energies for the two $^3T_{1g} \leftarrow {}^3T_{2g}$ transitions of $12F_2 - 60F_4$ and $10Dq + 13F_2 - 65F_4$. If configuration interaction is taken into account, the energies become the solutions of the secular determinant:

$$\begin{vmatrix} 10Dq + 5F_2 - 25F_4 & 6F_2 - 30F_4 \\ 6F_2 - 30F_4 & 4F_2 - 20F_4 \end{vmatrix} = 0$$

For some selected states, F_2 and F_4 are tabulated in Table 18.1.

With three d electrons, the Aufbau principle leads to the ground-state configuration t_{2g}^3, which is a quartet due to Hund's rule, and corresponds to a $^4A_{2g}$ state. The excited configuration $t_{2g}^2e_g$ has two quartet states, $^4T_{2g}$ and $^4T_{1g}$, and the configuration $t_{2g}e_g^2$ has one, $^4T_{1g}$; the last configuration, e_g^3, of course, has no quartet state. Thus, three quartet-quartet transitions, $^4T_{2g} \leftarrow {}^4A_{2g}$ and two $^4T_{1g} \leftarrow {}^4A_{2g}$, are predicted, and their energies again can be evaluated in terms of Dq, F_2, and F_4.

When the central atom of the complex has more than three d electrons, some new complications arise as pointed out above. In the absence of the ligand-field perturbation (i.e., in the atomic case) the four d electrons, according to the Aufbau principle and Hund's rule, would be assigned to four separate d orbitals with parallel spins. In the weak-field case (i.e., if Dq is small), the splitting is small, and the four electrons will still be

[4] C. E. Moore, "Atomic Energy Levels," Nat. Bur. Standards Circ., 467, Vol. I, 1949; Vol. II, 1952; Vol. III, 1958, Washington, D.C.

assigned to separate orbitals and give rise to a configuration $t_{2g}^3 e_g$ in a quintet state, ^5E_g. Excitation of one electron could give rise to the excited configurations t_{2g}^4, which, however, involves no quintet states, and $t_{2g}^2 e_g^2$ with the quintet state, $^5T_{2g}$. No further configurations have quintet states; hence only one quintet-quintet transition, $^5T_{2g} \leftarrow {}^5E_g$, is predicted.

When the perturbing ligand field is strong (Dq large), however, the configuration $t_{2g}^3 e_g$, favored by Hund's rule, is no longer the lowest one. Although electron repulsions are larger in t_{2g}^4 the difference is less than $10Dq$, and t_{2g}^4 is the lowest configuration. This is the *strong-field case*, and

TABLE 18.1

The Slater-Condon Parameters F_2 and F_4 for Selected Transition-Metal Ions[2b]

M	M²⁺		M³⁺	
	F_2	F_4	F_2	F_4
Ti	...	...	1100	80
V	1100	80	1170	85
Cr	1350	85	1290	110
Mn	1390	90	...	...
Fe	1480	115	1700	110
Co	...	...	1760	140
Ni	1600	110	...	...
Cu	1800	120	...	...

has as ground state a triplet, $^3T_{1g}$. Excited triplets are five $^3T_{2g}$, three ^3E_g, two $^3A_{2g}$, six $^3T_{1g}$, and a $^3A_{1g}(t_{2g}^3 e_g)$. In these cases, with so many states belonging to any one species, the various states can hardly be assigned to individual configurations, since configuration interaction (cf. Chapter 8) must be important. A large variety of transitions results, leading to very complex spectra.

For five d electrons, in the weak-field case the lowest configuration is $t_{2g}^3 e_g^2$, corresponding to a ground state $^6A_{1g}$. No other sextet states are possible; consequently only sextet-quartet transitions are observed, and these are of quite low intensity. In the strong-field case the lowest configuration is t_{2g}^5, the ground state is a doublet, and the number of excited doublets is so large that an adequate treatment becomes virtually impracticable.

The treatment of complexes with six and seven d electrons follows similar lines, and leads to different results for strong and weak fields. With eight or more electrons, all three t_{2g} orbitals are occupied, independently of field strength. Moreover, the behavior of a hole in an electron shell is quite analogous to that of an electron, except that it appears to have a positive charge. Consequently, configurations d^{10-n} are treated exactly like the complementary configurations d^n, except that the quantity Dq has a negative sign.

18.3   The Spectra of Octahedral Complexes

The method of LFT, as outlined in section 18.2, has been applied to a wide variety of complexes, for many of which more or less detailed calculations have been made. These calculations have involved various degrees of approximation: in some cases careful attention has been paid to spin-orbit coupling, and configuration interaction, where applicable, has usually been taken into account. Without going into the details of the calculations, which may become quite complex, some results will now be compared with experimentally observed spectra.[2b,5]

In configuration d^1 (Ti^{3+}), only one transition, $^2E_g \leftarrow {}^2T_{2g}$, is predicted, and only one is observed,[6] which occurs at 20,400 cm^{-1} in the hexaquo complex, corresponding to a Dq value of 2040 cm^{-1}. Some typical results for configuration d^2 (V^{3+}) are given in Table 18.2. In the case of these vanadium compounds, several triplet-singlet transitions are observed in addition to two of the expected triplet-triplet transitions; the third, $^3A_{2g} \leftarrow {}^3T_{1g}$, is completely obliterated by an allowed charge-transfer transition. Of the three quartet → quartet transitions predicted in the d^3 configuration (Cr^{3+}, V^{2+}), only two are observed; the third is again predicted in a range where more intense charge-transfer transitions occur. Some results are shown in Table 18.3.

As an example of a term diagram for a set of ligand-field states, the diagram for Cr^{3+} is given in Fig. 18.5, where the energy of each of the four quartet states is plotted as a function of Dq. Several interesting features are apparent. The lowest three states, at $Dq = 0$, coalesce into a single state, the ground state of Cr^{3+} (^4F), while the highest state ($^3T_{1g}$) is correlated with the ^4P state of the free ion. In the absence of configuration interaction and spin-orbit coupling, each state would be represented by a straight line; but the lines for the two $^4T_{1g}$ states would cross. Consequently, account of configuration interaction leads to the observed bending for these two states.

Very little information is available on configuration d^4. In d^5, the weak-field case involves a sextet ground state, $^6A_{1g}$, and no excited sextets exist. Consequently, any observed transitions are not only parity, but

[5] D. S. McClure, *Solid State Physics*, **9**, 399 (1959), gives a discussion of most of the available data, with special emphasis on solid spectra.

[6] H. Hartmann and H. L. Schläfer, *Z. physik. Chem.*, **197**, 116 (1951).

TABLE 18.2
Ligand-Field Spectra of Some Octahedral V^{3+} Complexes
(Configuration d^2; frequencies in cm.$^{-1}$)[a]

Transition	$V(aq)_6^{3+}$		VF_6^{3-} [b]		$VF_5(aq)^{2-}$ [b]	$VF_4(aq)_2^{-}$ [b]	$VF_3(aq)_3$ [b]	$V_3^{3+}:Al_2O_3$	
	Calc.	Obs.	Calc.	Obs.	Obs.	Obs.	Obs.	Calc.	Obs.
$^1E_g, {}^1T_{2g} \leftarrow {}^3T_{1g}$			9,200	10,200	10,500	12,000	11,500	9,100	$\begin{cases} 8,770 \\ 9,660 \end{cases}$
$^3T_{2g} \leftarrow {}^3T_{1g}$	(19,000)	19,000	(14,800)	14,800	15,500	16,000	16,200	(17,400)	17,400
$^1A_{1g} \leftarrow {}^3T_{1g}$								20,000	21,000
$^3T_{1g} \leftarrow {}^3T_{1g}$	28,500	25,000	23,200	23,000	23,500	23,800	24,500	25,400	25,200
$^1T_{1g} \leftarrow {}^3T_{1g}$			27,300			28,200			
$^3A_{2g} \leftarrow {}^3T_{1g}$								35,800	34,500

[a] C. J. Ballhausen and F. Winther, *Acta Chem. Scand.*, **13**, 1729 (1959); S. C. Furman and C. S. Garner, *J. Am. Chem. Soc.*, **72**, 1785 (1950); see also reference in footnote 2b.
[b] No separate calculations with different *Dq* are reported.

TABLE 18.3

The Spectra of Some Complexes of Configuration d^{3a}

Transition	$Cr(aq)_6^{3+}$		$Cr(am)_6^{3+}$		$V(aq)_6^{2+}$	
	Calc.	Obs.	Calc.	Obs.	Calc.	Obs.
$^4T_{2g} \leftarrow {}^4A_{2g}$	(17,200)	17,200	(21,500)	21,500	(12,200)	12,200
$^4T_{1g} \leftarrow {}^4A_{2g}$	25,700	25,600	30,500	28,500	18,700	17,900

[a] O. G. Holmes and D. S. McClure, *J. Chem. Phys.*, **26**, 1686 (1957); see also reference in footnote 2*b*.

also multiplicity, forbidden. Some such transitions have been observed in the crystalline halides of Mn^{2+}, in which the manganous ions are surrounded almost octahedrally by six halide ions. The data[7] for these compounds are given in Table 18.4. The agreement seems excellent, particularly considering that one empirical parameter is used to fit ten transitions. The ground state of configuration d^5 in the strong-field case is a doublet; the number of excited doublets is very large, and no careful analysis of any one system seems to have been made.

Although little experimental information is available for configuration d^7, it is instructive to compare its term diagram (Fig. 18.6) with that of the complementary configuration d^3 (Fig. 18.5). The right side of Fig. 18.6 is

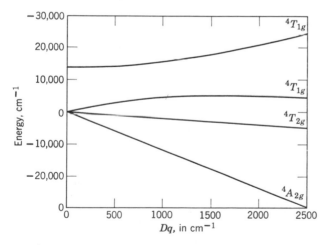

Fig. 18.5 Term-level diagram for Cr^{3+} (d^3). [Reprinted by permission from L. E. Orgel, *J. Chem. Phys.*, **23**, 1004 (1955).]

[7] R. Pappalardo, *J. Chem. Phys.*, **33**, 613 (1960); J. W. Stout, *J. Chem. Phys.*, **31**, 709 (1959).

TABLE 18.4

Ligand-Field Spectra of the Manganous Halides

(Configuration d^5, frequencies in cm^{-1})

Transition	MnCl$_2$ Crystal		MnBr$_2$ Crystal		MnF$_2$ Crystal	
	Calc.	Obs.	Calc.	Obs.	Calc.	Obs.
$^4T_{1g} \leftarrow {}^6A_{1g}$	18,500	18,500	18,740	18,450	(19,440)	19,440
$^4T_{2g} \leftarrow {}^6A_{1g}$	21,800	22,000	21,780	21,650	23,680	23,500
$^4A_{1g} \leftarrow {}^6A_{1g}$	(23,500)	23,590	(23,085)	23,084	25,190	25,190 25,300
$^4E_g \leftarrow {}^6A_{1g}$	23,700	23,825	23,150	23,550	25,480	25,500
$^4T_{2g} \leftarrow {}^6A_{1g}$	26,500	26,750	26,950	26,520	29,650	28,120 28,370
$^4E_g \leftarrow {}^6A_{1g}$	28,000	28,065	27,720	27,505	30,240	30,230
$^4T_{1g} \leftarrow {}^6A_{1g}$	34,000	36,000	31,620	29,950	32,960	33,060
$^4A_{2g} \leftarrow {}^6A_{1g}$	37,500	38,400	36,220	34,800	39,000	39,000
$^4T_{1g} \leftarrow {}^6A_{1g}$	39,000	40,650	39,160	37,400	43,200	41,400
$^4T_{2g} \leftarrow {}^6A_{1g}$	42,000	42,370	40,500	38,750	...	...

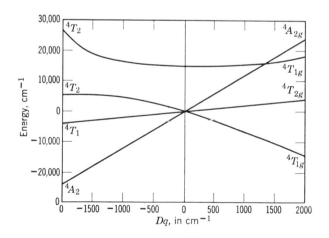

Fig. 18.6 Term-level diagram for Co^{2+} (d^7). [Reprinted by permission from L. E. Orgel, *J. Chem. Phys.*, **23**, 1004 (1955).]

applicable to the octahedral complex. The three states arising out of the atomic ground state (^4F) are seen to be just reversed from Fig. 18.5. The upper $^4T_{1g}$ state, however, remains above the others until it crosses the $^4A_{2g}$ state at about $Dq = 1300 \text{ cm}^{-1}$. Configuration interaction again affects the two $^4T_{1g}$ states.

The most widely investigated complexes are probably those of Ni^{2+} (d^8). Data for a series of octahedral complexes are given[8] in Table 18.5. Although not all predicted transitions are always observed, LFT seems amazingly successful in providing an interpretation of the observed spectra.

Finally, in configuration d^9 only one transition is predicted, and comparisons with one empirical parameter are useless. In this case, however, some very interesting calculations[9] based on a strictly electrostatic model have been made for a series of ammino aquo cupric complexes. Coordination in this case results in not quite octahedral symmetry, but a distorted octahedron of tetragonal symmetry. When no more than four ammino groups are present, they are assumed to lie in the xy plane, and the ligand (an aquo group except in the pentammine and hexammine complexes) is assumed to lie along the z axis slightly farther from the cupric ion than the ligands in the xy plane. The results of these calculations are shown in Table 18.6 and are seen to be amazingly accurate.

From data such as are shown in Tables 18.2–18.6, tables of Dq values may be assembled. Table 18.7 shows such a compilation.[2b,5] As shown before, if the basic concepts of LFT are correct, D should depend only on the central atom, q, on the ligand. That this is not so is readily obvious by examination of the table. The reason for failure lies, of course, in the tremendous oversimplifications of the theory, particularly in the assumption that the metal-ligand bonding is purely electrostatic. This assumption is examined further in section 18.4.

It is gratifying, however, to find that, as far as information is available, Dq values for a series of ligands generally fall in pretty much the same order, even in different configurations. Thus, Orgel[2b] quotes the order $Cl^- < H_2O <$ pyridine $< NH_3 < (CH_2NH_2)_2$ for Cu^{2+}, MeOH $< H_2O$ $<$ oxalate $<$ pyridine $< NH_3 < (CH_2NH_2)_2 < o$-phenanthroline for Ni^{2+}, $I^- < Br^- < Cl^- < CNS^- <$ oxalate $< H_2O < NH_3 < (CH_2NH_2)_2$ for Cr^{3+}, $CO_3^{2-} < OH^- < NO_3^- < SO_3^{2-} < CNS^- < H_2O <$ oxalate $< NH_3 <$ $(CH_2NH_2)_2 < NO_2^- < CN^-$ and $I^- < Br^- < Cl^- < N^- < RCOO^- <$ $F^- < NH_3 < NO_2^-$ for Co^{3+}. Thus, with the exception of the oxalate-water pair, there are no inversions of order in the five series.

    [8] A. D. Liehr and C. J. Ballhausen, *Ann. Phys.* (*N. Y.*), **6**, 134 (1959); references in footnote 2; G. Maki, *J. Chem. Phys.*, **29**, 170 (1958).

    [9] J. Bjerrum, C. J. Ballhausen, and C. K. Jørgensen, *Acta Chem. Scand.*, **8**, 1275 (1954).

TABLE 18.5

Ligand-Field Spectra of Octahedral Ni^{2+} Complexes

(Configuration d^8, frequencies in cm^{-1})

Transition	$Ni(aq)_6^{2+}$ Calc.	Obs.	$Ni(am)_6^{2+}$ Calc.	Obs.	$Ni(en)_3^{2+}$ Calc.	Obs.	$Ni(o\text{-phen})_3^{2+}$ Calc.	Obs.	$Ni^{2+}:MgO$ Calc.	Obs.
$^3T_{2g} \leftarrow {}^3A_{2g}$	(8,500)	8,500	11,000	10,750	11,600	11,400	12,000	11,550	8,500	8,600
$^3T_{1g} \leftarrow {}^3A_{2g}$	13,500	13,500	12,540	13,150	16,600	12,200	12,700	12,700	13,500	13,400
$^3T_{1g} \leftarrow {}^3A_{2g}$	14,500	15,400	17,200	17,500	19,900	18,600	18,700	19,300	14,500	14,800
$^3T_{1g} \leftarrow {}^3A_{2g}$	...	...	...	...	...	...	20,200	19,000	20,500	21,550
$^3T_{1g} \leftarrow {}^3A_{2g}$	24,000	25,300	27,900	28,200	30,400	29,200	...	...	24,000	24,500
$^1T_{1g} \leftarrow {}^3A_{2g}$	...	...	...	...	...	...	...	...	24,700	25,950
$^1E_g \leftarrow {}^3A_{2g}$	...	...	...	...	...	...	...	...	31,300	34,500

TABLE 18.6

The Ligand-Field Spectra of a Series of Ammino Aquo Cupric Ions

Complex	Wavelength, $m\mu$	
	Calc.	Obs.
Cu aq$_6^{2+}$	...	790
Cu am aq$_5^{2+}$	710	745
cis-Cu am$_2$aq$_4^{2+}$	670	680
trans-Cu am$_2$aq$_4^{2+}$	620	600
Cu am$_3$aq$_3^{2+}$	660	645
Cu am$_4$aq$_2^{2+}$	(590)	590
Cu am$_5$aq$_1^{2+}$	...	640
Cu am$_6^{2+}$	...	640

It may be concluded from Fig. 18.7, however, that the emphasis on electrostatic interaction made by LFT can be at best a crude approximation. According to the MO picture, Dq actually reflects a number of factors. When π bonding is ignored, Dq represents the antibonding contribution of $e_g{}^*$. Also, evaluation of multiplet splittings in terms of F_2 and F_4 can be only a first approximation, since the MO picture shows that e_g accepts a considerable contribution from ligand orbitals. When π

TABLE 18.7

Ligand-Field Splitting Dq in Some Octahedral Complexes
(in cm^{-1})

Central Ion	Ligand				
	$(H_2O)_6$	$(NH_3)_6$	$F_6{}^-$	$Cl_6{}^-$	$Br_6{}^-$
Ti^{3+}	2040				
V^{3+}	1900		1585		
V^{2+}	1220				
Cr^{3+}	1770	2150		1330	
Cr^{2+}	1260				
Mn^{3+}	2100				
Mn^{2+}	750		780	750	700
Fe^{3+}	2100				
Fe^{2+}	1050				
Co^{3+}	1910				
Co^{2+}	970	1100			
Ni^{2+}	850	1080			600
Cu^{2+}	1260	1510		650	

electrons are also considered, Dq must be reduced further by the anti-bonding contribution of t_{2g}. It is not at all surprising that this complicated mixture of effects does not readily lend itself to analysis into separate components D and q.

18.4   Relation of Ligand-Field Theory to Molecular-Orbital Theory

It may, at this time, be profitable to take a careful look at the consequence of the assumption of purely electrostatic bonding made at the beginning of section 18.1. This may be done most easily by comparing LFT with MO theory, and, consequently, the MO description of an octahedral complex will now be derived. The orbitals of the central atom to be considered are the s and p orbitals of the outer (valence) shell, and the d orbitals of the next inner shell. In the point group O_h the s orbital belongs to the species a_g, the three p orbitals to the species t_{1u}, and the d orbitals to t_{2g} and e_g as outlined above. Each ligand is assumed to have available for complex formation a single orbital pointed directly at the central atom. In order to transform the ligand orbitals into the symmetry appropriate to the problem, so-called GO's are formed as orthonormal linear combinations of the ligand orbitals, and it can readily be shown that these also occur as one of species a_g, a degenerate pair of species e_g, and a degenerate group of three of species t_{1u}. Interaction of the appropriate ligand GO's with the metal orbitals then forms the MO's shown in Fig. 18.7a. The bonding MO's a_{1g}, e_g, and t_{1u}, contain the twelve electrons forming the single bonds between the ligands and the central atom and are of no further interest. The t_{2g} orbitals are essentially nonbonding, and will contain most or all of the d electrons of the metal not involved in bonding. The e_g^*, t_{1u}^*, and a_g^* orbitals are antibonding. The t_{2g} and e_g^* orbitals of Fig. 18.7a are the ones previously considered as the ligand-field orbitals. The same treatment is given in Fig. 18.7b for the weak-field case. This is distinguished from the strong-field case of Fig. 18.7a in that the electrons are more tightly bound in the ligand, and hence the MO's involved in σ bonding are much more nearly pure ligand orbitals, and perturb the central atom orbital to a much lesser extent. It is readily seen that this corresponds to much smaller Dq, and much more closely to Pauling's concept of the ionic complex.

Many of the ligands involved in complex formation possess electrons in orbitals which have π character with respect to the ligand-central atom axis. Examples of such ligands are Cl^- and CN^-. There will, in general, be twelve such orbitals, two for each ligand. These again can be combined into GO's, which then belong to the symmetry species t_{1u}, t_{1g}, t_{2u}, and t_{2g}. The t_{1g} and t_{2u} orbitals have no counterpart on the central atom and hence represent nonbonding MO's in the complex. The t_{1u} orbital may interact

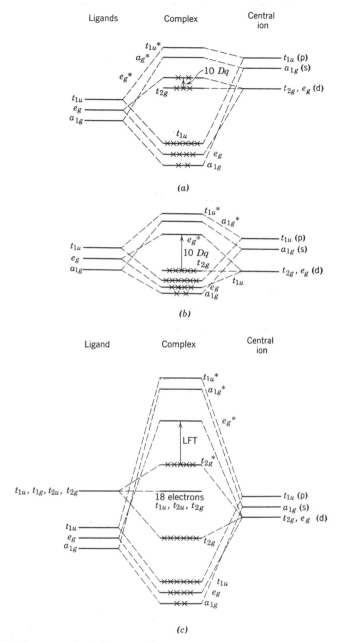

Fig. 18.7 The energy-level diagram of an octahedral complex: (a) the weak-field case, (b) the strong-field case, (c) including π interaction. The electrons corresponding to d^5 are shown.

slightly with the other two t_{1u} orbitals, but this is without serious consequence. However, the t_{2g} GO's of the ligands interact with the central atom t_{2g} orbitals, forming the π bonds often considered in the complex. The appropriate energy-level diagram is shown in Fig. 18.7c. Here the $t_{2g}*$ and e_g* orbitals correspond to the LFT orbitals considered in section 18.1.

The preceding discussion shows that the LFT represents a part of the much more complete MO representation of the complex. The tremendous power of the LFT lies in the fact that a number of qualitative or semi-quantitative conclusions are immediately possible, and that even quantitative calculations with only one empirical parameter, Dq, are astonishingly good. With adequate computation, the MO schemes of Fig. 18.7 should also permit good, possibly better quantitative predictions of the spectra of such complexes. Of course, such a complete treatment would give information, not only about the parity-forbidden so-called ligand-field transitions, but also about the allowed transitions usually occurring at somewhat shorter wavelengths, often called the *charge-transfer transitions*, which are further discussed later. However, even approximate quantitative calculations are almost impossible to achieve, since the number of orbitals and the number of integrals to be evaluated, either theoretically or empirically, are tremendous.

18.5   Square Planar (Tetragonal) Complexes

The ligand-field splitting in square planar (tetragonal) complexes was discussed in section 18.1 and shown graphically in Fig. 18.2c. The same arguments actually apply to any arrangement with tetragonal (D_{4h}) symmetry, e.g., to *trans*-ML_4X_2 complexes. The treatment of the aquo amino cupric complexes given at the end of section 18.3 is really an example of this situation.

At first sight such close relation between the octahedral and tetragonal cases may seem surprising. The much more complex level diagram of the tetragonal case might have suggested a more complicated term-level scheme. The situation is not quite so bad, however, since most levels of the tetragonal case have lower degeneracy, and hence the number of states belonging to any one configuration is much smaller. In fact, simple correlation diagrams, like the connection between Figs. 18.2b and 18.2c, can be given for states; some of the degenerate states split into separate ones of lower degeneracy, but otherwise no really new principles are involved.

Maki[10] has made an intensive study of a series of nickel(II) complexes.

[10] G. Maki, *J. Chem. Phys.*, **29**, 162, 1129 (1958).

She has, in particular, made calculations for a number of complexes of unknown geometry, assuming various different possible geometrics, such as tetrahedral, square planar, tetragonal bipyramidal, and octahedral, for complexes such as NiR_4X_2, and used the results to demonstrate which is the most probable geometry of the complex. Thus, in di-*o*-phenanthroline nickel(II)chloride, compound I, and bis(N,N′-diphenylethylene diammine)-

TABLE 18.8
Ligand-Field Transitions in Some Square Planar Nickel(II) Ions[10]
(in cm^{-1})

(a) Point Group D_{4h}

Transition	Compound I		Compound II		Compound III	
	Calc.	Obs.	Calc.	Obs.	Calc.	Obs.
$^3E_g \leftarrow {}^3B_{2g}$	(8,240)	8,240	...	...	...	...
$^3B_{1g} \leftarrow {}^3B_{2g}$	13,600	12,000	7,700	7,940	...	...
$^3A_{2g} \leftarrow {}^3B_{2g}$	...	...	10,200	9,800	8,000	8,900
$^1B_{2g} \leftarrow {}^3B_{2g}$	...	...	11,400	11,800	...	...
$^1A_{1g} \leftarrow {}^3B_{2g}$	14,900	12,700	...	...	...	...
$^3E_g \leftarrow {}^3B_{2g}$	17,300	17,500	12,200	14,900	14,800	15,100
$^1E_g \leftarrow {}^3B_{2g}$	...	...	20,100	19,900	...	...
$^3A_{2g} \leftarrow {}^3B_{2g}$	26,800	26,800	23,200	23,200	25,600	25,000

(b) Point Group D_{2h}

Transition	Compound IV		Compound V	
	Calc.	Obs.	Calc.	Obs.
$^3A_g \leftarrow {}^3B_{3g}$	7,000	9,200	...	...
$^1A_g \leftarrow {}^3B_{3g}$	10,500	10,500	8,100	8,800
$^3B_{1g} \leftarrow {}^3B_{3g}$	13,600	12,900	13,000	10,100
$^1B_{3g} \leftarrow {}^3B_{3g}$	...	...	16,600	13,400
$^3B_{2g} \leftarrow {}^3B_{3g}$	15,400	16,000	19,300	16,200
$^3B_{2g} \leftarrow {}^3B_{3g}$	23,200	23,800	27,000	27,200

nickel(II)chloride, compound II, a tetragonal bipyramid, with Cl⁻ ions at the apices, is concluded to be the best fit; data for these are given in Table 18.8*a*. Similar calculations for bisacetylacetone nickel(II), compound III, which may be assumed to be square planar, are given in the same table. It should be noted that, because of the chelating nature of the ligands, these complexes do not really have the D_{4h} symmetry assumed, but the ligand field, made up of the four equivalent coordinating nitrogen or oxygen atoms, closely approximates this symmetry. In the case of bissalicylaldehyde nickel(II), compound IV, and nickel(II)diglycinate, compound V, the coordinating oxygen atoms are nonequivalent, and the compound must have lower symmetry, presumably D_{2h}, i.e., a *trans*-planar arrangement. Calculations made on the basis of this symmetry are shown in Table 18.8*b*. In several of these cases, some of the assignments are to multiplicity-forbidden (triplet-singlet) transitions, and these are assigned to bands which were concluded on the basis of experimental observation to be of this type. Thus, the LFT seems to be able to interpret these spectra quite well, and to be actually useful in determining the geometry of the complexes.

Further calculations on *cis*- and *trans*-square planar complexes of nickel (II), of D_{2d} and D_{2h} symmetry, respectively, involved some glyoxime and salicylaldimine complexes.[10] It is of particular interest that the observed transitions from diamagnetic to paramagnetic behavior could be correlated with changes from stable singlet to triplet ground states, a case of strong and weak fields in square planar coordination.

18.6   Tetrahedral Complexes

The splittings of the degenerate d orbitals due to the tetrahedral field also were discussed in section 18.1 and shown in Fig. 18.2*d*. The situation quite closely resembles the one in the octahedral field, except that the direction of splitting is reversed. A typical term-level diagram for the quartet states of configuration d^7 is shown on the left half of Fig. 18.6. Although the term (state) designations are different, because of the different point group, it is seen that a direct correlation of states between octahedral and tetrahedral complexes is possible. However, the tetrahedral complexes involve one major complication: they have no center of symmetry. This fact immediately removes the parity forbiddenness of the ligand-field transitions, and so it is not surprising to find that they generally occur with much higher intensity than in octahedral complexes. On the other hand, the triply degenerate GO formed from the four σ-bonding hybrid ligand orbitals is of the same symmetry species (t_2) as the triply degenerate central ion d orbitals. Hence these orbitals mix, and the approximation of distinguishing between ligand-field transitions in the d shell of the central ion and charge-transfer transitions between the ligands and ion has much less validity. This fact also contributes to the intensity. As a result of these complications, the application of LFT to tetrahedral complexes has been much slower in developing. As late as 1955 Orgel[2b] found no indication that successful correlations had been made.

The situation has, however, considerably improved since then. Table

TABLE 18.9
Ligand-Field Transitions in Tetrahedral Ni^{2+} [11]
(in cm^{-1})

	Ni^{2+}:ZnO	
Transition	Calc.	Obs.
$^3T_2 \leftarrow {}^3T_1$	8,300	8,300
$^3T_2 \leftarrow {}^3T_1$	12,100	12,100
$^3T_2 \leftarrow {}^3T_1$	12,700	13,500
$^3T_2 \leftarrow {}^3T_1$	15,600	15,100
$^3T_1 \leftarrow {}^3T_1$	16,000	16,200
$^3A_2 \leftarrow {}^3T_1$	18,600	18,000

18.9 gives some highly encouraging results[8] for Ni^{2+}. Considerable success has also been obtained[11] in a series of chlorides, $MnCl_4^{2-}$, $CoCl_4^{2-}$, and $NiCl_4^{2-}$.

18.7 Intensities

Very little detailed work has been done on intensities of ligand-field transitions. This is not at all surprising, since all these transitions are forbidden and are of very low intensity, and high approximations must be used to obtain nonvanishing intensities. Wherever the complex has a center of symmetry, the parity selection rule ($g \leftrightarrow g$) makes the transitions forbidden. Even in the absence of a center of symmetry, however, the transitions are rather strictly forbidden because of symmetry selection rules. In addition, many of the potential transitions are forbidden by several selection rules. Thus, in all the complexes (except those of con-figurations d^1 and d^9) states of different multiplicity occur, which are forbidden, in addition to the above, by the multiplicity-selection rule. Accordingly, any calculation of intensity by the simple methods of Chapter 6 gives vanishing values, and any calculation which is to give different results must take into account the various possible perturbations.

The perturbation which comes to mind first when discussing observed forbidden transitions is distortion of the molecule by vibrations of low symmetry, i.e., vibronic interaction. Thus any change by one (or any odd number) of the vibrational quantum number of an ungerade vibration accompanying electronic excitation circumvenes the parity-selection rule, and permits absorption to occur in spite of this rule. Similarly, an odd-numbered change of vibrational quantum number of any vibration of

[11] S. Buffagni and T. M. Dunn, *Nature*, **188**, 937 (1960),

appropriate symmetry can avoid the operation of the symmetry selection rules. It is undoubtedly due to some such vibronic interactions that ligand-field spectra of octahedral and tetragonal complexes are observed. Multiplicity-forbidden transitions have also occasionally been observed; see Tables 18.2, 18.4, and 18.5 for examples. These transitions must derive their intensity from spin-orbit coupling (section 6.9). Symmetry species of vibrations important in removing forbiddenness, and combinations of states significantly involved in spin-orbit coupling, have been listed for the d^8 case.[10] Actually, spin-orbit coupling has been taken into account in a

TABLE 18.10

Intensities of Some Ligand-Field Transitions

(Expressed as $f \times 10^5$)[12]

Transition	$Ni(aq)_6^{2+}$		$Ni(am)_6^{2+}$		$V(aq)_6^{3+}$	
	Calc.	Obs.	Calc.	Obs.	Calc.	Obs.
$^3T_{2g} \leftarrow {}^3A_{2g}$	3.1	2.2	6.2	5.3	...	...
$^3T_{1g} \leftarrow {}^3A_{2g}$	4.3	3.5	10.0	7.0	...	...
$^3T_{1g} \leftarrow {}^3A_{2g}$	5.4	7.2	7.9	9.8	...	...
$^1E_g \leftarrow {}^3A_{2g}$	0.1	...	0.2	0.2	...	...
$^3T_{2g} \leftarrow {}^3T_{1g}$	...	...	...	...	1.9	9.3
$^3T_{1g} \leftarrow {}^3T_{1g}$	...	...	...	...	3.5	18

number of calculations of transition frequencies, has thereby been found not to be negligible, and is without doubt responsible for the appearance of multiplicity-forbidden transitions.

In complexes without a center of symmetry, in addition, configuration interaction with allowed transitions is important, to the extent that a strict distinction becomes impossible between the forbidden ligand-field transition and the allowed charge-transfer transition. This factor appears rather unimportant in octahedral complexes which are distorted because of either crystal distortions or an unsymmetrical set of ligands, since mixed aquo ammino and chloro ammino complexes appear to have spectra substantially like those of their symmetrical analogs. In tetrahedral complexes this factor is, however, of prime importance.

The intensities of some octahedral nickel complexes have been carefully examined,[12] taking account of vibronic interaction and spin-orbit coupling. The results are shown in Table 18.10, where calculated intensities are given only for those transitions for which experimental values are available. All the other transitions, presumably unobserved, of hexaquo nickel(II) ion have calculated f values less than 0.1 of the weakest observed transition,

[12] C. J. Ballhausen and A. D. Liehr, *Mol. Phys.*, **2**, 123 (1959).

and only the $^1T_{1g} \leftarrow {}^3T_{1g}$ transition, with $f = 0.2$, has an intensity as large as that of the very weak $^1E_g \leftarrow {}^1A_{2g}$ of hexammine nickel(II). Similar calculations for hexaquo vanadium(III) are somewhat less satisfactory. Again all unlisted transitions have vastly lower calculated intensity.

For the tetrahedral complexes $CoCl_4{}^{2-}$, $CuCl_4{}^{2-}$, $CrO_4{}^{2-}$, and $MnO_4{}^{-}$,[13] the theory is very much more complex and requires more assumptions; in particular, configuration interaction with states which are not pure d electron states, or hybridization of s, p, and d orbitals, must be taken into account. Under these circumstances, results obtained are in reasonable agreement with experiment.

Thus, it is encouraging to find that LFT, at least in complexes with a center of symmetry, not only is able to account qualitatively for the spectra and quantitatively for the wavelengths, but also gives reasonable approximations to intensities.

18.8   Charge-Transfer Absorption

Considering the complexity of the electronic structure of the complexes of transition elements, it is hardly to be expected that the ligand-field transitions discussed in the preceding sections of this chapter are the only observable transitions in the spectra of complexes. Examination of Fig. 18.7 indicates that quite a number of other transitions can be written, even in the absence of π electrons on the ligand, as, e.g., in the hexammine complexes. The most likely transition to be of importance is the $t_{1u} \rightarrow e_g$ excitation, which, because of the degeneracy of both levels, again gives rise to a series of possible bands. The lower, t_{1u} level is formed from hybrid orbitals of the ligand and p orbitals of the metal; since the hybrid orbitals of the ligand generally have lower energy than the metal p orbital, the t_{1u} molecular orbital receives a predominant contribution from the ligand; in terms of LFT, it is actually a pure ligand orbital. The e_g orbital, according to LFT, is a pure metal orbital; according to MO theory, it probably receives a predominant contribution from the metal. (Figure 18.7a may create the impression that this is not so; the relative positioning of metal and ligand orbitals in this figure is probably not quite realistic, but was drawn in this way to exaggerate and thereby illustrate more clearly the distinction between weak- and strong-field cases.) Thus, the $t_{1u} \rightarrow e_g$ transition involves a large degree of transfer of an electron from the ligands to the central ion; in terms of the pure LFT description it involves transfer of a whole electron. Consequently this transition and similar ones are frequently called *charge-transfer transitions*. They are either allowed or, at most, symmetry forbidden (aside from multiplicity-forbidden components, which may also occur at low intensity) and consequently are observed

[13] C. J. Ballhausen and A. D. Liehr, *Mol. Spectroscopy*, **2**, 343 (1958).

with relatively high intensity. They usually occur in the quartz ultraviolet and at shorter wavelengths; they occasionally extend into the visible. Whenever they occur, they obliterate any ligand-field transitions occurring in the same region.

In a vast number of complexes the ligands also have π orbitals available, which interact, as shown in Fig. 18.7c, with certain of the central ion orbitals. When the ligand π orbitals are completely filled, as in the halide ions, electrons from these orbitals can only be delocalized into the metal. In more complex ligands, such as CN^-, CO, and ethylene, delocalization of metal d electrons into antibonding π electrons of the ligand is also possible. In ligands such as PR_3, PX_3, and AsR_3, this is the only possible π-electron interaction. In other complexes such as aquo ions, the number of ligand π orbitals is more restricted. Each of these problems really requires careful and separate consideration which will, however, not be attempted here.

In octahedral halide or cyanide complexes, beyond the LFT transitions $t_{2g}{}^* \rightarrow e_g{}^*$, we would anticipate several $t_{1u} \rightarrow e_g{}^*$ and $t_{2u} \rightarrow e_g{}^*$ transitions, and some of these are observed. Since the t_{1u} and t_{2u} π orbitals (cf. Fig. 18.7c) are described as pure ligand orbitals, these transitions are again described as charge-transfer transitions.

In tetrahedral complexes, as was seen before, the separation into ligand-field transitions and charge-transfer transitions largely breaks down. Here, again, transitions involving ligand orbitals are possible.

An adequate description of the spectra due to all these transitions requires a more or less complete MO treatment of the molecules. Although some such treatments have been provided,[14] the magnitude of the problem is staggering, and the number of cases for which an adequate treatment is available is quite limited. Actually, the problems involved are qualitatively not different from the much less complex cases treated throughout earlier chapters of this book. Because of the quantitative difficulties, however, the charge-transfer spectra of complexes will not be discussed further.

GENERAL REFERENCES

The early work is reviewed by:

W. Moffitt and C. J. Ballhausen, *Ann. Rev. Phys. Chem.*, **7**, 107 (1956).

A careful, highly mathematical treatment is given by:

D. S. McClure, *Solid State Phys.*, **9**, 399 (1959).

A completely qualitative, but highly readable introduction is given by:

L. E. Orgel, *An Introduction to Transition-Metal Chemistry: Ligand-Field Theory*, Methuen and Co., London (John Wiley and Sons, New York), 1960.

Spectra are discussed by:

T. M. Dunn, in *Modern Coordination Chemistry*, edited by J. Lewis and R. G. Wilkins, Interscience Publishers, New York, 1960, Chapter 4.

[14] For example, M. Wolfsberg and L. Helmholz, *J. Chem. Phys.*, **20**, 837 (1952).

19 Spectroscopic properties of excited states; fluorescence and phosphorescence

19.1 Deactivation of Excited States

Previous chapters in this book, with the exception of early chapters concerned with a description of the electronic structures of the ground and excited states of molecules, have been devoted to absorption spectra. If it is recalled that light absorption occurs when molecules are excited from the ground to excited states, we may well inquire into the fate of the energy so absorbed. Although such an inquiry will produce little of interest in absorption spectroscopy, it leads to an insight into an entirely different realm of spectroscopic phenomena, the fluorescence and phosphorescence spectra. Consequently, preparatory to a discussion of these spectra, this section will deal with the different modes of deactivation of excited states.

Excited states reached by absorption of visible and ultraviolet light are states of quite high energy. Thus absorption of light at 400 mμ corresponds to absorption of 71.6 kcal/mole, and absorption at 200 mμ to 143.2 kcal/mole. It is hardly to be expected that molecules spend long times in such energy-rich states, and the usual excited states actually have half-lives which rarely exceed 10^{-6} sec, and more generally vary down to 10^{-8} or 10^{-9} sec.

The simplest mechanism by which we might expect an excited state to lose the excess energy is by re-emission as a light quantum of the same, or substantially the same, frequency as the quantum which produced the excitation. Such re-emission does frequently occur and gives rise to the phenomenon of fluorescence. That this mode of deactivation is not the only one, however, is clearly indicated by the fact that most compounds do not fluoresce, and that the amount of energy re-emitted by fluorescence in compounds that do fluoresce is usually considerably smaller than the amount of energy absorbed (i.e., the fluorescence yield, ϕ, is considerably below 1). The average decay period, τ, of fluorescing compounds (i.e., the time required for the intensity of the emitted light to fall to $1/e$ of its

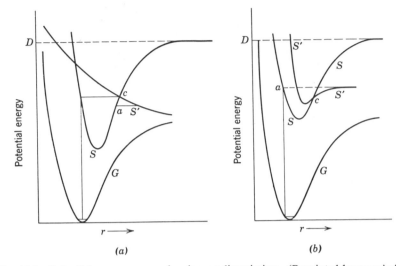

Fig. 19.1 Potential-energy curves showing predissociation. (Reprinted by permission from W. West, in Vol. IX of *Technique of Organic Chemistry*, edited by A. Weissberger, Interscience Publishers, New York, 1956.)

initial value) is of the order of 10^{-6} to 10^{-9} sec, thus indicating that this is the order of magnitude of the lifetime of excited molecules. Unless we wish to assume that the excited states of some compounds have considerably longer life (and it will be shown below that such an assumption would be unjustified for normal excited states), we must conclude that, for compounds which do not fluoresce, some other process occurs in a period shorter than these 10^{-6} to 10^{-9} sec. Several such processes are known.

One of these processes, known as predissociation,[1] is dependent on the existence of two excited states, S and S', which have crossing potential-energy curves, as shown in Fig. 19.1. Excitation from the ground state G leads to a molecule in state S which would be stable in the absence of the second excited state S'. If the excitation leads to a vibrational level of state S above its intersection with S', the molecule will, during its vibrational motion, pass through a point (c) at which the potential as well as the kinetic energies in the two states are equal. In the neighborhood of this point, there is a finite probability that the molecule will cross over to the state S', and then will dissociate, as implied by Fig. 19.1a, where S' is shown as a repulsive state. Even when S' is not repulsive, as shown in Fig. 19.1b, dissociation will occur after crossover, provided the vibrational level to which the molecule was excited (indicated by a in the figure)

[1] W. Kauzman, *Quantum Chemistry*, Academic Press, New York, 1957, pp. 542 ff; cf. also J. Franck and H. Levi, *Z. physik. Chem.*, **B27**, 409 (1935).

lies above the dissociation energy of S'. The crossover process between S and S' is not too well understood.

In polyatomic molecules, with their large number of vibrational degrees of freedom ($3n - 6$, where n is the number of atoms), such states S' very commonly exist, and the $3n - 6$ dimensional potential-energy surfaces very commonly cross. If the excitation energy to state S is larger than the bond-dissociation energy of some bond in the molecule, then it is very likely that a molecule excited to S crosses over to S', and that in this state dissociation occurs. This process is very rapid and is believed to occur in many molecules containing relatively weak bonds. The absence of fluorescence in nitro and iodo compounds, for example, is believed to be due to predissociation.[2]

Another, not uncommon, fate of the absorption energy is direct photodecomposition. This occurs when the vibrational level of S, reached by excitation of G, is one of the continuous set lying above the dissociation energy D of S (cf. Fig. 19.1), and is signaled by the fact that absorption in this region is continuous.

A further mechanism of deactivation of molecules consists in conversion of the excess energy into vibrational energy, so-called *internal conversion*. This process appears to be extremely rapid in very many molecules, maybe the vast majority, and to occur to some extent in all molecules. It is favored by great flexibility of the molecule (i.e., by the existence of many low-energy vibrations) and is counteracted by rigidity. For this reason, fluorescence is particularly apt to be observed in molecules which have rigid cyclic structures. A special case of internal conversion is encountered in *concentration quenching*, where the intensity of fluorescence actually decreases with increasing concentration. Although this phenomenon may be due to formation of nonfluorescent dimers in solution, it is believed to involve some quantum-mechanical (resonance) interaction between excited- and ground-state molecules.

A third mechanism of deactivation consists of energy transfer to other molecules, particularly solvent molecules in solution, and is called *external conversion*. This process undoubtedly plays an important role in deactivation in solution, where solute molecules are in virtually constant contact and continuous collision with solvent. The fact that fluorescence is generally more intense, and sometimes occurs only in, viscous media, and at low temperatures, suggests that internal and external conversions are very important, since both are apt to be inhibited by the restraint on free motion in viscous media and at low temperature.

A further mode of deactivation of excited molecules consists of their

[2] W. West, in *Chemical Applications of Spectroscopy*, Vol. IX of *Technique of Organic Chemistry*, edited by A. Weissberger, Interscience Publishers, New York, 1956, pp. 718 f.

return to a *lower excited state* by internal or external conversion. Such excited states may decay to the ground state by any of the routes discussed, although predissociation is unlikely. If the return is by emission of light, the resulting fluorescence has a wavelength substantially lower than that of the light absorbed. In some cases, the lower excited state may have a relatively long lifetime, presumably because it has different multiplicity from the ground state, and may emit light over a considerable period; in this case the emission is called *phosphorescence* (section 19.3).

19.2 Fluorescence Spectra

19.21 CONDITIONS FOR FLUORESCENCE. It was seen in section 19.1 that fluorescence may be expected to occur only if the molecule remains in the excited state for periods between 10^{-9} and 10^{-6} sec. Further discussion of the length of these time periods will be postponed to section 19.23. Accordingly a necessary condition for the existence of a fluorescence spectrum is that the other modes of deactivation of the excited state do not occur in shorter periods of time.

Predissociation is almost certain to occur when some bonds in the molecule, particularly in or adjacent to the chromophore, have a bond-dissociation energy appreciably lower than the energy corresponding to the wavelength of the absorbed light. Since a wavelength of 200 mμ corresponds to almost 150 kcal/mole, few molecules exist in which this amount of energy is insufficient to break some bonds, and hence predissociation makes fluorescence due to absorption in the far ultraviolet highly improbable. Accordingly it is not surprising that fluorescence is almost never observed in molecules absorbing only in the far ultraviolet, and that it is the more likely, the longer the wavelength of absorption. Even in molecules which absorb at long wavelength (i.e., which have low-lying excited states and which do fluoresce) it is observed that the fluorescence yield, ϕ, (i.e., the number of quanta re-emitted per quantum absorbed) decreases with decreasing wavelength of the absorbed raidation, presumably because, the shorter the absorbed radiation, the more likely is predissociation, and the more of the energy absorbed is dissipated in this way.

Internal conversion undoubtedly occurs to some extent for almost all compounds. It will inhibit fluorescence if it is fast enough, and it will be faster, the less rigid the vibrational modes of the compound. Consequently, fluorescence is most commonly observed in cyclic compounds having long-wavelength absorption, particularly the aromatic hydrocarbons and their derivatives, and in many dyes.

Once the conditions for fluorescence are met, and fluorescence is observed, a quantity of considerable interest is the fluorescence yield ϕ, which is quite equivalent to the quantum efficiency commonly used in photochemistry. The maximum theoretical value of ϕ is obviously 1, since each quantum absorbed excites only one molecule, which can emit only one quantum of light on return to the ground state. Since the quantum re-emitted is generally of longer wavelength than the one absorbed, the amount of energy re-emitted, even at $\phi = 1$, is less than the amount absorbed, and the excess is tranformed into heat. The fluorescence efficiency is usually considerably less than 1, indicating that predissociation and internal and external conversion compete with fluorescence, at least partly successfully, even when the latter is observed.

19.22 THE WAVELENGTHS AND VIBRATIONAL STRUCTURE OF FLUORESCENCE SPECTRA. If all molecules were always in the lowest vibrational level of the ground state, and were excited, by absorption of light, to the lowest vibrational level of the excited state, and if fluorescent re-emission were to occur between these same two levels, we would expect, except for second-order effects such as rotational structure, that the absorbed and emitted light would have the same wavelength. This ideal can be closely approximated in monatomic vapors at low pressure (e.g., sodium atoms), where no vibrations are possible, and emission occurs at the same frequency as absorption, but randomly in all directions and with a mean lifetime of 1.6×10^{-8} sec. This type of fluorescence is called *resonance radiation* because of a mistaken notion that it involved some sort of mechanical resonance between the frequencies of the light and the oscillation of the electrons.

A phenomenon similar to resonance radiation occurs in vapors of diatomic molecules at very low pressure. At a pressure which is low enough that practically no collisions occur during the lifetime of the fluorescence, and if internal conversion is slow, as it is in diatomic molecules which have only one relatively stiff vibration, excitation with strictly monochromatic light leads to a population of excited molecules in a particular rotational sublevel of a particular vibrational level of the excited state. These molecules may return to the ground state (lowest rotational and vibrational level) by emission of the same frequency as that absorbed, or may return to higher rotational and vibrational levels of the ground state by emission of light of lower frequency (i.e., longer wavelength). Thus the fluorescence spectrum consists of a series of lines, the spacings of which reflect the rotational and vibrational frequencies of the ground state only.

If, in the preceding experiment, the pressure is raised, collisions occur between excited molecules and other, usually ground-state molecules. Such collisions will lead to exchange of vibrational and rotational energy, and consequently the distribution of excited molecules among their vibrational and rotational levels will rapidly be similar to the distribution of ground-state molecules among its levels. This process, which may be

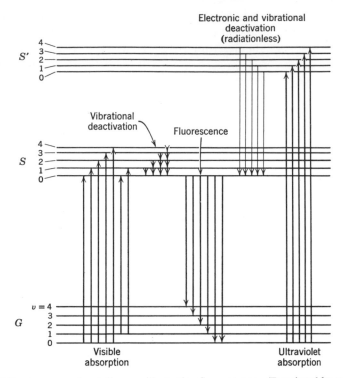

Fig. 19.2   An energy-level diagram illustrating fluorescence. (Reprinted by permission from W. West, in Vol. IX of *Technique of Organic Chemistry*, edited by A. Weissberger, Interscience Publishers, New York, 1956.)

called rotational and vibrational relaxation, is considerably faster than return to the ground state of excited molecules, and for all practical purposes we find the distribution of rotational and vibrational energy among excited states to be very similar to the same distribution in normal molecules. Since the vast majority of normal molecules are in the lowest vibrational state at room temperature, and particularly at the low temperatures often used for fluorescence measurements, the majority of fluorescence emission occurs from the lowest vibrational level of the excited state.

It is thus possible to have some understanding and clear picture of fluorescence emission. The processes involved are shown in Fig. 19.2. Heavy vertical arrows represent processes accompanied by emission or absorption of radiation; light arrows, radiationless processes. The figure assumes a ground state, *G*, a low excited state, *S*, and a higher excited state, *S'*. Absorption occurs from *G* to *S* or to *S'*, depending on the wavelength of the exciting radiation, and in each case to several vibrational levels of the excited state. Excited molecules in the S' state lose energy by some deactivation process, in one or more steps, and an appreciable fraction of them returns to state S, although a considerable number undergo other fates, such as predissociation, internal conversion, or radiationless transitions to other states. The molecules directly excited to the various levels of S, or those arriving there by various radiationless deactivations from S', also lose vibrational energy by collisions, till the majority is in the lowest vibrational level, whence they decay, with fluorescent emission, to various vibrational levels of the ground state.

A comparison of the upward and downward arrows connecting states G and S indicates that the two should overlap at the common frequency of the $0 \rightarrow 0$ band, and overlap to the extent that absorption and emission start from vibrationally excited states of the respective initial states. This occurs to some extent, the more the higher the temperature.

Some examples of the correspondence between absorption and fluorescence spectra are shown in Fig. 19.3. It is obvious that there is a

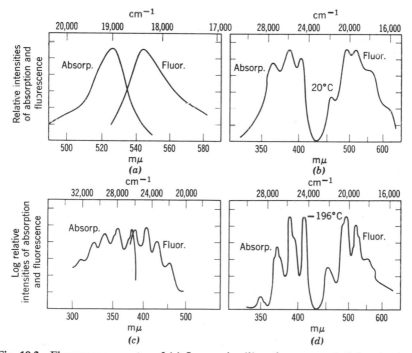

Fig. 19.3 Fluorescence spectra of (*a*) fluorescein, (*b*) anthracene, and diphenylcyclooctatetraene (*c*) at 20° and (*d*) at −196°. (Reprinted by permission from W. West, in Vol. IX of *Technique of Organic Chemistry*, edited by A. Weissberger, Interscience Publishers, New York, 1956.)

rough mirror-image relation.[3] This is due to two factors. (1) The vibrational frequencies of ground and excited states, although not identical, are usually quite similar, so that the spacings in the absorption spectrum (predominantly due to the vibrational structure of the excited state) and the fluorescence spectrum (ground-state vibrational structure) greatly resemble one another, although they are not generally identical. (2) The intensity distribution between the various vibrational components of the fluorescence spectrum is determined by the Franck-Condon principle (cf. next section), just as is the vibrational structure of the absorption spectrum. Given the similarity of the vibrational wave functions of the two interacting states, the intensity distribution can be expected to be similar. Hence the observed approximate mirror-image relation. The failure of this relation to be more accurately obeyed is probably due to the difference in ground- and excited-state vibration that does exist.

Figure 19.2 illustrates the common, though not universal, phenomenon that the same fluorescence spectrum is excited by light of quite different wavelengths. Although fluorescence spectra from higher excited states, such as S', are known (e.g., in azulene),[4] more commonly excitation to either S or S' leads to the same fluorescence spectrum, corresponding to the transition $S \rightarrow G$.

19.23 DECAY PERIODS.   The intensity of the emitted radiation after the exciting radiation is removed varies according to the equation

$$I(t) = I_0 e^{-t/\tau} \tag{19.1}$$

where $I(t)$ is the intensity at time t, I_0 the intensity during excitation, and τ the mean decay period, i.e., the time t at which $I(t)/I_0$ has fallen to $1/e$, as can be seen by substituting $t = \tau$ into equation (19.1) and rearranging. τ has been related to the dipole strength D (cf. section 6.2) of the transition[5] by the relation

$$\tau = \frac{3h}{64\pi^4 n \nu^3 e^2 G_j D} \tag{19.2}$$

where all symbols are as defined in section 6.2 except that n is the refractive index of the medium. Since thus τ is related to D, which also determines the intensity of absorption, it is obvious that absorption intensity and lifetime of fluorescent emission between a pair of states should be related

---

[3] E. L. Nichols and E. Merritt, *Phys. Rev.*, **31**, 376 (1910); W. L. Lewschin, *Z. Physik.*, **72**, 368, 382 (1931).

[4] J. Sidman and D. S. McClure, *J. Chem. Phys.*, **24**, 757 (1955).

[5] (a) R. S. Mulliken, *J. Chem. Phys.*, **7**, 14 (1939); (b) G. N. Lewis and M. Kasha, *J. Am. Chem. Soc.*, **67**, 994 (1945).

in a simple fashion, which, after substitution of universal constants, takes the form[5b]

$$\int \epsilon \, d\nu = 3.47 \times 10^8 \frac{1}{\nu^2 n^2} \cdot \frac{1}{\tau} \tag{19.3}$$

This relation is valid only as long as the fluorescent emission is the only process by which the excited state is deactivated, i.e., as long as the fluorescence yield is unity. Lewis and Kasha[5b] found that this relation actually holds to within a factor of about 2 for some compounds (fluorescein and rhodamine B).

19.24 SPECIAL EFFECTS IN FLUORESCENCE. It was indicated in section 19.1 that molecules in the excited state may be deactivated, not to the ground state, but to a metastable excited state, in which they remain trapped for considerable periods of time. If such metastable states are energetically rather close to the original excited state, the trapped molecules may be re-excited to the excited state, and give rise to a regular fluorescence spectrum, although one with an abnormally long decay period; such fluorescence is known as *slow fluorescence*. Since it depends on collisional re-excitation of the trapped molecules, it shows the typical temperature dependence of such processes.

Another rather abnormal fluorescence occurs in some very dilute solid solutions. As an example, both anthracene and naphthacene have characteristic absorption and fluorescence spectra. The fluorescences of the two compounds are readily distinguishable by their colors, blue and green, respectively. Irradiation of a very dilute solution (1 part in 10^4) of naphthacene in solid anthracene by light (365 mμ), absorbed by the anthracene but only very weakly by the naphthacene, gives rise to the green fluorescence of naphthacene with a high fluorescence yield. This indicates that in some way the energy absorbed by the anthracene molecules is transferred to the rare solute molecules (naphthacene) in a time period shorter than the decay period of anthracene, but is then trapped in the solute long enough for its fluorescence to be observed. The motion of the excitation energy through the crystal has been discussed by Franck and Teller.[6] The reverse process, i.e., transfer of energy from naphthacene to the solvent anthracene, does not take place.

Dilute solutions are also involved in another phenomenon characteristic of fluorescence. Many compounds have been observed to appear to fluoresce, and fluorescence was considered to be one of their characteristic properties until careful investigation showed that the fluorescence was not a property of the substance, but was due to a contamination consistently

[6] J. Franck and E. Teller, *J. Chem. Phys.*, **6**, 861 (1938); cf. also J. Franck and R. Livingston, *Revs. Modern Phys.*, **21**, 505 (1949).

occurring. Perhaps the most characteristic example of this phenomenon is fluorene, which actually derived its name from a strong visible fluorescence caused by impurities usually present, the most common being carbazole. Similar impurity fluorescence is observed with many condensed ring aromatics (e.g., anthracene and phenanthrene, which are commonly contaminated by naphthacene and anthracene, respectively). Such impurity contamination should be suspected when the usual mirror law between fluorescence and absorption spectra fails to hold, and very careful purification is a highly desirable safeguard. Failure of the mirror law, however, is insufficient to demonstrate that a fluorescence is due to impurity; at least one case where the law does not hold will be discussed below.

Another type of fluorescence invariably accompanying irradiation of some compounds but not due to the excited molecule occurs when the compound undergoes a photochemical reaction or decomposition. Many carbonyl compounds, for example, photochemically dissociate to form acyl radicals, which, in turn, dimerize. The dimeric biacyls themselves fluoresce in the visible, and give the appearance that the original carbonyl compound fluoresces. The first suggestion that the fluorescence is not due to the original carbonyl compound itself comes from the failure of the mirror law. Furthermore, the fluorescence intensity increases with time, suggesting that the fluorescing species is formed during irradiation. Also, the fluorescence spectra of several methyl ketones are identical in some wavelength regions, suggesting that the same photochemical product, biacetyl, is responsible. Finally, biacetyl itself has the same fluorescence spectrum. A complicating factor is that many carbonyl compounds also have characteristic fluorescence spectra of their own.[7] The situation is further complicated by the fact that the fluorescence spectrum of biacetyl is quenched by oxygen, a not-uncommon phenomenon which makes it advisable to operate in deaerated systems when studying fluorescence phenomena.

Photochemical reactions may give rise to yet another type of fluorescence. When the excited state breaks up, several fragments, usually free radicals, are formed. All or some of these are frequently formed as excited states and, in that case, may decay to their ground states. The light emitted in the process, of course, has no relation to the light absorbed, and the mirror law will not hold. On the other hand, no time dependence is to be expected. Examples of this behavior are the vapors of aliphatic alcohols and acids, the fluorescence of which is ascribed to OH radicals, and of amines, which give rise to NH_2 radicals.

A particularly interesting type of observation is possible with fluorescing compounds capable of undergoing acid-base reactions. The effects of pH

[7] R. E. Hunt and W. A. Noyes, Jr., *J. Am. Chem. Soc.*, **70**, 467 (1948).

changes on absorption spectra were discussed in section 9.7, and their use in the evaluation of pK will be considered in Chapter 20. When compounds capable of undergoing acid-base reactions are irradiated in aqueous solution, the spectrum depends characteristically on pH, depending on the species present in solution. The fluorescence spectrum also will be characteristic of the emitting molecular species. If the acidity or basicity of the excited state is different from that of the ground state, as usually is the case if the basic center is sufficiently close to the chromophore, or is part of it, and if the excited state persists long enough to permit the equilibrium to be reached, study of the pH dependence of the fluorescence permits determination of the prototropic equilibrium of the excited state. Furthermore, variation of the decay period by changes in medium permits determination of the time required for equilibrium to be established, i.e., the measurement of the rates of reactions which occur in 10^{-9} to 10^{-6} sec.[8]

19.25 TYPICAL EXAMPLES.   In general, compounds absorbing only in the far ultraviolet, or far out in the middle ultraviolet, do not fluoresce because predissociation deactivates excited states. Consequently, it is not surprising that aliphatic and simple nonconjugated olefinic hydrocarbons do not fluoresce. Most of the compounds derived from them by substitution also do not fluoresce. The fluorescence of the vapors of aliphatic aldehydes, acids, and amines is ascribed to excited OH and NH_2 radicals formed in the photochemical decomposition of these compounds.

It has already been pointed out that most carbonyl compounds apparently fluoresce because of the formation of biacyls. Most carbonyl compounds, however, also have a characteristic fluorescence of their own. The decay periods, however, are quite long (of the order of 10^{-3} sec for acetone) and probably are due to slow fluorescence (cf. section 19.24), where the metastable state is probably the triplet corresponding to n $\rightarrow$ π excitation.[9]

Since deactivation is possible by internal conversion, which is favored when the molecule is flexible, it is not surprising that even polyenes with relatively long-wavelength absorption do not usually fluoresce, although some carboxylic acids with five conjugated vinyl groups have visible fluorescence spectra.[10]

The conditions for fluorescence are much more favorable in aromatic and particularly in condensed hydrocarbons. These compounds absorb at relatively long wavelengths and have very rigid structure, making internal conversion quite difficult. Some of the experimental material has been assembled by West[11] and is reproduced in Table 19.1.

[9] T. Förster, Z. Elektrochem., 54, 42 (1950).
[9] G. N. Lewis and M. Kasha, J. Am. Chem. Soc., 67, 1001 (1945).
[10] K. W. Hausser, R. Kuhn, and E. Kuhn, Z. physik. Chem., B29, 417 (1935).
[11] W. West (see footnote 2).

Substitution in the aromatic hydrocarbon naturally shifts the wavelengths of fluorescence in agreement with the effect of the same substituent on the absorption spectrum. Since such effects have been treated in detail in Chapters 12 and 13, they need not be further discussed here. On the other hand, substituents also affect fluorescence yield and may completely inhibit fluorescence. Most of these effects are probably due to predissocia-

TABLE 19.1

Fluorescence Yields (ϕ) of Cyclic Hydrocarbons in Hexane Solution for Radiation of 253.7 mμ at 20°C (Deoxygenated Solutions)[11]

Compound	ϕ	Approximate λ of Fluorescence, mμ	Compound	ϕ	Approximate λ of Fluorescence, mμ
Benzene	0.11	270–310	Naphthalene	0.38	300–360
Toluene	0.23	270–310	Anthracene	0.46	370–460
o-Xylene	0.29	270–320	Phenanthrene	0.27	280–470
m-Xylene	0.30	270–320	Fluorene	1.0	300–370
p-Xylene	0.42	270–320	Acenaphthene	0.7	330–400
1,3,5-Trimethylbenzene	0.16	275–330	Biphenyl	0.23	290–360
1,2,4,5-Tetramethyl-benzene	0.52	280–330	Triphenylmethane	0.23	280–340
Hexamethylbenzene	0.04	280–330	Rubrene	1.0^a	545–623

^{a} Excitation by $\lambda = 436.0$ mμ. The fluorescence yield of rubrene is about 1.0 in hexane at 20° C, and, at $-60°$ C, is 0.73 in ethyl alcohol and 0.51 in acetone.

tion and are the more pronounced the weaker the bonds. Alkyl substituents, e.g., with bonds of strength similar to those of the parent hydrocarbon, have little effect. In the halogens, fluorine has little effect, chlorine and bromine weaken the fluorescence, and iodine completely inhibits it, undoubtedly because of predissociation, since iodobenzene is known to undergo photodecomposition. Also involved in the quenching by the heavier elements may be radiationless transitions to triplet states (cf. section 19.3), which are particularly favored by the presence of heavy atoms. Nitro groups also are very effective in quenching fluorescence, presumably because of predissociation. When nitro and iodo compounds, however, absorb at very long wavelengths, as do erythrosin or p-nitrodimethylaniline, the energy involved in the excitation is insufficient to lead to predissociation, and fluorescence occurs in such compounds. The azo group also inhibits fluorescence, even in compounds absorbing at quite long wavelength.

Table 19.2 lists experimental information on fluorescence spectra of some typical substituted benzenes.[12]

[12] W. West (see footnote 2), p. 730.

The simplest aromatic heterocyclics, pyridine, pyrrole, furan, and thiophene, do not fluoresce. The problem has been discussed for some pyridines and related compounds;[13] it is believed that radiationless transitions to a triplet compete successfully with fluorescence and lead to a

TABLE 19.2
Fluorescence of Substituted Benzenes in Ethyl Alcohol[12]

Compound	Formula	Wavelength Region of Fluorescence, $m\mu$	Relative Fluorescence Intensity
Benzene	C_6H_6	270–310	10
Toluene	$C_6H_5CH_3$	270–320	17
Propylbenzene	$C_6H_5C_3H_7$	270–320	17
Styrene	$C_6H_5CH{=}CH_2$	290–365	10
Fluorobenzene	C_6H_5F	270–320	10
Chlorobenzene	C_6H_5Cl	275–345	7
Bromobenzene	C_6H_5Br	290–380	5
Iodobenzene	C_6H_5I		0
Phenol	C_6H_5OH	285–365	18
Phenolate ion	$C_6H_5O^-$	310–400	10
Anisole	$C_6H_5OCH_3$	280–345	20
Aniline	$C_6H_5NH_2$	310–405	20
Anilinium ion	$C_6H_5NH_3{}^+$		0
Dimethylaniline	$C_6H_5N(CH_3)_2$	325–405	10
Benzoic acid	C_6H_5COOH	310–390	3
Benzonitrile	C_6H_5CN	280–360	20
Nitrobenzene	$C_6H_5NO_2$		0
o-Hydroxybenzoic acid	C_6H_5COOH	375–480	10
m-Hydroxybenzoic acid	C_6H_5COOH	340–450	8
p-Hydroxybenzoic acid	C_6H_5COOH	345–410	2

phosphorescent state. This may be generalized to the statement that a compound cannot strongly fluoresce and phosphoresce, since the two are competing processes, although phosphorescence is frequently, if not usually, accompanied by slow fluorescence. Heterocycles with fused ring systems frequently show extensive fluorescence.

19.3 Phosphorescence Spectra

Phosphorescence spectra resemble fluorescence spectra in that they represent re-emission of previously absorbed light, and persist for some time after the exciting radiation is turned off. But, whereas this time, the

[13] Quoted by M. Kasha, *Discussions Faraday Soc.*, **9**, 14 (1950).

decay period, is of the order of 10^{-9} to 10^{-6} sec for fluorescence, it is considerably longer, from 10^{-4} sec to whole seconds, and even longer, for phosphorescence. Also, in fluorescence there is a relation between the absorption and emission spectra, the mirror law, but in phosphorescence no such relation exists. The nature of phosphorescence has been elucidated by Lewis and Kasha,[14] who have demonstrated conclusively that phosphorescence involves radiative return to the ground state from a metastable state, which they have identified as a triplet level. On this basis, the identification of phosphorescence and fluorescence is not a matter of arbitrary distinction between the lifetimes of the excited states; rather the lifetimes are direct consequences of the different natures of these states.

Two rather different types of phosphorescence need to be distinguished. Many inorganic substances phosphoresce in the solid state. Almost universally the presence of certain "impurities," so-called activators, is required, and the phosphorescence is a function, not of the chemical properties of "solute" or "solvent" molecules, but of the energy levels of the crystal as a whole. The phosphorescence of organic compounds, on the other hand, is a true molecular property. Its wavelength is not generally appreciably affected by environment (except for second-order effects), and the intensity and decay period are affected because the environment has a large effect on the competing deactivation processes. The following discussion will be restricted to such phosphorescence of organic molecules.

It was shown in section 6.3 that transitions between singlet and triplet states (in general, states of different multiplicity) are forbidden by selection rules. In other words, in the first approximation, the probability of such transitions occurring is zero. In section 19.23 a relation between the absolute intensity of absorption and the decay period for emission between a pair of states was discussed. Since the absolute intensity for a transition from a singlet ground to an excited triplet state is small, it is not surprising that the decay period for re-emission from the triplet, returning to the ground state, is quite long.

The ground states of almost all stable organic molecules are singlets involving the electrons occupying MO's in pairs with opposite spin. Absorption of light is almost always accompanied by promotion of a single electron to a higher, previously unoccupied orbital. The excited state then involves all electrons occupying orbitals in pairs, and with paired spin, except two, the spins of which may be paired (singlet) or unpaired (triplet state). Consequently, to each excited singlet state reached by absorption there corresponds a triplet state. As will be shown below, the triplet state *always* has lower energy than the corresponding singlet, and

[14] G. N. Lewis and M. Kasha, *J. Am. Chem. Soc.*, **66**, 2100 (1944), cf. also A. Jablonski, *Z. Physik.*, **94**, 38 (1935).

hence phosphorescence spectra always occur at longer wavelength than either the exciting radiation or the corresponding fluorescence spectrum.

It will now be profitable to look more closely at the term-level diagram of a typical molecule. Figure 19.4 shows such a diagram. The ground state G, and the excited states S, S', etc., are singlets. Transitions between these, unless symmetry forbidden, occur readily and are observable as intense absorption spectra, and as fluorescence spectra, with short decay periods, unless some other mechanism of deactivation is even more rapid. To each excited singlet corresponds a triplet, T, T', etc. (except to some higher ones which involve multiple electron excitation and are of little spectroscopic interest). Transitions between these triplets also occur readily, unless forbidden. Transitions between the singlets and triplets, however, being multiplicity forbidden, occur only rarely and correspond to the inter-system connections of atomic spectra. In the normal process of phosphorescence, the molecule is excited from G to one of the S states, usually to a vibrationally excited level. It then drops to the T state by a single or a series of

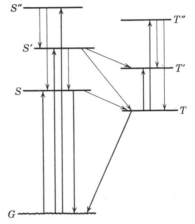

Fig. 19.4   Term-level diagram.

radiationless transitions, the nature of which is not too well understood. These transitions may depend, like predissociation, on crossing of potential-energy curves (cf. Fig. 19.1). Also, it is not known whether the path from S', for example, involves going through T' or through S. Once in T, and having lost excess vibrational energy, the molecule may remain trapped long enough for the phosphorescent transition $T \to G$ to occur. Also, the molecule may be re-excited by collisions to S, giving rise to the slow fluorescence discussed in section 19.24, and consequently phosphorescence is very commonly accompanied by slow fluorescence. Alternately, T may decay to G by radiationless transitions, in which case no phosphorescence is observed.

When the transitions from the higher triplet states (T', T'', etc.) to T are allowed, it is not surprising that no phosphorescence from these states is observed. However, no such phosphorescence is observed even if the transitions are symmetry forbidden. This is undoubtedly due to the fact that the decay period even for a symmetry-forbidden transition (such as $T' \to T$ could be) is much shorter than for a multiplicity-forbidden one ($T' \to G$).

19.31 DECAY PERIODS.   In the first approximation, all singlet-triplet or triplet-singlet transitions are forbidden. This approximation involves the assumption that the orbital and spin angular momenta of various electrons in atoms or molecules do not couple. Thus we generally assume that the orbital angular momenta of the electrons, l in atoms, couple to produce a total angular momentum L of the atoms, and similarly that the spin angular momenta s couple to produce the total spin S of the atom; then L and S couple to produce the total angular momentum J of the atom. This coupling scheme in atoms is known as Russell-Saunders (L-S) coupling and is valid for light atoms. Quite analogous coupling schemes are almost universally the basis of the treatment of molecules and were used in the discussion of linear molecules (e.g., acetylene, section 5.3) and cyclic molecules (the Platt FEM scheme for polynuclear hydrocarbons, section 13.2).

The assumption of Russell-Saunders coupling is not quite correct. Some interaction between spin and orbital angular momenta always occurs and was discussed in section 6.9. This spin-orbit coupling is probably the most important single factor making the intersystem transitions partially allowed.[15] If allowances are made for spin-orbit coupling and other perturbing effects, the transitions are of course no longer strictly forbidden, so that D in equation (19.2) no longer vanishes. Since the derivation of equations (19.2) and (19.3) is quite general, they hold for the relation between phosphorescence spectra and the corresponding singlet-triplet absorptions (but not the exciting singlet-singlet absorption) except for the modification necessary because of the triplet character of the excited state, which requires inclusion of the statistical weight of 3 of the upper state, and hence a factor of 3 in the right-hand side of equation (19.3). This equation has been tested by Lewis and Kaska[5b] and by McClure[15] by comparison with the very weak singlet-triplet absorptions; some of the latter's data are given in Table 19.3.

From atomic spectra it is well known that Russell-Saunders coupling holds best in very light atoms; in heavy atoms it has to be replaced by j-j coupling, where the individual l and s angular momenta of each electron couple to a total electronic angular momentum j, and the j of the individual electrons couple further to give J, the angular momentum of the atom. In the case of j-j coupling, no total spin angular momentum S exists for an atom, and hence we cannot legitimately speak of the multiplicity of an atomic state. In other words, in j-j coupling, spin-orbit coupling is complete. The situation in molecules is similar. The heavier the atoms in a molecule, the more important is spin-orbit coupling. Accordingly, Table 19.3 shows a considerable decrease in decay period for some typical halogen

[15] D. S. McClure, *J. Chem. Phys.*, **17**, 905 (1949).

compounds with increasing atomic weight of the halogen atom. The same effect of heavy atoms can be observed even when the heavy atom is not in the molecule, but only in its proximity, since Kasha[16] has shown that

TABLE 19.3

Lifetime of Phosphorescent Triplet State in Halogenated Naphthalenes and in Other Compounds

Compound	λ of Phosphorescence Band, mμ	τ, sec
α-Fluoronaphthalene	476.7	1.5
α-Chloronaphthalene	483	0.30
α-Bromonaphthalene	483	0.018
α-Iodonaphthalene	526	0.0025
β-Chloronaphthalene	476	0.47
β-Bromonaphthalene	473.8	0.021
β-Iodonaphthalene	475.2	0.0025
Benzene	340	7.0
Toluene	347	8.8
Phenol	350	2.9
Aniline	373	4.7
Benzoic acid	368	2.5
Acetophenone	384.5	0.008
Naphthalene	470	2.6
α-Aminonaphthalene	526	1.5
α-Nitronaphthalene	521	0.049
1,5-Dinitronaphthalene	502	0.11
Chrysene	505	2.5
Coronene	525	9.4
Triphenylene	420	15.9
Tetraphenylmethane	350	5.4
Tetraphenyllead	420	0.01

singlet-triplet absorption is enhanced by solvents containing heavy atoms, e.g., iodine. There is a further reason for this effect. Presence of heavy atoms, either in the molecule or in its vicinity, greatly enhances internal conversion from the excited singlet S to the lowest triplet T, and hence increases the phosphorescence yield, at the same time decreasing the fluorescence yield. Some typical examples[17] of phosphorescence quantum yields are given in Table 19.4. Both fluorescence and phosphorescence

[16] M. Kasha, *J. Chem. Phys.*, **20**, 71 (1952).
[17] E. H. Gilmore, G. E. Gibson, and D. S. McClure, *J. Chem. Phys.*, **20**, 829 (1952).

yields were found to be virtually independent of concentration and of the wavelength of the exciting radiation.[17]

It can be shown theoretically that the forbidden character of multiplicity-forbidden transitions disappears, at least partially, in an inhomogeneous magnetic field. Confirmation comes from an examination of a number of

TABLE 19.4

Fluorescence and Phosphorescence Quantum Yields (ϕ_F and ϕ_P, Respectively) in Solid Solutions at 77° K with Excitation at 253.7 mμ[17]

Compound	ϕ_F	ϕ_P
Benzene	0.18	0.18
Fluorobenzene	0.16	0
Chlorobenzene	0	0.03
Naphthalene	0.39	0.07
Benzophenone	. . .	0.56
Acetophenone	. . .	0.45
Acetone	. . .	0.03
Triphenylene	0.03	0.36

aetioporphyrins, phthalocyanines, and phaeophorbides.[18] In compounds with only diamagnetic metal ions (Mg^{2+}, Zn^{2+}) strong fluorescence was observed, whereas in paramagnetic Cu^{2+} and Ni^{2+} compounds fluorescence disappeared in favor of phosphorescence. This indicates that the paramagnetic ion permits much more ready conversion of the excited singlet to the phosphorescent triplet state. Presence of paramagnetic substances may, however, inhibit phosphorescence, because radiationless conversion of the triplet back to the ground state may also be facilitated. Thus, phosphorescence is frequently quenched by oxygen, a paramagnetic substance with a triplet ground state, and almost all phosphorescence experiments must be carried out in its absence.

19.32 THE WAVELENGTH OF PHOSPHORESCENCE. In the customary approximation of MO theory, the energies of the singlet and triplet states are the same. Only when electron correlation is considered is this degeneracy removed. The triplet state always has lower energy than the singlet, and hence phosphorescence spectra occur at longer wavelengths than fluorescence or the exciting radiation.

The proof of the foregoing statement depends on the evaluation of the electron-correlation energy, which depends in turn on the term $\Sigma_{ij} e^2/r_{ij}$ in the Hamiltonian operator. This term represents the Coulombic repulsion of two electrons i and j of charge e and at

[18] R. S. Becker and M. Kasha, *J. Am. Chem. Soc.*, **77**, 3669 (1955).

a distance r_{ij}, and involves a summation over all electron pairs. In the energy this gives rise to a term

$$W_{ij} = \Sigma_{ij}e^2 \int \Psi^* \frac{1}{r_{ij}} \Psi \, d\tau$$

where Ψ is the total wave function, i.e., a determinant of one-electron functions, including spin (cf. section 8.5). Substitution of these determinants and expansion give in a rather straightforward manner[19] the expression

$$W = \Sigma_{ij}(J_{ij} - \delta_{ij}K_{ij})$$

where

$$J_{ij} = \int \psi_i(1)\psi_j(2) \frac{1}{r_{12}} \psi_i(1)\psi_j(2) \, d\tau_1 \, d\tau_2$$

$$K_{ij} = \int \psi_i(1)\psi_j(2) \frac{1}{r_{12}} \psi_i(2)\psi_j(1) \, d\tau_1 \, d\tau_2 \qquad (19.4)$$

and $\psi_i(1)$ and $\psi_j(2)$ are the wave functions, with spin, of electrons 1 and 2, $d\tau_1$ and $d\tau_2$ are the volume elements in the coordinates of these electrons. δ_{ij} is a function which is equal to 1 if the wave functions i and j have equal spin (i.e., involve the same spin function) and to zero if the spins are different. The energies of the singlet and triplet states, belonging to the same configuration and having the same energy, omitting electron correlation, differ only in a single term, K, between the two electrons which are paired in the singlet, unpaired in the triplet. Since the term does not appear in the singlet, and appears as $-K$ in the triplet, and since K is an inherently positive quantity, it is obvious that the triplet always has lower energy than the singlet. The only thing that can change this relation is configuration interaction (cf. section 8.5), which might affect the two states differently.

An evaluation of the integral K then involves substituting the one-electron wave functions ψ_i and ψ_j in equation (19.4). This problem becomes quite laborious, since even in benzene each ψ is a linear combination of six atomic functions, giving a total of 6^4 or 1296 terms. However, theoretical estimates of these quantities have frequently been made in recent years.[20]

No qualitative or semiquantitative general rules about the singlet-triplet separation appear to exist, and consequently little can be said in general about where to expect the phosphorescence spectrum, either absolutely or in relation to the normal absorption or fluorescence. On the other hand, the phosphorescence spectrum has the same relation to the singlet-triplet absorption spectrum as the fluorescence spectrum has to the normal (singlet-singlet) absorption spectrum, and accordingly the same mirror law applies. It has some particular importance in the case of phosphorescence, since it may be used to verify that a particular very weak absorption is due to singlet-triplet absorption, not to impurities. The test best applied is that the $0 \rightarrow 0$ bands should coincide in absorption and emission. In

[19] See J. C. Slater, *Quantum Theory of Matter*, McGraw-Hill Book Co., New York, 1951, section 7.7, where the analogous case of an atom is treated in detail.

[20] R. Pariser and R. G. Parr, *J. Chem. Phys.*, **21**, 466, 767 (1953).

fluorescence, the mirror law is only approximate, since the absorption spectrum shows the vibrational structure of the excited state, the emission spectrum that of the ground state. The same is true in the phosphorescence case.

19.4   Triplet → Triplet Absorption

As seen in the preceding sections, molecules in excited singlet states have extremely short lifetimes, and consequently it is not surprising that sufficient concentrations have not been obtained to make any measurements on them, other than their decay to the ground state through fluorescence. The situation is considerably different with triplets, which have lifetimes up to and exceeding seconds. In this case it is conceivable that by strong irradiation with light of appropriate wavelengths sufficient concentrations of molecules in triplet states could be obtained to observe their spectra. The first authentic report of such a spectrum was made by G. N. Lewis and coworkers,[21] who observed a new spectrum of acid fluorescein, I,

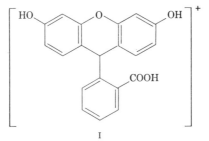

I

upon irradiation of the compound by intense light from a mercury arc. In Fig. 19.5 this spectrum is shown under near-saturation conditions, i.e., when most of the dye (88.5 per cent) is in the triplet state. That the absorbing state was really a triplet was demonstrated by measurement of its paramagnetism.[22] In some other cases (fluorescein, 1-hydroxy-2-naphthoic acid, and triphenylene) not only was the expected paramagnetism observed, but in addition the decay period of the magnetic susceptibility and of the absorption spectrum coincided.[23] This leaves little doubt that the observed absorption spectra originated from a triplet lower state; that the upper state also is a triplet appears unquestionable from the observed intensity, ϵ_{max} of 20,000 and 18,000 for the 650 and 505 mμ bands of acid fluorescein, respectively. Further observations of triplet-triplet absorptions have been

[21] G. N. Lewis, D. Lipkin, and T. T. Magel, *J. Am. Chem. Soc.*, **63**, 3005 (1941).

[22] G. N. Lewis and M. Calvin, *J. Am. Chem. Soc.*; **67**, 1232 (1945); G. N. Lewis, M. Calvin, and M. Kasha, *J. Chem. Phys.*, **17**, 804 (1949).

[23] D. F. Evans, *Nature*, **176**, 777 (1955).

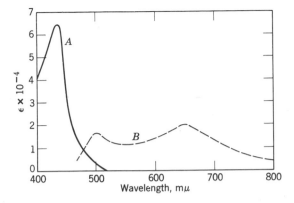

Fig. 19.5 The spectrum of acid fluorescein without (*A*) and with (*B*) irradiation. (Reprinted by permission from W. West, in Vol. IX of *Technique of Organic Chemistry*, edited by A. Weissberger, Interscience Publishers, New York, 1956.)

made on a number of other systems[24] in rigid glass solutions at low temperature. More recently another technique, flash photolysis, has become available to observe such spectra. This is substantially the same technique which has been so successful in observing short-lived fragments like small free radicals (cf. section 16.1). This technique has been used[25] to observe triplet-triplet absorptions on a wide variety of molecules. It is apt to prove increasingly successful, since, through synchronization of flash and observation, it enables the worker to observe effects in triplet states of much shorter lifetime than does the rigid glass technique. On the other hand, the flash technique, because of the extremely high light intensities involved, is apt to suffer from the difficulty that photodecomposition accompanies exposure, and that care must be taken that observed spectra are not due to decomposition products.

Two other phenomena, thermochromism and photochromism, have been interpreted frequently as triplet-triplet transitions. In thermochromism, a compound which is substantially uncolored at room temperature becomes progressively colored as the temperature is raised. In photochromism, an uncolored compound, as a result of irradiation, often

[24] G. N. Lewis and D. Lipkin, *J. Am. Chem. Soc.*, **64**, 2801 (1942); E. Clar, *J. Chem. Soc.*, 1823 (1950); D. S. McClure, *J. Chem. Phys.*, **19**, 670 (1951); D. P. Craig and I. G. Ross, *J. Chem. Soc.*, 1589 (1954).

[25] G. Porter and M. W. Windsor, *J. Chem. Phys.*, **21**, 2088 (1953); *Proc. Roy. Soc.* (*London*), **A245**, 238 (1958); G. Porter and F. J. Wright, *Trans Faraday Soc.*, **51**, 1205 (1955); R. Livingston, *J. Am. Chem. Soc.*, **77**, 2179 (1955); H. T. Witt, *Z. physik. Chem.* (*Frankfurt*), **4**, 120 (1955); D. S. McClure and P. L. Hunst, *J. Chem. Phys.*, **23**, 1722 (1955).

at low temperature as a solid or in a rigid glass, becomes colored. Thermochromism of bixanthylene, II,[26] bianthrone, III,[27] and many

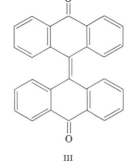

II   III

related compounds has been observed and interpreted as arising from excitation to a triplet state which absorbs in the visible. It has been assumed that thermal excitation of the singlet ground state, which deviates substantially from planarity because of steric hindrance, to the lowest triplet, in which the two *cata*-condensed three ring systems are in planes at 90°, is responsible for the thermochromism.

This view receives support from MO calculations[28] on the energy difference between the ground and excited states, and from paramagnetic resonance absorption measurements[29] which have demonstrated the presence of paramagnetic species in solution, with temperature-dependent concentration. This interpretation has been disputed by Kortüm,[30] who believes that the state absorbing in the visible represents a geometric isomer, also with a singlet ground state. His view is supported by magnetic susceptibility measurements on a thermochromic derivative of III, which was found to be diamagnetic at all temperatures, with constant diamagnetic susceptibility. The evidence that substituted derivatives of III, in which the steric hindrance of a planar ground state is increased, are not thermochromic appears to support Kortüm's view, since, in such compounds, the singlet should be further destabilized relative to the triplet. The controversy cannot be considered as resolved.

[26] A. Schönberg and O. Schutz, *Ber.*, **61**, 478 (1928); A. Schönberg, A. Mustafa, and M. E. E. Sobhy, *J. Am. Chem. Soc.*, **75**, 3377 (1953); A. Schönberg, A. Mustafa, and W. Asker, *J. Am. Chem. Soc.*, **76**, 4134 (1954); A. Mustafa and M. E. Sobhy, *J. Am. Chem. Soc.*, **77**, 5124 (1955).

[27] W. T. Grubb and G. B. Kistiakowsky, *J. Am. Chem. Soc.*, **72**, 419 (1950).

[28] S. L. Matlow, *J. Chem. Phys.*, **23**, 152 (1955).

[29] W. G. Nielsen and G. K. Fraenkel, *J. Chem. Phys.*, **21**, 1619 (1953).

[30] G. Kortüm, *Angew. Chem.* **70**, 14 (1958).

Photochromism has also been observed in bianthrone, III, derivatives[31] and has been ascribed to photoexcitation to the same absorbing triplet state as the thermochromism. Hirshberg claims that the thermochromic and photochromic spectra are identical. Kortüm again has questioned this conclusion and offered evidence suggesting that the two states are different. He proposes that the photoexcited state is a biradical with the halves of the molecules at right angles. Since this is equivalent to the lowest triplet discussed above, his conclusion that this is not a triplet is hard to understand.

A number of thermochromic and photochromic compounds other than those in the series discussed are known. However, in most cases the phenomenon probably does not involve a triplet-triplet absorption, but rather some form of bond breaking, fragmentation, dissociation, or other chemical reaction, or possibly a broadening of vibrational structure at higher temperature. An interesting example involves certain spiropyranes, IV,[32] which show reversible photochromism and in some cases thermo-

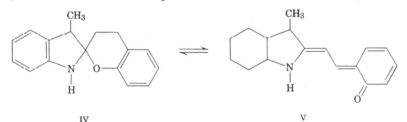

IV   V

chromism quite analogous to bianthrone. However, these phenomena are now believed to be due to a ring-opening mechanism, possibly leading to a structure like V. It is interesting that the photochromic color can be reversed; i.e., reaction V → IV can be produced, not only thermally, but also photochemically with visible light.

GENERAL REFERENCES

W. West in *Chemical Applications of Spectroscopy*, Vol. IX of *Technique of Organic Chemistry*, edited by A. Weissberger, Interscience Publishers, New York, 1956, Chapter 6.

E. J. Bowen and F. Wokes, *Fluorescence in Solutions*, Longmans, Green, London, 1953.

T. Förster, *Fluoreszenz organischer Verbindungen*, Vandenhoeck und Ruprecht, Gottingen, 1951.

P. Pringsheim, *Fluorescence and Phosphorescence*, Interscience Publishers, New York, 1949.

[31] Y. Hirshberg, *Compt. rend.*, **231**, 903 (1950); E. D. Bergmann and E. Fischer, *Bull. soc. chim. France*, **17**, 1084 (1950); Y. Hirshberg and E. Fischer, *J. Chem. Soc.*, 629 (1953).

[32] Y. Hirshberg and E. Fischer, *J. Chem. Soc.*, 4522 (1952); 2184 (1953); 297, 3129 (1954); *J. Chem. Phys.*, **21**, 1619 (1953).

20 Applications of spectra to quantitative analysis, and the determination of equilibrium constants

20.1 Quantitative Analysis

Ultraviolet spectra can be a powerful tool in a variety of analytical problems. Quantitative analysis is always concerned with the determination of concentration; and, if the sought-after species absorbs in the visible or ultraviolet, its concentration, even though very small, can frequently be determined with considerable accuracy by appropriate techniques. Entire books have been devoted exclusively to this aspect of absorption spectroscopy. Accordingly, the account which follows will be brief, and the reader may refer to the excellent books which cover the subject thoroughly.[1]

Quantitative analysis by spectrophotometric methods is based on Beer's law (cf. section 1.4):

$$\log I_0/I = A = abc \tag{20.1}$$

where I_0 is the intensity of the incident light; I is the intensity of the emergent light; A is the absorbance (or, as it has been called in the past, the optical density), which is the quantity indicated or recorded by the spectrophotometer; a is the absorptivity, a characteristic of the absorbing species; b is the cell length; and c is the concentration of the absorbing species. In some cases it has been shown that the absorbance is not proportional to concentration, i.e., that Beer's law is invalid; in such cases analysis by spectrophotometric methods is still possible but involves use of a calibration curve.

True deviations from Beer's law are probably quite rare; apparent deviations, caused by involvement of equilibria which are not accounted

[1] For example, M. G. Mellon, *Analytical Absorption Spectroscopy*, John Wiley and Sons, New York, 1950.

for, or by instrumental factors, however, may not be unusual. Consequently, construction of a calibration curve or verification of Beer's law is a necessary step in the development of an analytical method. For purposes of the following discussions, however, it will be assumed that the law holds. In addition, it will be assumed that there is no interaction of the absorbing species with each other, so that each makes an independent contribution to the absorbance.

The concentration of one absorbing compound in a mixture is easily determined if a wavelength can be chosen at which the desired compound is the only absorbing species. In such a case the absorbance of the mixture, A_m, is compared with that, A_0, of the pure compound in known concentration, c_0, at the same wavelength, and the concentration of the material in the mixture, c_m, can readily be calculated.

20.2   Analysis of Mixtures

If a mixture contains two substances each of which absorbs in the ultraviolet and no convenient wavelength can be selected at which one absorbs and the second does not or vice versa, then at any wavelength, λ', from equation (20.1):

$$A'(\text{obs}) = b(a_1'c_1 + a_2'c_2) \qquad (20.2)$$

where the primes refer to absorbance and absorptivities at λ', and the subscripts to species 1 and 2. Also at a second wavelength λ'',

$$A'' = b(a_1''c_1 + a_2''c_2) \qquad (20.3)$$

If the four absorptivities are known, the absorbance measurements at the two wavelengths are sufficient to determine the concentrations of each of the two components. In selecting the analytical wavelengths λ' and λ'', it is desirable to choose wavelength λ' where one component absorbs strongly and the other weakly (i.e., where a_1'/a_2' is a maximum) and to choose λ'' where the reverse situation holds (i.e., a_1''/a_2'' is a minimum).

Equations (20.2) and (20.3) can be used in three different ways, depending upon the knowledge that exists or is required about the *total* concentration of the components.[2]

If the actual (rather than the relative) concentration of each of the components is desired, simultaneous equations (20.2) and (20.3) are solved, giving

$$c_2 = \frac{(a_1''A' - a_1'A'')}{b(a_1''a_2' - a_1'a_2'')}$$

$$c_1 = \frac{-(a_2''A' - a_2'A'')}{b(a_1''a_2' - a_1a_2'')} \qquad (20.4)$$

[2] M. Ish-Shalom, J. D. Fitzpatrick, and M. Orchin, *J. Chem. Educ.*, **34**, 496 (1957).

It is apparent from an inspection of these equations that, if the four absorptivities and b are known and the two absorbances are measured, c_1 and c_2 can readily be calculated. The absorptivities are sometimes available in the literature, but it is decidedly advantageous to determine these values in the instrument being used for analysis. It is also apparent from an inspection of equations (20.2) and (20.3) that the total concentration need not be known; the sample need not be weighed before its dilution for the spectrometric determination if it is known that the mixture contains no other components, or only spectroscopically inactive ones.

If the sum of the concentrations ($c = c_1 + c_2$) of the two components is known, obviously one relation between the unknowns is available, and only one further relation is needed to determine both. Hence measurement at one wavelength is sufficient. Substitution of $c = c_1 + c_2$ into equation (20.2) gives, after rearrangement,

$$c_1 = \frac{A/b - a_2 c}{a_1 - a_2} \tag{20.5}$$

and hence c_1 and also $c_2 = c - c_1$ are readily obtained.

If the total concentration c is unknown, use can still be made of the above logic, provided there exists some wavelength, the *isoabsorptive* wavelength, λ^i, at which the absorbances $a_1{}^i$ and $a_2{}^i$ are equal.[3] Measurement at this wavelength immediately determines c, since

$$A^i = b(c_1 + c_2)a^i = a^i b c$$

where a^i is the common value $a_1{}^i = a_2{}^i$. Substitution into equation (20.5) gives

$$c_1 = \frac{A - a_2 A^i / a^i}{b(a_1 - a_2)} \tag{20.6}$$

Thus measurements at two wavelengths, λ, where a_1/a_2 is a maximum or minimum, and λ^i, where $a_1{}^i/a_2{}^i = 1$, are sufficient to give c and c_1, and hence also c_2.

The methods outlined are readily adaptable to use with graphic procedures. Equation (20.5) represents the equation of a straight line in a plot of c_1 versus A, and results can be directly read off such a line. A slight change in equation (20.6), dividing through by c, gives an equation

$$x_1 = \frac{a^i}{a_1 - a_2} \cdot \frac{A}{A^i} - \frac{a_2}{a_1 - a_2} \tag{20.7}$$

where x_1 is the weight fraction, c_1/c, of component 1; this is also a straight line. Thus, if the precision obtained in graphic interpolation is sufficient, these methods provide extremely convenient ways of obtaining c_1 and c_2, from two experimental measurements.

[3] R. C. Hirt, F. T. King, and R. G. Schmitt, *Anal. Chem.*, **26**, 1270 (1954).

The methods are, of course, subject to all the precautions customarily required of analytical methods, including particularly accurate determination of the required constants. Where repeated graphical determinations are desired, establishing the straight lines from a series of measurements on synthetic mixtures may be indicated. Even where duplicate analyses may not be readily possible, for instance, in kinetic experiments,[2,4] increased precision and reliability may be obtainable by making determinations at several wavelengths.

Methods for analysis of multicomponent systems follow the pattern discussed above. The measured absorbance at any particular wavelength for a mixture of absorbing compounds is given by

$$A = b(a_1c_1 + a_2c_2 + a_3c_3 + \cdots + a_nc_n)$$

If the absorptivities of all the absorbing species, a_n, are known, it is necessary only to measure A at n different wavelengths in order to secure the n unknown concentrations, c_n. As a matter of practice, this procedure is seldom used beyond a three-component system. In a three-component system, three simultaneous equations would be required and a total of nine calibration absorptivities is needed, the absorptivities, a, for each of the three compounds at the three chosen wavelengths.[5] Solution of the three simultaneous equations can be achieved by simple algebraic procedures, but for repeated calculation or for solution of four or more simultaneous equations a matrix inversion method is preferable.[6]

Use can again be made of a knowledge of total concentration to reduce the number of absorbance measurements required. Application to multicomponent systems is somewhat limited by the width of absorption bands, since it is necessary to find wavelengths at which the absorptivity ratios differ substantially. A method of analysis of two- and three-component mixtures based on the principles just discussed, but employing an ingenious averaging process using tristimulus colorimetry, has been suggested.[7]

A rather interesting application of spectrophotometry to qualitative analysis involves a series of measurements at several wavelengths on solutions, in which the ratios of several components vary, to determine the number of components.[8] This method is intended to detect how many absorbing species are present (e.g., in solutions of an ion with different concentrations of a complexing agent, or of an indicator at various pH's),

[4] J. D. Fitzpatrick and M. Orchin, *J. Org. Chem.*, **22**, 1177 (1957).

[5] For a detailed analysis of a three-component system see R. A. Friedel and M. Orchin, *Ultraviolet Spectra of Aromatic Compounds*, John Wiley and Sons, New York, 1951, pp. 30 f.

[6] P. D. Crout, *Trans. Am. Inst. Elec. Engrs.*, **60**, 1235 (1941).

[7] H. Flaschka, *Talanta*, **7**, 90 (1960).

[8] R. M. Wallace, *J. Phys. Chem.*, **64**, 899 (1960).

and may also be used to detect the presence of nonabsorbing species. The only assumption made is that Beer's law is valid for each component. The method is based on the construction of a matrix from the set of observations, and determination of the rank of this matrix. Use is made of a statistical test to determine which of the possible submatrices are singular. As an illustration it was shown that methyl red and methyl orange in the range of pH 2–6 each had two absorbing species, whereas mixtures of the two compounds had four.

20.3   Acid and Base Dissociation Constants

20.31 GENERAL THEORY.   The equilibrium constant for the reaction

$$\alpha A + \beta B + \cdots \rightleftharpoons \lambda L + \mu M \cdots \qquad (20.8)$$

is given by the expression

$$K = \frac{[L]^{\lambda}[M]^{\mu} \cdots}{[A]^{\alpha}[B]^{\beta} \cdots} \qquad (20.9)$$

where the quantities in brackets represent the concentrations, or better the activities of the respective species at equilibrium, and the Greek letters $\alpha, \beta, \cdots, \lambda, \mu, \cdots$ represent the coefficients with which the reactants and products enter into the balanced equation for the reaction. According to equation (20.9), evaluation of the equilibrium constant K requires only evaluation of the concentrations (or activities) of the components at equilibrium. Since it was seen in section 20.2 that spectrophotometry represents a powerful method for the determination of concentration of absorbing species, it obviously should provide a convenient method for the determination of equilibrium constants.

The widest application of spectrophotometry to the measurement of equilibrium constants probably is in the area of acid-base equilibria.[9] The acid dissociation constant, K_a, of an acid, HA, in a solvent, SH, is given by the expression

$$K_u = \frac{[A^-][SH_2^+]}{[HA]} \qquad (20.10)$$

where SH_2^+ is the solvated proton, and the dissociation reaction is

$$HA + SH \rightleftharpoons A^- + SH_2^+ \qquad (20.11)$$

The pK_a is defined as the negative logarithm of K_a, $pK_a = -\log K_a$. Basic dissociation constants are similarly defined:

$$K_b = \frac{[B^+][OH^-]}{[BOH]}$$

[9] L. A. Flexser, L. P. Hammett, and A. Dingwall, *J. Am. Chem. Soc.*, **57**, 2103 (1935).

Many bases, such as amines, do not contain OH groups or ions, and their basic dissociation constant is defined by

$$K_b = \frac{[BH^+][S^-]}{[B]} \tag{20.12}$$

corresponding to the reaction

$$B + SH \rightleftharpoons BH^+ + S^- \tag{20.13}$$

Since most acid-base reactions are measured in amphoteric solvents (i.e., solvents capable of acting as acids and bases), K_b of a base B can be related to the K_b of its conjugate acid BH^+ through the autoprotolysis constant K_p of the solvent (i.e., the equilibrium constant $K_p = [SH_2^+][S^-]$ for the reaction $2SH \rightleftharpoons SH_2^+ + S^-$). Substitution for S^- in equation (20.12) gives:

$$K_b = \frac{K_p[BH^+]}{[B][SH_2^+]} = \frac{K_p}{K_a} \tag{20.14}$$

or $K_a = K_p/K_b$. Although K_b appears extensively in the old literature, more recently the basicity of a base is usually expressed by the acidity (K_a or pK_a) of the conjugate acid.

Thus, according to equation (20.10), to determine K_a it is necessary only to determine the concentrations of HA, the acid; of A^-, its conjugate base; and of SH_2^+, the solvated proton. Where HA is the conjugate acid of a base, the same type of data is sufficient to determine the basicity, expressed as K_a of the conjugate acid, of any base. Knowledge of the autoprotolysis constant of the solvent then also permits calculation of the basic dissociation constant, K_b.

When dealing with acids having a pK_a in the range between 2 and 11 (or possibly 1 and 12) in aqueous solution, measurement of the activity of the solvated proton produces no difficulty, since, by definition, this is the pH, which can readily be determined by a pH meter. The determination of the concentrations of AH and A^- (or B and BH^+) also is no problem, provided solutions containing each one of the species to the exclusion of the other can be obtained. Since, in general, ultraviolet spectra are rather intense and detection methods are very sensitive, solubilities of the order of magnitude of 10^{-4} M are usually sufficient, and solubilities down to 10^{-5} or 2×10^{-5} M are occasionally used.

The procedure for the determination of K_a or K_b usually consists of determining the absorption spectrum of a series of solutions, each containing the same total concentration of the acid (HA) [or of the base (B)] but having different pH, which is adjusted by use of various buffers. A typical example of such a series of spectra is shown in Fig. 20.1. One of the characteristic features of a series of this type is the observation of an

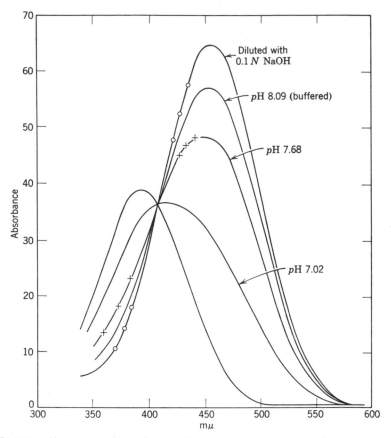

Fig. 20.1 The spectra of 4-methoxy-2-nitrophenol at various pH. (C. K. Hancock and M. Rapaport, private communication.)

isosbestic point, which is a special example of the isoabsorptive point discussed earlier. Whenever the spectra of pure acid and of pure conjugate base cross at some point, the spectra of all solutions containing various ratios of these two species (and no other absorbing species) must also go through this point, provided that the sum of the concentrations of both species is constant, and that the spectral characteristics (i.e., the absorption coefficients) of both species are insensitive to the effect of pH and of the buffer used. Assuming that $\epsilon_{AH}{}^{\lambda}$ and $\epsilon_{A^-}{}^{\lambda}$ are the molar absorptivities of AH and A$^-$, respectively, at the wavelength λ, the statement that the spectra cross at λ means that $\epsilon_{AH}{}^{\lambda} = \epsilon_{A^-}{}^{\lambda}$. The absorbance of a solution, using a 1 cm cell, containing both A$^-$ and AH is given by

$$A_{\lambda} = c_{A^-}\epsilon_{A^-}{}^{\lambda} + c_{AH}\epsilon_{AH}{}^{\lambda} \tag{20.15}$$

where c_{A^-} and c_{AH} are the concentrations in moles per liter of the two species. Hence, if $\epsilon_{A^-}{}^\lambda = \epsilon_{AH}{}^\lambda = \epsilon^\lambda$,

$$A = (c_{A^-} + c_{AH})\epsilon^\lambda = c\epsilon^\lambda$$

independent of c_{A^-}/c_{AH}, as long as $c_{A^-} + c_{AH} = c$. Thus, when $\epsilon_{A^-}{}^\lambda = \epsilon_{AH}{}^\lambda$, the point ϵ, λ is an isosbestic point. Measurement at this wavelength provides no information concerning the ratio of A^- to AH, but observation that an isosbestic point is present is desirable in order to verify that one is dealing with a simple acid-base reaction which is not complicated by further equilibria or other phenomena.

For the calculation of pK according to equation (20.10), a transformation is usually made. Taking logarithms on both sides, writing pK for $-\log K$ and pH for $-\log [H]$, we obtain

$$pK = pH - \log \frac{[A^-]}{[AH]} - \log \gamma_{H^+} \qquad (20.16)$$

But the absorbance A of a solution containing concentrations c_{A^-} of A^- and c_{AH} of AH is given by equation (20.15). If in addition

$$c_{A^-} + c_{AH} = c \qquad (20.17)$$

the ratio $[A^-]/[AH]$ is given by

$$\frac{[A^-]}{[AH]} = \frac{c_{A^-}}{c_{AH}} = \frac{A - A_{AH}}{A_{A^-} - A}$$

where A_{AH}, A_{A^-}, and A are the absorbances of the acid AH, the ion A^-, and the solution under investigation, all at the same concentration. Hence equation (20.16) becomes

$$pK = pH - \log \frac{(A - A_{AH})}{(A_{A^-} - A)} - \log \gamma_{H^+} \qquad (20.18)$$

The last term, $\log \gamma_{H^+}$, in equation (20.18) represents a correction for the hydrogen-ion activity coefficient and will be neglected in the following treatment. In working at known ionic strength, however, this term can be estimated and the appropriate correction made. For such work it is important to have series of buffers of known and constant ionic strength, and these buffers have been listed by Bates.[10]

Equation (20.18) is basic for all spectrophotometric pK determinations. It shows that the data required for the calculation of the pK of an acid are:

(1) The absorbances at some one selected wavelength of the free acid, and its conjugate base at some convenient, but equal, concentration, c.

[10] R. G. Bates, *Electrometric pH Determinations*, John Wiley and Sons, New York, 1954, pp. 116–117; *Ann. N.Y. Acad. Sci.* (in press).

(2) The absorbance of at least one solution of known pH in which both species are at equilibrium, at the same wavelength and total concentration as used in (1).

These minimum data are obviously available from a determination of the spectra discussed in connection with the isosbestic point. However, an adequate and reasonably accurate determination requires consideration of a number of additional points. Hence, the minimum data listed above are best supplemented by additional information more precise than that usually obtained from routine recording of a spectrum.

First, consider a plot of A versus pH for a single wavelength λ, such as might be obtained by reading values for A from successive curves in Fig. 20.1 and plotting against pH. In such a plot we may expect A to be constant above a certain pH, when substantially pure A^- is present in solution, and below some other pH, when the solute is completely in the AH form. A plot of this sort, but for the more complicated case of a dibasic acid, AH_2, is shown in Fig. 20.2. Constancy at low pH is approached asymptotically, but not reached at pH 0, where most of the acid present is in the free-acid, AH_2, form. Above pH 10 A is substantially constant, and all the solute is present as A^{2-}. In the intermediate range, pH 3–6, also, A is substantially constant, and the species in solution is substantially pure AH^-. Thus A values at pH 11 and 5 can be taken as A of A^{2-} and AH^-, respectively, but the A value for AH_2 must be obtained by extrapolation or by measurement in even stronger acid.

It is of interest to consider what range of pH values is necessary to ensure obtaining these constants. Rearrangement of equation (20.16) gives

$$\log \frac{[A^-]}{[AH]} = pH - pK$$

If a 1 per cent error is the largest to be tolerated in the determination of A, the ratio $[A^-]/[AH]$ must be less than $\frac{1}{100}$ and larger than 100, respectively, to ensure that the mixture contains not more than 1 per cent of the undesired species. This is equivalent to $\log ([A^-]/[AH]) = \pm 2$, and hence the pH of solutions in which values of A for free acid and conjugate base are determined should be $pK \pm \alpha$, with $\alpha \geq 2$. A rather accurate determination of these A values, A_{AH} and A_{A^-}, is necessary, since they enter the calculations repeatedly, and any error would affect each replicate calculation. In addition, it is assumed that these constants are themselves independent of pH, a property which is best verified in each case. Although such independence is usually observed, sometimes the extinction coefficients turn out to be pH dependent. This appears particularly likely in dealing with $n \rightarrow \pi$ transitions, which are notoriously solvent dependent. When

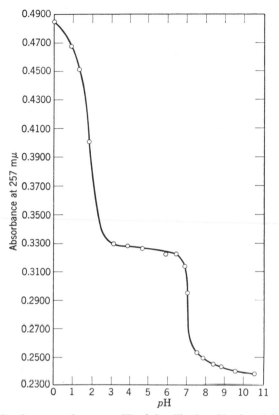

Fig. 20.2 A titration curve (ϵ versus pH) of the dibasic acid, phenylphosphonic acid. (Reprinted by permission from W. J. S. Polestak, "Determination of Dissociation Constants of Some Phenylphosphonic Acids from Ultraviolet Spectra," Thesis, Agricultural and Mechanical College of Texas, College Station, Tex., 1955.)

such cases occur, it is sometimes possible, by appropriate choice, to find a wavelength at which this pH dependence is absent or at least minimized. Sometimes, choice of a different absorption band may solve the problem. Finally, when no other correction has worked, a determination of the pH dependence and extrapolation method may be used to make needed corrections.

Equation (20.18) requires two differences, $A - A_{\mathrm{AH}}$ and $A_{\mathrm{A^-}} - A$. Reasonable accuracy in the ratio requires that neither of the differences be too small in magnitude. Other things being equal, the value obtained will be better, the more the ratio $A_{\mathrm{AH}}/A_{\mathrm{A^-}}$ differs from 1, in either direction. Thus, the spectra obtained in finding the isosbestic point will be used to determine the wavelength (or, better, wavelengths) at which this ratio is favorable, and all subsequent work can then be restricted to this wavelength or these wavelengths.

The single most accurate value of the pK is probably obtained when the two differences, $A - A_{AH}$ and $A_{A^-} - A$, are equal, which occurs at half-neutralization. However, use of only one solution, at half-neutralization, although frequently employed, is risky, since many difficulties do not become apparent unless several values of the pK are determined and compared. On the other hand, when either one or the other of the differences becomes too small, the uncertainties in the $[A^-]/[AH]$ ratio become large. Consequently it is desirable to make several measurements in the range of 0.1 or $0.2 < [A^-]/[AH] < 5$ or 10. Consistency between these determinations is generally indicative that the compound is of reasonable purity. Even contamination by an isomer of only moderately different pK usually leads to a systematic drift in such a series of results.

Another check on the consistency of results is frequently possible and often made by selection of several wavelengths as a basis for calculations. In particular, two wavelengths, one such that $\epsilon_{A^-} > \epsilon_{AH}$, the other such that $\epsilon_{A^-} < \epsilon_{AH}$, are highly desirable. The wavelengths chosen are often, but not necessarily, the λ_{max} of the two species. A difficulty with the use of two wavelengths is that the optimum concentration c is frequently not the same at both wavelengths, and consequently separate solutions may have to be used. The choice of an appropriate concentration for all measurements is also an important problem. The optimum value of absorbance for quantitative analysis has been carefully considered by a number of authors[11] and depends to some extent on instrument characteristics. Since equation (20.18) is based on a single total stoichiometric concentration for the sum of acid and conjugate base, it is obviously convenient to make the series of solutions by dilution of identical aliquots of a single appropriate stock solution of the acid with the desired buffers, thus assuring equality of concentrations. The optimum concentration is probably the highest concentration at which an accurate measurement can be made of the species with the higher A.

To ensure maximum accuracy, it is probably desirable to make the measurements with a manually operated instrument, such as the Beckman DU, rather than with a recording one, and to use an average of several measurements. Adequate accuracy in pH measurement is naturally also a requirement; this calls for measurement of the pH of the final solution rather than of the buffer used in diluting the stock. Good temperature control is necessary, since most pH's are temperature dependent.

The buffer solutions may also cause considerable difficulties. Many of

---

[11] This is discussed in most modern books on quantitative analysis and instrumental methods.

the substances used in common buffers themselves absorb considerably in the ultraviolet.[12] Thus phosphate and phthalate buffers have spectra of their own, and even acetate, carbonate, and borate buffers can cause some interference. Since the buffers usually are used in concentrations of 0.1–0.01 M, several powers of 10 more concentrated than the substrate, considerable difficulties may arise. Careful preparation of blanks for work in spectral regions where the buffers have even slight absorption is an absolute necessity; and, since the buffer spectra are also pH dependent, the pH of solution and blank must be carefully matched.

As outlined here, the method is directly applicable to the determination of the acid or base dissociation constant of any acid-base pair, provided that both acid and base are sufficiently soluble in water, that their spectra differ sufficiently, that no side reactions occur, and that the pK_a is in the range $1 < pK_a < 12$. The requirement that the spectra differ sufficiently has generally restricted the method to systems in which the acidic (or basic) function either is itself a chromophore or part of a chromophore, or is directly attached to a chromophore as an auxochrome. In spite of these restrictions, the method has been applied to a tremendous number of systems, and not even a selected list can reasonably be given. Its range of application is somewhat wider than that of the possibly more convenient potentiometric titration, since the required concentrations are usually lower by 1 or 2 powers of 10, and consequently the solubility requirements are less restrictive. Further, although neither method gives thermodynamic values, the spectrophotometric method permits the use of buffers of constant ionic strength,[10] and consequently activity corrections are made more readily.

20.32 VARIATIONS IN THE GENERAL METHOD.   The general method outlined in section 20.31 has many limitations, as discussed in the preceding paragraphs. A large number of variations and modifications have been proposed to overcome some of these limitations. A complete listing of all these modifications is impossible; only a few of the most important and most commonly encountered ones will be mentioned here.

A very large amount of work has been done with very weak bases,[9] i.e., bases the conjugate acids of which have a pK_a below 1 or 2. In such cases potentiometric titrations are inapplicable, and the spectrophotometric method is about the only one available. In work with such weak bases, pH measurement is impossible, since the limit of the pH meter lies somewhere about pH 1. Also, the concept of the pH breaks down. For more acidic solutions, Hammett has defined the so-called *acidity function* H_0.[13] The

---

[12] A list of buffers relatively free from absorption is given by R. A. Robinson, in *The Structure of Electrolytic Solutions*, edited by W. J. Hamer, John Wiley and Sons, New York, 1959, p. 256.

[13] M. A. Paul and F. A. Long, *Chem. Revs.*, **57**, 1 (1957).

definition of this function ensures that it becomes identical with pH in weakly acidic solutions, and measures the activity of solvated protons in strongly acidic solution. The acidity function has been measured for many solvent systems, particularly for aqueous solutions of strong acids,[13] but also for mixed aqueous alcoholic solutions of acids. Such measurements actually are based on pK measurements of series of indicators. With such H_0 functions available, it is a relatively simple matter to measure the basicity (i.e., the pK_a of the conjugate acids) of any weak base for which the spectra of free base and conjugate acid differ, using equation (20.18) as given above, but replacing pH by H_0:

$$pK = H_0 - \log \frac{(A - A_{BH^+})}{(A_B - A)} \qquad (20.19)$$

In this equation, unlike equations (20.16) and (20.18), the activity coefficient correction is absorbed in H_0. Unfortunately, however, the acidity function H_0 is applicable directly only to neutral bases in equilibrium with singly positively charged conjugate acids, and for such equilibria as $B^+ + H \rightleftharpoons BH^{2+}$ and $A^- + H^+ \rightleftharpoons AH$, special functions H_+ and H_- would be required, about which little or no information is available.

Another problem frequently encountered involves the matter of solubility. Many organic compounds are not sufficiently soluble in water to permit the use of the method described. A common technique has involved the preparation of a fairly concentrated stock solution in methanol or ethanol, and its dilution by aqueous buffers. It is then frequently assumed that the small concentration of the alcohol in the final solution may be neglected. In many such cases the compounds are actually sufficiently soluble in water to give the finally desired concentration, and the alcohol technique is needed only to permit the use of a more concentrated stock solution in order to ensure uniformity of final concentrations. In other cases the final solutions may be supersaturated, but rates of precipitation or crystallization are sufficiently low to allow completion of measurements before crystallization occurs.

An alternate method for water-insoluble compounds is the use of mixed solvents, such as aqueous (20, 50 or even 70 per cent) alcohol, dioxan, or the like. In such cases the assumption is made that pH measurements in these solvents are meaningful, i.e., that the glass electrode measures the activity of solvated protons. Since the same assumption is, however, equally implicit in the widely used potentiometric titration in such solvents, data obtained by this method are at least comparable with potentiometric ones; they should, however, not be considered as thermodynamic but as apparent equilibrium constants.

Another commonly encountered problem involves equilibria in which one or the other (or sometimes both) of the chemical species in equilibrium are unstable under the conditions of the experiment. Although such situations can be very complicated, the expedient of measuring the absorption of the appropriate solution as a function of time, and extrapolating back to the time of mixing of the solution, has sometimes produced usable results.

Occasionally it is not possible to obtain the value of A for either one or the other, or even both, of the species in equilibrium. This may be due to solubility relations, because of insufficient stability, but probably most often to interference from another equilibrium. Thus, if a dibasic acid undergoes two successive dissociations, $AH_2 \rightleftharpoons AH + H^+ \rightleftharpoons A^{2-} + 2H^+$, and the pK_a's of the successive steps are insufficiently separated, no solution can be obtained in which all the acid occurs as AH. When ΔpK, the difference between the two pK's, is 2, a solution having a pH halfway between the two pK values (i.e., the solution in which $[AH^-]$ is at a maximum) contains almost 10 per cent each of AH_2 and A^{2-}, and only about 80 per cent of AH^-, and thus cannot be used to determine A_{AH^-}. When ΔpK is 4, the corresponding solution contains about 98 per cent AH, 1 per cent each of AH_2 and A^-, and hence will give a reasonably accurate value of A_{AH^-}, provided this is not appreciably less than either ϵ_{AH_2} or $\epsilon_{A^{2-}}$. Furthermore, the absorbtivity of a very weak base sometimes cannot be obtained because sufficiently acidic solutions to convert it to the conjugate acid cannot be prepared.

Because of the extreme importance and frequent occurrence of these cases, a large variety of methods have been evolved to deal with them.[14] All of these depend, in one way or another, on the elimination or evaluation of the unobtainable A from equation (20.18) or (20.19). The various methods differ only in the particular mathematical tricks used to achieve this elimination; these are graphical in nature in some cases, or iterative analytic in others. Since the particular methods depend strongly on the specific problems involved in any given case, no general discussion of such methods will be presented.

Finally, a particularly elegant method merits brief mention. It involves the simultaneous use of any number of wavelengths desired, and conversion to a single straight line for any acid-base equilibrium.[15] Although originally set up for use with visible wavelengths and weighting in accordance with

[14] For example, D. H. Rosenblatt, *J. Phys. Chem.*, **58**, 40 (1954); H. Irving, H. S. Rossotti, and G. Harris, *Analyst*, **80**, 83 (1955); E. M. Arnett and C. Y. Wu, *J. Am. Chem. Soc.*, **82**, 5660 (1960); C. T. Davis and T. A. Geissman, *J. Am. Chem. Soc.*, **76**, 3507 (1954).

[15] C. N. Reilley and E. M. Smith, *Anal. Chem.*, **32**, 1233 (1960).

the tristimulus theory of color vision, the method is adaptable to the ultraviolet region and to any arbitrary weighting of wavelengths. In the case of overlapping equilibria, it permits derivation of the properties of the intermediate by *linear* extrapolation; however, the method also becomes impractical if the equilibria overlap too much.

A last consideration merits some comment. Because of the need for buffering, the spectrophotometric measurements on which the pK calculations are based are always made on solutions of relatively high ionic strength, even though the concentration of the test acid may be quite low. Consequently, the activity coefficients are distinctly different from unity, and the equilibrium constants obtained are apparent equilibrium constants, not thermodynamic ones. For many purposes these have either been considered adequate or been shown to be adequate. This is particularly true if one is interested in comparisons involving a series of structurally related compounds. Where thermodynamic equilibrium constants have been desired, either of two procedures has generally been used. Both depend on correction to infinite dilution. One applies the Debye-Hückel theory[16] to estimate the $\log \gamma_{H^+}$ term in equations (20.16) and (20.18), using theoretical parameters to achieve the correction; in this case all measurements are made at a single ionic strength,[10] and the results are corrected for the effect of the ionic strength. In the alternate procedure, measurements have been made at several ionic strengths, and correction to zero ionic strength has then been accomplished by use of an extrapolation which has the form dictated by the Debye-Hückel theory, but in which the parameters are evaluated empirically from data at the several ionic strengths.

20.33 ACID-BASE EQUILIBRIA IN NONAQUEOUS SOLVENTS. The methods discussed in the preceding sections are applicable to acid-base reactions in aqueous solution, and in mixed aqueous-nonaqueous solutions. They may also be applicable in nonaqueous prototropic media, such as liquid ammonia and alcohols. Measurements are also possible in solvents not involving autoprotolysis (e.g., chloroform) or having quite small autoprotolysis constants (e.g., acetic acid).

When there is a considerable difference between the spectra of the base and its conjugate acid, such measurements involve application of relatively straightforward equilibrium theory, such as will be discussed in detail in section 20.4. The reaction observed is between the acid and a reference base, or between the base and a reference acid. In this situation it is rather unimportant whether the reaction is followed by observation of the spectrum of the acid or base, or of the reference base or acid. A typical

---

[16] H. S. Harned and B. B. Owen, *The Physical Chemistry of Electrolytic Solutions*, Reinhold Publishing Co., New York, 1958, Chapters 2, 3, and 5.

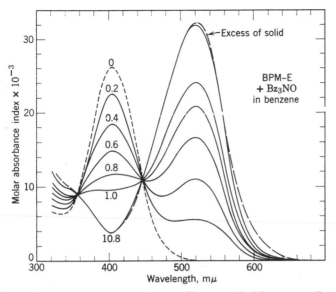

Fig. 20.3   The spectra of various mixtures of bromophthalein magenta E and tribenzyl-amine oxide in benzene. [Reprinted by permission from M. M. Davis and H. B. Hetzer, *J. Am. Chem. Soc.*, **76**, 4247 (1954).]

case is illustrated in Fig. 20.3, where data for the association of tribenzyl-amine oxide with bromophthalein magenta E are shown.[17] The only special problem which arises stems from the fact that in such media, which usually have low dielectric constants, dissociation into separate solvated ions does not generally occur, but ions are present as ion pairs (and possibly higher aggregates). The spectra of such ion pairs, even when the counter ion shows no absorption in the region under observation, are not necessarily independent of the nature of the counter ion. A particularly interesting case of this phenomenon has been investigated by Davis and Paabo,[18] whose data for bromophthalein magenta E are shown in Fig. 20.4. The most striking example of counter-ion effects is provided by ion pairs in which the cation-anion electrostatic interaction is enhanced by formation of a hydrogen bond, so-called *hydrogen-bonded ion pairs*.

Another interesting method for the investigation of acid-base reactions in nonaqueous media is due to Kolthoff and Bruckenstein,[19] who have investigated the behavior of a series of strong acids in anhydrous acetic acid. Use is made of an indicator which has different spectra in the acidic and basic forms, and which is allowed to react with various concentrations

[17] M. M. Davis and H. B. Hetzer, *J. Am. Chem. Soc.*, **76**, 4247 (1954).
[18] M. M. Davis and M. Paabo, *J. Am. Chem. Soc.*, **82**, 5081 (1960).
[19] I. M. Kolthoff and S. Bruckenstein, *J. Am. Chem. Soc.*, **78**, 1 (1956).

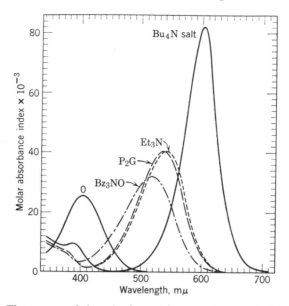

Fig. 20.4 The spectra of the salts formed between bromophthalein magenta E and tribenzylamine oxide (Bz_3NO), 1,3-diphenyl-guanidine (P_2G), triethylamine (Et_3N), and the tetrabutylammonium salt (Bu_4N); O is the spectrum without added base. [Reprinted by permission from M. M. Davis and M. Paabo, *J. Am. Chem. Soc.*, **82**, 5081 (1960).]

of the acid under investigation. The ratio of the acidic to the basic form of the indicator is evaluated spectrophotometrically, and is used to calculate not only the ionization constant into ion pairs, but also the ion-pair dissociation constant.

20.4 Polybasic Acids and Tautomeric Equilibria

In connection with the discussion of substituted pyridines in Chapter 14, reference was made to the special problems arising when a molecule contains two functional groups which can participate in acid-base equilibria. Since spectrophotometric methods have been widely used in the investigation of such systems, a rather detailed discussion is indicated. Three cases may be distinguished.

(1) The case of a dibasic acid H_2A undergoing successive dissociations:

$$H_2A \rightleftharpoons HA^- + H^+ \rightleftharpoons A^{2-} + 2H^+$$

(2) The case of a base (B) with two basic functional groups, such as amino groups undergoing the sequence of equilibria:

$$B + 2H^+ \rightleftharpoons BH^+ + H^+ \rightleftharpoons BH_2^{2+}$$

(3) A neutral molecule (AH) able to act as either an acid or a base:

$$AH_2^+ \rightleftharpoons AH + H^+ \rightleftharpoons A^- + 2H^+$$

Theoretically, these three cases are quite analogous except for the charges on the various species, and will be treated here in a single discussion which will largely ignore these charges.

Examples of case (1) are phthalic acid and p-hydroxybenzoic acid, of case (2) p-phenylenediamine and 4-aminopyridine, and of case (3) 4-hydroxypyridine and nicotinic acid.

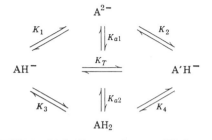

Fig. 20.5 Tautomeric equilibrium scheme.

For all three cases, a single equilibrium diagram may be written, which is shown as Fig. 20.5, where the charges assigned are those appropriate to case (1). A total of seven equilibrium constants can be defined in this system; of these only three are independent, the other four following from the first three. Their definitions are as follows:

$$K_{a1} = \frac{[A^{2-}][H^+]}{[AH^-] + [A'H^-]} \tag{20.20}$$

$$K_{a2} = \frac{[H^+]\{[AH^-] + [A'H^-]\}}{[AH_2]} \tag{20.21}$$

$$K_T = \frac{[A'H^-]}{[AH^-]} \tag{20.22}$$

$$K_1 = \frac{[A^{2-}][H^+]}{[AH^-]} \tag{20.23}$$

$$K_2 = \frac{[A^{2-}][H^+]}{[A'H^-]} \tag{20.24}$$

$$K_3 = \frac{[AH^-][H^+]}{[AH_2]} \tag{20.25}$$

$$K_4 = \frac{[A'H^-][H^+]}{[AH_2]} \tag{20.26}$$

where the square brackets, although strictly referring to activities, will be approximated by concentrations, except for $[H^+]$, and where AH^- and $A'H^-$ refer to two forms of the first anion of AH_2, as I and II for p-hydroxybenzoic acid. In the special case where AH^- and $A'H^-$ are

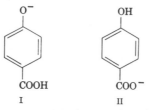

equivalent, as in phthalic acid (or p-phenylenediamine), $K_1 = K_2$, $K_3 = K_4$, $K_T = 1$, and

$$K_{a1} = \frac{[A^{2-}][H^+]}{2[AH^-]} \qquad (20.27)$$

$$K_{a2} = \frac{2[AH^-][H^+]}{[AH_2]} \qquad (20.28)$$

By substitution of (20.22)–(20.26) into (20.20) and (20.21) it can readily be shown that

$$K_{a1} = \frac{K_1}{(K_T + 1)} = \frac{K_2 K_T}{(K_T + 1)} \qquad (20.29)$$

$$K_{a2} = K_3(K_T + 1) = \frac{K_4(K_T + 1)}{K_T} \qquad (20.30)$$

Equations (20.29) and (20.30) represent four relations between the seven constants, and verify that only three are independent. Substitution of $K_T = 1$ into (20.29) and (20.30) shows that, for the case of equivalent acid (or basic) functions, (20.27) and (20.28) become

$$K_{a1} = \frac{K_1}{2} = \frac{K_2}{2} \qquad (20.31)$$

$$K_{a2} = 2K_3 = 2K_4 \qquad (20.32)$$

The factors $\frac{1}{2}$ in (20.31) and 2 in (20.32) are the *statistical factors* well known to physical organic chemists.

K_{a1} and K_{a2} are the first and second acid dissociation constants of AH_2, which can be evaluated experimentally by straight-forward experimental methods, such as potentiometric titration or the spectrophotometric methods of sections 20.31 and 20.32. K_1, K_2, K_3, K_4, and K_T are not readily evaluated experimentally without special assumptions; K_T in particular is of considerable interest, and a tremendous amount of work has gone into its determination. Again, the number of systems which have been studied is so tremendous that not even a partial listing will be attempted.

The simplest approach to a determination of K_T is a purely spectroscopic one. If the pH of a solution is adjusted so that practically no A^{2-} or

AH_2 is present, the spectrum of such a solution may be compared with the spectra of reference compounds which may reasonably be expected to have spectra identical with, or at least closely related to, AH^- and $A'H^-$. Thus, in the case of p-hydroxybenzoic acid, the anions derived from the methyl ester, III, and the methyl ether, IV, may reasonably be expected

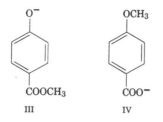

III   IV

to resemble greatly those of I and II, respectively. If $K_T < 0.01$, as it is in this example, the observed spectrum of the "equilibrium mixture" of I and II shown in Fig. 20.6 closely resembles that of IV, showing that the solution contains practically only II. If $K_T > 100$, similarly, the spectrum would closely resemble that of the reference compound for $A'H^-$. If $0.01 < K_T < 100$, the observed spectrum would show the bands characteristic of both AH^- and $A'H^-$. Provided it may be assumed that the spectra of these species are identical with those of their reference compounds, or that the spectra of both species can be evaluated theoretically, the concentration of both species can be calculated from the spectrum of the equilibrium mixture, and K_T can be determined.

An example of such a determination of K_T is provided by p-dimethylaminoazobenzene,[20] where comparison of the spectrum of the first conjugate acid (II in Fig. 20.7) with that of p-phenylazo-N,N,N-trimethyl anilinium ion, permitted evaluation of K_T as between 1.1 and 2.0, in fair agreement with other evidence.

Relations (20.29) and (20.30) also provide methods for the evaluation of K_T. Provided K_{a1} and/or K_{a2} have been or can be measured, any method of determining (or estimating) K_1 or K_2 [to be used in conjunction with K_{a1} and equation (21.29)] or K_3 or K_4 [in conjunction with K_{a2} and equation (21.30)] provides a way to estimate K_T. Although a large number of methods of estimating K_1–K_4 can be conceived, two merit special mention.

The first involves reference compounds similar to those used in the spectroscopic method just described. If it can be assumed that the change in going from AH^- to the reference compound, say ACH_3^-, does not affect the basicity of AH^-, measurement of the K_a for $AHCH_3 \rightleftharpoons ACH_3^- + H^+$ represents a direct determination of K_3. In similar ways, direct estimation

[20] S.-J. Yeh and H. H. Jaffé, J. Am. Chem. Soc., 81, 3283 (1959).

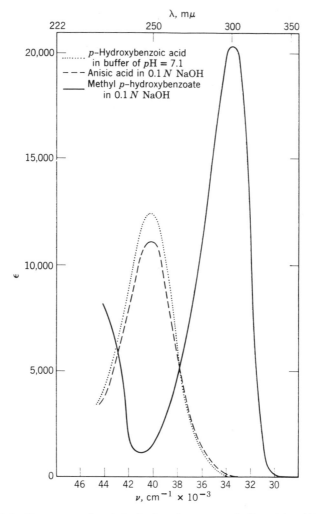

Fig. 20.6 The spectra of methyl p-hydroxybenzoate and of p-anisic acid in $0.1N$ NaOH, and of p-hydroxybenzoic acid at pH 7.

of K_4 is conceivable. Even if the assumption that the substitution does not affect the basicity of AH^- is not valid, it may be possible to estimate this effect and hence apply a correction to K_a.

The second method is based on any one of many available empirical relations, particularly the linear free-energy relations, such as the Hammett or Taft equation, which may be used to obtain reliable estimates of such constants as K_1–K_4. Measurements are then required only on series of compounds in which one or the other of the acidic functions, but not both, occurs in conjunction with other nonacidic substituents, the effect of which is well known.

Both these methods have been applied repeatedly and have produced reliable results. In some cases all three methods have been applied and have led to consistent results. The second and third methods have the advantage over the pure spectroscopic one of being capable of giving values of K_T outside the range $0.01 < K_T < 100$, and thus of providing information about free energy and possibly, although much less reliably, about enthalpy and entropy differences when one of the species never occurs in measurable quantities. Again, the tautomeric equilibrium in the conjugate acid of p-dimethylaminoazobenzene may be cited as an example of these methods.[20]

Methods permitting estimation of constants K_1–K_4 are capable of providing values for K_T even when K_{a1} and K_{a2} are not measurable. Division of equation (20.23) by (20.24), (20.26) by (20.25), and combination with (20.22) gives

$$K_T = \frac{K_1}{K_2} = \frac{K_4}{K_3}$$

so that estimation of either K_1 and K_2, or of K_3 and K_4, gives K_T. Also, multiplication of (20.20) and (20.21), of (20.23) and (20.24), and of (20.25) and (20.26), gives

$$K_{a1}K_{a2} = K_1K_2 = K_3K_4$$

and these equalities provide a check of the consistency of any set of data obtained.

Everything that has been said up to this point is applicable equally to any of the three cases discussed, which are differentiated by whether AH_2, A, or AH is the uncharged species. In the first two cases, some solvent

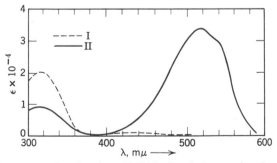

Fig. 20.7 The spectra of p-phenylazo-N,N,N-trimethylammonium ion and of the first conjugate acid of p-dimethylaminoazobenzene. [Reprinted by permission from S.-J. Yeh and H. H. Jaffé, *J. Org. Chem.*, **22**, 1281 (1957).

effects on K_T are likely to occur, since solvation of the singly charged ion is likely to differ with the nature of the charged group (e.g., O^- and COO^- in I and II, respectively, or $\geq NH^+$ or $-NH_3^+$ in 4-aminopyridine). In the third case, however, where the tautomeric equilibrium occurs in the uncharged species, solvent effects may be of particular importance. In 4-hydroxypyridine, where the species AH and A'H may be represented by the resonance hybrids V $\longleftrightarrow$ VI and VII $\longleftrightarrow$ VIII, respectively, solvent

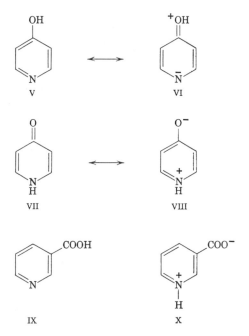

effects also are not likely to be too large. But in nicotinic acid, where AH, IX, is a chargeless species, but A'H, X, is a zwitterion, the latter must be stabilized with respect to the former by solvent polarity, and considerable solvent effects are to be expected and are actually observed[21] (see Fig. 9.10).

20.5   Complex Formation Equilibria

In the preceding sections, spectrophotometric methods for investigation of acid-base equilibria were discussed in some detail. Spectrophotometry is also of tremendous importance in the study of complexes. Two problems have received considerable attention: the determination of equilibrium constants, and the determination of the stoichiometry of the complexes.

---

[21] H. P. Stephenson and H. Sponer, *J. Am. Chem. Soc.*, **79**, 2050 (1957).

Although the two problems are usually examined simultaneously, the problem of the stoichiometry must be settled before meaningful data on equilibrium constants can be obtained. Only when the stoichiometry has been previously determined by other techniques can the spectrophotometric method be used for equilibrium constants without attention to stoichiometry. The spectrophotometric method is particularly powerful, since it does not require that the complex be capable of separate existence; evidence for the formation of quite unstable complexes can be obtained, and their stoichiometry, their free energies, and even their enthaplies and entropies of formation can be determined. Most of the work has been concerned with two types of complexes: (1) those between two neutral organic molecules, or one such molecule and a neutral inorganic molecule, e.g., the aromatic hydrocarbon-iodine and -polynitro compound complexes, and (2) the complexes of metallic cations with various ligands, which may be either anions or neutral compounds.

The simplest case of determination of the stoichiometry of a complex is well represented by the classical work of Benesi and Hildebrand,[22] who investigated the aromatic hydrocarbon-iodine system. By measuring the absorption spectra of solutions of iodine in benzene, these authors found at 297 mμ an absorption band, which is absent in iodine solutions in "inert" solvents such as carbon tetrachloride and hexane, and which was assigned to an iodine-benzene complex. This band is the so-called *charge-transfer band* discussed in section 12.6. The observation that the absorbance $A = \log (I_0/I)$ is proportional to the iodine concentration immediately suggested that the complex formed had the formula $C_6H_6 \cdot I_2$, i.e., was a 1:1 complex.

This determination is a simple example of a general method, proposed by Moore and Anderson,[23] and analogous to the method commonly used in kinetics for observing orders with respect to one reactant. In examining the equilibrium

$$\alpha A + \beta B \rightleftharpoons A_\alpha B_\beta$$

$$K = \frac{[A]^\alpha [B]^\beta}{[A_\alpha B_\beta]}$$

the log of the absorbance (proportional to log $[A_\alpha B_\beta]$) of a series of solutions with constant [A] and varying [B] is plotted against log [B], giving a straight line of slope β, and similarly with varying [A] and constant [B] a line with slope α is obtained. Constancy of [A] or [B] is readily achieved by use of a large excess of the constant component.

[22] H. A. Benesi and J. H. Hildebrand, *J. Am. Chem. Soc.*, **71**, 2703 (1949).
[23] R. L. Moore and R. C. Anderson, *J. Am. Chem. Soc.*, **67**, 168 (1945).

The preliminary estimate of the stoichiometry of the benzene-iodine complex was then checked by the empirical method mentioned. The equilibrium expression

$$K = \frac{[C_6H_6 \cdot I_2]}{[C_6H_6][I_2]}$$

$$= \frac{c}{(c_{I_2} - c)[c_A - c)} \tag{20.33}$$

was assumed, where c is the concentration of the complex, c_{I_2} and c_A are the initial concentrations of iodine and benzene, respectively, and, since $c_A \gg c_{I_2}$ was always used, c was negligible with respect to c_A. The extinction coefficient (ϵ_C) of the complex is naturally unknown, so that c cannot be evaluated directly. But c is related to ϵ_C by

$$\epsilon_C = \frac{A}{cb} \tag{20.34}$$

where b is the length of the cell used in the measurements. Combination of (20.34) and (20.33) gives

$$\frac{c_{I_2}b}{A} = \frac{1}{c_A K \epsilon_C} + \frac{1}{\epsilon_C} \tag{20.35}$$

This equation indicates that a plot of $c_{I_2}b/A$ versus $1/c_A$ should be linear with slope $1/K\epsilon_C$ and intercept $1/\epsilon_C$. The fact that such a plot is linear confirms the conclusion that the complex has the formula given, and permits the calculation of ϵ_C and K.

The method can be generalized to complexes of any other stoichiometry, except that different formulations analogous to equation (20.35) are necessary to transform the data into a linear relation which can be used to obtain ϵ_C and K. In substantially the form given, this method has been applied to a wide variety of molecular complexes. In one of the many applications of this method, the dissociation constants and free energies of a series of carcinogenic polycyclic hydrocarbon-trinitrofluorenone complexes were determined.[24]

The method outlined in the preceding paragraphs assumes that the absorbance of the components of the complex is negligible at the wavelength used for the determination. A modification which does not require this assumption has been proposed.[25] Application of this method to the

[24] K. H. Takemura, M. D. Cameron, and M. S. Newman, *J. Am. Chem. Soc.*, **75**, 3280 (1953).

[25] J. A. A. Ketelaar, C. van de Stolpe, A. Goudsmit, and W. Dzcubas, *Rec. trav. chim.*, **71**, 1104 (1952).

equilibrium just discussed leads to an equation identical in form to (20.35), except that ϵ_C is replaced by $\epsilon_C - \epsilon_{I_2}$, the difference between the extinction coefficients of the complex and iodine, and A by $A - A^0$, the difference between the absorbances of the test solution and one containing free iodine at the same total concentration. The treatment has been further generalized to eliminate the neglect to c compared to c_A.[26]

The empirical method just discussed involves the assumption that only a single complex is formed between the reactants, or that the formation constants for successive constants, if they do occur, differ by at least several powers of 10. The method can in principle also be generalized to systems of successive equilibrium constants,[27] differing by lesser amounts. However, even with two complexes the method becomes cumbersome and involves trial-and-error calculations, and the results are not highly reliable.

The empirical method of determining complex stoichiometry is widely used in investigating molecular complexes, where 1 : 1 ratios are by far the most common. In the field of ionic complexes, however, much higher ratios are usually encountered, and more systematic methods of determination of complex stoichiometry have been developed. The best known of these is Job's *method of continuous variation*.[28] This method has largely been designed for convenience in use, and accordingly is based on spectrophotometric analysis of mixtures in the ratio of $x:(1-x)$ volumes of equimolar solutions of concentration M of the two components A and B of the complex. It is assumed that no change in volume occurs when these solutions are mixed. The equilibrium is expressed by the general equation:

$$\alpha A + \beta B = A_\alpha B_\beta = C$$

$$K = \frac{[A]^\alpha [B]^\beta}{[C]} \tag{20.36}$$

where K is the instability constant of the complex C. Under the experimental conditions specified [i.e., equimolar solutions of A and B of concentration M mixed in proportion $x:(1-x)$]:

$$xM = [A] + \alpha[C] = c_A \tag{20.37}$$

$$(1-x)M = [B] + \beta[C] = c_B \tag{20.38}$$

where the quantities in square brackets are the actual concentrations, and c_A and c_B are the total concentrations of free plus complexed A and B,

[26] N. J. Rose and R. S. Drago, *J. Am. Chem. Soc.*, **81**, 6138 (1959).
[27] J. Landauer and H. McConnell, *J. Am. Chem. Soc.*, **74**, 1221 (1952).
[28] P. Job, *Ann. chim.* [9], **10**, 113 (1928).

respectively. Now it is assumed that all three species, A, B, and C, obey Beer's law at the wavelength chosen for investigation. Then the absorbance A of a given solution in a 1 cm cell is

$$A = \epsilon_C[C] + \epsilon_A[A] + \epsilon_B[B]$$

and

$$\Delta A = A - \epsilon_A[A] - \epsilon_B[B] = \epsilon_C[C] \qquad (20.39)$$

is the difference in absorbance of an actual solution and a mixture in which no complexing reaction occurs. ΔA is seen to be proportional to [C]. The wavelength must be so selected that ϵ_C is greatly different from ϵ_A and ϵ_B, and the most convenient choice is one where both ϵ_A and ϵ_B are zero. A plot of ΔA versus x is then a curve with a maximum, and it will be shown that this maximum corresponds to

$$x = \frac{\alpha}{(\alpha + \beta)} \qquad (20.40)$$

If equations (20.37) and (20.38) are solved for [A] and [B] and are substituted into (20.36),

$$K[C] = [xM - \alpha[C]]^x[(1 - x)M - \beta[C]]^\beta$$

which if written in logarithmic form is

$$\ln K + \ln [C] = \alpha \ln [xM - \alpha[C]] + \beta \ln [(1 - x(M - \beta[C]]$$

On differentiation with respect to x, we obtain

$$\frac{d \ln [C]}{dx} = \frac{\alpha \left[M - \alpha \dfrac{d[C]}{dx} \right]}{xM - \alpha[C]} + \frac{\beta \left[M - \beta \dfrac{d[C]}{dx} \right]}{(1 - x)M - \beta[C]} \qquad (20.41)$$

Since ΔA is proportional to [C], a plot of ΔA versus x will have a maximum at $d[C]/dx = 0$, and $[d \ln [C]]/dx = 0$ at the same point. Setting these derivatives to zero in equation (20.41) results in

$$\frac{\alpha M}{xM - \alpha[C]} = \frac{\beta M}{(1 - x)M - \beta[C]}$$

which reduces to equation (20.40).

Hence it is obvious that the stoichiometry can be evaluated by the simple expedient of plotting ΔA versus x for a series of solutions and obtaining the maximum of the plot.[29] Once the stoichiometry is established, the calculation of the equilibrium constant is a relatively simple matter. A special graphical method for determination of K is due to Hagenmuller.[30]

---

[29] Concerning the method for obtaining the maximum, cf. T. W. Gilbert, Jr., *J. Phys. Chem.*, **63**, 1788 (1959).

[30] P. Hagenmuller, *Compt. rend.*, **230**, 2190 (1950).

Although Job[28] stated that the method was applicable only when a single complex was formed between A and B, a method has been proposed which is applicable if a series of complexes is formed.[31] This method, however, has not proved very reliable and has not found wide application.

The most difficult problem is encountered in the equilibria between a cation A and anions (or neutral ligands) B, where frequently a whole series of complexes is formed which are usually partially dissociated in solution. The situation is described by a series of equilibria

$$A + B \rightleftharpoons AB \qquad K_1 = \frac{[A][B]}{[AB]}$$

$$AB + B \rightleftharpoons AB_2 \qquad K_2 = \frac{[AB][B]}{[AB_2]} \qquad (20.42)$$

$$AB_2 + B \rightleftharpoons AB_3 \qquad K_3 = \frac{[AB_2][B]}{[AB_3]}$$

etc.

where K_1, K_2, and K_3 are the instability constants of the complexes.

The problem has been treated spectrophotometrically by J. Bjerrum, using two auxiliary concepts, the *formation function*,[32] $\bar{n}$, and the *corresponding solution*.[33]

The formation function ($\bar{n}$) is defined as the concentration of B bound in the various complexes in a solution of total concentration c_A of A and c_B of B and is a function only of the concentration of free ligand and the various equilibrium constants:

$$\bar{n} = \frac{[B_{compl.}]}{[A_{total}]} = \frac{(c_B - [B])}{c_A}$$

Using the various equilibrium expressions given, it is readily shown that

$$\bar{n} = \frac{K_1[B] + 2K_1K_2[B]^2 + 3K_1K_2K_3[B]^3 + \cdots}{1 + K_1[B] + K_1K_2[B]^2 + K_1K_2K_3[B]^3 + \cdots}$$

A plot of log [B] versus $\bar{n}$ has the form of a typical titration curve. But whereas a titration curve becomes of little value when the ratio of successive equilibrium constants approaches 1, because the individual steps are no longer separated, in the log [B] vs. $\bar{n}$ plot successive steps

[31] W. C. Vosburgh and G. R. Cooper, *J. Am. Chem. Soc.*, **63**, 437 (1941).

[32] J. Bjerrum, *Metal Ammine Formation in Aqueous Solution*, P. Haase and Son, Copenhagen, 1941; cf. G. Charlot and R. Gauguin, *Les methodes d'analyse des reactions en solution*, Masson et Cie, Paris, 1951, pp. 65 f.

[33] J. Bjerrum, *Kgl. Danske Videnskab. Selskab*, **21**, 1 (1944); cf. G. Charlot and R. Gauguin, *Kgl. Danske Videnskab. Silskab*, pp. 67 f, 92 f.

remain well separated even for close equilibrium constants, and calculation of equilibrium constants by a method of successive approximations then becomes a relatively simple matter.

Calculation of $\bar{n}$ requires a determination of the amount of B that has been complexed or, alternately, the amount (concentration) that remains uncomplexed. This determination is achieved by the method of corresponding solutions. Each of equations (20.42) shows that, at constant [B], [A]/[AB], [AB]/[AB$_2$], etc., are constants. Also [A] + [AB] + [AB$_2$] + $\cdots = c_A$, and consequently, [A]/c_A, [AB]/c_A, [AB$_2$]/c_A are constants. Furthermore, since the absorbance A is given by

$$A = [A]\epsilon_A + [AB]\epsilon_{AB} + [AB_2]\epsilon_{AB_2} + \cdots$$

A/c_A is also a constant at any wavelength for all solutions of the same concentration [B], which are called corresponding solutions and also have identical $\bar{n}$. If two such solutions have concentrations $c_A{}'$ and $c_A{}''$ of A, $c_B{}'$ and $c_B{}''$ of B, respectively, then

$$\bar{n} = \frac{c_B{}' - [B]}{c_A{}'} = \frac{c_B{}'' - [B]}{c_A{}''} = \frac{c_B{}'' - c_B{}''}{c_A{}' - c_A{}''}$$

whence $\bar{n}$ and [B] are readily obtained.

Thus, determination of the equilibrium constants requires determination of a series of pairs of corresponding solutions. By choosing two concentrations $c_A{}'$ and $c_A{}''$, and determining the spectra as a function of the concentration c_B, all necessary data can readily be obtained. This method has found wide application in inorganic chemistry.

20.6 Kinetics

Another field of chemistry in which spectrophotometry has found wide application as an analytical tool is the area of kinetics. Since the basic problem of kinetics is that of determining concentration as a function of time, spectrophotometry is particularly well suited for the measurements. This is especially true if either one of the reactants or one of the products absorbs strongly, since then it is not necessary to destroy the sample for analysis. Reactants and products must, of course, have sufficiently different spectra so that the change can readily be followed.

Modern recording spectrophotometers in particular can be used to produce a continuous recording of concentration as a function of time, if simply the wavelength drive is disconnected or inactivated, and the chart is allowed to move while the wavelength is set at some specific, desired value.

With the tremendous advances made in electronic circuits, analog computers, and the like, it seems quite possible to force the recorder, or a unit interposed between amplifier and recorder, to serve the further function of translating the observed absorbance into the particular form, depending on reaction order and conditions, required by the kineticist, and thus obtain the linear plot desirable in the analysis of kinetic data directly from the spectrophotometer. No such experiments appear to have been reported to date.

The variety of uses of spectrophotometry is so vast that no attempt will be made to list even examples. Virtually every issue of every major chemical journal contains some cases.

GENERAL REFERENCES

M. G. Mellon, *Analytical Absorption Spectroscopy*, John Wiley and Sons, New York, 1950.

R. A. Robinson, in *The Structure of Electrolytic Solutions*, edited by W. J. Hamer, John Wiley and Sons, New York, 1959, Chapter 16.

Appendix 1   Glossary and definitions; spectral notation; conventions

Absorbance (A). For pure materials, the logarithm to the base 10 of the ratio of incident to transmitted light: $A = \log_{10}(I_0/I)$. In solution, the absorbance is the log of the ratio of the intensity of light transmitted through pure solvent to the intensity of light transmitted through the solution, both observed in identical cells.

Absorption band. A region of the absorption spectrum in which the absorptivity passes through a maximum or inflection. This term usually refers to all the absorption due to a single electronic transition, and includes all vibrational subbands.

Absorption maximum. The wavelength ($\lambda_{\max}$) at which a peak occurs in the absorption curve. There may be, and generally are, several such maxima in a curve.

Absorptivity (a). The absorbance divided by the product of concentration and path length: $a = A/bc$. It is the absorbance per unit concentration and thickness, i.e., the *specific* absorbance.

   molar (ϵ): the absorptivity expressed in units of liters per mole centimeter; the concentration in moles per liter and the cell length in centimeters.

Alternant hydrocarbon. Any conjugated system which does *not* possess an odd-membered carbon ring system.

   even alternant: an alternant with an even number of carbon atoms.

   odd alternant: an alternant with an odd number of carbon atoms, e.g., allyl or benzyl ions.

Auxochrome. An atom or group of atoms which, alone, does not give rise to absorption in the ultraviolet but which, when conjugated to a chromophore, causes a bathochromic shift and hyperchromic effect.

Bathochromic shift. A displacement of a particular band under discussion toward longer wavelength (lower frequency). It is also called a *red shift*.

Beer's law or **Beer-Lambert law** (absorption law). A statement that the absorbance for a beam of parallel, monochromatic light in a homogeneous, isotropic medium is proportional to the cell length, b, and to the concentration, c, of the absorbing species: $A = abc$. The constant of proportionality is the absorptivity, a.

Bond order (p). A number used to describe the degree of bond character in partial multiple bonds, usually in conjugated systems. Although defined in terms of both VB and MO theories, the two definitions are not equivalent, and numerical values from them do not coincide.

Character tables. Tables specifying the manner in which wave functions (or other properties) transform under the various symmetry operations of a given point group.

Charge density (q). A number indicating the number of electrons belonging to a given atom; defined in both MO and VB theory.

Charge-transfer spectra. Spectra involving an excited state which is formed from the ground state by transfer of an integral charge or the major portion of an integral charge. When the charge transfer occurs within a single molecule, the process is *intramolecular* charge transfer; when the transfer occurs between adjacent or loosely bonded separate molecules, *intermolecular* charge transfer.

Chromophore. An atom or group of atoms or electrons in a molecule which is chiefly responsible for an absorption band.

Configuration. The description of the electronic structure of an atom or molecule in terms of a product of one-electron functions.

Configuration interaction. In a complete quantum-mechanical treatment, the step, usually the last, in which wave functions having equal symmetry but belonging to different configurations are allowed to interact to lead to final states which can no longer be ascribed to a single electron configuration.

Coulomb integral (α). A parameter needed in MO treatment of molecules. It is assumed to be roughly proportional to electronegativity or ionization potential.

Eigenfunction. See **Wave function.**

Electron correlation. The interaction between electrons, which is generally neglected in descriptions of electronic structure in terms of configurations.

End absorption. The continuously rising intensity of absorption observed in solution spectra toward the far ultraviolet and usually attributable to Rydberg transitions, $n \rightarrow \sigma^*$ transitions, etc.

Even function. A function symmetric with respect to each of its variables: $y(x) = y(-x)$.

Essential double bond. A bond which is double in all principal resonance structures of the molecule which do not involve formal charges or "long" bonds, e.g., the 1,2 and 3,4 bonds of butadiene.

Essential single bond. A bond which is single in all principal resonance structures, e.g., the 2,3 bond in butadiene.

Franck-Condon principle. The statement that during an electronic transition the position and momentum of nuclei remain substantially unchanged because of the much greater speed of electronic motion relative to nuclear motion.

Free valence (F). A number, defined in both MO and VB theory, measuring the unfulfilled valences of an atom in a conjugated system; of particular interest in the description of reactivity of molecules.

Frequency (ν). Number of cycles per unit time. The same term is commonly loosely used to refer to wavenumbers.

Gerade. A function symmetric with respect to a center of symmetry.

Half-band width. The width of a particular absorption band at points where $\epsilon = \frac{1}{2}\epsilon_{\max}$, usually expressed in reciprocal centimeters, cm^{-1}, and indicated as $\Delta\nu$. This value is particularly useful in the comparison of the intensities of similar bands in the spectra of related compounds, since, approximately, $\int\epsilon \, d\nu \propto \epsilon_{\max}\Delta\nu$.

Hyperchromic effect. An increase in the intensity of a particular absorption band.

Hypochromic effect. A decrease in intensity of a particular absorption band.

Hypsochromic shift. A displacement of a particular absorption band under discussion toward shorter wavelength (higher frequency). It is also called a *blue shift*.

Inflection or **shoulder.** A slight halt on a curve of rising absorption, occurring at the point where the curve changes from concave to convex. It frequently indicates the presence of a submerged band.

Intensity. In analogy with emission spectroscopy, where the intensity is the relative amount of light emitted, in absorption the intensity is the relative amount of light absorbed. It is usually given in terms of molar absorptivity (ϵ) or as integrated intensity ($\int \epsilon_\nu \, d\nu$, where the integration extends over an entire absorption band). For comparison with theory the integrated intensity is often converted to oscillator strength by multiplication by 4.32×10^{-9}.

Ionization potential. The energy required to remove one electron from an atom or molecule.

Isoabsorptive point. The wavelength at which two (or more) compounds have equal absorptivities.

Isosbestic point. The wavelength at which two substances, which can be converted into one another, have equal absorptivity.

K-band (Burawoy classification). The high-intensity band present in the spectrum of conjugated systems and presumably associated with conjugation; from the German *konjugierte*—a loose assignment which should be abandoned.

LCAO (linear combination of atomic orbitals). The simplest approximation of MO theory, and the wave functions which are formed by linearly combining (i.e., forming weighted sums of) the AO's of the various atoms in the molecule.

Multiplicity. The existence of several degenerate wave functions distinguished only by the relative orientation of the spin angular momentum. Defined by the total spin angular momentum S, and given by $2S + 1$.

Nodal plane. A plane in which a wave function is zero.

Normalization. The process of determining the factor by which a satisfactory wave function must be multiplied so that its square reflects the probability.

Odd function. A function antisymmetric with respect to one of its variables, $y(x) = -y(-x)$.

One-electron levels or **functions.** Functions of the coordinates of a single electron only. Important because of the widespread assumption that the total electronic wave function of an atom or molecule can be factored into a product of functions, each of which depends on the coordinates of one electron only. A synonym for orbital.

Optical density. A term which should be considered obsolete; now replaced by absorbance, A, with which it is identical.

Orbital. A one-electron function.

degenerate: of equal energy.

bonding: having lower energy than the AO's from which it is formed.

antibonding: having higher energy than the corresponding AO's.

localized: an MO localized in one bond, i.e., between two atoms.

nonlocalized: an MO extending over more than two atoms.

nonbonding: an MO having energy equal to that of the corresponding AO's.

equivalent: orbitals formed from nonlocalized MO's by a linear transformation, making them as nearly as possible localized but still orthogonal.

group: an orbital extending over several atoms, not necessarily adjacent, in a molecule, which has the symmetry properties of the molecule. Usually extending over a number of atoms of the same element, and in equivalent position.

symmetry: same as group orbital.

Orthogonal. A term applied to two functions if the integral over all space of their product vanishes. Thus ψ_A and ψ_B are orthogonal if, for every positive value of $\psi_A\psi_B$, there is an equal but negative value of $\psi_A\psi_B$, i.e., $\int\psi_A\psi_B \, d\tau = 0$.

Oscillator strength. A theoretical measure of intensity obtained from the transition moment.

Overlap integral. The integral over the product of two orbitals over all space. It measures to a large extent the degree to which two orbitals interact.

Parity forbidden. Forbidden by the $g \nleftrightarrow g$ or $u \nleftrightarrow u$ selection rule.

Point group. A designation of molecules (or functions) possessing a particular combination of symmetry elements and only these.

Polarization. A molecule absorbs polarized light incident along one of its axes only, if there is an appropriate relation between the direction of polarization and the orientation of the molecule relative to the light. When the absorbed light is polarized in the direction of the long axis of the molecule, the absorption band is *longitudinally* polarized; when the light is polarized along the short axis, *transversely* polarized.

Primary band. The high-intensity short-wavelength band in the spectra of benzene derivatives related to the benzene band at 203 mμ; more appropriately designated as arising from the transition:

$$^1L_a \leftarrow {}^1A \text{ (Platt notation)} \quad \text{or} \quad {}^1B_{1u} \leftarrow {}^1A_{1g} \text{ (state notation)}$$

R band (Burawoy classification). The low-intensity, long-wavelength band in the spectrum of ketones and related compounds which shifts to shorter wavelengths with increasing solvent polarity; more appropriately designated as the n $\rightarrow \pi$ transition. When applied to long-wavelength, low-intensity bands of nonpolar compounds such as unsaturated hydrocarbons, the term R band refers to singlet-triplet absorption.

Resolution (resolving power). The ratio of the average wavelength (wavenumber or frequency) of two spectral lines which can just be detected as a doublet, to the difference in their wavelengths (wavenumbers or frequencies).

Resonance integral (β). An integral in MO theory measuring the degree of interaction between two orbitals. Approximately proportional to the overlap integral.

Rydberg bands or transitions. Transitions occurring between orbitals of a single atom in a molecule which are not involved in bond formation.

Second primary band. The allowed, high-intensity band in the spectra of benzene derivatives related to the 180 mμ band of benzene; more appropriately designated as arising from the transition:

$$^1E_{1u} \leftarrow {}^1A_{1g} \text{ (state notation)} \quad \text{or} \quad {}^1B \leftarrow {}^1A \text{ (Platt notation)}$$

Secondary band. The low-intensity forbidden band related to the 256 mμ band of benzene; more appropriately designated as arising from the transition:

$$^1L_b \leftarrow {}^1A \text{ (Platt notation)} \quad \text{or} \quad {}^1B_{2u} \leftarrow {}^1A_{1g} \text{ (state notation)}$$

Selection rule. A rule which states some condition under which the intensity of absorption in the lowest approximation is zero, and under which therefore the transition should not be observed.

Shoulder. See **Inflection.**

Spectroscopic moment. A number which reflects the effect of a substituent on the intensity of the spectrum of benzene and which is related to the electron-withdrawing or repelling character of the substituent.

Spin-orbit coupling. The coupling of spin and orbital angular momenta, and the consequent mixing of states of different multiplicity.

State. A possible condition of an atom or molecule.

ground state: the state of lowest energy.

excited state: any state energetically above the ground state.

singlet state: a state in which all electrons are paired, and hence there is no resulting spin angular momentum.

doublet state: A state in which there is $\frac{1}{2}$ unit of spin angular momentum.

Stray radiation. All the radiation reaching the detector at wavelengths which do not correspond to the spectral position under consideration.

Submerged band. An absorption band which underlies a stronger or more intense band and which is generally apparent as a *shoulder* or *inflection.*

Symmetry. The correspondence in position and magnitude of parts of a molecule (or function) in relation to a reference point (the center of gravity), axis, or plane.

symmetric with respect to a symmetry element: all properties of the molecule (or function) remain unchanged with respect to both magnitude and direction under the symmetry operation.

antisymmetric with respect to a symmetry element or operation: all properties of the molecule (or function) are unchanged with respect to magnitude but opposite with respect to direction or sign under the symmetry operation.

unsymmetric: no correspondence of the parts of a molecule or function with respect to any reference point or symmetry element.

dissymmetric: the mirror image of the object is nonsuperimposable on the original.

species: a classification of wave functions based on their symmetric or antisymmetric character with respect to particular symmetry operations.

local: the symmetry properties of a *part* of the molecule, such as a π-electron system, ignoring other parts. Thus acetaldehyde belongs to point group C_s, but the local symmetry of its CO group is C_{2v}, as in formaldehyde.

Term-level diagram. A diagram of the various states of an atom or molecule. The various states are shown as horizontal lines, the vertical direction measures energy.

Transition. The change of a molecule from one state to another, accompanied by absorption or emission of light.

allowed: a transition which is not forbidden by a selection rule.

forbidden: a transition which, according to some selection rule, should not occur.

Transition moment. A mathematical quantity of importance in treatment of the intensity of a transition. It is the square of the integral over all space of the product of the initial and final wave functions and the dipole moment vector

$\mathbf{M}$, where $\mathbf{M} = \Sigma e\vec{r}$ and $\vec{r}$ is the radius vector from the center of gravity of the positive charge to the electron.

Transmittance (T). The ratio of the intensity of the light transmitted by a sample (I) to that incident on the sample (I_0), both measured under identical conditions.

Ungerade. A function antisymmetric with respect to a center of symmetry.
Vibrational structure. The subbands associated with a single electronic
transition and arising from the small energy differences of various vibrational
levels of the molecules in both ground and excited states.
Wavelength (λ). The distance, measured along the line of propagation, between
two points on adjacent waves which are in phase.
Wave function. The solution of the Schrödinger equation, representing a
possible stationary state of a system. In the case of an electron, the wave
function is a function of the coordinates of the electron, and its square
represents the probability of finding the electron at a given point.
Wavenumber (ν). The number of waves per unit length in a vacuum, the
reciprocal of λ, usually measured in reciprocal centimeters, cm^{-1}.

Spectral Notation

A large number of systems of notation for spectral bands are currently
in use. Many of these are empirical in nature, and, while introduced at
their appropriate places in the text, have not been widely used here, since
an attempt was made to employ systematic notation wherever possible.

The simplest systematic notation describes a transition in terms of the
one-electron orbitals between which the electron jumps. The initial
orbital is given first, the final last, and the two are connected by an arrow.
The orbitals may be specified in a number of ways. Most satisfactory is to
designate them by the Schönflies symbols of the symmetry species to which
they belong, sometimes prefixed by a "quantum number." More crudely,
the orbitals may be referred to by the σ, π, δ notation, not only in the point
groups $C_{\infty v}$ and $D_{\infty h}$ to which it applies, but also in planar compounds
where it is commonly used. In this case, lone-pair electrons are designated
by n. Platt's system of using f for the highest occupied, g for the lowest
unoccupied, orbital, and subsequent lower and higher letters is sometimes useful. Finally, whatever other letters are chosen to designate
orbitals, e.g., ψ_i, *lower-case* letters are used to designate the one-electron
orbitals.

If a more sophisticated description of spectra is desired, state symbols are
used, and again Schönflies symmetry species symbols are often employed.
These have the disadvantage, however, of obscuring correlations between
analogous transitions in related molecules belonging to different point
groups. In this case Platt's scheme (Chapters 11 and 13) is helpful. In
both systems prefixed superscripts indicate multiplicity. In another
commonly used type of state notation, due to Mulliken, different *types* of
states are given different capital letters (N, V, T, R, etc.). In all state
notations, the letter designating the state is a capital, and the higher-energy
state is written first, with the arrow pointing toward the final state: thus
an arrow to the left indicates absorption, one to the right, emission.

General Conventions

A few general conventions, used systematically throughout this book, are collected here:

(1) Any wave function which is a function of the coordinates of only one electron, a one-electron function, is given by a *lower-case* Greek letter. Any wave function which is a function of *many* (more than one) electrons is indicated by a *capital* Greek letter.

(2) Any atomic wave function is indicated by the letter phi (ϕ or Φ); molecular electronic wave functions by psi (ψ or Ψ); vibrational functions [functions of the *internal* coordinates, ξ (xi)] of the *nuclei* in a molecule, by chi (χ); wave functions including both vibrational and electronic functions by capital xi (Ξ) .

(3) To distinguish it from an atomic one-electron function, the polar angle is indicated by an old-style, open phi (φ).

(4) Since molar extinction coefficients are usually indicated by Porson epsilon (ϵ), one-electron orbital energies are usually denoted by an old-style epsilon (ε).

(5) In MO's (molecular orbitals) which are expressed by the LCAO (linear combinations of atomic orbitals) method, the coefficients of the individual AO's (atomic orbitals) are variously expressed as c's (generally when there is a whole series of them), as λ's (as in $\psi = \phi_1 + \lambda\phi_2$, where λ is the *ratio* of two coefficients), or as sin α and cos α, if emphasis is placed on normalization.

Appendix 2   The variational principle and the LCAO method

Although the wave equation for the hydrogen atom can be solved exactly, only approximate solutions can be found for the much more complicated problems of molecules involving many electrons and nuclei. In the case of molecules it is almost universally customary to express the wave function (molecular orbital, ψ) of each electron as a linear combination of the hydrogen-like AO's (ϕ) of the constituent atoms:

$$\psi_j = \sum_r c_{jr}\phi_r \tag{1}$$

where the subscript r is used to define the individual atoms, and the subscript j identifies the different MO's. Once the decision is made that the wave functions ψ_j are to have this form, the problem remains to find the values of the coefficients c_{jr}, and to calculate the energy associated with the orbital. These calculations are generally made by use of a principle of quantum mechanics called the *variational principle*. This principle states that the energy ε calculated from the Schrödinger equation for any approximate wave function ψ is always larger than the energy $\varepsilon_0{}^0$, calculated from the correct wave function $\psi_0{}^0$ of lowest energy.[1] Consequently to find the c_{jr} in equation (1) it is necessary only to find those values for which ε is a minimum. The resulting ψ is then presumed to be the *best* wave function of the form of equation (1), though not necessarily, and actually never, the exact one.

The proof of the variational principle is not difficult, although the reader will have to accept certain mathematical truths which can be verified by reference to any text on mathematics or quantum mechanics. The Schrödinger equation reads

$$H\psi_j{}^0 = \varepsilon_j{}^0\psi_j{}^0 \tag{2}$$

---

[1] The restriction must be added that, in the evaluation of the energy, the complete Hamiltonian operator must be used.

where H is the Hamiltonian operator, the exact form of which will be of no interest in this discussion, and ψ_j^0 and ε_j^0 are the exact solutions (eigenfunctions) and the associated energies (eigenvalues). For an approximate solution ψ_j the corresponding equation,

$$H\psi_j = \varepsilon_j\psi_j \tag{3}$$

does not hold accurately at each point in space; however, if ψ_j is a reasonable approximation of ψ_j^0, equation (3) holds approximately, and the value ε_j is evaluated as an average value. This is accomplished[2] by the expedient of multiplying both sides by ψ_j and integrating over all space:

$$\int \psi_j H\psi_j \, d\tau = \int \psi_j\varepsilon_j\psi_j \, d\tau = \varepsilon_j \int \psi_j^2 \, d\tau = \varepsilon_j \tag{4}$$

where $d\tau$ is the element of volume. The second equality arises because ε_j, as an average value, is independent of the coordinates. The last equality is due to the fact that we always consider all ψ_j so chosen that they are normalized, i.e., that the integral following ε_j is equal to 1.

A fundamental theorem of mathematics states that it is always possible to expand any arbitrary function f of the variables $x_1, x_2, \ldots$, as a series of another set of functions g of the same variables, as long as the set of functions g is what is known as a complete set of orthogonal functions. Furthermore, it can be shown that the set of all the functions ψ_j^0 which are solutions of equation (2) is a complete set of orthogonal functions.[3] By using these two theorems, it is always possible to expand an arbitrary approximate ψ_j in terms of the exact ψ_j^0:

$$\psi_j = \sum_n a_n\psi_n^0 \tag{5}$$

The subscript n is used for the ψ_n^0 since the subscripts on the two sides of equation (5) are independent. In addition, the normalized character of ψ_j and of the ψ_n^0 implies

$$\sum_n a_n^2 = 1 \tag{6}$$

Substituting equation (5) into equation (4) leads to

$$\varepsilon_j = \int \sum_n a_n\psi_n^0 H \sum_{n'} a_{n'}\psi_{n'}^0 \, d\tau$$

$$= \sum_n \sum_{n'} a_n a_{n'} \int \psi_n^0 H\psi_{n'}^0 \, d\tau \tag{7}$$

[2] L. Pauling and E. B. Wilson, *Introduction to Quantum Mechanics*, McGraw-Hill Book Co., New York, 1935.

[3] The restriction must be made that among degenerate ψ_j^0's only orthogonal ones are chosen.

But since $H\psi_n{}^0 = \varepsilon_n{}^0 \psi_n{}^0$, by using the orthogonality condition $\int \psi_n{}^0 \psi_{n'}{}^0 = 0$ if $n \neq n'$, equation (7) reduces to

$$\varepsilon_j = \sum_n a_n{}^2 \varepsilon_n{}^0$$

Subtracting $\varepsilon_0{}^0$ from both sides, and remembering equation (6),

$$\varepsilon_j - \varepsilon_0{}^0 = \sum_n a_n{}^2 (\varepsilon_n{}^0 - \varepsilon_0{}^0) \tag{8}$$

But $\varepsilon_n{}^0 \geq \varepsilon_0{}^0$, and $a_n{}^2 \geq 0$, and therefore $\varepsilon_j - \varepsilon_0{}^0$ must be positive or 0, i.e., $\varepsilon_j \geq \varepsilon_0{}^0$. This proves the variational principle stated above.

   The calculation of the c_{jr} in equation (1) and of the associated ε_j now follows a rather straightforward course. Returning to equation (4), and substituting equation (1), we obtain

$$\int \sum_r c_r \phi_r H \sum_{r'} c_{r'} \, \phi_{r'} \, d\tau = \varepsilon \int \sum_r c_r \phi_r \sum_{r'} c_{r'} \phi_{r'} \, d\tau \tag{9}$$

where the subscripts j have been dropped temporarily because they are not needed. Rearrangement leads to

$$\sum_r \sum_{r'} c_r c_{r'} \int \phi_r H \phi_{r'} \, d\tau = \varepsilon \sum_r \sum_{r'} c_r c_{r'} \int \phi_r \phi_{r'} \, d\tau \tag{10}$$

To find the value of each c_r giving the minimum ε, equation (10) is successively differentiated partially with respect to each $c_{r'}$ and the partial differential coefficients $(\partial \varepsilon / \partial c_{r'})$ set equal to 0. The partial differentiations give equations

$$\sum_r c_r \int \phi_r H \phi_s \, d\tau = \frac{\partial \varepsilon}{\partial c_s} \sum_r \sum_s c_r c_s \int \phi_r \phi_s \, d\tau + \varepsilon \sum_r c_r \int \phi_r \phi_s \, d\tau \tag{11}$$

one such equation resulting for each possible value s of r'. A few simplifying symbols are now introduced:

$$\alpha_r = \int \phi_r H \phi_r \, d\tau \tag{12}$$

$$\beta_{rs} = \int \phi_r H \phi_s \, d\tau \quad (r \neq s) \tag{13}$$

$$S_{rs} = \int \phi_r \phi_s \, d\tau \tag{14}$$

α_r is called a Coulomb integral, β_{rs} a resonance integral, and S_{rs} an overlap integral. As long as the ϕ_r are normalized, $S_{rr} = 1$. Using these abbreviations, and setting $\partial \varepsilon / \partial s = 0$, equations (11) become

$$c_r \alpha_r + \sum_{s \neq r} c_s \beta_{rs} = \varepsilon \left(c_r + \sum_{s \neq r} c_s S_{rs} \right) \tag{15}$$

or

$$c_r (\alpha_r - \varepsilon) + \sum_{s \neq r} c_s (\beta_{rs} - \varepsilon S_{rs}) = 0 \tag{16}$$

and again there are as many such equations as there are atoms r. These equations are called the *secular equations*. They are a set of n linear homogeneous equations in n unknowns. Unlike a set of equations similar to (16), where the right-hand sides were constants other than 0, and which could be solved for the c_r, equations (16) do not, except for the trivial case of all $c_r = 0$, have solutions in general. Only for certain values of the energy ε can these equations be solved. These values of ε are given by the condition that the determinant D vanishes.

$$
D = \begin{vmatrix}
\alpha_1 - \varepsilon & \beta_{12} - \varepsilon S_{12} & \beta_{13} - \varepsilon S_{13} \cdots \\
\beta_{21} - \varepsilon S_{21} & \alpha_2 - \varepsilon & \beta_{23} - \varepsilon S_{23} \cdots \\
\beta_{31} - \varepsilon S_{31} & \beta_{32} - \varepsilon S_{32} & \alpha_3 - \varepsilon \quad \cdots \\
\cdots & \cdots & \cdots \quad \cdots \\
\cdots & \cdots & \cdots \quad \cdots
\end{vmatrix} = 0
$$

The determinant D, the so-called "secular determinant," has n rows and n columns, and can be expanded into an nth-order equation in ε, which can then be solved for n values of ε, the desired values ε_j. The corresponding c_{jr} are then obtained by successively substituting the ε_j back into all n of equations (16). Actually, all c_{jr} cannot be obtained, but only ratios of the c_{jr} for one j and all r. The last c_{jr} is finally obtained by normalization, i.e., by setting

$$
\int \psi_j{}^2 \, d\tau = \int \sum_r c_{jr}{}^2 \psi_r{}^2 \, d\tau = \sum_r c_{ir}{}^2 = 1
$$

This completes, in principle, the calculation of the orbitals using the variation method. In practice, some added approximations are generally made and are implied in all the work considered in this book. First, it is customary to neglect S_{rs} ($r \neq s$). This approximation greatly simplifies the calculations and has been shown to lead to results giving the same qualitative predictions and trends, although quantitatively different results. This approximation is commonly called the *neglect of overlap*. The second approximation which is almost universally made in all MO work is to neglect β_{rs} if r and s are not bonded.

Probably the most difficult part of MO calculations is the evaluation or estimation of the α and β integrals. The theory described here contains so many approximations and shortcuts that it is rarely profitable to go through the rather extensive computation required to compute these integrals theoretically. Rather, they are usually treated as empirical parameters and adjusted to produce agreement between experiment and calculation for one compound or one case, and then used in further calculations.

Appendix 3 Character tables

This appendix lists the character tables for all point groups commonly encountered in real molecules. The construction of these character tables was considered in section 4.4. Each table lists in the first column the various symmetry species applicable to the particular point group, in the body the characters for each of the important symmetry operations in columns headed by the operations, and in the final column the three elements of the dipole moment vector $\mathbf{M}$, M_x, M_y, and M_z, in the rows of the symmetry species to which they belong. The vector $\mathbf{M}$ is defined in section 6.2, is used extensively in Chapter 6, and is of importance wherever symmetry forbiddenness and polarization are discussed. The arrangement of the character tables follows Herzberg.[1]

TABLE A3.1

Symmetry Species and Characters for the Point Groups
$C_2,\ C_s,\ C_i \equiv S_2$

C_2	I	$C_2(z)$		C_s	I	$\sigma(xy)$		$C_i \equiv S_2$	I	i	
A	$+1$	$+1$	M_z	A'	$+1$	$+1$	M_x, M_y	A_g	$+1$	$+1$	$\cdots$
B	$+1$	-1	M_x, M_y	A''	$+1$	-1	M_z	A_u	$+1$	-1	M_x, M_y, M_z

[1] G. Herzberg, *Molecular Spectra and Molecular Structure*, D. Van Nostrand Co., Princeton, N.J., 1945.

TABLE A3.2

Symmetry Species and Characters for the Point Groups C_{2v}, C_{2h}, and $D_2 \equiv V$

C_{2v}	I	$C_2(z)$	$\sigma_v(xz)$	$\sigma_v(yz)$		C_{2h}	I	$C_2(z)$	$\sigma_h(xy)$	i	
A_1	+1	+1	+1	+1	M_z	A_g	+1	+1	+1	+1	...
A_2	+1	+1	−1	−1	...	A_u	+1	+1	−1	−1	M_z
B_1	+1	−1	+1	−1	M_x	B_g	+1	−1	−1	+1	...
B_2	+1	−1	−1	+1	M_y	B_u	+1	−1	+1	−1	M_x, M_y

$D_2 \equiv V$	I	$C_2(z)$	$C_2(y)$	$C_2(x)$	
A	+1	+1	+1	+1	...
B_1	+1	+1	−1	−1	M_z
B_2	+1	−1	+1	−1	M_y
B_3	+1	−1	−1	+1	M_x

TABLE A3.3

Symmetry Species and Characters for the Point Group
$D_{2h} \equiv V_h$

$D_{2h} \equiv V_h$	I	$\sigma(xy)$	$\sigma(xz)$	$\sigma(yz)$	i	$C_2(z)$	$C_2(y)$	$C_2(x)$	
A_g	+1	+1	+1	+1	+1	+1	+1	+1	...
A_u	+1	−1	−1	−1	−1	+1	+1	+1	...
B_{1g}	+1	+1	−1	−1	+1	+1	−1	−1	...
B_{1u}	+1	−1	+1	+1	−1	+1	−1	−1	M_z
B_{2g}	+1	−1	+1	−1	+1	−1	+1	−1	...
B_{2u}	+1	+1	−1	+1	−1	−1	+1	−1	M_y
B_{3g}	+1	−1	−1	+1	+1	−1	−1	+1	...
B_{3u}	+1	+1	+1	−1	−1	−1	−1	+1	M_x

TABLE A3.4

Symmetry Species and Characters
for the Point Group C_3

C_3	I	$2C_3$	
A	+1	+1	M_z
E	+2	−1	M_x, M_y

TABLE A3.5

Symmetry Species and Characters
for the Point Group C_{3h}

C_{3h}	I	C_3	σ_h	$2S_3$	
A'	+1	+1	+1	+1	...
A''	+1	+1	−1	−1	M_z
E'	+2	−1	+2	−1	M_x, M_y
E''	+2	−1	−2	+1	...

TABLE A3.6

Symmetry Species and Characters for the Point Groups C_{3v} and D_3

C_{3v}	I	$2C_3(z)$	$3\sigma_v$		D_3	I	$2C_3(z)$	$3C_2$	
A_1	+1	+1	+1	M_z	A_1	+1	+1	+1	...
A_2	+1	+1	−1	...	A_2	+1	+1	−1	M_z
E	+2	−1	0	M_x, M_y	E	+2	−1	0	M_x, M_y

TABLE A3.7

Symmetry Species and Characters for the Point Group D_{3h}

D_{3h}	I	$2C_3(z)$	$3C_2$	σ_h	$2S_3$	$3\sigma_v$	
A_1'	+1	+1	+1	+1	+1	+1	...
A_1''	+1	+1	+1	−1	−1	−1	...
A_2'	+1	+1	−1	+1	+1	−1	...
A_2''	+1	+1	−1	−1	−1	+1	M_z
E'	+2	−1	0	+2	−1	0	M_x, M_y
E''	+2	−1	0	−2	+1	0	...

TABLE A3.8

Symmetry Species and Characters for the Point Group $D_{3d}\ (\equiv S_{6v})$

D_{3d}	I	$2S_6(z)$	$2S_6^{\,2} \equiv 2C_3$	$S_6^{\,3} \equiv S_2 \equiv i$	$3C_2$	$3\sigma_d$	
A_{1g}	+1	+1	+1	+1	+1	+1	...
A_{1u}	+1	−1	+1	−1	+1	−1	...
A_{2g}	+1	+1	+1	+1	−1	−1	...
A_{2u}	+1	−1	+1	−1	−1	+1	M_z
E_g	+2	−1	−1	+2	0	0	...
E_u	+2	+1	−1	−2	0	0	M_x, M_y

TABLE A3.9

Symmetry Species and Characters for the Point Groups C_4, C_{4v}, D_4, and $D_{2d} \equiv V_d$

	I	$2C_4(z)$	$C_4^2 \equiv C_2''$	$2\sigma_v$	$2\sigma_d$	
C_{4v}	I	$2C_4(z)$	$C_4^2 \equiv C_2''$	$2\sigma_v$	$2\sigma_d$	
D_4	I	$2C_4(z)$	$C_4^2 \equiv C_2''$	$2C_2$	$2C_2'$	
$D_{2d} \equiv V_d \equiv S_4$	I	$2S_4(z)$	$S_4^2 \equiv C_2''$	$2C_2$	$2\sigma_d$	
A_1	$+1$	$+1$	$+1$	$+1$	$+1$	M_z for C_{4v}
A_2	$+1$	$+1$	$+1$	-1	-1	M_z for D_4
B_1	$+1$	-1	$+1$	$+1$	-1	$\dots$
B_2	$+1$	-1	$+1$	-1	$+1$	M_z for V_d
E	$+2$	0	-2	0	0	M_x, M_y

^{a} The species for C_4 are those listed, except that the absence of the elements σ_v and σ_d of C_{4v} eliminates the distinction between A_1 and A_2, making them A, and between B_1 and B_2, giving B.

TABLE A3.10

Symmetry Species and Characters for the Point Group C_{4h}

C_{4h}	I	$2C_4$	$C_4^2 \equiv C_2''$	σ_h	$2S_4$	$S_2 \equiv i$	
A_g	$+1$	$+1$	$+1$	$+1$	$+1$	$+1$	$\dots$
A_u	$+1$	$+1$	$+1$	-1	-1	-1	M_z
B_g	$+1$	-1	$+1$	$+1$	-1	$+1$	$\dots$
B_u	$+1$	-1	$+1$	-1	$+1$	-1	$\dots$
E_g	$+2$	0	-2	-2	0	$+2$	$\dots$
E_u	$+2$	0	-2	$+2$	0	-2	M_x, M_y

TABLE A3.11

Symmetry Species and Characters for the Point Group D_{4d} ($\equiv S_{8v}$)

D_{4d}	I	$2S_8(z)$	$2S_8^2 \equiv 2C_4$	$2S_8^3$	$S_8^4 \equiv C_2''$	$4C_2$	$4\sigma_d$	
A_1	$+1$	$+1$	$+1$	$+1$	$+1$	$+1$	$+1$	$\dots$
A_2	$+1$	$+1$	$+1$	$+1$	$+1$	-1	-1	$\dots$
B_1	$+1$	-1	$+1$	-1	$+1$	$+1$	-1	$\dots$
B_2	$+1$	-1	$+1$	-1	$+1$	-1	$+1$	M_z
E_1	$+2$	$+\sqrt{2}$	0	$-\sqrt{2}$	-2	0	0	M_x, M_y
E_2	$+2$	0	-2	0	$+2$	0	0	$\dots$
E_3	$+2$	$-\sqrt{2}$	0	$+\sqrt{2}$	-2	0	0	$\dots$

TABLE A3.12

Symmetry Species and Characters for the Point Group D_{4h}

D_{4h}	I	$2C_4(z)$	$C_4^2 \equiv C_2''$	$2C_2$	$2C_2'$	σ_h	$2\sigma_v$	$2\sigma_d$	$2S_4$	$S_2 \equiv i$	
A_{1g}	$+1$	$+1$	$+1$	$+1$	$+1$	$+1$	$+1$	$+1$	$+1$	$+1$	$\vdots$
A_{1u}	$+1$	$+1$	$+1$	$+1$	$+1$	-1	-1	-1	-1	-1	$\vdots$
A_{2g}	$+1$	$+1$	$+1$	-1	-1	$+1$	-1	-1	$+1$	$+1$	$\vdots$
A_{2u}	$+1$	$+1$	$+1$	-1	-1	-1	$+1$	$+1$	-1	-1	M_z
B_{1g}	$+1$	-1	$+1$	$+1$	-1	$+1$	$+1$	-1	-1	$+1$	$\vdots$
B_{1u}	$+1$	-1	$+1$	$+1$	-1	-1	-1	$+1$	$+1$	-1	$\vdots$
B_{2g}	$+1$	-1	$+1$	-1	$+1$	$+1$	-1	$+1$	-1	$+1$	$\vdots$
B_{2u}	$+1$	-1	$+1$	-1	$+1$	-1	$+1$	-1	$+1$	-1	$\vdots$
E_g	$+2$	0	-2	0	0	-2	0	0	0	$+2$	$\vdots$
E_u	$+2$	0	-2	0	0	$+2$	0	0	0	-2	M_x, M_y

TABLE A3.13

Symmetry Species and Characters for the Point Group D_{5h}

D_{5h}	I	$2C_5$	$2C_5^2$	σ_h	$5C_2$	$5\sigma_v$	$2S_5$	$2S_5^3$	
A_1'	+1	+1	+1	+1	+1	+1	+1	+1	⋮
A_1''	+1	+1	+1	−1	+1	−1	−1	−1	⋮
A_2'	+1	+1	+1	+1	−1	−1	+1	+1	⋮
A_2''	+1	+1	+1	−1	−1	+1	−1	−1	M_z
E_1'	+2	$2\cos 72°$	$2\cos 144°$	+2	0	0	$+2\cos 72°$	$+2\cos 144°$	M_x, M_y
E_1''	+2	$2\cos 72°$	$2\cos 144°$	−2	0	0	$-2\cos 72°$	$-2\cos 144°$	⋮
E_2'	+2	$2\cos 144°$	$2\cos 72°$	+2	0	0	$+2\cos 144°$	$+2\cos 72°$	⋮
E_2''	+2	$2\cos 144°$	$2\cos 72°$	−2	0	0	$-2\cos 144°$	$-2\cos 72°$	⋮

TABLE A3.14

Symmetry Species and Characters for the Point Groups
C_5, C_{5h}, C_{5v}, $D_5{}^a$

C_{5v}	I	$2C_5$	$2C_5{}^2$	$5\sigma_v{}^b$	
A_1	+1	+1	+1	+1	M_z
A_2	+1	+1	+1	−1	...
E_1	+2	2 cos 72°	2 cos 144°	0	M_x, M_y
E_2	+2	2 cos 144°	2 cos 72°	0	...

^{a} In C_5, A_1 and A_2 coalesce to form A, since there is no σ_v. For C_{5h}, add σ_h, separating A into A' (+1) and A'' (−1).
^{b} In D_5, replace $5\sigma_v$ by $5C_2$.

TABLE A3.15

Symmetry Species and Characters for the Point Groups
C_6 and $C_{6h}{}^a$

C_{6h}	I	$2C_6$	$2C_6{}^2 \equiv C_3$	$C_6{}^3 \equiv C_2''$	σ_h	$2S_6$	$2S_3$	$S_2 \equiv i$	
A_g	+1	+1	+1	+1	+1	+1	+1	+1	...
A_u	+1	+1	+1	+1	−1	−1	−1	−1	M_z
B_g	+1	−1	+1	−1	−1	+1	−1	+1	...
B_u	+1	−1	+1	−1	+1	−1	+1	−1	...
E_{1g}	+2	+1	−1	−2	−2	−1	+1	+2	...
E_{1u}	+2	+1	−1	−2	+2	+1	−1	−2	M_x, M_y
E_{2g}	+2	−1	−1	+2	+2	−1	−1	+2	...
E_{2u}	+2	−1	−1	+2	−2	+1	+1	−2	...

^{a} For C_6, absence of σ_h, S_6, S_3, and $S_2 \equiv i$ eliminates the g, u classification and reduces the species to A, B, E_1, and E_2.

TABLE A3.16

Symmetry Species and Characters for the Point Groups
C_{6v} and D_6

C_{6v} D_6	I I	$2C_6(z)$ $2C_6(z)$	$2C_6{}^2 \equiv 2C_3$ $2C_6{}^2 \equiv 2C_3$	$C_6{}^3 \equiv C_2''$ $C_6{}^3 \equiv C_2''$	$3\sigma_v$ $3C_2$	$3\sigma_d$ $3C_2'$	
A_1	+1	+1	+1	+1	+1	+1	M_z for C_{6v}
A_2	+1	+1	+1	+1	−1	−1	M_z for D_6
B_1	+1	−1	+1	−1	+1	−1	...
B_2	+1	−1	+1	−1	−1	+1	...
E_1	+2	+1	−1	−2	0	0	M_x, M_y
E_2	+2	−1	−1	+2	0	0	...

TABLE A3.17

Symmetry Species and Characters for the Point Group D_{6h}

D_{6h}	I	$2C_6(z)$	$2C_6^2 \equiv 2C_3$	$C_6^3 \equiv C_2''$	$3C_2$	$3C_2'$	σ_h	$3\sigma_v$	$3\sigma_d$	$2S_6$	$2S_3$	$S_6^3 \equiv S_2 \equiv i$	
A_{1g}	+1	+1	+1	+1	+1	+1	+1	+1	+1	+1	+1	+1	
A_{1u}	+1	+1	+1	+1	+1	+1	−1	−1	−1	−1	−1	−1	
A_{2g}	+1	+1	+1	+1	−1	−1	+1	−1	−1	+1	+1	+1	M_z
A_{2u}	+1	+1	+1	+1	−1	−1	−1	+1	+1	−1	−1	−1	
B_{1g}	+1	−1	+1	−1	+1	−1	−1	+1	−1	−1	+1	+1	
B_{1u}	+1	−1	+1	−1	+1	−1	+1	−1	+1	+1	−1	−1	
B_{2g}	+1	−1	+1	−1	−1	+1	−1	+1	−1	−1	+1	+1	
B_{2u}	+1	−1	+1	−1	−1	+1	+1	−1	+1	+1	−1	−1	
E_{1g}	+2	+1	−1	−2	0	0	−2	0	0	−1	+1	+2	
E_{1u}	+2	+1	−1	−2	0	0	+2	0	0	+1	−1	−2	M_x, M_y
E_{2g}	+2	−1	−1	+2	0	0	+2	0	0	−1	−1	+2	
E_{2u}	+2	−1	−1	+2	0	0	−2	0	0	+1	+1	−2	

TABLE A3.18
Symmetry Species and Characters for the Point Group $D_{\infty h}$

$D_{\infty h}$	I	$2C_\infty^\varphi$	$2C_\infty^{2\varphi}$	$2C_\infty^{3\varphi}$	$\ldots$	σ_h	∞C_2	$\infty \sigma_v$	$2S_\infty^\varphi$	$2S_\infty^{2\varphi}$	$\ldots$	$S_2 \equiv i$	
Σ_g^+	$+1$	$+1$	$+1$	$+1$	$\ldots$	$+1$	$+1$	$+1$	$+1$	$+1$	$\ldots$	$+1$	$\ldots$
Σ_u^+	$+1$	$+1$	$+1$	$+1$	$\ldots$	-1	-1	$+1$	-1	-1	$\ldots$	-1	M_z
Σ_g^-	$+1$	$+1$	$+1$	$+1$	$\ldots$	$+1$	-1	-1	$+1$	$+1$	$\ldots$	$+1$	$\ldots$
Σ_u^-	$+1$	$+1$	$+1$	$+1$	$\ldots$	-1	$+1$	-1	-1	-1	$\ldots$	-1	$\ldots$
Π_g	$+2$	$2\cos\varphi$	$2\cos 2\varphi$	$2\cos 3\varphi$	$\ldots$	-2	0	0	$-2\cos\varphi$	$-2\cos 2\varphi$	$\ldots$	$+2$	$\ldots$
Π_u	$+2$	$2\cos\varphi$	$2\cos 2\varphi$	$2\cos 3\varphi$	$\ldots$	$+2$	0	0	$+2\cos\varphi$	$+2\cos 2\varphi$	$\ldots$	-2	M_x, M_y
Δ_g	$+2$	$2\cos 2\varphi$	$2\cos 4\varphi$	$2\cos 6\varphi$	$\ldots$	$+2$	0	0	$+2\cos 2\varphi$	$+2\cos 4\varphi$	$\ldots$	$+2$	$\ldots$
Δ_u	$+2$	$2\cos 2\varphi$	$2\cos 4\varphi$	$2\cos 6\varphi$	$\ldots$	-2	0	0	$-2\cos 2\varphi$	$-2\cos 4\varphi$	$\ldots$	-2	$\ldots$
Φ_g	$+2$	$2\cos 3\varphi$	$2\cos 6\varphi$	$2\cos 9\varphi$	$\ldots$	-2	0	0	$-2\cos 3\varphi$	$-2\cos 4\varphi$	$\ldots$	$+2$	$\ldots$
Φ_u	$+2$	$2\cos 3\varphi$	$2\cos 6\varphi$	$2\cos 9\varphi$	$\ldots$	$+2$	0	0	$+2\cos 3\varphi$	$+2\cos 4\varphi$	$\ldots$	-2	$\ldots$
$\ldots$	$\ldots$	$\ldots$	$\ldots$	$\ldots$	$\ldots$	$\ldots$	$\ldots$	$\ldots$	$\ldots$	$\ldots$	$\ldots$	$\ldots$	$\ldots$

TABLE A3.19

Symmetry Species and Characters for the Point Group $C_{\infty v}$

$C_{\infty v}$	I	$2C_\infty^{\varphi}$	$2C_\infty^{2\varphi}$	$2C_\infty^{3\varphi}$	$\ldots$	$\infty \sigma_v$	
Σ^+	$+1$	$+1$	$+1$	$+1$	$\ldots$	$+1$	M_z
Σ^-	$+1$	$+1$	$+1$	$+1$	$\ldots$	-1	$\ldots$
Π	$+2$	$2\cos\varphi$	$2\cos 2\varphi$	$2\cos 3\varphi$	$\ldots$	0	M_x, M_y
Δ	$+2$	$2\cos 2\varphi$	$2\cos 2\cdot 2\varphi$	$2\cos 3\cdot 2\varphi$	$\ldots$	0	$\ldots$
Φ	$+2$	$2\cos 3\varphi$	$2\cos 2\cdot 3\varphi$	$2\cos 3\cdot 3\varphi$	$\ldots$	0	$\ldots$
$\ldots$	$\ldots$	$\ldots$	$\ldots$	$\ldots$	$\ldots$	$\ldots$	$\ldots$

TABLE A3.20

Symmetry Species and Characters for the Point Group T

T	I	$8C_3$	$3C_2$	
A	$+1$	$+1$	$+1$	$\ldots$
E	$+2$	-1	$+2$	$\ldots$
T	$+3$	0	-1	M_x, M_y, M_z

TABLE A3.21

Symmetry Species and Characters for the Point Groups T_d and O

T_d	I	$8C_3$	$6\sigma_d$	$6S_4$	$3S_4^2 \equiv 3C_2$	
O	I	$8C_3$	$6C_2$	$6C_4$	$3C_4^2 \equiv 3C_2''$	
A_1	$+1$	$+1$	$+1$	$+1$	$+1$	$\ldots$
A_2	$+1$	$+1$	-1	-1	$+1$	$\ldots$
E	$+2$	-1	0	0	$+2$	$\ldots$
T_1	$+3$	0	-1	$+1$	-1	M_x, M_y, M_z for O
T_2	$+3$	0	$+1$	-1	-1	M_x, M_y, M_z for T_d

TABLE A3.22

Symmetry Species and Characters for the Point Group O_h

O_h	I	$8C_3$	$6C_2$	$6C_4$	$3C_4^2 \equiv 3C_2''$	$S_2 \equiv i$	$6S_4$	$8S_6$	$3\sigma_h$	$6\sigma_d$	
A_{1g}	+1	+1	+1	+1	+1	+1	+1	+1	+1	+1	⋮
A_{1u}	+1	+1	+1	+1	+1	−1	−1	−1	−1	−1	⋮
A_{2g}	+1	+1	−1	−1	+1	+1	−1	+1	+1	−1	⋮
A_{2u}	+1	+1	−1	−1	+1	−1	+1	−1	−1	+1	⋮
E_g	+2	−1	0	0	+2	+2	0	−1	+2	0	⋮
E_u	+2	−1	0	0	+2	−2	0	+1	−2	0	⋮
T_{1g}	+3	0	−1	+1	−1	+3	+1	0	−1	−1	⋮
T_{1u}	+3	0	−1	+1	−1	−3	−1	0	+1	+1	M_x, M_y, M_z
T_{2g}	+3	0	+1	−1	−1	+3	−1	0	−1	+1	⋮
T_{2u}	+3	0	+1	−1	−1	−3	+1	0	+1	+1	⋮

Author index*

* Parentheses enclose the number of different literature references to the author on the indicated page.

Subject index